Organizational Behavior

Second Edition

Organizational Behavior

Second Edition

Robert P. Vecchio

Franklin D. Schurz Professor of Management
University of Notre Dame

The Dryden Press
Harcourt Brace Jovanovich College Publishers
Fort Worth   Philadelphia   San Diego
New York   Orlando   Austin   San Antonio
Toronto   Montreal   London   Sydney   Tokyo

Acquisitions Editor: Robert Gemin
Developmental Editor: Dan Coran
Project Editor: Teresa Chartos
Production Manager: Barb Bahnsen
Permissions Editor: Doris Milligan
Director of Editing, Design, and Production: Jane Perkins

Text and Cover Designer: Rebecca Lemna
Copy Editor: Carolyn Crabtree
Indexer: Leoni McVey
Compositor: Bi-Comp, Inc.
Text Type: 10/12 Sabon

Library of Congress Cataloging-in-Publication Data

Vecchio, Robert P.
     Organizational behavior / Robert P. Vecchio.—2nd ed.
        p.   cm.
     Includes bibliographical references and index.
     ISBN 0-03-033294-X
     1. Organizational behavior.   I.   Title.
HD58.7.V43   1991
658.3—dc20   90-3517
                                                                          CIP

Printed in the United States of America
  2-040-9876543
Copyright © 1991, 1987 by The Dryden Press

Requests for permission to make copies of any part of the work should be mailed
to: Copyrights and Permissions Department, Harcourt Brace Jovanovich, Publishers,
Orlando, Florida 32887.

Address orders:
The Dryden Press
Orlando, FL 32887

Harcourt Brace Jovanovich, Inc.
The Dryden Press
Saunders College Publishing

Cover Source: © Herb Comess.

To Betty, Julie, and Mark

The Dryden Press
Series in Management

Bartlett
Cases in Strategic Management for Business

Bedeian
Management
Second Edition

Bedeian and Zammuto
Organizations: Theory and Design

Boone and Kurtz
Contemporary Business
Sixth Edition

Bowman and Branchaw
Business Report Writing
Second Edition

Bracker, Montanari, and Morgan
Cases in Strategic Management

Cullinan
Business English for Industry and the Professions

Czinkota, Rivoli, and Ronkainen
International Business

Daft
Management
Second Edition

Efendioglu and Montanari
The Advantage Ski Company: A Strategic Simulation

Foegen
Business Plan Guidebook with Financial Spreadsheets

Forgionne
Quantitative Management

Gaither
Production and Operations Management: A Problem-Solving and Decision-Making Approach
Fourth Edition

Gatewood and Feild
Human Resource Selection
Second Edition

Greenhaus
Career Management

Higgins
Strategy: Formulation, Implementation, and Control

Higgins and Vincze
Strategic Management: Text and Cases
Fourth Edition

Hills
Compensation Decision Making

Hodgetts
Modern Human Relations at Work
Fourth Edition

Holley and Jennings
The Labor Relations Process
Fourth Edition

Huseman, Lahiff, and Penrose
Business Communication: Strategies and Skills
Fourth Edition

Jauch, Coltrin, and Bedeian
The Managerial Experience: Cases, Exercises, and Readings
Fifth Edition

Kemper
Experiencing Strategic Management

Kuehl and Lambing
Small Business: Planning and Management
Second Edition

Kuratko and Hodgetts
Entrepreneurship: A Contemporary Approach

Lee
Introduction to Management Science
Second Edition

Luthans and Hodgetts
Business

Montanari, Morgan, and Bracker
Strategic Management: A Choice Approach

Northcraft and Neale
Organizational Behavior: A Management Challenge

Tombari
Business and Society: Strategies for the Environment and Public Policy

Varner
Contemporary Business Report Writing
Second Edition

Vecchio
Organizational Behavior
Second Edition

Wolters and Holley
Labor Relations: An Experiential and Case Approach

Zikmund
Business Research Methods
Third Edition

Preface

My first encounter with a course in organizational behavior occurred many years ago. The topic fascinated me because I had held a number of different jobs up to that point in my life, and I could see the relevance and value of understanding the social dynamics that exist in the workplace. I began to read more about human behavior in organizations and ultimately came to teach courses in organizational behavior. In writing this text, I have attempted to share with you some of my interest and enthusiasm for the field by taking the research-related foundations of organizational behavior and making them understandable and accessible to the nonresearcher.

Level and Organization of the Text

Over the years, I have found that undergraduate- and MBA-level courses in organizational behavior are often similar in focus and content. Although I have prepared this text with the intention that it be appropriate for an undergraduate audience, it may be used with MBA students if suitable outside readings and additional assignments are provided. The topics covered in this text are fairly traditional; that is to say, I have not deviated far from the approach preferred by most instructors.

In preparing the second edition, I sought to maintain a balanced treatment of theory, research, and practice while presenting both the classic and current "cutting edge" theories. Important organizational behavior topics are covered, along with elements of human resources management, organizational development, and cross-cultural issues. In addition, several chapters are devoted to organizational theory.

In Part I the text begins with a consideration of how the field may be defined and a look at how it came into existence (Chapter 1). Next, the student is provided with an introductory treatment of how to understand the research base of the field of organizational behavior (Chapter 2). The substantive, topic-related chapters (Chapters 3 through 19) are organized and arranged so that the material progresses from a micro (individual) to a more macro (group and organizational) focus. The later chapters are grouped into three major sections, reflecting this progression: Part II, Individual Processes; Part III, Interpersonal and Work Group Processes; and Part IV, Organizational Structure and Processes. Under the heading of Individual Processes (Chapters 3 and 4 in Part II), topics in perception, personality, attitudes, and job satisfaction are explored. Interpersonal and Work Group Processes (Chapters 5 through 14 in Part III) include treatments of learning, motivation, job design, performance appraisal, power, leadership, decision making, group dynamics, conflict, and stress. The final section, Organizational Structure and Processes (Chapters 15 through 19 in Part IV), examines issues in communication, organizational design, environmental and cultural forces, and organizational change and development.

New to the Second Edition

While accommodating the suggestions of reviewers and users of the text, my goal for the second edition was to maintain the book's clear coverage of important classical and contemporary concepts in organizational behavior. New topic coverage has been added, Part IV on organizational structure and processes has been expanded, and the box items and opening vignettes were completely revised to tie them more closely to the chapter discussions. The following are some of the major new features of this edition:

- Conflict management and stress are now treated in separate chapters (Chapters 13 and 14). The conflict chapter now includes an extensive discussion of managing intergroup conflict, and the chapter on stress includes discussions of organizational factors that cause stress, views of job-related stress, time management, and wellness programs.

- An expanded discussion of ethics throughout the book includes coverage of Kohlberg's model of moral development in Chapter 3, the ethics of organizational politics and the incorporation of ethics into political behavior decisions in Chapter 9, and the ethics of managing organizational decline in Chapter 19.

- Greater coverage of international issues as they relate to organizational behavior includes discussions of Theory Z, doing business overseas, methods of cross-cultural training, teamwork in a global marketplace, and settling international trade conflicts.

- Environmental forces and cultural influences are now treated in separate chapters (Chapters 17 and 18). Chapter 17 includes a discussion of Thompson's typology of technology and new treatment of the relationship between organizational structure, environment, and strategy. Chapter 18 includes a major new section on understanding and analyzing organizational culture as well as a discussion of culture and strategy.

- To help students see how research and theory find expression in the real world, references to the experiences and programs of actual companies have been incorporated throughout the text.

- Other topics that are new to the second edition include selective perception and cognitive style (Chapter 3); Staw and Ross's work on job satisfaction (Chapter 4); the validity of the job characteristics model (Chapter 7); potential drawbacks of MBO programs (Chapter 8); consequences of using influence tactics (Chapter 9); cognitive resources theory and transformational and charismatic leadership (Chapter 10); decision making versus effective decision implementation (Chapter 11); barriers to effective communication (Chapter 15); and the future of organizational design (Chapter 19).

Pedagogy

The text includes a number of pedagogical features designed to enhance student learning and comprehension.

Learning Objectives   Eight-to-ten learning objectives at the beginning of each chapter direct and focus the reader's attention on the major issues within the chapter.

Opening Vignettes   Short stories based on real organizations at the beginning of each chapter give a true-to-life flavor to chapter topics.

Boxed Items   OB Focus and An Inside Look boxed features help illustrate the applications of organizational behavior principles. They provide current examples drawn from a variety of real corporations and businesses, and they emphasize aspects of ethics, technology, and international issues as they apply to the field of organizational behavior.

Summaries   At the end of each chapter a summary recaps chapter learning objectives and highlights critical points.

Key Terms   Each chapter contains a list of key terms for the student to use in sorting out and reviewing important concepts.

Questions for Discussion   At the end of each chapter interesting questions for discussion help stimulate application of concepts and foster greater understanding of the material.

Critical Incidents and Experiential Exercises   Each chapter is followed by a Critical Incident, a short case for discussion that applies chapter concepts. An Experiential Exercise is also included for each chapter. These exercises are a combination of classic favorites and all-new exercises; some are designed for individual use and some for group participation.

Video Cases   Closely tied to the text, these end-of-part cases relate chapter topics to the real world. The videos that accompany these cases feature the *Challenger* disaster and the opening of a McDonald's in Moscow.

Glossary   A glossary containing definitions of key terms appears at the end of the book. Key terms are boldfaced in the text where they first appear.

Ancillaries

A comprehensive set of ancillaries accompanies the second edition of *Organizational Behavior*.

Instructor's Manual   This manual includes extensive chapter outlines; class openers; suggested term projects; answers to discussion questions; additional experiential exercises; additional readings lists; examples from the popular press to help illustrate lectures; case notes for end-of-section video cases; a film guide; computer simulation guide; answers to in-text Critical Incidents and Experiential Exercises; additional cases; transparency masters; and guidelines for Experiential Exercises in the student learning guide. The *Instructor's Manual* was prepared by Susan Stites Doe, State University of New York at Buffalo.

Test Bank   Thoroughly revised and accuracy-tested, the *Test Bank* contains over 2,500 items to help gauge student comprehension. Its unique combination of question types includes true/false, multiple-choice, essay, and mini-case questions. Also, each question is classified according to level of difficulty and the chapter learning objective to which it pertains. The revised *Test Bank* was prepared by C. LaFaye Hargrove, University of South Carolina at Aiken, William Bommer, Bowling Green State University, and Wesley King, Jr., Miami University.

Computerized Test Bank   A computerized version of the printed test bank is available for IBM microcomputers.

Transparency Acetates   Color transparency acetates of key figures and concepts used in teaching organizational behavior and teaching notes for them are available. The acetates and teaching notes were prepared by William Bommer, Bowling Green State University.

Learning Guide/Experiential Exercise Book   This unique volume includes chapter review material and an Experiential Exercise for each chapter. The first part of each chapter helps students review key topics and prepare for class exams by testing their understanding of the text's material. It presents a thorough chapter overview and numerous sample test questions. The second half of each chapter includes an Experiential Exercise and a Critical Incident for both individual and class assignments. Instructors will find a variety of useful material here including role-playing and skills-building exercises, as well as other applications appropriate to key topics in organizational behavior. The *Learning Guide/Experiential Exercise Book* was written by Bruce Kemelgor, University of Louisville.

Video Package   Six videos, closely tied to the text, feature such real-world organizations and events as NASA's *Challenger* disaster and the opening of a McDonald's in Moscow. The videos focus on such topics as decision making, corporate culture, leadership, motivation, and enhancing employee performance. Complete teaching notes and discussion guidelines for each video are included in the *Instructor's Manual*. Please contact your Dryden Press sales representative for further information.

Acknowledgments

This book benefited from the efforts of many people. I must say a very special "thank you" to the following reviewers who made numerous suggestions on how to revise and improve the content of each chapter: Gail A. Ball, Pennsylvania State University; Richard R. Camp, Eastern Michigan University; Robert Cummins, University of Houston at Clear Lake; Arthur Darrow, Bowling Green State University; Allison Davis-Blake, Carnegie-Mellon University; William Hendrix, Clemson University; John Hollenbeck, Michigan State University; Charles Holloman, Augusta College; Bruce Kemelgor, University of Louisville; Wesley King, Jr., Miami University; Edward Miles, Georgia State University; Kevin Mossholder, Auburn University; Brian Niehoff, Kansas State University; Peter P. Poole, Lehigh University; Elizabeth Ravlin, University of South Carolina; Mark Sharfman, Pennsylvania State University; Sim Sitkin, University of Texas at Austin; Mark Turbin, University of Wyoming; David Vollrath, Indiana University at South Bend; and John Wissler, California State University at Fresno.

I am also indebted to the professionals at The Dryden Press who aided in the text's development, production, and design: Butch Gemin, Dan Coran, Becky Lemna, and Teresa Chartos. I am also grateful for the continued support of Jacqueline Marnocha. My wife, Betty, critiqued much of the writing and also helped to prepare the final manuscript. Without her support, suggestions, patience, and encouragement, this text would probably not have been published. A final note of appreciation goes to my children, Julie and Mark, who helped by sharpening pencils and, mostly, by staying away from "Daddy's big mess in the dining room."

Robert P. Vecchio
November 1990

About the Author

Robert P. Vecchio, Ph.D. (University of Illinois, Champaign-Urbana) is Franklin D. Schurz Professor of Management and former chairman of the Department of Management and Administrative Sciences at the University of Notre Dame. Since joining Notre Dame in 1976, he has taught undergraduate and graduate courses in organizational behavior and human resources management. Professor Vecchio is a frequent contributor to academic journals, such as the *Journal of Applied Psychology, Organizational Behavior and Human Decision Processes,* the *Academy of Management Journal,* and the *Academy of Management Review.* Dr. Vecchio is a member of the editorial review boards of the *Academy of Management Review,* the *Journal of Management,* and the *Employee Responsibilities and Rights Journal.* His current research interests include employee motivation, job satisfaction, and leadership.

Contents in Brief

Part I
Introduction to Organizational Behavior 1

Chapter 1 *An Introduction to Organizational Behavior: Overview and Origins* 2
Chapter 2 *Approaches to Studying Organizational Behavior* 32

Part II
Individual Processes 65

Chapter 3 *Perception and Personality* 66
Chapter 4 *Attitudes and Job Satisfaction* 106

Part III
Interpersonal and Work Group Processes 143

Chapter 5 *Changing Employee Behavior through Consequences: Learning and Punishment* 144
Chapter 6 *Motivation* 172
Chapter 7 *Enhancing Employee Motivation* 204
Chapter 8 *Performance Appraisal* 236
Chapter 9 *Power and Influence* 268
Chapter 10 *Leadership* 300
Chapter 11 *Decision Making* 340
Chapter 12 *Group Dynamics* 376
Chapter 13 *Conflict Management* 408
Chapter 14 *Stress* 434

Part IV
Organizational Structure and Processes 469

Chapter 15 *Communication* 470
Chapter 16 *Organizational Design* 498
Chapter 17 *Environmental Forces* 526
Chapter 18 *Cultural Influences* 548
Chapter 19 *Managing Organizational Change and Development* 578

Contents

■ **Part I**
Introduction to Organizational Behavior　　　　　　　　*1*

■ **Chapter 1**

An Introduction to Organizational Behavior:
Overview and Origins　　　　　　　　*2*

Building a Better Organization　　　　　　　　*3*

What is Organizational Behavior?　　　　　　　　4

Why Bother? Or Three Reasons for Studying
Organizational Behavior　　　　　　　　4

　Practical Applications 4　　Personal Growth 5
　Increased Knowledge 6

Organizational Behavior and Its Related Fields　　　　　　　　6

An Inside Look: Teamwork　　　　　　　　7

Studying the Behavior of People at Work:
Past and Present　　　　　　　　9

　Pre–Scientific Management Period (Before 1900) 9
　Scientific Management (1900–1945) 11　　Human
　Relations Approach (1927–1945): The Hawthorne
　Studies 13　　Contingency Approach
　(1945–Present) 17

Criticisms of the Field　　　　　　　　19

　It's So Obvious 19　　It's Only Common Sense 21

OB Focus: Discipline with a Twist　　　　　　　　22

A Framework for Studying Organizational Behavior　　　　　　　　22

Summary　　　　　　　　23

Critical Incident *You Just Can't Get Good Help Anymore*　　　　　　　　27

Experiential Exercise *What Do You "Know"*
about Human Behavior?　　　　　　　　28

■ **Chapter 2**

Approaches to Studying Organizational Behavior   32

An Experiment in Safety   33

Starting Assumptions   34
*Behavior Is Predictable 34   Behavior Is Caused
35   Behavior Has Many Causes 35
Generalities Can Be Drawn 35*

The Scientific Method in OB Research   35
Induction 36   Deduction 36   Verification 36

The Scientific Method in Practice   36
*Refining Theories 38   The Necessity of
Testability 38*

The Goals of Research   38

Research Terminology   39
*Independent and Dependent Variables 39
Hypotheses 40   Intervening Variables 40
Moderating Variables 40*

Two Major Research Methods   41
*The Correlational Method 41   The Experimental
Method 43*

Research Strategies and Settings   43
Case Studies 44   Surveys 44

OB Focus: Profile of a Management Scholar   45
*Field Experiments 46   Laboratory Experiments
47   Archival Research 49   Unobtrusive
Measures 50*

An Inside Look: High-Tech Observation or an Invasion
of Privacy?   51

Internal and External Validity   52

Ethics in Research   53

How to Read an OB Research Report   54
*Abstract 54   Introduction 54   Method 54
Results 54   Discussion 54*

Summary   55

Critical Incident *A Way to Manage Demand?*   60

Experiential Exercise *Approaches to Studying
Organizational Behavior*   61

Part II
Individual Processes

Individual Processes   65

Chapter 3

Perception and Personality   66
Seeking the Managerial Personality   67
The Perception of Others   68
    Accuracy in Perceiving Others 69   Perception of
    Personality Traits 71
An Inside Look: Personality and Management   72
    Mechanistic versus Impressionistic Prediction 73
    Obstacles to Accurate Perception 74   The Study of
    Attributions 78   Personality 79   The
    Determinants of Personality 80   Assessing
    Personality Traits 81
OB Focus: Perceptions and Success   82
    Important Dimensions of Personality 87   The
    Predictive Utility of Personality Measures 92
Summary   93
Critical Incident *A Questionable "Fit"*   97
Experiential Exercise *A Study in Attribution*   98

Chapter 4

Attitudes and Job Satisfaction   106
The View from the Middle   107
The Nature of Attitudes   108
    Measuring Attitudes 109   Attitude Formation
    110   Attitude Change 111
An Inside Look: Keeping Good Employees   117
    Attitudes and Actions 117
Job Satisfaction   118
    The Importance of Job Satisfaction 118
    Measuring Job Satisfaction 119   Sources of Job
    Satisfaction 121   The Search for Trends in Job
    Satisfaction 123   Consequences of Job
    Dissatisfaction 124
OB Focus: Cutting Absenteeism   125
    Job Satisfaction and Productivity 127
Summary   129
Critical Incident *When the Shoe Is on the Other Foot*   132
Experiential Exercise *Assessing Your Job Satisfaction*   133
Video Case *Quad Graphics, Inc. 139*

Part III
Interpersonal and Work Group Processes   143

Chapter 5

*Changing Employee Behavior through
Consequences: Learning and Punishment*   144

Changing Behavior from the Top Down   145

The Nature of Learning   146

Classical Conditioning   146

Observational Learning   148

Instrumental, or Operant, Conditioning   149
   Classical Conditioning versus Operant Conditioning 150

Using Operant Conditioning Principles in Organizational
Settings   150
   *Acquiring Complex Behaviors: Shaping 151
Maintaining Desired Behavior 151   Rules for
Applying Operant Conditioning Principles 154*

Setting Up an OB Mod Program   154

OB Focus: The Right Rewards   155
   *Does OB Mod Work? 156   Controversies
Surrounding OB Mod 156*

The Role of Punishment   158
   Alternatives to Punishment 158

Effective Punishment   159

An Inside Look: An Effective Punishment Strategy for
Spa Mechanics   160
   *Guidelines for Administering Discipline 160
Progressive Discipline 161   Conducting a
Disciplinary Meeting 162*

Termination   163
   *Conducting a Termination Meeting 163   Indirect
Approaches 164*

Summary   165

Critical Incident *The Wrong Reinforcement?*   167

Experiential Exercise *Handling Discipline—A Role Play*   168

Chapter 6

Motivation   172

Getting the Workers Involved   173

The Nature of Motivation   174
   *Hedonism 174   Instinctual Theories 175
Achievement Motivation Theory 175   Maslow's
Hierarchy of Needs 178   Two-Factor Theory 180*

OB Focus: AAL Finds the Factors That Motivate   *183*

Expectancy Theory 185   Reinforcement Theory 187

An Inside Look: Reinforcing the Use of New Technology   *188*

Equity Theory 189   Social Learning Theory 192

A Comprehensive Model of Motivation   *193*

Summary   *195*

Critical Incident *Salary versus Commission*   *198*

Experiential Exercise *What Do Employees Want
from Their Jobs?*   *199*

■ **Chapter 7**

Enhancing Employee Motivation   *204*

No Mistakes Allowed   *205*

Reward Systems   *206*

The Role of Compensation 206

Goal Setting   *211*

*Specificity 211   Difficulty 211   Acceptance
211   Management-by-Objectives 212*

Expectations   *214*

The Power of Self-fulfilling Prophecies 214

An Inside Look: Making Goal Setting Work   *215*

*The Constructive Management of Self-fulfilling
Prophecies 217*

Job Redesign   *219*

Methods of Job Redesign 220

OB Focus: Incentives for Hourly Workers   *221*

*Job Characteristics Theory 222   Other Job
Redesign Approaches 225   Obstacles to Job
Redesign 226*

Summary   *227*

Critical Incident *Is Job Redesign Needed?*   *230*

Experiential Exercise *Goal Setting and Performance*   *230*

■ **Chapter 8**

Performance Appraisal   *236*

Coping with Poor Performance   *237*

Why Appraise Performance?   *238*

When Should Performance Be Appraised?   *239*

Who Should Appraise Performance?   *240*

*The Immediate Supervisor 240   Self-appraisal
240   Peers or Coworkers 241   Subordinates
242   Other Sources of Appraisal 243*

What Should Be Appraised?   244

How Should Appraisals Be Conducted?   244
Graphic Rating Scales 245

An Inside Look: Accuracy of Appraisals   246
*Rankings 246   Behaviorally Anchored Rating
Scales 248   Behavioral Observation Scales 249
Management-by-Objectives 250   Assessment
Centers 251*

The Feedback Interview   253
Conducting a Feedback Interview 253

OB Focus: Firing Practices   256

Legal Aspects of Performance Appraisal   256
*Adverse Impact 257   Penalties 258   Legally
Defensible Appraisal Systems 258*

Summary   259

Critical Incident *Is an Improvement Needed?*   262

Experiential Exercise *Designing Behaviorally
Anchored Rating Scales*   262

■ Chapter 9

Power and Influence   268

Ways to Wield Power   269

Distinguishing Power and Influence   270

Interpersonal Influence Processes   270

The Five Bases of Power   271
Interplay among the Power Bases 273

An Organizational Analysis of Power   274

An Inside Look: Unexpected Influence   275

Tying It All Together   276
A Social Influence View of Supervisor Behavior 277

Politics: The Facts of Organizational Life   277
*Political Tactics 278   Devious Political Tactics
279   Political Blunders 280   Coping with
Organizational Politics 281   Machiavellianism
282   Consequences of Using Influence Tactics
283   The Ethics of Organizational Politics 284*

Responding to Social Influence: Conformity   286

Responding to Authority: Obedience   288

OB Focus: Obeying Unethical Orders   292

Summary   293

Critical Incident *Warner Memorial Hospital*   296

Experiential Exercise *Who Has Power?*   297

■ **Chapter 10**

Leadership   *300*

Creating Peak Performance   *301*

The Nature of Leadership   *302*

What Do Managers Actually Do?   *303*

Approaches to Leadership   *304*
  The Trait Approach 304   The Behavioral
  Approach 305

An Inside Look: Team Leadership   *307*
  Contingency Approaches 311

OB Focus: Seeking the Best Leadership Style   *312*

A Comparison of the Major Leadership Models   *323*

Substitutes for Leadership   *325*

Summary   *326*

Critical Incident *Hal's Halo*   *329*

Experiential Exercise *Leadership Style Profile*   *330*

■ **Chapter 11**

Decision Making   *340*

Who Decides?   *341*

Types of Organizational Decisions   *342*
  Personal versus Organizational Decisions 342
  Programmed versus Nonprogrammed Decisions 343

Classical Decision Theory   *344*

A Behavioral Theory of Decision Making   *346*
  The Influence of Judgmental Strategies 348

Obstacles to Effective Decision Making   *349*
  Escalation of Commitment 349   Groupthink 350

An Inside Look: Stirring Up Good Decisions   *353*
  Risk Taking within Groups 354

Techniques for Improving Decision Making   *355*
  Individual versus Group Decision Making 355

OB Focus: Letting Workers Decide Their Fate   *357*
  The Nominal Group Technique 358   The Delphi
  Technique 358   Bootstrapping 360

Creativity and Decision Making   *361*
  Characteristics of Creative Individuals 361
  Measuring Individual Creativity 362   Steps in the
  Creative Process 363   Methods of Enhancing
  Creativity 363   Establishing a Climate for
  Creativity 365

Summary   365

Critical Incident *The Root of All Evil*   368

Experiential Exercise *How Creative Are You?*   370

◼ Chapter 12

Group Dynamics   376

Family Ties   377

The Nature of Groups   378
   Formal versus Informal Groups 378   Open versus
   Closed Groups 379

Reasons for Joining Groups   380

Interpersonal Attraction   381
   Physical and Psychological Distance 381
   Similarity 382

Stages in Group Development   384

Impact of Group Properties on Performance   385
   The Mere Presence of Others 385   Size 385

An Inside Look: Group Illusions   387
   Composition 387   Roles 388   Status 390
   Norms 391   Cohesiveness 393

Use of Groups in Organizations   395
   Task Forces and Committees 395   Boards and
   Commissions 395   Increasing the Effectiveness of
   Meetings 396   Quality Circles 397

OB Focus: Teamwork in a Global Marketplace   398

Summary   400

Critical Incident *A Difficult Task Force*   403

Experiential Exercise *Participating in and*
Observing Group Processes   404

◼ Chapter 13

Conflict Management   408

Conflict at the Top   409

Conflict   410
   Changing Views of Conflict 411

Sources of Conflict   412
   Communication Factors 412   Structural Factors
   412   Personal Behavior Factors 414

Levels of Conflict   415
   Intrapersonal Conflict 415

An Inside Look: An Ethical Dilemma   416
   Interpersonal Conflict 418

Strategies for Reducing Conflict   420
   Superordinate Goals 420   Structural Approaches
   421   Styles of Conflict Management 422

OB Focus: Settling International Trade Conflicts   424

Intergroup Conflict   424

Stimulating Conflict   427

Summary   427

Critical Incident *A Manager's Nightmare*   429

Experiential Exercise *How Well Do You Manage Conflict?*   431

■ **Chapter 14**

Stress   434

The High Cost of Stress   435

Views of Job-related Stress   436

Causes of Stress   438
  Personal Factors 438   Organizational Factors 439

An Inside Look: Entrepreneurial Couples: Double the
Stress   442

Reactions to Stress   443
  *Physical Problems 443   Alcoholism and Drug
  Abuse 444   Absenteeism, Turnover, and
  Dissatisfaction 445   Mass Psychogenic Illness
  445   Burnout—A Companion Problem 446*

Coping with Stress   446
  *Flight or Fight 447   Exercise 447   Social
  Support 447   Job Redesign 447   Relaxation
  Techniques 448   Developing a New Philosophy of
  Life 448   Time Management: A Practical
  Approach to Reducing Stress 448*

Wellness Programs   450

OB Focus: Rubbing Stress Away   450

Summary   451

Critical Incident *No Response from Monitor 23*   453

Experiential Exercise *Health Risk Appraisal*   455

Video Cases *Patagonia 462   Ethical Decision Making:
  Morton Thiokol and the Space Shuttle* Challenger *Disaster 464*

■ **Part IV**
Organizational Structure and Processes   469

■ **Chapter 15**

Communication   470

Listen to Me!   471

A Model of the Communication Process   472

Types of Communication   474

Communication Networks   474

The Direction of Communication   476
  Downward Communication 476   Upward
  Communication 477

An Inside Look: Westinghouse's High-Tech Network   477
  Horizontal Communication 478

Communication Roles   478
  Gatekeepers 478   Liaisons 479   Isolates 479
  Cosmopolites 479

Transactional Analysis   480
  The Child 480   The Adult 480   The Parent
  480

Nonverbal Communication   482
  Dimensions of Nonverbal Communication 482

OB Focus: Comic Communication   483
  Proxemics 484   Spatial Arrangements 485
  Time 486

Individual Barriers to Communication   486
  Differences in Status 486   The Credibility of the
  Source 487   Perceptual Biases 487

Organizational Barriers to Communication   487
  Information Overload 487   Time Pressures 487
  Organizational Climate 487

Informal Communication   488

Improving Organizational Communications   489

Summary   490

Critical Incident *A Failure to Communicate*   493

Experiential Exercise *Are You Really Listening?*   494

■ Chapter 16

Organizational Design   498

P&G's Redesign   499

Principles of Organizing   500
  Decentralization versus Centralization 500
  Tall versus Flat Structures 502

OB Focus: Centralized Structure Positions Ford for
Changes in Europe   503
  Unity and Chain of Command 505

The Classical Approach to Organizational Design   506
  An Assessment of Weber's View 507

The Behavioral Approach to Organizational Design   509

An Inside Look: Restructuring for Customer Service — *511*

The Sociotechnical Systems Approach — *511*

A Look at Some Modern Organization Designs — *513*
*Functional Form 513   Product Form 514
Hybrid Form 514*

Summary — *518*

Critical Incident *A Structural Straightjacket at Wild Wear* — *521*

Experiential Exercise *City of Brookside Redesign* — *522*

■ **Chapter 17**

Environmental Forces — *526*

Coping with Peace — *527*

Dimensions of External Environments — *528*
*Simplicity–Complexity 528   Static–Dynamic
529   Environmental Uncertainty 529   The
Population Ecology Perspective 529   The Resource
Dependence Model 532*

Managing the External Environment — *533*
*Establishing Favorable Linkages 533   Controlling
Environmental Domains 533*

An Inside Look: Management Style in a Changing
Environment — *534*

The Contingency View of Organizational Design — *534*

OB Focus: McDonald's in Moscow — *535*
*Burns and Stalker's Mechanistic and Organic
Systems 536   Lawrence and Lorsch's Contingency
Research 537   Woodward's Studies of
Technology 538   Thompson's Typology of
Technology 540*

Structure and Strategy — *540*

Summary — *541*

Critical Incident *Environmental Pressures
Intensify at Health-Rite* — *543*

Experiential Exercise *Assessing Some Dimensions of an
External Environment* — *544*

■ **Chapter 18**

Cultural Influences — *548*

Mistakes Welcome — *549*

Organizational Culture — *550*
*Rituals and Stories 551   The Measurement and
Change of Organizational Culture 551   The
Creation and Maintenance of Organizational Culture 552*

A Framework for Understanding Organizational Culture   *553*

  *Critical Decisions of the Entrepreneur or Founding
  Members 553*

OB Focus: Neurotic Corporations   *554*

  *Guiding Ideas and Mission 554   Social Structure
  554   Norms and Values 555   Remembered
  History and Symbolism 555   Institutionalized
  Arrangements 555*

Culture and Strategy   *555*

Cross-Cultural Research   *556*

  *Cultural Differences 557   Dimensions of Cultural
  Differences 559   Japanese Management 561*

Doing Business Overseas   *563*

An Inside Look: The Perils of Uninformed Travel   *565*

  Methods of Cross-Cultural Training 566

Summary   *568*

Critical Incident *Keeping Things the Same*   *570*

Experiential Exercise *Is Your Culture Gap Showing?*   *571*

■ Chapter 19

*Managing Organizational Change and
Development*   *578*

Life Cycles of an Organization   *579*

Sources of Change   *580*

Organizational Growth and Decline   *581*

  *Growth through Creativity 581   Growth through
  Direction 582   Growth through Delegation 582
  Growth through Coordination 583   Continued
  Growth through Collaboration 583*

OB Focus: Ethics in Managing Decline   *584*

Critical Determinants of Organizational Success and
Failure   *585*

  *Factors That Lead to Success 586   Factors That
  Lead to Failure 586*

An Inside Look: Coping with Technological Change   *587*

Organizational Development   *588*

  *Phases in the OD Process 588   Resistance to
  Change 589   Determining Whether an
  Organization Is Ready for Change 590   OD
  Techniques 590   Conditions for the Successful
  Adoption of OD 593*

Evaluating OD Interventions   *594*

Does OD Work?   *598*

OD in Perspective   *599*

Summary 601

Critical Incident *Staunch Resistance at Metropolitan Police Department* 604

Experiential Exercise *Introducing a Change—A Role Play* 606

Video Cases *Lakeway Resort 608   Moscow McDonald's Golden Arches: Gateway to the West 610*

Glossary 615
Name Index 629
Subject Index 635
Organization Index 643

I

Introduction to Organizational Behavior

■ **Chapter 1**
An Introduction to Organizational Behavior:
Overview and Origins

■ **Chapter 2**
Approaches to Studying Organizational Behavior

Management is the
art of getting other
people to do all the
work.

—Anonymous

Learning Objectives

After studying this chapter, you should be able to:

1. *Define the purpose and nature of the field of organizational behavior.*

2. *Tell why organizational behavior is an important field of study for managers.*

3. *Distinguish organizational behavior from organizational theory, human resources management, and organizational development.*

4. *Cite several significant applications of behavioral principles that occurred before 1900.*

5. *Outline the basic principles of scientific management and discuss the shortcomings of this approach to dealing with worker behavior.*

6. *Relate the findings of the Hawthorne Studies to the development of the human relations approach.*

7. *Explain why believers in the contingency approach rarely give a simple answer to a seemingly simple question.*

8. *Respond to critics who contend that most principles of organizational behavior are obvious and based on common sense.*

An Introduction to Organizational Behavior
Overview and Origins

■ Building a Better Organization

What is the best way to manage an organization? Someone is always ready with an answer. In the early part of this century, it was popular to think of running a business as more of a science than an art. Some managers adopted the principles of Frederick Winslow Taylor, who popularized time-and-motion studies. These people used observation, experimentation, and specific reasoning plus quantitative analysis to make their businesses more productive. Many of these managers also found themselves bogged down in the paperwork of this so-called "scientific management."

Then the pendulum began to swing. The 1960s saw the rise of people-oriented management theories. For example, trainers proposed to teach managers sensitivity and self-awareness by bringing together a group of people with no leader or agenda and waiting to see what would happen.

As a new, young manager for Pillsbury, John Clemens attended a T-Group (or training group) session with about 20 colleagues. Clemens recalls that their trainer, a psychiatrist, told them to sit on the floor and to remove their ties, shoes, and name tags. Then someone turned out the lights. Says Clemens, "We began crawling on the floor in the dark when I bumped into our president. It was atrocious. We would have done better by ourselves, figuring out how to sell more brownie mix."

Other theorists have attempted to help companies make the most of their human resources. Some executives have become concerned that employees keep fit in order to perform their best. For example, PA Executive Search Group tells potential clients that managers who smoke cost their companies $4,000 a year in higher absenteeism and lower productivity. In the face of such numbers, it is no wonder that companies have tried instituting wellness programs that encourage employees to eat right, exercise, and quit smoking. The question is whether the companies stay with these programs until they get results. Robert G. Cox, PA Executive Search's president, estimates that a wellness program "probably has a two-to-three-year life cycle."

A currently popular approach to running a company is to focus on its "organizational culture," that is, the values, goals, rituals, and heroes that characterize the company's style. Allan A. Kennedy, author of *Corporate Cultures*, tells of the enthusiasm his ideas have generated. He delivered a talk on organizational cultures to the top executives of an industrial-service corporation. At the dinner following the talk, the company chairman exclaimed, "This culture stuff is great!" Turning to the company president, the chairman added, "I want a culture by Monday."

Scientific management, T-Groups, wellness programs, and organizational culture are only a few of the many ways people have tried to understand and improve the workings of organizations.

Where does a manager begin to sort out all these ideas? Perhaps the best place is with an understanding of the general principles of organizational behavior. This chapter will introduce you to what organizational behavior is all about and how it can help managers be more effective.

Source: John A. Byrne, "Business Fads: What's In — And Out," *Business Week*, January 20, 1986, 52–55, 58, 60, 61.

What Is Organizational Behavior?

All of us have wondered why some people succeed and others fail in the world of work. Most of us have also marveled at how some people seem to possess a bottomless well of enthusiasm for their work, while others regard their work as something slightly better than torture. Although most of us often do nothing more than speculate on the factors that affect our work lives, behavioral scientists have established a relatively new field of inquiry concerned with the scientific study of the behavioral processes that occur in work settings, the field of *organizational behavior*. The content of this field is quite broad. It encompasses such topics as employee attitudes, motivation, and performance, to name a few. And it extends to larger organizational and societal factors, such as the structure of organizations and environmental pressures, that influence an individual's behavior and attitudes.

The field of organizational behavior borrows many concepts and methods from the behavioral and social sciences, such as psychology, sociology, political science, and anthropology, because all are relevant to understanding people's behavior in organizational settings. Consequently, issues and topics touching on many academic disciplines may become the subject of study in the field of organizational behavior. Thus, in the course of this book, we will examine sociological topics, such as the importance of organizational structure; psychological questions, such as the importance of personality factors in explaining employee behavior; anthropological concerns with the meaning and influence of culture; and political science topics, such as the distribution and use of power in an organization. In general, however, organizational behavior draws most heavily from the field of psychology. In fact, many of the major theorists in the field are psychologists (e.g., Maslow, Herzberg, and Skinner).

Why Bother? Or Three Reasons for Studying Organizational Behavior

Practical Applications

There are important practical benefits to understanding the principles of organizational behavior. For example, the development of a personal style of leadership can be guided by knowledge of the results of studies that have attempted to relate leadership style to situational requirements (Chapter 10). The choice of a problem-solving strategy (Chapter 11) or the selection of an appropriate employee appraisal format (Chapter 8) can be guided by an understanding of the results of studies in the associated topic areas. Especially in the area of performance enhancement (Chapters 5 to 7), there are benefits to be gained by applying the knowledge that has been gathered in the field of organizational behavior.

It is difficult to overstate the practical importance of being able to deal effectively with others in organizational settings. Attracting and developing talented individuals are two critically important issues to the survival and prosperity of an organization. Emphasis on the *human element* (instead of on technical, financial, and other tangible resources) often separates competing organizations when it comes to organizational performance. This occurs be- cause all serious competitors in a given industry are likely to have attained nearly the same level of technical sophistication. Thus, other things being equal, organizations that have talented and dedicated employees are likely to be more effective. Furthermore, within a given industry, the variability on human dimensions across organizations is likely to be greater than the variabil- ity on technical dimensions. Consequently, we can argue that the element that is most important to an organization's welfare — and the one that may be most neglected because of its less tangible nature — is the behavioral element.

As an illustration of how crucial the human element is to organizational excellence, consider the various professional football teams. All have much the same equipment and facilities. For example, each team has a stadium, a staff of trainers, practice facilities, state-of-the-art equipment, and the like. In addi- tion, each team has the same number of members and essentially the same structure. Therefore, what distinguishes one team from another in the eyes of sports enthusiasts and on the record book is largely traceable to the human element: the talent of the players and coaches, the ability of coaches to develop their players' talents, and the ability of the coaches and players to motivate themselves to high levels of accomplishment.

A similar illustration can be made for the reputations of universities and colleges. Generally speaking, colleges that seek to have prestigious reputations have much the same facilities (e.g., classrooms, dormitories, and attractive landscaping). However, those institutions having faculty members who possess strong reputations in their fields and students who are more competitively admitted have more solid reputations. The separation of institutions on the dimension of reputation is based largely on the human element.

Personal Growth

The second reason for studying organizational behavior is the personal fulfill- ment we gain from understanding our fellow humans. Understanding others may also lead to greater self-knowledge and self-insight. Such personal growth is an aspect of education that is often cited as the greatest benefit of studying the liberal arts and sciences. Some may question the practical value of this feature in the business world. But it can, in fact, make a difference when it comes to advancing beyond an entry-level position. Entry-level hirings are based largely on technical competency, such as certification in a specialized area by a BBA, CPA, or MBA. Promotions, however, are often based on more than mere technical competency. They are often based on demonstrated abilities to understand and work effectively with superiors, peers, and subordinates. In short, an understanding of organizational behavior may not be a "union card" that helps you get your first job in any obvious way, but it will be invaluable to you once you have that first job and seek to distinguish yourself.

Students who are taking an introductory organizational behavior (OB) course should understand that the purpose of such a course is to provide a framework into which later personal organizational experiences can be integrated. The course material, therefore, forms a foundation for increasing the extent to which they can learn from experience. In short, *what* one learns in an OB course is not as critical as *how* the course prepares one to learn (and thereby to grow) in an organization. The material in an OB course is relevant to personal growth whether one works for a large, established corporation (such as a General Motors, an IBM, or a Du Pont) or a relatively small, fledgling organization.

As a field, organizational behavior is constantly opening new frontiers of knowledge. Most of the researchers in the field are young and recently trained. In fact, it is a fairly safe bet that the vast majority of professionals who have ever claimed an affiliation with the field of organizational behavior are still alive today. Many of the journals that publish the findings of OB research are relatively new. As you will notice in reading this text, the dates of the studies that are cited are all fairly recent, covering only the last few decades. Yet the widespread acceptance of organizational behavior as an important subject for future managers is evidenced by the fact that an OB course is included in the curriculum of virtually every business school.

Increased Knowledge

The third goal of organizational behavior is to gather knowledge about people in work settings. At a minimum, the field seeks to gather knowledge for its own sake. As evidenced by the progress of many "pure science" fields, such as physics, space research, and chemistry, the practical use of certain findings may not be apparent for years.

A similar process occurs in the field of organizational behavior. For example, early research on leadership processes identified two major dimensions of leadership (to be discussed fully in Chapter 10). Training specialists who followed this research came to apply the findings in the design of the leadership training programs that are now offered to organizations.

Organizational Behavior and Its Related Fields

Larry Cummings, a professor at the University of Minnesota, contends that organizational behavior can be distinguished from related fields.[1] **Organizational behavior** is the systematic study of the behavior and attitudes of both individuals and groups within organizations. This may be termed a micro-level perspective. At the micro level, an organization's organizationwide attributes, such as size and structure, are usually taken as givens that have uniform effects

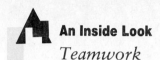

An Inside Look
Teamwork

Two interesting teamwork stories come from First Security Service Co., a bank based in Salt Lake City, and Milbar Corp., a Chagrin Falls, Ohio, manufacturer of specialty mechanics hand tools.

First Security instituted a product-knowledge competition called "SuperKnowledge." Two hundred teams and 3,000 employees in bank branches in the western United States were involved. Each branch had at least one team. Employees studied product-knowledge materials that enabled them to refer customers to salespeople. Then, each week, the team had to handle phoned-in questions about bank policies, products, and sales skills.

Participation in the contest was gradually narrowed down to area, division, and state competitions. Each winner of the final contest

received $500, with preliminary prizes awarded throughout the competition. First Security reports that employee response to the contest was enthusiastic. Employees studied, held side competitions, and even gave parties devoted to question-and-answer practice.

Milbar Corp. used teams in a somewhat different way. Jack A. Bares, the company's president, had been struggling with two difficult problems: (1) how to reduce the production costs of one of the company's most popular tools, specialized pliers that were losing market share to cheaper pliers made in Asia, and (2) how to develop hand tools that could effectively penetrate international markets.

Bares turned his problems into a contest. He created four teams,

each composed of six employees from the design, engineering, production, quality control, and accounting departments. Two teams were assigned to address each problem. At the end of the contest, the company held a banquet for the teams, at which a plaque and $50 were awarded to each winning team member.

Again, the response was enthusiastic. Team members met two or three times each week to brainstorm, and some worked nights and weekends. Reports Bares, "There was a phenomenal amount of team spirit. It got so competitive that some team members were actually spreading 'disinformation' around to confuse their rivals." Perhaps most important, the winning teams came up with ideas that are vital to the company's survival.

Sources: "In-House Product Promotion Turns Tellers into Sellers of Bank Services," *Marketing News*, July 4, 1986, 7; John F. Persinos, "Double Teaming," *Inc.*, May 1984, 206.

on behavior in a particular situation. The focus or unit of analysis for the micro perspective is primarily the individual.

Organizational theory focuses on the organization as the unit of analysis. Organizational attributes, such as goals, technology, and culture, are the objects of study. Organizational theory often uses an across-organizations approach, or macro-level perspective, in gathering new knowledge. Organizational behavior and organizational theory use distinctly different research methods. Organizational behavior usually relies on laboratory and field experimentation for gathering information, while organizational theory tends to rely more on surveys and case studies. Nonetheless, it would be an oversimplification to assume that organizational behavior is oriented solely to understanding individual behavior, just as it would be a mistake to conclude that organizational theory is concerned exclusively with theory.

The field of **human resources management** (or personnel management) attempts to apply the principles of the behavioral sciences in the workplace.

■   **Figure 1.1**

Four Fields in the Organizational Sciences

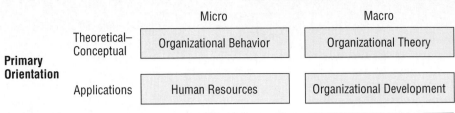

While organizational behavior is somewhat more concept oriented, human resources management is more concerned with applied techniques and behavioral technology. Human resources management tries to provide a link between the individual and the organization by designing and implementing systems for attracting, developing, and motivating individuals within an organization.

Organizational development is concerned with the introduction of successful changes in organizations. Organizational development specialists sometimes approach the task of change from a macro perspective focusing on changing the structure and values of the organization. Ultimately, these efforts are intended to enhance organizational effectiveness.

One can distinguish organizational behavior from other closely related fields by its emphasis on the scientific study of behavioral phenomena at the individual and group levels. Organizational theory focuses largely on organizational and environmental phenomena, human resources management focuses on the application of behavioral knowledge in selecting and placing personnel, and organizational development focuses on enhancing organizational performance. A useful but perhaps somewhat oversimplified way of understanding these four fields is to distinguish among them on two dimensions: the micro versus macro level of analysis, and theory versus application. A consideration of the combinations that result from crossing these two dimensions suggests that organizational behavior is a "micro/theory-oriented" field, human resources management is a "micro/application-oriented" field, organizational theory is a "macro/theory-oriented" field, and organizational development is a "macro/application-oriented" field. (Figure 1.1 summarizes the results of a crossing of these two dimensions.) In this text, you will notice that the related fields of organizational theory, human resources management, and organizational development will also be occasionally discussed.

In summary, the field of organizational behavior is characterized by *diversity*, as a consequence of drawing from many different disciplines; *newness*, as evidenced by its relatively recent emergence on the scientific scene; and *vitality*, as demonstrated by the growing number of members in the field, the growth of new publications, and the intensity of scientific debate within the field.

■ **Figure 1.2**

Major Periods in the Development of the Field of Organizational Behavior

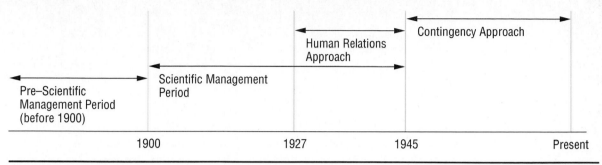

Studying the Behavior of People at Work: Past and Present

Today, organizational behavior is a growing field that is rich in its variety of approaches. It is interesting to examine the various ways of viewing worker behavior that have emerged over the years (Figure 1.2). Taking a historical perspective on attitudes toward worker behavior helps us both to understand where organizational behavior stands today and to visualize the directions it may take in the future.

Pre–Scientific Management Period (Before 1900)

Perhaps the earliest application of a behavioral principle occurred during prehistoric times, when the principle of division of labor was probably applied for the first time. Anthropologists suggest that one of the simplest devices for improving a family unit's chances of survival lies in assigning specialized roles to individuals who are best able to perform them. Consequently, it is likely that sex-typed behaviors emerged during the prehistoric era in response to certain biological necessities. While the women stayed back to guard the campsite and children, the men took the role of chasing game.*

The earliest written evidence of a deliberate concern about managing workers' behavior appears in accounts provided by the Chinese and Mesopotamians between 3000 and 4000 B.C., relating to the importance of the specialization of labor and hierarchy of authority. Unfortunately, these writings do not provide a cumulative body of knowledge that would benefit today's managers.[2] Similarly, the ancient Romans wrote about the results of their efforts to reorganize the lines of communication in the legions and to decentralize decision making in an empire of over 50 million people.[3] These reports suggest that the problems of effectively managing people are perennial and that humans have long felt the need to develop a systemized body of knowledge about such

---

* With a high rate of infant mortality and little or no knowledge of contraception, a state of virtual perpetual pregnancy also probably hindered female mobility.

■ **Table 1.1**

Some Important Events During the
Pre–Scientific Management Period

Approximate Year	Individual or Group	Major Managerial Contributions
5000 B.C.	Sumerians	Record keeping
4000 B.C.	Egyptians	Recognition of need for fair play in management; allowing workers to vent complaints
1800 B.C.	Hammurabi	Establishment of minimum wage
400 B.C.	Cyrus	Use of motion study, layout, materials handling
A.D. 20	Jesus Christ	Golden Rule, human relations perspective
late 1400s	Venetians	Numbering of inventoried parts, interchangeability of parts, assembly-line technique, inventory control
1776	Adam Smith	Application of principle of specialization to manufacturing workers
1832	Charles Babbage	Time-and-motion study, division of labor, effects of colors on employee efficiency
1881	Joseph Wharton	Established college course in business management

Source: Claude S. George, *The History of Management Thought,* Englewood Cliffs, N.J., Prentice-Hall, 1972.

issues.† Table 1.1 lists some important contributions to management during the pre-scientific era.

Historical documents do not provide much further insight on managing others until the time of Nicolo Machiavelli, a sixteenth-century Italian philosopher and politician. Machiavelli is probably best known for his suggestions of extreme political pragmatism. He endorsed such ethically questionable principles as the "ends justify the means." Machiavelli's place in history is nonetheless secure in that he called attention to the use of deception in manipulating others for one's own purposes. In Chapter 9, we will examine more closely some of Machiavelli's notions.

At much the same time that Machiavelli was writing his treatises on political realism, an important event took place in Venice. The then-powerful city-state created a shipyard for building and refitting its naval war fleet. The arsenal at Venice became one of the largest industrial plants of the time (see Figure 1.3). Due to its size, its managers developed a focus on efficiency; in fact, many of their methods would be familiar to modern businesspeople. For example, the Venetians devised an assembly-line system that is roughly similar to modern assembly lines. Galleys were sailed up canals, which were bordered by warehouses that were stocked with the necessary equipment for refitting a damaged galley or building a new one. As a galley was sailed past each warehouse, the appropriate fittings were brought out and immediately attached. In

† It is interesting to note that the earliest recorded labor dispute concerned monotony of diet and working conditions in ancient Egypt (1153 B.C.), while the earliest recorded strike, which concerned meal breaks, was led by an orchestra leader named Aristos in ancient Rome (309 B.C.).[4]

■ **Figure 1.3**

The Arsenal at Venice

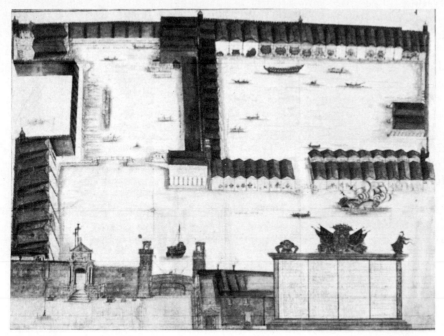

From a watercolor plan by Antonio di Natale. The largest industrial complex in
Europe at the time, the arsenal employed 5,000 workers and sheltered 150 galleys.

Source: Pegli Museo Navale.

addition to devising an early form of assembly line, the Venetians introduced
routine beverage breaks for their personnel: wine was provided six times a
day.‡ They used a merit-rating plan to review employees' contributions and to
assign pay raises based on performance. They also invented new accounting
systems to keep track of all expenditures and systems for controlling inventory.
Unfortunately, many of the Venetians' innovations were not widely adopted at
the time (except for their advances in accounting, which spread throughout
Europe). The notion of a *formal* beverage break for workers was not reintroduced until the twentieth century.

Scientific Management (1900–1945)

The Industrial Revolution of the nineteenth century brought about many radical changes in the management of workers. In contrast to the work of crafts-
people of prior times, work became centrally located in factories. Also, jobs

‡ Because of this frequent use of wine, it is likely that the quality of work done on ships toward the
end of the day was less than the quality of work done earlier in the day.

required less skill because machines controlled production processes. Though production increased dramatically, other results of these sweeping changes were not all positive. Some writers, most notably Adam Smith and Karl Marx, pointed out that simplification of work processes beyond a certain point could have diminishing returns and produce feelings of alienation in workers.

Although we recognize the significance of these criticisms of work simplification today, the industrialists of the early twentieth century were not yet ready to do so. They preferred an engineering approach to managing worker behavior called **scientific management**. Scientific management, which was developed by Frederick Taylor, called for the careful analysis of tasks and time-and-motion studies in conjunction with piece-rate pay schemes in order to improve productivity.§ Believers in scientific management searched for the "one best way" to perform a task. They introduced standard parts and procedures. In the extreme, the scientific management approach subscribes to the belief that one single best solution exists for a given situation.

The scientific management approach to dealing with worker behavior has been criticized on a number of counts. A major shortcoming is that much time and effort must be devoted to establishing work standards, closely monitoring many aspects of the work process, and calculating rates of pay. The cost of these activities may offset the expected benefits. A further problem lies in worker resistance to attempts to measure effort and productivity. This resistance may be manifested in slowdowns when workers are aware that they are being observed.

Workers also oppose changes in pay schemes because they suspect that the new rates may be designed to speed up production. For example, Taylor advocated pay schemes that only gave workers a maximum wage increase of roughly 60 percent regardless of how much worker productivity increased. Taylor's 1911 description of his handling of a worker at the Bethlehem Steel Works provides an illustration of the inequity that can result from such a pay scheme.[5] The job of Schmidt, a pig-iron handler, was to move large, 100-pound slabs ("pigs") of iron from a loading dock onto a railroad car (Figure 1.4). While employed by Bethlehem Steel as a consultant, Taylor designed an incentive pay scheme (coupled with rest periods) that encouraged Schmidt to haul substantially more iron in a given day. Schmidt responded to the incentive plan by raising his efforts so that his wages increased from $1.15 per day to $1.85 per day. In order to obtain this higher wage, Schmidt hauled $47\frac{1}{2}$ tons of iron per day, whereas he had previously hauled only $12\frac{1}{2}$ tons of iron per day. The inequity that exists in this situation can be understood by calculating and comparing the relative percentage increases in pay and productivity. Schmidt's pay increased 61 percent while his productivity increased 280 percent. Clearly, the company was benefiting more from Schmidt's increased productivity than was Schmidt himself. Taylor's belief that workers should be limited to a 60 percent increase in wages was based on his assumption that greater rewards would make workers more defiant and difficult to manage. This conclusion

§ In addition to his contributions to time-and-motion study, Fred Taylor was also the U.S. tennis doubles champion in 1881.

■ **Figure 1.4**

Bethlehem Steel Pig-Iron Handlers

Source: Courtesy of Bethlehem Steel.

was based not on scientifically gathered evidence but on untested personal assumptions about human nature. Furthermore, Taylor believed that management was entitled to substantial profits because management bore the responsibility and costs of designing new production techniques.

Taylor's concepts of time-and-motion studies, elemental analysis of tasks, and standards for productivity were partly a reflection of his training as an engineer. A legacy of these concepts is that many jobs are still designed with the goal of maximizing short-run efficiency. The negative implications of workers performing simplified, repetitive tasks did not concern the advocates of scientific management.**

Human Relations Approach (1927–1945): The Hawthorne Studies

During the same period that scientific management was popular, another largely separate school of thought emerged, the **human relations approach**. The human relations approach, which partially grew out of the field of psychology, emphasized the importance of motivation and attitudes in explaining worker behavior. The approach drew much of its strength and following from the results of a series of studies conducted at the Hawthorne plant of the

** As a counterpoint to these criticisms, some recent writers have argued that Taylor has been much maligned and that his techniques of time study, standardization, goal setting, and monetary incentives may have been based on fundamentally correct concepts for dealing with numerous situations.[6]

Western Electric Company, located in the western suburbs of Chicago. The **Hawthorne Studies** were begun in 1927 and spanned 12 years.[7] The Hawthorne experiments were important because they demonstrated that in addition to the job itself certain factors can influence workers' behavior. Informal social groups, management-employee relations, and the interrelatedness among the many facets of work settings were found to be quite influential.

The Hawthorne Studies represented a major step forward in the attempt to systematically study worker behavior. Although the studies can be grouped into at least five major efforts or divisions, three are of particular interest: the Illumination Experiments, the Relay Assembly Room Study, and the Bank Wiring Room Study.

The Illumination Experiments   In the **Illumination Experiments**, the researchers investigated the effects of increased illumination on worker productivity. At the time, electric lighting was becoming more widely available in factories, and a scientifically based demonstration of the beneficial effects of lighting was desired by both managers and researchers. In one illumination experiment, one group of workers were selected to work under a constant intensity of light while three other groups worked under varying intensities of light. The results were surprising in that both the group under a uniform intensity and the test groups showed appreciable gains in productivity. In one extreme condition, the illumination intensity was reduced to the equivalent of working by moonlight. Despite this apparent handicap, the workers maintained production levels and reported no eyestrain and less fatigue than they had when working in a more illuminated condition.

Because these results defied reason, the researchers considered the possibility that something besides light intensity had affected the workers' reactions. To find out what other factors could have influenced the outcomes, the researchers designed a yet more elaborate series of studies.

The Relay Assembly Room Study   In the **Relay Assembly Room Study**, a small group of female employees was taken from its regular workplace and assigned to assemble small telephone relays in an arrangement that was very similar to that of the actual Relay Assembly Department. The decision to separate the women from the remainder of the work force was based on the researchers' desire to maintain total control over the experimental working environment. Of special interest to the investigators was whether changes in the work setting would influence the women's productivity. Among the changes that the investigators tried were the introduction of rest periods, a free midmorning lunch, a workday that was a half-hour shorter, a five-day workweek (an idea that was novel at that time), and variations in methods of payment.

The researchers hoped that their studies would show that the introduction of 15-minute rest periods produced a 10 percent increase in productivity, while a five-day workweek decreased productivity by 16 percent, and so on. But once again, the results were perplexing. Instead of finding that some conditions increased productivity while others decreased it, the researchers found that productivity followed a gradual upward trend over the course of the entire study, regardless of the condition instituted. In addition, when the women were in the test room, their rate of absenteeism was lower than in their original job setting.

These results, as well as the results of the illumination studies, led the Hawthorne researchers to consider the psychological aspects of the work setting in addition to its more objective features. Careful analysis suggested that the positive outcomes were partially attributable to the fact that the workers enjoyed the attention and recognition that the researchers had been showing them. For example, during the illumination studies, the workers commented favorably on all the changes that were made in the lighting. And in the relay assembly test room, the workers displayed positive attitudes toward the entire research enterprise. In response to the favorable treatment that they received in the test situations, compared to the usual treatment of workers in that era,†† the workers reciprocated by providing the results that they thought the researchers wanted. This phenomenon, in which the alteration of social and psychological aspects of a work setting results in enhanced performance largely because the employees realize they are being observed, has been termed the **Hawthorne effect**. The Hawthorne effect often explains many instances in which the mere study of people at work, in and of itself, can be responsible for an observed set of results.‡‡

The Bank Wiring Room Study Another important Hawthorne study, the **Bank Wiring Room Study**, sought to gather more information about the social nature of work groups. For this study, a group of 14 men who wired telephone banks was observed in a standard shop condition (Figure 1.5). An observer was stationed in the room with instructions to take continuous notes on the workers' actions. The observer was not allowed to give orders or become involved in conversations with the workers. Although the workers were initially very apprehensive about the observer, they settled into more natural and relaxed behavior after roughly three weeks. Because the foreman for the work group also supervised other workers in another room, and because the observer was deliberately unobtrusive, the workers were relatively free from constant supervision.

Although the workers were paid according to their output, the observer soon noted that the workers had established an informal daily norm of 6,600

†† In a follow-up interview conducted in the 1970s with one of the women who actually participated in the study, it was reported that it was not uncommon at that time for supervisors to punish a group of operators who failed to meet their assigned standard. One form of this punishment consisted of not permitting the operators to use the elevators.

‡‡ Recently, there has been much debate over whether the actual results of the Hawthorne studies in fact showed substantial and incontrovertible evidence of improved performance due to the workers' being observed.[8] The criticisms stem partly from the lack of extremely tight controls in the study (e.g., some of the workers who were studied initially were replaced by other workers for various reasons during the long course of the study). Nonetheless, the vast majority of scholars who study organizational behavior accept the general conclusions of the Hawthorne researchers and acknowledge the likely existence of such a phenomenon as the Hawthorne effect.

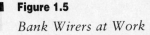

■ **Figure 1.5**

Bank Wirers at Work

Source: Reprinted by permission of Pitman Publishing Ltd., London.

units per person. Typically, the men would pace their work so that they reached the norm near the end of the day. Of course, some of the men could do more than 6,600 units. But if they indicated that they would prefer to be more productive, they risked becoming the victims of various schemes for controlling production.

The two most frequent schemes consisted of minor verbal and physical harassment. Verbal harassment took the form of name calling. More productive individuals were labeled "speed king," "company man," and "Phar Lap" (a prize-winning racehorse of the time).

Physical harassment sometimes took the form of a game called "binging." A "bing" was a sharp blow to the muscle of the upper arm. The game of binging would be played in rounds. At first, one worker would hit a very productive individual on the arm. As the fellow who was struck was obligated to defend his manhood, he would hit the aggressor back in a like manner. The aggressor would then strike the victim on the same arm as before, and so on. After several rounds of exchanging blows to each other's arms, the two would eventually stop from exhaustion or pain. The game was always carried off in a good-natured fashion. And after it was finished, the two participants would usually laugh and make friendly remarks about the power of each other's punches.

Binging served several purposes for those who wished to see production restricted in the work unit. First, the game interrupted the production routine within the group at the same time that it disrupted the routine of the highly productive individual. It created an additional hindrance for the productive individual in that he had to finish the rest of the workday with a sore arm. The alleged good humor of the game was also an important element. The aggressor always offered his friendship at the conclusion of the contest. This friendship could then be used as the basis for further attempts to influence the ambitious worker to restrict his efforts. If the contest ended on a bitter note, the door would be closed to future attempts to dissuade the worker via verbal or physical methods.

In other observations, the Hawthorne researchers noted that a social order existed within the work unit that was based on clique membership rather than job function. Cliques could be identified by their membership criteria: one should not be a rate buster (someone who produces too much), a chiseler (someone who produces below the unit's informal work norm), or a squealer (someone who passes to a supervisor information that could harm a co-worker). In short, an intricate social arrangement was identified within the work unit that maintained its existence through such mechanisms as ridicule, sarcasm, and binging.

Many scholars believe that the Hawthorne studies show the importance of the social nature of workers. This would seem to contradict the economic or rational approach to worker behavior that is implicit in the principles of scientific management. But just as the scientific management approach possesses problems of application, so does the human relations approach. The greatest difficulties stem from an unproven assumption that is the cornerstone of the human relations approach: the belief that workers who are satisfied with their jobs will feel indebted to their employers and will show their appreciation by being more productive. This suggests a reciprocal relationship between management and labor — that greater concern for improving the condition of workers will pay dividends to employers through greater productivity from happier and more appreciative workers.

Unfortunately, this simple *quid pro quo* relationship has not been firmly established. Studies have not found clear evidence of a relationship between worker satisfaction and productivity.§§ Due to this lack of evidence, it is difficult to endorse the position that managers should worry about their workers' level of contentment in the hope that workers will return the favor. Nonetheless, managers cannot ignore the issue of worker well-being for other solid, defensible reasons, as we shall demonstrate in Chapter 4.

Contingency Approach (1945–Present)

Following World War II, a new perspective on organizational behavior began to develop. Called the **contingency approach**, it acknowledged the difficulty of offering simple general principles to explain or predict behavior in organiza-

---

§§ As we shall see in Chapter 4, the entire issue of the relationship between worker satisfaction and worker productivity is a complex one.

tional settings. Nonetheless, the contingency approach did not abandon the search for principles, but instead sought to specify the conditions under which we can expect to find certain relationships. As such, it represented a search for the factors that would aid in predicting and explaining behavior. Organizational behavior researchers who subscribe to the contingency approach believe that employee behavior is too complex to be explained by only a few simple and straightforward principles. Instead, they seek to identify the factors that are jointly necessary for a given principle to hold. Contingency researchers recognize the *interdependency* of personal and situational factors in the determination of employee behavior.

If you ask a contingency researcher for a simple answer to a seemingly simple question, you should expect to be given a fairly complex and highly qualified answer. Because human behavior is itself complex, a statement of behavioral principles must also be complex.

For example, consider the seemingly simple question, which is the better way to behave as a manager, autocratically or democratically? Contingency researchers would not simply pick one alternative over the other, but would try to identify a set of conditions in which one style of supervision could be expected to yield superior results compared to the other style. They would consider such issues as subordinates' expectations and preferences for different styles of leadership. To be sure, if you are in charge of a band of fascists, your subordinates might well expect and desire that you rule with an iron fist.

Cultural differences would also be taken into account in choosing a style of supervision. For example, in the United States, democratic and participative supervision is endorsed, while an autocratic supervisory style is generally frowned on. But in other countries, a leader who shows empathy and is willing to be influenced by subordinates might be viewed as being weak. In addition, the leader's ability to enact a particular supervisory style would be an important consideration, as would the nature of the task to be performed.

Finally, a contingency researcher would want to know what criteria will be used to measure the success of a leadership style. Will the leader be judged according to subordinates' satisfaction, quantity or quality of unit performance, the leader's satisfaction, organizational survival, or some other criterion?

In most cases, a contingency researcher's answer can be summarized in two words: "It depends." But this two-word answer is not meant to be evasive, as a contingency researcher will then attempt to identify precisely what the important dependencies are. Contingency researchers assume that the number of important dependencies can be specified. On the basis of this, they then search for a valid representation of worker behavior. Today, most specialists in the field of organizational behavior subscribe to the contingency approach. The need to establish the validity of behavioral principles by using a truly scientific approach is also widely accepted. The questions surrounding how one can forcefully make such demonstrations will be the focus of Chapter 2.

It should be noted that the contingency approach did not integrate the two previous approaches, scientific management and human relations, but instead replaced them as the clearly dominant perspective for the study of organizational behavior. The two earlier approaches have not gone the way of the dinosaurs, however. Although the fervor that surrounded them has clearly waned, they still have some advocates. The human relations adherents tend to be associated with a humanistically oriented, altruistic philosophical camp, while the latter-day scientific management advocates are often found in close association with schools of engineering.

Criticisms of the Field

Although the field of organizational behavior is relatively new, it has created quite a bit of controversy, drawing criticism from scholars in the field itself, as well as from students and managers. The fact that organizational behavior generates such debate is evidence that the field is truly alive and developing.

The two most frequent criticisms of organizational behavior as a field of study are raised by students in introductory courses. They often say that much of what they learned in their organizational behavior course is fairly obvious and that most of it could be derived from common sense. We will consider each of these comments in turn.

It's So Obvious

The observation that most of the content of organizational behavior is obvious usually arises in response to reading the results of studies that have been conducted in the field. For example, consider the following behavioral principles that have frequently been demonstrated in behavioral studies: "Rewarding workers on the basis of their past performance is likely to improve their subsequent performance," or "An employee will tend to like a coworker who has indicated a liking for her or him."*** Some people may think that these statements are ridiculously self-evident and that anyone could make these observations without going through the trouble of scientific studies. And since any one of us could predict such principles, why bother to develop a field around such clichés?

To examine the criticism that organizational researchers do little more than restate the obvious, consider the following case. As part of the effort to win World War II, the U.S. Army set up a research branch of the War Department. During the course of the war, the research branch conducted several hundred studies on such issues as soldiers' attitudes, morale, and feelings of frustration. In the process, over 600,000 soldiers were interviewed. The results of these studies were so extensive that their final summary required four volumes. When these volumes were finally published in 1949, they were widely criticized in the popular press. One criticism was that many of the findings were terribly obvious. For example, a major conclusion of the report was that many soldiers were unhappy during the war. This conclusion seemed so self-

*** These statements are variations on the "law of effect" and "the reciprocity principle of interpersonal attraction."

evident that it raised questions about the legitimacy of investing energy and time in attitude surveys that generate such obvious findings.

In a review of the four-volume work, Paul Lazarsfeld, a sociologist, provided a brief list of typical findings.[9] How would you rate the novelty of each of the following statements taken from his review?

1.   As long as the war continued, enlisted men were more desirous of returning home to the United States than they were after the collapse of the Nazi regime. (Would anyone be surprised to find that soldiers do not want to be killed?)

2.   Soldiers from the southern states were better able to tolerate the tropical climate in the South Pacific than were soldiers from the northern states. (Given differences in upbringing and adjustment to climate, this too could be easily predicted.)

3.   White enlisted men were more desirous of promotions than were black enlisted men. (Given the lack of real opportunities for blacks in the U.S. military at that time, this is not unexpected.)

4.   Highly educated men had more difficulty adjusting to army life, especially as manifested by minor psychological disorders, than did men who were less well educated. (The highly cerebral individual might easily be expected to have difficulty adjusting to a situation requiring obedience and unquestioning acceptance of a difficult daily regimen.)

5.   Blacks from the southern states preferred to serve under white officers who were also from the southern states, versus officers from the northern states. (Similarity in backgrounds and values could easily explain this result.)

6.   Soldiers who had grown up in rural areas were better able to adjust to army life than were soldiers from urban areas. (Sleeping under the stars might be a difficult adjustment for someone who had rarely, if ever, stepped off a slab of concrete.)

If we acknowledge the obvious nature of these findings, we must question the entire enterprise of research on people in organizational settings. If these are the basic data that serve to develop principles in the field, then the average person is already fairly sophisticated about organizational behavior.

These statements would be true except for one important fact. The previous list presents the exact *opposite* of the actual findings. In truth, soldiers preferred to remain overseas until the war was concluded and wanted to return home afterwards. Southerners had no greater tolerance for the heat of the South Pacific, blacks were more desirous of promotion, poorly educated men had more difficulties in adjusting to army life, and so forth. In each instance, we can now generate an explanation that once again is seemingly obvious. For example, the soldiers' desire to remain overseas could be explained by their commitment to completing the war effort and by their patriotism, while homesickness became strong after their mission was complete; blacks were more desirous of promotion because they were relatively deprived of opportunities as a group; and so on. Had the true findings been presented initially, our reaction would be that they too were obvious.

The notion that behavioral phenomena are obvious is therefore something of a delusion. It may well be that when we are presented with a statement concerning human behavior, we engage in a defensive reaction in which we state, "Oh sure, I would have guessed it." This reaction may be very self-satisfying (after all, it suggests we are well in control of our surroundings), but clearly it also can be very much in error. As every manner of human behavior is at least conceivable, we must not fall into the trap of self-deception by relying on intuition and armchair theorizing in place of an empirical search for evidence. Also, we must search for the joint factors, both personal and situational, that are responsible for a particular regularity in human behavior. Healthy skepticism is necessary because nearly every explanation of human behavior, regardless of its truth or falsity, can be dismissed as obvious after we have heard it.

It's Only Common Sense

The criticism that much of organizational behavior is deducible from common sense is also without foundation. Consider that common sense is, when you cite examples, reducible to a series of widely accepted truisms. If you follow the tenets of common sense, you presumably will make judgments based on the collected wisdom of past generations. But, over the years, this collected wisdom has generated a truism for every conceivable situation, so that common sense can be cited as the basis for following contradictory courses of action.

For example, consider a hiring decision involving several competing applicants. Common sense would advise that you thoroughly investigate the credentials of all candidates: "Look before you leap." Therefore, let us assume that you prolong your search until you have more data on the candidates. In the meantime, your two best candidates take offers from other companies. Your taking time to gather more information can then be criticized for violating another common-sense truism: "He who hesitates is lost." Since common sense places its bets on both sides of an issue, it can be easily cited, *after* the fact, to explain any success or failure. Consequently, common sense has no value as a means of predicting future events because it never backs one outcome over another.†††

As further evidence of this point, consider the following pairs of commonsense truisms:

1a. If at first you don't succeed, try, try again.
 b. Don't beat your head against a brick wall.

2a. You're never too old to learn.
 b. You can't teach an old dog new tricks.

---

††† For a more esoteric examination of the relationships between the behavioral sciences and common sense, see Note 10.

OB Focus

Discipline with a Twist

Some approaches to management don't seem reasonable at first glance. For example, John Huberman, a Canadian industrial psychologist, promotes the idea of giving problem employees a day off.

Does that sound like a reward for poor behavior? When Bruce Withers, a construction worker for the highway department in Pinellas County, Florida, was given a paid day off to think about his absenteeism, he didn't think so. "I was embarrassed in front of everyone," he says. "I didn't want that to happen again." He mended his ways. Since his experience, Withers has received two promotions and a 50 percent raise.

This is how this unusual discipline technique works: The problem employee first gets an oral "reminder" (not called a reprimand). If that doesn't work, the supervisor tries a written reminder. Finally, if the employee's behavior does not improve, the company gives the employee a paid day off. The day is called a decision-making leave day, and the employee is supposed to use it to decide whether to shape up or leave. After the leave day, the employee must agree, usually in writing, to be on his or her best behavior for the next year. If the employee does not agree, he or she is then fired.

A number of companies have adopted this approach in the hope

that it will improve morale and reduce turnover. Tampa Electric Co. reports that in its first eight years of using this approach to discipline, more employees have improved than have left the company. When Frito-Lay Inc. adopted such a program, terminations at the company's plant fell from 58 to 19 per year.

Dean Broome, manager of a Tampa Electric power station, likes the approach's results. He tried giving a lazy mechanic a day off to decide whether he wanted to keep his job. Says Broome of the mechanic, "We sure got his attention. He turned around on his own."

Source: Laurie Baum, "Punishing Workers with a Day Off," *Business Week,* June 16, 1986, 80.

3a. Nothing ventured, nothing gained.
 b. It's better to be safe than sorry.

4a. Nice guys finish last.
 b. Do unto others as you would have others do unto you.

5a. Haste makes waste.
 b. Time waits for no one.

6a. Out of sight, out of mind.
 b. Absence makes the heart grow fonder.

7a. Two heads are better than one.
 b. Too many cooks spoil the broth.‡‡‡

A Framework for Studying Organizational Behavior

In practice, managers and researchers who are interested in organizational behavior tend to group issues and topics within a number of more or less common categories, such as performance appraisal, communication, attitudes,

‡‡‡ Psychologist Karl Halvor Teigen created a clever experiment wherein he converted 24 proverbs into their opposites. For example, "Fear is stronger than love" became "Love is stronger than fear," and "Truth needs no colors" became "Truth needs colors." Students given lists containing some authentic proverbs and some reversed proverbs judged both sets to be equally true.[11]

■ Figure 1.6

A Framework for Studying Organizational Behavior

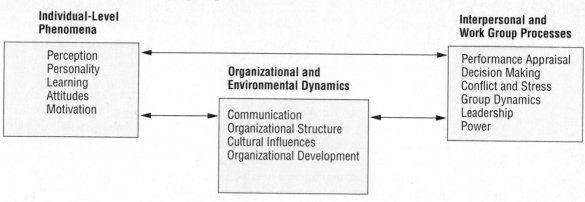

**Individual-Level
Phenomena**

Perception
Personality
Learning
Attitudes
Motivation

**Organizational and
Environmental Dynamics**

Communication
Organizational Structure
Cultural Influences
Organizational Development

**Interpersonal and
Work Group Processes**

Performance Appraisal
Decision Making
Conflict and Stress
Group Dynamics
Leadership
Power

leadership, and the like. These commonly used categories form the basis for the chapter topics of this book. The order of the chapters follows a logical flow from within-individual issues to between-individual issues, and ultimately to individual–organizational issues. Thus, the chapters flow from micro (smaller) to macro (larger) levels of analysis and discussion.

Figure 1.6 summarizes the organization of these topics by grouping many of the chapter headings within three larger categories. Initially, we will consider individual-level topics, such as perception, personality, learning, and attitudes. Afterwards, we will examine interpersonal and work-group processes, such as leadership and group dynamics. Last, we will consider organizational and environmental forces, such as structural and cultural influences.

In essence, we will start with the upper-left cluster of topics in Figure 1.6 and proceed clockwise through the framework. An important feature of the framework is the interconnectedness of the clusters (as noted by the use of the ever-popular two-headed arrow). These interconnections denote the interplay, or mutual influence, that exists among the topics. That is to say, interpersonal processes are influenced by both individual and organizational factors, and vice versa. For example, the actual design of a performance appraisal system will be partly a product of individual and organizational forces. The appraisal system, in turn, will influence both individual-level and organizationwide activities. Behavioral processes do not occur in a vacuum. Instead, they should be thought of as potential causes and consequences of other processes.

Summary

1. Define the purpose and nature of the field of organizational behavior.
Organizational behavior (OB) is a relatively new field of inquiry concerned with the scientific study of the behavioral processes that occur in work settings. Borrowing many of its concepts and methods from the behavioral and social sciences, OB explores a wide range of subjects that span (1) individually based

phenomena, such as perception and personality, (2) interpersonal and work-group processes, such as motivation and leadership, and (3) organizational and environmental forces, such as structural and cultural influences. Due to its newness, OB is a dynamic and promising field characterized by diversity and vitality.

2. Tell why organizational behavior is an important field of study for managers.

Understanding OB will help managers in at least three ways. First, through OB, managers can learn to better understand and enhance their subordinates', their superiors', and their own performance. Second, managers will find that studying OB can lead to personal growth. Better understanding of others can be highly fulfilling and contribute to greater self-knowledge and self-insight. Third, OB offers managers knowledge for its own sake. Although some OB findings may not yet have practical applications, they are nonetheless valuable additions to the cumulative store of human knowledge.

3. Distinguish organizational behavior from organizational theory, human resources management, and organizational development.

Strictly speaking, organizational behavior is the systematic study of the behavior of individuals and groups within organizations. In contrast, organizational theory focuses on the organization as the unit of analysis, and organizational attributes such as goals, technology, and culture are the objects of study. The field of human resources management attempts to apply the principles of the behavioral sciences in the workplace by designing and implementing systems for attracting, developing, and motivating individuals within an organization. Finally, organizational development seeks to enhance organizational performance through instituting systematic changes in the structure and values of an organization.

4. Cite several significant applications of behavioral principles that occurred before 1900.

Prehistoric humans were probably the first to recognize the benefits of division of labor. To increase their chances of survival, family units assigned specialized roles to the individuals who were best able to perform them. As far back as 4000 B.C., the Chinese and Mesopotamians wrote about the importance of specialized labor and hierarchy of authority, while somewhat later the ancient Romans wrote about their efforts to reorganize the lines of communication in the legions and decentralize decision making throughout their empire. In the sixteenth century, the Italian philosopher and politician Machiavelli provided insights into managing others, contending that in any situation the ends justify the means and advocating the use of deception and manipulation to further one's own purposes. At much the same time, the city-state of Venice developed a sophisticated and efficient assembly-line system of repairing damaged ships and building new ones. The Venetians were also the first to allow their workers to take regular beverage breaks. In addition, they used a merit-rating plan to assign pay raises and devised sophisticated accounting systems to track expenditures and control inventory.

5. Outline the basic principles of scientific management and discuss the shortcomings of this approach to dealing with worker behavior.

Essentially an approach to controlling worker behavior developed by Frederick Taylor, an engineer, scientific management used detailed task analysis and time-and-motion studies in conjunction with piece-rate pay schemes to increase productivity. In their search for the single best way to perform a given task, the proponents of scientific management imposed standard parts and standard procedures on manufacturing processes. This approach had many critics. Among its shortcomings was the huge amount of time and effort required to establish work standards, monitor the work process, and calculate rates of pay. Fearing that the new pay rates were an attempt to speed up production, many workers used deliberate slowdowns to resist attempts to measure their effort and productivity. In fact, the pay schemes recommended by Taylor could lead to dramatic inequities in pay.

6. Relate the findings of the Hawthorne Studies to the development of the human relations approach.

The human relations approach, which partially grew out of the field of psychology, emphasized the importance of motivation and attitudes in explaining worker behavior. This philosophy drew many of its beliefs from the findings of the Hawthorne Studies, a series of studies conducted at a single manufacturing plant over the course of twelve years. Three of the studies yielded especially compelling results. The Illumination Experiments first signaled the possibility that factors other than the job itself can influence workers' behavior. The Relay Assembly Room Study, in turn, led researchers to recognize the Hawthorne effect, while the Bank Wiring Room Study showed how peer pressure could affect individual productivity. The Hawthorne Studies represented a major step forward in the attempt to systematically study worker behavior and demonstrated that informal social groups, management–employee relations, and the interrelatedness of many other factors all contribute to on-the-job performance.

7. Explain why believers in the contingency approach rarely give a simple answer to a seemingly simple question.

Proponents of the contingency approach contend that the complexity of worker behavior defies simple explanations. They seek to identify the many personal and situational factors that are jointly necessary to explain and predict behavior. Today, most specialists in the field of OB subscribe to the contingency approach.

8. Respond to critics who contend that most principles of organizational behavior are obvious and based on common sense.

Because every manner of human behavior is at least conceivable, we have a tendency to believe that many OB findings appear to be obvious. Such a reaction could lead to a reliance on intuition and armchair theorizing in place of empirical research. No matter how obvious a statement about behavior may be, OB researchers do not accept it as fact until it is scientifically proven. We might also assume that much of OB is deducible from common sense. Since common sense often backs both sides of an issue, it can easily be cited after the fact to explain any success or failure and has no value in predicting future events.

Key Terms

Organizational behavior	Hawthorne Studies
Organizational theory	Illumination Experiments
Human resources management	Relay Assembly Room Study
Organizational development	Hawthorne Effect
Scientific management	Bank Wiring Room Study
Human relations approach	Contingency Approach

Review and Discussion Questions

1. Organizational behavior is a relatively young field of study that borrows many concepts and methods from the behavioral and social sciences. What advantages and disadvantages can you see in such youth and diversity?

2. Having graduated from college with a degree in organizational behavior, you are now seeking your first full-time job. The recruiter for Harold Guaranty Trust, where you'd like to work, tells you that only accounting majors are accepted into their management training program. What would you say to persuade the recruiter that your studies should qualify you for management training as well?

3. You are an assembly-line worker at a small auto parts manufacturer in Michigan that has called in four consultants who each specialize in a different field—organizational behavior, organizational theory, human resources management, and organizational development. Which consultant's efforts will probably affect you most? Which will most affect your supervisor? Which will most affect the president of the company? Explain your responses.

4. Although we have written records of ancient Chinese and Mesopotamian thoughts on the importance of specialized labor and the hierarchy of authority, modern managers may not find these accounts very helpful. Why not?

5. How would you explain the former popularity of scientific management? Why do you think this movement eventually lost its following? What aspects of scientific management would account for this approach's enduring popularity in certain schools of engineering?

6. After reading about the Relay Assembly Room Study, the supervisor of a typing pool decides that her subordinates will perform better if they know that she is observing them. Therefore, every day at 10 A.M. and 2 P.M. she walks up and down the rows of desks, pausing to watch each typist. Is this situation likely to produce the Hawthorne effect?

What other effects are possible? How would you explain these outcomes to the supervisor?

7. To earn extra money, you and three friends organize a free-lance yard crew to sell lawn mowing, leaf raking, and similar household services to the homeowners near your campus. Although you only work after school and on weekends, there is immediately great demand for your services because you are so conscientious, courteous, and efficient. After a few weeks, however, one of your partners starts arriving late every day, another rarely comes to work at all, and the third sits and watches while you do all the mowing and raking. How would you use the contingency approach to explain your partners' behavior? What factors would you consider? What conclusions would you draw?

8. The recruiter from Harold Guaranty Trust (see Question 2) remains unconvinced of the value of your degree in organizational behavior. "After all," he says, "most findings in OB are obvious and the rest are common sense." What would you say to change his mind?

Critical Incident

You Just Can't Get Good Help Anymore

The Greenley Corporation's profit over the last five years had increased at an annual rate of 13.5 percent. Most of this increase was a direct result of subcontracts the firm had secured from other companies.

Six months ago, to deal with its 90-day backlog of orders, Greenley introduced an incentive plan to increase output. There were several versions of the plan, each tailored to specific jobs. The one for assemblers and packers offered a bonus of 25 percent for all work over standard. The average assembler-packer was making $5.75 an hour and was expected to assemble and pack 10 units within this time period. With time allowed for lunch and rest breaks, people put in seven hours of work and were expected to produce 70 units, resulting in a base of 57.5¢ per unit.

If the assembler-packer chose to work on Saturday, the rate was time and a half, and management also promised to pay the 25 percent bonus for output over standard. One of the assembler-packers who turned out 82 units a day received a weekly gross pay of $317.70. The calculations were as follows:

Average weekly pay (7 hours × $5.75 per hour × 5 days)	$201.25
Bonus for 12 extra units per day (57.5¢ per unit × 1.25 percent bonus × 12 extra units × 5 days)	43.13
Saturday overtime (7 hours × $8.625 [$5.75 per hour ×1.5 for overtime])	60.38

Saturday bonus for 12 extra units
      (57.5¢ per unit × 1.5 for overtime × 1.25 $\underline{12.94}$
      percent for incentive × 12 units) $\$317.70$

Last week the production department reported that there was a 100-day backlog of orders. The vice-president in charge of production told the president that he would like to start finding subcontractors for some of these orders. The president gave his consent but urged the manager to try to get as much of the work as possible done in-house. "If necessary," he said, "raise the incentive to 35 percent of base pay." The vice-president agreed to do so, but pointed out to the president that only 6 percent of the total plant work force was willing to work on Saturday. "I don't think we're having much success with our incentive program. If you ask me, you just can't get good help anymore."

Questions

1. Does the Greenley management think that money motivates people? Explain.

2. Why is the incentive plan not proving effective?

3. Based on the vice-president's last comment, how would you characterize his view of human nature?

Altman, Valenzi, and Hodgetts, *Organizational Behavior* (Academic Press, 1985), p. 29.

■ Experiential Exercise

What Do You "Know" about Human Behavior?

Chapter 1 discussed various approaches to the study of organizational behavior. Implicit in the discussion was the point that organizational behavior is an empirically based social science. As such, behavioral researchers must rely on various methods to collect data. Yet much of what we "know" about interacting with others is not derived from data gathering. We develop opinions, hunches, and so forth in our daily lives that help us decide what to do.

The following exercise is designed to give you some feedback about what you think you may "know" about human behavior.

Mark T (true) or F (false) next to each statement to indicate your agreement with it. The correct answers are provided at the end.

_____ 1. People are inherently social.

_____ 2. People who are often silent are usually deep thinkers.

_____ 3. On average, men are better drivers than women.

_____ 4. Most managers prefer to use written communication (e.g., memos).

_____ 5. There are certain aspects of personality that are common to all people.

_____ 6. More people who are high achievers come from an upper-middle-class background.

_____ 7. Women apparently have more intuition than men.

_____ 8. Introverts are more sensitive to abstract ideas and feelings than are extroverts.

_____ 9. Most people who are highly intelligent seem to be physically weak.

_____ 10. High-risk takers also seem to be high achievers.

_____ 11. People are more likely to attribute success to luck or "breaks."

_____ 12. Those who smoke appear to take more sick days off from work than nonsmokers.

_____ 13. An appreciation for art or music appears to be inherited.

_____ 14. It appears that most people primarily work for money.

_____ 15. It seems that most great athletes are of below-average intelligence.

_____ 16. Very religious people seem to come mostly from poor backgrounds.

_____ 17. Seventy-five percent of the U.S. population apparently prefers to gather information through intuition.

_____ 18. It appears that most blind people possess excellent hearing.

_____ 19. Most people who go to work for the government are low-risk takers.

_____ 20. University professors have higher self-esteem than do members of any other occupational group.

_____ 21. The best workers in an organization often produce two or three times as much work as the poorest workers.

_____ 22. In social interactions, women look more at the other person than do men.

_____ 23. In the United States there seems to be a greater emphasis on "fitting in" rather than on "standing out" in social situations.

_____ 24. Good leaders have become quite common in most organizations.

_____ 25. Attempting to influence the behavior of others is a natural human tendency.

_____ 26. Top-level executives appear to have a greater need for money than for power.

_____ 27. History suggests that most famous people were born of poor, hard-working parents.

_____ 28. One's experiences as an infant and child tend to determine behavior in later life.

_____ 29.   Work stress is undesirable and should be avoided whenever possible.

_____ 30.   Most successful relationships support the notion that opposites attract.

Below are the answers to the questionnaire. Check your answers to see how well you "know" human behavior. Most students get between 16 and 22 right; how did you do?

You may recall that, in introducing this exercise, the point was made that much of what you "know" about human behavior is not based on research. As such, it tends to be in error.

Organizational behavior, however, is based on more than opinion and intuition. It is a science. Therefore, as you begin reading and studying the following chapters, remember that the information is empirically based.

1. T	11. F	21. T
2. F	12. T	22. T
3. F	13. F	23. F
4. F	14. F	24. F
5. T	15. F	25. T
6. T	16. F	26. F
7. F	17. F	27. F
8. T	18. F	28. T
9. F	19. F	29. F
10. F	20. T	30. F

Source: Written by Bruce Kemelgor, University of Louisville; used by permission.

Notes

1. L.L. Cummings, "Toward Organizational Behavior," *Academy of Management Review* 3 (1978): 90–98.
2. D.A. Wren, *The Evolution of Management Thought* (New York: Wiley, 1979).
3. C. George, *The History of Management Thought* (Englewood Cliffs, N.J.: Prentice-Hall, 1972).
4. A. Russell (ed.), *Guinness Book of World Records* (New York: Bantam Books, 1988), p. 403.
5. F.W. Taylor, *The Principles of Scientific Management* (New York: Norton, 1911).
6. L.W. Fry, "The Maligned F.W. Taylor: A Reply to His Many Critics," *Academy of Management Review* 30 (1976): 124–139; E.A. Locke, "The Ideas of Frederick W. Taylor: An Evaluation," *Academy of Management Review* 7 (1982): 14–24.
7. F.J. Roethlisberger and W.J. Dickson, *Management and the Worker: An Account of a Research Program Conducted by the Western Electric Company, Hawthorne Works, Chicago* (Cambridge, Mass.: Harvard University Press, 1939).
8. D. Bramel and R. Friend, "Hawthorne, the Myth of the Docile Worker, and Class Bias in Psychology," *American Psychologist* 36 (1981): 867–878; E.A. Locke, "Critique of Bramel and Friend," *American Psychologist* 37 (1982): 858–859; H.M. Parsons, "What Caused the Hawthorne Effect? A Scientific Detective Story," *Administration and Society* 10 (1978): 259–283; J. Feldman, "Ideology Without Data," *American Psychologist* 37 (1982): 857–858; R. Stagner, "The Importance of Historical Context," *American Psychologist* 37 (1982): 856.
9. P.F. Lazarsfeld, "The American Soldier— An Expository Review," *Public Opinion Quarterly* 13 (1949): 377–404.
10. G.J. Fletcher, "Psychology and Common Sense," *American Psychologist* 39 (1984): 203–213; R.P. Vecchio, "Some Popular (But Misguided) Criticisms of the Organizational Sciences," *Organizational Behavior Teaching Review* 11 (1987): 28–34.
11. A. Kohn, "You Know What They Say . . . ," *Psychology Today* 22 (1988): 36–41.

If all the behavioral scientists in the world were laid end to end, it would be a good thing.

—Anonymous

Science is a means whereby noncreative people can create.

—Abe Maslow

Learning Objectives

After studying this chapter, you should be able to:

1. *Summarize the starting assumptions that enable organizational behavior researchers to systematize their studies.*

2. *Define the essential steps in the scientific research process.*

3. *Enumerate the fundamental goals of OB research.*

4. *Distinguish an independent variable from a dependent variable, an intervening variable, and a moderating variable.*

5. *Differentiate the correlational method of research from the experimental method and assess the strengths and weaknesses of each approach.*

6. *Identify the most frequently used strategies and settings of OB research.*

7. *Discuss why the design of research studies requires a trade-off between internal and external validity.*

8. *Cite the most important ethical issues that OB researchers must bear in mind.*

9. *Outline the basic format of a typical OB research report.*

Approaches to Studying
Organizational Behavior

■ An Experiment in Safety

Concern about employee safety led a Washington state lumber mill to conduct an experiment into worker behavior. The company determined that mill workers were being exposed to small amounts of a preservative called tetrachlorophenol, which prevents fungi from growing on green wood. Exposure occurred even though the company had instructed workers on safety precautions, and employees wore gloves and other protective clothing.

According to Sanford Horstman, associate professor at the University of Washington's School of Public Health, who was called in to supervise the experiment, the exposure resulted from work habits and working conditions. Some employees, for example, used their legs to push lumber into position. When the lumber containing the chemical repeatedly touched their pants in the same place, the chemical eventually soaked through to the skin. And in the summer, employees often elected to wear short-sleeved shirts, even though this meant that the chemical would get on their forearms.

"None of the workers was being exposed to dangerous levels of the chemical," said Horstman, "but obviously no exposure at all is the ideal."

Horstman and Randy Bentley, who directed the study while a graduate student, considered this information and hypothesized that workers were engaging in unsafe practices because they weren't getting immediate feedback that told them they had done something unsafe. To test this hypothesis, Horstman and Bentley devised a way to provide that feedback. They mixed a harmless fluorescent dye with the preservative and installed a bank of ultraviolet lights at the work site. When

employees finished work, they exposed themselves to the light, which caused the dye in the preservative to glow. Twenty workers were involved in the experiment; nine of them were monitored closely, and the remainder were permitted to use the lights on their own if they chose to.

The employee response supported the researchers' hypothesis. All the employees involved in the experiment showed reduced exposure levels. The most effective response was wearing long-sleeved shirts even on warm days, which led to a 25–50 percent drop in exposure levels. Employees also found they could reduce exposure by laundering their work clothes daily and washing carefully at the end of the day.

The results of an experiment such as this provide a means for better understanding employee behavior. Such results can help to improve the quality of decisions we may make concerning the well-being of employees. For the results of research to be useful, studies must be well-designed.

This chapter examines the principles and methods of research into organizational behavior. Understanding these will enable

you to evaluate the research you read about and will assist you in approaching problems involving organizational behavior.

Source: Allan Halcrow, "Safety: Seeing Is Believing," *Personnel Journal*, August 1988, pp. 22, 24.

In the previous chapter, we defined organizational behavior (OB) as the systematic study of human behavior within organizational settings. The actual approach by which we study employees in work settings constitutes a behavioral science. As such, it stresses the importance of careful logic, attention to measurement, and reliance on empirical evidence. Evidence that is empirical is based on observation and is, therefore, verifiable. By limiting OB studies to empirical evidence, we eliminate potentially fruitless debates on the nature of behavior and focus instead on hard evidence obtained from research studies. The final words for an empiricist who is engaged in a philosophical debate are, "Show me your data."

Before we can examine the information that the field of OB has to offer, we need to consider the ways in which such information is gathered and interpreted. Consequently, this chapter presents the purposes, rationale, and methods of organizational behavior research — that is, the "how" of OB research. It is not the goal of this chapter to train researchers; rather, the information in the chapter is intended to aid readers in becoming enlightened consumers of management literature.

Starting Assumptions

Behavioral phenomena are unlike many phenomena we might study in that they influence, and are influenced by, many processes. As a result, OB researchers accept several starting assumptions that enable them to systematize their research efforts. These assumptions are summarized in Table 2.1.

Behavior Is Predictable

First, OB researchers assume that behavior is predictable. In essence, they assume that the entire effort to study employee behavior will be successful. The reverse of this assumption — that is, that behavior is unpredictable — would

Table 2.1

Four Assumptions of OB Research

1. Behavior can be predicted
2. Behavior is caused
3. Behavior has a finite number of causes
4. Generalities can be reasonably drawn

negate the value of systematically studying employee behavior. Our own day-to-day experience, however, suggests that behavior is often predictable due to certain regularities that we observe in our own and others' behavior. For example, you may have noticed that unhappy workers are more likely to quit their jobs in favor of employment elsewhere. Or you may have noticed that new employees tend to cling together as a group until they feel that they are assimilated into the workplace. If human behavior were random or capricious, the conduct of our daily affairs would be virtually impossible. Therefore, the assumption of predictability appears reasonable.

Behavior Is Caused

A second assumption is that behavior is caused. This assumption is crucial to the study of behavior because otherwise we could not draw connections between behavior and the observable influences that affect it. Almost everyone would agree that there are causes for much of human behavior. The simplest example is a reflex response, such as pulling your hand away from an overheated piece of machinery. For more sophisticated behaviors, the causes are more complex. Sophisticated behaviors should, nonetheless, be subject to causal influences.*

Behavior Has Many Causes

In the study of organizational behavior, we must further assume that behavior has multiple but limited causes. Simply stated, this means that human action is typically the result of a set of forces, the total number of which is finite. Given the assumption of multiple but limited causality, we approach the study of employee behavior with a recognition that our explanations will need to be complex in order to represent the complexity of the causal processes. But we can also be reassured that the number of important causal factors will probably not be endless.

Generalities Can Be Drawn

Finally, researchers assume that despite the fundamental uniqueness of every situation, generalities can nonetheless be drawn. For example, all employees are different, and all have basically different job experiences, but they can be expected to react similarly to certain situations. Thus, when faced with the prospect of a pay cut or give-back of benefits, most employees will react similarly, regardless of their position within the company.

The Scientific Method in OB Research

Scientific research follows a particular process, as shown in Figure 2.1. The process consists of three essential steps: induction, deduction, and verification.

---

* As Voltaire wrote, "It would be very singular that all nature, all the planets, should obey eternal laws, and that there should be a little animal, five feet high, who, in contempt of these laws, could act as he pleased."[1]

■ **Figure 2.1**

The Scientific Method

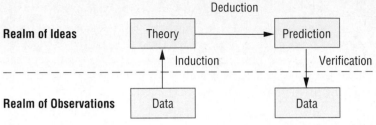

Induction

In the first step, **induction,** we start with a set of observations or facts and generate a theoretical statement that can explain them. In this way, we move from a set of very specific observations to a general explanatory principle, or theory. A theory is a statement of interrelated principles, assumptions, and definitions that is generated by a researcher in an attempt to explain a set of observations. As you might suspect, many possible theories can be constructed to explain a set of observations. Some, of course, will be better than others. Demonstrating which theories are better is an important part of the scientific approach.

Deduction

Deduction, the second step, is part of the process for determining whether a particular theory is a good representation. The use of logic guides us in deducing (from a theory) a prediction of what to expect under specified circumstances.

Verification

As the final step in the process, **verification,** we attempt to determine the truth or falsehood of a prediction — and by inference, the adequacy of the underlying theory — by gathering new data and checking to see if they support or refute the deduced predictions. Support for a prediction suggests that our theoretical constructions are on the right track. A failure to find support for a prediction, assuming that our research methods and deductive logic are sound, suggests that the theoretical basis of the prediction is in need of revision.

The Scientific Method in Practice

As an illustration, consider the question of how workers respond to unfair or inequitable situations. Many observers have commented on the importance of feelings of justice or fairness in determining workers' performance and satisfaction. From these observations J. Stacy Adams generated a set of propositions to explain the major issues that individuals focus on when judging their relative state of equity.[2] The theory that Adams generated is, in fact, quite elaborate, but one facet of it concerns the quality and quantity of output that an individual can be expected to produce under a piece-rate pay scheme. Specifically, Adams predicted that an individual who feels overpaid on such a pay scheme will increase the quality of each unit of production but decrease the quantity of units produced. This prediction is based on the principle that people will try to maximize equity by adjusting their efforts and also attempting to control their rewards. Clearly, this prediction is somewhat counterintuitive in that most of us would predict that people who feel overpaid would probably be very productive.

In a study designed to test this prediction, two groups of workers were paid on a piece-rate basis to conduct interviews.[3] One group was paid a reasonable rate per interview, while the other group was paid a much higher rate. As Adams predicted, the highly paid group actually conducted fewer interviews than did the more reasonably paid workers. However, the quality of the interviews, as measured by the number of words recorded by each interviewer, was greater for the workers who were overpaid. Because these results support Adams's predictions for worker performance in an overpaid setting, by inference they suggest that his theoretical formulations are correct.

In this example, we see the major steps of the research process:

1. Adams made a number of observations about inequity: he collected anecdotal and research-based accounts of worker behavior in inequitable settings. From his observations, he induced (developed) a fairly detailed and complete set of theoretical propositions about people's psychological and behavioral reactions to inequity.

2. From his propositions, Adams deduced the "if–then" prediction that the maximization of equity is more important to most people than is the raw maximization of pay, so that if workers feel overpaid, then certain changes in performance will occur.

3. As part of the verification process, the "if" aspects of Adams's prediction were set up in a controlled situation that satisfied the logical requirements for testing them. The results of the study, therefore, corroborated the theoretically based expectation, that is, the "then" part of the "if–then" statement.

This illustration helps to show the importance of theory in OB research. If Adams had not carefully formulated and articulated his theory, we might have simply followed our intuitive impulses regarding the likely behavior of employees who are overcompensated. The results indicate that our impulses would have misguided us to believe that quantity would be higher and quality would be lower, when actually the opposite is true. As noted in Chapter 1, all varieties of human behavior are conceivable. Therefore, we use theory to guide our study of employee behavior and data to guide our further refinement of our theoretical constructions.

Refining Theories

At this point, you may be thinking that it is still likely that overcompensated employees will increase their quantity of output and sacrifice the quality. It is difficult to give up the notion that people act primarily out of self-interest. Therefore, you may argue that only under certain conditions and with certain types of people would we be more likely to find an altruistic response to overcompensation. Through this thought process, you generate further refinements and qualifications of the theoretical propositions in light of your own personal experience and observation. They, in turn, suggest the need for further research. If you wished to test your refinements, you would carefully lay out the logic and the associated predictions. Next, you would design and conduct an experiment to see if your hunches are correct. If they are, the original theoretical propositions would require revision. If they are not, you would have to consider why your predictions were not supported. Were there errors in your initial observations of behavior? Were there errors in logic? Errors in designing the study? Errors in analyzing the data from your study?

Theories are set forth to be revised or refuted. Although a theory may be supported time and again, if it is static or self-contained, it is of little value in obtaining new knowledge. In other words, a theory should suggest and direct further research. Other things being equal, a theory that suggests new ideas (or new "rocks to be looked under") is preferable to a theory that is stated in a very complete or closed fashion.

The Necessity of Testability

A scientific theory must be testable. A set of propositions, however logical and appealing, that does not generate a specific prediction that can be tested for truth or falsehood is of no real value to the search for new knowledge. For example, an organizational consultant whose training program I once attended professed to believe a set of theoretical propositions that included the notion that all people are born with the knowledge of what life is like on other planets in the galaxy. Over time, so the thesis went, people lose this knowledge. When challenged by his audience to show evidence of his claims, the speaker stated that proof could not be provided because, as children learn to speak, the very process of learning a language conflicts with and eliminates their prior knowledge of other planets.

In analyzing this proposal carefully, you will note that it is stated in an untestable fashion. It is evident that one can make any outlandish claim if it is defined in a way that renders it untestable. Thus, the requirement that propositions be testable is absolutely essential for separating pipe dreams from real processes.

The Goals of Research

In organizational behavior, as in other fields, the research process has four major goals. The first goal is *description*. Describing behavior or events leads to a classification system that paves the way for attaining the other three goals. The second goal is simple *prediction* of behavior or events. Prediction may consist of nothing more than an extrapolation from past events. *Explanation*, the third goal, involves the statement of the underlying processes that produce or are responsible for events or behaviors. Lastly, *control* of some behavior or events is desirable as the ultimate goal of research.

As an example of how these four goals are pursued, consider how OB has approached the subject of employee turnover. Early on, researchers recognized the need to classify turnover into at least two major divisions: voluntary (or quitting based on personal choice) and involuntary (or forced termination). Researchers then turned their attention to predicting the different kinds of turnover from a knowledge of employee attributes, such as sex, expressed dissatisfaction, number of children, and so on. After these findings were established, researchers focused on developing theoretical models to explain the antecedents and consequences of turnover. Still more recently, research has been directed toward controlling or managing turnover so that poor performers are encouraged to leave while superior performers are discouraged from leaving.

Research Terminology

Researchers in OB, as well as in other fields, employ a common set of terms to describe their work. To fully understand their writings, one must be familiar with the most commonly used terms, such as hypotheses and four types of variables (summarized in Table 2.2).

Independent and Dependent Variables

An **independent variable** is a set of values (i.e., measurements) that is believed to cause changes in another set of values. For example, the different values obtained by employees on an intelligence test can serve as an index of an important influence on employee learning in a training program. In this instance, intelligence would be an independent variable if one chose to study its influence. A value that is affected by the independent variable is a **dependent variable.** The specific values of this second set are "dependent" on the specific values of the independent variable.

■ **Table 2.2**

Four Types of Variables in OB Research

Type	Definition
Independent Variable	A suspected cause of or influence on another variable
Dependent Variable	An outcome or consequence that is attributable to the independent variable
Intervening Variable	A useful concept for explaining the link between the independent variable and the dependent variable
Moderating Variable	A factor influencing the form of the relationship between the independent variable and the dependent variable

As an illustration, consider a study on the effects of seating arrangements on feelings of success in two-person negotiations. A researcher might set up several different seating arrangements around a table of a given size. For instance, she might first place two seats side-by-side, then arrange them kitty-corner, and finally put them on opposite sides of the table. The researcher chooses these seating arrangements because they are suspected to cause or contribute to feelings of success in negotiations. Thus, the seating arrangement is the independent variable.

After groups of two are given an exercise in negotiating a difficult confrontational issue, they are asked to complete a questionnaire that indicates the extent to which they feel satisfied that they reached a mutually acceptable resolution. The researcher suspects that the responses will be influenced by the seating arrangement to which the people were assigned. Because the responses are assumed to depend on the seating arrangements, they are the dependent variable.

Hypotheses

A **hypothesis** is a prediction or hunch. It is a statement of how the independent and dependent variables are related. A researcher tests whether a hypothesis should be accepted or rejected by examining the results of a study. In the seating example, one hypothesis might be that the seating arrangement in which the negotiators sit across from each other at the table leads to the lowest degree of reported satisfaction, while the side-by-side arrangement leads to the highest. The data gathered would dictate whether to accept or reject the hypothesis that seating arrangement affects feelings of satisfaction.

Intervening Variables

Sometimes researchers find it useful to propose **intervening variables** in their theories. An intervening variable is an unobservable state or process that helps to explain the link between an independent variable and a dependent variable. An example of an intervening variable in OB theorizing would be "attitudes." Attitudes are not directly observable but must be inferred from measurements of other variables that are assumed to be closely related to them. In the seating-arrangement example, a theorist might propose that any relationship between seating and feelings of success in negotiation occurs because seating arrangements arouse attitudes of cooperation or competition in participants. These attitudes in turn might influence reactions to the experience of negotiation.

Moderating Variables

Another notion that is sometimes used in OB research is that of moderating variables. A **moderating variable** is one that is responsible for a change in the relationship between an independent and a dependent variable.[4] That is to say, the relationship between the independent and dependent variables varies in association with the values of a third variable, the moderating variable. If you recall the discussion of the contingency approach in Chapter 1, you will recognize that a moderating variable represents a dependency, in that the nature of the relationship between two variables depends on the status of a third dimension. In a sense, the contingency approach centers on identifying important moderating variables.

Organizational researchers generally believe that moderators, or interdependencies, are very important for describing and explaining behavioral phenomena. As an illustration, consider the proposal that gender may moderate the relationship between seating arrangement and feelings of success in negotiations. Stated as a hypothesis, one might predict that males are likely to respond that they experienced lower feelings of success than did females when placed in a confrontational seating arrangement (i.e., on opposite sides of a table).

Another example would be the proposal that the relationship between employee intelligence and job satisfaction might be moderated by the level of a job, so that the relationship is positive for high-level jobs but negative (or inverse) for low-level jobs. This example suggests that more intelligent employees respond favorably to challenging and responsible jobs, but respond negatively to jobs that do not tap their abilities. Less intelligent employees might be frustrated by highly challenging jobs, yet find jobs requiring less mental exercise to be more satisfying.

Two Major Research Methods
OB research may employ either a correlational or an experimental method.

The Correlational Method
The **correlational method** of research is concerned with the relationship between two variables, particularly whether changes in one variable are associated with changes in another variable. As variable A increases, does variable B also increase? If so, a positive association or correlation would be indicated. Or, as variable A increases, does variable B decrease? In such cases, a negative, or inverse, correlation is implied.

Although the results of correlational studies may tell us whether and how two variables are associated, they can provide no more than a descriptive summary of a relationship. In a sense, the results of correlational research provide a snapshot of a relationship and do not really tell why or how the relationship was produced.

A study reported by Kasl and French employed the correlational method.[5] Their results identified a positive correlation between the occupational status of industrial workers and measures of physical and emotional health. In their study, the researchers did not manipulate occupational status or degree of health.† They merely correlated values of these two measures in their search for an association. If we attempt to find a causal relationship between the two variables, one shortcoming of the correlational method becomes apparent: Does health influence attainment of a high- or low-status job?

---

† In fact, one cannot conceive of an ethical study in which either status or health would be manipulated in order to study their effects.

Or does attainment of a particular kind of job influence health? Does another factor vary in association with both status and health (for instance, prior education), so that this third variable is in fact responsible for the observed correlation? These three alternative explanations — (1) that variable A causes B, (2) that variable B causes A, and (3) that a third variable causes changes in both variables A and B — are all possible interpretations for an observed correlation. No firm conclusions about causality can be drawn from purely correlational evidence.

As a further illustration, consider a hypothetical positive correlation between daily ice cream sales and the number of daily drownings that occur at seaside resorts. Three causal explanations are possible here: (1) ice cream consumption could lead to drownings (in accordance with our grandmothers' warnings about the danger of getting cramps if we eat before we swim); (2) drownings could lead to increased ice cream consumption (crowds might gather to watch rescue efforts and subsequently frequent ice cream stands); (3) daily temperature could influence both ice cream consumption and drownings (when the temperature rises, people tend to eat more ice cream and venture more often into the water).

In addition to these three causal explanations for an observed correlation, there is also a fourth: *spuriousness*. Spuriousness occurs when an apparently nontrivial correlation is due to chance alone. This fourth explanation is always a possibility. However, researchers attempt to reduce the likelihood of spuriousness by gathering a large number of observations.

A well-known example of a correlation that is probably spurious is the correlation between the overall yearly performance of the Dow Jones Industrial Average and the league affiliation of the winning football team in the Super Bowl. Throughout the first 22 Super Bowls, the league affiliation of the winning team has been a perfect predictor of whether the Dow Jones Average would rise or fall during the coming year. If the winning team was a member of the National Football League, the Dow Jones Average would rise; if the winning team was a member of the American Football League, the average would fall. Therefore, in years when the Packers, Redskins, Colts, and Forty-Niners were winners, the economy generally improved. In the years when the Dolphins and Chiefs won, the economy suffered. It is difficult to offer a causal explanation for this perfect correlation. Yet the correlation cannot be completely dismissed by saying that it is the likely result of chance.‡ It is likely that in additional years we will see a breakdown in this pattern of perfect prediction. That is to say, the use of a large number of observations helps to ensure that correlational results are not due to spuriousness.§

‡ Based on statistical probability, the probability of this association occurring in 22 of 22 instances (assuming chance is the only factor operating) is less than one in a million!

§ It is possible that in the future some people who are aware that the league affiliation of the Super Bowl winner is a predictor of economic activity may consciously use the outcome of the game as a forecast of future economic prosperity. If they do, they may conduct their financial affairs in ways that bring about fulfillment of their own prophecy.

Despite its shortcoming, correlational research can be valuable. In fact, certain questions can be addressed only through the use of a correlational method. For example, the relationship between economic depressions and employee attitudes can only be studied correlationally, since it is not feasible to create an economic depression for research purposes. Also, correlational studies may be a productive first step in analyzing certain events, as a prelude to more controlled studies. It is important to remember, however, that it is impossible to infer causality from correlational evidence with a high degree of confidence.

The Experimental Method

When feasible, the experimental method is the preferred method for studying cause-and-effect relationships. In the **experimental method,** a researcher manipulates a particular variable (the independent variable) in the hope of observing corresponding changes in another measure (the dependent variable). Other variables that might also influence the results but that are not of immediate interest to the researcher are controlled or eliminated through the careful design of the study.

The experimental method was used in the seating-arrangement study discussed earlier. In the example, seating arrangements were deliberately manipulated in order to study their effects. The researcher attributed differences in the measures (that is, the reported emotional reactions) to the only major manipulated difference that existed across the conditions (that is, the different seating arrangements).

Researchers must make certain assumptions in order to draw causal inferences from studies based on the experimental method. For example, researchers infer that an independent variable produced changes in a dependent variable because they assume that if one event precedes another, the only accepted order of causality is that the earlier event caused the later event. Similarly, there is no substitute for a personal understanding of the phenomenon under investigation. Without this understanding, an investigator could seem to follow the experimental method closely and yet reach ridiculous conclusions. As an example, you may recall the story about the scientist who cut off the hind legs of a trained jumping frog. After removing the legs, he commanded the frog to jump. Since the frog now failed to jump on command, the scientist recorded in his log, "Removal of a frog's hind legs induces deafness."**

Research Strategies and Settings

A variety of strategies and settings are used in carrying out the two major methods of OB research. Among the most frequently employed are case stud-

---

** This story is actually an illustration of the danger of making inferences that are beyond the available data (in that the scientist did not actually measure deafness).

ies, surveys, field experiments, laboratory experiments, and archival research, as well as unobtrusive measures.

Case Studies

The simplest and least rigorous approach to studying organizational behavior is to gather information informally. In a **case study,** an investigator closely examines the goings-on in an organization but makes no effort to control or eliminate alternative causal explanations for what is observed. The observations gathered for a case study can also vary, ranging from casual personal recollections of the researcher's own experience to more elaborate routines that involve interviewing others or making daily entries in a diary. Case studies are typically based on the intense study of only one organization, although several organizations are sometimes examined. In a recent case-study approach, Witte examined the introduction of industrial democracy in a company manufacturing stereo equipment on the West Coast.[6]†† The industrial-democracy project involved the creation of autonomous, or self-regulating, work groups; the frequent use of voting to decide issues; worker representation on high-level decision-making committees; and so on. To assess the effects of these efforts, Witte gathered data from tape recordings of committee meetings, the outcomes of votes, a personal diary, several sets of interviews, and casual remarks from employees. Witte's role in the situation was that of a participant-observer, in that he was employed by the firm to administer some of these radical changes.

The results that Witte reported are difficult to interpret in terms of the effectiveness of introducing industrial democracy. Because a formal comparison group was not available and because he did not obtain hard data on questions such as whether changes in productivity were due to the impact of the democratic experiment, one cannot reach solid conclusions on the likely effects of introducing industrial democracy. Also, Witte's role as a participant-observer who had a personal interest in the success or failure of industrial democracy could lead to questions about his objectivity. Case studies do possess several important positive features. Their results can be useful in generating hypotheses for further testing in more controlled studies. Also, case studies can provide insights that aid in theorizing. Finally, the results of case studies may suggest causal variables that help to explain a process.

Surveys

Researchers often use surveys to gather data about organizational behavior. A **survey** is a set of questions, either oral or written, designed to collect people's personal responses to a subject of interest to a researcher. Some phenomena, such as workers' attitudes toward their supervisor, are especially well suited to survey studies. But other phenomena, such as worker effort, may be better

†† Industrial democracy is a system of administration that attempts to institute political equality for all members of a firm by the use of certain decision-making mechanisms such as referenda, mass assemblies, and election of representatives to councils and committees.

OB Focus

Profile of a Management Scholar

What's it like to be a management researcher and consultant? For some, it can be life on the fast track.

Take the case of Harvard University sociologist Rosabeth Moss Kanter, who is also a partner in the consulting firm called Goodmeasure. IBM flew Kanter to London for a day. CBS Inc. sent its jet to Martha's Vineyard to pick her up. And when Kanter was eight months pregnant, General Electric offered to place an obstetrician on call so she wouldn't miss a speech.

Kanter's research background is in productivity in the labor force. She has written four books and coauthored still more. She is also a popular lecturer; in 1984,

she received 440 speaking requests and made 107 speeches.

Kanter uses concrete examples to drive home her productivity message. She encourages companies to experiment with new products and not to hesitate to challenge the status quo. She tells executives to get everyone in their companies involved in developing ideas. Taking a narrow view of problems, she says, only fosters workers' attitudes that solving problems is not their job. As an example of what happens when people get involved, Kanter refers to Data General, where 30 engineers developed a new computer in record time.

Kanter has other success stories to relate. At Xerox, she helped

develop a philosophy for the company's employee-involvement program. With her assistance, Honeywell structured guidelines for quality circles, which bring managers and workers together to solve company problems. Another company started an internal venture capital fund at Kanter's suggestion. Kanter once suggested that a Midwest electronics company consider combining two divisions; when she said this, an executive ran out of the room. He had been urging this very idea unsuccessfully, and Kanter had given him the argument he needed.

Kanter sums up her value to her clients succinctly: "I try to tell executives how to be ahead of change instead of victims of it."

Source: "Scholar on a Fast Track," *U.S. News and World Report,* December 2, 1985, pp. 59–60.

studied through observation or experimentation. Researchers must decide on a case-by-case basis whether a survey will serve their purposes.

When constructing a survey, the researcher must consider a number of potential problems, most of them related to respondents' reactions. For example, the questions must be designed so that respondents can answer easily and accurately, even if their responses are unlikely or rare. Otherwise, the collected data may be unreliable. Questions must also be worded in such a way that they do not bias the respondents' answers. Respondents may also react to the personal attributes of an interviewer or the general appearance of a questionnaire and, as a result, offer answers that they might not otherwise endorse. Respondents may also show response tendencies, or biases. Several common forms of bias are (1) *social desirability,* the tendency to give the answers that are believed to be most socially acceptable, (2) *acquiescence/defiance,* the tendency to agree or disagree with whatever question is posed, regardless of its content, and (3) *extremism,* the tendency to either rely on or avoid extreme options when responding to a question.

In a study of the relationship between race and job satisfaction, data were gathered from a national sample of 2,600 full-time workers.[7] The data were gathered through interviews over a period of several years by the National Opinion Research Center of the University of Chicago. Among the many questions put to the respondents were items about level of job satisfaction with present employment, job title, years of education, and self-classification of race. The results indicated that job satisfaction was higher for people who had more education and were in higher-status jobs, regardless of race. Education and job status were closely related, as one might readily predict. On the average, blacks were significantly less satisfied with their work than were whites. However, most of the black workers also occupied jobs of lesser status and had less formal education. These results, of course, are descriptive and do not tell whether blacks and whites differ in job satisfaction independently of education and job status. Although we implicitly assume that education leads to higher job status, we do not know from these results whether race in itself influences satisfaction, job status, and education. This illustration is fairly typical of the advantages as well as the limitations associated with survey research. Although the results of survey research tell us something we may not have known, the results may be of somewhat limited value because we cannot easily draw firm causal inferences.

Field Experiments

Another strategy for studying organizational behavior topics is the field experiment. It permits cause-and-effect inferences if several reasonable assumptions can be made. A **field experiment** is a study in which a variable is manipulated in one setting while the same variable remains unchanged in another, similar setting. If we can assume that the two settings were identical on all potentially important dimensions and that no other changes were introduced in the two settings during the course of the study, then any differences in a dependent variable that may be observed between the two settings can be *at least partially* attributed to the one variable that was deliberately manipulated, the independent variable.

It is necessary to be very cautious in making causal inferences based on field experiments because many *seemingly* trivial variables may not be controlled. Thus, when we say that differences are *at least partially due* to the one variable that was changed, we acknowledge that other influences may also be operating to produce the obtained results.

As an example of a field experiment, consider a study by Muczyk on the effects of a management-by-objectives (MBO) program in a multibranch bank.[8]‡‡ In order to test for the influence of MBO on bank-branch performance, Muczyk introduced the program in 13 branches (the treatment group), but did not introduce it in a small group of comparable branches (the comparison group). Because the branches were geographically separated, Muczyk

---

‡‡ Management by objectives (MBO) is an organizational program wherein a supervisor and subordinate meet on a regular basis to engage in setting specific, measurable performance goals. It is a relatively popular management technique that is designed to improve employee motivation and performance. MBO is discussed in greater detail in Chapter 7.

could reasonably assume that employees would not be overly conscious of their different working conditions.

After monitoring branch performance for a one-year period, Muczyk observed an increase in performance at the branches that had been given the MBO program. If this were the only evidence available, we would probably conclude that the MBO program was highly effective. But performance results for the comparison group led to a very different conclusion. Over the course of the year-long study, the comparison group also showed a gain in performance. Because both the treatment and the comparison groups manifested the same pattern of results, we must conclude that the MBO program did not have an appreciable impact.

The ability to reach firmer conclusions about the impact of variables is a major advantage of a field experiment. Another advantage is that such a study's results can easily be generalized to the population of interest. For example, if you want to study the hiring-decision process in large accounting firms, you can do a field experiment using a sample of personnel specialists from the appropriate firms and, based on the results, draw conclusions about the entire population with relative ease. A field experiment may also create less suspicion among participants than would a survey because a field experiment can often be more subtly integrated into the ongoing activities of an organization. Finally, through field experiments, situations can be studied in the real world that, for ethical reasons, could not be created in a laboratory environment. For example, the behavior of people in such interesting situations as exit interviews (after they have given notice that they are quitting), hospital emergency rooms, and military crises can only be reasonably studied in their actual settings.

Field experiments also have several disadvantages. Perhaps the most notable is the researcher's lack of control over all potentially important variables. Because we cannot be certain which factors in a situation need to be controlled in order to draw strong inferences and because we face real-world constraints on our control of some factors, we cannot have complete confidence in the causal inferences we may draw from field experiments.

A further obstacle to drawing causal inferences arises because the employees we study in organizations are, in a sense, "contaminated" by their roles or positions. Organizational members are typically selected for specific reasons, have been through some form of training, and have consciously chosen to remain with the organization rather than seek employment elsewhere. Consequently, the members of an organization may have unique perspectives and abilities that could interact with other variables we may choose to experiment with, and, in the process, enhance or diminish their effects.

Laboratory Experiments

The epitome of scientific inquiry is the laboratory experiment. In such a study, the researcher has total control over the design of the study and the selection of variables to be manipulated and measured. A **laboratory experiment** involves the careful creation of conditions in which only the factors of interest to the researcher are permitted to vary. Even the selection of the types of individuals to be studied is controlled by the researcher.

As an illustration, imagine an investigation into the effects of different pay schemes on goal setting. In an experimental laboratory study, the researcher would decide on the various pay schemes to be contrasted, such as piece rate, hourly rate, and salary. Then he or she would choose the exact rates, after careful consideration of regional differences in pay and the subjects' expectations based on the task to be performed. Next, the researcher would select the precise task to be performed, for example, assembly work, paper handling, or problem solving, as well as the kind of individual to be studied, such as college students, housewives, or the hardcore unemployed.

Each participant would then be assigned to one of the pay schemes and asked to set a target number of units to be produced in a given period of time. This target number would serve as the primary measure of the effect of the incentive pay scheme. With all possible extraneous factors controlled, the investigator could reasonably conclude that differences in goal setting across the various pay schemes were due to differing incentive qualities of the pay schemes.

The powerful advantage of control, or precision, that is afforded by the laboratory experiment is offset by several potential disadvantages. An important one is that the results are obtained in a fairly unrealistic setting; that is, people do not typically report to laboratory settings to engage in brief exercises. Also, the people who are readily available to participate in laboratory experiments are not often the people to whom the investigator wishes to generalize the conclusions of a study. For example, many studies are conducted with samples of undergraduate or MBA students, while the population of ultimate interest may actually be executives, campus recruiters, or first-level supervisors.[9] The students may not be directly comparable to the group of interest because their responses to experimental procedures and their prior work experience may predispose them to act in ways that are not typical of people in the workaday world. The nonrepresentative nature of both the setting and the sample in most laboratory experiments, therefore, limits the ability to generalize the results that are obtained.

A further problem is that the laboratory setting may encourage subjects to behave in a particular, unrealistic fashion. The cues and signals of an experimental setting that indicate to the subject how to respond are called **demand characteristics.** One need only recall the behavior of the relay assembly workers in the Hawthorne studies (Chapter 1) to recognize the potentially disruptive influence of a subject's awareness that he or she is being studied. In that study, the workers' awareness of their being studied led them to behave as they thought they were expected to behave, rather than as they might have behaved if the changes in their work setting had occurred more naturally. This example underscores one of the perplexing problems of studying behavior in a laboratory: humans react to the knowledge that they are under scrutiny. This does not negate the value of lab studies for examining phenomena that are not likely to be affected by subject awareness — for example, studies that involve highly absorbing and personally motivating tasks, or studies crafted so that the subjects are not aware of being studied. But studies that do not or cannot reduce subjects' awareness of being monitored must be scrutinized to determine if that awareness in any way affected the results.§§

In defense of laboratory experiments, two points need to be highlighted. First, behavior in the lab is still behavior. It is no less human than behavior in organizational settings. Although the conditions created in a lab may never occur in precisely the same way in an organization, the predisposition to behave in a certain way remains a potentiality for organizational settings. As a potentiality, the response must be considered in any full explanation of what occurs in an organizational setting.

Second, laboratory experiments provide the opportunity to assign subjects randomly to experimental conditions. This feature is especially important for the study of human behavior because all humans possess attitudes and acquired habits that can have unpredictable effects on the results of an experiment. **Random assignment,** in which individuals have an equal likelihood of being placed in an experimental group or a comparison group, overcomes the problem of these potentially confounding (i.e., extraneous but important) factors. By randomly assigning people to experimental conditions, we can be certain that equal proportions of confounding influences will be present in each group. This will ensure that the effects of such influences will also be equal from group to group. Therefore, there should be no expected difference between groups other than that which is due to the experimental manipulation.

Laboratory research and field research are not mutually exclusive alternatives. A researcher is not restricted to studying a form of behavior in either one or the other setting. Rather, the approaches are complementary. A program of research may begin with the uncovering of a behavioral process in a field setting. Because this original evidence is from an uncontrolled setting, a laboratory study may be conducted in order to minimize extraneous influences. The results of the lab study may then suggest other directions for research that can only be studied in field settings. In short, the research process requires moving from one setting to the other, with each setting offering answers that can only be obtained in that particular setting.

Archival Research

Archival research uses already existing information to study behavioral processes. The sources of data for archival research are endlessly diverse, ranging from scholarly books and journals to newspaper and magazine articles, stock

§§ The entire problem of the object of study responding to the process of being studied is not unique to the behavioral sciences; it is a potential problem in all sciences. The problem lies in the issue of the degree to which the measurement process alters the thing being measured. To some degree, the measurement process will always have some effect, however trivial or irrelevant. For example, if we measure the width of a table with a yardstick, we will alter (to a trivial degree) the top of the table. The surface of the table will be changed because a portion of it will be shaded by the ruler (and, therefore, the temperature of the surface will be changed slightly). While these changes in temperature (and therefore molecular motion) and weight are assumed to be irrelevant to the constancy of the table's width, the table has nonetheless been affected by the measurement process. In brief, the very act of measuring an object can — to some small degree, it is hoped — influence the object. This is a potential problem for all forms of measurement.

market quotations, and personal correspondence. One outstanding example of archival research is provided by David McClelland's work on achievement motivation.[10] McClelland hypothesized that a strong emphasis on achievement in the upbringing of children would be predictive of a nation's economic growth. In order to measure the variable of emphasis on achievement in childhood, McClelland examined the achievement imagery presented in grade-school readers (reading textbooks) from 23 countries during the 1920s. He assigned scores to the readers according to a previously defined set of rules that counted references to standards of excellence and the importance of hard work. To measure economic growth, McClelland looked at the increase in the amount of electricity that was produced per capita in each country during the two following decades. Intriguingly, McClelland identified a significant positive correlation between the level of achievement emphasis in the 1920s and the per capita growth in electrical production in subsequent decades.

Unobtrusive Measures

As we have already noted, humans tend to change their behavior when they know they are being observed. Thus, using an **unobtrusive measure,** a research approach that does not interfere with employees' usual behavior, is highly desirable.

In addition to using high technology to unobtrusively measure employee behavior (for example, the ethically debatable use of hidden cameras and tape recorders), one can also employ an unobtrusive approach by looking for evidence of past behavior. For example, the degree of selective wear or use of some item or the deposit of materials can provide evidence of past behavior.[11] An automobile dealer, Z-Frank Chevrolet of Chicago, has used the technique of having mechanics record the position of radio dials when cars are brought in for service. From this evidence, the dealer was able to estimate the popularity of various radio stations and thereby decide which stations to use for advertising.

The directors of the Chicago Museum of Science and Industry wanted to determine which of their exhibits were the most popular. Many of the exhibits are fascinating because they employ lights, motion, and models that illustrate various principles. But many of the exhibits illustrate principles that museum visitors do not understand. Therefore, you can foresee the potential problems of simply stopping visitors as they leave the museum to ask them which exhibit they enjoyed the most. Because of a desire not to reveal their lack of understanding, respondents might answer that the "nuclear fission exhibit" was most enjoyable, when in fact the "captured Nazi U-boat" was their favorite exhibit. To avoid the potential problems of identifying how visitors felt about the exhibits, investigators checked the frequency with which floor tiles had to be replaced around the various exhibits. This selective wear was taken as a measure of the relative popularity of exhibits. Results revealed that while most exhibits only required tile replacement after a period of years, a chick-hatching incubator exhibit required tile replacement every six weeks.

An Inside Look

High-Tech Observation or an Invasion of Privacy?

Technology is enabling today's managers to collect more information about employee behavior. Besides such standard devices as bugs and wiretaps, bosses now can use special chairs to measure how much the person in the chair is wiggling — the assumption being that someone who is wiggling isn't working. General Electric Company has installed tiny fish-eye lenses behind pinholes in walls and ceilings to watch employees suspected of crimes. At Du Pont, hidden long-distance cameras monitor the loading docks.

A modern technique for monitoring work is to have computers keep track of the performance of the employees using them. For example, at many airlines, computers measure the number of reservations written by each employee. Managers at Chicago-based Management Recruiters Inc. surreptitiously monitor computerized schedules that indicate which recruiters interview the most job candidates. Safeway Stores Inc. in Oakland, California, has installed dashboard computers on its trucks. The computers record driving speed, oil pressure, engine RPMs, idling time, and the number and length of times the truck is stopped. If the record for a driver is abnormal, the company's management investigates, thereby saving money spent on maintenance and fuel and encouraging drivers to be more careful.

Not surprisingly, employees tend to object to such monitoring when they learn about it. According to George Sveum, secretary of Teamsters Local 350 in Martinez, California, the union has filed a number of grievances when Safeway has used its computer data as the basis for suspending or discharging drivers. Says Sveum, "If a trucker is just two minutes late, he can be brought up on charges." Office workers who are subjected to computerized monitoring complain that it creates a sweatshop environment and invades their privacy.

Despite the complaints, the law has generally tended to give employers wide latitude in monitoring worker activities.

Employers may eavesdrop on office telephone conversations, observe employees through cameras, and go through employees' offices, desks, lockers, and mail. In 1987, in fact, approximately 14,000 employers listened in on the telephone conversations of almost 1.5 million workers, most of whom were not told they were being monitored. To win a lawsuit for invasion of privacy, workers must prove that their "reasonable expectations of privacy" outweigh a company's reasons for eavesdropping. Even then, the company can justify its actions if it has informed its employees of its surveillance policies.

As technology strengthens management's hand, Congress may give a boost to privacy advocates. The legislature is considering bills that would require more notification when a person is being monitored. Such attention is making workplace privacy, in the words of corporate lawyer Eric H. Joss, "the hottest employment law topic of the 1990s."

Source: Jeffrey Rothfeder and Michele Galen, "Is Your Boss Spying on You?" *Business Week*, January 15, 1990, pp. 74–75.

As these examples show, unobtrusive measures have the distinctive feature of not requiring the cooperation of the respondent, while simultaneously reducing the possible contamination of the measurement process itself. Also, the design of unobtrusive measures requires a good deal of creativity and ingenuity.

In addition to such actuarial records as voting patterns, budgets, and judicial records, various organizational records are often possible sources of data (for example, records of sales, absenteeism, and productivity). It has been

■ **Table 2.3**

Research Strategies and Settings: Advantages and Disadvantages

	Advantages	Disadvantages
Case Study	Provides insights Suggests hypotheses	Little rigor or control Simplistic
Survey	Informative Best for studying attitudes	Response tendencies Correlational evidence
Field Experiment	Permits causal inferences Easier to generalize results Greater realism Can arouse less employee suspicion	Limited degree of control Employees are not randomly selected
Laboratory Experiment	High degree of control and precision Permits strong causal inferences Random assignment is possible	Often artificial and unrealistic Limited generalizability of results Arouses subject suspicion
Archival Research	Unobtrusive Relevant to the topic of interest	Limited to using available data Correlational evidence

proposed that unobtrusive measures of job satisfaction might even be possible. For example, one might monitor trips to the water cooler and the number of toilet flushes as indices of employee dissatisfaction across departments, in the perhaps reasonable assumption that unhappy employees spend relatively more time away from their jobs and proportionately more time around the water cooler or in the restrooms.

Internal and External Validity

Now that we have reviewed a number of research strategies and settings, it is useful to consider two larger questions. The first question concerns whether the treatment variable had the hypothesized or predicted effect. This is a question of whether a study possesses **internal validity.** The second question concerns whether the results of a study can be generalized beyond the immediate sample, measures, and situation. The extent to which a study's results can be generalized is termed **external validity.**

One might reason that an ideal study would be both highly internally valid (that is, so tightly and rigorously controlled that one could easily make inferences about the independent variable's effects) and highly externally valid (designed so that one could easily generalize the results to settings and samples of interest). Unfortunately, the design of studies usually involves a trade-off between these two features: the more internally valid a study is, the less externally valid it is likely to be, and vice versa. A study that is designed to be internally valid usually involves creating a very artificial and unrealistic situation such that one has difficulty in drawing inferences for naturally occurring situations. On the other hand, if we study samples and settings of primary interest to us, we are likely to be examining conditions that lack the control necessary to draw causal inferences about the independent variable. Therefore, as we attempt to maximize the internal validity of a study, we sacrifice generalizability. If we strive to maximize external validity, we sacrifice control over important variables. This trade-off is partly due to the inclusion of certain features in studies, such as random assignment, which have mutually exclusive implications. While the control feature of random assignment leads to the internal validity of a study, it creates an unrealistic circumstance. Without random assignment, we may enhance external validity, but we would reduce internal validity.

The research strategies that have been considered can be judged in terms of how each contributes to enhancing internal and external validity. The least internally valid research approach is the case study, while the most internally valid is the laboratory experiment. Conversely, the least externally valid approach is the laboratory experiment, while one has difficulty attributing any internal validity to the results of a case study. This last statement suggests an important point: if a study is not at least internally valid to a minimal level (such that one cannot comfortably draw any inferences about an independent variable), then a discussion of external validity is moot. Internal validity may, therefore, be considered a more critical concern than external validity. Perhaps the best one can hope to achieve for a single study in the way of a compromise between the goals of internal and external validity is represented by a field experiment. A field experiment involves conditions of primary interest to the researcher (as evidenced by the selection of a particular site), while also striving for a degree of control over major variables.

Ethics in Research

The study of employee behavior in organizational settings sometimes raises ethical questions. While most studies in organizational behavior are relatively innocuous (compared, say, to medical research), the possibility of ethical violations nonetheless exists.[12]

Researchers in organizational behavior need to be aware of potential ethical problems. For instance, they should respect an individual's freedom to choose whether to participate in a study. They should also respect an individual's right to be fully informed about a study when deciding whether to participate. It is highly unethical to place people in a situation where they could be psychologically harmed without giving them a full explanation of any potential danger and assuring them that they can withdraw from participation at their discretion.[13]

Another ethical issue is the participant's right to privacy. A researcher may violate this right in different ways. For example, people may be observed without their knowledge. Also, highly personal questions may be posed on questionnaires or asked of friends and coworkers without the participant's knowledge. Another potential form of invasion of privacy is the use of a participant-observer in a study. In such an instance, the observer may be pretending to be essentially a coworker while hiding his true identity and goals from his colleagues.

A researcher who fails to treat data (especially personal-opinion data) confidentially may be accused of unethical behavior. One way to avoid this is to provide participants with an option to answer questions anonymously. A researcher must also be careful not to injure the reputation of individuals or organizations when reporting results from a study. One ethical question should guide researchers' behavior: Does a proposed study raise even a slight possibility that individual rights could be violated? If the answer is yes, the study should not be conducted. If there is any doubt about the reasonableness of conducting a study, the codes of ethics of the American Psychological Association, the American Sociological Association, and the U.S. Department of Health and Human Services should be consulted.[14]

How to Read an OB Research Report

Since much information about organizational behavior is presented in journal articles and technical reports, it is useful to understand the format in which reports are presented. The typical research report contains five major sections: abstract, introduction, method, results, and discussion.

Abstract

An *abstract* is a summary that appears at the beginning of a report. It gives a brief, one-paragraph overview of the major features of the study. It provides a descriptive outline of the study's purpose, methods, results, and conclusions.

Introduction

The first major portion of the report is the *introduction*, which explains the rationale or purpose of the study. It usually begins with a review of past research on the topic and justifies the need for the present study. The hypotheses to be tested and the logic by which the hypotheses were deduced are presented in the introduction.

Method

The *method* section describes the sample, measuring instruments, setting, and procedures used in conducting the study. These features are extremely important because they often contain points that would limit the study's generalizability or raise questions about its internal validity.

Results

Analyses of the data, especially statistical tests and graphs, are presented in the *results* section. The results are usually presented in highly technical terms that presuppose a substantial familiarity with statistical techniques. For most readers, the results are the most difficult part of the report to read and understand.

Discussion

The last section of a research report, the *discussion*, reviews the major points of the study and draws conclusions from the results. It usually includes a statement about the limitations of the study and other qualifying aspects, and

■ **Figure 2.2**

Major Journals and Magazines Devoted to Topics in the Field of Organizational Behavior

Journals	Magazines
Academy of Management Journal	Business Horizons
Academy of Management Review	California Management Review
Administrative Science Quarterly	Harvard Business Review
Human Relations	Human Resources Management
Journal of Applied Psychology	Management Review
Journal of Management	Organizational Dynamics
Journal of Organizational Behavior	Personnel Journal
Journal of Vocational Behavior	Supervisory Management
Organizational Behavior and Human Decision Processes	Training and Development Journal
Personnel Psychology	

presents insights and suggestions about how future research in the topic should be conducted. Finally, the discussion examines the possible importance of the study for a given area of research and the implications of the results in light of past research.***

At first, you may find OB research reports difficult to understand because they are often written in highly technical terms. Although you may need some persistence to develop the ability to read such reports, the rewards for your effort will be a fuller understanding of employee behavior.

Figure 2.2 lists the major journals and magazines devoted to topics in the field of organizational behavior. The journals tend to be more technical in nature, while the magazines are more comprehensible to the layperson.

Summary

1. Summarize the starting assumptions that enable organizational behavior researchers to systematize their studies.
Behavioral phenomena are complex in that they influence, and are influenced by, many processes. Thus, to systematize their studies, OB researchers accept four key assumptions: (1) behavior is predictable, (2) behavior is caused, (3) behavior has many causes but the total number of possible causes is limited, and (4) it is possible to draw generalities about behavior.

2. The scientific research process follows three steps. Define the essential steps in the scientific research process.
In the first step, induction, the researcher starts with a set of observations or

*** For more information on how to read as well as write a research report in the behavioral sciences, consult the Publication Manual of the American Psychological Association.[15]

facts and generates a theory that explains them. In the second step, deduction, the researcher makes logical predictions of what to expect under specified circumstances in an effort to determine whether the theory is a good representation of the behavior it seeks to explain. In the third step, verification, the researcher checks the truth or falsehood of a prediction by gathering new data to see if they refute or support prior assumptions.

3. Enumerate the fundamental goals of OB research.
In OB, as in other fields, the research process has four main goals: (1) description of behavior and events in order to create a classification system that paves the way for attaining the other three goals, (2) prediction of behavior and events, (3) explanation of the underlying processes that produce behavior and events, and (4) control of some behavior and events.

4. Distinguish an independent variable from a dependent variable, an intervening variable, and a moderating variable.
To understand a specific behavior or event, researchers must study the relationships among its basic elements, or variables. Thus, they start with a hypothesis, or prediction, about how a change in one variable will affect another variable. The factor or event that they believe will cause a change is called the independent variable, while the factor or event that is expected to be affected is called the dependent variable. The dependent variable is the phenomenon that the researchers seek to explain.

The relationship between an independent and a dependent variable is not always simple and direct. Consequently, researchers may include some intervening variables in their explanations. An intervening variable is an unobservable state or process that helps to explain the link between an independent and a dependent variable. In addition, the relationship between two variables may be influenced by a third variable, called a moderating variable.

5. Differentiate the correlational method of research from the experimental method and assess the strengths and weaknesses of each approach.
An OB study may employ either a correlational or an experimental method. The correlational method focuses on the relationship between two variables, seeking to determine if changes in one variable will produce changes in another. Although the results of correlational studies may tell whether and how two variables are related, they will not indicate why or how the relationship was produced. Despite this limitation, correlational research can be a productive first step in analyzing certain events and may be the only appropriate technique in some cases.

When researchers want to study cause-and-effect relationships, they usually prefer to use the experimental method. In this approach, a researcher manipulates an independent variable in the hope of observing corresponding changes in a dependent variable. Through careful design, other variables that might influence the results but are not of interest are controlled or eliminated. Despite the greater rigor of the experimental method, researchers must keep in mind two limitations of the experimental approach. First, they can only *infer* that an independent variable caused changes in a dependent variable because the independent event preceded the dependent event—they cannot *prove* that it did. Second, in order to avoid reaching distorted conclusions, the researchers must have an adequate understanding of the phenomenon under investigation.

6. Identify the most frequently used strategies and settings of OB research.
Five basic strategies and settings are used in OB research. In a case study, an investigator closely examines the goings-on in an organization through, for example, personal recollections, interviews with others, and daily diary entries. The researcher makes no attempt to control variables or eliminate alternative causal explanations for what is observed. Although case studies rarely produce hard data, they can be useful in generating hypotheses, providing insights that aid theorizing, and suggesting causal variables that help explain a process.

A survey is a set of questions, either oral or written, designed to collect personal responses to a topic of research. A survey must be carefully designed so that it will be easy to answer accurately and will compensate for or avoid respondents' biases. Although survey research may uncover new information, it rarely offers insights into cause-and-effect relationships.

When researchers want to make inferences about causes and effects, they may prefer to use field experiments. In this approach, an independent variable is manipulated in one setting while the same variable remains unchanged in another, similar setting. Assuming that the two settings are identical and that no other changes are introduced, the researcher should be able to assume that any changes in the dependent variable are at least partially attributable to manipulation of the independent variable. However, some variables may be beyond the researcher's control. In addition, participants in the experiment are not necessarily representative and may have unique perspectives that could influence the results.

Researchers can often avoid the pitfalls of field experiments through the use of laboratory experiments, in which the researcher carefully creates conditions in which only the factors of interest are permitted to vary. Such vastly increased control is highly desirable, but it is offset by a number of disadvantages. Because the laboratory conditions are artificially created, both the setting and the participants may bear little resemblance to the real-world situation of interest. Moreover, the specialized laboratory setting may encourage subjects to behave unrealistically.

Finally, researchers may do archival research, using already existing information in scholarly books and journals, newspapers, popular magazines, government documents, and the like to study a behavioral phenomenon of interest. Researchers may also employ unobtrusive measures to gather desired information. Because unobtrusive measures do not interfere with subjects' usual behavior, they often provide evidence that is insightful.

7. Discuss why the design of research studies requires a
trade-off between internal and external validity.
In interpreting any study, we must evaluate both its internal and its external validity. Internal validity is concerned with whether one can draw inferences

about the effect of the independent variable, while external validity is gauged by the extent to which the study's results can be generalized beyond the immediate research setting. In reality, the more internally valid a study is, the less externally valid it is likely to be, and vice versa. This occurs because a study designed to be internally valid (e.g., a laboratory experiment) usually requires the creation of an artificial setting that may not have many parallels to naturally occurring situations. On the other hand, when researchers study a phenomenon in its natural environment (e.g., a case study), they often lack the control necessary to draw causal inferences about the independent variable. Given this double bind, a trade-off between internal and external validity is unavoidable.

8. Cite the most important ethical issues that OB researchers must bear in mind.
Because OB research focuses on human beings, investigators must be highly ethical in their choice of methods and treatment of participants. For example, a researcher should always respect an individual's right to privacy and rights to be physically and psychologically safe, fully informed, and free to choose whether to take part in a study. A researcher should treat all information confidentially and meticulously avoid injuring the reputation of any individual or organization when reporting the results of a study. The overriding question for every researcher should be, Does a proposed study raise even the remote possibility that individual rights could be violated? If there is any doubt, the study should not be conducted.

9. Outline the basic format of a typical OB research report. The typical research report contains five key sections.
The abstract is a brief overview of the study's significant features. The introduction explains the purpose of the study, reviews the relevant past research, justifies the need for the current study, and presents and explains the hypotheses to be tested. The method section describes the sample, measuring instruments, setting, and procedures used, while the results section presents analyses of the data, especially statistical tests and graphs. Finally, the discussion section reviews the main points of the study and draws conclusions from the results.

Key Terms

Induction	Case study
Deduction	Survey
Verification	Field experiment
Independent variable	Laboratory experiment
Dependent variable	Demand characteristics
Hypothesis	Random assignment
Intervening variable	Archival research
Moderating variable	Unobtrusive measure
Correlational method	Internal validity
Experimental method	External validity

Review and Discussion Questions

1.   In your opinion, how reasonable are the four starting assumptions of OB research? Do they cover every eventuality? Should some of the assumptions be eliminated? Should other assumptions be added? Be specific in your criticisms and suggestions.

2.   Explain in your own words the scientific method as depicted in Figure 2.1. How does each element of the model fit into the total process?

3.   The research goals of OB are the same as the research goals of any other scientific field. Should they be? Why or why not?

4.   Two OB students, Archie Stack and Val Marion, plan to investigate the relationship between the number of hours their fellow OB students study and the final grades they receive. Their prediction is that students who spend more time studying will receive higher grades. What are the independent and dependent variables in this situation? What intervening and moderating variables should Archie and Val anticipate?

5.   Should the student researchers in Question 4 use a correlational or an experimental method of investigation? What elements of the situation should influence their decision? What advantages and disadvantages should they expect from the method they choose?

6.   What research strategy or setting would you recommend for each of the following situations? Why? (You may suggest more than one approach if you think that a combination would yield better results.)

     a.   The human resources department at a large manufacturing firm wants to know how assembly-line employees feel about a newly instituted piece-rate scheme.

     b.   A nationwide hospital chain asks a consultant in organizational behavior to determine if providing on-site day-care facilities at each of its 30 branches will reduce absenteeism among employees who are parents of preschoolers.

     c.   An OB researcher hopes to prove that there is a definite link between workers' productivity and the amount of encouragement they receive from their supervisor.

     d.   A consultant who specializes in organizational behavior is hired by a fast-food chain to discover why a competitor's employees seem to be more productive than the client's employees.

     e.   The president of an American auto manufacturer is considering a joint venture with a Japanese firm. If the plan goes through, a new plant will be built in the United States, with day-to-day operations managed by the Japanese. The president wants to know what adjustments such a system would demand of American workers.

7.   Discuss the trade-offs between internal and external validity that Archie and Val will have to make in conducting the study described in

Question 4. Will their results ultimately have greater internal validity or greater external validity? Why?

8.   What ethical issues should Archie and Val keep in mind as they plan and conduct their research? What ethical objections might their subjects raise? Might the two be forced to abandon their project for ethical reasons?

9.   Assume that Archie and Val have completed their research and are ready to present their findings. What format should they use? What information should they include in each section?

Critical Incident

A Way to Manage Demand?

At Southeastern State University, the Principles of Management course has always been taught in small lecture–discussion classes of approximately 40 students each. Because of the very high demand for this course, and the fact that resources for hiring additional faculty to teach more sections were not available, the departmental faculty suggested that some alternative teaching methods be explored.

Three alternative methods of presenting the course were proposed. One method was to retain the traditional lecture–discussion format with 40 students per class. A second approach was to combine several sections into a large lecture format. Approximately 160 students would attend this lecture twice a week, followed by a question-and-answer lab session with a graduate teaching assistant. The third approach involved the use of videotape. The students assigned to this approach would attend the videotaped lectures and, if they had questions, they could direct them to a graduate assistant who would meet with them once per week for a lab session.

Each student was to be randomly assigned to one of the three conditions. At the end of the semester, the results of student performance were to be evaluated. Average scores on a multiple-choice exam were to be used as the measure of each approach's effectiveness.

As Dean of the Business School, you have several questions to ask of the departmental faculty before giving your consent.

1.   Should the students be randomly assigned to the various conditions or should they be allowed to choose their own sections?

2.   Is the proposed measure of effectiveness a reasonable way of deciding which approach is best? What other ways could be used to determine which teaching format is most effective?

3.   Explain the type of research design that is being proposed.

Experiential Exercise

Approaches to Studying Organizational Behavior

Step 1.   Please read the following case and respond to the questions that follow.

Step 2.   Form small groups of four to seven members to discuss the questions and formulate one cohesive plan of action based on the consensus.

Brockport Foundry Inc.

Brockport Foundry has been in operation for 75 years. It is a family-owned business operated by President and Chief Executive Officer Peter O'Shay. Peter took the helm as CEO following the sudden death of his father last year. Old Mr. O'Shay was 85 at the time of his death. Mr. O'Shay had built the company up from nothing over the course of 55 years.

Today the company employs 150 people. A handful of them have worked for Brockport Foundry for their entire adult lives. Most of them have been with the foundry for five years or more. The majority work as laborers on the foundry floor, pouring molten metal into molds in the manufacture of cast products. An insurance salesperson was shocked recently to learn that some of the employees are functionally illiterate. They could not complete application forms, nor could they sign their names to essential documents. The foundry has never been unionized.

The company is now in a dramatic stage of transition. Even though Peter, aged 48, is well known to foundry employees (he was chief operating officer at the time of his father's death), his style of management is different from that of his father. He is beginning to make changes that he deems to be essential to the long-term viability of the company, and not everyone agrees with those changes.

The 1980s were not kind to U.S. foundries. Competition from foreign automakers and an overall recessionary business climate proved to be fatal to many foundries whose crafted works simply couldn't measure up against the products of some foreign competitors. The Japanese, for example, used robotics and advanced technologies to produce very high quality products at prices much lower than those offered by U.S. foundries whose equipment dated back to the early 1900s. At one point during the early 1980s, U.S. foundries were closing at the rate of one per week.

Peter knew that changes had to be made to ensure that the Brockport Foundry would not be added to the list of casualties. He immediately set out to streamline the production process to allow for cost savings and production efficiencies. He joined a national trade association that provided a wealth of market research to the company. He even laid off 25 workers with the promise of rehiring them should business improve.

Yesterday, Greg Barnhardt, the plant manager, approached Peter. He reported that employees seem to be exhibiting signs of work-related stress and are anxious about their futures with the company. One man even admitted that a union representative has asked if he could meet with employees, and they have consented. Greg adds that employees are not fully participating in weekly problem-solving meetings, that they appear to be showing up just because they have to.

Peter wants to find out what's going on and he has hired you, an employee of a consulting firm that specializes in OB research, to get to the bottom of the problem.

Individual Questions

1. In light of the issues discussed in the chapter, what research strategy would you use? Why?

2. Explain exactly how you would work with this strategy.

Additional Group Assignment

Reach a consensus regarding the appropriate research strategy to use, and develop it as fully as you can in the time given.

Optional Group Assignment

Greg thinks he can do a better job of researching this situation than you can. He has developed a survey that he administered to employees and is working on gathering the results. Neither you nor Peter knew anything of the survey before it was administered.

Greg handed the survey exactly as it appears below to employees as they stood in line to punch the time clock at the close of a business day (the easiest place to gain access to them all at once). They were not told anything about its purpose, nor were they offered any information about how the results would be used. They were simply asked to fill it out and bring it in to work the next day. An empty box was set up to receive surveys.

Questions

1. What do you think of Greg's idea of administering a survey?

2. What objectives does the survey serve?

3. How could you improve the survey?

4. What impact might the administration of a survey have on the situation?

Survey for All Employees

1. How long have you worked at Brockport Foundry? (check one answer)

    _____ less than 1 year   _____ 1 to 3 years   _____ 3 to 5 years
    _____ 5 to 10 years   _____ 10 to 15 years   _____ over 15 years

2. On a scale of one to ten, with one being the lowest and ten being the highest, please tell me how satisfied you are with your job. _____

3. Why do you feel this way?

    _____
    _____
    _____

4. Do your feelings of satisfaction relate to any of the following factors? (Please check all that apply.)

_____ work hours   _____ your workstation   _____ supervision
_____ goal clarity   _____ top management   _____ your pay
_____ your coworkers   _____ your work quota

Other comments:

_____

_____

_____

_____

_____

Source: Written by Susan Stites Doe, State University of New York College at Buffalo.

Notes

1. W.C. Dampier, *A History of Science and Its Relations with Philosophy and Religion* (London: Cambridge University Press, 1949), p. 197.
2. J.S. Adams, "Toward an Understanding of Inequity," *Journal of Abnormal and Social Psychology* 67 (1963): 422–436.
3. R.P. Vecchio, "An Individual-Differences Interpretation of the Conflicting Predictions Generated by Equity Theory and Expectancy Theory," *Journal of Applied Psychology* 66 (1981): 470–481.
4. L.H. Peters, E.J. O'Connor, and S.L. Wise, "The Specification and Testing of Useful Moderator Variable Hypotheses," in *Method and Analysis in Organizational Research*, ed. T.S. Bateman and G.R. Ferris (Reston, Va.: Reston, 1984).
5. S.V. Kasl and J.R.P. French, Jr., "The Effects of Occupational Status on Physical and Mental Health," *Journal of Social Issues* 18 (1962): 67–89.
6. J.F. Witte, *Democracy, Authority, and Alienation in Work: Worker Participation in an American Corporation* (University of Chicago Press, 1980).
7. R.P. Vecchio, "Worker Alienation as a Moderator of the Job Quality–Job Satisfaction Relationship: The Case of Racial Differences," *Academy of Management Journal* 23 (1980): 479–486.
8. J.P. Muczyk, "A Controlled Field Experiment Measuring the Impact of MBO on Performance Data" (Unpublished paper, Cleveland State University, 1976).
9. M.E. Gordon, L.A. Slade, and N. Schmitt, "The Science of the Sophomore Revisited: From Conjecture to Empiricism," *Academy of Management Review* 11 (1986): 191–207; J. Greenberg, "The College Sophomore as Guinea Pig," *Academy of Management Review* 12 (1987): 157–159.
10. D.C. McClelland, *The Achieving Society* (Princeton, N.J.: Van Nostrand, 1961).
11. E.J. Webb, D.T. Campbell, R.D. Schwartz, and L. Sechrest, *Unobtrusive Measures: Nonreactive Research in the Social Sciences* (Chicago: Rand-McNally, 1966); E.J. Webb and K.E. Weick, "Unobtrusive Measures in Organizational Theory: A Reminder," *Administrative Science Quarterly* 24 (1979): 650–659.
12. P.H. Mirvis and S.E. Seashore, "Being Ethical in Organizational Research," *American Psychologist* 34 (1979): 766–780.
13. P.J. Runkel and J.E. McGrath, *Research on Human Behavior* (New York: Holt, Rinehart and Winston, 1972).
14. American Psychological Association, *Ethical Principles in the Conduct of Research with Human Participants* (Washington, D.C.: APA, 1973); American Sociological Association, *Code of Ethics* (Washington, D.C.: ASA, 1971); U.S. Department of Health, Education, and Welfare, *The Institutional Guide to DHEW Policy on Protection of Human Subjects* (Washington, D.C.: Government Printing Office, 1971).
15. *Publication Manual of the American Psychological Association*, 3d ed. (Washington, D.C.: APA, 1983).

II

Individual Processes

■ **Chapter 3**
Perception and Personality

■ **Chapter 4**
Attitudes and Job Satisfaction

Success is simply a
matter of luck. Ask
any failure.

—Earl Wilson

If you take a
starving dog, and
feed him, and make
him prosperous, he
will never bite you.
That is the
difference between
a dog and a man.

—Mark Twain

Learning Objectives

*After studying this chapter,
you should be able to:*

1. *Defend the notion that
   perception is a complex
   and active process.*

2. *Explain how facial
   expressions and other
   nonverbal cues affect the
   accuracy of our
   perceptions.*

3. *Identify the most common
   obstacles to accurate
   perception.*

4. *Outline the basic principles
   of attribution theory.*

5. *Discuss the concept of
   personality and the factors
   that affect its development.*

6. *Describe the most
   commonly used techniques
   for measuring personality
   attributes.*

7. *Specify and define several
   dimensions of personality
   that are especially relevant
   to organizational behavior.*

Perception and Personality

■ Seeking the Managerial Personality

Every year, Super Valu, a food wholesaler, sends hundreds of its current and prospective managers to be tested at Personnel Decisions Inc. (PDI) of Minneapolis. A day's battery of tests includes two and one-half hours of exercises including role playing to measure skills in reasoning, analysis, and problem solving; ninety minutes of an "in-basket exercise," in which the person demonstrates decision-making habits by handling a series of memos that call for immediate action; and an interview with a psychologist.

Following such a session, PDI reports to Super Valu about various aspects of the employee's personality, including motivation, judgment and decision making, leadership skills, and adjustment. This report also predicts the employee's long-term strengths and weaknesses and his or her suitability for advancement. Super Valu uses this information to judge whether to promote employees

and what career path would best mesh with their skills.

For example, Tina Moore, a data-processing manager who started with the company as a clerk, took PDI's tests for career development, that is, to see what positions she might hold in the future. She typifies Super Valu's management in that she rose through the ranks to a management position, rather than being recruited from a business school or another company. As part of the testing, Moore role-plays the boss of a deceitful and aggressive sales manager who disappoints customers by promising more than he can deliver. The psychologists who watch Moore perform conclude that she "probed well" but "could have been more specific in her recommendations." Overall, they score Moore high on motivation but relatively low on conceptual skills — a rating Moore considers accurate and not inconsistent with her hopes for future promotions.

PDI has found that certain personality characteristics tend to be correlated with success as a manager. For example, most managers tend to rely on thinking more than feeling; that is, understanding other people seems to be more helpful than empathizing with them. The desire to make a good impression works against success at top levels of management, where people are expected to make tough decisions. And successful managers tend to be somewhat flexible.

The tests are embraced as useful by the highest levels of Super Valu's management. According to Michael W. Wright, the company's chief executive officer, psychological testing "has helped us identify the people within the organization who warrant promotion." Before Super Valu began using the PDI tests, the company had been filling 60 percent of management positions with people from outside the company, but more than one-third of them quit within two years. The testing information has helped Super Valu to fill 80 percent of all management openings through promotion, and the failure rate of new managers has been halved.

Recognizing personality differ- ences not only helps with promotion decisions but also enables managers to understand relationships within groups, to achieve cooperation, and to benefit from the variety of strengths people bring to the workplace. This chap- ter supplies some guidance in understanding how people perceive one another. It also discusses some dimensions of personality that can help to explain behavior in organizations.

Source: Edmund L. Andrews, "Mind Reading," *Business Month*, January 1990, pp. 36–39.

Being able to accurately perceive and understand others is an important ability for any manager. How we come to know others and understand their behavior are related to perception and personality, two topics that we will consider in this chapter.

The Perception of Others

Although our experience of those around us seems very direct and immediate, careful analysis of what is involved in perceiving others indicates that the process of recognizing and understanding others (i.e., person **perception**) is quite complex. For example, imagine that you are looking at a person seated at another desk (in a work or school setting). You will likely notice that the individual is of a certain sex and age, with a particular hair color, and so forth. These attributes all seem to be quite clear and inherent in the person being viewed. But a careful analysis of this hypothetical episode reveals that much more is involved. In actuality, cells in the retina of your eyes were activated by light waves reflected off the person. These retinal cells triggered neural impulses that traveled via the optic nerve to various locations in the brain. The impulses that reached the higher centers of the brain were then constructed into the experience of viewing the person at the next desk. In considering the chain of events that are involved in perception, we recognize that we do not have direct and immediate experience with the object, but instead rely on neural transmissions and electrochemical translations of stimuli. As perception researchers prefer to say, we are only dealing with our own neural activities, not with the actual person.

Most people also erroneously assume that the perceptual process is a largely passive, or totally receptive, process dictated by attributes of the observed object. Yet the process of viewing a person involves an active, directed focus on the part of the perceiver. For example, when you are viewing another person you are simultaneously being bombarded with other stimuli. The sounds in the room, the weight of your clothes, and the pressure of the chair in which you may be seated are all competing for your attention. However, you actively select and process specific information from your environment. Thus, it is clear that the perceiver is actively involved in the construction of his or her experiences. Alluding to this active involvement in selecting, structuring, and interpreting experiences, perception researchers are fond of saying, "There's more to the issue of perception than actually meets the eye."

■ **Figure 3.1**

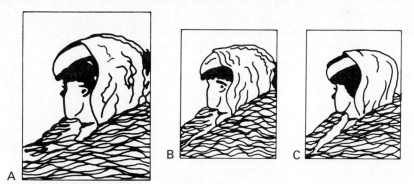

Note: The interpretation of the picture in A depends on whether one has been previously exposed to the picture in B or C.

In a well-known demonstration of the active role of the perceiver in the perceptual process, Leeper devised a clever means for displaying this natural predisposition.[1] As stimuli, Leeper prepared three drawings of a woman (Figure 3.1). One version of the drawing clearly shows a young woman looking over her shoulder, while a second depicts a much older woman. The third version of the drawing was created to be fairly ambiguous — that is, either the old woman or the young woman could be seen, depending on the observer's point of view. In his study, Leeper presented the picture of either the young woman or the old woman to two groups of subjects. Following this initial exposure, he presented the subjects with the ambiguous drawing. All of the subjects who were initially exposed to the old woman reported seeing her when they first viewed the ambiguous picture. Meanwhile, the vast majority (95 percent) of subjects who had initially viewed the drawing of the young woman thought that the ambiguous drawing was a likeness of a young woman.

In this illustrative study, the subjects processed the information in accordance with a prepared mental set. In essence, the subjects structured the information to be consistent with their previous experience. Clearly, perception is not a passive or simple process. It is influenced by individual dispositions and prior experience.

Accuracy in Perceiving Others

There is great value in being able to accurately assess the emotions and personality characteristics of others. Being able to tell whether others are experiencing a particular emotion enables us to gauge the effects of our words and actions. Knowing something about an individual's personality traits can be highly useful in interpersonal relations. All of us, to some extent, engage in "reading" the emotional styles and personality traits of others. When we approach a new coworker, we are likely to try to accurately assess that person's feelings and traits. The success of salespeople, among others, depends in large part on their ability to accurately assess others.

Facial Expressions   Research findings suggest that most of us are able to identify certain emotional states from facial expressions. Several of these facial expressions are universally recognized. For example, smiles and frowns convey the same meaning regardless of an individual's culture.[2]*

Although much research has shown that we can generally read facial expressions in research settings where participants are likely to be fairly honest in their behavior, the "real world" presents many more problems. As anyone who has dealt with a used car salesperson or a politician knows, facial expressions can be very deceiving. Some people are masters of deception who are skilled not only in concealing their feelings but also in falsifying their facial expressions.

But such behavior is not foolproof. Based on their research, Ekman and Friesen identified several clues that can help a viewer determine the sincerity of someone's facial expressions.[4] The researchers found that if the time between an emotionally arousing event and a person's facial reaction is too great, the reaction is probably dishonest. Also, if all aspects of a person's facial expression do not agree, deceit may be involved. For example, consider a facial reaction in which a person's eyebrows are raised as if in amazement, but his mouth is closed. A perceptive viewer might suspect the sincerity of the expression, because in a genuinely amazed reaction, a person's mouth is likely to be open. A third clue is provided by very brief facial expressions that appear on a person's face for a fraction of a second. These microexpressions are likely to convey genuine emotions that emerge just before the person exercises facial control.

Another indication of deception is a subtle shift in the tone or pitch of a person's speaking voice.[5] When someone is lying, there is often a detectable rise in the pitch of his or her voice. **Nonverbal cues,** such as posture shifts, scratching, and frequent licking of the lips, can provide subtle indications of nervousness and, by inference, of possible deceit.[6] Also, increased eye blinking is associated with psychological stress in that people blink more often when excited or angry.

Other Nonverbal Cues   Nonverbal cues are important in situations in which people are formally evaluated. For example, employment interviews are one important arena in which people attempt to control the impressions they transmit to each other. In a study of the impact of nonverbal cues, Imada and

---

* Charles Darwin was one of the first researchers to study the judgment of emotional states seriously.[3] He contended that the facial expressions associated with emotions were remnants of muscular movements that had functional value in our species' history. As an illustration, consider that the facial posture for displaying disgust is quite similar to the facial expression that occurs during regurgitating. He further argued that certain facial expressions are invariably correlated with specific emotional reactions. For example, a smile would indicate that a person is experiencing a pleasant or happy reaction.

Hakel[7] hired undergraduates to conduct employment interviews with a stranger. The interviewee, in fact, was a trained accomplice (confederate) of the researchers, who behaved in one of two possible nonverbal styles. In one condition, the confederate behaved in a style intended to evoke a positive evaluation. Specifically, the interviewee maintained substantial eye contact with the interviewer, sat up straight, smiled a good deal, and frequently leaned toward the interviewer. In the other condition, the confederate's behavior involved slouching in the chair, having little eye contact, smiling not at all, and leaning away from the interviewer. The interviewers' ratings differed significantly as a function of the confederate's nonverbal cues. In particular, they gave the interviewee higher ratings for competence, motivation, and recommendation for hiring when they experienced the nonverbal cues that were deliberately designed to evoke a positive reaction.

A primary implication of these results is that nonverbal cues have powerful effects on our appraisals of each other. Job interviewers are likely to be swayed by such cues when other facets of competing individuals, such as educational qualifications and experience, are equal. Partly because nonverbal cues can be confusing, the actual success rate for interviewers in predicting performance has been fairly poor.[8]

Of all the nonverbal cues that are used in perceiving and judging others, eye contact is among the most important. Generally, the more eye contact that occurs between two people, the more favorably the relationship is likely to be judged by others.[9] People typically conclude that when others avoid eye contact, it is due to a negative state, such as guilt or depression.[10]

Eye contact that is carried to extremes, however, such as staring, is socially arousing but disruptive. In instances of such staring, the nonverbal message is typically inferred to be that of hatred and potential aggression.[11] Most often, staring has the effect of driving others away (i.e., people normally leave a situation when they have been stared at). In organizational settings, staring is sometimes used as a device for extracting compliance from a coworker. For example, if a coworker is having trouble unloading a heavy parcel, he or she may stare at you in order to induce a sense of guilt, which in turn might motivate you to offer your assistance. Given that overt aggression is not socially acceptable in organizations, staring is one of the more powerful social devices for communicating hostility.

Perception of Personality Traits

While much research has been conducted to determine whether some individuals excel in judging others, the efforts have been hampered by several problems. The most notable problem has been the difficulty of determining a specific unquestionable criterion against which to compare an evaluator's judgment. Many criteria have been proposed (e.g., test scores, self-assessments, and peer assessments), but all can be criticized for having possible flaws. For example, test scores do not capture actual behavior, while self-assessments of personality traits may be biased in a favorable direction. Other problems for studying accuracy in personality assessment have arisen from methodological shortcomings in the definition of accuracy.[12]

An Inside Look

Personality and Management

Consultant Jason Leigh thinks an executive's success is largely determined by personality. The personality factor outweighs experience, education, luck, business acumen, and the latest popular formula for success.

Many people have tried to describe personality. More than 2,000 years ago, Greek physician and philosopher Hippocrates identified four personality types, which he named sanguine, choleric, melancholy, and phlegmatic. In modern times, psychologists Katherine Briggs and Isabel Briggs-Myers developed a questionnaire to measure personality types.

Based on his experience with the Myers Briggs Type Indicator, Leigh identified four types of business personalities roughly corresponding to those named by Hippocrates. Leigh's types are the Hard Charger (melancholy), the Power Broker (phlegmatic), the

People Catalyst (choleric), and the Fast Track (sanguine).

The Hard Charger adheres to tradition and rules and follows a prescribed pattern. Such a person tends to be stubborn. As an example of a Hard Charger, Leigh cites August A. Busch III, head of Anheuser-Busch. When Busch learned that Miller Beer was mounting an aggressive campaign against Anheuser-Busch, he reportedly replied, "Tell Miller to come along but to bring lots of money."

Chrysler executive Lee Iacocca is an example of a Power Broker. Power Brokers are typically visionaries and love challenges. They tend to be resourceful and skillful at motivating others.

The People Catalyst thrives on involvement with other people and often views serving others as a life goal. Feelings, subjective values, and reputation are important to such a person. Leigh calls real estate tycoon Trammel Crow a

People Catalyst. During a recent recession, Crow had cash-flow difficulties, but lenders carried him through because he had a reputation for trustworthiness.

Finally, Leigh calls Steve Wozniak a Fast Track executive. When Wozniak and Steven Jobs created Apple Computer, they staked out the territory they felt they had a right to: the personal computer business. This illustrates Fast Track executives' love of a good fight. These people see risk as a challenge and easily get caught up in a project.

Personality types contradict what Leigh sees as a contemporary emphasis on sameness. He objects to the idea that a few principles of management can apply equally well to every person or situation. According to Leigh, "There are no right or wrong personality types. However, there are types that have unique abilities and insights that come naturally."

Source: Jason Leigh, "Executives and the Personality Factor," *Sky*, May 1985, p. 34.

Despite these research problems, it is nonetheless possible to draw several guarded conclusions about the characteristics of people who are good judges of others. According to one researcher, they typically possess high intelligence, esthetic and dramatic interests, good emotional adjustment, and a specialization in the physical sciences rather than in the social sciences.[13] These findings generally make sense, except that we would probably expect specialists in the social sciences to be good judges of personality. One reasonable explanation for the reverse finding is the possible tendency for people who are interested in social relations to be overly sensitive to small differences among people. Sensitivity can lead to overdifferentiation in a judgment task (i.e., the tendency to overestimate the importance of small differences). Given that most human attributes (e.g., height, weight, etc., as well as personality traits) follow a bell-shaped, normal distribution, one can be accurate a large percentage of the time when judging others by simply sticking close to the center (or average) of the distribution. Using extreme assessments of others to make judgments can lead to a larger number of errors.

When people try to predict others' behavior from subjective assessments of personality, they are not particularly successful. This has far-reaching ramifications in the workplace, because such predictions are made many times a day by people who are responsible for hiring employees. When other, more objective qualifications, such as experience and education, are equal, assessors often make subjective personality judgments in predicting performance.

Mechanistic versus Impressionistic Prediction

Evidence on the ability of human judges to make use of personality assessments in forecasting the behavior of others shows that people generally are not adept at the task. Something of a debate has been waged for several decades over whether the task of predicting behavior from personality indices is better done with a **mechanistic** combination of the data or an **impressionistic** (human judge) approach. In a thorough literature review, Jerry Wiggins has summarized much of the debate.[14] According to Wiggins, the impressionistic approach relies on an intuitive, or subjective, combination of information about an individual when attempting to predict behavior (e.g., worker performance, absenteeism, or sales). The mechanistic, or statistical, approach involves combining information mathematically in an optimal manner. The typical statistical device is regression analysis, which uses a mathematical technique to optimally weight data to minimize the magnitude of error in prediction. When the two approaches to predicting behavior have been applied to the same set of data, the mechanistic approach has been found to be equal or superior to the impressionistic approach. The mechanistic approach has been found to be superior whether the judges are students, managers, or social scientists.

Although these results suggest that statistical manipulations of data produce more accurate predictions of human behavior, it would be erroneous to conclude that there is no place for humans in the field. Instead, the role of humans should be viewed as one of devising and validating statistical prediction systems. Once a statistical prediction system is devised and validated, it is perhaps best for the humans to be removed from the prediction process. The superiority of the mechanical process is largely due to the fact that a mathematically optimal combination of data cannot easily be beaten by an error-prone and inconsistent judge (i.e., a human).

In addition to being the creative force behind a statistical prediction scheme, humans have one other advantage over the mechanistic approach. Because the mechanistic approach requires large sets of data (i.e., a large sample size, to generate the optimal weights under the mathematical assumptions of statistical devices), there are many situations in which the statistical approach cannot be used; for example, in unique or one-of-a-kind situations in which no data are available for generating a regression analysis, or where only a single prediction is to be made for one individual (and/or the cost does not warrant the development of a regression analysis). In such circumstances, the impressionistic approach is the only recourse.

■ **Table 3.1**

Common Obstacles to Perception

Stereotyping
Halo Effect
Projection
Perceptual Distortion
Subliminal Influences
Selective Perception

Obstacles to Accurate Perception

There are many barriers to the precise perception of others' behavior. Each barrier is a possible source of misleading or distorted information. Table 3.1 summarizes these barriers.

Stereotyping   **Stereotypes** are judgments of others that are based on group membership. Such attributes as sex, race, ethnic group, and age are the basis of commonly held stereotypes. For example, the beliefs that older workers are not capable of being trained for new tasks and that younger workers cannot handle responsibility are commonly held stereotypes. Occupational groupings also frequently serve as the basis for stereotypes. For example, consider your own views of, say, police officers, top-level corporate executives, and union officials. Even relatively superficial attributes can be the basis of stereotypes, as evidenced by such clichés as "redheads are short-tempered."

This is not to say that stereotypes are totally worthless and inaccurate. In some instances, stereotypes can provide a useful shortcut for quick evaluation. But the potential costs of erroneous evaluations must always be considered.

In the aggregate, stereotypes may, in fact, be based on group characteristics; this is the "kernel of truth" notion of stereotypes.[15] The proposal argues that some stereotypical beliefs are based on an element of truth, in that the beliefs are derived from observations that hold for an entire group but that do not hold with much accuracy for given individuals in the group. While the stereotype of, say, police officers may have some accuracy, the variability of the traits of individual police officers is so great that it is extremely difficult to classify an individual officer accurately from the stereotypical information alone.

The Halo Effect   The **halo effect** occurs when a perceiver uses a general impression of favorableness or unfavorableness as the basis for judgments about more specific traits. In essence, the perceiver's evaluation is influenced by an overall impression. The halo effect explains why a subordinate who is liked by a superior can do no wrong in the superior's eyes, while a subordinate who is disliked may have difficulty obtaining a favorable review from the same superior.

Most students have witnessed the phenomenon in classroom settings, where an instructor might rate a student highly on participation because of a prior favorable impression of that student, when an actual tally of participation in the class might reveal that the favored student spoke no more frequently than other less highly rated students. One study revealed that U.S. Army officers who were liked were judged to be more intelligent than officers who were disliked, while an examination of scores on intelligence tests revealed no differences between the two groups of officers.[16]

It has also been observed that judges tend to link certain traits. For example, when a person is judged to be aggressive, he or she is also likely to be seen as highly energetic. The trait of industriousness tends to be linked to that of honesty. Someone who is a churchgoer is likely to be viewed as clean or neat. This phenomenon has come to be termed **implicit personality theory.** Simply stated, it is the tendency to perceive trait X in an individual given that trait Y exists. Because the consistency of correlations or clusterings of traits is not that substantial, assessments of others that are grounded in an implicit personality approach are likely to be in error.

A somewhat related concept is the notion of **central traits**. In a now famous study, Solomon Asch observed that certain specific traits of a person being judged were particularly powerful in influencing the judgment of other traits.[17] Asch presented two groups of students with differing lists of character traits. One group heard a stimulus person described as intelligent, skillful, industrious, warm, determined, practical, and cautious, while a second group heard the same list with the simple substitution of the word *cold* for *warm*. When the students were asked to rate the stimulus person on other traits (such as generous, wise, happy, reliable), the two groups of raters provided very different assessments. From these results, Asch concluded that warm and cold acted as central traits that had substantial responsibility for organizing the development of impressions. Other traits that Asch studied, such as polite and blunt, did not appear to influence impression formation to nearly the same extent.

These studies suggest that our impressions of others are often based on very skimpy information. Our readiness to "fill in the gaps" is partly a matter of expediency and convenience, and partly due to learned associations of traits such as stereotyping and the halo effect.

Projection   We have a tendency to ascribe our own feelings and attributes to others. This is known as **projection.** It is a defense mechanism that helps us to protect ourselves from unpleasant or unacceptable truths. An individual's emotional state has been shown to influence his or her perception of that emotional state in others. In one study, fear was aroused in a group of subjects by telling them that they would later receive an electric shock.[18] Before any shock was administered, members of the group were asked to evaluate the fearfulness of other subjects. Compared to a control group, which had not been threatened with electric shock, the shock-threatened subjects tended to describe others as more fearful and aggressive.

In another study, individuals who were rated high on such unattractive traits as obstinacy, stinginess, and disorderliness tended to rate others as being higher on these same traits.[19] These results suggest the possibility of projecting one's own undesirable traits onto others. Consequently, it is easy to imagine a situation in which a manager who is fearful of organizational change and

■ **Figure 3.2**

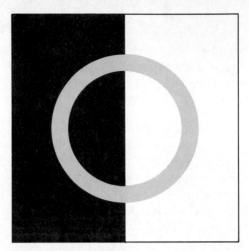

Note: Notice that the grey circle or ring is uniform in brightness. Now, place a pencil along the vertical line that is the border between the light and dark sections of the square. Has the apparent brightness of each half of the circle changed?

distrustful of others would project these attributes onto his coworkers, believing that they are fearful and cannot be trusted.

Perceptual Distortion   In addition to defending our ego by projecting feelings and attributes onto others, we may simply deny that something occurred or that we witnessed something. Similarly, we may modify or distort what we report in an attempt to avoid an unpleasant reality. Or we may deliberately pay attention only to what we want to see. These acts are forms of **perceptual distortion**.

Illusions are another form of perceptual distortion. We are all familiar with the notion of an illusion, in which our perception of something does not reflect its reality. Consider, for example, the well-known illusion of perceptual contrast shown in Figure 3.2. The grey area is of uniform color, yet when judged within a context, the grey ring appears to have differing tones. The context influences our perception and creates an illusion of difference that does not exist. So too in social relations, an individual may give a particular impression due to the context in which he or she is being judged. For example, an individual of moderate intelligence might be judged as being of substantially higher intelligence because of a prior belief that workers in his job classification are not typically very intelligent. This social misperception is based on an illusion influenced by context.

Subliminal Influences   Lastly, our perception of others may be affected by factors that we are not fully aware of. Influences that are below our threshold of awareness are called **subliminal influences**. Studies have shown that some

■ **Figure 3.3**

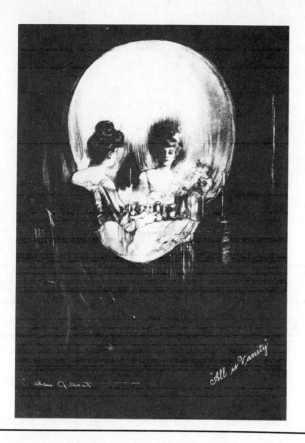

"All is Vanity"

degree of perceptual detection can occur even when people are unaware of having seen anything.[20] However, the effectiveness of attempts at deliberately designed subliminal influence appears to be overrated. Generally, stimuli of greater intensity have greater influence.

The existence of subliminal influences can be demonstrated by the successful use of posthypnotic suggestions. In such cases, a person is hypnotized and told that when he awakes, he will respond in a specific way to a specific cue, such as whistling when he hears the word *bird*. The individual later responds to the cue when not hypnotized, but cannot recall the origin of the suggestion or the motive for his action. Also, if two sharp pins are placed very near each other on the skin of a person's back, most individuals cannot consciously distinguish whether there are two pins or only one. Yet, when forced to guess, most subjects correctly guess the number of pins.

As another illustration, consider that a configuration of people or objects can create a sense of uneasiness in a perceiver even though the perceiver may be unaware of the origin of the feelings. For example, Figure 3.3 might create a feeling of dread in viewers without their being able to articulate exactly what they find upsetting. However, further examination of the picture (held either close up or at a distance) reveals that a disturbing image is embedded in the scene. Such influences in social perception and in day-to-day life are likely to be very subtle.

Selective Perception   Yet another obstacle to accurate perception arises from the tendency to be influenced by our own interests. As it is not possible to take in all stimuli we receive, we tend to select out certain elements. As an illustration of this, consider the experience that follows the purchase of a car. Suddenly you begin to notice that type of car on the street much more frequently. **Selective perception** occurs in organizations when managers tend to interpret problem situations in light of their own background and interest. For example, given an ambiguous problematic situation, a sales manager will be inclined to see sales issues as the underlying cause while a production manager will be inclined to see manufacturing-related issues.

The Study of Attributions

Within the area of perceptual research, one of the more widely studied topics is the process of attribution. Initially popularized by Fritz Heider, **attribution theory** focuses on the inference process that is used to deduce another's dispositions or traits from observations of their behavior.[21] Central to Heider's theory is the proposal that people perceive behavior as being caused, either by the individual in question or by the environment. This is a distinction between internal causality and external causality, that is, whether people initiate actions or merely react to their environment. In addition, Heider proposed that the outcome of a particular action is perceived to be the result of environmental and personal forces as well as the influences of personal power (ability) and effort (trying).

Consider the demolition of a building. Either an earthquake or a person with a wrecking ball could achieve the same result. The environmental force (the earthquake) could aid the personal force (the person with a wrecking ball), or either force could produce the same result with the other force absent. Personal and environmental forces conceivably can also work against each other and thereby cancel out one another.

The theory's components of personal power and effort are also important. If either of these components is absent, the strength of the personal force is reduced to zero. An observer of a set of actions must be able to take these various factors into account in order to make a correct attribution about a person.

Another variable of importance in the attribution process is the notion of noncommon effects. A given action may reflect several dispositions. Therefore, in order to sort out the underlying dispositions, it is necessary for the observer to have evidence that clearly points to a particular disposition. For example, someone may run several personal errands for his boss, who is ill, and also make an anonymous contribution to a charity. Running errands could be motivated both by altruism and by a desire for approval. The charitable donation could be motivated by altruism, but also by a desire to have a larger tax deduction on income taxes. The common effect is the aid of another, while approval and a tax deduction are noncommon effects. The conclusion to be reached is that the person under observation is altruistic.

Social status is often viewed as determining the extent to which an individual acts freely versus being controlled by the environment. In a study by Thibaut and Riecken, student subjects were assigned the task of convincing either a high-status individual or a low-status individual that a choice of materials for a project was a good one.[22] The high- and low-status individuals were confederates of the investigators who accepted the subjects' attempts at influence and conceded the wisdom of each subject's choice of materials. When the subjects were later asked to rate the extent to which the compliance they received from their listeners was freely given, differences were observed that favored the high-status individual (i.e., the compliance of the high-status individual was seen as more internally caused or freely given, relative to that of the low-status individual). Subjects also reported a greater amount of attraction for the high-status individual. High-status individuals, therefore, are viewed as acting more freely and, perhaps as a consequence, are more subject to praise as well as censure.

A related argument can be made that the perception of being externally controlled is partly a function of the perceived strength of environmental forces. In a study by Strickland, two subjects served as subordinates for a supervisor-subject.[23] The two subordinates performed a task for ten trials. The supervisor-subject was permitted to monitor the performance of subordinate A for nine trials and subordinate B for two trials. Although the investigator arranged the situation so that both subordinates had nearly identical performance records, the supervisor-subject indicated that he trusted subordinate B (the less-supervised worker) more than subordinate A. Subordinate A's performance was also viewed as being more externally controlled than subordinate B's. Since the supervisors saw their monitoring of A as relatively high, A's behavior was viewed as being more externally controlled.

Personality

Thus far in this chapter, we have considered the difficulties of accurately perceiving others. Let us now turn our attention to how individuals differ. Such differences are what make social life stimulating and sometimes frustrating. First, we will consider the nature of personality and the determinants of personality. Next, we will examine the techniques used to measure differences in personality. And last, we will look at several important dimensions of individual differences.

Personality is defined here as the relatively enduring individual traits and dispositions that form a pattern distinguishing one person from all others. This is by no means a universally accepted definition. In fact, there are nearly as many definitions of personality as there are theories of personality. Nonetheless, for our purposes, this definition will suffice.†

---

† It should be noted that some writers have questioned whether the notion of personality is even necessary. They contend that individual attributes can be easily explained by reducing the observations of an individual's "personality" to more basic concepts, such as habits, conditioned reflexes, attitudes, and so on. In other words, "personality" is something akin to the canals on Mars: It may

The concept of personality represents stylistic differences in the behavior of people. Let us suppose, for example, that you have closely observed the behavior of one of your coworkers. This person rarely speaks in group meetings, has virtually no friends at work, and seems to prefer to be alone most of the time. From these observations, you would likely infer that this individual is introverted. This would help to explain the individual's past and present behavior and predict his behavior in future situations. Our definition of personality includes the notion that the traits are relatively enduring, which implies consistency of behavior across situations and over time. To be sure, people do change over time, but the rate of such change is typically very gradual. Normal maturation processes are sufficiently slow that we can usefully assess individual traits with a fair certainty of their stability.

The Determinants of Personality

There has been considerable debate about the origins of an individual's personality. One point of view argues that personality is largely determined at conception by each individual's unique complement of genes. In essence, this perspective holds that personality traits, such as temperament and sociability, are determined in much the same way as hair color and facial features.

The counterpoint to the heredity position is an environmental argument. Environmentalists contend that the results of experience can shape and alter an individual's personality. For example, whether an individual is lethargic or industrious would be determined by whether she was rewarded or punished by parents, teachers, and friends for displaying related behaviors in the past. If the notion of the work ethic was ingrained in an individual at an early age and she repeatedly encountered situations in which hard work paid off, she would be inclined to espouse values that support the work ethic.

Some evidence shows that heredity can determine personality. Perhaps the most intriguing indication of the importance of genetic predisposition comes from studies of identical twins who have been separated at birth and raised apart. Even though many of the twins were raised by families from different social classes, and sometimes in different countries, each set shared many common traits. For example, they sometimes married spouses with the same first name and gave their children similar names. Food and clothing preferences and such personal habits as smoking, fingernail biting, and the sporting of moustaches were often shared by the separately raised pairs.[24]

A considerable amount of evidence also suggests that the situations to which a person is exposed influence personality traits. The most striking illustration arises from cross-cultural comparisons. As many people have noted, the personality traits of Westerners are often distinct from traits of people raised in other cultures, such as Orientals and Asian Indians. Also, people who

be more in the eye of the beholder (as part of the observer's structuring of what is being observed) than it is an actual feature. There may be some truth to this criticism of the entire enterprise of studying personality. However, the *consistency* that we find within an individual's behavior suggests that it may well be worthwhile to infer the existence of traits and dispositions that can partially account for and thereby help explain employee behavior.

are raised in a new culture from an early age often reflect the influence of their experiences within that new culture.

One can also find evidence of a link between personality and more immediate environmental influences. For example, research on the relationship of birth order to personality has revealed some interesting findings. Firstborn children are more dependent, more influenced by social pressure, and more prone to schizophrenia than are later-born children.[25] Compared to later-borns, firstborns view the world as more predictable, rational, and orderly. In addition, firstborns are less likely to defy authority, more ambitious, more cooperative, and more concerned with being socially accepted. A disproportionate number of firstborns are listed in *Who's Who*. In one interesting study, it was found that the U.S. voting population has tended to elect firstborns to the presidency during years of relative crisis, for example, in an election year before the outbreak of a war.[26]

The personality differences that have been identified between firstborn and later-born children are believed to result from the differing experiences to which the children are exposed. Firstborns are generally treated differently by parents. Compared to later-borns, they tend to receive more attention at first but are then expected to behave more responsibly in looking after younger children.

For most students of the topic, the heredity–environment debate is resolved by recognizing the importance of *both* heredity and environment as determinants of personality. Heredity may predispose an individual to certain patterns of behavior, while environmental forces may precipitate more specific patterns of action. Both sets of factors are necessary for a fuller accounting of individual behavior.

One of the more perplexing aspects of personality is its general resistance to modification. Studies of attempts to change an individual's personality typically show that it is very difficult, if not impossible, to do so for many individuals. This difficulty does not negate the possibility of personality change via environmental forces, but instead argues that the magnitude of such forces for change and the inclination of individuals to change are typically not sufficient. This resistance to change is significant because it suggests that managers must learn to deal with people's personality traits in the work setting. In short, a manager's hope of dramatically altering a worker's personality traits is not great. It may be more realistic to try to accept people as they are or to try for only modest accommodations between personality features and job requirements.

Assessing Personality Traits

There are many different techniques for measuring personality attributes. Among them are personality ratings, situational tests, inventories, and projective techniques.

Personality Ratings   A well-known device for assessing personality is the use of **ratings.** The most frequently used formats of such ratings are five-point and seven-point scales, with adjectives as endpoints, or anchors, for the scales (see

OB Focus

Perceptions and Success

How we view our abilities can affect how well we do a job. For example, researchers have found that when women work alone or with other women, they have the same expectations for succeeding as men do. However, when women work in a group with men, the women's expectations and achievements are lower than those of the men.

Two researchers, Joan LaNoue and Rebecca Curtis, investigated what it is about the way women tend to perceive their performance that diminishes their achievement. LaNoue and Curtis found that when women do poorly at work they frequently see the cause as being bad luck or an overall lack of ability. Therefore, they often give up. This is self-defeating, because high achievement depends

on trying harder, even after repeated failures.

LaNoue and Curtis decided to see whether changing women's perceptions of what caused them to fail would inspire them to exert more effort. The researchers had 72 men and 72 women work on a routine numerical task in same-sex groups, mixed-sex groups, or alone. LaNoue and Curtis checked the results, then told all the subjects that they had done poorly. They asked the subjects to pay themselves as they deserved. Overall, the women not only paid themselves less than the men did, they also attributed their "poor" work to lack of ability more often than the men did. The next part of the experiment involved doing an anagram test. First LaNoue and Curtis divided the subjects

into two groups. They told one group only that they would be doing an anagram test. The other group received a kind of pep talk; they were told that their performance on the next test would depend on their concentration and perseverance, not on luck or ability.

For all of the men and for the women who worked in same-sex groups, the talk made no difference in performance. However, for the women from the mixed-sex groups, the task raised their expectations and performance, as well as the level at which they rewarded themselves. Changing the women's perceptions of their ability to succeed affected how well they did.

Source: Carol Tavris, "Do Women Work Better Without Men?" *Vogue*, July, 1986, p. 84.

Chapter 4 for examples of rating scales). Such rating scales may not yield reliable assessments because the meanings associated with the endpoints and midpoints are not clearly defined. Thus, different raters may interpret the same scale differently.

This approach can be improved upon by using rating scales whose scale points are clearly defined by specific behavioral indicators. For example, consider the following example of a scale for measuring the trait of competitiveness.[27]

1. _____ Sensitive to the presence of competitive situations but becomes disorganized, let down, or unproductive, or flees from them. Discouraged about own abilities or appears to seek defeat compulsively.

2. _____ No real competitive interest; enjoys games for the fun of playing them but relatively unimportant who wins.

3. _____ Is stimulated by competitive situations and enjoys excelling, but can accept defeat without much strain. Periodic competitive sprees but not persistent and pervasive.

4. _____ Enjoys excelling competitors to the point of being upset when faced with a loss, takes failure very hard, or can't restrain an overt expression of satisfaction after winning. Competitive drive is very pronounced in several fields or has one field in which it is terribly important to excel.

5. _____ Extreme drive to excel competitors, won't play if can't win, always picks inferior opponents, or cheats to win. Beating competitors is primary or only satisfaction in work or play situations. Competitive drives extend to many situations that most individuals would not define as competitive.

As this example implies, it is important that a rater be in a position to observe the traits in question. The rater must also be unbiased and frank.‡ Typically, evaluators are reluctant to use the extreme negative positions on rating scales. As a consequence, ratings are often clustered toward the positive end of the scale, with the result that ratings do not discriminate among individuals and are, therefore, not informative.

Situational Tests **Situational tests** (or behavioral tests) involve the direct observation of an individual's behavior in a setting that is designed to provide information about personality. The earliest situational tests were used to assess personality in children. For example, to assess the trait of honesty, students were asked to grade their own papers. A later check of the papers indicated how honest each student was. In an assessment of charitableness, children were invited to anonymously donate small gifts, such as school supplies, to less fortunate children. Because the individual items were surreptitiously marked, it was possible to identify how much each child donated.

As part of a situational test of honesty in adults, conducted by the military during World War II, soldiers were placed in isolation in a test situation in which a series of numerical problems were to be solved. The answer book was available in the room, but each individual was instructed to not open the book. By secretly observing the individual from behind a screen, the assessors were able to determine the individual's level of honesty.[28]

Another illustration of situational testing is provided by Toyota's screening program at its Georgetown, Kentucky, auto-assembly plant. As part of this program, the problem-solving ability of applicants is tested by putting them through a flawed mock-up of an assembly line and asking them to suggest improvements in the line's procedures.[29]

Situational tests offer many advantages. They are less subjective than rating scales, and the trait in question can sometimes be assessed in a fairly natural setting. This suggests that the results of the assessment will be more

---

‡ Unfortunately, raters are sometimes asked to perform evaluations without having an opportunity to observe the necessary traits. For example, university professors are often asked to provide evaluations of students who apply to MBA programs or law school. Many times these evaluations include ratings of such personality traits as maturity, social ascendency, and dependability. Most faculty members, however, have only superficial contact with the students that they are asked to evaluate and oftentimes are very generous in their ratings.

valid. Unfortunately, situational tests are very expensive to create and administer. Additionally, certain traits, such as self-esteem, do not readily lend themselves to situational assessment.

Personality Inventories   **Personality inventories** are perhaps the most widely used method of assessing personality characteristics. Typically, inventories ask the respondent to indicate whether a statement pertains to or is true of himself or herself. A typical inventory question would be, "Do you find it easy to make friends?" The first concerted effort to use a personality inventory occurred during World War I when the U.S. Army attempted to identify men who were likely to have severe adverse emotional reactions to the rigors of trench warfare. Rather than screen the men with interviews, Woodworth devised a lengthy questionnaire, called the Personal Data Sheet, in which an individual would essentially interview himself.[30] Among the 116 items in the Personal Data Sheet were:

1.   Have you ever had a vision?

2.   Do you sometimes feel that you are being watched?

3.   Have you ever had dizzy spells?

4.   Do you feel that you have hurt yourself by taking drugs?

5.   Did you have a happy childhood?

Individuals were screened out if they answered a specified number of questions in the "neurotic" direction.

Today, many devices are used to assess literally hundreds of personality characteristics. As aids in determining whether a suitable inventory is available and whether the device has acceptable measurement characteristics, the researcher can consult such reference sources as *Mental Measurements Yearbook* and *Tests in Print*.[31]

Although inventories have the clear advantage of ease of administration, there remains the problem of the possible "faking" of answers and the related issue of the "approval motive"—the respondent's tendency to answer in a socially desirable fashion.[32] Some of the more sophisticated inventories, however, provide checks for faking. Items are included in the inventory that do not measure personality traits per se but instead act as "flags" that a respondent is answering dishonestly.§

Projective Techniques   **Projective techniques** are designed to probe the more subtle aspects of an individual's personality. The most commonly used forms of projectives are inkblot tests, story-telling devices, and sentence completions.

---

§ Faking scales are typically devised by paying people to fake their answers deliberately in a specific direction (either "fake good" or "fake bad"). Their responses to the questions are then analyzed to identify the items that discriminate between intentional fakers and others who are paid to answer honestly.

■ **Figure 3.4**

An Inkblot of the Type Employed in the Rorschach Technique

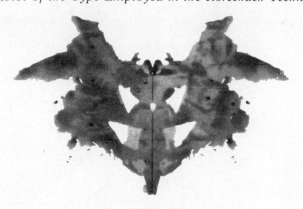

The Rorschach Test   Projective techniques are based on the belief that a person will provide a highly individualistic interpretation of an ambiguous stimulus (Figure 3.4).** This notion was used by Hermann Rorschach, a Swiss psychiatrist, when he created his well-known inkblot test called the **Rorschach test.** Individuals are scored as much on *why* they report seeing something as they are on *what* they report seeing. Responses are typically scored in accordance with one of several schemes. However, the interpretation of the scoring is far less standard.

Another drawback of the Rorschach is the lack of evidence about its reliability and validity. Nonetheless, it is one of the most widely used devices in personality assessment. Its popularity stems from its frequent use as a probe into personality rather than as a definitive assessment.

Story-telling   **Story-telling** devices have a better track record than the Rorschach test in terms of standardized interpretation, reliability, and usefulness as a predictor of behavior. The most widely used story-telling technique is the **Thematic Apperception Test,** or TAT.[34] The TAT is composed of 20 pictures, each of which portrays a social setting of ambiguous meaning. For example, one picture shows a boy staring wistfully at a violin. For each picture, the respondent is asked to provide a story that contains the following elements: a description of the characters in the story, a statement about what is presently

** This tendency to interpret ambiguous stimuli in a unique, personalized manner was first noted by Leonardo da Vinci. As the story goes, one day during a playful moment, da Vinci threw a paint-soaked sponge at an apprentice. The apprentice ducked and the sponge struck a wall, leaving a smudge. Da Vinci noticed that the smudge, on various occasions, reminded him of different objects. More interesting was his observation that when visitors to his workshop were asked what they saw in the smudge, they reported seeing things that made sense in light of their occupations or past experiences.[33]

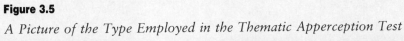

Figure 3.5

A Picture of the Type Employed in the Thematic Apperception Test

going on in the picture, and explanations of what led up to the current situation as well as how the story is likely to conclude. The 20 stories are then analyzed for recurring themes. Assuming that people identify with the protagonist of their stories, it is possible to draw inferences about a respondent's attitudes, needs, aspirations, and self-perception. Figure 3.5 presents a picture of the type used in the TAT.

Sentence Completions   **Sentence completions** are a third popular variety of projective technique in which respondents are asked to supply the endings for a series of partial sentences. The format of sentence completions is fairly straightforward. For example,

1.   I wish my boss would _____.
2.   I feel good about myself when _____.
3.   The trouble with my coworkers is _____.

In some instances, standardized scoring schemes have been developed to aid in interpreting the responses. Because the intent of sentence completions is relatively transparent and respondents are usually given unlimited time to answer, this test format is best used when respondents have little to gain by faking their answers. Appropriate situations might include sensitivity-training sessions and team-building exercises. When people answer honestly, their responses to incomplete sentences can be very enlightening.

Important Dimensions of Personality

There is an enormous number of human traits. It has been estimated that there may be as many as 5,000 adjectives that could be used to describe personality traits. In terms of relevance to organizational behavior, however, the number of important personality traits is much smaller. Consequently, for now we will limit our discussion to five dimensions of personality: locus of control, authoritarianism, the work ethic, cognitive style, and moral maturity. In organizational behavior research, these five dimensions have received much more attention than others. Throughout this text, however, we will consider other personality dimensions as they pertain to behavior in the workplace.

Locus of Control   Psychologist Julian Rotter proposed that the likelihood of an individual's engaging in a particular act is a function of (1) the person's expectancy that the act will yield rewards and (2) the personal value of those rewards to the individual.[35] In essence, Rotter's proposal rests on the notion of locus of control. **Locus of control** is the extent to which individuals believe that control over their lives lies within their own control or in environmental forces beyond their control. Someone who strongly believes that she controls events has a high *internal locus of control,* while someone who feels that she is at the mercy of fate has a high *external locus of control.*

Rotter developed a scale for measuring the extent to which an individual is internally or externally oriented. The Internal–External Control Scale asks the respondent to choose one of two possible interpretations as the cause of an event. The alternatives reflect internal versus external control. The following are sample items from the scale:[36]

1a. In the long run, people get the respect they deserve in this world.
 b. Unfortunately, an individual's worth often passes unrecognized, no matter how hard he tries.

2a. In my case, getting what I want has little or nothing to do with luck.
 b. Many times, we might just as well decide what to do by flipping a coin.

3a. By taking an active part in political and social affairs, people can control world events.
 b. Many times, I feel that I have little influence over the things that happen to me.

As you can see from these items, choice "a" in these examples indicates an internal response, while choice "b" exemplifies an external response.

Research based on the locus-of-control concept has yielded interesting results. It has been found, for example, that internally oriented individuals are less likely to respond to group pressures or persuasive communications.[37] Furthermore, a number of studies have observed that internal orientation is associated with success in school. For black students in particular, locus of control was a better predictor of academic achievement than was any other variable studied, including school location and quality.[38]

Social class and racial differences in locus of control have also been reported, in that upper-class individuals and whites tend to score as more

internally oriented relative to lower-class individuals and blacks.[39] Because
social class is correlated with race, it is difficult to say whether poverty or
discrimination is a more important cause of an external locus of control. To be
sure, the experience of powerlessness and the lack of personal evidence that
hard work leads to success contribute to the external orientation that is found
in certain segments of society.[40]

It is perhaps not surprising that compared to externally oriented individuals, internally oriented individuals have higher incomes, hold jobs of higher
status, and advance more rapidly in their careers.[41] What perhaps is surprising
is that scores on Rotter's scale have been shifting over the past two decades,
with test scores revealing that Americans appear to be becoming more externally oriented.[42]

Finally, it should be noted that internally and externally oriented individuals differ in the kinds of rewards they prefer. Externally oriented individuals,
who believe that forces beyond their control are responsible for success, tend
to prefer such extrinsic rewards as increased pay and job security. In contrast,
internally oriented individuals usually prefer intrinsic (self-supplied) rewards
such as a feeling of accomplishment and sense of achievement.[43] The implication is fairly clear: managers who understand their subordinates' loci of control can better tailor their reward systems to reflect individual needs.

Authoritarianism   Another frequently studied personality dimension is **authoritarianism** (i.e., a blind acceptance of authority). Given the importance of
power relations in organizational settings, the topic of authoritarianism is
clearly a pertinent one.

The study of authoritarianism was begun during World War II by a
group of researchers who fled Hitler's campaign of antisemitism. These researchers, who collaborated throughout the 1940s, conducted a program of
research culminating in the publication of the book *The Authoritarian Personality*.[44] As part of their research efforts, they produced scales for measuring
four facets of authoritarianism: fascism, ethnocentrism, antisemitism, and political-economic conservatism. Sample items from each of the four respective
scales follow:

- Obedience and respect for authority are the most important virtues
  children should learn (fascism scale).

- There will always be wars because, for one thing, there will always be
  races who ruthlessly try to grab more than their share (ethnocentrism
  scale).

- Jews tend to remain a foreign element in American society, to preserve
  their old social standards, and to resist the American way of life (antisemitism scale).

- A political candidate, to be worth voting for, must first and foremost
  have a good character, one that will fight inefficiency, graft, and vice
  (political-economic conservatism scale).

Researchers have found that highly authoritarian individuals tend to reject minority group members;[45] view others in relatively simplistic terms;[46] vote for conservative political candidates, such as MacArthur and Goldwater;[47] endorse strong parental control as a way of making family decisions;[48] and are less well educated.[49] In addition, it has been found that workers who are rated as highly authoritarian are more productive under authoritarian supervision.[50]

Early research on the authoritarian personality has been criticized for being a liberal polemic against political conservatism in the guise of a politically neutral analysis of personality. In order to correct this point, Rokeach proposed the more general but related construct of dogmatism.[51] **Dogmatism** is defined as a system of beliefs that is organized around an acceptance of absolute authority and intolerance toward others. By this definition, a left-wing radical, such as an extreme Marxist-communist, could be judged to be as dogmatic as a right-wing radical, such as a follower of Nazism.

Dogmatic individuals tend to be closed-minded and inflexible. Highly dogmatic managers are likely to reach decisions in relatively little time, after a limited search for data. They are also likely to be extremely confident about the quality of their decisions.[52] In addition, highly dogmatic employees report substantial differences between how they spend their time on the job and how they would prefer to spend their time.[53]

The Work Ethic   The work ethic embodies a cluster of beliefs, including a belief in the dignity of all work, contempt for idleness and self-indulgence, and a belief that if you work hard, you will be rewarded. Personality research seems to indicate that a stable predisposition toward the work ethic can be identified. The measurement of this predisposition is typically done through inventories asking respondents to describe their own beliefs and behaviors. Individuals who subscribe to the work ethic have been found to be more accepting of authoritarian leadership.[54] They also tend to have an interest in jobs that can be characterized as concrete as opposed to abstract; for example, they may prefer carpentry to journalism. When asked to perform simple, dull, and repetitive tasks without financial incentive, endorsers of the work ethic are more persistent and productive.[55] When told that they are doing poorly on a boring task in comparison to other performers, endorsers of the work ethic respond by increasing their efforts, while others reduce their efforts.[56] In response to positive feedback, both endorsers and nonendorsers of the work ethic increase their effort.

Recent evidence suggests that the work ethic may be waning in the United States. For example, Cherrington reported that older workers are more prone to endorse the work ethic than are younger workers.[57] If we assume that the work ethic's belief system is learned early in life, this finding suggests the work ethic may be eroding. In a study of workers' desire to continue working even if they no longer had the financial need to do so, it was found that the number of people who would choose early retirement increased in the past decades.[58] In 1955, only 20 percent of the respondents indicated that they would quit working if they did not need the money. But by the late 1970s, this

■ **Table 3.2**

Characteristics of Four Cognitive Styles

	Cognitive Style			
Characteristics	Sensing/Thinking (ST)	Intuiting/Thinking (NT)	Sensing/Feeling (SF)	Intuiting/Feeling (NF)
Is interested in:	Facts	Possibilities	Facts	Possibilities
Tendency to be:	Pragmatic, down-to-earth	Logical, but ingenious	Sympathetic, sociable	Energetic, insightful
Strengths:	Technical skills involving facts	Theoretical problem solving	Providing help and services to others	Understanding and communicating with others
Typical Occupations:	Physician, accountant, computer programmer	Scientist, corporate planner, mathematician	Salesperson, social worker, psychologist	Artist, writer, entertainer

percentage had increased to 28 percent. From such evidence, we may conclude that adherence to the work ethic is diminishing and that it is gradually being replaced by a leisure ethic. The unprecedented current affluence of the United States in comparison to all other countries and all other times is a likely contributing factor to this attitudinal shift. It should be noted, however, that such cultural value shifts are not new and that the present shift may reflect a more fundamental process of gradual cultural maturation.[59]

Cognitive Style Carl Gustav Jung, a famous European psychoanalyst, proposed a model of **cognitive styles,** or modes of problem solving. He suggested four types of psychological functioning that involve information gathering and evaluation: sensing, intuiting, thinking, and feeling. Sensing and intuiting are viewed as opposite styles in that a person tends to be oriented to one more than the other. Similarly, thinking and feeling are viewed as opposites. Sensing types prefer to deal with hard facts in a structured setting, while intuitive types prefer to deal with possibilities and dislike routine activities. Feeling-oriented individuals tend to be sympathetic, to prefer social harmony, and to get along well with others. In contrast, thinking-oriented people prefer logical or analytical rationales for decision making and are less interested in the feelings of others. For any individual, one of the four cognitive styles is considered dominant, with one of the two remaining opposites serving as a "back-up" or secondary defining style. From this scheme, four combinations can be created: Sensing/Thinking (ST), Intuiting/Thinking (NT), Sensing/Feeling (SF), and Intuiting/Feeling (NF). Each of these four combinations can be thought of as epitomizing a particular problem-solving style.

The measurement of these cognitive styles has relied heavily on a paper-and-pencil test developed by Katherine Briggs and Isabel Briggs-Myers (known as the Myers–Briggs Type Indicator). Research using this instrument has generally supported the typology and shown that people of differing cognitive styles prefer different occupations. Table 3.2 summarizes some of the characteristics found to be associated with these different cognitive styles.[60]

■ **Table 3.3**

Six Stages of Moral Development

Stage	What is considered to be proper
Preconventional Level	
Stage One: Obedience and punishment orientation	Sticking to rules to avoid punishment. Obedience for its own sake.
Stage Two: Instrumental purpose and exchange	Following rules only when it is in one's immediate interest. Right is an equal exchange, a fair deal.
Conventional Level	
Stage Three: Interpersonal accord, conformity, mutual expectations	Stereotypical "good" behavior. Living up to what is expected by people close to you.
Stage Four: Social accord and system maintenance	Fulfilling duties and obligations to which one has agreed. Upholding laws except in extreme cases where they conflict with fixed social duties. Contributing to the society, group.
Principled Level	
Stage Five: Social contract and individual rights	Being aware that people hold a variety of values; that rules are relative to the group. Upholding rules because they are the social contract. Upholding nonrelative values and rights regardless of majority opinion.
Stage Six: Universal ethical principles	Following self-chosen ethical principles. When laws violate these principles, act in accord with principles.

Adapted from Kohlberg, L. (1969) Moral Stages and Moralization: The Cognitive-Developmental Approach. In. T. Lickona (Ed.), *Moral Development and Behavior: Theory, Research, and Social Issues* (pp. 34–35). Holt, Rinehart & Winston.

Moral Maturity   The topic of ethical decision making in organizations has received increasing attention in recent years. Surveys of managers who are lower in an organization's structure report more pressure to compromise their personal values in order to achieve company goals.[61] One *Wall Street Journal* survey reported that 4 out of 20 executives reported that they had been asked to behave unethically.[62]

Lawrence Kohlberg, a Harvard University psychologist, has developed and tested a model of moral judgment.[63] This model emphasizes the cognitive, or reasoning, processes that can be used to characterize individuals when making ethical decisions. Kohlberg's research identified six stages of moral development. Moral development is reflected in movement from stage to stage in a fixed, or invariant, and irreversible sequence. Any individual's reasoning can be said to be operating in a manner that is characteristic of one of these stages. Table 3.3 outlines the six stages of Kohlberg's model. At stages one and two (termed the preconventional level), a person is focused on such concrete consequences as rewards and punishments, and personal interest. At stages three and four (the conventional level), correct behavior and judgment are defined by the expectations of good behavior of one's family and society. At stages five and six (the principled level), correct behavior or judgment is defined in terms of universal values and principles.

Kohlberg and his research associates have developed several tests for measuring a person's stage of moral maturity. Studies of behavior and decision making reveal that individuals of higher moral maturity are less likely to cheat in laboratory experiments and less likely to follow the orders of an authority figure if the directives are likely to injure another individual. Highly moral individuals are more likely to help another individual who is in need of assistance.[64] More highly morally mature individuals also are less likely to engage in padding an expense account.[65] Kohlberg's model of the stages of moral development has been found to be a reasonable representation of people in non-Western cultures as well.[66]

Although an individual may be inclined to behave morally as a function of an important predisposition, the context in which an individual is operating can also have a powerful influence on ethical conduct. As noted by Linda Trevino of Penn State University, ethical decision making and behavior can be better explained and predicted by the interaction of both individual and situational factors.[67]

Other Dimensions of Personality   Five other personality dimensions are also relevant to behavior in the workplace. Because they are frequently studied in connection with other topics, we will consider them later in the text. Specifically, need motivation will be considered in the chapter on motivation (Chapter 6), Machiavellianism will be examined in the chapter on power and influence (Chapter 9), cognitive complexity will be related to the topic of leadership (Chapter 10), and risk taking and creativity will be discussed in the chapter on decision making (Chapter 11).

The Predictive Utility of Personality Measures

A number of studies have been conducted that use personality data to predict employees' performance. The results of these studies typically are modest.[68] Usually, the correlation between a personality trait and performance is low, but positive. Given our daily observations of the strong presence of personality and its role in daily interpersonal behavior, the lack of a stronger relationship between personality and performance may seem surprising. But there are several reasons for this occurrence. First, personality measurement usually involves only a few aspects of an individual's make-up. Also, the measured dimensions may not be particularly relevant to the specific work situation. Thus, if researchers knew more about the specific requirements of a given job, they might be able to demonstrate the role of specific personality dimensions more convincingly.

Furthermore, the measurement of performance itself is not simple. Often, performance measures address only part of the total picture, omitting qualitative features of performance in favor of more easily quantified features. For example, customer satisfaction with bank tellers is likely to be influenced by the teller's personality traits. However, banks typically assess tellers on the single dimension of whether their cash drawers balance at the end of the day. Also, customers are not surveyed about their impressions of the teller following a transaction. As salespeople will testify, the impressions they make on customers are important to their performance. However, this critical qualitative element of sales is not often measured; instead, sales volume, a quantitative element, is the standard. It is interesting to note that in a study of sales performance that examined personality traits as predictors, it was found that a composite of such personality traits as social dominance, gregariousness, and altruistic interest in serving others was a useful predictor of sales success.[69]

Last, it should be noted that single studies attempting to predict performance from personality measures are often limited by a number of research design problems such as restriction of possible ranges on predictors and criteria, and unreliability of measures. These problems, however, can be overcome by cumulating results across studies and applying statistical corrections.[70] It must be noted that none of the difficulties associated with measuring and attempting to use personality dimensions as predictors lead one to conclude that personality is an unimportant topic.

Summary

1. Defend the notion that perception is a complex and active process.
Perception is the process by which an individual selects, organizes, and interprets information about the environment and thus gives it personal meaning. Because the environment and the individual's physiological and psychological systems are so complicated, perception is an extremely complex process. The individual takes an active role in screening out irrelevant stimuli and carefully structuring the relevant stimuli into meaningful messages that apply to the immediate situation. This is done in accordance with a prepared mental set based on previous experiences. In this way, the perceiver actually constructs his or her own version of the environment.

2. Explain how facial expressions and other nonverbal cues affect the accuracy of our perceptions.
People's facial expressions and other nonverbal cues help us to gauge the effects of our words and actions. When a person's words, facial expression, and nonverbal cues are all in agreement, they reinforce our perceptions. However, because people are masters at disguising their true intentions and feelings, it is important to watch for discrepancies between verbal and nonverbal cues. Nonverbal cues, such as amount of eye contact, frequency of smiling, and posture, can influence our perceptions of others.

3. Identify the most common obstacles to accurate perception.
There are many barriers to precise perception, each a possible source of misleading or distorted information. Among the most common are stereotyping, the halo effect, projection, perceptual distortion, and subliminal influences. A stereotype is a judgment of an individual based on certain characteristics attributed to a specific group. A person who has been thus categorized is expected to behave in fixed, preconceived ways, without regard to individual differences. The halo effect occurs when a perceiver's evaluation of specific traits is influenced by an overall impression, either favorable or unfavorable. Projection is the tendency to ascribe our own feelings and traits to others in order to protect ourselves from unpleasant or unacceptable truths. A related defense mechanism is perceptual distortion, the altering of a perception in order to avoid an unpleasant reality. Another obstacle arises from selective perception, or the tendency to be influenced by our own interests. Finally, our perception may be misled by subliminal influences, factors that are below our

threshold of awareness. In such cases, an individual reacts without realizing the source of influence.

4. Outline the basic principles of attribution theory.

According to attribution theory, when we observe an event, we try to understand its cause, assess responsibility for its outcome, and evaluate the personal qualities of the people involved. A key factor in attribution is whether the observer believes that the event is caused by an individual (internal causality) or by the environment (external causality). For example, a supervisor may attribute an employee's poor performance either to the worker's own laziness or to substandard working conditions. The cause that the supervisor infers will greatly influence his perception of the individual, the traits he attributes to her, and the steps taken to deal with the situation.

5. Discuss the concept of personality and the factors that affect its development.

Personality is the relatively enduring pattern of individual traits and dispositions that distinguishes one person from all others. The origin of individual personality is the subject of considerable debate, with one point of view contending that personality is largely determined by heredity, and another holding that personality is primarily the product of environment. In fact, both heredity and environment are important determinants of personality. Heredity may predispose an individual to certain patterns of behavior, while environmental forces may cause more specific patterns of behavior.

6. Describe the most commonly used techniques of measuring personality attributes.

While there are many different techniques for measuring personality attributes, the most frequently used are ratings, situational tests, inventories, and projective techniques. Ratings usually take the form of five- or seven-point scales with adjectives describing personality traits as endpoints, or anchors. Some ratings include specific definitions for each point on the scale. In situational tests, an individual's behavior is directly observed in a setting that is specifically designed to reveal personality. Although they are expensive to create and administer, the results of situational tests are less subjective and therefore more valid than the results of ratings. Personality inventories, a widely used method of measuring personality traits, ask an individual to respond to a series of statements by indicating whether the statement describes himself. Projective techniques are designed to probe the more subtle aspects of personality by asking the individual to respond to deliberately ambiguous stimuli. Included in this category are inkblot tests, story-telling, and sentence completions.

7. Specify and define several dimensions of personality that are especially relevant to organizational behavior.

Five dimensions of personality have received substantial attention in OB research: locus of control, authoritarianism, the work ethic, cognitive style, and moral maturity. Locus of control identifies where an individual feels that control over his life lies: within his own control or in environmental forces beyond his control. Internally oriented persons differ from externally oriented individuals in terms of responsiveness to group pressures, success in school, income, job status, speed of career advancement, and preference for specific kinds of rewards. Authoritarianism is the extent to which an individual favors blind submission to authority and believes that power should be concentrated in a leader or an elite class. This dimension has far-ranging implications for an individual's behavior as both a leader and a group member. The work ethic embodies a cluster of beliefs, including respect for the dignity of all work, contempt for idleness and self-indulgence, and faith that hard work will be rewarded. Recent evidence suggests that the work ethic may be waning in the United States. Cognitive style refers to four modes of gathering and evaluating information: sensing, intuiting, feeling, and thinking. Moral maturity refers to one's stage of ethical judgment.

Key Terms

Perception	Situational tests
Nonverbal cues	Personality inventories
Mechanistic or statistical prediction	Projective techniques
Impressionistic prediction	Rorschach test
Stereotypes	Story-telling
Halo effect	Thematic Apperception
Implicit personality theory	Test (TAT)
Central traits	Sentence completion
Projection	Locus of control
Perceptual distortion	Authoritarianism
Subliminal influences	Dogmatism
Selective perception	Work ethic
Attribution theory	Cognitive style
Personality	Moral maturity
Ratings	

Review and Discussion Questions

1. Hal, Sara, and Mike all attended the same sales meeting at which a new breakfast cereal — Nummy Flakes — was introduced. Afterwards, they discussed their reactions. "What a drag!" said Hal. "Meetings are such a waste of time. That new product manager is really ignorant. And 'Nummy Flakes'? What a dumb name!" "Wait a minute," replied Mike. "I thought the new manager was really dynamic — and cute, too. With her masterminding the marketing campaign, I bet Nummy Flakes will be a terrific success." "All right, you guys," chimed in Sara. "Rather than jumping to conclusions, why don't you give both the new product manager and Nummy Flakes time to rise or fall on their own merits?" How does the complexity of the perceptual process help to explain these three persons' different reactions to the same event?

2. If you were interviewing candidates for a job, what verbal and nonverbal cues would most likely leave you with a positive impression of an

individual? Which cues would most likely leave you with a negative impression? Would the cues and their interpretations change if you were the interviewee instead of the interviewer? How and why?

3.   In the sales meeting situation presented in Question 1, how are stereo-typing, the halo effect, projection, perceptual distortion, selective perception, and subliminal influences reflected in Hal's, Mike's, and Sara's reactions?

4.   How would attribution theory account for Hal's, Mike's, and Sara's responses to the new product manager?

5.   "All this psychology stuff just makes excuses for people's weaknesses," observed Mr. Tuggle, the supervisor of the customer service department. "I say that if workers can do their jobs, then fine — keep them. And if they can't do their jobs, then it's their problem — fire them. What does some academic notion like personality and its development have to do with the real world of work?" Answer Mr. Tuggle's question, helping him to see how an understanding of individual personality differences can improve both his own effectiveness and that of his subordinates.

6.   The personnel director of Graycote, Inc., a medium-sized paint manufacturer where you are serving a summer internship, thinks it might be a good idea to use some form of personality assessment when screening job applicants. Since Graycote is too small to have a psychologist on staff, the director asks you to look into the available possibilities. Prepare a report that summarizes the characteristics of the most commonly used personality measures, reviews their pros and cons, and recommends a course of action based on Graycote's limited financial and personnel resources.

7.   Define each of the following dimensions of personality and explain why they are especially important for managers to understand. Based on your personal experience, either at work or at school, cite examples of behavior that strike you as typifying the extremes as well as the midpoint of each dimension.
- locus of control
- authoritarianism
- the work ethic
- cognitive style
- moral maturity

Critical Incident

A Questionable "Fit"

Irene Long was recently promoted to department manager of accounting for the Badger Manufacturing Company. Badger produces metal toolboxes and related items under its own brand and for private labels. Irene has worked in the finance area and then in accounting with Badger for twelve years. When the previous manager retired, she was asked to fill the position.

Several problems have arisen over the past two months between Irene and her manager Wayne, the vice-president of finance and accounting. Wayne wants Irene to "run" the accounting department. This involves handling all the day-to-day issues, staying on top of what needs to be done, and so on. When you, the consultant, met with Wayne, he described Irene as too laid-back and not assertive enough in assuming her new responsibilities. Wayne provided you with some examples of Irene's failing to get things done on time, not following up on other people's duties to provide her with information, and always waiting to be told what to do instead of initiating action.

In meeting with Irene, you find that she feels that Wayne does not appreciate her and her abilities. She claims that she is willing to do whatever needs to be done but Wayne does not provide good direction. Irene says she wants to do a good job, but that she is not going to be a dictator. When you ask if she likes her new job, Irene replies that she thinks so, but she's not sure.

You decide that it would be helpful to assess Irene's personality type and you administer the Myers–Briggs Type Indicator. Irene's score indicates that she is more of a Sensing/Thinking type (ST). Giving Wayne the same test, you discover that he is an Intuiting/Thinking type (NT).

Using the type information, and what you know about the working relationship between Wayne and Irene, address each of the following questions:

Questions

1.   What are the major difficulties Irene and Wayne have in trying to develop a working relationship?

2.   What should be the major issues each must consider in trying to work together?

3.   Using the Myers–Briggs information, what strategy would you propose for resolving the difficulties between Irene and Wayne?

■ **Experiential Exercise**

A Study in Attribution

Step 1. Read the following news article.

Hours Before Blasts, Workers Fought to Contain Hexane
(Courier-Journal, *February 16, 1981*)

Hours before Louisville's sewers exploded Friday, six workers at the Ralston Purina plant used a five-gallon pail on a rope to try to scoop up excess amounts of the toxic chemical hexane that had begun to back up into the plant.

In interviews, Ralston employees described struggles to contain the volatile chemical.

The workers shut down the plant about 11 p.m. when they discovered a backup of hexane from the sewer.

The efforts failed: A few hours later miles of the city's sewer began to explode.

The preliminary findings of the state fire marshal's office are that the explosive solvent hexane escaped from the Ralston Purina plant and that it overwhelmed the containment basin, the plant's final line of defense to keep any hexane from going in the city's sewers.

While all of the problems may not be known, in interviews with Ralston employees and some government officials, The Courier-Journal has pieced together a version of last week's difficulties at the plant leading up to the sewer blasts that did at least $42 million in damage to public property.

Their version suggests that mechanical failure, rather than human error, may have been principally at fault in the incident.

About 8 a.m. Wednesday, a stirring arm broke in a vat filled with soybean meal. Before repairs could be made and production resumed, a surge of near-zero weather swept into the Louisville area, freezing pipes in the plant's solvent building.

Not until 5 or 5:30 p.m. Thursday was an attempt made to resume the plant's operation.

About 8 p.m., employees noticed that more than the normal amount of hexane was being used by the processing system. Some company officials have said that when the plant is starting up after a shut-down, more hexane is needed — but employees who knew that expressed concern nevertheless.

The employees also noticed that a wastewater evaporator, through which small amounts of hexane flow to be vaporized for recovery, was not heating close to its normal temperature of 180 to 200 degrees.

The employees tried to correct that problem by using an extra steam hose to heat the evaporator. But for some reason, that didn't work.

The employees called a supervisor at his home about 9:15, and he told them that if they could not increase the temperature in the evaporator, they should call him back.

About 11 p.m., it was discovered that hexane and water were backing up from the containment basin to the solvent building. The liquid mixture at that point was visible through an open sewer grating.

Almost simultaneously, the employees shut down the system and tried to call the supervisor. His line was busy and another supervisor was called.

After a series of calls, two supervisors came to the plant and notified the Metropolitan Sewer District (MSD) of a possible hexane spill.

By employees' accounts, that call was made about midnight. That contradicts the MSD version, which put the call at about 1 a.m.

It was discovered that excessive amounts of hexane were in the containment basin — the last line of defense designed to hold any excess hexane and keep it from getting into the sewer.

When workers discovered how much hexane was in the basin, they bailed it out of the basin with a five-gallon drum on a rope.

Between about midnight and 2 a.m. the workers filled six or seven 55-gallon drums with the chemical. They quit when they ran out of empty drums.

The two operators on duty in the six-story solvent building had been told to fine-tune the complex system of pipes, heaters, pumps, and condensors to bring the system into balance. But it became clear that something was seriously wrong.

Jim Reed, the company spokesman, said last night that "cold temperatures may have led to a malfunction of certain operating equipment."

Reed said that company investigators suspect that is the case but that it hasn't been determined.

Apparently, the answer is locked inside the now-idle equipment in the solvent building.

Investigators apparently have not found any simple explanation, such as a broken pipe producing an obvious spill, although that possibility has not been ruled out.

Reed, the company spokesman, said last night that the company was operated safely and in accordance with regulations.

Some employees say that, because of the cold weather, or because of freeze-damage to some equipment, the recovery process may have failed — flooding the system with liquid hexane.

Investigators say they have turned up nothing yet to substantiate that theory.

Step 2.   Either individually or in small groups, as directed by your instructor, answer the following question: According to the article, who or what was responsible for the explosion?

Step 3.   Now read the following article about the sewer explosion.

Fire Officials Say They Had a Way to Prevent Blasts
(Louisville Times, *February 17, 1981*)

The explosions that wracked Old Louisville early Friday might have been defused if the extent of a chemical leak had been discovered during the night, fire officials say.

The established procedure whenever potentially explosive or flammable chemicals spill into the sewers is to open fire hydrants along the line, flooding the sewers with water to dilute the chemical.

And that's what the fire department would have done along the sewer line from the Ralston Purina Co. plant of Floyd Street if fire officials had been notified of the extent of the leak that they suspect fueled the explosions.

Instead, several hundred — or maybe as much as thousands — of gallons of hexane flowed through the line during the night until a spark ignited the chemical vapors. The chain of explosions that followed tore up streets and caused up to $42 million in damage.

The key to whether the explosions could have been prevented is that the MSD (Metropolitan Sewer District) inspector, who responded to a call from the Ralston Purina plant at approximately 1:30 a.m., didn't find any signs of explosive fumes in the sewers when he checked them.

His findings have puzzled investigators and some Ralston Purina workers have said the MSD inspector conducted only a cursory investigation of the leak when he came to the plant.

However, MSD officials have refused to allow the inspector, Jim Surace, to respond to those allegations or say publicly what testing he did at the plant.

Ralston Purina officials called MSD — as the law requires — because they suspected that some hexane had leaked into the sewers because of a malfunction in their equipment.

Initially, company officials told MSD that up to 500 gallons of hexane may have spilled into the sewers. Since the explosions, investigators have speculated that the force of the blasts indicates that much more of the chemical — perhaps thousands of gallons — had to have been in the sewers.

Ralston Purina officials continued yesterday to assert that no definite link has been established between their plant and the explosions.

Ralston Purina's statement yesterday also seemed to be aimed at countering statements from some workers at the plant that officials hesitated — perhaps dangerously long — before they shut the plant because they didn't want to lose production time.

Charles Chapman, business representative for Local 604 of the Chemical Workers Union, said some of his union members who worked at the plant that night told him workers realized the hexane back-up was serious as early as 6 p.m., but supervisors didn't want to shut down.

The plant had been shut down the day before because of problems caused by cold weather. Workers were attempting to start it up again Thursday night when the hexane problem arose.

Company spokesmen have declined to comment on why MSD was not called earlier than 1 a.m., at least an hour and a half after the first leak was apparently suspected.

State fire marshals suspect that the hexane from the first leak may have already passed through the sewers before the MSD inspector left around 3 a.m. That leak eventually produced the explosion, according to the fire marshal's scenario.

Judging from water marks on the basin from which the hexane flowed into the sewers, one specialist in hazardous materials now believes that as many as 8,000 gallons of the highly explosive chemical may have leaked into the sewers last Thursday night and Friday morning.

That conflicts with the 500 gallons initially reported to the Metropolitan Sewer District by the company.

The specialist said he believes workers pumped as much hexane into the plant's system that night as it ordinarily uses in 10 to 20 days — possibly as many as 20,000 gallons.

"Once they used that much, they should have known something was screwy," he said. "Everybody there was well aware it was going in the sewer system."

A federal investigator added, "They were very fortunate the plant didn't blow up."

Two sources — one an MSD official and the other a local investigator — said Surace's report on that night indicates that plant officials did not tell him hexane was flooding the basin that feeds into the sewers.

"As I understand it, if it was in the basin, theoretically it was contained. He wouldn't look in the basin," the MSD official said. "Normally, if it's in the basin, it meant they had a handle on it."

A local investigator said Surace would have realized a dangerous spill was imminent if the company had told him it had lost seven or eight thousand gallons. But, he said, "It would indicate from Jim's report that they did not."

The same source said even if plant officials didn't realize the seriousness of the leak when they first called MSD — or while Surace was there — they should have called back as soon as they did.

Even immediately after the explosions, another investigator said, "The easy thing would have been to call the fire department and MSD and say, 'We've got a problem.'"

"The fire department would have come and pumped more water in [the basin] or put dirt down the sewer to block it or something. But they [Ralston Purina] did not do that."

Step 4. Either individually or in small groups, as directed by your instructor, answer the following question: Based on this story, who or what was responsible for the sewer explosion?

Step 5. In small groups or with the entire class, answer the following questions:

Questions

1. How do the two accounts of the sewer explosion differ?
2. Who is responsible for this accident?
3. How does our knowledge of attributional biases allow us to predict the differences between the two versions?
4. What do you believe is the most likely cause of the accident?
5. How could we and those involved in the situation more accurately attribute the cause of the explosion?

Notes

1. R. Leeper, "The Role of Motivation in Learning: A Study of the Phenomenon of Differential Motivation Control of the Utilization of Habits," *Journal of Genetic Psychology* 46 (1935): 3–40.
2. R. Buck, *Nonverbal Behavior and the Communication of Effect* (New York: Guilford Press, 1983); P. Ekman, "Cross-cultural Studies of Facial Expression," in *Darwin and Facial Expression,* ed. P. Ekman (New York: Academic Press, 1973).
3. C. Darwin, *The Expression of the Emotions in Man and Animals* (London: Murray, 1872).
4. P. Ekman and W.V. Friesen, *Unmasking the Face* (Englewood Cliffs, N.J.: Prentice-Hall, 1975).
5. L.A. Streeter, R.M. Krauss, V. Galler, C. Olson, and W. Apple, "Pitch Changes During Attempted Deception," *Journal of Personality and Social Psychology* 35 (1977): 345–350.
6. R.E. Kraut, "Verbal and Nonverbal Cues in the Perception of Lying," *Journal of Personality and Social Psychology* 36 (1978): 388–391; S. Chollar, "In the Blink of an Eye," *Psychology Today* 22 (1988): 8–10.
7. A.S. Imada and M.D. Hakel, "Influence of Nonverbal Communication and Rater Proximity on Impressions and Decisions in Simulated Employment Interviews," *Journal of Applied Psychology* 62 (1977): 295–300.
8. L. Ulrich and D. Trumbo, "The Selection Interview Since 1949," *Psychological Bulletin* 63 (1965): 100–116.
9. C.L. Kleinke, F.B. Meeker, and C. La-Fong, "Effects of Gaze, Touch, and Use of Name on Evaluation of 'Engaged' Couples," *Journal of Research in Personality* 1 (1974): 368–373.
10. M.L. Knapp, *Nonverbal Communication in Human Interaction,* 2d ed. (New York: Holt, Rinehart and Winston, 1978).
11. P.C. Ellsworth and J.M. Carlsmith, "Eye Contact and Gaze Aversion in an Aggressive Encounter," *Journal of Personality and Social Psychology* 28 (1973): 280–292; P.C. Ellsworth and E.J. Langer, "Staring and Approach: An Interpretation of the Stare as a Nonspecific Activator," *Journal of Personality and Social Psychology* 33 (1976): 117–122.
12. L.J. Cronbach, "Processes Affecting Scores on 'understanding of others' and 'assumed similarity,'" *Psychological Bulletin* 52 (1955): 177–193.
13. R. Taft, "The Ability to Judge People," *Psychological Bulletin* 52 (1955): 1–23.
14. J.S. Wiggins, *Personality and Prediction: Principles of Personality Assessment* (Reading, Mass.: Addison-Wesley, 1973); B. Kleinmuntz, "Why We Still Use Our Heads Instead of Formulas: Toward an Integrative Approach," *Psychological Bulletin* (1990): 296–310.
15. H.C. Triandis and V. Vassiliou, "Frequency of Contact and Stereotyping," *Journal of Personality and Social Psychology* 7 (1967): 316–328.
16. S.S. Zalkind and T.W. Costello, "Perception: Some Recent Research and Implications for Administration," *Administrative Science Quarterly* 7 (1962): 218–235.
17. S.E. Asch, "Forming Impressions of Personality," *Journal of Abnormal and Social Psychology* 41 (1946): 258–290.
18. S. Feshback and R.D. Singer, "The Effects of Fear Arousal upon Social Perception," *Journal of Abnormal and Social Psychology* 55 (1957): 283–288.
19. S.S. Sears, "Experimental Studies of Perception, I. Attribution of Traits," *Journal of Social Psychology* 7 (1936): 151–163.
20. J.V. McConnell, R.L. Cutler, and E.B. McNeil, "Subliminal Stimulation: An Overview," *American Psychologist* 13 (1958): 229–242; J.V. McConnell, "Reinvention of Subliminal Perception," *Skeptical Inquirer* 13 (1989): 427–429.
21. F. Heider, "Social Perception and Phenomenal Causality," *Psychological Review* 51 (1944): 358–374; F. Heider, *The Psychology of Interpersonal Relations* (New York: Wiley, 1958).
22. J.W. Thibaut and H.W. Riecken, "Some Determinants and Consequences of the Perception of Social Causality," *Journal of Personality* 24 (1955): 113–133.
23. L.H. Strickland, "Surveillance and Trust," *Journal of Personality* 26 (1958): 200–215.
24. C. Holden, "Identical Twins Reared Apart," *Science* (March 1980): 1323–1324.
25. J.R. Warren, "Birth Order and Social Behavior," *Psychological Bulletin* 65 (1966): 38–49.
26. L.H. Stewart, "Birth Order and Political Leadership: I. The American Presidents" (paper presented at the annual meeting of the American Psychological Association, 1970).
27. J.W. Macfarlane, L. Allen, and M.P. Honzik, "A Developmental Study of the Behavior Problems of Normal Children Between 21 Months and 14 Years," *University of California Publications in Child Development* 2 (1954): 483.

28. D.W. Mackinnon, "Violation of Prohibitions," in *Explorations in Personality*, ed. H. Murray (New York: Oxford University Press, 1938).

29. R. Koenig, "Toyota Takes Pains, and Time, Filling Jobs at Its Kentucky Plant," *The Wall Street Journal*, December 1, 1987, p. 1.

30. R.S. Woodworth, *Personal Data Sheet* (Chicago: Stoelting, 1918).

31. J.C. Nunnally, *Psychometric Theory* (New York: McGraw-Hill, 1967); O.K. Buros, ed., *Tests in Print III* (University of Nebraska, 1983); O.K. Buros, ed., *Mental Measurements Yearbook* (University of Nebraska, 1941–).

32. D.P. Crowne and D. Marlowe, *The Approval Motive: Studies in Evaluative Dependence* (New York: Wiley, 1964).

33. A.I. Rabin, "Projective Methods: An Historical Introduction," in *Projective Techniques in Personality Assessment*, ed. A. Rabin (New York: Springer, 1958), 3.

34. C.D. Morgan and H.A. Murray, "A Method of Investigating Fantasies: The Thematic Apperception Test," *Archives of Neurological Psychiatry* 34 (1935): 289–306.

35. J.B. Rotter, "Level of Aspiration as a Method of Studying Personality, III. Group Validity Studies," *Character and Personality* 11 (1943): 254–274; J.B. Rotter, "Generalized Expectancies for Internal Versus External Control of Reinforcement," *Psychological Monographs* 80, no. 609 (1966).

36. Rotter, "Generalized Expectancies," 11–12.

37. H.M. Lefcourt, "Recent Developments in the Study of Locus of Control," in *Progress in Experimental Personality Research*, ed. B. Maher (New York: Academic Press, 1972), 1–39.

38. J.S. Coleman, E.Q. Campbell, L.J. Hobson, J. McPartland, A.M. Mood, F.D. Weinfeld, and R.L. York, *Equality of Educational Opportunity* (Washington, D.C.: Government Printing Office, 1966).

39. R.P. Vecchio, "Workers' Belief in Internal versus External Determinants of Success," *Journal of Social Psychology* 114 (1981): 199–207.

40. M. Seeman, "On the Meaning of Alienation," *American Sociological Review* 24 (1959): 782–791; M. Seeman, "Alienation and Social Learning in a Reformatory," *American Sociological Review* 69 (1963): 270–284.

41. P.J. Andrisani and C. Nestel, "Internal-External Control as a Contributor to and Outcome of Work Experience," *Journal of Applied Psychology* 61 (1976): 156–165.

42. J.B. Rotter, "Some Problems and Misconceptions Related to the Construct of Internal versus External Control of Reinforcement," *Journal of Consulting and Clinical Psychology* 43 (1975): 56–67.

43. R.M. Baron and R.L. Ganz, "Effects of Locus of Control and Type of Feedback on the Task Performance of Lower-Class Black Children," *Journal of Personality and Social Psychology* 21 (1972): 124–130.

44. T. Adorno, E. Frenkel-Brunswik, D. Levinson, and N. Sanford, *The Authoritarian Personality* (New York: Harper and Row, 1950).

45. J.G. Martin and F.R. Westie, "The Tolerant Personality," *American Sociological Review* 24 (1959): 521–528.

46. I. Steiner and H. Johnson, "Authoritarianism and 'tolerance of trait inconsistency,'" *Journal of Abnormal and Social Psychology* 67 (1963): 388–391.

47. O. Milton, "Presidential Choice and Performance on a Scale of Authoritarianism," *American Psychologist* 7 (1952): 597–598; L.S. Wrightsman, "Attitudinal and Personality Correlates of Presidential Voting Preferences" (paper presented at the annual meeting of the American Psychological Association, 1965).

48. D.J. Levinson and P.E. Huffman, "Traditional Family Ideology and its Relation to Personality," *Journal of Personality* 23 (1955): 251–273.

49. L.S. Wrightsman, *Social Psychology in the Seventies* (Belmont, Calif.: Wadsworth, 1972).

50. V.H. Vroom, "Some Personality Determinants of the Effects of Participation" *Journal of Abnormal and Social Psychology* 59 (1959): 322–327.

51. M. Rokeach, *The Open and Closed Mind* (New York: Basic Books, 1960).

52. R.N. Taylor and M.D. Dunnette, "Influence of Dogmatism, Risk-taking Propensity, and Intelligence on Decision-making Strategies for a Sample of Industrial Managers," *Journal of Applied Psychology* 59 (1974): 420–423.

53. J.P. Esposito and H.C. Richards, "Dogmatism and the Congruence between Self-reported Job Preference and Performance among School Supervisors," *Journal of Applied Psychology* 59 (1974): 389–391.

54. J.M. Minelo and J. Garrett, "The Protestant Ethic as a Personality Variable," *Journal of Counseling and Clinical Psychology* 36 (1971): 40–44.

55. M. Merrens and J. Garrett, "The Protestant Ethic Scale as a Predictor of Effective Work Performance," *Journal of Applied Psychology* 60 (1975): 125–127.

56. J. Greenberg, "The Protestant Work Ethic

and Reactions to Negative Performance Evaluation on a Laboratory Task," *Journal of Applied Psychology* 62 (1977): 682–690.

57. O. Cherrington, "The Values of Younger Workers," *Business Horizons* 20 (1977): 18–20.

58. R.P. Vecchio, "The Function and Meaning of Work and the Job: Morse and Weiss (1955) Revisited," *Academy of Management Journal* 23 (1980): 361–367.

59. P.A. Sorokin, *The Crisis of Our Age: The Social and Cultural Outlook* (New York: Dutton, 1941).

60. I.B. Myers and K.C. Briggs, *Myers-Briggs Type Indicator* (Princeton, N.J.: Educational Testing Service, 1962); W. Taggert and D. Robey, "Minds and Managers: On the Dual Nature of Human Information Processing and Management," *Academy of Management Review* 6 (1981): 187–195; J.W. Slocum and D. Hellriegel, "A Look At How Managers' Minds Work," *Business Horizons* 26 (1983): 58–68.

61. A.B. Carroll, "Linking Business Ethics to Behavior in Organizations," *SAM Advanced Management Journal* 43 (1978): 4–11.

62. R. Ricklees, "Ethics in America," *The Wall Street Journal,* October 31, 1983, p. 33.

63. L. Kohlberg, "Stage and Sequence: The Cognitive-Developmental Approach to Socialization," in *Handbook of Socialization Theory and Research,* ed., D.A. Goslin (Chicago: Rand-McNally, 1969), 347–400.

64. L. Kohlberg and D. Candee, "The Relationship of Moral Judgment to Moral Action," in *Morality, Moral Behavior and Moral Development,* ed. W. Kurtines and J. Gerwitz (New York: Wiley, 1984), 52–73.

65. W.E. Stratton, W. Flynn, and G. Johnson, "Moral Development and Decision Making: A Study of Student Ethics," *Journal of Enterprise Management* 3 (1981): 35–41.

66. J.R. Snarey, "Cross-cultural Universality of Social-Moral Development: A Critical Review of Kohlbergian Research," *Psychological Bulletin* 97 (1985): 202–232.

67. L.K. Trevino, "Ethical Decision Making in Organizations: A Person-Situation Interactionist Model," *Academy of Management Review* 11 (1986): 601–617.

68. E.E. Ghiselli, "The Validity of Aptitude Tests in Personnel Selection," *Personnel Psychology* 26 (1973): 461–477.

69. J.L. Hughes, "Expressed Personality Needs as Predictors of Sales Success," *Personnel Psychology* 9 (1956): 347–357.

70. F.L. Schmidt and J.E. Hunter, "Development of a General Solution to the Problem of Validity Generalization," *Journal of Applied Psychology* 62 (1977): 529–540; J.E. Hunter, F.L. Schmidt, and K. Pearlman, "History and Accuracy of Validity Generalization Equations: A Response to the Callender and Osburn Reply," *Journal of Applied Psychology* 67 (1982): 853–858.

You may fool all of the people some of the time, you can even fool some of the people all of the time, but you can't fool all of the people all of the time.

— Abraham "Honest Abe" Lincoln

Work is a four-letter word.

— Abbie Hoffman

Job satisfaction? I didn't know the two words went together!

— A steelworker

Learning Objectives

After studying this chapter, you should be able to:

1. *Explain the nature of attitudes and their essential components.*

2. *Outline the most widely used methods of measuring attitudes.*

3. *Identify the means through which attitudes are formed.*

4. *Specify the components of attitude change and trace the steps in the change process.*

5. *Tell why management should take an interest in workers' job satisfaction.*

6. *Note the principal methods of measuring job satisfaction.*

7. *Cite the most frequent sources of job satisfaction.*

8. *Describe some typical employee responses to low job satisfaction.*

Attitudes and Job Satisfaction

■ The View from the Middle

The restructuring and streamlining of corporations that became so popular during the past decade have affected the attitudes of middle managers toward their jobs and employers. Often, it has been in the ranks of middle management that companies look for "dead wood" to eliminate, leaving the remaining managers as busy as they are nervous about the future of their careers.

One attitude that results is cynicism. Says a middle manager at Manufacturers Hanover Trust Company, "If I'm cynical, it's for a good reason. I've seen too many people thrown out on the street. And yet the same basic management team that got us in the predicament — whether it's bad foreign loans, bad energy loans, or the failure to move ahead in investment banking — is still there."

Another common attitude is fear, which leads many of the remaining middle managers to occupy themselves with self-protection more than with the duties of their job. For example, the Manufacturers Hanover manager observes, "Instead of trying to get work done, people are constantly covering their ass. You make sure you document everything, to the point where you wonder that guys might have tape recorders in their pockets at meetings." A manager who survived the massive cutbacks at General Motors says, "Any time we had a bad period in the past, you could see the light at the end of the tunnel, and you could usually guess what it would take to turn things around. This is the first time I can't see a light."

In this environment, middle managers often feel burdened by carrying a load of work formerly handled by several people. The GM manager says, "I ended up with a job description that was roughly twice the scope of my old responsibilities." At General Electric, a middle manager observes, "I feel overworked. I work hard, and sometimes I don't enjoy it anymore." This manager finds that he is too busy with paperwork to spend enough time with subordinates, which makes him feel like a poor manager.

Not surprisingly, such attitudes translate into low levels of job satisfaction. A middle manager at Georgia-Pacific Corporation says, "I would take early retirement today if I could live off of it." Nevertheless, many managers remain loyal to their employer. Says one, "The Organization Man isn't dead, he's disillusioned."

If, as expected, companies continue to seek ways to operate with lower administrative costs, these concerns will continue through the end of the century. This chapter describes why companies should be concerned about the attitudes and job satisfaction of employees — first-line workers as well as managers. It begins by exploring the nature and formation of attitudes in general, then turns to the more specific issue of job satisfaction.

Source: John A. Byrne, "Caught in the Middle: Six Managers Speak Out on Corporate Life," *Business Week*, September 12, 1988, pp. 80–88.

Much of the excitement and fascination of organizational life stems from differences of opinion. One member of a work group may feel that the supervisor is overbearing, while another may find the same supervisor highly likable. People also have different attitudes toward the quality of their jobs, the adequacy of their pay, and so on. These attitudes help to explain a good deal of the behavior that occurs in organizational settings. For example, attitudes toward supervisors and company policies predict workers' endorsement of unionization. Also, attitudinal differences can explain why people have different reactions to essentially the same work experiences.

The Nature of Attitudes

When we use the term attitude in daily speech, such as when we speak of our attitude toward the space program or our attitude toward social welfare, we are usually referring to our feelings about something. But organizational behavior researchers prefer a more precise definition. In organizational behavior, an **attitude** is an idea charged with emotion that predisposes a set of actions to a specific group of stimuli.[1] This definition covers the three essential components of an attitude: the cognitive, the affective, and the behavioral.

The **cognitive**, or knowing, **component** of an attitude is represented in our definition by the word "idea." By an idea, we mean that some category we use in our thinking is an essential feature of an attitude. For example, we would infer the category "authority figures" from observing the responses of a friend to teachers, police officers, parents, and supervisors. The **affective**, or emotional, **component** of an attitude is noted in the phrase "charged with emotion." The emotional component of an attitude is its most critical feature and is reflected in such comments as "I like . . . ," "I dislike . . . ," and "I hope . . . . "

The **behavioral component** of an attitude refers to a predisposition to act in a particular way. In our definition of an attitude, the behavioral component is represented by the phrase "predisposes a set of actions to a specific group of stimuli." The behavioral component is demonstrated by such actions as seeking or avoiding certain people and situations, purchasing a particular product, and so on.

It is important to note that the behavioral predisposition is determined to some extent by the cognitive and the affective components.* Consider, for example, someone who believes that her job offers no opportunity for advancement (the cognitive aspect). She states that being in a dead-end job is very distasteful to her (the emotional component). Consequently, she says that she is going to begin searching for another job (the behavioral predisposition).

---

* Imagine a South Sea Islander who is seeing a helicopter for the first time in his life. Since he does not have the category "helicopter" in his mental repertoire, he may possibly categorize the stimulus as a monster. Given the emotion associated with the category "monster," he will likely throw rocks at the helicopter or flee from it. Upon learning that the object is not threatening and given encouragement to approach, he will come to develop a new category for the object. It would be erroneous to infer that the islander had an initially unfavorable attitude toward helicopters, because he did not truly possess the category of helicopter.

Measuring Attitudes

Attitudes are not directly observable. Their existence and nature must be inferred. Thus, people who study attitudes (such as organizational behavior researchers, social psychologists, marketing researchers, political scientists, communication researchers, and pollsters) cannot examine attitudes directly, but must instead consider the three aspects of attitudes.

Attempts to study attitudes focus most frequently on the affective component. Measures of the affective component can be physiological (heart rate, blood pressure, and pupil dilation, for example) or verbal (as in the use of survey questions). The cognitive component can be measured through verbal statements of belief (such as personal estimates that an outcome will follow an event) or reports of categorizations and attributes (for example, whether a person classifies others directly as liberals or conservatives, versus recognizing the existence of many gradations of political beliefs). The behavioral component can be measured by studying actual behavior (whether employees request job transfers, or how they vote in an election) or by studying statements of intention to act in a particular way.

Graphic Scales   The most commonly used device for studying attitudes is the **graphic scale.** Since Rensis Likert first advocated such scales in 1932, they have become exceedingly popular.[2] A graphic, or Likert, scale asks a person to indicate his degree of agreement with a statement by checking one of five possible positions: strongly agree, agree, undecided, disagree, or strongly disagree. A sample Likert scale question would be:

**Trade unions have too great an
effect on the economy.**

Strongly   :_____ :_____ :_____ :_____ :_____: Strongly
Disagree   1   2   3   4   5   Agree

It is not absolutely necessary to have five possible positions for responding. The simplest response format would consist of only two options:

Agree_____   Disagree_____.

But research indicates that the reliability of rating scales increases with the number of steps in the scale.†

Semantic Differential Scales   **Semantic differential scales** are another useful attitude measure. These scales ask for ratings based on a pair of adjectives that are opposite in meaning.[4] The following semantic differential scale items could be used to assess a person's feelings toward the movement for women's equality.

---

† The increase in reliability is fairly rapid as we move from 2 to 20 steps, with the gain in reliability leveling off at 7 steps. After 11 steps, there is fairly little gain in reliability for the additional refinement.[3] As a result, many attitude researchers prefer to use scales with 7 or 11 steps.

Women's Equality Movement

Ineffective :___:___:___:___:___:___:___: Effective
         1   2   3   4   5   6   7

Foolish   :___:___:___:___:___:___:___: Wise
         1   2   3   4   5   6   7

Weak   :___:___:___:___:___:___:___: Strong
         1   2   3   4   5   6   7

Useless   :___:___:___:___:___:___:___: Useful
         1   2   3   4   5   6   7

Bad   :___:___:___:___:___:___:___: Good
         1   2   3   4   5   6   7

Attitude Formation

Attitudes are acquired through learning.‡ Their sources can be divided into three categories: direct experience, social communication, and emotional conditioning.

Direct Experience   Our direct and personal involvement with the objects in our environment create our attitudes, both positive or negative. It is difficult to like someone who ignores you or is overbearing, and it is difficult to dislike someone who is warm and responsive to you or who pays you compliments. On the other hand, lack of contact can facilitate the development of negative attitudes. This principle is suggested by the sometimes deliberate maintenance of distance between soldiers and their enemies in order to reduce the possibility of interpersonal liking.

Interestingly, simple exposure to an object can lead to positive evaluations.[5] Repeated exposure to an object having no strong prior emotional value attached to it is sufficient to enhance one's attitude toward the object. These findings suggest that "familiarity breeds attraction." Based on these findings, Milgram proposed the notion of the "familiar stranger" — that is, a person you see with some regularity, but never interact with socially.[6] Examples of familiar strangers are people with whom you wait each morning to catch a bus, fellow students in a classroom with whom you do not speak, and office workers with whom you share an elevator each day. If by chance you meet one of these people outside of their typical setting, you are likely to develop a positive interpersonal relationship quickly.

Social Communication   We also develop attitudes from social communication. Few of us have ever actually met the president of a Fortune 500 company or a union official. Yet all of us have attitudes toward such individuals that are based on messages transmitted to us by others. For example, parents influence their children's attitudes toward people of other races and ethnic origins. Politicians and the managers of the mass media can also control the information we receive, which in turn influences attitudes. Coworkers can also greatly

‡ Alternative explanations for the origin of attitudes (e.g., inborn or genetic explanations) are difficult to defend. However, it is not inconceivable that there may be genetic differences in individual susceptibility to persuasion.

■ **Table 4.1**

Influences and Steps in Attitude Change

Factors That Influence Attitude Change (Independent Variables)	Steps in the Attitude Change Process (Dependent Variables)
Source	Attention
Message	Comprehension
Medium	Yielding
Audience	Retention
	Action

influence an employee's attitudes toward a job. This process occurs when employees attempt to influence a coworker to share their view (positive, negative, or indifferent) of many of the features of their work setting.[7]

Emotional Conditioning   Attitudes also can be formed via emotional conditioning. As will be discussed in Chapter 5, physiological reactions can be aroused by pairing a neutral stimulus with a positive or negative event. This process suggests that attitudes are sometimes formed for reasons not always rational. For example, we may come to endorse a particular point of view in part because the source of the message is highly attractive or entertaining.

Because we encounter objects and persons in contexts that have their own rewarding or punishing features, our attitudes toward them are susceptible to a wide variety of contaminating influences. Janis, Kaye, and Kirschner reported an intriguing study that demonstrated the influence of context in shaping attitudes.[8] As part of a study of the effects of persuasive communication, they provided soft drinks for some subjects to enjoy while reading specific material. The results showed that the individuals who had been provided soft drinks were persuaded by what they had read to a greater degree than individuals who had not been given soft drinks. This set of results suggests that seemingly trivial factors within a given setting can have discernible effects.

Attitude Change

People are constantly trying to change each other's attitudes. Advertisers want to change the public's attitudes toward their clients' products. Union leaders, managers, and employees attempt to influence others' attitudes in favor of their points of view. Over the years, a good deal of research has been conducted on the topic of attitude change by people in the fields of marketing, communications, social psychology, and political science as well as in the field of organizational behavior. Despite the diversity of the approaches of these researchers, the research findings are generally accepted by most students of the topic, regardless of their discipline.

The Components of Attitude Change   Four factors are involved in attitude change: the source, the message, the medium, and the audience. The process of attitude change follows five steps: attention, comprehension, yielding, retention, and action (Table 4.1).

Source factors refer to aspects of the presenter of an attitude change attempt (intent to persuade, attractiveness, etc.). **Message factors** are the specific structure and content of what is transmitted in a persuasive appeal (e.g., whether or not one or two sides of an issue are presented). **Medium factors** involve the effects of the channel that is employed (printed material, a face-to-face appeal, etc.). **Audience factors** deal with the influence of individual characteristics (e.g., aspects of the personality of the target person).

The five steps in the process of attitude change focus on the target person's attention (whether the person is attentive to and receiving the persuasive appeal), comprehension (whether the appeal is understood as it was intended to be), yielding (whether the individual truly surrenders to the persuasion), retention (whether the individual's attitude change is more than merely transitory), and action (whether the attitude change attempt alters subsequent behavior).

Most researchers believe that an individual must go through all five steps in the process of attitude change. But researchers who believe in the possibility of subliminal influences contend that messages that are not attended to or comprehended can still influence attitudes and later behavior. Subliminal messages that are sometimes embedded in background music in department stores in an effort to discourage shoplifting are based on this premise.

The most prevalent approach to studying attitudes labels the four sets of factors (source, message, medium, and audience) as *independent variables* — factors to be manipulated by researchers in order to study their influence — and views the five steps in the process as *dependent variables* — outcomes or measures of the effects of changes in the independent variable. As an introductory overview of the topic of attitude change, some of the major findings associated with each of the four factors will be discussed.

Source Factors   The source of an attempt at attitude change can have a significant influence on the magnitude and direction of the change. Research shows that people are more likely to be influenced by sources that seem more expert and attractive. People also respond better to sources who are similar to themselves. That is why politicians often try to emphasize the traits and experiences that they have in common with their audience.

The initial degree of liking that an audience feels for the source is also important. Generally, the more a person likes the source of a persuasive appeal, the greater the likelihood of attitude change in the hoped-for direction. This can be explained from the perspective of **balance theory**.[9] Balance theory proposes that we try to maintain a fair degree of order or consistency among our beliefs. We can portray many simple situations involving attitude change attempts using a triangular model (Figure 4.1).

Imagine a source whose opinion you highly value (for example, your secretary) tells you he or she strongly dislikes another secretary whom you like somewhat. This places you in a socially difficult situation. Such a situation is unbalanced in that you probably feel a psychological tension or strain (see Figure 4.1a). Balance theory predicts you will probably attempt to restore harmony or balance by altering your feelings on the weakest of three links. In

■ Figure 4.1

Representations of Unbalanced and Balanced Situations

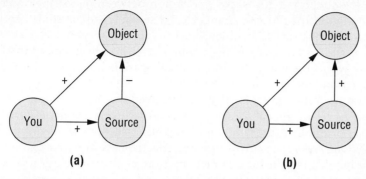

(a)   (b)

Positive and negative signs represent comfortable and uncomfortable psychological states.

our example, your attraction to the source is likely to be the strongest link. Assuming that the source's dislike for the other secretary is substantial (and not likely to be changed by simple persuasion), it is likely your favorable evaluation of the other secretary will be diminished. However, if your evaluation of the other secretary is extremely positive, you may exert substantial effort to change your secretary's attitude.

An ideal balanced situation, of course, is one where all three links are positive (see Figure 4.1b). Situations in which any two links are negative — such as hearing a person you dislike making a statement that you find distasteful — are also balanced or consistent. When diagramming social situations, an odd number of negative signs is an indication of unbalance, while an even number signifies balance.

The use of highly attractive sources for endorsing products is based on the same logic that underlies balance theory. Advertisers hope that the linkage between the target person and the initially neutral object will produce a positive response by virtue of the other linkages being positive. In interpersonal relations, we sometimes rely on a similar ploy by telling others that a prestigious or attractive individual has endorsed some object or course of action. This tactic is occasionally used to steer the target person away from a course of action or an object by citing a disliked person's endorsement.

Message Factors   The influence of both the content and the structure of messages has been heavily researched. One content factor that has been intensely studied is the power of playing on people's fears. Portraying fearful situations is a potent means of inducing attitude change. For example, attempts to sell life insurance via the media typically rely on fear appeals, as do attempts to sell such products as radial tires and motor oil. By increasing the level of the threat, one could expect to encourage individuals to surrender to an endorsed position. However, one can also imagine appeals to fear having an opposite effect, in which people respond by becoming more resistant to the persuasive appeal (i.e., by putting up blinders). Research on the topic, which has examined the influence of fear appeals in many diverse contexts, has uncovered evidence of the existence of both attitude change and audience resistance (although most studies have reported a positive association between increasing levels of fear and the amount of attitude change[10]). For purposes of attitude change, it is likely that there is an optimal level of fear arousal, beyond which the appeal can have an adverse effect. This optimal level, however, may be difficult to pinpoint without conducting an empirical search, since the level is likely to vary across individuals and topic areas.

Another message factor that has received considerable study is whether conclusions in an appeal are more persuasive when explicit (stated for the audience) or implicit (unstated but derivable from the arguments made in the appeal). One can argue for the greater effectiveness of either explicit conclusions or implicit conclusions. For example, an explicit conclusion would aid in audience comprehension. On the other hand, an implicit conclusion would allow people to discover the main point by themselves, with greater acceptance of the conclusion possibly resulting. The results of research on the topic suggest that the explicit approach is generally more effective than the implicit approach, perhaps because the explicit approach improves message receptivity (i.e., audience comprehension). However, the implicit approach may be more effective in producing attitude change if the topic is one that is highly ego-involving. Since most of the topics studied have not been ego-involving (as is also true of most media advertising), it is possible that the potential usefulness of the implicit approach has been understated.

Considerable research has also been conducted on the effectiveness of presenting both sides of an argument as opposed to presenting a one-sided argument that ignores the opposing point of view. Controlled studies contrasting two-sided and one-sided presentations suggest that success of either appeal depends on other factors. Ignoring the opposing point of view tends to be more effective with individuals who initially favor the presenter's conclusion (it appears that they do not wish to have any doubts raised). Those initially opposed to the presenter's conclusion are more likely to be persuaded by a presentation showing both sides of an issue. The intelligence of the audience is an additional consideration, in that individuals who are more intelligent are likely to expect an even-handed (two-sided) presentation of an issue before they will form an opinion. The level of familiarity or controversy surrounding an issue is also important; topics that are relatively unknown to an audience can be more easily handled by merely ignoring the unpublicized or unfamiliar point of view, since the audience may be unaware of opposing arguments.

Medium Factors   During the 1960s and early 1970s, attitude researchers were greatly interested in the ways that media affected people's attitudes.[11] More recently, researchers have become more skeptical about the once-popular notion that the medium has greater impact on an audience than has the message itself. Research suggests that people find spoken appeals more influential than written appeals, even though they comprehend written appeals better, and they are more likely to be persuaded by face-to-face appeals. The greater effectiveness of face-to-face appeals may be due to the social pressure that a listener feels to avoid being rude and to comply with a speaker's explicit or implied request.

In comparison to other channels of communication, the mass media appear to be relatively ineffective in significantly altering attitudes. The mass media can, however, instruct and inform the public about the existence and the availability of objects and issues. The public's resistance to the influence of mass media appears to stem from a lack of strong involvement in media presentations. Generally speaking, the more immediate and personalized the attitude change attempt, the greater the degree of audience compliance.

Audience Factors   Individual differences have been examined in connection with the magnitude of attitude change. The more commonly studied audience factors include age (both chronological age and mental age), sex, self-esteem, and prior beliefs.

There is a fairly consistent relationship between chronological age and persuasibility. Suggestibility peaks at about age 8 or 9 and then decreases.§ The decline in suggestibility with age may be steeper, however, for males than females. Mental age (i.e., intelligence) bears a far less consistent relationship with susceptibility to persuasion. It appears that intelligence is also generally related to a greater degree of attention and comprehension, but inversely related to degree of yielding.

Sex and persuasibility have long been assumed to be related; females are generally regarded as being more easily influenced by attitude change attempts. Evidence of sex effects has been reported in many different studies.[12] Typically, this effect has been attributed to greater cultural pressure on females to be conforming and compliant. More recently, a review of the sex effect literature has called into question the accuracy of the simple statement concerning female compliance.[13] The sex of the influencer and influencee may affect the level of influence. Also, female compliance with attitude change attempts may be diminishing as the societal norm of accepting and encouraging female noncompliance becomes more widely endorsed.

Intuitively, we would expect that self-esteem would be related to an individual's susceptibility to persuasion, with high self-esteem individuals less easily persuasible than low self-esteem individuals. However, the relation of self-esteem and ease of persuasibility may be different for males and females. Low self-esteem females appear to be alienated from and rejecting of attempts to influence their attitudes, while an inverse relationship exists for males.[14]

A person's prior beliefs play an important role in determining his or her response to an attitude change attempt. As mentioned earlier in our discussion of balance theory, people desire to have consistency among their beliefs. Inconsistency, or dissonance (to borrow the musical analogy of a dissonant chord), is stressful.

One of the interesting aspects of dissonance is the influence it can have on altering our attitudes. Leon Festinger has argued that when individuals behave in ways that run counter to their private beliefs, and little external justification

§ It was probably more than coincidence that Hitler's Youth Corps was directed toward young people in this age range.

exists to explain or rationalize away their behavior in light of their original beliefs, then their attitudes are likely to be altered in order to bring about consistency between their beliefs and behavior.[15]

As a test of the principle of **cognitive (or mental) dissonance**, Festinger and Carlsmith conducted a now well-known experiment.[16] College students were asked to perform a boring task (repeatedly turning wooden pegs). After two hours of tedium, the subject was asked to tell the next subject that the experiment was fun and exciting (clearly, a request to make a statement that the subject did not believe in). Ostensibly, the subject was being asked to help create a mental set in the mind of the next subject in order to study the performance effects of being given a positive expectation about a task. Each subject was offered either $1.00 or $20.00 for serving as an assistant to the researcher by lying to the next subject. After attempting to deceive the next subject during a brief conversation in a waiting room, each subject was then asked to complete a lengthy questionnaire.

Of interest to the researchers was the evaluation of the boring task by the subjects who were paid to say something that they did not believe. The results showed that those subjects who were offered $20.00 for advocating something they did not initially believe in continued to hold a low opinion of the attractiveness of the task (i.e., they had an external justification for having lied — they did it for the money). As predicted by Festinger's theory of cognitive dissonance, those subjects who were offered only $1.00 rated the task as being enjoyable. This attitude change resulted from the subjects' felt need to justify the inconsistency of their earlier actions and their prior beliefs. Since the subjects offered $1.00 could not explain away their behavior by attributing it to a financial incentive (and since they could not change the historical fact that they had endorsed a statement they did not believe was truthful), they were under a degree of psychological pressure to alter their attitude toward the task (i.e., they actually came to view it as enjoyable).

This finding, and other related dissonance study findings, are all the more intriguing because of the counterintuitive nature of the dissonance reduction process. The principles of learning theory, a view to be discussed in Chapter 5, would predict that the subjects who received the larger reward ($20.00) would be more likely to change their attitude in a favorable direction.

In a related study of the dissonance phenomenon, Aronson and Mills studied the evaluations of social groups after a price had been paid to gain membership to the group.[17] Specifically, they required college women to undergo the equivalent of initiation rites in order to gain admission to a highly desirable social group. The results suggested that the greater the cost to the individual (the more severe the price of initiation), the more dissonance the individual experienced when she later learned that the group was, objectively, quite uninteresting and socially unattractive. The reduction of dissonance was manifested by the initiates who paid the "higher price" for admission to the group by their providing more favorable evaluations of the social group. A clear implication of this finding is that the more that people can be made to "pay" for admission to a group (be it membership in a fraternity or a corporation), the more likely they are to value eventual acceptance into that group.

An Inside Look
Keeping Good Employees

One company that has a record of keeping and benefiting from good employees is 3M. The company uses programs that are designed to keep its employees innovative. As a result, its employees have developed more than 45,000 different products. Says Bruce Hoeffel, 3M's director of staffing and employee resources, "If we provide people with challenges on the job, the company will be compensated."

An example of how the company encourages innovation involves fluorochemicals. For more than seven years, over 100 people worked on the fluorochemical project, but the company had no earnings to show for this investment. Top management considered canceling the project. The vice president for research quizzed 50 members of the research team individually, asking whether the project should continue; 48 said it should, and the project continued.

Shortly thereafter, a laboratory technician spilled a sample of fluorochemicals on her tennis shoes. It would not wash out, and the technician made a surprising discovery. The affected parts of her shoes stayed much cleaner than the rest. The result: Scotchguard fabric protection and a whole line of additional products.

Another 3M technique for keeping valuable employees is a so-called dual ladder of advancement for employees with special skills (say, in science or in sales). If such an employee's next career step is management, the employee is offered a choice: moving into administration or continuing to work in his area of specialty with heightened status and a higher salary. 3M executives recognize that a move into management is not a reward for every employee. In Hoeffel's words, "An important thing at 3M is sensitivity."

3M further demonstrates its sensitivity by conducting an employee survey of its management style every three years. The company also has a policy of promoting from within.

John Mirtz, an executive recruiter and management consultant with Byrnes, Elsom, Mirtz, Morice, Inc., observes that high performers "are like gifted children," and companies often do not know how to handle them. 3M is clearly an exception.

Source: Henry Eason, "Keeping Good People," *Nation's Business*, July 1984, pp. 37–39.

Attitudes and Actions

The link between verbal statements and behaviors is not simple, or always direct. In some situations you may notice a good deal of inconsistency between what people say and what they do.

Mental states and behaviors may be controlled by different mechanisms.[18] Verbal statements are often made in response to very different constraints and pressures than are behavioral expressions. Actions are influenced by such additional forces as norms, changes in group affiliation and salience, and the opportunity to engage in specific behaviors. When the strength of a group's norms and the strength of an individual's desire to comply with such influences are taken into account, attitudes can be used to predict actions with surprising accuracy.[19] The degree of accuracy is especially great if the time horizon for the prediction is not extremely distant.

The need for individuals to have specific knowledge about how to comply with an attempt to change their attitudes is also important for explaining subsequent behavior. In a study of the effectiveness of an attempt to persuade college students to get tetanus shots, one group of subjects merely received information on the importance of obtaining the shot, while another group received the same appeal plus specific information on how to reach the campus infirmary, whom to see, the best hours to visit the infirmary, a campus map, and so on. Although students in both groups were apparently favorably influenced by the persuasive appeal, the percentage of students in each group who actually obtained the shot differed, with the students who had gotten the specific information about how to obtain the shot being far more likely to receive it.

Generally, it can be stated that attitudes often do affect behavior. Available evidence suggests that attitudes that are very specific in nature and that are developed from direct experience with a person or an object do affect many forms of behavior.[20]

Job Satisfaction

Emotional reactions to work experiences are inevitable. One's thinking, feeling, and action tendencies (that is, one's attitude) toward work is termed **job satisfaction**. As is true of all attitudes, a person's level of job satisfaction is formed via experience. While a worker's attitudes are influenced by the job itself, communications from others can also play an important role. Furthermore, a worker's expectations about a job can greatly influence his or her interpretation and evaluation of work-related experiences.[21]

The Importance of Job Satisfaction

Modern managers recognize that an organization's performance should be measured in human dimensions as well as in terms of return on investment, market share, profit after taxes, and the like. A variety of reasons support the desirability of attending to workers' satisfaction. Perhaps the foremost reason is a moral one. Consider that working is a requirement for most people. The alternative, a subsistence-level existence based on government and charitable support, is unacceptable to most people. Given that most people must work, and that most people will spend the majority of their adult lives at work, it can be argued that employers have a *moral obligation* to make the experience personally rewarding (or, at a minimum, not painful or dehumanizing.)**

Workers' *physical and mental well-being* appear to be correlated with job satisfaction in that more highly satisfied workers have better physical and mental health records.[22] This evidence, however, is strictly correlational in nature. As a consequence, it is difficult to say in what direction the "causal arrow" is pointing. It is also conceivable that other factors that may come into

---

** It is an interesting exercise to calculate the proportion of one's life that is spent at work. Consider that the average adult will live to a predicted actuarial age. The number of years, in fact hours, of life that a person has left can then be determined. This finite number of hours can be further divided into unconscious time (spent sleeping), conscious but uninteresting and nonproductive time (when engaging in routine activities such as brushing teeth, dressing, and commuting), and conscious productive time. As a percentage, the majority of conscious productive time will be spent working.

play (e.g., educational level and income) could be largely responsible for the observed correlations. Nonetheless, serious job dissatisfaction, as manifested by stress, can lead to a variety of physiological disorders, including ulcers and arterial disease.

Job satisfaction can also play an important role in a company's *ability to attract and retain qualified workers.* An organization's very survival rests heavily on this ability, and a company that is known to mistreat its personnel will have difficulty in drawing the best people to staff its positions.

Low levels of job satisfaction have been related to such problems as turnover,[23] absenteeism,[24] union-organizing activity,[25] and the *filing of grievances.*[26] Because such problems can be costly and disruptive to an organization, they cannot be lightly dismissed. Thus, job satisfaction is exceedingly important for the well-being of the organization as well as for the individual.

Measuring Job Satisfaction

In recognition of the importance of job satisfaction, many organizations monitor employee attitudes. Though many large organizations, such as General Electric, Hewlett-Packard, and Sears, routinely conduct their own surveys of employee satisfaction, others, such as Wells Fargo and Leaseway Transportation, hire consulting firms to handle the task of assessing employee attitudes.[27]

Although in-depth interviews and questionnaires are sometimes used to measure job satisfaction, the most commonly used method is the anonymous survey. The variety of attitude scales that are employed in surveys reflects the diversity of approaches to conceptualizing job satisfaction (Figure 4.2). The earliest approaches characterized job satisfaction in global terms, that is, satisfaction was viewed as an overall reaction to one's job in its entirety.†† Scales such as the GM Faces Scale[28] and the Brayfield-Rothe Job Satisfaction Questionnaire[29] exemplify the **global approach.** More recently a faceted approach to studying employee satisfaction has emerged. The **faceted approach** attempts to study employee reactions to each of several aspects, or facets, of the job (e.g., one's supervisor, pay, or coworkers). Two outstanding examples of the faceted approach are the Job Descriptive Index[30] and the Minnesota Satisfaction Questionnaire.[31]

Global or facet-free scales offer the advantages of being relatively brief and easy to administer. In fact, if a set of simple instructions is read to the participants, the GM Faces Scale can be administered to employees who are illiterate. The faceted scales tend to be more lengthy; the Minnesota Satisfaction Questionnaire, or MSQ, has 100 items covering a total of 20 different facets. The Job Descriptive Index, or JDI, offers something of a compromise between length, ease of administration, required level of education of the respondent, and number of job facets (i.e., pay, coworkers, supervision, oppor-

†† Perhaps the earliest report of a study of job satisfaction was a treatise by Rammizzini in Modeno, Italy, in the early 1600s. Having noted a look of disgust on the faces of cesspool cleaners, he decided to question them on their feelings about their work. In the mid-1800s, Karl Marx developed a satisfaction questionnaire. However, the early forms of surveys more often asked *supervisors* to state what they believed workers felt about their jobs, rather than asking the workers themselves.

■ **Figure 4.2**

Sample Items from Various Job Satisfaction Scales

Brayfield-Rothe Satisfaction Scale

My job is like a hobby to me.

Strongly Agree   Agree   Undecided   Disagree   Strongly Disagree

I enjoy my work more than my leisure time.

Strongly Agree   Agree   Undecided   Disagree   Strongly Disagree

---

Job Descriptive Index

How well does each word describe your pay? Circle Y if it does describe your pay, N if it does not describe your pay, or ? if you cannot decide

Less than I deserve   Y   N   ?   Insecure   Y   N   ?   Highly paid   Y   N   ?

G M Faces Scale

Consider all aspects of your job. Circle the face which best describes your feelings about your job in general.

7   6   5   4   3   2   1

Minnesota Satisfaction Questionnaire

On my present job, this is how I feel about . . .

1. Being able to keep busy all the time.

Very Dissatisfied   Dissatisfied   Neutral   Satisfied   Very Satisfied

2. The praise I get for doing a good job.

Very Dissatisfied   Dissatisfied   Neutral   Satisfied   Very Satisfied

---

tunities for promotion, and the work itself). For these reasons (along with evidence of its reliability and validity), the JDI is one of the most widely known and commonly used devices for measuring job satisfaction.

The faceted approach is logically superior to the global approach, in that one can easily imagine instances in which an employee might be dissatisfied with her coworkers but extremely satisfied with the work itself. As previously mentioned, such scales as the JDI and the MSQ permit the independent assessment of attitudes on a number of distinct dimensions. In practice, the responses of people to these different facets tend to be positively correlated, so that people who are satisfied with their supervisor also tend to be satisfied with their coworkers, and so on. This evidence suggests that it may be reasonable to conclude that a general or global factor underlies the responses. In summary, most researchers acknowledge the need to use faceted scales, since they yield more specific information. However, most respondents in satisfaction surveys do not appear to compartmentalize their feelings.

■ **Table 4.2**

Causes and Consequences of Job Satisfaction

Causes		Consequences	
Pay and Benefits	Autonomy	Absenteeism	Mental Well-being
Coworkers	Job Challenge	Tardiness	Grievances
Supervisors	Working Conditions	Turnover	
Opportunities for Promotion	Job Security	Early Retirement	
Job Level	Sense of Recognition	Union Activity	
	Initial Expectations	Physical Well-being	

Sources of Job Satisfaction

Over 3,000 studies have been conducted on the topic of job satisfaction, or morale as it was more frequently termed in previous years.‡‡ Their results tend to point to much the same conclusions. For example, certain variables are consistently correlated with job satisfaction (Table 4.2). One of the most important variables is job level. Satisfaction is higher among workers in higher-level positions, while satisfaction tends to be lowest among holders of jobs that can be characterized as hot, heavy, or dangerous, such as work in steel mills and unskilled jobs.

Length of service and race are also frequently correlated with job satisfaction. Individuals with less time on the job and black workers are, in the aggregate, somewhat more dissatisfied than "long-termers" and white workers. Of course, it is difficult to draw any firm conclusions from such correlational evidence because job level is also associated with length of service and race. Long-termers tend to be in higher-level jobs, and black workers tend to be less educated and are more likely to hold unskilled positions.[33]

Females are also more likely to be found in lower-level jobs. Historically, lower female expectations for employment opportunities have been fairly consistent with the lack of opportunities for women. Evidence of sex differences in job satisfaction levels has been mixed. It is likely, however, that rising expectations of women in the labor force will produce differences in job satisfaction between the sexes. It is also likely that differences in job satisfaction between younger and older women will become more evident as a result of the growing disparity in expectations between generations.

Finally, organizational size has been identified as a correlate of job satisfaction. Employees in smaller organizations tend to be more satisfied than employees in larger organizations.[34] The size of an organization may not in and of itself affect job satisfaction, but size is associated with more specific sources of satisfaction.

‡‡ Blum and Naylor, however, maintain that the terms *satisfaction* and *morale* should not be used interchangeably, since satisfaction is an individual phenomenon, while morale is a by-product of personal experiences in a group setting.[32]

Intrinsic versus Extrinsic Sources of Satisfaction   All sources of job satisfaction fall into two categories: intrinsic and extrinsic. Intrinsic sources originate from within the individual and have psychological value. Such satisfactions are essentially self-administered. Autonomy (that is, independence, such as the ability to choose one's own work pace) is one source of intrinsic satisfaction. Other intrinsic sources include a sense of challenge and feelings of recognition.

Extrinsic sources of satisfaction originate from outside the individual; they come from his or her environment. Forces beyond the individual's control determine the frequency and magnitude of extrinsic sources of satisfaction. Working conditions and opportunities to interact with coworkers are sources of extrinsic satisfaction, as are job security and fringe benefits.

In addition, some sources of satisfaction serve a dual purpose in that they can be extrinsic, or tangible, in nature while having intrinsic, or psychological, value because of what they symbolize. Both a high salary and rapid career progress would offer dual sources of satisfaction.

Expectations   Satisfaction is a very personal experience that depends heavily on an individual's expectations. For example, imagine that you have just been offered an executive position that pays $150,000 a year. It sounds attractive, of course. In the abstract, it's difficult to conceive of how someone could be dissatisfied with such a salary. Suppose, however, that you discover that other people who have much the same job are receiving $500,000 to $900,000 per year. What formerly seemed to be an attractive salary would suddenly become unsatisfactory.

Expectations can have a powerful influence on a person's level of satisfaction. For example, new employees often have unrealistically high expectations. In the time between being offered a job and the first day of work, new employees may fantasize about how rapidly they will rise in the new organization, what immediate working conditions will be like, and so on. Once on the job, however, they may experience a shock when confronted with a number of harsh realities. They may discover that no promotion ladder extends from their current position, that their coworkers are not very pleasant, or that the lunch room and restrooms are delapidated. The unrealistic expectations of new employees may be generated partly by personal fantasy and by the media. But company recruiters may also play a role by deceiving prospective employees about the nature of their future employment.

Companies can counter the potential problem of unrealistic expectations by providing job-orientation programs that present a more realistic point of view. The effects of realistic job previews on individuals' reactions to their work have been extensively studied. With minor exceptions,[35] the results have generally shown that individuals who are told both the bad and the good features of their new jobs before they begin working have higher levels of job satisfaction, lower initial expectations about the job, and a lower rate of early turnover.[36],§§ Some organizations (for example, Nissan Motor Manufacturing

§§ The importance of creating realistic expectations is increasingly being recognized. In addition to profit-oriented organizations, nonprofit organizations such as religious orders are employing realistic job previews. One group of religious women provides a realistic preview to young women

at its Smyrna, Tennessee, facility) modify the concept of providing realistic previews by having prospective employees participate in "preemployment" programs that are essentially "job tryouts." During a job tryout, an applicant completes a variety of exercises that simulate job-related tasks. Although the tryout is of value to the employer as it serves as both a screening and an indoctrination experience, the employee also gains an appreciation of what the actual job is likely to entail.[37]

Dispositional Influences Although much work in the area of job satisfaction indicates that external influences, such as job design, affect employee attitudes, some recent research suggests that individual job attitudes may be fairly consistent over time and jobs. In a nationwide longitudinal study of the job satisfaction of 5,000 middle-aged men, Staw and Ross found significant stability over a 5-year time period. Even when individuals changed employers and/or occupations, prior attitudes continued to be a strong predictor of later job satisfaction. These findings suggest that individuals may be predisposed to feel good or bad about their employment situation, regardless of the actual specifics of the situation. These results help to explain why some people seem to be perpetually unhappy with their work or life and others appear generally content and good-natured regardless of changes in their surroundings. In short, people may carry with them, across jobs, predispositions to feel good or bad about work.[38]

A perhaps even more surprising finding in this area comes from research on the possible influence of genetics on job satisfaction. Specifically, researchers at the University of Minnesota studied the reported job satisfaction of identical twins who had been reared apart. These researchers reported that a significant proportion of the variance in the job satisfaction responses could be attributed to genetics. Similarities across pairs of twins existed despite differences in jobs.[39] These findings suggest that organizations may have less control over employee satisfaction than previously thought. However, the likelihood that genetics is a contributing factor to job satisfaction does not mean that job satisfaction is not influenced by environmental factors.[40]

The Search for Trends in Job Satisfaction

Based on magazine articles, television, and movies, we might be tempted to conclude that most workers are dissatisfied with their jobs. However, available evidence indicates that such a conclusion would be in error. Surveys of workers in the United States show that the vast majority are fairly satisfied with their jobs. One set of surveys that spanned a 20-year period revealed that satisfied workers comprised 80 to 90 percent of the labor force in a given year.[41] Other representative samplings reveal much the same pattern.

Despite this reassuring evidence, some alarmists argue that worker satisfaction is declining and that the resulting rise in worker alienation could lead

---

who are considering joining their convent. The preview is designed to show the drabness of the individual rooms and the hardships of daily chores. It is hoped that such previews will diminish attrition in the order by reducing the occasional expectation that life in the order will be a *Sound of Music*–type experience.

to worker revolt. It is perhaps the implicit threat of a worker revolution that makes the prospect of declining satisfaction a topic of widespread concern.***

Due to increasing levels of education, expectations in the work force are rising. If better educated workers do not obtain better jobs, it is conceivable that job satisfaction could decline over the coming years. The unprecedented affluence of recent decades may also contribute to the creation of a more defiant work force that is less concerned with traditional extrinsic rewards and incentives, such as job security, and more concerned with intrinsic rewards, such as having a challenging and interesting job.

Studies over the years that have asked employees to rank the features of employment they most prefer suggest that such a change has already taken place.[42] Other evidence indicates that interest in work itself may be diminishing. Based on a study that they conducted in 1954, Morse and Weiss reported that 80 percent of the work force said that they would prefer to continue working even if they did not have a financial need to do so.[43] In a similar survey conducted during the 1970s, it was reported that only 72 percent of the work force would continue to work if they did not have the financial need to do so.[44] This and other evidence suggests that the work ethic may be giving way to a leisure ethic in the United States. In the future, managers may well face the added challenge of directing a work force that may be more demanding, more highly educated, and less interested in work as an end in itself. Surprisingly, these changes will take place at a time when the quality of working and living conditions has never been better.

Consequences of Job Dissatisfaction

Withdrawal Behaviors   Individuals are usually drawn to situations that are rewarding, while they tend to withdraw from situations that are unrewarding or painful. This principle of reward and punishment appears to underlie much of the evidence on the relationship between job satisfaction and employee behavior.

Absenteeism   Each year, more work time is lost due to absenteeism than to strikes and lockouts. Absenteeism's direct costs to business are estimated at up to $30 billion. Studies of absenteeism have often found that less satisfied employees are more likely to miss work.[45] When studying absenteeism, it is important to distinguish between avoidable (or voluntary) absenteeism and unavoidable (or involuntary) absenteeism. Unavoidable absenteeism — for example, that due to illness or family emergency — is largely unrelated to level of job satisfaction.

*** The evidence of fairly high general job satisfaction should not be interpreted as indicating that working conditions (in factories, for example) are not in need of improvement. Such problems are overlooked when one examines aggregate data for the entire work force. Also, people are remarkably adaptive to many unpleasant situations, and they often find alternative sources of satisfaction in otherwise adverse conditions. For example, social relations can be a major source of satisfaction in a dull and repetitive job. As evidence that many workers desire better positions, consider that only 24 percent of blue-collar employees report that they would choose the same type of work again. For white-collar employees, the figure only rises to 41 percent. Therefore, many people probably aspire to better conditions, although they are reasonably content with their present situation.

OB Focus

Cutting Absenteeism

The Maid Bess Corporation, a garment manufacturer based in Salem, Virginia, tried an experiment that focused on a common problem — worker absenteeism. Its absenteeism rate of about 6 percent was common for the garment industry but costly for Maid Bess. Even though the company doesn't pay workers who stay away from work, the company spent more than $700,000 a year in lost sales and production, overtime pay, added overhead, and extra employees.

The usual approaches of warnings, threats, and docked pay were not working.

The company decided to address the problem with an experiment in positive reinforcement. At one of the company's 400-person plants, Maid Bess instituted an attendance recognition program. At the end of each quarter, employees who had a perfect attendance record or only one absence received a card signed by the manager congratulating them. At the end of each year,

employees who missed no more than two days received a custom-designed piece of jewelry. At other plants, Maid Bess tried reward programs that offered only financial incentives or only management recognition.

In the plants with only one kind of reward, attendance did not increase significantly. But in the plant that gave both types of reward, absenteeism fell by almost 40 percent. Although the program cost the company $10,000, it saved $58,000 in direct labor.

Source: "Want to Cut Absenteeism? Try the Carrot, Not the Stick," *Working Woman*, January 1986, p. 18.

To examine the relationship between satisfaction and absenteeism, Frank Smith studied the attendance rate of office employees at the Chicago headquarters of Sears, Roebuck on the day of a severe blizzard.[46] As a comparison group, Smith examined the attendance rate of employees in a New York City office, where, on the same day, the weather was pleasant. By relating absenteeism to individual job satisfaction data, Smith found that absenteeism in Chicago was more variable, that is, highly satisfied employees were far more likely to make the extra effort to report to work despite the blizzard, while dissatisfied employees were more likely to remain home.

Tardiness   It is also generally believed that chronic tardiness tends to reflect employee dissatisfaction.[47] Of course, it cannot be assumed that chronic tardiness is invariably due to dissatisfaction, because intervening factors, such as car pooling or preparing a large family for school each morning, often play a role. Nonetheless, certain forms of employee tardiness, such as that caused by lingering in the parking lot or restroom, may be attributed to such attitudinal factors as dissatisfaction, low job involvement, or low professional commitment. Over and above attitudinal factors, the existence of formal organizational penalties and incentives related to tardiness, as well as social pressures, can play a role in an individual's decision to be tardy.[48]

Turnover   Studies have shown, with a fair degree of consistency, that dissatisfied employees are more likely to quit. The specific influence of dissatisfaction on the decision to quit may be only moderate, however, because a variety of other factors are also involved. Perhaps of greatest influence is the availability of alternative employment opportunities. For example, general economic conditions and an employee's sense of confidence in the marketability of personal skills probably play major roles in the decision to seek a new job.[49] Fluctuations in quit rates, for example, are strongly associated with changes in job opportunities (as during periods of rising employment). In fact, the majority of the variation in quit rates may be explained by the simple factor of the business cycle.[50]

Although we might be tempted to think that managers should try to reduce employee turnover, it has been suggested that turnover may not be inherently undesirable. In fact, the desirability of turnover depends on who is leaving. If the people who are quitting are generally superior performers, turnover needs to be reduced or eliminated. But if turnover is great among poor performers, the change is actually in the best interests of the organization. The notion that high turnover among poor performers can benefit an organization is termed **functional turnover**.[51] Attempts to document the prevalence of functional turnover, in which quit rates are analyzed separately for high and low performers, are fairly new. Thus, it is difficult to say as yet how prevalent functional turnover may be or to identify the precise mechanisms through which organizations can foster functional turnover.

Early Retirement   Another topic of recent interest is the relationship between job satisfaction and the decision to take early retirement. One might expect that the choice of whether to take early retirement would be influenced by level of job satisfaction. In a study of state civil servants, Schmitt and McLane found supportive evidence that employees who chose early retirement held less positive attitudes toward their positions than did those who chose to remain working.[52] Job level was also associated with early retirement in that individuals in lower-level jobs were more likely to take advantage of the opportunity to retire than were individuals in higher-level positions.

Union Activity   Increased interest in union activity has long been accepted as a consequence of employee dissatisfaction,[53] but empirical evidence in support of this notion has been obtained only recently. In an attitude survey of over 62,000 employees, Clay Hamner and Frank Smith observed that roughly one-third of the variance in union activity could be predicted from job-satisfaction information.[54] The single most important predictor of union activity was dissatisfaction with supervision. While dissatisfaction with other facets of the job contributed to the level of union activity, dissatisfaction with pay had no significant relationship.

Studies by Getman, Goldberg, and Herman and by Schriesheim have provided evidence that attitudes regarding job satisfaction and toward unions in general can predict voting behavior in union elections.[55] Pro-union voting was associated with concern for economic issues (such as security and working conditions) rather than noneconomic issues (such as the desire for creativity and independence). In the Getman, Goldberg, and Herman study, information on job satisfaction permitted the prediction of employee voting with an accuracy rate of 75 percent. In addition to voting behavior, other forms of union activity (such as the frequency of strikes and grievance rates within departments) have been found to be correlated with job dissatisfaction.[56] Therefore, some organizations, such as Sears, Roebuck, deliberately use periodic attitude surveys as an early-warning system to spot problems that may lead to union organizing activity.[57]

Job Satisfaction and Productivity

Most people believe that satisfied workers are more productive workers. They reason that satisfied employees are inclined to be more involved with their work and, therefore, are more productive. Empirical research, however, has not identified much support for this proposal. In fact, the available evidence suggests that the relationship between job satisfaction and productivity is a very weak one. In a review of a large variety of job satisfaction–productivity studies, Vroom concluded that the median correlation between satisfaction and productivity is .14 (i.e., very low, but positive).[58] This correlation suggests that very little variance in performance can be attributed to job satisfaction.

Because people tend to overestimate the influence of job satisfaction, they underestimate other factors that contribute to productivity. Among these other factors are informal work norms, task interdependence, and machine pacing of productivity. These forces often restrict the range of individual productivity. For example, coworkers usually will not allow an individual to work too fast or too slow, since a worker who is too productive will create a logjam at the next workstation and one who is not productive enough will create a bottleneck for other workers who supply materials to the individual. Furthermore, machine pacing and production planning are designed to reduce uncertainty and maintain strong control over the production process. These factors serve to limit employees' freedom to vary their performance to match their personal desires.

While these factors help explain the lack of strong empirical support for a relationship between performance and satisfaction, they do not refute the proposition that such a relationship exists. The belief that these variables are related, or at least influence each other, is still widely held by the business community and debated by researchers. Some researchers have suggested that the two dimensions will be correlated only when satisfaction can have a direct impact on performance.[59] For example, in situations where there is little pressure to be productive, the two dimensions are more likely to be correlated. In situations with high pressure to produce (perhaps the majority of situations), employees will be fairly productive by necessity, and the two variables are unlikely to be correlated.

Other researchers have argued that satisfaction and performance are potentially correlated as a consequence of their being causally related. Three variations on this argument have been raised. The first viewpoint contends that *satisfaction causes performance*. This proposal was the underlying premise for the human relations approach, which assumes that if you make workers happy, they will reciprocate by being more productive. To date, no evidence clearly demonstrates that workers feel a strong urge to reciprocate with high performance in exchange for a felt concern for their feelings.

■ **Figure 4.3**

The "Performance Causes Satisfaction" View

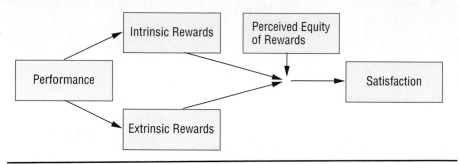

Source: E.E. Lawler and L.W. Porter, *Industrial Relations*, 1967.

The second viewpoint holds that *performance causes satisfaction*. That is, high performers tend to be more satisfied than low performers. It is usually suggested that performance influences satisfaction via the receipt of *equitable rewards*. In other words, satisfaction can be viewed as a reaction to rewards rather than simply a reaction to job performance in itself.

Figure 4.3 summarizes the view of those who believe that performance causes satisfaction. Job satisfaction is seen as a reaction to the rewards generated by performance. Whether the rewards are perceived as equitable is also a consideration. The definition of equitable rewards, in turn, is partially influenced by perception of one's own performance and resulting deservedness. According to this point of view, the failure to find a stronger association between satisfaction and productivity lies partly in the failure of many organizations to tie rewards to performance. As we will see in Chapter 5, wages and salaries are often not clearly based on performance.

A third viewpoint contends that *satisfaction and performance influence each other*.[60] According to this viewpoint, the impact of job satisfaction on performance is probably very indirect. For example, satisfaction may indirectly influence performance via the belief that performance will be rewarded equitably. The impact of performance on satisfaction is perhaps greater than the impact of satisfaction on performance since, as noted earlier, there are potentially more intervening factors between the experience of satisfaction and later performance than there are between performance and later satisfaction.

The Importance of a Positive Correlation between Job Satisfaction and Productivity   If superior performers are receiving greater rewards than poor performers, satisfaction levels should be higher among superior performers. The consequence of such a state of affairs is that satisfaction and performance will be positively correlated. Therefore, the extent to which satisfaction and performance are positively correlated within an organization is a partial indication of the extent to which an organization is "healthy." Consider the converse situation of an organization in which satisfaction and performance are inversely related. Such a situation would be one in which poorer performers are more satisfied than higher performers and in which functional turnover is probably low. Clearly, this situation, as well as a situation in which satisfaction and performance are totally uncorrelated, is not in the best long-term interest of the organization. Managers should therefore strive to create linkages between performance and satisfaction by offering highly attractive, equitable rewards that are tied to performance.

Summary

1. Explain the nature of attitudes and their essential components.
An attitude is an idea charged with emotion that predisposes an individual to react in a particular way when confronted with a specific situation. Thus, an attitude has three basic components: (1) the cognitive component, (2) the affective component, and (3) the behavioral component. It is important to note that the behavioral predisposition is determined to some extent by the cognitive and the affective components.

2. Outline the most widely used methods of measuring attitudes.
Because attitudes are not directly observable, they cannot be directly studied. Consequently, in their attempts at greater understanding, researchers examine the three basic components. The affective component is measured with physiological and verbal tests, the cognitive component is measured through statements of belief or reports of categorizations or beliefs, and the behavioral component is measured by studying actual behavior. The two most common written tests of attitudes are graphic scales, which ask an individual to indicate his degree of agreement with a series of statements, and semantic differential scales, which ask for ratings based on pairs of adjectives that are opposite in meaning.

3. Identify the means through which attitudes are formed.
We acquire our attitudes through three kinds of learning. For example, we may develop either positive or negative attitudes through direct experience — our own personal involvement with people and things in our environment. Our attitudes may also grow out of our social communication with others — we will be influenced by the information we receive from parents, friends, coworkers, managers, and personal acquaintances as well as by information culled from public figures and mass media. And we form attitudes through emotional conditioning — a process which suggests that our attitudes are not always based on rational grounds.

4. Specify the components of attitude change and trace the steps in the change process.
Four factors are involved in attitude change: (1) source factors are the characteristics of the originator of an attempted attitude change, (2) message factors are the specific structure and content of the persuasive appeal, (3) medium factors are the characteristics and effects of the channel of communication, and (4) audience factors are the characteristics of the target of the attitude change. These are the four key influences on an individual's process of changing atti-

tudes. To achieve a lasting change in attitude, most researchers believe that an individual must go through five required phases: (1) attention to the attempt to persuade, (2) comprehension of the persuasive appeal, (3) yielding to persuasion, (4) retention of the new attitude, and (5) action in keeping with the new attitude.

5. Tell why management should take an interest in workers' job satisfaction.

Job satisfaction is the product of an individual's thoughts, feelings, and attitudes toward work. Because organizational performance should be measured in human as well as financial terms, management cannot ignore the significance of job satisfaction. Some might argue that because most people must work and consequently spend much of their adult lives doing so, companies have a moral obligation to make work rewarding. The company also benefits, however, because studies show that satisfied workers enjoy better physical and mental health and that job satisfaction plays a significant role in a firm's ability to attract and retain qualified workers. Furthermore, low levels of job satisfaction have been related to such problems as turnover, absenteeism, union organizing, and the filing of grievances. Thus, job satisfaction is a crucial issue for both individuals and organizations.

6. Note the principle methods of measuring job satisfaction.

In-depth interviews and questionnaires are sometimes used to measure job satisfaction, but the most common method uses anonymous surveys employing attitude scales. Global, or facet-free, scales look at satisfaction in terms of a worker's overall reaction to his or her job. They are relatively brief and easy to administer. More recently, faceted scales that examine employees' reactions to specific aspects of a job have gained popularity. While such scales yield more detailed information than do global scales, they are also more lengthy and complicated to administer.

7. Cite the most frequent sources of job satisfaction.

The results of numerous studies indicate that certain variables are consistently correlated with job satisfaction, among them job level, length of service, and size of organization. In addition, satisfaction strongly depends on the individual's expectations. While surveys of the U.S. work force indicate that the vast majority of workers are fairly satisfied with their jobs, recent trends indicate that, in the future, managers may well be challenged by a work force that is more demanding, more educated, and less interested in work as an end in itself.

8. Describe some typical employee responses to low job satisfaction.

Among the most common reactions to low job satisfaction are withdrawal behaviors, such as absenteeism, tardiness, turnover, and early retirement. Employees may also express their dissatisfaction through increased union activity. While numerous studies have investigated the relationship between job satisfaction and productivity, there is little empirical evidence to support the pervasive notion that satisfied workers are more productive.

Key Terms

Attitude	Medium factors
Cognitive component	Audience factors
Affective component	Balance theory
Behavioral component	Cognitive dissonance
Graphic scale	Job satisfaction
Semantic differential scale	Global approach
Source factors	Faceted approach
Message factors	Functional turnover

Review and Discussion Questions

1. Ralph, one of your subordinates, took an instant dislike to Myra, a new coworker, because he thinks that her clothes are too informal and her hair is too long. "You know," he complains to you, "her work is just as sloppy as her appearance." In fact, you know that Myra's work is excellent, so you reply, "Ralph, I think your attitude toward Myra is clouding your judgment." "Attitude?" he asks. "What do you mean by attitude?" Explain exactly what you mean.

2. You have been called in as a consultant by the operations department of a mail order company that wants to measure order takers' attitudes toward their jobs. Explain why attitudes cannot be directly measured, review the alternatives, and describe some likely test formats.

3. As a result of your explanation in response to Question 1, your subordinate Ralph is growing increasingly interested in the subject of attitudes. "Where do you think I got this attitude?" he asks. Tell him how attitudes are formed.

4. Having won Ralph's confidence with your explanations of attitudes and their formation, you think you may be able to persuade him to change his attitude toward Myra. How would you accomplish this goal? What source, message, medium, and audience factors would you have to consider? What specific steps would you lead Ralph through? How successful do you think you would be?

5. Both in the past and in many other countries today employers have paid little attention to their employees' job satisfaction. Why should employers be interested in job satisfaction? In your opinion, why is job satisfaction primarily a modern and Western concern?

6. What approach would you use to measure the job satisfaction of each of the following groups? Why?
   a. coal miners
   b. computer programmers
   c. dentists
   d. migrant farmworkers

7. Were you surprised to learn that 80 to 90 percent of workers in the

United States are satisfied with their jobs? Why or why not? How would you account for this high level of job satisfaction? Would you expect this trend to continue?

8. If you were a manager, what clues would help you identify employees who were dissatisfied with their jobs? As long as your workers were productive, could you assume that they were satisfied? Could you assume that greater satisfaction would lead to greater productivity? Why or why not?

Critical Incident

When the Shoe Is on the Other Foot

Underhill Packing Co. is a meat-processing firm that has been growing over the past 10 years. Phil had worked on the processing line for almost 8 years. During that time, the union had gone on strike three times, with each incident lasting 4 to 6 weeks.

Approximately 6 months ago, Phil was promoted to a supervisor's position. The job offered several thousand dollars more in salary and the opportunity was too good to pass up. Phil had always supported the union but now he was part of the management group.

Over the past couple of months, two incidents have occurred that have Phil thinking. One concerned a disagreement he had with a union steward who accused Phil of harassing a worker. Phil maintained that he had to tell the worker several times one day to keep busy and get back to work. Nevertheless, a grievance was filed and later withdrawn only after Phil was asked to apologize.

The second incident involved a worker who was repeatedly late to work. Phil documented each occurrence and, after the third time in two weeks, he sent the worker home without pay as stipulated in the labor–management contract. Again, a grievance was filed claiming that Phil was overstepping his authority and harassing the worker. The time card indicated that the worker had clocked-in on time, but Phil insisted that he was 10 to 15 minutes late each time.

Phil has become upset and angry over these situations and believes that the union is trying to discredit him. He likes his job as supervisor, but wishes someone had told him more about union–management relations and how to deal with them.

Questions

1. How would you characterize Phil's attitude toward the union when he first became a supervisor?

2. Do you believe his attitude has changed? To what do you attribute this change?

3. What factors are likely to affect the attitudes of those who move from being a worker to being a supervisor?

Experiential Exercise

Assessing Your Job Satisfaction

As discussed in this chapter, job satisfaction is an extremely important factor for the well-being of both the individual and the organization. In this exercise, you are asked to assess your feelings of job satisfaction in terms of your present job or in the kind of job you think you will have when you complete this aspect of your education.

If you are currently employed, either part-time or full-time, respond in terms of your present job. If you are not currently employed, describe your last job. If you have never worked, respond in terms of the kind of job you realistically think you will have when you start working.

Step 1   Presented below are 20 statements concerning characteristics or attributes of your job. For each statement, provide two ratings:

a.   How much of the characteristic *is there now* associated with your job?

b.   How much of the characteristic *should there be* associated with your job?

Circle the number on the scale that represents the amount of the characteristic being rated. That is, low numbers represent minimum amounts and high numbers represent maximum amounts. Thus, if you think there is very little of the characteristic associated with your job, circle 1. If you think there's a little, circle 2. If you think there is a lot of the characteristic, circle 4, and so on. For each scale, circle only one number; please do all of the scales.

1.   The extent to which my job is challenging:

   a.   How much is there now?   (min)   1   2   3   4   5   (max)
   b.   How much should there be?   1   2   3   4   5

2.   The feeling of personal accomplishment one gets from being in my job position:

   a.   How much is there now?   (min)   1   2   3   4   5   (max)
   b.   How much should there be?   1   2   3   4   5

3.   The extent to which the pay associated with my job is appropriate:

   a.   How much is there now?   (min)   1   2   3   4   5   (max)
   b.   How much should there be?   1   2   3   4   5

4.   The feeling of security one has in my job:

   a.   How much is there now?   (min)   1   2   3   4   5   (max)
   b.   How much should there be?   1   2   3   4   5

5.   The opportunity one has to work closely with others and develop close friendships:

   a.   How much is there now?   (min)   1   2   3   4   5   (max)
   b.   How much should there be?   1   2   3   4   5

6.   The extent to which one is recognized for achievements in performing my job:

a. How much is there now?   (min) 1 2 3 4 5 (max)
b. How much should there be?   1 2 3 4 5

7. The extent to which my job gives me prestige and status within the organization:

a. How much is there now?   (min) 1 2 3 4 5 (max)
b. How much should there be?   1 2 3 4 5

8. The opportunity my job provides for developing a sense of responsibility:

a. How much is there now?   (min) 1 2 3 4 5 (max)
b. How much should there be?   1 2 3 4 5

9. The extent to which my job provides an appropriate set of fringe benefits:

a. How much is there now?   (min) 1 2 3 4 5 (max)
b. How much should there be?   1 2 3 4 5

10. The opportunity my job provides for being involved in making decisions:

a. How much is there now?   (min) 1 2 3 4 5 (max)
b. How much should there be?   1 2 3 4 5

11. The extent to which my job provides appropriate working conditions:

a. How much is there now?   (min) 1 2 3 4 5 (max)
b. How much should there be?   1 2 3 4 5

12. The opportunity for autonomy (i.e., independent thought and action) in my job:

a. How much is there now?   (min) 1 2 3 4 5 (max)
b. How much should there be?   1 2 3 4 5

13. The feeling of being "in the know," that is, having access to important or useful information in my job:

a. How much is there now?   (min) 1 2 3 4 5 (max)
b. How much should there be?   1 2 3 4 5

14. The opportunity for participating in establishing goals and objectives for my job:

a. How much is there now?   (min) 1 2 3 4 5 (max)
b. How much should there be?   1 2 3 4 5

15. The extent to which my job is governed by appropriate rules and procedures:

a. How much is there now?   (min) 1 2 3 4 5 (max)
b. How much should there be?   1 2 3 4 5

16. The opportunity my job provides for meeting challenges and solving problems:
    a.   How much is there now?   (min)   1   2   3   4   5   (max)
    b.   How much should there be?   1   2   3   4   5

17. The opportunity to earn additional income (e.g., bonus, overtime) in my job beyond the normal wages:
    a.   How much is there now?   (min)   1   2   3   4   5   (max)
    b.   How much should there be?   1   2   3   4   5

18. The feeling of being able to use my unique abilities in performing my job:
    a.   How much is there now?   (min)   1   2   3   4   5   (max)
    b.   How much should there be?   1   2   3   4   5

19. The extent to which policies and procedures governing advancement are appropriate in my job:
    a.   How much is there now?   (min)   1   2   3   4   5   (max)
    b.   How much should there be?   1   2   3   4   5

20. The extent to which my supervisor sees to it that every person does a fair day's work:
    a.   How much is there now?   (min)   1   2   3   4   5   (max)
    b.   How much should there be?   1   2   3   4   5

Step 2   Compute your satisfaction/dissatisfaction score for each of the items using the table below. The extent of your satisfaction/dissatisfaction with each job characteristic is scored as the rating for (b) minus the rating for (a); that is, "how much should there be" minus "how much is there now."

1.   For each question, subtract part (a)'s rating from part (b)'s rating, that is, (b) − (a).

2.   Enter the (b) − (a) value for each question in the space next to the number of that question in the columns below. If (a) is greater than (b), be sure to retain the minus sign for the difference.

3.   Next, add up the numbers in each column to obtain a total for each category. Again, be sure to retain any minus signs.

4.   Divide this total by the number of questions used to measure each category.

Remember, this adjusted score is a measure of dissatisfaction. The lower it is, the more satisfied you are. The higher it is, the more dissatisfied you are.

Intrinsic Factors	Extrinsic Factors
1b − 1a = _____	3b − 3a = _____
2b − 2a = _____	4b − 4a = _____
6b − 6a = _____	5b − 5a = _____
7b − 7a = _____	9b − 9a = _____
8b − 8a = _____	11b − 11a = _____
10b − 10a = _____	15b − 15a = _____
12b − 12a = _____	17b − 17a = _____
13b − 13a = _____	19b − 19a = _____
14b − 14a = _____	20b − 20a = _____
16b − 16a = _____	
18b − 18a = _____	
Total: _____	Total: _____
Divide by: 11	Divide by: 9
Adjusted Score: _____	Adjusted Score: _____

Step 3   Your instructor will ask you to form groups of three to five people. Each group should discuss the members' satisfaction scores in terms of:

1. The features of the job that could be viewed as responsible for each person's high and low satisfaction scores.

2. What might be done to change each job so as to lessen the dissatisfaction.

3. What type of job, for each individual, might lead to improved job satisfaction.

Step 4   Be prepared to share your responses to the previous questions with the entire class. In addition, you could discuss the implications of these findings for career planning. That is, what attributes of your job are significant in terms of satisfaction/dissatisfaction? How can such information assist you in making career decisions?

Notes

1. H.C. Triandis, "A Critique and Experimental Design for the Study of the Relationship Between Productivity and Job Satisfaction," *Psychological Bulletin 56* (1959): 309–316.

2. R.A. Likert, "A Technique for the Measurement of Attitudes," *Archives of Psychology* 140 (1982): 44–53.

3. J.C. Nunnally, *Psychometric Theory* (New York: McGraw-Hill, 1967).

4. C.E. Osgood, G.J. Suci, and P.H. Tannenbaum, *The Measurement of Meaning* (Urbana, Ill.: University of Illinois Press, 1957).

5. R.B. Zajonc, "Attitudinal Effects of Mere Exposure," *Journal of Personality and Social Psychology Monograph Supplement 9* (1968): 1–27.

6. S. Milgram, "The Experience of Living in Cities," *Science* 167 (1970): 1461–1468.

7. G.J. Blau and R.D. Katerberg, "Toward Enhancing Research with the Social Information Processing Approach to Job Design," *Academy of Management Journal 7* (1982): 543–550.

8. I. Janis, D. Kaye, and P. Kirschner, "Facilitating Effects of 'Eating-While-Reading' on Responsiveness to Persuasive Communications," *Journal of Personality and Social Psychology 1* (1965): 181–186.

9. F. Heider, *The Psychology of Interpersonal Relations* (New York: Wiley, 1958).

10. H. Leventhal, "Fear — for Your Health," in *Readings in Psychology Today*, 2d ed.

(Del Mar, Calif.: CRM Books, 1972), 627–631.

11. M. McLuhan, *Understanding Media* (New York: McGraw-Hill, 1964).

12. K. Gergen and D. Marlowe, eds., *Personality and Social Psychology* (Reading, Mass.: Addison-Wesley, 1969).

13. A.H. Eagley and L.L. Carli, "Sex of Researchers and Sex-typed Communications as Determinants of Sex Differences in Influenceability: A Meta-analysis of Social Influence Studies," *Psychological Bulletin* 90 (1981): 1–20.

14. K. Gergen and R. Bauer, "The Interactive Effects of Self-esteem and Task Difficulty in Social Conformity," *Journal of Personality and Social Psychology* 6 (1967): 16–22.

15. L. Festinger, *A Theory of Cognitive Dissonance* (Stanford, Calif.: Stanford University Press, 1957).

16. L. Festinger and J.M. Carlsmith, "Cognitive Consequences of Forced Compliance," *Journal of Abnormal and Social Psychology* 58 (1959): 203–210.

17. E. Aronson and J. Mills. "The Effect of Severity of Initiation on Liking for a Group," *Journal of Abnormal and Social Psychology* 59 (1959): 177–181.

18. R.P. Abelson, "Are Attitudes Necessary?" in *Attitudes, Conflict, and Social Change,* ed. B.T. King and E. McGinnis (New York: Academic Press, 1972), 19–32.

19. M. Fishbein, "Attitude and the Prediction of Behavior," in *Readings in Attitude Theory and Measurement,* ed. M. Fishbein (New York: Wiley, 1967), 477–492.

20. R.H. Fazio and M.P. Zanna, "Direct Experience and Attitude-Behavior Consistency," in *Advances in Experimental Social Psychology,* vol. 14, ed. L. Berkowitz (New York: Academic Press, 1981).

21. Blau and Katerberg, "Toward Enhancing Research with the Social Information Processing Approach."

22. E. Palmore, "Predicting Longevity: A Follow-up Controlling for Age," *Gerontology* (Winter 1969); A.W. Kornhauser, *Mental Health of the Industrial Worker: A Detroit Study* (New York: Wiley, 1965).

23. H.J. Arnold and D.C. Feldman, "A Multivariate Model of Job Turnover," *Journal of Applied Psychology* 67 (1981): 350–360.

24. J.A. Breaugh, "Predicting Absenteeism from Prior Absenteeism and Work Attitudes," *Journal of Applied Psychology* 66 (1981): 555–560.

25. J.M. Brett, "Why Employees Want Unions," *Organizational Dynamics* (Spring 1980): 847–859.

26. R.B. Dunham and F.J. Smith, *Organizational Surveys* (Glenview, Ill.: Scott, Foresman, 1979).

27. "A Finger on the Pulse: Companies Expand Use of Employee Surveys," *Wall Street Journal,* October 27, 1986, 23.

28. F.J. Landy, "The Early Years of I/O: J.D. Houser and J.D.I.," *Industrial Psychologist* 26 (1989): 63–64; T. Kunin, "The Construction of a New Type of Attitude Measure," *Personnel Psychology* 8 (1955): 65–78.

29. A.H. Brayfield and H.F. Rothe, "An Index of Job Satisfaction," *Journal of Applied Psychology* 35 (1951): 307–311.

30. P.C. Smith, L.N. Kendall, and C.L. Hulin, *The Measurement of Satisfaction in Work and Retirement* (Chicago: Rand-McNally, 1969).

31. D.J. Weiss, R.V. David, G.W. England, and L.H. Lofquist, *Manual for the Minnesota Satisfaction Questionnaire,* Minnesota Studies in Vocational Rehabilitation: 22 (Minneapolis: University of Minnesota Industrial Relations Center, 1967).

32. M.L. Blum and J.C. Naylor, *Industrial Psychology* (New York: Harper and Row, 1968).

33. R.P. Vecchio, "Worker Alienation as a Moderator of the Job Quality–Job Satisfaction Relationship: The Case of Racial Differences," *Academy of Management Journal* 23 (1980): 479–486.

34. L.W. Porter and E.E. Lawler, "Properties of Organization Structure in Relation to Job Attitudes and Job Behavior," *Psychological Bulletin* 64 (1965): 23–51.

35. R. Katerberg, "A Study of Met Expectations in an Organization" (master's thesis, University of Illinois–Urbana, 1976).

36. S.M. Colarelli, "Methods of Communication and Mediating Processes in Realistic Job Previews," *Journal of Applied Psychology* 69 (1984): 633–642; J.P. Wanous, "Tell It Like It Is at Realistic Job Previews," *Personnel* 52 (1975): 50–60.

37. S.L. Premack and J.P. Wanous, "A Meta-analysis of Realistic Job Preview Experiments," *Journal of Applied Psychology* 69 (1985): 706–719.

38. B.M. Staw and J. Ross, "Stability in the Midst of Change: A Dispositional Approach to Job Attitudes," *Journal of Applied Psychology* 70 (1985): 469–480; B.M. Staw, N.E. Bell, and J.A. Clausen, "The Dispositional Approach to Job Attitudes: A Lifetime Longitudinal Test," *Administrative Science Quarterly* 31 (1986): 56–77.

39. R.D. Arvey, T.J. Bouchard, H.L. Segal, and L.M. Abraham, "Job Satisfaction: Environmental and Genetic Components," *Journal of Applied Psychology* 74 (1989): 187–192.

40. A. Davis-Blake and J. Pfeffer, "Just a Mirage: The Search for Dispositional

Effects in Organizational Research," *Academy of Management Review* 14 (1989): 385–400; I. Levin and J. Stokes "Dispositional Approach to Job Satisfaction," *Journal of Applied Psychology* 74 (1989): 752–758.

41. R.P. Quinn and G.L. Staines, *The 1977 Quality of Employment Survey* (Ann Arbor: Institute for Social Research, University of Michigan, 1979).

42. H.L. Sheppard and N. Herrick, *Where Have All the Robots Gone?* (New York: Free Press, 1972).

43. M.C. Morse and R.S. Weiss, "The Function and Meaning of Work and the Job," *American Sociological Review* 20 (1955): 191–198.

44. R.P. Vecchio, "The Function and Meaning of Work and the Job: Morse and Weiss (1955) Revisited," *Academy of Management Journal* 23 (1980): 361–367.

45. G. Johns, "The Great Escape," *Psychology Today*, October, 1987, 30–33; L.R. Waters and D. Roach, "Relationship Between Job Attitudes and Two Forms of Withdrawal from the Work Situation," *Journal of Applied Psychology* 55 (1971): 92–94; R. Hackett and R.M. Guion, "A Reevaluation of the Absenteeism–Job Satisfaction Relationship," *Organizational Behavior and Human Decision Processes* (1985): 340–381; K.D. Scott and G.S. Taylor, "An Examination of Conflicting Findings on the Relationship Between Job Satisfaction and Absenteeism: A Meta-analysis," *Academy of Management Journal* 28 (1985): 588–612.

46. F.J. Smith, "Work Attitudes as Predictors of Attendance on a Specific Day," *Journal of Applied Psychology* 62 (1977): 16–19.

47. L.W. Porter and R.M. Steers, "Organizational, Work, and Personal Factors in Employee Turnover and Absenteeism," *Psychological Bulletin* 80 (1973): 151–176.

48. R.M. Steers and S.R. Rhodes, "Major Influences on Employee Attendance: A Process Model," *Journal of Applied Psychology* 63 (1978): 391–407.

49. R.P. Vecchio, "Workers' Perceptions of Job Market Favorability and Job Insecurity," *Mid-Atlantic Journal of Business* 21 (1983): 9–16.

50. H. Wool, "What's Wrong with Work in America?: A Review Essay," *Monthly Labor Review* 96 (1973): 38–44.

51. D.R. Dalton and W.D. Todor, "Turnover Turned Over: An Expanded and Positive Perspective," *Academy of Management Review* 4 (1979): 225–236; D.R. Dalton, W.D. Todor, and D.M. Krachhardt, "Turnover Overstated: The Functional Toxonomy," *Academy of Management Review* 7 (1982): 117–123; M.B. Staw, "The Consequences of Turnover," *Journal of Occupational Behavior* (1980): 253–273.

52. N. Schmitt and J.T. McLane, "The Relationship Between Job Attitudes and the Decision to Retire," *Academy of Management Journal* 24 (1981): 795–802.

53. R. Stagner and H. Rosen, *Psychology of Union-Management Relations* (Monterey, Calif.: Brooks-Cole, 1965).

54. W.C. Hamner and F.J. Smith, "Work Attitudes as Predictors of Unionization Activity," *Journal of Applied Psychology* 63 (1978): 415–421.

55. J.G. Getman, S.B. Goldberg, and J.B. Herman, *Union Representation Elections: Law and Reality* (New York: Russell Sage Foundation, 1976); C.A. Schriesheim, "Job Satisfaction, Attitudes Toward Unions, and Voting in a Union Representation Election," *Journal of Applied Psychology* 63 (1978): 548–552; M.D. Zalesny, "Comparison of Economic and Noneconomic Factors in Predicting Faculty Vote Preference in a Union Representation Election," *Journal of Applied Psychology* 70 (1985): 243–256.

56. E.A. Fleishman and E.F. Harris, "Patterns of Leadership Behavior Related to Employee Grievances and Turnover," *Personnel Psychology* 15 (1962): 54–56; E.A. Fleishman, E.F. Harris, and H.E. Burtt, *Leadership and Supervision in Individuals* (Columbus: Ohio State University Personnel Research Board, 1955).

57. D. Buss, "Job Tryouts Without Pay Get More Testing in U.S. Auto Plants," *Wall Street Journal*, January 10, 1985, 31.

58. V.H. Vroom, *Work and Motivation* (New York: Purley, 1964).

59. R.B. Ewen, "Pressure for Production, Task Difficulty, and the Correlation Between Job Satisfaction and Job Performance," *Journal of Applied Psychology* 58 (1973): 378–380; R.S. Bhagat, "Conditions under Which Stronger Job Performance–Job Satisfaction Relationships May Be Observed: A Closer Look at Two Situational Contingencies," *Academy of Management Journal* 25 (1982): 772–789; Triandis, "A Critique and Experimental Design."

60. E.E. Lawler and L.W. Porter, "The Effect of Performance on Job Satisfaction," *Industrial Relations* 7 (1967): 20–28.

Case

Quad Graphics, Inc.

Harry Quadracci's daydreams about his career after law school probably didn't include a vision of himself on stage leading amateur performers in songs from *Pirates of Penzance*. He found himself performing as part of his role as the C.E.O. of Quad Graphics, the full-color printing company he started in 1970 when he quit his position as a labor negotiator for a large Wisconsin printing company owned by his father. The annual stage performance is an integral part of the company's spirited, team-oriented culture. Quad Graphics had grown to employ approximately 3,300 people and generated annual sales of one-half billion dollars. Its clients included *Newsweek, Time, U.S. News & World Report, Playboy, Lillian Vernon,* and *James River Traders.*

Quadracci had always resisted hard-nosed, antilabor management tactics. In starting his own firm, he was anxious to employ an entirely new strategy for human resource management.

He built his organization based firmly on trust. The book *The 100 Best Companies to Work for in America* (Signet 1987) honors Quad Graphics, highlighting the ways it implements trust to form the backbone of its culture:

- Trust in teamwork. Employees trust that together they will accomplish more than they would individually.

- Trust in responsibility. Employers trust that each worker will carry his/her fair share of the load.

- Trust in productivity. Customers trust that Quad Graphics' work will represent the most competitive levels of pricing, quality, and innovation available.

- Trust in management. Shareholders, customers, and employees trust that the company will make decisive judgments for long-term success rather than focusing only on short-term goals like today's profit.

- Trust in Thinking Small. Quad Graphics people all trust in each other: they regard each other as persons of equal value; they respect the dignity of individuals by recognizing individual accomplishments, as well as the feelings and needs of individuals and their families; they all share the same goals and purposes in life.

These principles illustrate that, at Quad Graphics, trust is more than an empty promise.

Quad Graphics has far fewer rules and regulations than most companies of its size, and that's no accident. It's the way the founder likes to run the show. Quadracci calls his personal and direct style of management, expressly avoiding formalized rules and regulations, "Theory Q." As opposed to the traditional American top-down "Theory X" style or the Japanese participatory "Theory Z," Quadracci maintains the attitude that communications should be personal, vocal, and spontaneous, and that one should avoid the shelter of more formal, traditional limits such as job descriptions, time clocks, policies, and procedures.

Quadracci works to ensure that employees are happy and satisfied in their work, and also that they are challenged. Most of Quad's employees have completed high school educations at most. Quadracci believes that the key to corporate growth is these individuals' growth via on-going training and development. The burden of this training and development falls mostly on peers. Employees train one another.

Nearly 1,000 people complete the various training courses that Quad Graphics sponsors each week in a remodeled former elementary school building. With the exception of new recruits, who are paid to attend what amounts to basic training, the vast majority attend classes on their own time. Graduates of previous Quad classes teach their peers.

After completing basic training, part of an employee's job is to begin learning other jobs. This way all employees can contribute to improving the firm's management and productivity. This sense of shared purpose driven by individual responsibility nurtures a vital, creative work environment. Passing knowledge among fellow workers makes everyone's job easier and stimulates employees' growth in new directions. As many decisions are made on the plant floor as possible in the belief that the best ideas come from the people doing the work.

Each division operates as a separate company. Most divisions hire their own workers to suit their own needs, and most newly hired employees are referred by current employees. In 1984, the in-house newspaper reported that 39.5 percent of all employees were somehow related to other employees. This was called the "ouchi rating," taken from a Japanese term that translates roughly as "part of the family." At the time of the in-house article, the median age of Quad Graphics employees was 27 years old.

The sharing of authority that brings decision making to the ground floor of the organization attracts and holds these employees, as do the foundation of trust and the focus on education. A number of other conditions keep employment at Quad Graphics attractive. For one, employees own approximately 40 percent of the company. They share in its profits via a plan that links take-home pay to efficiency.

Quad Graphics' unusual shift schedule is attractive, as well. Each employee works three 12-hour shifts a week and every other Sunday (at double salary). This amounts to pay for 48 hours per week while working 42 hours.

The culture of equality among peers also helps individuals flourish. Plant managers wear the same uniforms everyone else does. Every employee gets a clean, dark blue uniform daily.

The company welcomes individual advice and input, encouraging employees to "get big by thinking small." Quad employees have developed improvements in production equipment and generated new business ideas, as well. Employees have even initiated entire new operating units like ink manufacturing, equipment repair,

and Quad Tech, a high-tech division that develops new printing technologies for sale to other printers.

The company allows all managers to use its 57th Street apartment in Manhattan for visits to New York City. The company even picks up the air fare for two. This exposes young managers from Wisconsin to the home turf and daily operations of most of their clients.

Harry Quadracci pays close attention to the physical environment of the company, believing that it can be an important tool to promote employee creativity and voluntarism. These attitudes can deteriorate when employees run machines that run machines. Most Quad Graphics employees monitor computers that take over many of the mechanical tasks once performed by people. To combat boredom this separation from the work might cause and to promote a joyful work place, a popcorn machine on the shop floor is available to anyone at any time. Overhead pipes and machines throughout the factory are painted in a rainbow of colors.

The company supports workers' interests outside the narrow limits of their jobs as well. Employees have set up child-care facilities and food service facilities at Quad. They built up physical fitness programs that encourage teamwork and comradeship along with better health. Also, Quad pays employees $30 to attend a seminar to help them quit smoking. Those who quit for a year receive a bonus of $200.

A symbol of the firm's convivial team atmosphere, the stage show led by Quadracci has become a traditional part of the annual Christmas party. All managers participate, and the performers rehearse on their own time. The affairs have centered on a number of themes. In 1984, the party took the form of a sit-down dinner for 2,200 employees and their guests at the firm's new Sussex, Wisconsin plant. The show that year followed a circus parade theme, with all managers dressed as clowns and Quadracci, dressed as a ringmaster, riding in on an elephant.

Quad Graphics' state-of-the-art printing plants, phenomenal growth, and unique philosophy of management promote employees' sense of shared purpose. Besides churning out the product, technology helps the firm create a better, happier, more satisfying work environment for its workers. This combination of personal vision and technical development has made Quad Graphics a very successful company, and one employees like to work for.

Questions

1. What medium factors does Quadracci consider appropriate? Does he favor any particular medium factor over others? Why?

2. Quad Graphics promotes employee job satisfaction in many ways. What benefits does this create?

3. To what factors do you attribute the company's high degree of job satisfaction?

4. Do you foresee any potential problems related to the high ouchi factor at Quad? (Hint: Might this create barriers to effective perception?)

5. Could Harry Quadracci's personality be described in terms of the Myers-Briggs typology?

Source: Written by Susan Stites Doe, State University of New York College at Buffalo.

III

Interpersonal and Work Group Processes

■ **Chapter 5**
Changing Employee Behavior through Consequences: Learning and Punishment

■ **Chapter 6**
Motivation

■ **Chapter 7**
Enhancing Employee Motivation

■ **Chapter 8**
Performance Appraisal

■ **Chapter 9**
Power and Influence

■ **Chapter 10**
Leadership

■ **Chapter 11**
Decision Making

■ **Chapter 12**
Group Dynamics

■ **Chapter 13**
Conflict Management

■ **Chapter 14**
Stress

**Experience is what
enables you to
recognize a mistake
when you make it
again.**

— Earl Wilson

Learning Objectives

*After studying this chapter, you
should be able to:*

1. *Explain what learning is
   and why managers need to
   understand the learning
   process.*

2. *Describe the process of
   classical conditioning and
   cite several examples of
   this form of learning in the
   workplace.*

3. *Tell what observational
   learning is and how it
   occurs in the workplace.*

4. *Discuss the nature of
   operant conditioning and
   cite four rules for applying
   operant conditioning
   principles to enhance
   employee performance.*

5. *Summarize the advantages
   and disadvantages of OB
   Mod.*

6. *Analyze the role of
   punishment in shaping
   employee behavior.*

Changing Employee Behavior through Consequences
Learning and Punishment

■ Changing Behavior from the Top Down

At Thermwood Corporation, Ken Susnjara, the chairman, president, and chief executive officer, knew that something had to change. The small manufacturer of robots and automation equipment, which Susnjara had founded in 1969, was losing money fast. Susnjara decided that he needed to learn a new way of operating.

He temporarily turned over leadership of Thermwood to the company's sales manager and became a salesman for Thermwood's products. Listening to customers quickly taught Susnjara what was wrong.

About 60 percent of Thermwood's sales are to small and medium-sized companies, for which the equipment is often the biggest purchase they ever make. Therefore, the customers want reliability more than anything else. And because small companies often cannot afford employees with sophisticated technical skills, the customers are also looking for equipment that is easy to use.

However, Thermwood, like its competitors, was focused instead on developing the leading technology. Says Susnjara, "We had gotten caught up in the industry hype. We were very engineering- and R&D-oriented. We were developing all sorts of fancy systems that nobody really had any use for." He concluded that the company must begin to focus more on reliability.

Back at the helm, Susnjara restructured the company along product lines, then set out to find a way of leading his managers to change their behavior so that they focused more on the customer. He cut the top executives' salaries by two-thirds to three-fourths, which would be supplemented by a bonus plan based on each division's profits. Says Susnjara, "The formula was such that, if you were even marginally successful, you could make a fortune."

With rewards like that dangled in front of them, the managers came around quickly. According to Susnjara, the company regained popularity after only about two weeks under this new arrangement. "It is almost unbelievable," he says, "when people are handling their own money, how well they do with it. Instantly, it was as though a fog lifted." The top managers began restructuring and cutting out unneeded expenses.

To keep management focused on the customer, the company has begun requiring that every officer of Thermwood meet with customers at least four times a month. Explains Susnjara, "We need to make sure that we don't lose sight of the fundamental values that got us back to where we are today."

At Thermwood, Ken Susnjara changed his behavior by learning ways to satisfy customers. In turn, he used a system of rewards to change the behavior of his man- agers. This chapter introduces the process of learning, examining what learning is and the ways in which it takes place. The chapter explores how learning occurs in the workplace and how managers use various learning techniques to shape employee behavior.

Source: John H. Sheridan, "Out of the Isolation Booth," *Industry Week,* June 19, 1989, 18–19.

Learning, one of the most fundamental behavioral processes, involves both the development and the modification of thoughts and behaviors. Other concepts and aspects of organizational behavior (for example, motivation and supervi- sion) that we will discuss in later chapters can be more fully explained with the use of learning principles.

New employees bring with them a set of previously learned ways of behaving. They are then expected to learn additional information that applies to their jobs. Established employees continue to develop their job-related skills and abilities. Therefore, learning is a never-ending process for all employees. The process is also very complex. For example, an employee who has already learned one way to perform a job may have trouble learning a second, albeit better, way.

An employee's motivation to perform is closely linked to learning. There- fore, a manager who understands the learning process can use the principles of learning to guide employee behavior and performance. To be successful, em- ployee training and development programs must be based on sound learning principles.

The Nature of Learning

Learning is a fairly permanent change in behavior that occurs as a result of experience.[1] A distinctive feature of this definition is the term *change*. In order to say that learning has occurred, a change, or modification, of behavior must be evident. The change in behavior must also be more than temporary. It should also be possible to attribute this change to the occurrence of an event. Thus, while learning is a process that we cannot observe directly, we can infer that learning has occurred when we observe a fairly permanent change in behavior.

Only in this century have researchers begun to systematically study the learning process. Their efforts have produced three approaches to the explana- tion of learning: classical conditioning; observational, or vicarious, learning; and operant, or instrumental, conditioning.

Classical Conditioning

Early in the twentieth century, Ivan Pavlov, a Russian physiologist, conducted research on digestive glands. In the course of his research, Pavlov discovered that a laboratory dog's secretions of saliva were controlled by both learning

Figure 5.1

Pavlov and Assistants at the Soviet Military Academy

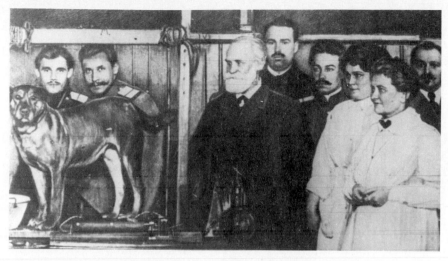

processes and direct physiological stimulation. He noted that the sound of approaching footsteps, as well as the simple sight of food, would cause a dog to salivate (Figure 5.1).

In later research, Pavlov focused even more closely on how various stimuli could be used to produce a desired response. Specifically, he paired the ringing of a bell with the presentation of food to a dog. After a number of pairings, the sound of the bell alone (that is, without the food) was sufficient to produce salivation. Based on his experiments, Pavlov developed the notion of classical conditioning.

In **classical conditioning,** an **unconditioned stimulus (UCS)** — or stimulus that has the capacity to reliably evoke a naturally occurring reflexive or **unconditioned response (UR)** — is paired with the occurrence of a neutral stimulus, one that does not have an initial capacity to evoke the response of interest. Following a number of simultaneous presentations of the unconditioned stimulus and the neutral stimulus, the mere presence of the neutral stimulus will evoke a reflexive response. This reflex-like response is termed the **conditioned response (CR).** When a neutral stimulus attains this capacity, it is termed a **conditioned stimulus (CS).** In Pavlov's experiments, the sight of food was the unconditioned stimulus that evoked the unconditioned response of salivation. The sound of the bell was the neutral stimulus that attained the power of a conditioned stimulus; that is, the bell gained power to evoke the conditioned, or learned, response of salivation. In classical conditioning, the initial relationship of UCS→ UR is replaced by CS→ CR (Figure 5.2).*

* In an early demonstration of the power of classical conditioning, John Watson used Pavlovian techniques with an 11-month-old boy to condition a phobic (fear) reaction to white furry objects.[2] The conditioning sequence consisted of pairing the presence of a white lab rat with a loud noise. After a number of pairings, the mere presence of white furry objects (such as a man's white beard)

■ Figure 5.2

A Summary of Classical Conditioning

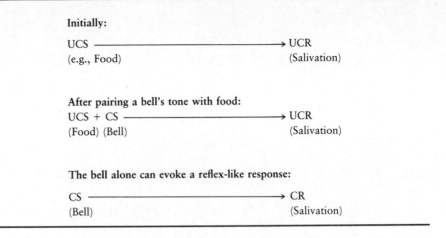

Initially:

UCS ──────────────────────→ UCR
(e.g., Food)   (Salivation)

After pairing a bell's tone with food:
UCS + CS ──────────────────→ UCR
(Food) (Bell)   (Salivation)

The bell alone can evoke a reflex-like response:

CS ───────────────────────→ CR
(Bell)   (Salivation)

Many jobs require conditioned responses. For example, driving a 40-foot tractor trailer or a forklift calls for reflexive behaviors. The driver's ability to apply the brakes quickly and firmly or otherwise react appropriately depends on conditioned responses to previously neutral stimuli, such as warning lights.† A manager's goal of training personnel to the point where they do not require continual monitoring and feedback also calls for classical conditioning.

Observational Learning

Much of the learning that occurs in organizations is based on observation. For example, a new employee may observe a skilled employee performing a task. After simply observing the activities, the new employee is able to model her behavior after her observations. **Observational learning** occurs when a person witnesses the behavior of another and vicariously experiences the consequences of the other person's actions.[3] When tasks are fairly simple, observational learning can be immediate and complete; numerous trials and rehearsals are unnecessary. Furthermore, no apparent reward is administered in observational learning. Quick mastery of behavior and the lack of a visible reward for correct responses are unique to observational learning.

---

was sufficient to produce a fearful reaction in the boy. In a sense, the boy had developed a seemingly irrational fear of white furry objects. Before Watson could desensitize the boy (for instance, by pairing white furry objects with the presence of food), the boy's mother left town, taking the boy along. Whether the boy may have overcome the phobic reaction on his own is debatable. This case represents one of the first ethically questionable uses of conditioning techniques. After this experience, Watson abandoned research along these lines and went into advertising.

† If you normally drive a car with a manual transmission but later switch to a car with an automatic transmission, you may notice your left foot reflexively stomping on a nonexistent clutch pedal. This is an example of a conditioned response encountered in everyday life.

Some contend that the reward in observational learning is purely psychological. In essence, the individual engages in *self-rewarding,* perhaps by congratulating himself or herself each time a correct action occurs. If we accept this suggestion, then we must consider the existence of a competency motive, that is, the desire to feel in control of one's surroundings and, therefore, self-sufficient.[4] In contrast to classical conditioning, in which the learner is totally dependent on someone else to set up the scheme for learning, observational learning is largely self-regulated. The choice of what to attend to, as well as how, when, and where to respond, is a matter of personal choice.

As previously noted, much of the learning that takes place in organizational settings is observational. In addition to informal observational learning, employees sometimes undergo formal training programs that rely on the same process. For example, the use of training films presumes that the observers will imitate the desirable forms of conduct portrayed on the screen. Training manuals and lectures are based on the premise that trainees will absorb, retain, and enact the preferred forms of conduct in their jobs. At Xerox, for example, managerial training seminars often involve learning by watching films or videotapes of desired activities, as well as by role playing. These seminars cover such topics as interviewing, selling, listening, and reading effectively.[5] At a minimum, such training experiences can increase employee awareness of the existence of alternative ways of responding to problem situations.

Many advocates of observational learning contend that it is most successful when external rewards are provided.[6] Thus, they join observational learning principles with conditioning principles and recognize the importance of both individual cognition (that is, mental events) and external rewards.

Instrumental, or Operant, Conditioning

Much of human behavior in organizations is instrumental, in the sense that people act on their surroundings as well as deliberately move into and out of different situations. In other words, the behavior of employees is often instrumental in bringing about a desired outcome. When a desired outcome is obtained, the likelihood of that behavior recurring is enhanced. These principles are summarized in Thorndike's **Law of Effect,** which states that responses that are followed by a desirable experience will be more likely to occur in the future, while responses that are followed by undesirable experiences will be less likely to occur.[7] More loosely stated, the law proposes that behavior that produces pleasant outcomes is more likely to recur, while behavior that produces unpleasant outcomes is less likely to recur.

In **operant conditioning,** reinforcement is used in conjunction with a response. There are two kinds of reinforcements: positive and negative. **Positive reinforcement** is any event used to increase the frequency of a response (for example, praise from a supervisor for the successful completion of a task). **Negative reinforcement** is any event that, when removed, increases the frequency of a response (for example, a loud buzzer that sounds when a worker fails to monitor a machine's operation and that shuts off only when the worker responds appropriately, or the criticism of a supervisor, which the worker can learn to avoid by performing a task correctly).

Both positive and negative reinforcement can increase the strength and frequency of the behaviors they follow. However, these two types of reinforcement will create work environments with very different characteristics and behavioral dynamics. Positive reinforcement will lead to people performing in order to seek positive outcomes, while negative reinforcement will lead to people responding out of fear and anxiety.

Classical Conditioning versus Operant Conditioning

Classical conditioning and operant conditioning possess some interesting similarities and differences. The similarities stem from the shared perspective that performance is enhanced by pairing desirable outcomes with behavior and diminished with the removal of such associated outcomes. One major difference between the two types of learning lies in classical conditioning's focus on relatively reflexive and simple responses. By contrast, operant conditioning focuses on fairly voluntary and complex responses. In essence, classical conditioning is concerned with training a person to produce a particular response (that is, a reflexive action), while operant conditioning is concerned with eliciting the response from a person (that is, a voluntary action).

It was once widely believed that the two types of conditioning represented two separate learning processes, with operant conditioning under the control of the central nervous system (i.e., primarily the brain itself), and classical conditioning under the control of the other parts of the nervous system (primarily the chains of nerves running along the sides of the spinal cord that influence glandular activity). The correctness of this distinction, however, has recently been seriously questioned in light of studies suggesting that certain reflexive responses (for example, one's own blood pressure and heart rate) can be brought under voluntary control. Also, many apparently voluntary responses can be classically conditioned.[8] Such evidence suggests that learning may be fundamentally a single process. The two types of conditioning should perhaps be viewed as different manifestations of a more basic phenomenon. It would therefore be inappropriate to state that one type of conditioning provides a superior understanding of learning relative to the other.

Using Operant Conditioning Principles in Organizational Settings

B. F. Skinner and his associates have elaborated on the principles of operant conditioning to the point where a systematic approach to the modification of human behavior has now been developed.[9] Although Skinner has not dealt with the topic of organizational behavior in his research, a number of OB researchers have adapted his principles to the field. The application of Skinner's principles to organizational settings is called organizational behavior modification, or **OB Mod.**

Acquiring Complex Behaviors: Shaping

One particularly powerful technique used to modify behavior is termed *shaping*. **Shaping** involves reinforcing small approximations of the final desired behavior. As shaping progresses, the reward is gradually withheld until larger portions of the complete task are performed. Many times, the desired worker behavior involves a set of responses so complex that the complete pattern of correct behavior is not likely to occur all at once. When shaping is used the individual receives reinforcement for small, successive approximations of the desired behavior. For example, learning to operate a complex piece of machinery is likely to take a long period of time. In applying the principle of shaping, a trainer would praise a worker for each gradual improvement in operating the machine. Praise would then be withheld until more complex patterns of behavior were successfully performed.

Maintaining Desired Behavior

Because a manager cannot always be available to administer reinforcement, it is highly desirable that subordinates learn to perform at high levels without continual reward. To achieve this, the manager must increase the strength of the desired response to the point where it will not disappear if reinforcement is not provided. The elimination of a response due to the discontinuation of reinforcement is called **extinction.** For desired behaviors, extinction should be avoided, while for inappropriate behaviors, such as tardiness and insubordination, extinction may be actively sought.

A manager wants to increase a desired behavior's **resistance to extinction,** that is, he or she wants to ensure the response's persistence in the absence of reinforcement. Increased resistance to extinction can be achieved through **partial reinforcement.** When partial, or intermittent, reinforcement is used, a response is rewarded in a noncontinuous, or variable, manner. An alternative approach would be to praise a subordinate for every correct response, an approach termed **continuous reinforcement.** Behavior learned under a partial reinforcement scheme is more resistant to extinction than behavior learned under a continuous reinforcement scheme.

Schedules of Reinforcement   The scheduling of reinforcement is a particularly important aspect of OB Mod. There are four major kinds of partial reinforcement schedules: (1) fixed interval, (2) variable interval, (3) fixed ratio, and (4) variable ratio. **Interval schedules** reinforce behavior on the basis of time elapsed, while **ratio schedules** are based on the number of times the behavior is performed. In a **fixed schedule,** the amount of time or number of behaviors is specified in advance, while in a **variable schedule,** the amount of time or number of behaviors varies.

Fixed Interval Schedule   A **fixed interval schedule** reinforces individuals for their response after a predetermined period of time has elapsed. Although the response must meet minimal standards, performance beyond the minimum does not lead to greater rewards. Performance under a fixed interval schedule of reinforcement tends to be poor. As one might expect, the lack of a direct relationship between rewards and level of performance leads to only the minimal amount of effort necessary to meet the standard. In essence, a fixed interval scheme offers workers little incentive. Nonetheless, most organizations rely on such a schedule when they compensate employees on a weekly or hourly basis and ignore performance as long as it meets minimal standards. Research with both animal and human subjects indicates that responses learned under fixed interval schedules of reinforcement diminish or extinguish very rapidly when rewards are withheld.

Variable Interval Schedule   With a **variable interval schedule,** reinforcement is administered after varying periods of time have elapsed. Although the average period of time may be calculated, an individual cannot predict in advance how much time will elapse between reinforcement. (Recall that in a fixed interval scheme, the time period can be predicted precisely.)

As an example of such a scheme, consider a top-level manager's unannounced but fairly regular twice-monthly visits to a loading dock. Although the employees cannot say precisely when the manager will visit, they can nonetheless assume that *on the average* he will make an inspection every two weeks or so. Because of the controlling influence of the evaluative experience, it is possible that performance will drop somewhat after reinforcement is administered.

Fixed Ratio Schedule   In a **fixed ratio schedule,** reinforcement is given in exchange for a predetermined number of responses. The most common business use of a fixed ratio schedule is the piece-rate pay scheme. Under such a scheme, fruit pickers might be paid a set amount of money for every 10 pounds of fruit that they harvest. Performance tends to be higher under fixed ratio schedules than it is under interval schedules, but performance is likely to drop temporarily immediately after reinforcement. Thus, on the average, performance is high, but it tends to be variable. In such a scheme, employees are likely to exert effort in spurts in order to attain a given specified level of output.

Variable Ratio Schedule   Under a **variable ratio schedule,** reinforcement is provided after an individual has produced a number of desired responses. The desired number of responses, or standard, however, is not precisely stated, but instead varies around an average number. To receive reinforcement, an individual might have to correctly perform a behavior 18 times in one instance, 8 times the next, 15 times the next, and so on, with the average number being perhaps 12.

Although very few, if any, companies use a variable ratio schedule as their primary wage-payment method, many organizations use the scheme in other ways. For example, managers commonly praise employees via a variable ratio schedule. Thus, employees can rarely be certain beforehand that their actions will be rewarded. Other examples include the intermittent use of cash bonuses, public recognition, and other awards for good performance.

Comparing Schedules of Reinforcement   When these methods of reinforcement are compared (Table 5.1), the variable ratio schedule is clearly the most

■ **Table 5.1**

A Comparison of Schedules of Partial Reinforcement

| | SCHEDULE | | | |
	Fixed Interval	Variable Interval	Fixed Ratio	Variable Ratio
Form of Reward	Reward after a specific time period	Reward after a varying time period	Reward after a specific number of responses	Reward after an average number of responses
Influence on Behavior	Mediocre performance	Fairly high, somewhat unstable performance	Fairly high and stable performance	Very high performance
Influence on Extinction	Little resistance to extinction	Somewhat resistant to extinction	Little resistance to extinction	Very resistant to extinction
Organizational Examples	Hourly and weekly pay schemes	Unannounced inspections, informal appraisals of performance	Piece-rate pay schemes, bonuses	Awards, praise, bonuses tied to variable standard of output

Source: Adapted from *Introduction to Organizational Behavior* by R. M. Steers, p. 137. Copyright © 1981 by Scott, Foresman and Company. Reprinted by permission.

effective in producing a consistently high level of performance. Behaviors rewarded under a variable ratio schedule are also the most resistant to extinction. As two illustrations, consider gambling and intimidating behavior. In gambling (say, playing slot machines or betting on horse races), one is rewarded on a variable ratio schedule in that one only wins occasionally. Despite the fact that in the long run gambling does not pay, the activity has an addictive quality in that it is always possible that the next play will be the lucky one that pays off.

An example of a negative behavior that is rewarded on a variable ratio schedule is a senior employee's threats and intimidating behavior. As most young managers find, it is difficult to ignore such posturing. By *occasionally* giving in to the angry senior employee, however, a manager is rewarding the employee on a variable ratio schedule. A likely consequence of such intermittent rewarding is that the employee will persist in his intimidating behaviors, given that he cannot be certain beforehand whether a particular instance will be the "lucky one" that pays off (in an analogous fashion to gambling). In general, a variable ratio reward schedule will enhance a response's resistance to extinction.

By contrast, the fixed interval schedule is the least effective scheme when judged against the criteria of performance enhancement and resistance to extinction. Perhaps because of their ease of administration, fixed interval schedules of reinforcement are the most commonly used in organizations. Relative to the fixed interval and variable ratio schedules, the two other schedules (fixed ratio and variable interval) can be judged as intermediate in effectiveness.

Rules for Applying Operant Conditioning Principles

Hamner and Hamner have outlined a number of rules for application of the principles of operant conditioning.[10] If a manager follows these rules in dealing with subordinates, their performance should be enhanced. With some modification, the rules offered by Hamner and Hamner can be summarized as follows:

1. *Use differential rewarding.* Many managers try to treat all subordinates alike. Although this sounds noble, it tends to encourage mediocrity. When all employees receive equal rewards, superior performers begin to feel that their efforts are unappreciated, while poorer performers recognize that they will not be penalized for minimal effort. In response, over time, most above-average performers will drop their performance to the minimal level. A few superior performers may, of course, persist, but most will lower their efforts to the level that they feel equals their rewards.

    When rewards are commensurate with performance, however, subordinates receive a quite different message. Superior performers get the signal that their efforts are valued, and potentially high performers are encouraged to try harder.

2. *Identify valued rewards for individuals.* If a manager hopes to influence an employee's behavior through the use of rewards, the rewards must have value to the employee. One of the best ways to obtain such information is simply to ask employees what rewards they would like to receive. Younger workers may prefer more paid vacation days or greater involvement in decision making, while older workers may choose better medical insurance or a larger contribution to their pension plan.

3. *Instruct subordinates on how rewards are tied to performance.* In order for operant conditioning principles to be maximally effective, employees must clearly understand how rewards and performance are connected. When specific information is lacking, subordinates may try to second-guess their manager's intentions by constructing their own imagined system of rewards. Thus, much confusion and counterproductivity can be avoided if a manager clearly states goals for performance and explains how rewards will be related to performance.

4. *Provide informative feedback on performance.* In order to meet their manager's standards of performance, employees must have instructive feedback. Their manager must evaluate and interpret their performance for them, indicating how well or how poorly they are doing and suggesting specific ways to improve. In addition to providing guidance, feedback can also serve as an additional form of reinforcement.

Setting Up an OB Mod Program

Advocates of OB Mod principles have laid out five basic steps necessary to establish an OB Mod program (Figure 5.3).[11] First, performance must be defined in purely behavioral terms. This means that performance must be

OB Focus

The Right Rewards

Two key principles of rewarding employees are to tie rewards to performance and to find rewards that the employees value. One organization that does this well is Mary Kay Cosmetics.

Company founder and president Mary Kay Ash specifically set out to develop an organization that would put its employees first and reward them appropriately and generously. Her own experience inspired her to do this. As an achievement-oriented sales representative for Stanley Home Products, she entered every sales contest. The top prize in the first contest she won was a flounder light, used in fishing. For a single mother of 40 years ago, that reward was actually a crushing disappointment. Said Ash, "I made up my mind that if I ever ran a company, one thing I would never do was give someone a fish light."

What Ash did do was set up a company based on a sales force of women who were encouraged to work hours that accommodated their families. Rewards are structured to be exciting and inspiring. At carefully planned Pageant Nights, top achievers receive prizes that include cars, trips, jewels, and fur coats. Mary Kay's consultants testify that these prizes work. Patsy Williams, who started out selling Mary Kay products during lunch hours at the textile mill where she worked, won a pearl and ruby ring shortly after she started. Said Williams, "From the moment I won that ring, I began thinking of myself as a person who deserved a better standard of living. I built a new life to go with the ring."

Rewards are based on performance, and many Mary Kay consultants are inspired to perform. *The Wall Street Journal* reports that in one year Mary Kay had considerably more women earning over $50,000 in annual commissions than any other company in the United States. Mary Kay also claims that more black and Hispanic women earn annual commissions of over $50,000 with Mary Kay than at any other corporation in the world.

Source: Kim Wright Wiley, "Cold Cream and Hard Cash," *Savvy*, June 1985, pp. 36–41.

reducible to observable and measurable events. Second, an estimate of typical or baseline performance is taken by conducting an assessment of performance by a simple tallying. The goal of this tallying is to obtain an objective measure of the current level of performance. The third step involves the establishment of specific, reasonable performance goals for each employee and communicating these goals to the employee. The fourth step consists of each employee

■ Figure 5.3

Essential Steps in Setting Up an OB Mod Program

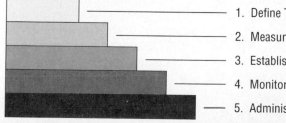

1. Define Target Behavior
2. Measure Frequency of Behavior
3. Establish and Communicate Behavior Goals
4. Monitor Behavior
5. Administer Rewards

performing his or her job while keeping personal records of performance. The employees' maintenance of their own performance records provides constant self-feedback. Finally, the fifth step, the administration of rewards (such as praise, recognition, or bonuses), is considered the key element in OB Mod. Positive reinforcement from the supervisor is intended to strengthen the desired actions, while withholding reinforcement is intended to extinguish undesirable action.

Does OB Mod Work?

Studies of the effectiveness of OB Mod programs have generally indicated that they constitute a useful approach to improving employee performance. In a review of research on OB Mod programs, Hamner and Hamner identified ten organizations that had experimented with OB Mod.[12] In nine of the ten cases, the introduction of OB Mod was judged as having had a positive effect. Many other recent examples (some involving control or comparison groups) also point to the success of OB Mod. Most instances in which OB Mod was applied shared several common characteristics. The typical OB Mod program attempts to improve either the performance or the attendance of blue-collar workers by providing immediate feedback about behavior and employing praise or recognition from superiors as reinforcers. Interestingly, the programs do not commonly use money as a reinforcer of superior performance. More typically, such social rewards as praise and recognition are used. The use of these less costly rewards may be partially responsible for the appeal of OB Mod to many managers.

Controversies Surrounding OB Mod

Although much of the available evidence suggests that many OB Mod programs have been successful, there is a good deal of controversy surrounding the application of operant principles in organizations.[13]

Opponents of OB Mod accuse it of being manipulative, charging that OB Mod programs suggest a deliberate and calculated effort to control the behavior of others, sometimes at the cost of the individuals who are being controlled. Opponents argue that OB Mod smacks of a "Big Brother" approach to management, in which an all-knowing, all-powerful overseer attempts to maintain control and forced dependency by unilaterally defining the rules of the game.

Advocates of OB Mod acknowledge that the potential for misuse does exist, but they contend that good judgment is likely to prevail because deception and exploitation are apt to meet with worker resistance. Advocates of operant conditioning point out that while the term *manipulation* may have negative connotations, it is ultimately a manager's responsibility to ensure that employee behavior contributes to the larger mission of an enterprise. Thus, managers must be aware of the factors that influence employee behavior and use them to fulfill their responsibilities to the company.

Another criticism of OB Mod is that it is not an original technique for managing employees. In some respects, OB Mod has much in common with Frederick W. Taylor's principles of scientific management (see Chapter 1). For example, OB Mod programs require closer supervision of employees, more specific definitions of job activities, frequent evaluation and feedback, and the distribution of rewards based on output. The reliance of OB Mod on such rewards as praise and recognition can also be viewed as merely taking a page out of the human relations approach to management. At the least, it is fair to say that the OB Mod approach does borrow from other traditions in the field of organizational behavior.

An added criticism of OB Mod surrounds the faithfulness of OB Mod programs to operant principles. Many programs employ only a watered-down version of the principles of operant conditioning. For example, in programs relying heavily on self-feedback (in which employees maintain their own performance records), an alternative explanation of positive performance results — one based on the notion of self-reinforcement — can be posited.[14]

Conversely, in programs that are in closer conformity with operant conditioning principles, unpleasant questions arise as to whether an organization should be condoning such programs. For example, the following OB Mod program was designed to reduce high absenteeism in a manufacturing facility.[15] On every day an employee attended work, he or she drew a card from a deck of playing cards. After a week's time, each employee would have drawn five cards, a poker hand. The employee with the best hand received, say, a $40 bonus. This program employs the principle of intermittent rewards using a variable ratio schedule. The reward is both externally administered and contingent on behavior. In fact, such programs do reduce absenteeism rates. Unfortunately, they also raise two questions: (1) should an organization endorse a form of gambling, the aim of which is to develop an addictive behavior in employees? and (2) should employees be enticed to work at a presumably distasteful job that most likely is responsible for the high absenteeism? In short, it might be more appropriate and more compassionate to first investigate the *causes* of high absenteeism and then remedy the causes by modifying the job, rather than focusing on the superficial manifestation of an underlying problem.

Operant conditioning has also been criticized for ignoring the importance of internally mediated rewards, for example, the motivation that results from the inherent enjoyment of performing certain attractive tasks. Deci suggests that the emphasis of OB Mod on externally administered, contingent rewards focuses attention on only one of the important features of motivation.[16] Furthermore, he argues that the use of such rewards for performing tasks that are intrinsically rewarding can undercut the motivation that a task may offer.

A final criticism of OB Mod is its lack of concern for mental processes. Because operant conditioning grew out of early work with animals and partly because of a reaction against early research attempts to study mental events, advocates of OB Mod have downplayed the importance of dealing with thought processes. To be sure, cognitive experiences are an important aspect of being human that cannot be totally ignored in any complete explanation of employee behavior.

■ **Figure 5.4**

Frequently Used Rewards and Punishments

Rewards	Punishments
Bonuses	Reprimands
Promotions	Oral warnings
Pay increases	Ostracism
Vacation time	Probation
Time off	Criticism from superiors
Use of company car	Suspension
Awards	Citations
Praise and recognition	Disciplinary hearing
Increase in formal responsibility	Written warning
	Pay cut
Increase in department budget	Demotion
	Reduced authority
Sense of accomplishment	Undesired transfer
Self-recognition	Termination

The Role of Punishment

So far, we have focused primarily on the use of reward as a means of altering behavior, but the use of punishment must also be considered (Figure 5.4). For purposes of discussion, we will define **punishment** as an undesirable event that follows a behavior it intends to eliminate. Punishment's role in shaping employee behavior is quite complex. Often, in response to its administration, an employee will not eliminate the undesirable behavior but instead will seek other ways of engaging in the behavior as well as ways of getting even with the punisher. In most cases, punishment leads to only a temporary suppression of the punished behavior. Consequently, any proposal to use punishment must be carefully thought out.

Alternatives to Punishment

Before using punishment to eliminate undesired behavior, managers should consider several other strategies. One alternative is to rearrange the work setting so that the undesired response cannot occur. For example, if unauthorized individuals are using a copying machine, the installation of a lock and a meter will prevent further misuse.

A second strategy is extinction. As noted earlier, a response can be extinguished if the reward with which it is usually paired is eliminated. Identifying the reward that undesired behavior generates for an employee is often not too difficult. In some instances, the reward may actually be the satisfaction of knowing that a peer or supervisor has been annoyed. Extinction in such cases might consist of ignoring the irksome behavior, thereby reducing the probability that it will recur.

To be sure, ignoring undesirable behaviors is a form of inaction. However, many managers will attest that doing nothing about certain minor prob-

■ **Figure 5.5**

Features of Effective Punishment

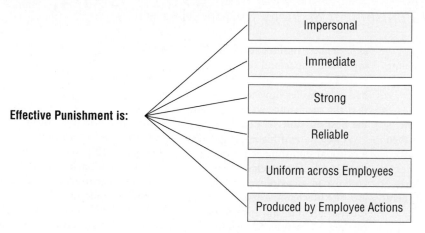

Effective Punishment is:

- Impersonal
- Immediate
- Strong
- Reliable
- Uniform across Employees
- Produced by Employee Actions

lem situations can sometimes be the best way to deal with them. For example, a problem may arise that seems to demand that some form of elaborate and detailed managerial action be taken (for example, an employee may frequently complain that a company policy is unfair to him). Sometimes, merely postponing discussion of the problem will coincide with the elimination of the origin of the problem (for instance, a problem employee may quit) or the diminution of its importance over time.

Effective Punishment

In some instances, none of these alternatives may be feasible. It may be too costly or physically impossible to change a situation to prevent the undesired behavior. Possibly the undesired behavior may provide its own reward and thus resist extinction. Or the undesired behavior may be so serious that it warrants some form of punishment. Advocates of the *reasoned* use of punishment contend that punishment can work under very specific conditions.[17] The features of effective punishment in the workplace are similar to those we have all encountered in daily life. For example, we have all learned to be careful in dealing with electricity and fire without personally resenting them. We accept the punishing aspects of natural forces due to certain common features: The punishment is impersonal, fairly immediate and strong, reliable over time, uniform from person to person, and specifically produced in response to an individual's own actions. Figure 5.5 lists the features of effective punishment.

Effective punishment in an organizational setting should possess the same attributes. The recipient should recognize that the punishment is not directed toward his or her character or sense of self-worth. The punishment should be given as soon as possible after the undesired behavior. It should be sufficiently severe that it cannot be ignored. It should be administered with consistency across instances and across people. Finally, it should be extremely

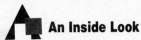

An Inside Look

An Effective Punishment Strategy for Spa Mechanics

The inspiration for Barry Fribush's business, Bubbling Bath Spa and Tub Works, Inc. — and for its style of managing workers — came from his experience as a customer. In the late 1970s, Fribush, who was then running a printing business and advertising agency, bought a hot tub. "It was terrible," he reports. "It kept breaking down, and there was no easy way to get it repaired. I figured I could do a better job selling and servicing them."

When Fribush founded Bubbling Bath, he set out to make sure that his customers wouldn't have to share his negative experiences. Besides stocking top-quality spas and hiring experienced mechanics, Fribush had to consider how to ensure that the mechanics were providing the best possible service.

A key part of his approach was a rational punishment for doing poor work: If a mechanic has to go back to a customer to redo a job, the mechanic doesn't get paid for that second call. Instead of earning a generous $25 an hour, he or she earns nothing. Mechanics are aware of this policy in advance, so they can control the consequences of their behavior. The policy also means that the consequences of poor work are immediate and consistent among mechanics.

Perhaps it is because this policy meets the criteria of effective punishment that it has worked so well. According to Fribush, when he started Bubbling Bath, an average of 30 percent of all repair jobs were callbacks. Since the company instituted the policy of no pay for redoing a job, callbacks have almost been eliminated. Furthermore, customer referrals have helped place Bubbling Bath on *Inc.* magazine's listing of the fastest-growing small private companies in 1989.

Source: Paul B. Brown, "For You, Our Valued Customer," *Inc.*, January 1990, 108–109.

clear that the punishment was caused by the specific actions of the transgressor. As a result, the punishment is informative in that the recipient can see the connection between behavior and punishment.

In organizations, many factors undermine these principles and thereby reduce the effectiveness of punishment. For example, some managers may ignore an occasional transgression in the hopes of extinguishing it. But as a result, they may seem inconsistent in dealing with the undesired behavior, and the occasional attention that they do give may seem capricious. Some managers may delay administering punishment due to indecision. Others may feel guilty after punishing an employee. If a manager then responds to his or her guilt feelings by showering the employee with positive attention, the intended effects of the punishment may be greatly diluted.

Guidelines for Administering Discipline

Given that some situations require the use of discipline, the question is how to deliver it and in what form. The answer depends on several major considerations. An important one is a supervisor's personal style of leadership. Leadership style (see Chapter 10) influences both the preferred method of discipline and the practicality of other methods. For example, a manager who subscribes to the human relations approach may prefer to avoid punishment and in fact may be unable to enforce a strict approach.

Employees' backgrounds also determine which approaches to punishment will be most effective. Highly educated employees or professionals may object to a strict approach, while blue-collar workers might readily accept the same approach. The size of an organization is another influence of the nature of discipline. Larger organizations have more formal systems of discipline. Given the difficulties inherent in coordinating larger enterprises, employees are often willing to accept a more formal system of discipline.

Progressive Discipline

Discipline should ultimately be a tool to improve performance. Its foremost goal should be to *change* behavior rather than simply to punish it. One very popular approach is **progressive discipline,** a system in which penalties are increased according to the frequency and severity of infractions. The rules are known in advance and are imposed objectively. Repeated transgressions ultimately lead to an employee's termination. A positive feature of progressive discipline is that it provides individuals with the opportunity to alter their own behavior; that is, it gives a person another chance if the infraction is not severe. Punishment is designed to be informative and to lead to a modification of the undesired behavior.

Progressive discipline programs consist of a series of steps that gradually impose increasingly severe penalties. For example, consider an employee who is repeatedly late to work by one or two hours. With a progressive discipline scheme, the employee would receive an informal verbal warning from the supervisor for the first offense. A second offense within a specified period of time would result in a meeting between the employee, the immediate supervisor, and a shift supervisor at which the employee would receive a formal oral warning. If the employee violated the same rule again, he would receive a formal written warning that would become part of his permanent record. A fourth infraction would lead to the employee being suspended without pay for the remainder of the workday. This fourth step might be coupled with the technique of mailing a letter to the employee's spouse. The letter would describe the seriousness of the situation (i.e., the danger of the employee being ultimately terminated) and seek to enlist the spouse's cooperation in "turning around" the employee. If after all this, the employee was late to work on a fifth occasion, he would be terminated.

It should be noted that at every step in this process the employee is aware that a company policy is being enforced and that the superior's actions are not based on personal malice. Another benefit of such a program is that it provides guidance to supervisors about how to deal with infractions of company rules. A supervisor need not debate whether or how to discipline employees because the course of action is clearly spelled out. Unions are also more likely to accept the outcome of progressive discipline because union stewards often attend disciplinary meetings and are kept informed of the disciplinary actions.

Most progressive discipline programs can be tailored to the severity of the offense. For such serious offenses as gambling in the locker room or fighting, the discipline might begin at step four (suspension). For an unconscionable

■ Table 5.2

Suggested Steps for Disciplinary Action

A. *Offenses resulting in first, oral warning; second, written warning; and third, immediate discharge*
    1. Uncivil conduct
    2. Tardiness
    3. Failure to punch the time clock
    4. Foul language
    5. Incompetence or inefficiency in performing job
    6. Unauthorized absence

B. *Offenses resulting in first, written warning; then, immediate discharge*
    1. Sleeping on the job
    2. Gambling
    3. Negligent use of property
    4. Failure to comply with published rules, regulations, or executive order
    5. Failing to report to work without notification for one or two days

C. *Offenses resulting in immediate discharge*
    1. Theft
    2. Destruction of property
    3. Fighting
    4. Use of drugs
    5. Gross insubordination
    6. Conduct unbecoming an employee
    7. Falsifying time cards
    8. Falsification of information in applying for position
    9. Failing to report to work without notification for three or more days
    10. Failure to maintain current license or certification
    11. Refusal to work
    12. Actions that endanger the safety, health, or well-being of others

Source: R. L. Oberle, "Administering Disciplinary Actions," *Personnel Journal*, 1978, p. 30.

offense, such as theft of a large sum of money from the organization, discipline might skip to step five (termination).

Many companies post a list of how various infractions will be treated within a progressive discipline scheme (Table 5.2). For example, category A offenses might consist of such minor infractions as tardiness, category B offenses might cover such actions as sleeping on the job, and category C offenses might include major transgressions. All employees would understand that each category is associated with a different step in the progressive discipline program.

Conducting a Disciplinary Meeting

One of the most distasteful tasks a supervisor can face is conducting a meeting devoted to disciplining a subordinate. Given the emotions involved, and win/lose implications for both parties, it is easy to understand why some supervisors are reluctant to administer punishment.

From the reports of actual experiences of supervisors, there are certain ground rules that can make disciplinary meetings more effective.

1. *Have a private meeting with the offender.* There's an old saying of managers, "Praise in public, punish in private." In the interests of protecting the individual's dignity, it is necessary that criticism and punishment be administered behind closed doors.

2. *Don't lose your cool.* Of course, this is more easily said than done. If it becomes impossible for the supervisor to control rage during a disciplinary meeting, it is perhaps best to break it off and set another time to complete the meeting. Words that are exchanged in anger are invariably regretted later on. If a subordinate displays anger, it is important not to respond in kind, but instead to remain calm.

3. *Be certain of your facts.* Some supervisors jump the gun when disciplining subordinates in that they are prepared to discipline an individual (for a variety of reasons) but do not have the facts to back up their charges. For example, imagine a supervisor who starts disciplinary action against an employee who is late returning from lunch. A subsequent investigation might reveal that the employee was late to work because he had to take his sick child to the hospital.

4. *Select an appropriate punishment.* The severity of the punishment should match the severity of the offense. It is perhaps best if a progressive discipline system has been previously worked out. Such a system can then be consulted when deciding on the most appropriate action.

5. *Accomplish the following three objectives: (a) state what is wrong, (b) state what you expect, and (c) state what happens if you don't get what you expect.* When stating the problem, your expectations, and the possible consequences, it is important to be very clear and specific. It is likely to be a mistake to diminish the seriousness of a problem in the mere hope of social harmony. During the course of the meeting, the employee should be asked to indicate that he or she understands your expectations and the possible consequences of further infractions.

6. *Keep records.* It is almost a cliché to say that employees are becoming more litigious. Because you may be required to present evidence in court or at a grievance hearing, it is essential that records be maintained on the nature and content of all disciplinary meetings. One advantage to keeping records is that it will add strength to your case if your actions are ever contested. When keeping records, it is best to follow the rules of journalism: Answer the questions of who, what, when, where, and how as they pertain to a behavioral incident.

Termination

Conducting a Termination Meeting

Managers rarely discharge an employee, primarily because they find the psychological pressures of doing so too unpleasant. Some managers will try to delegate the responsibility to someone else in the organization, such as a personnel officer. However, it is more professionally correct for the immediate supervisor to conduct the termination meeting. If the discharge does not need to occur immediately, it is recommended that the meeting be scheduled for the end of the workday or at the end of the week.[18] Because these are times when other employees are usually gone, it saves the parties involved from possible embarrassment. It also avoids the potential problems that can arise when a disgruntled employee remains on the premises with a long workday left to be completed.

The reasons for the discharge should be laid out within the first few minutes of the meeting. This is not a time to get involved in an argument over details. The finality of the decision must be conveyed. It is also not a good time to lecture the employee on his or her character flaws or to attempt to play psychotherapist. The session need not last longer than 10 minutes — in fact, the longer the meeting continues, the more likely the parties are to say something they may later regret.

Following a discharge meeting, it is recommended that the matter not be discussed with employees who are not in a "need to know" position. This may seem counterproductive — after all, if the discharge were just, wouldn't it be best to emphasize that the person had been terminated and that justice had prevailed? But given the litigious nature of employer–employee relations, it is best that nothing be said that could be construed as criticism or defamation of the discharged employee's character.

Consider the following case of the manager of a Sears, Roebuck auto-repair department who resigned after being charged with stealing parts and money from his employer. He gave his resignation in exchange for the employer's promise not to take the case to court. (It's a fairly common practice in such instances to offer employees a choice between resignation and prosecution.) When the discharged employee's subordinates demanded to know why he had been terminated, the employer revealed that the supervisor had resigned rather than be prosecuted and further implied that he was guilty of various criminal acts. When the former supervisor learned that he had been labeled a thief by his former employer, he sued for slander (recall that he resigned but did not sign a confession or admit any wrongdoing) and won.[19]‡ In hindsight, it would have been wiser for the employer not to have discussed the reason for the termination with the remaining employees. One disadvantage of refusing to discuss termination, however, is that damage can be done to morale if employees suspect that their employer dismisses workers arbitrarily.

Indirect Approaches

A fair number of organizations rely on indirect approaches to termination. One such approach is the indefinite layoff, in which a worker is told that he or she will be recalled when business picks up. While the worker is laid off, however, the employer redefines the job by changing the work process in some manner. This redefinition is intended to disqualify the former jobholder from

‡ The settlement was for $50,000.

reapplying for the new job. Because the process of indefinite layoff is done in slow steps, it minimizes worker awareness and possible protest.

Another indirect (and likewise questionable) approach to termination is to force an employee to resign by reducing his or her responsibilities. This approach is more commonly taken with management-level employees. Being reassigned to a job in the corporation's equivalent of Siberia or having various perquisites taken away are fairly clear signs that a resignation is expected.

Another example of an indirect approach taken with management-level employees is to ask a manager to prepare a letter of resignation, ostensibly as a show of good faith and in the hopes of extracting a quicker decision from superiors on a promotion or reappointment. The employer then turns around and actually accepts the resignation even though it was previously implied that the offer to resign would be rejected at a higher level.

Ideally, an organization should rely less on external devices for disciplining its employees and more on an employee's own self-discipline. Developing the desire for self-discipline and the identification of individuals who possess this desire will be topics of discussion throughout the remaining chapters.

Summary

1. Explain what learning is and why managers need to understand the learning process.
Learning is a fairly permanent change in behavior that occurs as a result of experience. It is a complex and never-ending process for all employees that can greatly affect both performance and motivation. Consequently, a manager who understands the learning process can use its principles to guide employee behavior and achieve organizational goals.

2. Describe the process of classical conditioning and cite several examples of this form of learning in the workplace.
In classical conditioning, an unconditioned stimulus is repeatedly paired with a neutral stimulus until the neutral stimulus alone can elicit the same response that was evoked by the unconditioned stimulus. When this occurs, the neutral stimulus is termed a conditioned stimulus and the response, a conditioned response. Many jobs require conditioned responses. For example, a truck driver's ability to apply the brakes quickly and firmly depends on a conditioned response to a conditioned stimulus, such as a warning light. A manager's attempt to train personnel to the point where they no longer require continual monitoring may also involve classical conditioning.

3. Tell what observational learning is and how it occurs in the workplace.
Observational learning occurs when a person witnesses the behavior of another and vicariously experiences the consequence of that person's behavior. This form of learning is very common in organizations. For example, a new employee may observe an experienced employee performing a task and then model her own behavior on the observations. Employees who attend training programs also learn from observation by viewing films, reading manuals, and attending lectures.

4. Discuss the nature of operant conditioning and cite four rules for applying operant conditioning principles to enhance employee performance. Operant conditioning is based on the notion that behavior is a function of its outcomes. Thus, behavior that produces a pleasant outcome is more likely to be repeated, while behavior that produces an unpleasant outcome is likely not to recur. To use the principles of operant conditioning to encourage desired behavior in the workplace, managers should follow four basic rules: (1) Match the reward to the performance, so that superior performers receive greater rewards. (2) Match the reward to the individual's preferences. (3) Be sure that subordinates understand how rewards are tied to performance. (4) Give employees informative feedback about their performance.

5. Summarize the advantages and disadvantages of OB Mod.
Organizational behavior modification, or OB Mod, is the application of the principles of operant conditioning to organizational settings in the attempt to alter employee behavior. The typical OB Mod intervention seeks to improve either the performance or the attendance of blue-collar workers by providing immediate feedback about behavior and by employing praise or recognition as reinforcers. Studies have indicated that such programs are generally quite effective. Nonetheless, OB Mod has many critics who contend that it is manipulative, unoriginal, and of questionable faithfulness to true operant conditioning principles, and that it ignores the role of mental processes in behavior.

6. Analyze the role of punishment in shaping employee behavior.
Punishment is an undesirable event that follows a behavior it intends to eliminate. Its role in shaping employee behavior is quite complex and its administration often does not eliminate the undesirable behavior. Consequently, any proposal to use punishment should be carefully thought out in light of the available alternatives. For punishment to be effective, (1) the recipient must recognize that it is not directed at his or her character or self-worth, (2) it should be given as soon as possible after the undesired behavior, (3) it should be sufficiently severe that it cannot be ignored, (4) it should be administered consistently across instances and people, and (5) it should be extremely clear that the punishment was caused by the specific actions of the transgressor. Ultimately, punishment should be used as a tool to change behavior and improve performance rather than as an end in itself. A well-planned progressive discipline program, consisting of a series of steps imposing increasingly severe penalties, can often accomplish this purpose.

Key Terms

Learning	Resistance to extinction
Classical conditioning	Partial reinforcement
Unconditioned stimulus	Continuous reinforcement
Unconditioned response	Interval schedule
Conditioned response	Ratio schedule
Conditioned stimulus	Fixed schedule
Observational learning	Variable schedule
Law of Effect	Fixed interval schedule

Operant conditioning
Positive reinforcement
Negative reinforcement
OB Mod
Shaping
Extinction

Variable interval schedule
Fixed ratio schedule
Variable ratio schedule
Punishment
Progressive discipline

Review and Discussion Questions

1. American corporations spend an estimated $60 billion annually on employee training. In your opinion, why are businesses willing to spend so much money on educating workers?

2. Some people contend that the principles of classical conditioning are more applicable to animals in laboratories than to humans in the workplace. Do you agree or disagree? Why?

3. Describe a situation in which you learned a new skill through observation. In what other ways might you have picked up the same skill? Compare the strengths and weaknesses of each approach, select the most effective one, and defend your choice.

4. In your opinion, is the assigning of grades at the end of each school term a form of operant conditioning? Why or why not?

5. Imagine that your school is planning to institute an OB Mod program to reduce tardiness for early morning classes. How would you recommend that such a program be set up? What reinforcers would you suggest? Do you think that such a program would be effective in reducing tardiness? Would you participate in it yourself? Explain your responses.

6. Some people contend that because its negative side effects may outweigh its potential benefits, punishment should not be used in the modern workplace. Furthermore, they claim that a manager who is truly on top of things need not fall back on punishment in order to guide subordinates. Do you agree with this position? Why or why not?

Critical Incident
The Wrong Reinforcement?

Royal Coach Corporation is a large manufacturer of school buses and related small vehicles that are used by tour groups, airport shuttle services, and so forth. A large warehouse operation is crucial to the success of the production process as many different parts are stored and then moved to the line as needed.

Charles Hodges has worked for Royal for almost four years. He is 26, single, and lives at home with his parents. His job in the warehouse involves moving raw materials to various assembly lines as they are needed. His work is steady and he uses both a forklift and motorized hand truck to transport parts.

Charles has had a history of sporadic absences from work over the past few years. These absences usually last two or three days at a time. Charles has also been late to work many times.

It is after 7:00 A.M. and Charles has not shown up for work. The warehouse crew is shorthanded once again. Charles's supervisor pulls his file while trying to decide what to do. This is the fourth supervisor for whom Charles has worked while at Royal. Each of the previous supervisors had placed written comments about Charles in the folder. Each had noted that after several periods of being absent, Charles would be called in for a meeting and promise to improve his attendance. Thereafter, he usually did.

Charles was generally a good worker. He did his job, but was not exceptional. He earned good wages and always seemed to have plenty of spending money. Two of his previous supervisors were fairly laid-back and permitted their employees to do their jobs with a minimum of supervision. A third was more autocratic and provided close supervision. He was the type who offered both help and criticism, and monitored everyone. According to the attendance record, Charles had missed more days under this supervisor than under any of the others.

It appeared to the present supervisor that Charles might be starting another period of absenteeism. He had already missed one day that week. The supervisor decided that something had to be done.

Questions

1. What principles of reinforcement have Charles's previous supervisors used? Why hasn't this reinforcement been effective?

2. What type of behavior modification program might the present supervisor try to use?

3. If a behavior modification approach does not seem to work, what should the supervisor do?

Experiential Exercise
Handling Discipline — A Role Play

I. Introduction   The text discussion focused on the importance of reinforcing appropriate behavior and recognizing the need to confront actions that are ill-suited to the workplace. It is often easier for a manager to reinforce or reward positive actions than it is to discipline or punish negative ones. This activity provides you with an opportunity to apply some of these concepts in a no-risk situation. What you learn from the experience will enable you to be more skillful when you must handle a real situation.

II. Procedure

1. Your instructor may assign individuals or ask for volunteers to play the three roles in this situation. All others in the class may function as observers.

2. Everyone should read the following description of the situation:

     Jim Turner and Bill Evans, mechanics in the service department, had been told to clean some large service equipment in the rear of the garage. When their supervisor checked on them, they were tossing pennies at a line they had drawn on the floor, clearly gambling. This is the second problem this week with Turner, a new employee who has been with the company only eight months. On the other occasion, he was found sitting in the rest room looking at a comic book when he should have been putting away his tools and reading a manual he was asked to look over. Bill Evans has been with the company for seven years and is considered one of the most reliable and hard-working employees. He has never given any trouble.

3. The two persons playing the roles of Jim and Bill can begin to enact their parts (tossing pennies at a line, etc.). The individual who is playing the part of their supervisor should think of responses to the following questions. The supervisor should then begin the role play at the point of walking in and discovering the gambling. The supervisor's role play should demonstrate how he or she chose to answer these questions.

     a. How would you handle this situation?

     b. What penalties would you impose?

     c. Would you impose the same penalty for each employee?

4. Continue the role play until everyone understands what is going to occur in terms of any sanctions. When that point is reached, the activity can be terminated.

III. Discussion

1. How do the observers feel about the way the situation was handled?

2. Do the observers feel that a reasonable conclusion was reached?

3. Analyze any face-saving behaviors that were evidenced.

4. How did the supervisor feel in dealing with the situation? How did Jim and Bill feel?

5. Did the supervisor attempt to apply progressive discipline concepts in this situation? What were they?

6. Is a disciplinary meeting warranted? With whom and why? How should it be handled?

Source: Written by Bruce Kemelgor, University of Louisville; used by permission.

Notes

1. G.A. Kimble and N. Garmezy, *Principles of General Psychology* (New York: Ronald Press, 1963).

2. J.B. Watson and R. Rayner, "Conditioned Emotional Reactions," *Journal of Experimental Psychology* 3 (1920): 1–14.

3. A. Bandura, *Social Learning Theory* (Englewood Cliffs, N.J.: Prentice-Hall, 1977).

4. R.W. White, "Motivation Reconsidered: The Concept of Competence," *Psychological Review* 66 (1959): 297–333.

5. T.J. Peters and R.H. Waterman, Jr., *In Search of Excellence: Lessons from America's Best-Run Companies* (New York: Harper and Row, 1982).

6. A.P. Goldstein and M. Sorcher, *Changing Supervisor Behavior* (New York: Pergamon, 1974).

7. E.L. Thorndike, *Animal Intelligence* (New York: Macmillan, 1911).

8. N.E. Miller and B.R. Dvorkin, "Visceral Learning," in *Contemporary Trends in Cardiovascular Psychophysiology*, ed. P.A. Obrist et al. (Chicago: Aldine, 1973); B.T. Engel, "Operant Conditioning of Cardiac Function: A Status Report," *Psychophysiology* 9 (1972): 161–177.

9. B.F. Skinner, *The Behavior of Organisms* (New York: Appleton, 1938).

10. W.C. Hamner and E.P. Hamner, "Behavior Modification on the Bottom Line," *Organizational Dynamics* 4 (1976): 3–21.

11. W.C. Hamner, "Worker Motivation Programs: The Importance of Climate, Structure, and Performance Consequences," in *Contemporary Problems in Personnel*, ed. W.C. Hamner and F.L. Schmidt (Chicago: St. Clair Press, 1977); F. Luthans and R. Kreitner, *Organizational Behavior Modification* (Glenview, Ill.: Scott, Foresman, 1975).

12. Hamner and Hamner, "Behavior Modification on the Bottom Line."

13. E.A. Locke, "The Myths of Behavior Mod in Organizations," *Academy of Management Review* 2 (1977): 543–553.

14. F.H. Kanfer and P. Karoly, "Self-control: A Behavioristic Excursion into the Lion's Den," *Behavior Therapy* 3 (1972): 398–416.

15. E. Pedalino and V. Gamboa, "Behavior Modification and Absenteeism: Intervention in One Industrial Setting," *Journal of Applied Psychology* 59 (1974): 694–698.

16. E.L. Deci, "The Effects of Contingent and Noncontingent Rewards and Controls on Intrinsic Motivation," *Organizational Behavior and Human Performance* 8 (1972): 217–229; P.C. Jordan, "Effects of Extrinsic Reward on Intrinsic Motivation: A Field Experiment," *Academy of Management Journal* 29 (1986): 405–411.

17. R.L. Solomon, "Punishment," *American Psychologist* 19 (1964): 239–253.

18. R.D. Buchanan, "How to Apply Constructive Discipline," *Food Service Marketing* 40 (October 1978): 63–67.

19. *Haddad v. Sears, Roebuck and Co.*, 526 F.2d 83 (6th Cir. 1975).

**Work is the price
you pay for money.**

— Anonymous

**If hard work were
such a wonderful
thing, surely the
rich would have
kept it all to
themselves.**

**— Lane Kirkland,
AFL – CIO President**

Learning Objectives

After studying this chapter, you should be able to:

1. *Describe how hedonism explains behavior and state limitations of this explanation.*

2. *Summarize the impact of instinctual theories on the understanding of motivation.*

3. *Describe a technique for uncovering a person's dominant needs.*

4. *Describe Maslow's hierarchy of needs.*

5. *Compare the ways motivator factors and hygiene factors may influence employees.*

6. *Describe how expectations can influence an employee's efforts.*

7. *Explain how behavior modification affects behavior in organizations.*

8. *Explain how employees' sense of equity affects their motivation.*

9. *Describe how social learning influences behavior.*

10. *Identify steps managers can take to motivate employees.*

Motivation

■ Getting the Workers Involved

A decade ago, there was plenty of room for improvement at A. O. Smith Corporation's automotive works in Milwaukee. Workers were bored with jobs that required them to perform routine tasks in which they welded and riveted car and truck frames, repeating the same task every 20 seconds. Workers' pay was based partly on the number of pieces produced, so they hurried to move parts through without regard to quality. As a result, quality was so poor that the company stationed workers at the end of the assembly lines to repair frames that were built improperly the first time. In 1981, 20 percent of the frames produced on a Ford Ranger line had to be repaired before they could be shipped out. Furthermore, absenteeism some days was as high as 20 percent.

To motivate the workers to do better, A. O. Smith sought to get them more involved in running the company. However, the various committees and discussion groups Smith formed, with and without union involvement, just didn't seem to make much of a difference. Finally, in 1987, Smith decided it would have to make a radical change.

The company decided to involve workers in decision making in a more significant way. Smith reorganized them into production teams that effectively were to manage themselves. Each team comprises five to seven workers, who rotate from one job to another. The team members elect team leaders, who take on many managerial duties, including scheduling production and overtime, ordering maintenance work, and stopping the assembly line to

correct defects. The company also eliminated the piecework pay system, initially freezing employees' wages (rather than simply effectively cutting compensation by eliminating the piecework incentives).

Although the additional responsibilities might seem to be simply an added burden for workers, A. O. Smith hoped that the changes would make jobs more interesting, thereby motivating employees to do better. Some evidence suggests that the plan may be working. By 1988, the rate of productivity growth had doubled, and defects on the Ranger line had fallen to 3 percent. Shop steward Charles Perkins is an enthusiastic convert to the new program. "They just turned control of the shops over to us," he explains. "Our destiny is in our own hands. I love it!"

Involving workers in managing and decision making is just one of many approaches to motivating an organization's employees. This chapter explores the concepts behind such efforts. It begins by discussing basic knowledge of how people are motivated, then goes on to describe ways these principles apply to the organization. The chapter closes with some ideas managers can use in creating an environment that motivates.

Source: John Hoerr, "The Cultural Revolution at A. O. Smith," *Business Week*, May 29, 1989, 66, 68.

Recently, I took a tour of a large manufacturing plant on the East Coast. My guide, a first-level supervisor, highlighted the size and capabilities of the facility. Since I was very much impressed by the large number of people who were employed in the plant, I asked my guide, "How many people work here?" Not knowing the intent of my question, he answered, "About half!"

This experience underscores one of the major concerns of all managers: How to motivate others to higher levels of performance. In one survey of over 4,000 adults, 57 percent reported that they could easily be more productive in their jobs if they wanted to.[1] As this evidence suggests, there is an untapped potential for greater productivity. The key to motivating others lies in somehow arousing and channeling their desire to produce.

The Nature of Motivation

Exactly how to motivate others is difficult to determine because motivation itself is such a complex phenomenon. For example, specific behavior may be the result of several motives, rather than a single motive. Furthermore, people who express essentially the same motive may engage in very different behaviors, while people who express very different motives may engage in very similar behavior.

Motives cannot be directly observed; they can only be inferred from the behavior of others. This difficulty can easily lead to errors in interpretation. In addition, motives are dynamic, or constantly changing. The changes result from the rise and fall of a motive's importance as it is variously satisfied or unsatisfied. To complicate things further, some motives do not decrease in importance when a desired goal is attained. Perhaps the best example of this is the reaction that may accompany a pay raise. Often, the raise increases, rather than decreases, an employee's desire for more money.

The complexity of motivational processes is perhaps matched by the complexity and variety of approaches that have been offered to explain motivation. In this chapter, we will review the major approaches to explaining worker behavior and consider a possible integration of these views.

Hedonism

One of the earliest attempts to explain individual motivation occurs in the writings of utilitarian, or hedonistic, philosophers. In the 1800s, philosophers such as Jeremy Bentham and John Stuart Mill proposed that most, if not all, individual behavior could be explained by the principle of **hedonism.**[2] This principle holds that people will seek pleasure and avoid pain. According to Bentham and Mill, people are fairly rational when choosing between alternative courses of action, and their decisions reflect a careful weighing of costs and benefits.*

The principle of hedonism tends to be too vague and general to be of much use in explaining worker behavior. The hedonistic perspective is most accurate in explaining behavior *after the fact*. That is, after a person engages in a behavior, we can say that he or she acted in order to attain pleasure and/or to avoid pain. All actions, however, can be described as hedonistic. Even such altruistic behavior as sacrificing your life to save the lives of others in a combat situation can be viewed as selfishly motivated. One can reason, after the event, that the apparently altruistic act was performed in order to avoid a later sense of guilt. Because hedonistic explanations work best in explaining actions after they occur, they are not useful in predicting behavior.

Instinctual Theories

From about 1890 to 1920, instinctual views of motivation were popular. The writings of William James and Sigmund Freud endorsed the view that **instincts** (that is, inborn or innate predispositions) largely determine an individual's interpretation of and response to situations.[3] One of Freud's major contributions to this discussion was his emphasis on the role of unconscious motives (motives of which an individual is unaware). Although unconscious motives may play a role in behavior (the existence of unconscious motives can be demonstrated by verbal "slips," dream symbolism, and hypnotic suggestions), the impact of unconscious motives is probably not great.

Instinctual views continued to gain acceptance until the number of proposed instincts reached approximately 6,000! Included among them were the needs for autonomy, deference, dominance, exhibitionism, harm avoidance, order, play, and sex. The large number of identified instincts reflected the wide variety of possible human behaviors. But, like hedonism, instincts can be proposed, after the fact, to explain any act. Because of its own enormity and lack of a practical framework for deciphering the growing list of instincts, the instinctual approach lost its following.

Achievement Motivation Theory

The Thematic Apperception Test   One legacy of the instinctual approach is the use of story-telling techniques to uncover dominant needs (that is, recurring concerns for goal attainment). While devising his own lengthy instinct-related list, Henry A. Murray created a test for establishing the presence and strength of various needs.[4] Specifically, Murray compiled a set of drawings cut out of stories in magazines. Even without their associated stories, the drawings

---

* As an explanatory framework, hedonism is actually a very old approach. Epicurus, an early Greek philosopher, proposed essentially much the same viewpoint many centuries before Bentham and Mill. The real legacy of Bentham and Mill has been the subsequent generation of more specific explanations of human behavior that were laid on the foundations of hedonistic principles.

were intriguing and provocative. For example, one drawing showed a man who was apparently outraged and about to run out of a room, while a woman attempted to restrain him from committing what might be a rash act.

Murray used a set of 20 drawings as a projective story-telling device (see Figure 3.5 for an example). In administering his test, called the Thematic Apperception Test, or TAT, Murray would ask the respondent to look at each drawing and offer a story to explain it.[5] Each story was to include a description of the main characters as well as summaries of what led up to the situation, what was currently going on, and what would be a likely outcome. Murray observed that people's stories tended to reflect their dominant needs. For example, the stories that people create when they are placed in need-heightening situations (such as when they are deprived of food, sleep, or social contact) typically contain themes devoted to the heightened need. Thus, in a food deprivation study, the stories may involve people going to a banquet or returning from a hamburger stand.

The McClelland Studies   David McClelland, a successor of Murray, continued to use story-telling techniques to understand dominant needs.[6] McClelland, however, focused on a more limited set of needs: the **need for achievement,** the **need for affiliation,** and the **need for power.**[7]

McClelland's research on the need for achievement has received the greatest attention in organizational behavior literature. In his studies, McClelland sought first to identify persons with a high need to achieve. He interpreted recurring themes of hard work and success in their stories as signs of a high need to achieve. He then studied these high-achievement individuals in a variety of natural and laboratory settings.

Based on these studies, McClelland and his colleagues were able to identify some factors that indicated a predisposition to strive for success.[8] In general, high performance levels and executive success appear to be correlated with a high need for achievement. Individuals with a relatively high need for achievement tend to prefer situations that involve moderate risk and personal responsibility for success rather than luck, and they desire specific feedback on their performance.

The need for achievement partly determines how employees will respond to challenging job assignments, because task persistence and the acceptance of challenge are closely related to this need. High achievers are driven by the prospect of performance-based satisfaction rather than by monetary gain. For these individuals, money is primarily a source of feedback on personal performance rather than an end in itself. Other evidence suggests that high-achievement individuals are more likely to set clocks and watches ahead by 10 or more minutes to avoid being late for appointments and that they doodle in a distinctive style (making clear symbols and filling up the bottom of a page, seldom retracing a line).

The need for achievement is an important explanation of individual success and failure, but it can be overemphasized. Though having the drive to succeed is desirable in many situations, it is not always appropriate to every job in every organization. Furthermore, individuals who are dominated by the need for achievement may have difficulties in getting along with coworkers.

In fact, a manager's effectiveness depends not on a single dimension but on a pattern of needs and the appropriateness of the pattern for a given work setting (for example, manufacturing versus social service). Managers should have a reasonably high need for power in order to function effectively as leaders.[9] A moderate level of need for affiliation can also be useful in many settings. In a recent study of the promotion histories of 237 managers at AT&T, McClelland and Boyatzis found that a moderate-to-high need for power and a low need for affiliation were associated with managerial success for nontechnical (nonengineering) managers.[10] Also, high need for achievement was associated with career advancement, but only at lower level positions, where individual contributions may be more important than the ability to influence others. The career success of technical managers with engineering responsibilities, however, could not be predicted from the same measures.

Individuals who have a high need for affiliation tend to be warm and friendly in their relationships. But unless their affiliation needs are balanced by the needs for achievement and power, they are likely to be seen as relatively ineffective in many settings.[11] Their ineffectiveness may stem from the fear of disrupting social relations by being direct and confrontational, even though a forthright approach may be the most appropriate.

McClelland's research on the need for achievement has moved into two further directions: the origins and the economic consequences of achievement motivation. The origin of achievement motivation appears to lie in one's socialization during childhood. Parents who encourage early self-reliance in their children (for example, by training a child to cross the street alone at a relatively early age) produce children who are more achievement-oriented later in life. However, early independence training must also be coupled with supportiveness. Warmth or supportiveness is crucial in that the self-reliant child must not feel that he or she has been abandoned.

Religious differences in emphasis on personal achievement have also been identified.[12] These differences may largely be due to parental emphasis on personal striving versus obedience to authority. Research suggests that Protestant and Jewish parents generally emphasize striving and independence, whereas Catholic parents are more likely to emphasize obedience.[13] These differences are reflected in later life. For example, a comparison of the average level of educational attainment for the three major religious groups in the United States revealed that Jews attain higher than average educational levels.[14] The same study notes that Jews and Protestants, as compared to Catholics, also respond to job challenge and responsibility in more positive ways by displaying higher levels of job satisfaction in higher-quality jobs. These differences, of course, are based on aggregate, or large-sample, findings. Therefore, a specific individual's religion is not necessarily an accurate predictor, given the wide variability that occurs for all three major religious groups. The continuing assimilation of religious groups into the mainstream culture is also believed to be diminishing differences among the groups.

McClelland proposed that a culture's growth is due to the level of need for achievement inherent in its population.[15] His research indicates that increases in the level of need for achievement precede increases in economic activity. An analysis of the literature of various cultures (including an analysis of popular themes in children's readers and the folklore of preliterate tribes) suggests that an increase in achievement themes may precede an increase in economic growth.

McClelland also proposed that achievement motivation can be enhanced in adults who otherwise lack a high level.[16] Training programs have been designed to heighten achievement motivation by having participants focus on goal setting and on thinking and acting in a high-achievement manner. The results of such programs have reportedly been successful; participants are likely to have greater subsequent success in their careers, as measured by rates of promotion, salary progress, and business expansion. One program, run by the Metropolitan Economic Development Association in Minneapolis-St. Paul for small-business owners and potential entrepreneurs, required participants to complete and interpret their responses to the Thematic Apperception Test as well as to engage in goal setting. Follow-up data revealed that participants experienced significant increases in personal income and expanded business activity.[17] However, because many participants in such training programs are selected for their entrepreneurial predisposition, it is difficult to say with certainty that the training program in itself was responsible for their later success. It is altogether possible that a placebo, or guinea pig, effect accounts for the reported enhancement in personal performance. More carefully controlled studies are needed in this area before we can firmly conclude that an individual's need for achievement can be substantially modified by training programs.

Maslow's Hierarchy of Needs

At much the same time that Murray and McClelland were formulating their views of motivation, Abraham Maslow was developing a more complete view of individual motivation.[18] From his work as a clinical psychologist, Maslow devised a model for explaining the essential needs for healthy psychological development. Maslow incorporated McClelland's emphasis on the importance of social acceptance, personal control, recognition, and achievement, but he went several steps further by proposing additional sets of needs and suggesting a rational order for them.

According to Maslow, needs can be classified into a hierarchy, with the needs that are lower in the hierarchy being more essential to survival. Maslow's **hierarchy of needs** is illustrated in Figure 6.1. Lower-order needs, called **deficiency needs,** must be satisfied to ensure an individual's very existence and security. Higher-order needs, or **growth needs,** are concerned with personal development and realization of one's potential. The specific needs under each general category are then arranged into a five-step hierarchy reflecting the increasingly psychological nature of each set.

Deficiency Needs

1.   *Physiological needs.* This most basic level of Maslow's hierarchy includes the needs for food, water, sleep, oxygen, warmth, and freedom from pain. If these needs are unsatisfied, an individual's actions will be dominated by attempts to fulfill them. If these needs are sufficiently met, the second set of needs will emerge.

▇ Figure 6.1

Maslow's Hierarchy of Needs

2. *Safety needs.* These needs relate to obtaining a secure environment in which an individual is free from threats. Society provides many devices for meeting these needs: insurance policies, job-tenure arrangements, savings accounts, and police and fire departments. If a person is reasonably safe and secure, a third set of needs will probably emerge.

3. *Social needs.* The third set includes the needs for affection, love, and sexual expression. The absence of friends or loved ones can lead to serious psychological maladjustment.

Growth Needs

4. *Esteem needs.* If the deficiency needs are reasonably satisfied, a concern for self-respect and the esteem of others may arise. Esteem needs include the desires for achievement, prestige, and recognition as well as appreciation and attention from others.

5. *Self-actualization needs.* This category includes the desire for self-fulfillment. Personal development may be expressed in many different ways — for example, maternally, athletically, artistically, or occupationally. Some individuals may never experience the desire to develop their own potential. An individual who attains self-actualization will occasionally have peak experiences. A peak experience can best be described as a sense of euphoria that is not chemically induced. It can be felt as a sense of completeness or of oneness with the universe.

One of Maslow's basic premises was that the five categories of needs followed a hierarchical ordering in terms of potency. By this he meant that if a deficiency arises, a lower-order need can supersede a higher-order need to demand its fulfillment. For instance, imagine that you are engaged in a pleasant conversation with a group of coworkers (you are satisfying your social needs) when suddenly your oxygen is cut off. It would, of course, be very difficult to think of anything else at that time except the restoration of oxygen, a lower-level need. This capacity of lower-order needs to assert themselves is termed **prepotency.**

More typically, needs emerge gradually rather than suddenly. These unsatisfied needs produce an internal tension that must be reduced. Generally, needs are not 100 percent satisfied; partial satisfaction is more common. For example, physiological needs may be 95 percent satisfied, safety needs 65 percent, social 45 percent, and so on.[19]

Most organizations probably do a fairly good job of satisfying employees' lower-order needs either directly (by opportunities to feel warm, safe, and part of a work group) or indirectly (by wages that can be used to purchase goods that will satisfy various needs). But organizations are not nearly so successful at providing opportunities to satisfy the higher-order needs for esteem and self-actualization. Research by Lyman Porter suggested that upper-level employees are often concerned with esteem and self-actualization needs that may go unmet.[20]

Maslow believed that managers should strive to create the climate necessary to develop employees' potentials to their fullest. Ideal organizational climates would provide opportunities for independence, recognition, and responsibility. Poor work climates, Maslow contended, lead to high levels of employee frustration, low job satisfaction, and high rates of turnover. Maslow's theory, therefore, is of greatest importance in establishing organizational policies.

Research findings on the validity of Maslow's hierarchy of needs have not always been supportive. For example, the proposed notion of prepotency has been difficult to verify. The measurement of various features of the model has also been problematic.[21] Because certain concepts that Maslow proposed (such as self-actualization) were derived from his work with neurotic clients in his practice as a psychologist, we cannot be certain to what extent the various principles can be generalized to the normal adult work force. While the notion of self-actualization may be important to a person who is struggling with his self-identity, it may have little meaning or importance to an unskilled laborer who has made a personal accommodation to the limits of his current position. As is generally true of the humanistic perspective, much of Maslow's writing also suffers from a degree of imprecision and fuzziness in terminology and conceptualization.† Despite these problems, Maslow nonetheless deserves credit for being one of the first to espouse a humanistic approach to the treatment of employees.

Two-Factor Theory

One of the most widely known and influential views of work motivation is Fred Herzberg's **two-factor theory**.[23] As part of a study of job satisfaction, Herzberg and his colleagues conducted in-depth interviews with 203 engineers and accountants in the Pittsburgh area. The researchers asked respondents to recall two separate job-related events in which their work satisfaction had improved or declined. The responses suggested that the work-related factors

---

† The number of needs that Maslow proposed (five sets) may be an over-refinement. Alderfer has proposed a three-step hierarchical theory: ERG theory.[22] Alderfer's view argues for the three broad need categories of Existence, Relatedness, and Growth. ERG theory also allows for the simultaneous importance of various needs (as does Maslow's view) and attempts to explain movement down (as well as up) the hierarchy by factors related to frustration and psychological regression.

that led to feelings of satisfaction were different from those factors that led to dissatisfaction. The satisfiers usually pertained to the content of the job and included such factors as career advancement, recognition, sense of responsibility, and feelings of achievement. Herzberg called these **motivator factors.** The dissatisfiers more often stemmed from the context in which the job was performed. They related to job security, company policies, interpersonal relations, and working conditions. Herzberg called these **hygiene factors.**

Herzberg reasoned that motivator factors had the potential to motivate workers to higher levels of performance because they provided opportunities for personal satisfaction. While the absence of these factors would not make employees *unhappy,* it would leave them feeling somewhat neutral toward their jobs.

Although they could not induce a worker to higher levels of performance, hygiene factors could create great dissatisfaction if they were not attended to. Hygiene factors could make a worker very unhappy, but they could not create more than a neutral feeling toward the job even if they were ideally modified.

Herzberg's argument is unique in that it differentiates the factors that motivate employees from those that lead to dissatisfaction. Furthermore, two-factor theory (or motivator–hygiene theory, as it is sometimes called) contends that improving physical working conditions may help to reduce worker discontent, but will not provide sufficient incentive for most workers to strive for superior performance. As a hypothetical illustration, consider the removal of your garbage from the front of your home every week. This issue is a hygiene factor in that it has the capacity to make one very unhappy if it is not attended to (imagine your unhappiness if the trash were not removed for a period of several weeks). Alternatively, if your trash is removed with complete regularity, you are not likely to turn cartwheels upon seeing that the garbage has been taken away sometime during the day. Trash removal, like poor working conditions, is something that we expect to have taken care of, but take little interest in once it is remedied. Motivator (or psychological) aspects of many jobs, in turn, tend to be neglected.

In essence, Herzberg contends that attraction toward work and dissatisfaction leading to the avoidance of work are not opposite ends of a single bipolar continuum. Instead, two separate, unipolar continua should be used to represent the independent influences of the motivator and hygiene factors. Graphically, the influence of motivator factors can range from neutral to positive,

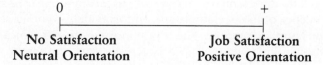

while the influence of hygiene factors can range from neutral to negative.

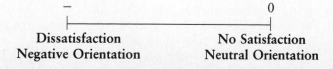

Figure 6.2

Predicted Relationships Between Level of Job Factors and Worker Orientation/Satisfaction

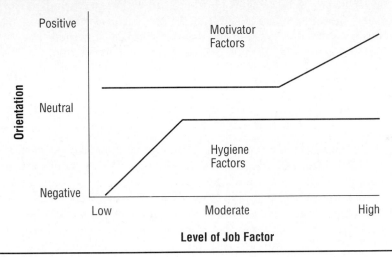

Another way of expressing two-factor theory is to graph the relationships between increasing levels of job factors (motivators and hygienes) and orientation toward work satisfaction. As Figure 6.2 shows, inattention to hygiene factors can lead to serious dissatisfaction, while beyond a moderate level, increased attention to hygiene factors brings no further increase in satisfaction. Conversely, low levels of motivator factors can at worst only lead to neutrality. But high levels of motivator factors can yield significant gains in satisfaction.

The extremes on each factor and the combination of these extremes are worth considering. A job that combines high levels of motivator and hygiene factors would be ideal, while the combination of low levels on both would be undesirable. The combination of a high level of motivator factors with a very low level of hygiene factors yields the situation like that of the "starving artist," that is, a person who greatly enjoys working but is unhappy with poor working conditions, wages, and the like. According to Herzberg, the opposite situation — a combination of a high level of hygiene factors with a low level of motivator factors — would produce a state of total neutrality.

If two-factor theory is valid, we can expect to find evidence for the curvilinear relations presented in Figure 6.2. In fact, a number of studies have provided evidence of these relationships. Unfortunately, another set of studies has not found similar support. The nonsupportive studies typically report a linear (or straight-line) relationship between the level of a factor and worker satisfaction. Figure 6.3 summarizes these linear associations, in which the motivator or psychological factors appear to be more important in determining worker response than the hygiene or environmental factors (this is indicated by the line for motivator factors being above the line for hygiene factors). Most studies of the two-factor theory reveal the relatively greater importance of psychological factors versus environmental factors.

A comparison of conflicting studies suggests that the method used to

OB Focus

AAL Finds the Factors That Motivate

As businesses have learned that it takes more than money to motivate workers, many of them have sought to introduce more of the factors that Herzberg terms *motivators*. This has been the case particularly in manufacturing settings, where businesses have employed a variety of tactics to give workers more autonomy and responsibility in doing their jobs. A service business that has sought to motivate workers through similar means is Aid Association for Lutherans (AAL), an 84-year-old fraternal insurance company (that is, an insurance company where profits are used to do charitable works and to benefit members — the people who buy policies — through such means as scholarships to attend college).

At AAL, these changes took the form of organizing workers into teams. Typically, the workers at an insurance agency do simple, repetitive tasks that require little thinking or awareness of

customers. AAL was organized to facilitate such division of labor, with specialized workers in three divisions handling either health insurance, life insurance, or support services. If a field agent contacted the home office to make a policy change or to find out the status of a complex case, he or she might get bounced around from one person to another, because one person would know only about the claims being processed through a policy, whereas someone else would be responsible for making changes to the policy. This system did not foster a sense of responsibility or achievement in satisfying customers.

Under its new system, AAL set up five groups to provide complete services for the agents in a particular region. Each group consists of three or four teams of 20 to 30 employees who can perform all of the 167 tasks that previously were divided among the functional sections. As a team, employees are responsible for

scheduling their own hours within the company's flextime program, assigning themselves tasks, and rotating jobs. The field agents deal solely with their assigned team, thereby enabling them to know the employees on that team, which helps everyone to provide better service to customers and to enjoy a sense of achievement from working as a team to solve a customer's problem.

The change was difficult for many employees, who found themselves leaving friends to work with a whole new group. But the autonomy is appealing. In the words of Diana Stephani, a processing clerk training to be an underwriter, "The team idea lets you grow, and you don't always have a supervisor sitting over you." The numbers also look good for AAL: a 20 percent increase in productivity and a case-processing time that has fallen by as much as 75 percent.

Source: John Hoerr, "Work Teams Can Rev Up Paper-Pushers, Too," *Business Week*, November 28, 1988, 64ff.

study the theory is related to the degree of support that the theory receives. Typically, studies using the interview method (which Herzberg employed in his original study) have obtained evidence that the theory is valid, whereas studies employing other methods (such as questionnaires) have failed to find support for the theory's principles. This suggests that the theory may be **method-bound,** that is, the theory can only be supported by a particular method.[24]‡

‡ Method-bound theories represent interesting traps for scientists. A couple of centuries ago, researchers suggested the notion of "phylgistin" to explain why things burned as long as they did. So the reasoning went, paper had a lot of phylgistin, water had none, and some rocks (coal) amazingly contained phylgistin. The way to measure the amount of this strange substance was simply to burn the object. The longer it burned, the more phylgistin it contained. Phylgistin was conveniently defined as being odorless, colorless, tasteless, and weightless, so that the only method for measuring its volume was to time how long an object burned. Clearly, our ancestors were deceiving themselves (with a forerunner of the concept of oxygen) by constructing a theory that could be tested with only a single method.

■ **Figure 6.3**

Frequently Observed Relationships Between Level of Job Factors and Worker Orientation/Satisfaction

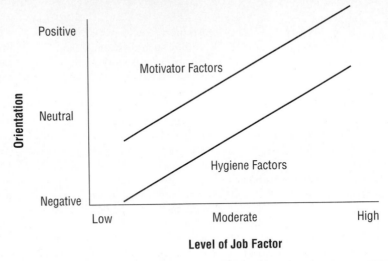

Critics of the two-factor theory argue that respondents in an interview setting may be providing answers in an ego-defensive manner. According to this argument, respondents are inclined to report that the good things that happen to them at work are related to their own efforts, while the bad things are due to external or environmental forces. It is easier to blame coworkers and company policy when things go poorly than it is to blame oneself. In addition, critics point out that many of the job factors that are rather neatly compartmentalized as motivators or hygienes within the theory are not exclusively members of one set or the other. For example, salary is certainly a potential source of dissatisfaction, and salary is externally administered (a hygiene factor). However, salary can be a source of personal pride and, therefore, serves as a source of psychological reward (a motivator factor).

Despite these shortcomings, two-factor theory has had a substantial influence on the thinking of managers and researchers. It is probably safe to say that two-factor theory is one of the most widely known theories of motivation (rightly or wrongly) in managerial circles. The theory's influence continues through its prescriptions for job redesign.

Two-factor theory can be seen as building on the work of Maslow. Table 6.1 compares the factors from the two theories. As the table shows, both theories focus on much the same facets of work life. Herzberg's contribution has been to refine and extend the work of Maslow by (1) suggesting different dynamics and interplay among the facets, and (2) underscoring the significance of higher-order factors in the determination of worker motivation.

■ **Table 6.1**

A Comparison of Factors in Maslow's Hierarchy of Needs and Herzberg's Two-Factor Theory

Hierarchy of Needs	Two-Factor Theory
Growth Needs	*Motivators (Satisfiers)*
Self-actualization	Responsibility
	Work itself
	Achievement
	Advancement
Esteem	Recognition
	Advancement opportunities
Deficiency Needs	*Hygienes (Dissatisfiers)*
Social	Supervision
	Interpersonal relations
	Status
	Salary
Safety	Company policy
	Job security
Physiological	Working conditions

Expectancy Theory

Expectancy theory (or perhaps more properly, theories, since a variety of expectancy approaches have emerged during recent decades) represents an attempt to explain worker motivation in terms of anticipated rewards. These theoretical models assume that people make rational decisions based on economic realities. Many researchers are attracted to expectancy theory because it tries to bring together both personal and situational influences.

Although many variations of expectancy theory have been proposed, the most widely cited version was proposed by Victor Vroom of Yale University.[25] Vroom's model argues that the psychological force on an employee to exert effort is a function of his or her expectancies about the future and the valence (or attractiveness) of specific future outcomes. Two kinds of expectations are important in the model: the expectation that effort will lead to performance and the expectation that performance will lead to rewards.§

Effort–Performance Expectancy (E→P)   In deciding on a course of action, employees will consider whether their effort will translate into a desired accomplishment. If the obstacles are such that they cannot reasonably expect their effort to lead to an acceptable level of performance, their motivation to perform will be diminished.

Performance–Outcome Expectancy (P→O)   Another consideration is whether a given level of performance will result in the obtainment of a particular

§ What follows is essentially a "bare-bones" or introductory-level discussion of expectancy theory.

outcome. The more strongly a person believes that performance will lead to a positive outcome (or the avoidance of a negative outcome), the more likely it is that he or she will be motivated to higher levels of performance.

Valence (V)   The outcomes that an employee receives can be evaluated in terms of their value or attractiveness. Expectancy theorists, however, prefer to use the special term **valence** to denote this attractiveness. The valence that an individual attaches to an outcome is a very personal matter that cannot be accurately predicted by other people. Thus, it is essential to ask an individual about the valences that he or she attaches to anticipated outcomes. The valence of a given outcome may also vary in relation to how recently the individual has been rewarded.

The linkages of effort–performance expectancy and performance–outcome expectancy can be measured by questioning individuals on the subjective probabilities that they believe characterize the linkages. **Subjective probabilities** are estimates of the likelihood that one event will follow another. In this case, respondents would be asked to report their personal probability estimates that effort will lead to performance and that performance will lead to a given outcome. These probabilities can range from 0, indicating a belief that one event will definitely *not* follow the other, to 1.0, indicating complete confidence that one event *will* follow the other. The valence of an outcome is assessed by having respondents provide an associated value that can range from −1.0 (highly unattractive) to +1.0 (highly attractive).

The probability estimates can be multiplied together to yield an overall expectancy value. This value can then be multiplied by the associated valence to yield a summary index of the psychological force on an individual to exert effort. In summary, the mathematics involved are:

$$(E{\rightarrow}P) \times (P{\rightarrow}O) \times (V) = \text{Motivational Force}$$

As an example, consider a salesperson who is deciding whether to make additional sales calls. She believes that the additional calls (effort) will lead to additional sales (performance) and that the additional sales will lead to a bonus (outcome). The size, or magnitude, of the bonus (valence) must also be considered. For illustrative purposes, imagine that the salesperson's probability estimate of $E{\rightarrow}P$ is .8, and the estimate of $P{\rightarrow}O$ is .7. Also, the anticipated bonus has a valence of +.6. The motivational force that is exerted on the salesperson is given by $(.8) \times (.7) \times (.6) = .34$. If she had valued the bonus more highly, so that its valence were +.9, the motivational force would have been $(.8) \times (.7) \times (.9) = .50$. If she felt that the bonus was trivial, the valence portion of the equation would significantly reduce her motivational force.

Several clear implications for motivating others can be derived from expectancy theory. First, it is important for employees to recognize that effort and performance are closely related. A manager's job should include the establishment of conditions that help to translate effort into performance. This may involve the removal of obstacles and the creation of production systems that help employees see the link between effort and performance.

Managers also need to create linkages between rewards and performance. To establish this connection, the creation and maintenance of reward systems are necessary. Furthermore, the rewards that are offered should be tailored to the values of the individual employee. This may require surveying employees in order to determine individual preferences among reward options. Lastly, conflicting expectancies and rewards need to be eliminated. Conflicting influences may arise when coworkers attempt to restrict another's performance or when conflicting demands are made by different supervisors.

Research on the principles of expectancy theory has generally been supportive.[26] However, expectancy theory has become exceedingly complex. Careful readings of Vroom's work have also led many researchers in quite different research directions.[27] A true test of the complete expectancy model would require an enormous effort on the part of participants to answer a very large number of questions. The resulting information would also have to be combined in a matrix-algebra format in order to include the many combinations of *multiple* levels of effort, performance, and reward that could be anticipated.[28] In addition, expectancy theory's relevance is limited to settings where a conscious, reward-maximization decision-making process is operating. For individuals who do not follow such a process (or in settings that induce different decision-making processes), an expectancy theory view may not be appropriate. Yet despite its esoteric character and the doubtfulness of the proposition that employees actually engage in a cognitive calculus before making decisions, expectancy theory remains a popular framework for explaining employee motivation.[29]

Reinforcement Theory

The principles of operant conditioning, presented in Chapter 5, can also be used to explain work motivation. The allocation of rewards in exchange for specific behaviors can have a powerful effect on subsequent behavior. The design of specific reward systems will be considered further in Chapter 7.

Operant conditioning, or **behavior modification** as its applied version is termed, is particularly influential in directing behavior if rewards are (1) substantial and highly desired, (2) administered intermittently, and (3) differentially distributed so that higher levels of performance lead to proportionally larger increases in reward.[30]

Proponents of organizational behavior modification (OB Mod) prefer to diagnose situations in terms of an "antecedent–behavior–consequence" or A–B–C framework.[31] Antecedents are stimuli that precede behaviors. Consequences are the outcomes, or rewards and punishments, that follow from behaviors. These consequences, in turn, serve as antecedents for subsequent behavior. By managing the consequences of behavior, OB Mod specialists seek to modify later behavior.

Reinforcement theory and expectancy theory have a similar conceptual foundation. Both approaches derive from a simple hedonistic base. However, **reinforcement theory** focuses on the influence of past rewards in shaping present behavior, while expectancy theory focuses on the influence of anticipated rewards on present behavior. Reinforcement theory has been character-

An Inside Look

Reinforcing the Use of New Technology

When Sandoz Pharmaceuticals set out to introduce its salespeople to using computers, the company made sure that the employees would feel well rewarded for learning the new system, which uses laptop computers to link sales reps with headquarters. The positive reinforcement took the form of ease of use, company approval, and more free time for salespeople.

First, the company made sure that the system would fit the needs of the salespeople and that they would benefit from any information they entered into the system. The system's designers gave the sales reps access to the information they entered. The designers also sent teams to meet with sales reps and regional managers, studying their routines and requirements to ensure that

the system would be easy to use in the field.

After developing the system, the company initiated an internal promotional campaign, which included a humorous videotape showing how the system would help a salesperson on a typical day. This program taught the sales reps to use the system and also showed that doing so was important to the company, meaning that employees who learned the system would meet with company approval.

The company instituted a pilot program to test the new system, and the sales reps began reaping the major reward: the savings in time that resulted from not doing as much paperwork as they had been. The sales reps who tried the new system began to have time to call on one additional physician

every two days. Also, said one salesperson, "The weekends are now my own. On Friday evening, I used to begin writing my weekly report. Now, by just entering a comment on my day's activities, my report is prepared each week for me."

Thus, Sandoz used a form of OB Mod to motivate its salespeople to use the company's new technology. The promotional campaign, company approval, and training program served as antecedents stimulating the behavior of using the laptop computers. A variety of rewards ensued, including ease of use, access to information, and time freed from paperwork. These consequences subsequently served as antecedents for future behavior involving use of the computer system.

Source: Sharon Faber, "When Employees Ask: 'What's in It for Me?'" *Business Month*, September 1989, 79.

ized as *hedonism of the past,* whereas expectancy theory has been described as *hedonism of the future.*[32] The historical emphasis of reinforcement theory partly stems from the approach's initial focus on studying nonverbal animals of limited mental ability (such as rats and pigeons). In contrast, expectancy theory research has been devoted to studying the behavior of humans. Despite their differing origins, both expectancy and reinforcement theories generate essentially identical predictions for behavior in a variety of settings.

The two approaches do differ, however, in their predictions of what effects will result from a change in the scheduling of rewards. If a person is rewarded continuously (that is, with an expectancy of 1.0) and then rewards are shifted so that they are administered less often (that is, on an intermittent schedule), expectancy theory predicts a decline in motivation, while reinforcement theory predicts that motivation will persist. Although a formal competitive test of these differing predictions has not been reported as yet for employee samples, persistence in the absence of rewards could reasonably be expected (based on day-to-day observations of employees). Because of its relative sim-

■ Table 6.2

Examples of Inputs and Outcomes in Adams's Theory of Equity

Inputs	Outcomes
Effort	Salary
Education	Fringe benefits
Training	Travel allowance
Experience	Number of subordinates
Loyalty	Autonomy
Age	Titles
	Status symbols
	Job assignments
	Time off
	Opportunities for overtime

plicity and ease of application, reinforcement theory appears to have more followers within the field of applied work motivation than expectancy theory.

Equity Theory

Feelings of fairness, or equity, can serve as a powerful stimulus to increase or decrease effort. J. Stacy Adams has proposed a theory that attempts to explain the influence of such feelings on employee behavior.[33] Adams's **equity theory** assumes that people will strive to restore equity if they feel an imbalance exists.

Basic to equity theory is the belief that employees continuously monitor the degree of equity or inequity that exists in their working relations by comparing their own outcomes and inputs with those of another highly similar person. In the context of equity theory, *outcomes* are anything that employees view as being provided by their jobs or the organization. Outcomes include pay, an office with a window, access to the executive washroom, the size of one's ashtrays, use of a company car, and so on. *Inputs* include all the contributions that a person makes to the employment relationship. Examples of inputs include personal effort, years and kind of education, prior work experience, training, and the like. Generally speaking, an input is anything that a person believes he or she should be compensated for. Table 6.2 provides a list of inputs and outcomes that employees typically consider important.

The inputs and outputs that a person views as relevant are very personal choices. According to equity theory, it is essential to ask individuals their reactions to possible outcomes and inputs when attempting to assess the degree of equity or inequity that they feel exists.

Adams contends that an individual will estimate the ratio of outcomes to inputs, but this ratio is of only partial importance. Each person also calculates a similar ratio for a person whom he or she judges to be in a similar position. This second person is called the *comparison other*. Adams predicts that an employee will be relatively satisfied if his or her own ratio of outcomes to inputs is equivalent to the ratio for the comparison other. This condition may be summarized as follows:

$$\frac{\text{Outcomes A}}{\text{Inputs A}} = \frac{\text{Outcomes B}}{\text{Inputs B}} \qquad (1)$$

If person A feels that his ratio is either higher or lower than person B's, he should experience a sense of inequity. The magnitude of this feeling will be proportional to the size of the gap between the ratios. Feelings of inequity produce a psychological tension that requires reduction.

$$\frac{\text{Outcomes A}}{\text{Inputs A}} < \frac{\text{Outcomes B}}{\text{Inputs B}} \qquad (2)$$

If person A is undercompensated in comparison to person B (equation 2), he may attempt to restore equity by working on one of the four components in the two ratios:

1. He may increase his own outcomes by asking for a raise.
2. He may decrease his own inputs by being less productive.
3. He may decrease person B's outcomes by persuading his boss to alter B's pay.
4. He may increase B's inputs by pressuring her to work harder.

    If person B is undercompensated in comparison to person A (equation 3), equity theory predicts that person A will experience guilt and will attempt to restore equity by altering one or more of the four components of the two ratios. For example, person A may attempt to reduce his own outcomes or increase person B's outcomes by appealing to his boss for an adjustment. Also, person A may increase his inputs by exerting greater effort on the job. Lastly, person A may help person B to decrease her input, perhaps by coaching her in how to work more efficiently.

$$\frac{\text{Outcomes A}}{\text{Inputs A}} > \frac{\text{Outcomes B}}{\text{Inputs B}} \qquad (3)$$

If the four components of the ratios cannot be altered and if the magnitude of inequity is substantial, person A would be forced to choose another course of action. He might:

1. Alter his perceptions of the situation so that the inequity no longer seems unjustified, saying, for example, "I deserve to earn more money because I work harder than most people."
2. Leave the field by quitting or obtaining a transfer.
3. Choose a different comparison other, someone whose ratio provides a less uncomfortable contrast.

    Much of the initial research on equity theory focused on demonstrating that the desire to restore equity would occur in work settings. Generally, the results supported the theory.[34] One of the more frequently used research designs for studying equity processes has been to create a short-term work situa-

■ **Figure 6.4**

*Predicted Changes in Quantity and Quality of Performance
as a Function of Inequity Condition and Rate of Pay for
Expectancy Theory and Equity Theory*

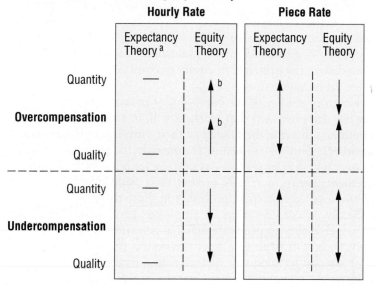

[a] Expectancy theory does not make rigid predictions for these settings in that effort and performance may not be correlated in some situations.

[b] These predictions may also be inversely stated depending on whether quality and quantity are inversely related for a given task.

tion for college students wherein their rate of pay (hourly versus piece-rate) is fixed. A comparison other is created in the mind of the employee, and a belief that one is equitably paid, overpaid, or underpaid is then induced. By virtue of controlling the design of these situations, the only readily available avenue for restoring equity is to alter effort (i.e., the employee cannot alter the inputs or outcomes of the comparison other, and so on).

The theory's specific predictions for such highly controlled conditions are very clear. Figure 6.4 displays the predicted changes in quantity and quality of performance (compared to an equitable condition) in relative overcompensation and undercompensation, under hourly and piece-rate pay conditions. The predictions also reflect the interdependency of effort, quantity, and outcomes in piece-rate schemes. For example, increases in quantity in a piece-rate scheme lead to greater rewards — an undesirable situation for someone who already feels overcompensated.

Figure 6.4 also summarizes the predictions that expectancy theory would generate for the various conditions. In certain conditions, equity theory and expectancy clearly disagree. For example, one of the most interesting aspects of equity theory is its prediction for worker performance in a condition of overcompensation on a piece-rate pay scheme (as when someone is paid 40 cents per unit of output, while the comparison other receives only 20 cents per unit).

In such a situation, the more units that the overcompensated employee produces, the more inequity he or she will generate. Therefore, to restore equity, the overcompensated individual should produce relatively fewer units of output. However, the quality of each unit should increase as a result of the individual's desire to exert greater effort and thereby restore equity by increasing the inputs portion of his or her ratio. This prediction is quite different from what would be predicted from an expectancy theory perspective. Expectancy theory, of course, is grounded in the philosophy of hedonism, while equity theory is founded on the principle of equity maximization, which takes a more altruistic view of human nature.

Evidence from studies of the condition of overcompensation on a piece-rate scheme has demonstrated that workers will, in fact, decrease the quantity of their output and increase the quality of their output relative to more equitably paid workers. This phenomenon is somewhat transitory, however, and diminishes over a period of several days.[35] The inability of expectancy theory or reinforcement theory to readily predict this result largely stems from the absence of employee comparison processes in these theories as originally formulated. Clearly, a consideration of employee comparison processes adds something to our ability to predict employee behavior accurately.

Intuitively, it is difficult to accept the notion that people who are overpaid will not attempt to maximize quantity. In a study that sought to identify individual differences in the desire to restore equity versus maximization of reward, the performance of overpaid individuals and that of equitably paid individuals were compared under a piece-rate scheme.[36] Results suggested that actions of individuals who were measured as being more altruistic (that is, more morally mature) were more likely to follow the predictions of equity theory (decreasing quantity of output and increasing quality) than actions of individuals who were measured as being less altruistic. Therefore, equity theory may provide a better description of the behavior of more principled individuals, while expectancy theory may provide a better description of the behavior of less principled individuals.

Although equity theory has been criticized for not explicitly predicting which method an employee will select in order to restore equity,[37] the theory presents a unique perspective on a major facet of work motivation. The perception of fairness is an important determinant of the impact of any reward system. Furthermore, the equity theory perspective continues to generate additional research initiatives. For example, alternative versions of Adams's original ratios and the process that underlies the selection of a comparison other are currently being investigated.[38]

Social Learning Theory

Social learning theory is another approach to motivation.[39] The desire to imitate models can be very powerful. Modeling first manifests itself in childhood, when children imitate adults and other siblings. In organizations, a desire to imitate superior performers or supervisors may be strong in some individuals. Certainly, the taking of roles and the imitation of previously witnessed behavior illustrate the subtle influences of social learning.

Social learning theory contends that people develop expectancies about their capacity to behave in certain ways and the probability that such behavior will result in rewards. The first of these expectancies relates to how they perceive their own competence, while the second pertains to outcomes and is analogous to the concepts of expectancy theory. Therefore, organizational training programs that rely on films, lectures, and role-playing techniques (i.e., the vast majority of organization-sponsored training programs) are using an approach based on social learning theory principles. The self-administration of rewards is also an important part of social learning theory. Modeling, or imitative behavior, serves as a standard for administering self-reinforcement in the form of increased personal satisfaction and enhanced self-image. The direct instruction of employees by peers, supervisors, or trainers on how to set personal standards for performance can also be used, but whether employees accept such direct instruction probably depends on such factors as the power and attractiveness of the instructors.[40] The use of social learning theory principles in conjunction with extrinsic rewards for performance may provide a most effective combination of motivational approaches.

A Comprehensive Model of Motivation

So far we have examined a number of different perspectives on work motivation. Although each perspective takes a somewhat different approach to motivation, it is possible to identify similarities among them and to integrate them into a larger conceptual framework.

Each approach falls into one of two categories: content theories or process theories. **Content theories** focus on *what* motivates people to perform. They are concerned with identifying the different rewards that people seek in their work. The theories of Maslow, Herzberg, and McClelland are essentially content theories. The other theories that we have examined are more concerned with *how* rewards control behavior. These theories focus on the dynamics, or process aspects, of work motivation. Expectancy, equity, reinforcement, and social learning theories are examples of **process theories.**

The content and process theories can be integrated into a still broader conceptual framework. Figure 6.5 presents a well-known and accepted framework proposed by Lyman Porter and Edward E. Lawler.[41] In essence, they outlined a dynamic model of motivation — the **Porter-Lawler model** — that includes many of the aforementioned theories as components of a larger process.

Beginning on the left-hand side of the model, the expected value of a reward combines with the expectation that effort will result in a reward. These two influences determine the level of effort that an employee exerts. Effort, however, does not simply or easily convert into performance (or accomplishment). The employee's abilities and role perceptions interact in determining the level of accomplishment. Unless a person has a minimum level of ability and the correct understanding of just how to perform a job, his or her effort will not yield an acceptable level of performance.

■ **Figure 6.5**

The Porter-Lawler Model of Motivation

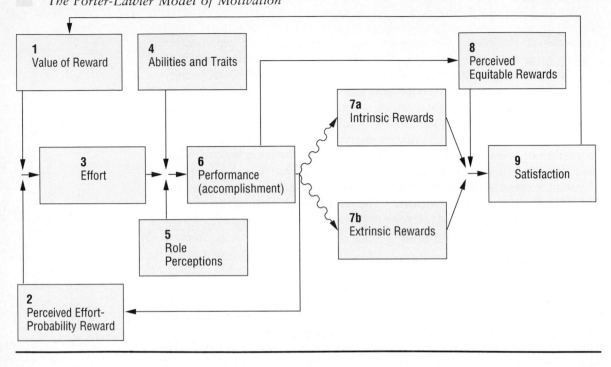

Performance may or may not be linked to rewards in a given situation, hence the wavy lines between rewards and performance. The employee's expectations of what is equitable in the way of rewards is influenced by the awareness of his or her own performance. Perceptions of equity or inequity interact with the rewards actually received to determine the level of satisfaction.

The model includes two feedback loops. The first links satisfaction to subsequent estimates of the value of rewards. If an employee feels that rewards received for past performance are not particularly satisfying, he or she will diminish future efforts. The second feedback loop runs from the performance–rewards linkages to the expectation that future effort will result in rewards. Here again, the employee's future effort will be influenced by his or her past experiences.

If we consider the various theories of motivation in light of the Porter-Lawler model, we see that each can be incorporated within this larger framework. Maslow's distinction between higher- and lower-order needs, as well as Herzberg's distinction between motivator factors (intrinsic factors) and hygiene factors (extrinsic factors), are represented by boxes 7a and 7b in the model. McClelland's principles regarding needs for achievement, affiliation, and power are contained in the intrinsic reward aspect of the model. Expectancy theory's principles are incorporated in the valence and expectancy features of the model, boxes 1 and 2. The concepts of equity theory are contained in box 8. Their influence is reflected in the interaction of equity perceptions and rewards in determining satisfaction.

The linkage between rewards and performance is a primary theme in reinforcement theory. The conversion of the wavy lines that connect rewards to performance into straight lines is a goal of OB Mod advocates. The feedback loop from the performance–reward linkage to the expectancy estimate of box 2 incorporates a major operant conditioning principle (the importance of consequences for future behavior). Imitation and proper role conduct, important features of social learning theory, are implicit in box 5, role perceptions.

Several of the boxes in the model were not discussed in this chapter. However, job satisfaction (box 9) was considered in Chapter 4. Abilities and traits (box 4) are in the province of human resources (or personnel) specialists, who attempt to select individuals who possess the requisite abilities and traits for successful job performance. Effort (box 3) is a topic that is typically considered by students of human factors engineering or work design.

The Porter-Lawler model does a good job of summarizing the major approaches to studying work behavior. From the perspective of the model, it is clear that the field of organizational behavior, which might appear fragmented because of the diversity of the topics it investigates, is not in disarray or segmented in its efforts to understand work behavior. Each of the various investigative lines of research can be viewed as examining different pieces of a larger puzzle. While the Porter-Lawler model may not be the final word in describing work behavior, it nicely summarizes and integrates a good deal of what is already known about individual behavior in work settings.

The importance of the Porter-Lawler model for managers is substantial. The model underscores the many facets of the motivational process, each of which must be understood and attended to if a manager wishes to be successful in motivating subordinates. The complexity of the model also emphasizes the fact that many things can go wrong and thereby undermine a manager's efforts. The following checklist, derived from the model, suggests that to be successful managers should:

1. Offer valued rewards
2. Create perceptions that effort will lead to rewards
3. Design jobs so that effort leads to high performance
4. Hire qualified employees
5. Train employees in the correct manner for performing their tasks
6. Design tasks so that performance is measurable
7. Design reward systems so that rewards are tied to performance
8. Ensure that rewards are viewed as fair and equitable.

Summary

1. Describe how hedonism explains behavior and state limitations of this explanation.

The principle of hedonism states that people will seek pleasure and avoid pain. They make rational choices based on a careful weighing of costs and benefits. In explaining motivation, hedonism tends to be vague and is most accurate in explaining behavior after the fact. Thus, it is not often useful for predicting behavior.

2.　Summarize the impact of instinctual theories
on the understanding of motivation.
Freud and others focused on the role of unconscious motivations for human behavior. Use of the instinctual theory grew, along with the number of instincts proposed. Ultimately, the theory was difficult to apply.

3.　Describe a technique for uncovering a person's dominant needs.
The Thematic Apperception Test uses drawings to uncover an individual's dominant needs. When a person tells stories about the drawings, he or she is likely to refer to a heightened need. Other researchers have used similar techniques to focus on specific needs.

4.　Describe Maslow's hierarchy of needs.
Maslow grouped needs into deficiency (lower-order) and growth (higher-order) needs. From lowest to highest, deficiency needs are physiological needs, safety needs, and social needs; growth needs are esteem needs and self-actualization needs.

5.　Compare the ways motivator factors and hygiene
factors may influence employees.
Motivator factors lead to feelings of satisfaction. These factors include career advancement, recognition, a sense of responsibility, and a feeling of achievement. The absence of hygiene factors leads to dissatisfaction. These factors involve job security, company policies, interpersonal relations, and working conditions. In theory, the absence of motivator factors does not make employees dissatisfied, nor do high levels of hygiene factors serve to increase employee satisfaction.

6.　Describe how expectations can influence an employee's efforts.
Employees consider whether their effort will translate into a desired accomplishment (effort–performance expectancy) and whether a given level of performance will result in obtaining a particular outcome (performance–outcome expectancy). Employees are predicted to make the greatest effort when these expectancies are high.

7.　Explain how behavior modification affects behavior in organizations.
Behavior modification interprets actions in terms of antecedents, behaviors, and consequences. Antecedents are stimuli that precede behaviors. Consequences are the rewards or punishments that follow from behaviors and become antecedents for subsequent behavior. Behavior modification involves managing the consequences of behavior, which can influence future behavior.

8.　Explain how employees' sense of equity affects their motivation.
Employees continuously monitor the degree of equity in their working rela-

tions. An employee will be relatively satisfied if his or her own ratio of outcomes to inputs is equivalent to the ratio for a comparison employee. Employees will strive to restore equity if they feel an imbalance exists.

9. Describe how social learning influences behavior.

People develop expectations about their capacity to behave in certain ways and the probability that their behavior will result in rewards. When a person meets a standard of behavior, that person rewards himself or herself with increased personal satisfaction and enhanced self-image.

10. Identify steps managers can take to motivate employees.

To motivate employees, managers should offer valued rewards, create perceptions that effort will lead to rewards, design jobs so that effort leads to high performance, hire qualified employees, train employees to do their tasks correctly, design tasks so that performance is measurable, design reward systems that tie rewards to performance, and ensure that rewards are seen as fair and equitable.

Key Terms

Hedonism	Hygiene factors
Method-bound	Expectancy theory
Instincts	Valence
Need for achievement	Subjective probabilities
Need for affiliation	Behavior modification
Need for power	Reinforcement theory
Hierarchy of needs	Equity theory
Growth needs	Social learning theory
Prepotency	Content theories
Two-factor theory	Process theories
Motivator factors	Porter-Lawler model

Review and Discussion Questions

1. Why is it difficult to determine how to motivate other people?

2. The Thematic Apperception Test grew out of instinctual theories. What do these two approaches have in common?

3. Al Ambitious has interviewed the applicants for a management trainee position and narrowed them down to five. He just read about a new psychological test that measures individual need for achievement, and he wonders whether it would be a good way to decide which of the five candidates to hire. Would this test alone be a good basis for Al's hiring decision? Why or why not?

4. From lowest to highest, what are the categories of needs in Maslow's hierarchy? Might a person strive to fulfill a higher need before all the lower ones are totally met?

5. What are motivator factors and hygiene factors? How might workers likely feel about jobs that lacked motivator factors but provided hygiene factors? Based on the two-factor theory, would enhancing job security make workers satisfied?

6. Which factors in two-factor theory correspond to Maslow's deficiency needs? Which factors correspond to growth needs? Give some examples of job attributes that could fulfill what Maslow calls the need for self-actualization.

7. Eva Adams has just been assigned to the sales territory for Montana, Washington, and Alaska. Sales for this territory have tended to lag behind the rest of the nation, and Eva's manager has promised her a bonus if she can increase sales by 15 percent for this year. Much as Eva wants the bonus, she believes her territory is just a bad one. What can Eva's manager do to motivate her?

8. Adam Evers, MBA, has spent 20 years with Advanced Extrusion, remaining loyal even through the cutbacks of the last recession. Because the workload has grown in recent years. Advanced Extrusion hired Ned New, a recent college graduate, to assist Adam in the finance department. Adam is shocked to learn that Ned will have the same title as he does and that they will be sharing the office Adam formerly had to himself. According to equity theory, what responses might Adam make to this situation?

9. What are content theories and process theories? Give examples of each.

10. In what ways can managers create a work environment that motivates employees? Do these actions constitute exploitation of employees or are they justified? Explain your answer.

Critical Incident

Salary versus Commission

Jerry Palmer was not an outstanding marketing student in college and felt very fortunate to have secured a sales position with a pharmaceutical firm. The pay appeared to be competitive and, best of all, he was going to be working with a fixed salary rather than on commission.

During the first year, Jerry had a hard time making sales. But as he kept working at improving his sales techniques, his sales began to rise. By the end of his third year, and based on discussions with other salespeople, Jerry believed he had become one of the top sales representatives in the company. However, since the company never revealed how its salespeople performed (no sales data, etc.), Jerry never knew if he was a top seller or not.

Last year was an excellent one for Jerry. His manager called him in for a brief meeting in October and praised him for his efforts. He was even told that if the company had ten more people like him they would probably be number 1 in the industry. Jerry took these comments to mean he was an excellent sales representative. He had exceeded his sales goals by over 20 percent and was looking forward to another great year.

This year he is off to a good start and appears well on his way to exceeding the sales goal once again. However, Jerry has begun having some motivational problems. He has heard that competitors annually have sales contests and that they recognize top performers as salesperson of the month. He knows that they also give out awards and hold banquets. Jerry has begun to get upset with his company. He asked his manager about considering such incentives or even having a salary plus commission program. He was told "that's not how this company does things" and that he "shouldn't worry about it."

Jerry is starting to look around for another position with a competitor. He is convinced that pay should be tied to performance.

Questions

1. Why do you believe Jerry came to be dissatisfied with his company's fixed-salary payment policy?

2. In light of McClelland's notion of need for achievement, how would you characterize Jerry?

3. What is now motivating Jerry? What type of incentive program would probably be attractive to him?

Experiential Exercise

What Do Employees Want from Their Jobs?

This activity is designed to help you think about the above question and to help you better understand the factors that influence an employee to perform. Because it can be difficult to motivate, it is vital to recognize and understand the factors that employees seek on the job. By providing opportunities to have various needs satisfied, one can provide employees with a motivating environment.

1. Examine the list of factors presented below and think of how employees (i.e., people you've worked with or supervised) would rank them. Remember, you are looking at this list from the employees' perspective. Your ranking should reflect what you think they would say they wanted from their jobs. Place a 1 after the factor you believe they would want most from their job, a 2 after the next most wanted factor, and so on.

Factors	Ranking	Supervisors' Rankings*	Employees' Rankings*
a. Interesting, challenging work			
b. A feeling of being "in" on things			
c. Job security			
d. Competent supervisor			
e. Good working conditions			
f. Tactful discipline			
g. Promotion and growth in organization			
h. Appreciation of work well done			
i. Sympathetic understanding of personal problems			
j. Good wages			
k. Involvement in plans or decisions			
l. Loyalty and support from management			
m. Relevant and timely feedback on performance			
n. Clear goals and objectives			

* Will be provided by your instructor.

2. After you have completed ranking these factors, your instructor will provide you with the supervisors' rankings from a study. Record these rankings in the appropriate column.

3. Looking at the supervisors' rankings compared to yours:
    a. Are you and the supervisors making similar assumptions about the workers' job satisfaction?
    b. Do you notice any areas or clusters of work factors to which there are similar rankings?
    c. (If asked to do by your instructor) Was the average class ranking on selected factors similar to that of the supervisors? How do you account for the differences?

4. Your instructor will now provide you with the employees' rankings. Given this information, the following discussion questions are of interest:
    a. Is there generally good agreement between the employees' rankings and those of their supervisors? And your ranking?
    b. On what factors or clusters of factors is there general agreement or disagreement?
    c. If there are some large differences, to what do you attribute them? What role might perception play?

5. Your instructor will ask you to form groups of 4 to 6 people. As a group, discuss the following questions:
    a. Why do you believe the supervisors and employees ranked the factors as they did?
    b. What are some implications of the data for managers?
    c. What should managers do to create motivating environments?

Source: Written by Bruce Kemelgor, University of Louisville; used by permission.

Notes

1. "America's Growing Anti-business Mood," *Business Week*, June 17, 1972, 101.

2. J.S. Mill, *Utilitarianism* (New York: Liberal Arts Press, 1949).

3. W. James, *The Principles of Psychology* (New York: Holt, 1890); S. Freud, *Civilization and Its Discontents* (London: Hogarth Press, 1930).

4. H.A. Murray, *Explorations in Personality* (New York: Oxford University Press, 1938).

5. H.A. Murray, *Thematic Apperception Test Manual* (Cambridge, Mass.: Harvard University Press, 1943).

6. D.C. McClelland, *The Achieving Society* (Princeton: Van Nostrand, 1961); D.C. McClelland, "Toward a Theory of Motive Acquisition," *American Psychologist* 23 (1965): 321–333.

7. D.C. McClelland, J.W. Atkinson, R.A. Clark, and E.L. Lowell, *The Achievement Motive* (New York: Appleton-Century-Crofts, 1953).

8. D.C. McClelland and D.G. Winter, *Motivating Economic Achievement* (New York: Free Press, 1969); G.A. Steiner and J.B. Miner, *Management Policy and Strategy* (New York: Macmillan, 1977).

9. H.A. Wainer and I.M. Rubin, "Motivation of Research and Development Entrepreneurs: Determinants of Company Success," *Journal of Applied Psychology* 53 (1969): 178–184.

10. D.C. McClelland and R.E. Boyatzis, "Leadership Motive Pattern and Long-term Success in Management," *Journal of Applied Psychology* 67 (1967): 737–743.

11. D.A. Kolb and R. Boyatzis, "On the Dynamics of the Helping Relationship," *Journal of Applied Behavioral Science* 6 (1970): 230–237.

12. R.F. Berdie, *After High School — What?* (Minneapolis: University of Minnesota, 1954).

13. G.H. Elder, Jr., "Structural Variations in the Child Rearing Relationship," *Sociometry* 25 (1962): 241–262.

14. R.P. Vecchio, "A Test of a Moderator of the Job Satisfaction — Job Quality Relationship: The Case of Religious Affiliation," *Journal of Applied Psychology* 65 (1980): 195–201.

15. McClelland, *The Achieving Society*.

16. McClelland, "Toward a Theory of Motive Acquisition."

17. D.E. Durand, "Effects of Achievement Motivation and Skill Training on the Entrepreneurial Behavior of Black Businessmen," *Organizational Behavior and Human Performance* 14 (1975): 76–90;

J.A. Timmons, "Black is Beautiful — Is it Bountiful?" *Harvard Business Review* 49 (1971): 81–94; Metropolitan Economic Development Association, "Business Leadership Training — What's Happening," *MEDA Reports* 5, no. 1 (1977): 1–7.

18. A.H. Maslow, *Motivation and Personality* (New York: Harper, 1954); A.H. Maslow, *Toward a Psychology of Being* (New York: Van Nostrand, 1968).

19. A.H. Maslow, "A Theory of Human Motivation," *Psychological Review* 50 (1943): 370–396.

20. L.W. Porter, "A Study of Perceived Need Satisfaction in Bottom and Middle Management Jobs," *Journal of Applied Psychology* 45 (1961): 1–10.

21. M.A. Wahba and L.G. Bridwell, "Maslow Reconsidered: A Review of Research on the Need Hierarchy Theory," *Organizational Behavior and Human Performance* 15 (1976): 212–240; E.E. Lawler and J.L. Suttle, "A Causal Correlational Test of the Need Hierarchy Concept," *Organizational Behavior and Human Performance* 7 (1972): 265–287; D.T. Hall and K.E. Nougaim, "An Examination of Maslow's Need Hierarchy in an Organizational Setting," *Organizational Behavior and Human Performance* 3 (1968): 12–35.

22. C.P. Alderfer, *Existence, Relatedness, and Growth* (New York: Free Press, 1972).

23. F. Herzberg, B. Mausner, and B. Synderman, *The Motivation to Work* (New York: Wiley, 1959).

24. H.M. Soliman, "Motivation–Hygiene Theory of Job Attitudes," *Journal of Applied Psychology* 55 (1970): 452–461; J. Schneider and E.A. Locke, "A Critique of Herzberg's Classification System and a Suggested Revision," *Organizational Behavior and Human Performance* 12 (1971): 441–458.

25. J. Galbraith and L.L. Cummings, "An Empirical Investigation of the Motivational Determinants of Task Performance: Interactive Effects Between Valence–Instrumentality and Motivation–Ability," *Organizational Behavior and Human Performance* 2 (1967): 237–258; L.W. Porter and E.E. Lawler, *Managerial Attitudes and Performance* (Homewood, Ill.: Irwin, 1968); J.P. Campbell, M.D. Dunnette, E.E. Lawler, and K.E. Weick, *Managerial Behavior, Performance, and Effectiveness* (New York: McGraw-Hill, 1970); M. Sussmann and R.P. Vecchio, "Conceptualizations of Valence and Instrumentality: A Fourfold Model,"

Organizational Behavior and Human Performance 36 (1985): 96–112; V.H. Vroom, *Work and Motivation* (New York: Wiley, 1964).

26. T.R. Mitchell, "Expectancy Models of Job Satisfaction, Occupational Preference and Effort: A Theoretical, Methodological, and Empirical Appraisal," *Psychological Bulletin* 81 (1974): 1096–1112; J.P. Campbell and R.D. Pritchard, "Motivation Theory in Industrial and Organizational Psychology," in *Handbook of Industrial and Organizational Psychology*, ed. M. Dunnette (Chicago: Rand McNally, 1976), 63–130.

27. Sussmann and Vecchio, "Conceptualizations of Valence and Instrumentality."

28. J. Hollenback, "A Matrix Method for Expectancy Research," *Academy of Management Review* 4 (1979): 579–587.

29. B.M. Staw and G.R. Salancik, eds., *New Directions in Organizational Behavior* (Chicago: St. Clair Press, 1976), 77.

30. B.F. Skinner and W.F. Dowling, "Conversation with B.F. Skinner," *Organizational Dynamics* 1 (1973): 31–40.

31. F. Luthans and R. Kreitner, *Organizational Behavior Modification* (Glenview, Ill.: Scott, Foresman, 1975); F. Luthans, *Organizational Behavior* (New York: McGraw-Hill, 1977).

32. Vroom, *Work and Motivation*.

33. J.S. Adams, "Injustice in Social Exchange," in *Advances in Experimental Social Psychology*, vol. 2, ed. L. Berkowitz (New York: Academic Press, 1965).

34. P.S. Goodman and A. Friedman, "An Examination of Adams' Theory of Inequity," *Administrative Science Quarterly* 16 (1971): 271–288; J.S. Adams and S. Freedman, "Equity Theory Revisited: Comments and Annotated Bibliography," in *Advances in Experimental Social Psychology*, vol. 9, ed. L. Berkowitz and E. Walster (New York: Academic Press, 1976); Campbell and Pritchard, "Motivation Theory in Industrial and Organizational Psychology."

35. E.E. Lawler, C.A. Koplin, T.E. Young, and J.A. Faden, "Inequity Reduction Over Time in an Induced Overpayment Situation," *Organizational Behavior and Human Performance* 3 (1968): 253–268.

36. R.P. Vecchio, "An Individual Differences Interpretation of the Conflicting Predictions Generated by Equity Theory and Expectancy Theory," *Journal of Applied Psychology* 66 (1981): 470–481.

37. R. Mowday, "Equity Theory Predictions of Behavior in Organizations," in *Motivation and Work Behavior*, 2d ed., ed. R.M. Steers and L.W. Porter (New York: McGraw-Hill, 1979); M.R. Carrell and J.E. Dittrich, "Equity Theory: The Recent Literature, Methodological Considerations and New Directions," *Academy of Management Review* 3 (1978): 202–210; R.W. Griffeth, R.P. Vecchio, and J.W. Logan, "Equity Theory and Interpersonal Attraction," *Journal of Applied Psychology* 74 (1989): 394–401; R. Huseman, J. Hatfield, and E. Miles, "A New Perspective on Equity Theory," *Academy of Management Review* 12 (1987): 222–234.

38. P.S. Goodman, "Social Comparison Processes in Organizations," in *New Directions in Organizational Behavior*, ed. B.M. Staw and G.R. Salancik (Chicago: St. Clair Press, 1976); R.P. Vecchio, "Predicting Worker Performance in Inequitable Settings," *Academy of Management Review* 7 (1982): 103–110; R.P. Vecchio, "Models of Psychological Inequity," *Organizational Behavior and Human Performance* 34 (1984): 266–282.

39. A Bandura, *Social Learning Theory* (Englewood Cliffs, N.J.: Prentice-Hall, 1977).

40. A.P. Goldstein and M. Sorcher, *Changing Supervisor Behavior* (New York: Pergamon, 1974).

41. Porter and Lawler, *Managerial Attitudes and Performance*.

All work and no play
makes Jack a dull
boy.
All work and no play
makes jack.

— Anonymous

Choose a job you
love, and you will
never have to work
a day in your life.

— Confucius

Learning Objectives

After studying this chapter, you should be able to:

1. *Distinguish between extrinsic and intrinsic rewards.*

2. *Compare various types of rewards on the dimensions of average importance, flexibility, frequency, and visibility.*

3. *Evaluate the merits of different pay-for-performance schemes.*

4. *Explain why incentive plans have lost popularity.*

5. *Describe three attributes of goals that are important for improving performance.*

6. *Describe management-by-objectives and some of its advantages and possible problems.*

7. *Give some examples of the power of self-fulfilling prophecies.*

8. *Describe some ways of constructively managing self-fulfilling prophecies.*

9. *Describe methods of job redesign used to reduce worker discontent.*

10. *List the job characteristics that enhance a sense of the meaningfulness of one's work, a sense of responsibility, and knowledge of the results of one's work.*

11. *Discuss some obstacles to job redesign.*

Enhancing Employee Motivation

■ No Mistakes Allowed

*I*n the early 1980s, Motorola was struggling to keep up with stiff competition. The company had already lost out to Japanese companies, notably Toshiba and NEC, in the global competition for color television and car radios. It seemed that an important problem was that Japan was winning the quality war, using an emphasis on producing goods with zero defects. At the same time, observed Arthur Sundry, whose two-way radio division was then the best at Motorola, "Our quality levels really stink."

To reverse this decline, Motorola's top management decided to boost quality. Chairman Bob Galvin began by asking managers in the Communications Sector to seek a tenfold improvement in quality. The managers replied with an even more ambitious proposal: zero defects.

The managers called their plan Six Sigma, with sigma referring to the common symbol for standard deviation in statistics. The idea was thât if all of production were described by a normal distribution curve, the defect-free products should fall within six standard deviations, which would include almost all of the products. In other words, products would be perfect 99.9999998 percent of the time.

Impressed, Chairman Galvin charged the Communications Sector with achieving this objective within six years. He then began expanding the program to the rest of the company. In 1989, Motorola began linking most performance review and bonus incentives to the Six Sigma requirements.

As sales and profits shot up and employees began earning quality-related bonuses, Motorolans began to credit the Six Sigma program with the company's and their better fortunes. At the Communications Sector, a 27-person unit recently celebrated its 255th straight week without a defect. An enthusiastic proponent of Six Sigma in the Communications Sector is Kim Fudge, the sector's

manager of operations. "We have some large data-communications systems with tens of thousands of parts," he explains, "so you can see how reckless it is to operate at three sigma [99.7 percent error-free performance]." His remark refers to the fact that if just 0.3 percent of 10,000 parts contain errors, the system has 30 defects.

While zero-defects management is becoming a buzzword in American business, what makes Motorola's program unusual is that it extends to white-collar workers, such as sales and staff positions. For example, to motivate quality order taking, Motorola inserts cards with its products that customers are to fill out if they receive an incorrect order. To make a quarterly bonus, a phone sales-person must have no more than one card returned per 2,000 orders.

In the marketing services department, where brochures and manuals are prepared, Six Sigma poses challenges in developing measurable standards. The department measures whatever it can: errors in photography, pricing, and grammar, for example. Enthusiasm for Six Sigma has led management to seek other measures as well, such as whether publications contain too much jargon.

Motorola's ultimate objective? "We will continue to improve quality," says Richard Buetow, vice-president and director of quality, "till we become the perfect company."

Establishing goals such as zero

defects is one way to motivate employees to do better. This chapter discusses ways to motivate employees through such techniques as offering rewards, setting goals, managing expectations, and redesigning jobs.

Source: Mark Stuart Gill, "Stalking Six Sigma," *Business Month*, January 1990, 42–46.

In Chapter 6, we considered a variety of perspectives on the topic of work motivation. As shown by the Porter-Lawler model at the conclusion of the chapter, each of these perspectives offers insights into the process by which employees are motivated to perform. In this chapter, we will examine four ways to apply our knowledge of the motivational process in order to enhance employee performance: through reward systems, goal setting, management of expectations, and job redesign.

Reward Systems

Motivational theorists often distinguish between extrinsic and intrinsic rewards. **Extrinsic rewards** come from sources that are outside of, or external to, the individual, while **intrinsic rewards** may be more accurately characterized as self-administered. Examples of extrinsic rewards include pay, fringe benefits, promotions, and perquisites. Examples of intrinsic rewards are feelings of competence, accomplishment, responsibility, and personal growth. Although we typically think of extrinsic rewards as the primary means by which managers attempt to influence subordinates to perform well, intrinsics can also be used. In particular, the design of a job plays an important role in creating opportunities for intrinsic rewards. We will consider the redesign of work later in this chapter and, for the moment, will focus only on extrinsic reward systems.

The Role of Compensation

Edward E. Lawler III is one of the strongest advocates of tying rewards to performance. Although Lawler has studied the use of a number of different types of rewards, he is perhaps best known for his writings on how to use pay as a means of motivating employees.[1] Although organizations can use a variety of rewards, they tend to rely on only a few. Pay is used most frequently because it possesses certain optimal characteristics.

First, a good reward should be valued by its recipient — and there is no question that pay is highly important to most people. Second, the size of a reward should be flexible. Some rewards, such as promotions, cannot be divided into various-sized portions, but the size of a pay raise can be easily manipulated. Third, the value of a reward should remain relatively constant.

■ **Table 7.1**

A Comparison of Five Major Organizational Rewards

	Average Importance	Flexibility in Amount	Frequency	Visibility
Pay	High	High	High	Potentially high
Promotion	High	Low	Low	High
Fringe Benefits	High	Moderate	Low	Moderate
Status Symbols	Moderate	High	Low	High
Awards and Certificates	Low	High	Low	High

Source: Adapted from E.E. Lawler III, "Reward Systems," in J.R. Hackman and J.L. Suttle (eds.) *Improving Life at Work.* Glenview, Ill.: Scott, Foresman, 1977.

Some rewards, such as verbal praise, may lose their value if used repeatedly, but pay can be given frequently without diminishing its worth. Finally, for a reward to be effective (as noted in our discussion of expectancy theory in Chapter 6), the relationship of a reward to performance must be obvious. Because pay is so visible, employees can easily see the relationship between it and their performance. Thus, if we compare pay with other major organizational rewards on the dimensions of importance, flexibility, frequency, and visibility, pay is clearly one of the strongest resources available for improving performance (Table 7.1).

As has been noted several times in this text, the linking of rewards to performance is critical. Many managers think that performance and pay are closely linked in the units that they administer. However, in one survey, Lawler found that only 22 percent of workers in the United States believe that there is a direct link between how hard they work and how much they are paid.[2] There are a number of reasons for this disturbing perception. How hard one works, of course, may not be related to one's level of accomplishment. Intervening forces, such as uncooperative coworkers, unanticipated interruptions, and faulty equipment, can all conspire to undercut an employee's best intentions. Determining an employee's level of accomplishment is also an imprecise technology. Performance appraisal systems (a topic to be considered more fully in Chapter 8) need to be designed to foster the perception that the measurement of performance is both objective and fair.

Attempts to relate pay and performance vary widely across organizations. These pay-for-performance schemes differ on three major dimensions: (1) the organizational unit, (2) the method of measuring performance, and (3) the form of monetary reward. One of three organizational units usually serves as the basis for comparing performance: the individual, the work group, or the total organization. The methods of measuring performance are more diverse and vary in terms of subjectivity. Ratings by supervisors are clearly the most

■ **Table 7.2**

*Ratings of Pay-for-Performance Schemes**

	Method of Measuring Performance	Ties Pay to Performance	Reduces Negative Side Effects	Encourages Cooperation	Employee Acceptance
Salary Reward					
Individual	Productivity	4	1	1	4
	Cost Effectiveness	3	1	1	4
	Supervisor Rating	3	1	1	3
Group	Productivity	3	1	2	4
	Cost Effectiveness	3	1	2	4
	Supervisor Rating	2	1	2	3
Organizationwide	Productivity	2	1	3	4
	Cost Effectiveness	2	1	2	4
Bonus					
Individual	Productivity	5	3	1	2
	Cost Effectiveness	4	2	1	2
	Supervisor Rating	4	2	1	2
Group	Productivity	4	1	3	3
	Cost Effectiveness	3	1	3	3
	Supervisor Rating	3	1	3	3
Organizationwide	Productivity	3	1	3	4
	Cost Effectiveness	3	1	3	4
	Profit	2	1	3	3

* Ratings can range from 1 to 5, with 5 denoting a scheme is higher on that dimension.

Source: Adapted from E.E. Lawler III, "Reward Systems," in J.R. Hackman and J.L. Suttle (eds.) *Improving Life at Work*. Glenview, Ill.: Scott, Foresman, 1977.

widely used but most subjective device. Hard productivity data, such as sales figures and the number of units a person produces, are very objective. Other indexes of cost effectiveness and profitability (for example, number of errors and wastage) are also sometimes used. The two most common forms of monetary rewards are the bonus, which is a one-time, lump-sum reward, and the salary increment, which is a cumulative reward. Some organizations, for example Lincoln Electric, pay employees on a piecework system with an annual bonus based on the quality of output.[3]

　　Lawler has examined the combinations of the three dimensions of unit, performance, and pay, and offered an assessment of the effectiveness of each.[4] Table 7.2 summarizes his ratings of the pay-for-performance schemes. Note that the ratings reveal several patterns. The perception that pay is tied to performance is enhanced when rewards are administered on the basis of individual performance. Bonus schemes receive higher ratings on this dimension than do salary schemes. Objective measures of performance (productivity, cost effectiveness) also elicit higher ratings. The most successful pay schemes are, therefore, likely to be individually based bonus plans that rely on objective measures of performance. Such schemes do have some negative side effects, according to Lawler; for example, social ostracism of superior performers and falsification of performance reports are more likely to occur with individually based bonus schemes.

Cooperation among group members tends to be greater with group and organizationwide pay plans. Such schemes foster the desire to help coworkers because of the perception that success is mutually beneficial. Individual schemes, on the other hand, encourage a greater sense of competitiveness.

On the dimension of employee acceptance, most of the pay plans rated moderately well. Individually based bonus plans, however, received a somewhat lower rating, possibly because the increased competition and the potential for falsification of performance reports produce the belief that the scheme is unfair.

In general, Lawler's analysis suggests that there is no single best pay incentive plan. Instead, each situation must be examined in terms of its unique characteristics. It is also important to note that these pay plans are not mutually exclusive. It is entirely possible to set up multiple or overlapping pay plans.

How Effective Are Incentive Plans?   Although available research indicates that incentive pay plans can increase productivity by 15 to 35 percent, the popularity of such plans has declined in recent decades.[5] Piece-rate schemes in particular have lost their appeal. Incentive plans have run into problems because of a variety of factors, including adversarial relationships, class consciousness, and societal changes.

Adversarial Relationships   When faced with incentive pay schemes, employees may use a number of ploys to lower production rates. When being observed, workers may produce at a very slow rate in order to deceive time-study consultants. And they may be reluctant to suggest improved methods for performing a task. Furthermore, informal norms will sometimes overpower individual initiative (see, for example, the Bank Wiring Room Study in Chapter 1). As an additional tactic for dealing with the establishment of incentive schemes, employees may turn to collective bargaining by electing a union to negotiate on their behalf.

Class Consciousness   Because the tasks involved in higher-level jobs (such as administrative and supervisory positions) do not lend themselves to easy quantification, incentive schemes are used more often for workers than for managers. This distinction can lead to a sense of "us versus them" within an organization's work force. The sense of being discriminated against can, in turn, feed otherwise latent hostilities. The consciousness of class differences coupled with the adversarial tactics mentioned above may produce protectionism, little sharing of information, a narrow definition of loyalty, and little trust. In general, an unhealthy organizational culture can be expected to emerge.

Societal Changes   The nature of work has changed significantly since the beginning of this century. At present, many jobs involve service or information delivery. High technology has gained increasing importance in many otherwise simple jobs. The stand-alone jobs that involved simple manufacturing are being replaced by interdependent jobs that require the use of more complex equipment in more continuous process-type operations.

In addition, there has been a movement in some settings to redesign work to make it less simple and repetitive, and thus to increase worker satisfaction, reduce turnover, and improve the quality of output. These attempts to enrich the nature of the work experience by offering more meaningful, complex, and interdependent tasks often create situations in which it is extremely difficult to measure performance in a simple, accurate, and fair manner.

The Future   Lawler foresees no major social changes that might increase the popularity of incentive pay.[6] Our country's recent poor growth in national productivity and its competitive disadvantage as a manufacturer in international circles suggest, however, that incentive pay as a means of improving performance should not be abandoned. Interestingly, a majority of workers (61 percent) express a desire for their pay to be tied to performance.

As a strategy for the future, Lawler suggests some combination of profit sharing, stock ownership, and gain sharing. At present, the use of all three types of plans appears to be increasing. Profit sharing and stock ownership are more commonly used than gain sharing. As a motivator, the link between reward and performance may be too weak to be effective, since one's on-the-job efforts are not immediately and visibly tied to the organization's performance. However, profit sharing and stock ownership emphasize the long-term benefits of joint efforts, and therefore may be ideal for directing the behavior of higher-level employees in ways that are beneficial to the entire organization. These two incentive schemes also can have significant symbolic value for employees in that they may develop a greater sense of identification with the organization.

The earliest **gain-sharing** plans were devised by union leader Joseph Scanlon over 30 years ago, but this approach is still considered relatively new. Essentially, gain sharing ties an individual's bonuses to the performance of a business unit. Specifically, such a plan might provide monthly bonuses to all members of a department or plant if a predetermined formula indicates that there has been a measurable decrease in the cost of materials, supplies, operations, or labor. For example, Herman Miller, a furniture manufacturer with a long involvement in gain sharing, offers a bonus system plus opportunities for employees to participate in decision making.[7] Similarly, such diverse organizations as Cummins Engine Company, TWA, and ROLM have gain-sharing plans.

The growing popularity of gain sharing appears to be due to several factors. Gain sharing is often introduced in a participative fashion, with employees being given a say in the design of the plan. Also, all employees — both managers and workers — are likely to be covered in the plan. In addition, because the setting of individual work standards and the calculation of individual compensation are not necessary in a gain-sharing plan, workers perceive the system as fairer.

Although Lawler foresees an increase in the use of gain-sharing plans, there may be limits to their use. For example, their implementation in such nonmanufacturing settings as hospitals may prove problematic because of the difficulty of establishing and measuring costs. As a recommendation, Lawler advocates the implementation of *multiple* pay systems in order to improve productivity and profitability. He further suggests that motivation will be at its maximum when employees have both a psychological stake and a financial stake in unit success.[8]

Goal Setting

Managers and employees need to understand each other's goals. In addition, managers are responsible for helping employees in setting goals or objectives. With a clear understanding of explicit goals or objectives, managers and employees can work together to achieve specific outcomes. Research on employee goals for performing a task suggests that several attributes of goals are especially important for improving performance: goal specificity, goal difficulty, and goal acceptance.[9]

Specificity

Goal specificity refers to the preciseness with which a goal or objective is stated. Increases in goal specificity are positively related to increases in performance. Very specific goals that are quantifiable reduce ambiguity and thereby help to focus employees' efforts.[10] Therefore, it is generally a good idea to avoid developing or stating goals in very broad or ambiguous terms.

Difficulty

Increasing **goal difficulty** can also result in superior performance. The more difficult the goal is, so the research results suggest, the more challenging the task is perceived as being. Greater task challenge, in turn, results in greater effort being put forth by an employee. One major limitation to this argument, however, is that the goals must be feasible. Setting outlandish goals or goals that are unquestionably out of the reach of the employee will more likely lead to frustration and rejection of the goal.

Acceptance

Employees must also accept the goals that are set. **Goal acceptance** is most likely to occur when assigned goals correspond with personal aspirations. Difficult, specific goals that are accepted by an employee will therefore result in superior performance. This line of reasoning suggests that managers must encourage employees to focus on measurable and challenging goals while trying to elicit employee commitment to the goals.

■ Figure 7.1

An Outline of the Steps in the MBO Process

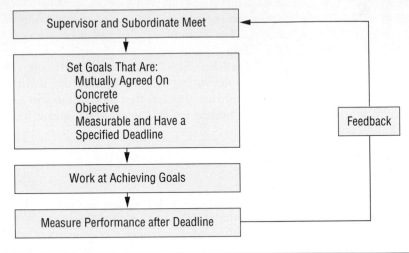

Management-by-Objectives

Management-by-objectives (MBO) is a practical application of the reasoning behind the notion of goal-setting theory. MBO is a process in which employees participate with management in the setting of goals, or objectives.[11] An essential feature of an MBO program is that it involves a one-on-one negotiation session between a supervisor and a subordinate in order to set concrete, objective goals for the employee's performance. During the session, a deadline is set for the measurement of accomplishment, and the paths to the desired goals and the removal of possible obstacles are discussed. After an established period of time has elapsed (typically six months or a year), the supervisor and subordinate meet again to review the subordinate's performance using the agreed-upon goals as a measuring stick. Figure 7.1 summarizes the essential steps in the MBO process.

A positive feature of an MBO system lies in its emphasis on establishing specific, measurable goals. In fact, a goal is unacceptable or inadmissible in an MBO system unless it is measurable. You may think that this is impossible for all goals, especially those of top-level executives. Although it is difficult to set measurable goals at the higher levels of an organization, it is nonetheless possible. For example, one such quantifiable goal might be that an institution will be ranked in the top ten by an annual polling of executives in the same industry. Or, the head coach of a college football team may set a goal of making the top 20 in the Associated Press's coaches' poll within the next five years. Some more typical goals would be to increase market share from 45 to 55 percent by the end of the next fiscal year, to increase annual production by 10 percent, or to increase profits after taxes by 3 percent. Some goals can be measured in simple yes or no fashion. For example, the goal of establishing a training program for sales personnel or completing a feasibility study by a certain date can be judged in a simple success or failure fashion when the deadline arises. Either such a project has been completed or it has not.

Advocates of MBO believe that everyone in an organization could and should be involved in goal setting. This includes all personnel, from the chief executive officer (who may set goals in consultation with the board of directors) to the newest member of the clean-up crew. In practice, however, middle-level managers and first-line supervisors are more commonly involved in such goal-setting systems.

Proponents of MBO systems also believe that supervisors must play a special role in the goal-setting process. Supervisors should view themselves as coaches or counselors whose role is to aid their subordinates in goal attainment. This role of coach/counselor extends beyond merely helping to identify and remove obstacles to goal attainment (for example, using personal influence to expedite shipments from another department). It also implies that the supervisor will serve as a mentor — someone to whom subordinates can go with their work-related problems and assume that they will be treated with respect and support.

Do MBO Systems Work?   Research at such organizations as Black and Decker, Wells Fargo, and General Electric has shown that, on the whole, MBO programs can succeed.[12] Because MBO relies on the established principles of goal setting, it has great potential for improving performance. Real-world constraints, however, can sometimes reduce the positive impact of a goal-setting system.

One major obstacle to the success of an MBO program can be lack of support from top-level executives. If key people in the organization — especially the president and vice-presidents — do not fully endorse MBO, their lack of support will likely be felt and responded to at lower levels. The net effect will be a decided lack of enthusiasm for the program.

Problems may also arise if managers are not interested in having subordinates participate in the goal-setting process. Some managers prefer to retain an evaluative and superior posture and are uncomfortable with the notion of being a coach or counselor to their subordinates.

Personality conflicts between superiors and subordinates are another potential problem for goal-setting systems, as is competitiveness. A superior who feels threatened by talented subordinates may do little to help them be more successful and, consequently, more visible. In addition, subordinates may hesitate to set challenging goals for fear of failure and its consequences.

MBO systems also tend to emphasize the quantifiable aspects of performance while ignoring the more qualitative aspects. This is an understandable tendency, since participants in MBO systems are encouraged to focus on measurable dimensions of performance. Qualitative aspects of performance, which are often more difficult to identify and measure, are likely to be overlooked or de-emphasized. For example, how can the quality of service that an organization provides or an organization's image in the local community be defined and measured?

Because the success of an MBO system rests heavily on the quality of the relationship between supervisor and subordinates, the degree of trust and supportiveness that exists in a work unit is a central concern. For an MBO system to be highly successful, these elements are critical prerequisites. The absence of trust and supportiveness severely restricts the system's effectiveness.*

MBO has passed through several phases since its introduction in the 1950s. Initially, MBO was greeted with much enthusiasm by managers and management scholars. During the late 1960s and early 1970s, MBO appeared to be "sweeping the nation." Presently, MBO is viewed more objectively by scholars and practitioners as a tool that (like any tool) can be most effective under specific favorable conditions. It is now becoming passé even to invoke the initials MBO. In fact, the principles and philosophies of MBO have become so emotion-laden in the minds of managers that an organization will often introduce an MBO system under a different label. For example, an organization may establish a program called START (an acronym for Set Targets and Review Them) or GAP (Goal Acceptance Program). The mechanics of such programs are likely to borrow heavily, if not totally, from the MBO approach. In short, the trend is toward putting old wine into new bottles, with a recognition that mutual goal setting is not a panacea for all organizational problems under all possible circumstances.

Expectations

One of the more subtle approaches to influencing employee performance is through expectations.[13] People communicate their performance expectations both verbally and nonverbally. Often, we send cues revealing that we either approve or disapprove of another's conduct. This approach to influencing employee performance is often employed without deliberate intent in that few of us consciously try to influence others by our transmitted expectations. The use of expectations to change performance, however, is receiving increasing recognition in the field of organizational behavior as a powerful force in influencing employee effort and performance.

The Power of Self-fulfilling Prophecies

Perhaps the clearest examples of the power of expectations can be seen in the responsiveness of children to the expectations of parents and teachers. All of us have seen children who are labeled as "little devils" or "star pupils" respond exactly as expected. It can be said more generally that an individual often responds to expectations in a manner that supports the beliefs of the person who transmits the cues.

Robert Rosenthal of Harvard University is the foremost researcher of the power of expectations. In one investigation, Rosenthal and Jacobson studied

---

* This point prompts the paradoxical observation that MBO systems work best in situations where they may be needed the least (that is, where good supervisor–subordinate relations already exist), and MBO systems work least well in situations where they are needed most desperately (where divisiveness and conflict exist)!

An Inside Look
Making Goal Setting Work

Managers don't always find it easy to set goals for their department. Sometimes they go to great lengths to involve employees in the process, try to set workable goals, and still find that the system isn't working. The following are some pitfalls managers should avoid.

1. *Too many goals.* This could mean either that no priorities are set for the goals or that there are simply more goals than people can keep track of. A task that is performed regularly probably need not be defined as a goal.

2. *Insufficient accountability.* Sometimes, a manager and employee set goals but don't follow them through. This gives the impression that the manager was not serious about the goal or goal setting to begin with. Once a goal is set, the manager should display interest, although not to the extent of directing every step. Managers should only set

goals they are prepared to follow through on.

3. *Too much forgiveness.* Sometimes a manager follows up on goals, but if an employee does not achieve them, the manager "forgives" him or her. This is another way to teach employees not to take goals seriously. If goals are not met, the manager should explore the reasons for this. Were the goals realistic? Was performance adequate? Were there extenuating circumstances?

4. *Too few subgoals.* While some objectives may be best accomplished over a long term, managers should avoid waiting too long to measure progress. They can do this by setting and tracking subgoals and readjusting goals as necessary. Employees are reinforced when they achieve subgoals.

5. *Conflicting priorities.* Sometimes managers impose priorities that are important

to them but not to employees. For example, some managers insist that desks be cleared of all material before employees leave for the night. If employees think this requirement takes time away from truly productive work, they will take such goals less seriously.

6. *Ego goals.* Managers may come up with projects that seem important to them and would, if achieved, earn them prestige. But if employees see no benefit to themselves, they will not commit themselves.

7. *Withholding managerial resources.* A manager who has the time, knowledge, experience, or skill that would help employees achieve their objectives should offer his or her resources. Otherwise, employees may feel stranded or on the firing line. Their resentment and hesitation to take risks may hinder their achievement.

Source: Thomas L. Quick, *Managing People at Work Desk Guide,* © 1983 by Executive Enterprises, Inc., New York.

the influence of elementary school teachers' expectations on their pupils.[14] At the start of the school year, pupils were given an academic aptitude test. The investigators then provided false feedback to the teachers, identifying 20 percent of the children as likely to bloom academically during the coming school year. In fact, the likely "bloomers" had been selected by a random process. At the end of the school year, all pupils were again tested. The results showed that the so-called bloomers did in fact bloom, as evidenced by significant gains in IQ in comparison to their classmates. Because the teachers' expectations were the only deliberately manipulated aspect in this study, the investigators concluded that the changes in student performance were largely due to qualitative differences in how the teachers related to individual students.

In their report of this study, entitled *Pygmalion in the Classroom,* Rosenthal and Jacobson argued that the teachers probably conveyed messages of expected success and failure to individual students.† The students, in turn, responded by living up to the teachers' expectations. In essence, each teacher held a prophecy, or expectation, for each student, and each student then behaved to fulfill the expectation. This process is called a **self-fulfilling prophecy (SFP)**.

The relevance of the SFP phenomenon for organizations is straightforward. Employees, like all people, desire approval from their superiors. To some degree, supervisors transmit cues, or expectations, that an individual has the potential to succeed or, alternatively, will never succeed. Employees then typically respond by conforming to the communicated prophecy. An employee who receives positive cues can seemingly do no wrong, while an employee who receives negative cues can rarely do anything right. When faced with negative expectations, part of an employee's failure stems from the fear of being evaluated harshly by a supervisor. This obsession distracts the individual from performing well and encourages him or her to interpret ambiguous situations in a more negative light.

In a study that paralleled that of Rosenthal and Jacobson, King studied the performance of a group of hard-core unemployed men who were enrolled in a welding course.[15] Initially, King gave the men a test of mechanical aptitude. The classroom supervisors were then given false feedback about the students' test performances, with some of the men arbitrarily labeled as "high-aptitude" students. As in the Pygmalion study, the only real difference lay in the minds of the observers. At the end of the course, the men were given a comprehensive test of welding knowledge. The so-called high-aptitude individuals did in fact do better on the test than their classmates. In addition, these same individuals were absent fewer times during the course and completed many of the exercises ahead of their peers. A confidential poll of the men regarding the popularity of their classmates revealed that the "high-aptitude" men were the most popular members of the class (that is, they were rated "most preferred to be with" by their classmates).

A more controlled study of the SFP phenomenon was reported by Eden and Shani in a study entitled "Pygmalion Goes to Boot Camp."[16] In their study, Eden and Shani randomly labeled soldiers in the Israeli army as having "high command potential." These soldiers were then assigned to various instructors who were familiar with their alleged potential. Although the soldiers had different instructors, the results were much the same: soldiers who had been randomly labeled as having high potential displayed superior performance during their training experience when compared to other trainees.‡

† Pygmalion, a character in Greek mythology, is said to have sculpted a stone statue of a lovely maiden. Because he fell in love with the statue and wished strongly for it to be a living person, the gods took pity on him and brought the statue to life, hence fulfilling his aspirations.

‡ The statistical magnitude of the SFP effects was also substantial: the percentage of variability in subsequent performance that could be accounted for or explained by the SFP phenomenon was 73 percent, while 66 percent of the variability in attitudinal data could be attributed to the phenomenon.

From these examples, it is clear that the SFP phenomenon is not limited to young children or animals.§ Other examples of the SFP effect can also be cited. A bank run, in which the depositors flock to a bank and demand their money, is a classic illustration of a self-fulfilling prophecy. In a bank run, the depositors act collectively on a rumor of insolvency and thereby convert the rumor into reality. To some extent, the rate of inflation is partially due to an SFP. Consider a situation in which union bargaining representatives expect that inflation in the coming year will be around 4 percent. With this expectation, they will feel obligated to demand at least a 4 percent increase in wages in order to keep up with inflation. Manufacturing firms will, in turn, see their labor costs rising by at least 4 percent because of the workers' demands and will raise their prices accordingly. Thus, the expectation that the cost of everything will go up at least 4 percent in the coming year helps to create a situation in which the prophecy is fulfilled.**

The Constructive Management of Self-fulfilling Prophecies

All too often we are unwitting participants in self-fulfilling prophecies, either as the perpetrator (cue sender) or benefactor/victim (cue receiver). In organizations, the effects of this influence process can be substantial. Rather than lament the traps of SFPs, it is perhaps best to think about how we can control this process to positive ends. Since we cannot avoid influencing one another's actions, it is important to consider how we can use SFP to encourage optimal performance from all organizational members.

A primary consideration in using SFP for benevolent purposes is to be more sensitive to how others perceive us. That is to say, we should strive to be more aware of how subtle aspects of our own behavior and speech communicate our thoughts to others. Small factors, such as amount of eye contact, tone of voice, phrasing of sentences, and so on, can speak volumes about how we truly feel. Thus, we must pay greater attention to controlling our own actions in order to communicate positive expectations to all individuals.

Many times, managers honestly feel that they treat all subordinates equally, but they communicate personal biases nonetheless. Workers rarely feel that their supervisors treat all subordinates alike. Most commonly, they claim that some subordinates are members of the boss's inner circle, while others are viewed as outsiders.

Managers can also use SFP to foster motivation. One technique for doing so is to display enthusiasm for the work unit's mission. Such enthusiasm will usually be contagious and spread to subordinates. A contagious enthusiasm

§ As an example of how humans and animals communicate expectations, consider how a dog typically reacts when we convey cues of fear versus confidence: fear typically evokes an aggressive response, while confidence and relaxation elicit acceptance. In a dramatic illustration of the potential for subtle communication between humans and animals, Rosenthal and Fode told college students that individual lab rats they were asked to train in a maze were "bright" (allegedly based on past maze performance) or "dull."[17] The bright rats in fact outperformed the dull rats when the college students actually trained them to run a maze. Without knowing it, the college students had related to the rats in ways that conveyed positive or negative performance expectations. The rats were able to sense and respond to the students' cues.

** It should be apparent that inflation is not solely attributable to an SFP process. Other factors (such as changes in oil prices, oil shortages, and the size of the money supply) can also play a role.

that focuses on task accomplishment also draws attention away from interpersonal concerns of relative likes and dislikes.

SFPs may also play a role when performance appraisal schemes rely too heavily on subjective appraisals. In such cases, personal bias can be introduced. One common safeguard against this potential problem is the use of more objective indexes of performance. Sales figures or widgets produced per day should provide less biased measures of performance. Yet, even the perception of seemingly simple objective indexes such as these can be influenced by prior expectations.

To illustrate the point that even the perception of simple objective events can be biased by prior expectations, consider a study done in the area of extrasensory perception (ESP) research.[18] Researchers surveyed a group of college students on the extent to which they believed in ESP and related phenomena (e.g., psychokinesis). Based on their responses, the students were sorted into two groups: "believers" and "skeptics." Members of the two groups were then invited to participate in a study that was purportedly being made of the ability of a well-known psychic who tried to influence a set of over 50 dice to turn up a large number of 6s. In truth, no one directly handled the dice spilling — it was done by machine, and a camera was positioned over the table to film the outcomes of 20 spillings of the dice. Also, no psychic was involved in the study. Upon viewing the film, the students were asked to record the number of times that they saw the number 6 appear on the screen. A third group of observers (a control group that was not asked any questions about belief in ESP) was later asked to view the same film without being given any cover story concerning a well-known psychic (that is, they were simply asked to count the number of 6s on the dice after each of the 20 tosses onto the table).

The average results for the three groups revealed that the believers counted a large number of 6s (significantly more than statistical theory would predict), the skeptics counted very few 6s (significantly less than would be predicted statistically), and the control group reported an intermediate number of 6s (within a predicted range derived from statistical theory). Thus, the believers reported evidence of psychokinesis, while the skeptics found evidence of a reverse psychokinesis! Clearly, prior expectations do influence the perception of seemingly simple objective events. The arousal of prior expectations, therefore, can be a powerful distorter of one's perception. This example should not lead one to despair of the possibility of accurate perception, but instead should caution one as to the power and prevalence of expectations.

In summary, our expectations influence both our perception of others and the behavior of others. In order to optimize the performance of every subordinate, it is essential that managers pay great attention to their prior expectations and the transmission of those expectations. This is not to advocate the manipulation of others by conveying deceptive cues. Rather, it is to advocate bringing out the best in others by treating them supportively and optimistically. The principle of using expectations to maximize performance may be summarized as follows: "Do not treat others as you may believe they are — treat them as if they are already what you hope they will become."

Job Redesign

A portion of the material wealth of our culture stems from the application of the principle of division of labor. The division of labor was recognized as an important factor in increasing productivity during the Industrial Revolution, when mechanization and job fragmentation began to emerge most strongly. Although Adam Smith, in his book *An Inquiry into the Nature and Causes of the Wealth of Nations,* identified division of labor as an important factor in improving productivity, he also suggested it had the potential to "corrupt" the worker via repetition and drudgery.[19] Karl Marx also observed that the trend toward industrialization in the West was creating a less than ideal set of circumstances for workers. As a solution, Marx advocated the overthrow of the capitalist system and the creation of a state in which factories and products were owned collectively by the workers.

Despite these concerns, job specialization and greater division of labor continued. The productivity gains of job specialization resulted from decreased time spent changing tasks, decreased training time for employees, and increased skill due to repetition. Labor was also less able to claim that important skills were involved in the tasks and, therefore, was less able to demand higher wages. The early decades of this century witnessed a continuing drive toward job simplification, with the principles of scientific management (Chapter 1) helping to spur on the trend.††

More recently, management scholars have recognized that job simplification can improve productivity *up to a point*. Beyond that point, worker dissatisfaction can set in (Figure 7.2). Workers then become hostile toward the task and the employer, and consequently reduce their efforts or increase labor costs through absenteeism or turnover. The challenge, as many managers see it, is to find the ideal level of simplification that maximizes productivity without risking worker discontent. In practice, most managers have been more likely to focus on increasing productivity at some cost to worker satisfaction. To be sure, a level of worker discontent that risks causing a wildcat strike or serious insubordination is to be avoided. But levels short of that extreme may be incurred in order to increase short-run production.

For numerous reasons, working conditions continue to improve. Since the emergence of the organized labor movement in the 1930s, management has rarely used work speed-ups — a tactic in which the pace of an assembly line is drastically increased for a short period of time. Workers (especially younger, better educated workers) are also more likely to express a desire for more challenging work. And due to larger societal trends respecting individual rights and liberties, a movement toward the enrichment, or humanization, of work is gaining strength. In the opinion of Filley, House, and Kerr, this movement

†† One of the dullest and most repetitious jobs with which I am familiar is that of bottle capper in a perfume factory. The job entails screwing on small perfume bottle caps for eight hours a day. These workers cannot leave their workstation unless a relief person is present. Also, if a worker is running out of caps, it is a different person's sole responsibility to see that the bin of bottle caps is replenished. For the record, the longest substantiated industrial career in a single job was that of Polly Gadsby, who began work at the age of 9 and wrapped elastic for the same company until her death at the age of 95.

■ **Figure 7.2**

Relationship of Job Simplification to Productivity

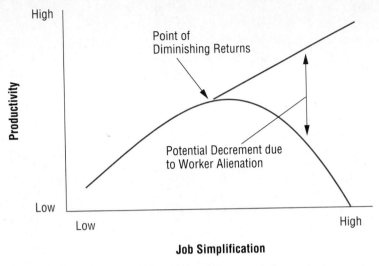

represents something akin to the return swing of the pendulum.[20] For many centuries, craftsperson-type jobs (where job simplification is low) were prevalent. In the nineteenth century, the trend moved toward more simplified work, and now the trend appears to be heading back toward jobs with less simplification (although the era of the craftsperson may not fully return). In a sense, the world of work has been passing through a period of relative dehumanization. More recently, the trend is toward the rehumanization of work.

Methods of Job Redesign

The first serious attempt to break from the principles of job simplification occurred during the 1940s and 1950s. This approach, called **job enlargement**, involves an increase in the variety of an employee's activities. In essence, a job is extended to include additional elements without really altering its content. For example, a worker may solder the red wires as well as the black wires. On the whole, job enlargement tends to improve worker satisfaction and the quality of production. The quantity of production, however, does not appear to be clearly or directly affected.

Job rotation is a related notion in the area of job redesign. In job rotation, the task stays the same, but the personnel who perform the task are systematically changed. Many organizations use job rotation as a training device to improve workers' flexibility. But the available evidence suggests that it does not aid either worker satisfaction or performance. Nonetheless, job rotation may be the only available means for introducing variety into jobs that cannot be redesigned to make them more meaningful or challenging.

Fred Herzberg was one of the first people to make an important observation about job-redesign efforts.[21] He noted that many redesign efforts focused

OB Focus

Incentives for Hourly Workers

Providing pay incentives for hourly workers poses special challenges. Management must determine what incentives hourly workers will respond to and how to tie these incentives to the things hourly workers can control.

A company that has come up with a successful scheme for compensating hourly workers is Parsons Pine Products, Inc., of Ashland, Oregon. Parsons has instituted a four-point plan for giving hourly workers positive reinforcement.

First is safety pay. An employee who goes for a month without a lost-time accident receives a bonus equal to four hours' pay.

Second is retro pay. When its workers' compensation premiums decline as a result of a reduced accident rate, the company divides the money it saves among its employees.

Third is well pay. Instead of sick days, employees receive "well pay" each month. This is equal to eight hours' worth of wages. Employees receive well pay if they have been neither absent nor tardy.

Finally, hourly employees receive profit pay. Parsons uses a bonus pool, into which it puts all the company's earnings over 4 percent after taxes. Each employee gets a share. The share is determined by multiplying the employee's wages or salary by a job rating based on attendance, productivity, and leadership. Employees receive the bonus twice a year, at Christmas and in July, when the plant shuts down for vacations.

Since the company instituted the program, its accident rate fell from 86 percent above the state average to 32 percent below the state average. Turnover, tardiness, and absenteeism have also fallen.

Source: Patricia Amend, "Creating Incentives for Hourly Workers," *Inc.*, July 1986, 89–90.

on changing the *variety* of activities without changing their content. Also, the new designs did not give workers control over their jobs. Often, workers' efforts were paced by the rate of an assembly-line process instead of being self-paced. Herzberg proposed that autonomy and self-regulation are important causes of positive changes in worker behavior. He also felt that job-redesign efforts should focus on giving more decision-making responsibility to workers, rather than merely expanding the number of tasks performed. A distinction can thus be made between vertical and horizontal expansions of a job. Vertical expansion represents **job enrichment**, while horizontal expansion represents job enlargement. The specific job factors that have the potential to enrich work are drawn from the list of motivators that Herzberg proposed in his two-factor theory of work motivation (see Chapter 6).

Studies of job enrichment processes have tended to be success stories.[22] One of the more widely known examples of job enrichment programs is provided by Volvo's Ralmar plant in Sweden. The program changed the conventional assembly-line method of manufacturing to a more employee-centered system of controlling the assembly process. The assembly system relies on computer-controlled trolleys that carry partially assembled automobiles through the plant. However, reports of this experience and other job enrichment programs (such as those at Texas Instruments, General Foods, and Polaroid) have tended to be informal and lacking in rigor, so drawing a conclusive assessment of the value of job enrichment efforts is difficult.[23]

In what may be viewed as something of a backlash to the job enrichment movement, it has been argued that not everyone is interested in an enriched job. This position has been presented with several variations. The most extreme statement is that people are very adaptable and will adjust to most situations. Taking what may seem to be a callous perspective, the head of a human resources division of one large firm recently stated that it was not important to worry about the pay level of the organization's lower-level employees because these people are "accustomed to managing financial hardship."

A more moderate view is that only certain people desire enriched work, while others actually prefer the freedom from hassles resulting from an unchallenging job. Similarly, some claim that the high walls created by being "in a rut" offer a certain degree of insulation and security from potentially threatening surroundings.

Charles Hulin and Milton Blood have best expressed the moderate position on the need to consider individual differences.[24] They contend that a further important consideration is whether workers are from urban or rural areas. Rural workers may be more likely to subscribe to middle-class work norms, such as a belief in the Protestant work ethic and a positive view of achievement. In contrast, urban workers are more likely to be alienated from the work norms of the middle class and instead subscribe to the norms of a more heterogeneous urban subculture.

In analyzing data from over 1,300 blue-collar workers in 21 plants in the eastern United States, Blood and Hulin found that a worker's degree of urbanization tended to influence the relationship between job level and job satisfaction.[25] Specifically, they reported that employees in more urbanized settings responded with less job satisfaction to jobs of greater responsibility, whereas employees in less urbanized communities responded with increasing levels of job satisfaction to jobs of greater responsibility.

Although the consideration of individual differences seems to be intuitively reasonable, and one can easily imagine situations in which specific individuals may prefer nonchallenging work, more recent evidence from a national sample suggests that the magnitude of the differences among workers is not that great.[26] These data suggest that the vast majority of people respond positively to jobs of increasing quality (i.e., greater challenge, autonomy, and responsibility), but that the strength of this desire is greater in some segments of the population. Blood and Hulin's study notwithstanding, it appears that workers rarely report negative reactions to increases in job quality.[27]

Job Characteristics Theory

J. Richard Hackman and Greg Oldham have proposed a comprehensive theory of job enrichment that attempts to explain how various job dimensions affect worker behavior.[28] Their **job characteristics theory** also accounts for the possible influence of individual differences on the desire for enriched work. To their credit, Hackman and Oldham have tried to establish empirically the accuracy of their model and have designed measures of key variables.

■ Figure 7.3

The Job Characteristics Model of Job Enrichment

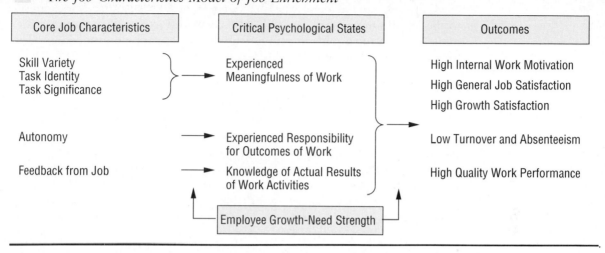

Source: Adapted from J.R. Hackman and G.R. Oldham, *Work Redesign* (Reading, Mass.: Addison-Wesley, 1980), 77.

The main components of their model and the links among them are portrayed in Figure 7.3. According to the model, a number of work outcomes, such as desire to perform well (that is, high internal work motivation) and satisfaction, are influenced by the experience of three critical psychological states. These three states — the meaningfulness of work, felt responsibility, and knowledge of results of job — are all "critical" in the sense that the absence of any one of them will not foster the desired outcomes. Each of the three states is influenced in turn by the various core job characteristics. Specifically, a sense of the meaningfulness of work is enhanced by the presence of

1. Skill variety: the extent to which a job requires that different duties be performed involving a number of different skills

2. Task identity: the extent to which a person is permitted to complete a "whole" or identifiable piece of work from start to finish

3. Task significance: the extent to which a job affects the lives of others (i.e., is the job of some value to others in the organization or the world?).

Responsibility is enhanced by the presence of

4. Autonomy: the extent to which a job offers independence and self-determination for the scheduling of work and the performance of associated tasks.

And knowledge of results is determined by

5. Feedback from the job: the extent to which the conduct of the job provides clear and direct information on the effectiveness of the worker's performance.

To assess the degree to which a job is enriched, Hackman and Oldham developed a series of questions that determine the extent to which a worker views his or her job as possessing each of the five job characteristics. Responses to the **job diagnostic survey** can then be combined in accordance with a formula for assessing a job's overall potential for motivating an individual. The Motivating Potential Score, or MPS, is given by:

$$\text{Motivating Potential Score (MPS)} = \left(\frac{\text{Skill Variety} + \text{Task Identity} + \text{Task Significance}}{3} \right) \times \text{Autonomy} \times \text{Feedback}$$

Because the formula involves the multiplication of terms, it suggests that a low or near-zero value on the job characteristics that define a critical psychological state will also lead to a total MPS value of near zero. The MPS formula is particularly useful for comparing different jobs and for assessing the same job over time (as might be done in a study of the effects of a job enrichment effort).

To illustrate the importance of the core job characteristics, consider almost any recreational activity that people engage in. The game of golf provides a particularly useful example. Golf involves a variety of skills and requires the use of personal judgment, as in deciding which club to use. A player completes the entire course, as opposed to only a portion. The game also possesses a form of significance, in that players keep a tally of the number of strokes they take to move the ball from the tee to the cup. This tally permits players to compare their performance against several standards: their own past performance on the hole, the par (or standard) for the hole, and the performance of their competitors. Autonomy is involved in that players are personally responsible for their performance. They are in charge of their own conduct and, consequently, their own success or failure. Finally, feedback is immediate. A player learns instantly if his or her shot hooks, slices, or lands in the sand. Clearly, the game of golf is highly "enriched," which explains why many people spend much of their spare time on the links.

It is interesting to consider what the game of golf would be like with any of the core characteristics removed. Suppose that feedback were eliminated, so that a player could not watch the flight of the ball to see how far it went or where it landed. Or imagine that autonomy were removed, so that a player had to follow someone else's directions on how to play each shot. In both cases, a great deal of the game's interest would be lost. If we failed to keep a tally of strokes (or a score of performance) and simply hit the ball around the course, we would also make the game less meaningful. In short, the removal of any of the critical psychological states would diminish the experience of enrichment or fulfillment and tend to make the activities seem more like "work" (in the most negative sense of the word).

To complete our discussion of the job characteristics model, we need to consider one additional component: the strength of an employee's desire for personal growth experiences in the work setting. Clearly, not everyone responds positively to challenging work. Some individuals prefer to be given assignments that are very clear-cut and offer little challenge. An attempt to enrich such people's jobs may be futile. In recognition of this fact, Hackman and Oldham have incorporated the notion of an individual differences moderator variable into their model (see Chapter 2 for a discussion of the concept of moderator variables). **Employee growth-need strength** enters the enrichment experience in two places: (1) it moderates the experience of psychological states in reaction to job characteristics (i.e., individuals who are higher on growth-need strength tend to experience the states more fully), and (2) it moderates the relationship between the psychological states and worker outcomes (i.e., individuals who are higher on growth-need strength tend to have more positive outcomes in response to the psychological states). In short, the job characteristics model holds that the enrichment process will succeed only with individuals who are predisposed to benefit from the enrichment experience.

Evidence on the Validity of the Job Characteristics Model   The job characteristics model has been tested extensively in recent years. By and large, the results support the model's predictions.[29] The model appears to predict internal work motivation and job satisfaction quite well, and absenteeism less well. Predicting performance has proven to be more problematic. Quality enhancement is somewhat more certain, while quantity enhancement is not very reliable. It seems that the further one moves from psychological variables to job behaviors, the less successful the model is as a predictor.

Other Job Redesign Approaches

In addition to job enrichment, two other work redesign techniques are also growing in popularity: flextime and the modified workweek.

Flextime refers to a work schedule that gives employees some discretion in arranging their working hours. Most frequently, the employer specifies a period of time during the day when all employees must be present — the core time. Employees may then schedule the rest of their work hours according to their own preferences. In most cases, the earliest starting time and latest stopping time are prescribed, as is the total number of hours that an employee must complete every week. Many flextime plans also hold an employee to a two-hour maximum time limit for lunch. But within these constraints, employees are free to select starting and finishing times each day. To be sure, flextime does not redesign the actual tasks that workers perform, but it does offer each employee a means of balancing work and home life.

Research on flextime has yielded generally positive results. For example, Cohen and Gadon reported that absenteeism and turnover were lowered, while performance increased following the introduction of flextime.[30] Significant increases in productivity were also reported in a study by Schein, Maurer, and Novak.[31] Other experiments have also tended to find positive effects, especially in reduced absenteeism and turnover.[32]

Modified workweek plans attempt to design alternatives for the currently prevalent 8-hour day, 5-day workweek. The most commonly adopted design is the 4-day, 10 hours per day workweek, or 4-40 scheme. Because the rest of the business world still follows a 5-day workweek (and therefore expects to communicate and send goods on a 5-day schedule), many experimenting organizations have had to stagger their 4-day plans so that part of the company will be open on any given workday.

The impact of the 4-40 schedule has been mixed. While employees can enjoy longer stretches of uninterrupted leisure time and less commuting, they are more likely to be fatigued from working longer shifts. Absenteeism, however, is often reduced due to the potentially greater cost that a lost workday has for the individual employee. Informal evidence of the productivity gains of 4-40 programs, such as surveys based on managers' impressions, has tended to be positive.[33] But other evidence tends to be mixed. Ivancevich and Lyon found that while performance and satisfaction increased following the introduction of a 4-40 scheme, both outcomes returned to original levels after about two years.[34] A survey by Cohen and Gadon suggests that some companies that have experimented with 4-40 schemes are returning to a traditional workweek.[35] Despite such mixed findings, most social forecasters predict that a 4-40 workweek lies in our future.[36] Most of these predictions, which were made during the late 1970s and early 1980s, assumed a continuing, long-term energy crisis. So the reasoning goes, substantial start-up and heating/cooling costs for manufacturing and office facilities, as well as reduced commuting costs, could be realized by the nationwide adoption of a 4-40 workweek.

Obstacles to Job Redesign

The introduction of a job redesign program, like any change effort, is seldom a simple task. Numerous obstacles are likely to arise, and some of the greatest resistance is likely to come from the employees themselves. Frequently, employees, as well as managers, are comfortable with the informal power systems that already exist. They thus view job redesign as an intrusion on the existing social order. Unions also tend to oppose job redesign, perceiving such efforts as schemes for extracting greater work from employees without providing hard compensation in exchange. As one union member once said, "If you want to make me feel proud or tell me I'm doing a good job, say it with money!"

Supervisors often fear job redesign efforts as well. Their fears are grounded in the belief that an increase in employee self-control or self-monitoring will result in a need for fewer supervisors. This fear is valid in that a successful job enrichment program will reduce the need to monitor employee performance closely.‡‡

Further problems may arise if employees are not personally involved in the job redesign effort. Including employees in the redesign process can be a powerful means of gaining their commitment to the program's success.

A final, and less easily remedied, limitation of job redesign involves the diminishment of the impact of redesign programs on successive "generations" of employees. Due to naturally occurring turnover, the employees who witnessed a work redesign change will eventually be replaced by employees who did not experience the change. These newer employees may take their now-

---

‡‡ One consultant who specializes in the introduction of job enrichment programs told me that the greatest initial protest to such proposed programs is likely to come from first-level supervisors, who typically argue that *their employees* will not like the new situation.

enriched jobs for granted because they lack the perspective of long-time employees, who clearly recognize the before–after contrast. Merely telling a recently hired employee that his job is much better than it used to be, thanks to a redesign program, is unlikely to have much real impact on his feelings and behavior. Thus, job redesign efforts may have their strongest positive effects on employees who experience the change personally and are therefore sensitive to the changes. The natural attrition and replacement of workers may tend to diminish the positive impact of redesign efforts over time. As yet, this suspected process of diminished impact has received only informal consideration by job redesign specialists. The magnitude of this potential limitation and the possible remedies remain to be explored.

Summary

1. Distinguish between extrinsic and intrinsic rewards.
Extrinsic rewards come from sources outside of the individual, while intrinsic rewards are self-administered.

2. Compare various types of rewards on the dimensions of average importance, flexibility, frequency, and visibility.
Table 7.1 summarizes ratings along these dimensions for pay, promotion, fringe benefits, status symbols, and awards and certificates.

3. Evaluate the merits of different pay-for-performance schemes.
Table 7.2 summarizes the merits of salary and bonus rewards when productivity, cost effectiveness, and supervisor rating methods are used to rate employees in relation to the individual, group, or organization.

4. Explain why incentive plans have lost popularity.
Incentive plans have run into problems because they may foster an adversarial attitude in employees; because they can lead to a sense of class distinctions between workers and managers; and because of the impact of societal changes, such as the increasingly interdependent nature of jobs and workers' desires for more challenging and meaningful work.

5. Describe three attributes of goals that are important for improving performance.
Three goal attributes that are especially important for improving performance are (1) the specificity of the goal, or the preciseness with which a goal or objective is stated; (2) the difficulty of the goal; and (3) the acceptance of the goal by employees.

6. Describe management-by-objectives and some of its advantages and possible problems.
MBO is a process in which employees participate with management in setting goals for the employee's performance. After an established period of time, employee and supervisor meet again to review the employee's performance based on the goals. Advantages are that goals are specific and measurable and that MBO programs have the potential to improve performance. However, problems can arise from lack of top-level support, management's discomfort

with employee participation, personality conflicts between employee and manager, and the potential for neglect of the qualitative aspects of performance.

7. Give some examples of the power of self-fulfilling prophecies.

Children develop in response to the expectations of parents and teachers. In one study, children performed in school according to their teachers' beliefs about their aptitude. Similarly, a group of men in a welding course performed in accordance with their teacher's expectations. Soldiers labeled as having high potential displayed superior performance. In all these studies, the labels were assigned randomly. A bank run is another example of the power of expectations.

8. Describe some ways of constructively managing self-fulfilling prophecies.

People can manage SFPs by being more sensitive to how others perceive their behavior. They can also pay more attention to controlling their behavior and speech so as to communicate positive expectations to everyone. Displaying enthusiasm for the group's goals is another way to manage SFPs constructively, as is attempting to help poorer performers.

9. Describe methods of job redesign used to reduce worker discontent.

Some methods of job redesign are job enlargement, which increases the variety of an employee's activities; job rotation, which rotates personnel in various tasks; and job enrichment, which is an expansion of an employee's autonomy and self-regulation in a job. Other methods include flextime and modified workweeks.

10. List the job characteristics that enhance a sense of the meaningfulness of one's work, a sense of responsibility, and knowledge of the results of one's work.

The job characteristics that enhance a sense of meaningfulness are skill variety, task identity, and task significance. A sense of responsibility is enhanced by autonomy, while knowledge of results is enhanced by feedback from the job.

11. Discuss some obstacles to job redesign.

Employees often are comfortable with the existing informal power systems. Unions may see job redesign as a way to extract more work from employees without an increase in pay. Supervisors fear that giving employees more self-control or self-monitoring will reduce the need for supervisors. Failure to involve employees in the planning can also lead to problems. Other problems can arise when new employees are hired; they have not experienced the initial impact of the program and take the present conditions for granted.

Key Terms

Extrinsic reward
Intrinsic reward
Gain sharing
Goal specificity
Goal difficulty
Goal acceptance
Management-by-objectives (MBO)
Self-fulfilling prophecy (SFP)

Job enlargement
Job rotation
Job enrichment
Job characteristics theory
Job diagnostic survey
Employee growth-need strength
Flextime
Modified workweek

Review and Discussion Questions

1. Give two examples of extrinsic rewards and two examples of intrinsic rewards.

2. What are some advantages of using pay as a reward for employees? Only a small percentage of workers in the United States see a link between how much they are paid and how hard they work. What are some possible reasons for this discrepancy?

3. Based on Table 7.2, what kind of pay schemes are likely to be most successful? What kind of pay schemes are likely to enhance cooperation among group members?

4. Explain the reasons incentive pay schemes have lost their appeal. Do you think incentive pay will become more popular in the future? Why or why not?

5. What are some advantages of compensating employees with profit sharing, gain sharing, and stock ownership?

6. Martha Wilson is the manager of Best Foot Forward, a shoe store in a neighborhood shopping center. She is concerned that all her sales personnel feel motivated to work together and do their best. She meets privately with each of her salespeople and says, "I have set a goal for you that you increase your sales performance each month. I know you can do an excellent job, and if you need any help, please come talk to me." Does Martha's goal have the attributes of a goal that will improve performance? Explain your answer.

7. Acme Ace Company has instituted a new MBO system. Some goals developed by members of the accounting department follow. State whether these are good MBO goals and support your answer.

   - Process accounts receivable records faster.
   - Reduce paperwork costs by June 15.
   - Increase sales by 5 percent by the end of the fiscal year.
   - Institute a training program for bookkeepers by May 1.

8. Bert Burton, marketing vice-president for Dynamo Power Tools, likes to give all his personnel helpful guidance. He had been watching Winston Brash, a sales rep who broke all the sales records but also disrupted most meetings by talking constantly. One day Bert called Winston into his office. "Winston," he said, "You're a fine sales rep, but I'm afraid you're just not cut out to be a manager." That afternoon at a sales meeting, Winston was about to make a suggestion, but caught himself as he remembered Bert's words to him. Two weeks later, Winston left Dynamo Power Tools for a sales job at another company. How did Bert's expectations affect Winston? How could Bert have used his influence positively?

9. How does a company benefit from job specialization? What are some limitations of this approach?

10. Explain the differences between job enlargement, job rotation, and job enrichment as job redesign strategies.

11.   What characteristics of a job enrich it? Should a company be responsible for enriching jobs and using techniques such as flextime and modified workweeks, even if doing so hurts profitability? Why or why not?

Critical Incident

Is Job Redesign Needed?

Healthcare America, Inc. is a large health insurance company that operates in 46 states. At its corporate headquarters, there is a great deal of reliance on a word processing department. There are 22 people working in this department, with one supervisor and an assistant supervisor. They type a wide variety of documents that are supplied by the various departments. Some of the work involves forms and letters while other work centers around lengthy manuscripts. Most of the work is performed against a deadline.

The work is given to the individual typist by the supervisor. The supervisor attempts to equally distribute the work and monitor progress. The supervisor also checks to make sure everything is in order before giving it to the typist. If it is not, it is sent back to the originator.

Because of the importance surrounding the exactness of the work, completed documents are sent to proofreaders for review. These people then forward the documents or return them for corrections. However, many complaints are still received about an excessive amount of errors and deadlines not being met. In addition, the department has experienced high absenteeism and turnover.

As a consultant, you have been asked to analyze this situation and offer some recommendations.

1.   What do you believe is causing the problems in this department? Why?

2.   Consider redesigning the job of the word processor/typist according to the principles of job enlargement and job enrichment.

3.   What are the advantages and disadvantages of each approach?

Source: Written by Bruce Kemelgor, University of Louisville; used by permission.

Experiential Exercise

Goal Setting and Performance

This activity is designed to help you understand and examine the relationship between the process of setting goals and the resulting performance of an individual in an organization. To the extent that the process of goal setting contributes to organizational behavior, this activity seeks to have you analyze the methods used by your manager to use objectives in relation to your job.

1.   Think of your present job or a job you held recently. If you have not been employed, use your "job" as a student and consider one of your instructors as the manager. The following statements refer to that job and to the objectives associated with it. Please read each statement carefully and then circle the appropriate number indicating how true or untrue you believe each statement to be.

	Definitely Not True	Generally Not True	Slightly Not True	Uncertain	Slightly True	Generally True	Definitely True
1. Management encourages employees to define job objectives.	−3	−2	−1	0	1	2	3
2. If I achieve my objectives, I receive adequate recognition from my supervisor.	−3	−2	−1	0	1	2	3
3. My objectives are clearly stated with respect to the results expected.	−3	−2	−1	0	1	2	3
4. I have the support I need to accomplish my objectives.	−3	−2	−1	0	1	2	3
5. Achieving my objectives increases my chances for promotion.	−3	−2	−1	0	1	2	3
6. My supervisor dictates my job objectives to me.	−3	−2	−1	0	1	2	3
7. I need more feedback on whether I'm achieving my objectives.	−3	−2	−1	0	1	2	3
8. My supervisor will "get on my back" if I fail to achieve my objectives.	−3	−2	−1	0	1	2	3
9. My job objectives are very challenging.	−3	−2	−1	0	1	2	3
10. Management wants to know whether I set objectives for my job.	−3	−2	−1	0	1	2	3
11. My supervisor will compliment me if I achieve my job objectives.	−3	−2	−1	0	1	2	3
12. My objectives are very ambiguous and unclear.	−3	−2	−1	0	1	2	3
13. I lack the authority to accomplish my objectives.	−3	−2	−1	0	1	2	3
14. Achievement of objectives is rewarded with higher pay.	−3	−2	−1	0	1	2	3
15. My supervisor encourages me to establish my own objectives.	−3	−2	−1	0	1	2	3
16. I always have knowledge of my progress toward my objectives.	−3	−2	−1	0	1	2	3
17. My supervisor will reprimand me if I'm not making progress toward my objectives.	−3	−2	−1	0	1	2	3
18. My objectives seldom require my full interest and effort.	−3	−2	−1	0	1	2	3
19. Management makes it clear that defining job objectives is favorably regarded.	−3	−2	−1	0	1	2	3
20. My supervisor gives me more recognition when I achieve my objectives.	−3	−2	−1	0	1	2	3
21. My objectives are very concrete.	−3	−2	−1	0	1	2	3
22. I have sufficient resources to achieve my objectives.	−3	−2	−1	0	1	2	3

(*continued*)

	Definitely Not True	Generally Not True	Slightly Not True	Uncertain	Slightly True	Generally True	Definitely True
23. My pay is more likely to be increased if I achieve my objectives.	-3	-2	-1	0	1	2	3
24. My supervisor has more influence than I do in setting my objectives.	-3	-2	-1	0	1	2	3
25. I wish I had better knowledge of whether I'm achieving my objectives.	-3	-2	-1	0	1	2	3
26. If I fail to meet my objectives, my supervisor will reprimand me.	-3	-2	-1	0	1	2	3
27. Attaining my objectives requires all my skills and know-how.	-3	-2	-1	0	1	2	3

2.   For each of the nine subscales (A through I), compute a total score by summing the answers to the appropriate questions. Be sure to subtract minus scores.

A. Question
  1. +( )
  10. +( )
  19. +( )
  Total

B. Question
  3. +( )
  12. +( )
  21. +( )
  Total

C. Question
  6. +( )
  15. +( )
  24. +( )
  Total

D. Question
  4. +( )
  13. +( )
  22. +( )
  Total

E. Question
  7. +( )
  16. +( )
  25. +( )
  Total

F. Question
  9. +( )
  18. +( )
  27. +( )
  Total

G. Question
  5. +( )
  14. +( )
  23. +( )
  Total

H. Question
  2. +( )
  11. +( )
  20. +( )
  Total

I. Question
  8. +( )
  17. +( )
  26. +( )
  Total

3.   Plot the score from each of the subscales on the graph below. Use an X to indicate the appropriate scale value. Next, connect the nine subscale values by drawing a line from value A to value I. This provides you with a profile of your responses.

Subscale

A	-9	-7	-5	-3	-1	$+1$	$+3$	$+5$	$+7$	$+9$
B	-9	-7	-5	-3	-1	$+1$	$+3$	$+5$	$+7$	$+9$
C	-9	-7	-5	-3	-1	$+1$	$+3$	$+5$	$+7$	$+9$
D	-9	-7	-5	-3	-1	$+1$	$+3$	$+5$	$+7$	$+9$
E	-9	-7	-5	-3	-1	$+1$	$+3$	$+5$	$+7$	$+9$
F	-9	-7	-5	-3	-1	$+1$	$+3$	$+5$	$+7$	$+9$
G	-9	-7	-5	-3	-1	$+1$	$+3$	$+5$	$+7$	$+9$
H	-9	-7	-5	-3	-1	$+1$	$+3$	$+5$	$+7$	$+9$
I	-9	-7	-5	-3	-1	$+1$	$+3$	$+5$	$+7$	$+9$

4. Answer the following question: How satisfied are you with this job?
    a. highly satisfied
    b. satisfied
    c. it's OK
    d. somewhat dissatisfied
    e. very dissatisfied

    Form small groups based on your (honest) response to this question. As a group, address the following questions:

    a. Is there a common pattern in your questionnaire responses?
    b. Do certain subscale values (A through I) suggest appropriate managerial use of objectives? Which one(s)?
    c. Are certain subscales representative of the characteristics of objectives? Which one(s)?

5. Remain in your small group. Your instructor will ask each group for a representative to describe its predominate profile. Look for similarities among and differences between the group responses.

    What do you believe accounts for these differences? What characteristics of objectives and the managerial use of objectives contribute to satisfaction within organizations?

Source: Based in part on P. Lorenzi, H.P. Sims, Jr., and E.A. Slusher, "Goal Setting, Performance and Satisfaction: A Behavioral Demonstration," *Exchange: The Organizational Behavior Teaching Journal* 7, no. 1 (1982): 38–42.

Notes

1. E.E. Lawler III, *Pay and Organizational Effectiveness* (New York: McGraw-Hill, 1971); E.E. Lawler III, "New Approaches to Pay: Innovations that Work," *Personnel* 53 (1976): 11–23; E.E. Lawler III, *Pay and Organization Development* (Reading, Mass.: Addison-Wesley, 1981); E.E. Lawler III, "Whatever Happened to Incentive Pay?" *New Management* 1 (1984): 37–41.

2. Lawler, "Whatever Happened to Incentive Pay?"

3. "Lincoln Electric's Past Enhances the Future," *Management Review* (1984): 40–41.

4. E.E. Lawler III, "Reward Systems," in *Improving Life at Work*, ed. J.R. Hackman and J.L. Suttle (Glenview, Ill.: Scott, Foresman, 1977).

5. Lawler, "Whatever Happened to Incentive Pay?"

6. Ibid.

7. J. Ramquist, "Labor-Management Cooperation," *Sloan Management Review* 23 (1982): 49–55; E. Leefeldt, "Profit-Sharing Plans Reward Productivity," *Wall Street Journal*, November 15, 1984, 1.

8. Lawler, "Whatever Happened to Incentive Pay?"

9. G.P. Latham and G. Yukl, "A Review of Research on the Application of Goal-Setting in Organizations," *Academy of Management Journal* 18 (1975): 824–845; E.A. Locke, "The Relationship of Intentions to Level of Performance," *Journal of Applied Psychology* 50 (1966): 60–66; E.A. Locke, "Toward a Theory of Task Performance and Incentives," *Organizational Behavior and Human Performance* 3 (1968): 157–189; E.A. Locke, "What Is Job Satisfaction?" *Organizational Behavior and Human Performance* 4 (1969): 309–336; E.A. Locke, "Job Satisfaction and Job Performance: A Theoretical Analysis," *Organizational Behavior and Human Performance* 5 (1970): 484–500; P.M. Wright, "Test of the Mediating Role of Goals in the Incentive–Performance Relationship," *Journal of Applied Psychology* 74 (1989): 699–705; J. Hollenbeck, C. Williams, and H. Klein, "An Empirical Examination of the Antecedents of Commitment to Difficult Goals," *Journal of Applied Psychology* 74 (1989): 18–23; P.C. Earley, T. Connolly, and G. Ekegren, "Goals, Strategy Development, and Task Performance," *Journal of Applied Psychology* 74 (1989): 24–33;

M. Tubbs, "Goal Setting: A Meta-analytic Examination of the Empirical Evidence," *Journal of Applied Psychology* 71 (1986): 474–483; A.J. Mento, R.P. Steel, and R.J. Karren, "A Meta-analytic Study of the Effects of Goal Setting on Task Performance," *Organizational Behavior and Human Decision Processes* 39 (1987): 52–83.

10. S.E. White, T.R. Mitchell, and C.H. Bell, "Goal Setting, Evaluation Apprehension, and Social Cues as Determinants of Job Performance and Job Satisfaction in a Simulated Organization," *Journal of Applied Psychology* 62 (1977): 665–673.

11. H. Tosi, J.R. Rizzo, and S. Carroll, "Setting Goals in Management-By-Objectives," *California Management Review* 12 (1970): 70–78.

12. P.F. Drucker, *The Practice of Management* (New York: Harper, 1954); A.P. Raia, *Managing by Objectives* (Glenview, Ill.: Scott, Foresman, 1974); S.J. Carroll and H.L. Tosi, *Management by Objectives: Applications and Research* (New York: Macmillan, 1973); J. Kondrasuk, "Studies in MBO Effectiveness," *Academy of Management Review* 6 (1981): 419–430.

13. R.A. Jones, *Self-Fulfilling Prophecies: Social, Psychological, and Physiological Effects of Expectancies* (Hillsdale, N.J.: Erlbaum, 1977); J.S. Livingston, "Pygmalion in Management," *Harvard Business Review* 47 (1969): 81–89.

14. R. Rosenthal and L. Jacobson, *Pygmalion in the Classroom: Teachers' Expectations and Pupil Intellectual Development* (New York: Holt, Rinehart & Winston, 1968).

15. A.S. King, "Managerial Relations with Disadvantaged Work Groups: Supervisory Expectations of the Underprivileged Worker" (Ph.D. diss., Texas Tech University, 1970).

16. D. Eden and A.B. Shani, "Pygmalion Goes to Boot Camp: Expectancy, Leadership, and Trainee Performance," *Journal of Applied Psychology* 67 (1982): 194–199.

17. R. Rosenthal and K. Fode, "The Effect of Experimental Bias on the Performance of the Albino Rat," *Behavioral Science* 8 (1963): 183–189.

18. R.S. Kaufman and F.D. Sheffield, "A Methodological Flow in ESP Experiments" (paper presented at the Annual Meeting of the Eastern Psychological Association, 1952).

19. A. Smith, *An Inquiry into the Nature and Causes of the Wealth of Nations* (New York: Modern Library, 1937; first published in 1776).

20. A.C. Filley, R.J. House, and S. Kerr, *Managerial Process and Organizational Behavior* (Dallas: Scott, Foresman, 1987).

21. F. Herzberg, B. Mausner, and B. Snyderman, *The Motivation to Work* (New York: Wiley, 1959).

22. L.E. Davis and A.B. Cherns, *The Quality of Working Life. Volume Two: Cases and Commentary* (New York: Free Press, 1975).

23. M. Fein, "Job Enrichment: A Reevaluation," *Sloan Management Review* (Winter 1974): 69–88; S.A. Levitan and W.B. Johnston, "Job Redesign, Enrichment — Exploring the Limitations," *Monthly Labor Review* (July 1973): 35–41; E.E. Lawler, "Job Design and Employee Motivation," *Personnel Psychology* (1969): 426–438; W. Paul, K.B. Robertson, and F. Herzberg, "Job Enrichment Pays Off," *Harvard Business Review* (1969): 83–98.

24. C.L. Hulin and M.R. Blood, "Job Enlargement, Individual Differences, and Worker Responses," *Psychological Bulletin* 69 (1968): 41–55.

25. M.R. Blood and C.L. Hulin, "Alienation, Environmental Characteristics and Worker Responses," *Journal of Applied Psychology* 51 (1967): 284–290.

26. R.P. Vecchio, "Individual Differences as a Moderator of the Job Quality–Job Satisfaction Relationship: Evidence from a National Sample," *Organizational Behavior and Human Performance* 26 (1980): 305–325.

27. J.K. White, "Individual Differences and the Job Quality–Worker Response Relationship: Review, Integration, and Comments," *Academy of Management Review* 3 (1978): 267–280.

28. J.R. Hackman and G.R. Oldham, "Motivation Through the Design of Work: Test of a Theory," *Organizational Behavior and Human Performance* 16 (1976): 250–279; J.R. Hackman and G.R. Oldham, *Work Redesign* (Reading, Mass.: Addison-Wesley, 1980).

29. J.B. Miner, *Theories of Organizational Behavior* (Hinsdale, Ill.: The Dryden Press, 1980).

30. A.R. Cohen and H. Gadon, *Alternative Work Schedules: Integrating Individual and Organizational Needs* (Reading, Mass.: Addison-Wesley, 1978).

31. V.E. Schein, E.H. Maurer, and J.F. Novak, "Impact of Flexible Working Hours on Productivity," *Journal of Applied Psychology* 62 (1977): 463–465.

32. R.T. Golembiewski and C.W. Proehl, "A Survey of the Empirical Literature on

Flexible Workhours: Character and Consequences of a Major Innovation," *Academy of Management Review* 3 (1978): 837–855.

33. P. Dickson, *The Future of the Workplace* (New York: Wybright and Talley, 1975).

34. J.M. Ivancevich and H.C. Lyon, "The Shortened Workweek: A Field Experi-ment," *Journal of Applied Psychology* 62 (1977): 34–37.

35. Cohen and Gadon, *Alternative Work Schedules*.

36. D. Wallechinsky, A. Wallace, and I. Wallace, *The Book of Predictions* (New York: William-Morrow, 1981).

It is only when one
is pursued that one
becomes swift.

— *Kahlil Gibran*

Let us be thankful
for the fools. But for
them, the rest of us
could not succeed.

— *Mark Twain*

Learning Objectives

After studying this chapter, you should be able to:

1. *List reasons for appraising performance.*

2. *Describe different timetables for performance appraisals.*

3. *Discuss the relative merits of performance appraisal by the immediate supervisor, the employee being appraised, peers or coworkers, subordinates, and people outside the work unit.*

4. *Describe the process of job analysis.*

5. *Explain why performance appraisal cannot be totally objective.*

6. *List methods of performance appraisal.*

7. *Describe sources of tension in feedback interviews.*

8. *List the elements of a successful feedback interview.*

9. *Describe how courts evaluate whether a company's actions have had an adverse impact on a group.*

10. *Describe the characteristics of a legally defensible appraisal system.*

Performance Appraisal

■ Coping with Poor Performance

The founder of a Massachusetts company that manufactures heavy machinery encountered a dramatic drop in profitability and market share. The consultant who was called in recommended that the manufacturing manager be replaced immediately. The situation was urgent and disastrous.

The manufacturing manager had been with the company for 25 years. He had risen in the ranks from machinist to lead man to supervisor to superintendent to vice-president of manufacturing. Everyone liked him, but he lacked managerial skill. A colleague reported, "As a machinist, he is excellent. As a manufacturing executive, he is an excellent machinist."

The company's founder felt unable to ignore the manager's work history. The manager was a devoted employee who had worked long hours and had remained loyal through the vagaries of company politics. The founder decided to organize the company around the manager rather than fire him.

The manager was relieved of his title as vice-president and was put in charge of production planning and scheduling. He was given a highly capable assistant whose strengths were expected to make up for the manager's weaknesses in planning and scheduling. The manager's salary was retained, but he became ineligible for future increases. (In effect, this is a way of saying that the person is overpaid. This system also creates the problem of hiring an assistant who is more capable than his or her boss but who is paid considerably less.)

The company pulled out of its problems, but not to the extent it might have. In his new position, the manager is now the weak link in the planning and scheduling chain, which was actually set up to solve some of the company's problems. Also, the manager is left hanging, in charge of an assistant he knows is better at the job. The company's founder has sent the employees a message that he values long service but not performance.

It can be unpleasant to address an employee's poor performance directly, but it is often necessary. Management counselor King MacRury says supervisors with loyal but unproductive employees have five choices:

1. Refuse to do anything, in which case the problem is likely to intensify.

2. Move the employee to a different, but parallel, position. MacRury says this rarely works.

3. Put the individual on notice with a grace period for finding another job. In this case, the employee is likely to avoid confronting the issue until the last minute.

4. Use the person as a consultant, which makes little sense if he or she is incompetent.

5. Face the matter squarely!

This last approach requires a cool head and advance preparation, but, according to MacRury, it is generally the only way to go. Keeping an unproductive person in a key position can hurt other employees' morale.

Evaluating an employee's performance and discussing it with him or her can be a difficult task. Done poorly, it can hurt performance or even expose an organization to discrimination lawsuits. However, understanding the theory and methods of performance appraisal can enable supervisors to motivate employees and improve their performance.

This chapter discusses the purposes of performance appraisal and ways to appraise performance effectively. It includes some suggestions for conducting appraisal interviews and guidelines for developing appraisals that are fair and can help the organization avoid discrimination suits.

Source: King MacRury, "Between a Rock and a Hard Place," *Inc.,* July 1986, 101–102.

Productivity is a function of the ways in which monetary, technical, and human resources are managed. While monetary and technical resources can be managed by specialists in finance, accounting, and engineering, the management of human resources is the responsibility of all those who supervise others, regardless of function specialty. In order to develop human resources with an eye toward maximizing productivity, it is essential that supervisors periodically assess the performance of each subordinate. The results of the performance assessment, or appraisal, should then be shared with the subordinate in a constructive manner that can help the individual to correct any deficiencies or maintain excellence.

The topic of performance appraisal is central to the field of organizational behavior. Because performance appraisal involves aspects of learning, perception, personality, motivation, and incentive systems, it integrates many of the topics that we have considered in previous chapters. In this chapter, we will approach the notion of performance appraisal much as a newspaper reporter would, by asking why, when, what, how, and by whom performance appraisal is, and should be, conducted. Finally, we will conclude by considering some legal issues that currently surround the topic of performance appraisal.

Why Appraise Performance?

We have already suggested that performance appraisals are done with the goal of maintaining or improving performance. Beyond this important consideration, there are several additional reasons for conducting formal periodic appraisals. Chief among these is to aid supervisors in making decisions about relative compensation. Any organization that uses a pay-for-performance scheme should deliberately design its compensation plans around its performance appraisal system. The appraisal process should convey a sense of equity to all who are involved.

Periodic appraisals also help managers evaluate subordinates' suitability for training and development and for job changes, such as promotions, transfers, demotions, or dismissals. Sending a subordinate to a training program can be costly; as a result, supervisors need to be selective. Similarly, supervisors must make wise decisions about whom to promote or transfer. During harsh economic times, performance appraisals can also be used to decide who to demote or temporarily lay off.

A further reason for conducting performance appraisals is to open lines of communication between supervisors and subordinates. Communication about performance-related topics is an essential first step in any program that is designed to enhance productivity. Of course, simply having a superior and a subordinate discuss their perspectives on performance issues is not a guarantee that performance will be enhanced. A subordinate, for example, may not accept the supervisor's views or interpretations of the current state of affairs. Reaching agreement on the need for performance enhancement, as well as the manner in which it can be achieved, is a critical part of a performance appraisal session. Later in this chapter, we will consider how to conduct a performance appraisal session in order to avoid potential communication problems.

Finally, performance appraisals provide subordinates with useful feedback about how they are doing in their jobs. Virtually all employees want to know how their superiors view their performance. Unfortunately, in many organizations there is often little time or inclination for both parties to sit down and discuss personal strengths and weaknesses. Performance appraisal sessions, in a sense, force a superior to meet with each subordinate and provide concrete feedback.

A performance appraisal system serves many important functions within an organization. As we shall see, however, there are many potential obstacles to the conduct of proper appraisals.

When Should Performance Be Appraised?

In most organizations, formal performance reviews are carried out on an annual basis. To be sure, one can argue that *informal* performance feedback from superiors should be a daily affair. But an important distinction must be made between formal and informal reviews. Informal feedback can, and should, be given with great frequency. Formal feedback, however, involves greater preparation from the evaluator and requires more time.

Annual reviews for all employees are often done on a common review date. This format is widespread because many organizations set their budgets on an annual basis. As a consequence, raises (which are tied to performance reviews) are associated with a particular time of each year. Some organizations, however, conduct annual reviews based on the anniversary date of the subordinate's hiring or entering a particular job. With this system, evaluation can be spread throughout the year so that supervisors are not swamped by the task of conducting numerous appraisals in a short period of time.

In some cases, naturally occurring events mark the need for a formal appraisal. One of these is the completion of an initial probationary period. In entry-level positions, when a person is hired without much relevant work experience, a probationary period of one or more months may be required. At the end of this probationary period, a formal appraisal is conducted and a decision made about whether to continue the individual's employment. The completion of a major project that has spanned many months or years can also prompt a formal appraisal. Top-level employees are especially likely to be evaluated on such a basis.

Who Should Appraise Performance?

Initially, one might think that the only answer to this question is a subordinate's immediate supervisor. However, there are a number of perspectives from which to assess subordinate performance, each of which has certain advantages and disadvantages.

The Immediate Supervisor

On logical grounds, one can argue that it is most fitting for an employee's immediate superior to evaluate his or her performance. According to the reasoning, the immediate superior is in the best position to observe each subordinate. Furthermore, it is the immediate supervisor's responsibility to direct the behavior of subordinates. Thus, the immediate supervisor should, by virtue of his or her position, be able to judge the relative contribution of each subordinate to the overall performance of the organizational unit.

Upon careful reflection, however, it becomes clear that supervisors are often *not* in the best position to observe subordinate behavior. In fact, supervisors are frequently too far removed from their subordinates. They may actually spend a great deal of their time on activities such as meeting with other unit leaders, traveling, preparing budgets, and writing reports rather than on the direct monitoring of their subordinates. In addition, subordinates' activities may remove them from their superior's direct supervision, as in the case of traveling sales representatives.

Despite these possible disadvantages, employees are most frequently evaluated by their immediate superiors. As reported by Lazer and Wikstrom, roughly 95 percent of all performance appraisals involve the immediate supervisor as a rater.[1] In addition, some appraisal systems involve evaluations by (1) the individual subordinate (13 percent), (2) groups or committees (6 percent), and (3) personnel department officers (6 percent).* Although they constituted less than 1 percent each, other sources of appraisal include consultants, coworkers (or peers), and subordinates.

Self-appraisal

Many people are surprised to learn that self-appraisals are sometimes used in organizations. To be sure, such self-ratings are likely to be inflated and show little agreement with supervisor ratings, but in certain situations and with reasonable caution, self-ratings can be helpful.[2] One possibility is to combine self-ratings with supervisor ratings.[3] In such a situation, the subordinate and the superior complete identical appraisal forms. At a subsequent formal inter-

---

* The percentages represent frequency of use and total more than 100 percent because of the occasional use of multiple sources of evaluation.

view session, the two then compare their responses. For each question, the supervisor and subordinate discuss why they agree or disagree in their perceptions of the individual's conduct. If such a discussion can be carried out in a nonthreatening and supportive manner, it can provide a rich opportunity for the subordinate to gain insights and suggestions about his or her workplace behavior. In addition, the supervisor may gain understanding of the subordinate's behavior. In the process, both the supervisor and the subordinate can gain an enhanced sense of working together to improve performance.

A second use of self-rating is in conjunction with participative goal setting. In management-by-objectives (MBO) programs (see Chapter 7), a subordinate will be asked to appraise his or her own performance periodically with respect to attaining specific performance goals. Such required self-appraisals can help subordinates view their own accomplishments more honestly.

Self-ratings are also useful in self-development. In training settings, where self-insight is a primary goal, self-ratings can help a subordinate to gauge the degree of learning that has occurred.

Despite their usefulness in certain settings, self-ratings rarely have much influence on decisions about promotions, raises, transfers, and the like.

Peers or Coworkers

Appraisals by peers are rarely used, but their worth should not be ignored.[4] As you might imagine, peers are frequently able to observe a given subordinate for a longer period of time and in a wider variety of situations than is an immediate supervisor. As one result of this greater contact, peers are likely to generate more accurate assessments and predictions of each other's performance.[5] As an illustration, consider that your classmates probably know you better as a student (in terms of your study habits, interest in coursework, personal mores, and so on) than your instructors know you. Yet your instructors, with whom you usually have only very limited and formal contact (much like an immediate supervisor), will ultimately evaluate your academic performance by assigning a grade to you.

In comparison to self-ratings, peer ratings are generally less inflated.[6] Not too surprisingly, peer ratings and ratings by superiors show little agreement.[7] This lack of agreement probably occurs because subordinates tend to change their behavior when in the presence of their superior.

Peer ratings are not used in most organizations because they are susceptible to a number of potential biases. Their vulnerability to friendship effects constitutes one major liability: people are likely to rate their friends more highly.[8] Also, raters are likely to rate members of their own race more highly.[9] When there is serious competition for promotions and raises, better performers may receive harsher evaluations due to their peers' attempts to improve their own chances of obtaining rewards.

Despite these shortcomings, peer appraisals can be useful in certain situations. Most notable among these is when a group of coworkers is completing a training program (or other period of close contact) and is about to be assigned to geographically dispersed locations or distinct job assignments. If the assign-

■ **Figure 8.1**

Sources of Performance Appraisal Information

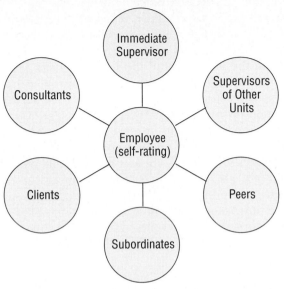

ments are predetermined and therefore independent of the appraisal exercise, peer evaluations may yield useful and accurate information for making forecasts of subsequent success or failure.

Subordinates

Another intriguing but rarely used approach to appraisal is to request anonymous performance evaluations from an individual's subordinates. Subordinates do, in fact, have a very different perspective on a supervisor's performance, although their impressions may not be uniform.[10] Of course, subordinates are likely to resist being involved in such appraisals out of fear of reprisal; when a work group is small, anonymity may be difficult to safeguard. Most subordinates also feel that it is not their responsibility to evaluate their boss, or that they are not in the best position to observe the boss's performance.

Despite these and other very rational objections, a number of organizations, including Exxon and Weyerhauser, have experimented with subordinate appraisal systems.[11] Generally, the problems inherent in such appraisals outweigh their limited potential value. Nonetheless, they should not be totally dismissed. When used as a source of personal feedback, with the intent of improving performance or self-diagnosis, subordinate appraisals may be of some value. For example, college teachers typically ask their students to complete evaluation forms at the end of a course. The resulting information can

■ **Table 8.1**

Advantages and Disadvantages of Different Appraisal Sources

Source of Appraisal	Advantages	Disadvantages
Immediate supervisor	Makes decisions on rewards	Personal bias possible
	Has perspectives on all subordinates	Supervisor may be removed from subordinates
Self	Unique perspective	Likely to be too lenient
	A useful basis for comparison	
	Useful for self-insight	
Peers	Greater exposure to appraisee	Competitive atmosphere confounds usage
	More accurate assessment	
Subordinates	Can give diagnostic-type feedback	Can subvert the leader's authority
Superiors of other units	Can be less subjective	Too removed from the individual
Customers or clients	Gives input from immediate client group	Only sees limited facet of appraisee
Consultants	Complete, thorough appraisal	Too expensive for use with all employees

help both instructors and college administrators to identify areas of deficiency. However, when students' evaluations are used for making major decisions related to promotions and raises, as they are used at some schools, there is a real danger that academic standards may slip as a result of the instructors' attempts to curry favor with their evaluators.

Other Sources of Appraisal

In addition to superiors, workers themselves, peers, and subordinates, people outside of the immediate work unit may be asked to assist in performance appraisal. These may include customers or clients, who may be surveyed for their impressions, and committees composed of managers who are one level above the individual being appraised. Sometimes an external consultant or group of consultants may be hired to conduct performance appraisals. Because of the inherent cost, this practice is usually limited to the evaluation of higher-level managers. When consultants are brought in, they usually canvass a variety of sources including the employee, peers, subordinates, superiors, and external clients before finalizing their assessment. In essence, all who would have information on the employee in question would be queried.

Figure 8.1 summarizes the common sources of information for appraising performance, and Table 8.1 lists the advantages and disadvantages of these sources. As this table suggests, no single rater or group of raters can be endorsed as satisfactory for all settings. Instead, a careful judgment must be made in each work setting.

What Should Be Appraised?

Before considering the actual appraisal process, we must examine what an evaluator will be asked to appraise. Since performance is complex and multifaceted, it cannot be assumed to have any simple or general meaning. Rather, performance must be defined in terms of the actual behaviors that an employee is expected to display in a given job. Only after performance has been defined for a given job can assessment of an employee's performance be attempted in a meaningful way.

Defining the major dimensions of performance requires a job analysis. Although there are a number of different approaches to conducting such an analysis, the common goal of each is a precise statement of the activities that constitute a job.[12] Typically, a job analysis is performed by an observer who carefully examines all available data on a given job. In the course of gathering data, the observer will usually interview the current holders of the job and the immediate supervisor. The outcome is a **job description**, a concise summary of the duties to be performed by someone who occupies the job in question. The job description consists of a series of simple descriptive statements defining the responsibilities of the job holder. For example, the job description of a secretary might include such statements as "Answers the telephone promptly" and "Handles requests for price quotations from outside vendors." A statement from the job description of a sheet-metal worker might be "Sets the cutting blades of the splicer to meet customer's requested specifications" and "Cleans up workstation area at the end of the day." As these examples suggest, the focus in a job description is on actual behaviors that are central to the conduct of the job. Job descriptions play an important role in designing an effective appraisal system because appraisals that are based on job descriptions possess greater relevance.†

How Should Appraisals Be Conducted?

Intuitively, one might think that the best appraisal system is one that is *totally objective*. In fact, such a system is not obtainable. Consider the study on psychokinesis cited in Chapter 7 that showed that even the perception of simple objective events is influenced by prior expectations. Results of that study suggest that a strong belief in an employee's ability (or lack of ability) can influence the way in which performance is observed, and ultimately interpreted. One might still argue that a "hard" measure of performance, such as annual sales, is beyond question an index of performance. However, as any salesperson will quickly tell you, sales volume is in large part a function of the quality of a territory and the quality of the product line that one is given to sell. The interpretation of sales figures, therefore, requires consideration of the extent to which external factors affect individual performance.

In addition, performance encompasses many aspects and cannot easily be assessed by a single quantifiable measure. For example, bank tellers are typi-

† Also, if challenged in court as being discriminatory, an appraisal system that is not based on a job analysis is more likely to be judged unfair (*Kirkland* v. *New York Department of Correctional Services,* 1974).

cally assessed on a performance measure called "daily over-or-short balancing," that is, whether their drawer is over or short by any amount of money at the end of the workday. Most bank tellers strongly protest the use of this measure as an index of performance. Nonetheless, the banking industry prefers it because it is relatively "hard" and summarizes a single aspect of performance — accuracy in monetary transactions. Other aspects of teller performance, such as courteousness and the speed or volume of transactions, are ignored. As this example suggests, the "hardness" of a performance measure does not ensure its relevance.

Given the need to rely on a subjective appraisal of a range of job behaviors, which are condensed over time into an overall impression in the mind of an evaluator, let us consider the major methods of performance appraisal. Each of these methods has both strengths and limitations.

Graphic Rating Scales

The most widely used performance appraisal device is the **graphic rating scale**. Such scales typically consist of a continuum of points that are anchored by mutually exclusive descriptive adjectives. For example:

Cooperative :_____:_____:_____:_____:_____: Uncooperative
             1   2   3   4   5

Industrious :_____:_____:_____:_____:_____: Lazy
             1   2   3   4   5

The evaluator places a check over the position on each continuum that best reflects his or her appraisal of an employee on that dimension.

Such rating scales are widely used, largely because they are easy to construct and complete. Unfortunately, they are also plagued by a variety of problems. One major shortcoming is the common reliance on anchors that are of little or no relevance to the actual conduct of a given job. As a result, such scales may provide little more than a format for recording a supervisor's general like or dislike of an employee. Furthermore, relying on anchors that are not explicitly tied to job behaviors may result in ratings that largely reflect sexual or racial biases. Although the research results are mixed, bias in rating does, nonetheless, appear to be quite possible.[13] A reliance on ratings that are based on behavior-specific rating formats can, however, reduce bias.[14]

When using graphic rating scales (as well as some other devices that we will consider), raters are also prone to commit a variety of reporting errors. Among the most common are halo, central tendency, leniency, and harshness errors. **Halo errors** occur when an evaluator completes all rating scales in accord with an overall impression based on only one aspect of the employee's performance, instead of judging each scale independently. In a sense, the rater's overall impression of the employee shades the entire evaluation.

Central tendency, leniency, and harshness errors are three examples of a rater's tendency to restrict his or her evaluation to a limited part of the scale. In a **central tendency error**, the rater uses only values that are in the middle range of each scale. In **leniency** and **harshness errors**, the rater generally gives extremely favorable or extremely unfavorable appraisals to the employees being

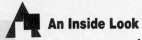

An Inside Look
Accuracy of Appraisals

Employees often complain that performance appraisals are unfair. Appraisal forms are often based on performance traits or vague qualities such as initiative, leadership, or reliability. Managers, too, often feel overwhelmed by performance appraisals. Many managers feel they need more training in how to conduct them, but few companies help.

However, researcher and trainer David DeVries claims that most managers "are much more sophisticated than the researchers realize. I think they understand the appraisal process pretty well because they are the ones who have to live with the results."

According to a study by management professor H. John Bernardin, inaccuracy in performance ratings arises more

from intentional distortions than from rating error. For example, when times are tough, managers may inflate ratings to make sure their subordinates qualify for raises, to prevent cuts to their departments, or to keep valued employees from leaving. Or consider central tendency error: From an administrative point of view, it could make sense to lump most of one's subordinates in the middle range, for by doing so, the manager might avoid unwanted comparisons and arguments with or among employees.

Psychologist Kevin Murphy says companies do not need improved rating forms as much as they need to train managers in how to be better observers. Observation skills might include gathering and recording supporting evidence, discriminating between relevant

and irrelevant information, doing selective work sampling if there is little opportunity to observe workers directly, and deciding which aspects of performance are measurable.

Ultimately, the manager has to accept that all rating techniques have limitations and select the approach that works best for him or her. For example, DeVries says, "Take traits like integrity, initiative, optimism, energy, and intelligence. Researchers today feel such traits shouldn't be used in performance reviews . . . but in business those traits are very important, subjective or not. Executives make personnel decisions based on them all the time. If they do, then those traits should be evaluated, and we researchers can't afford to ignore them."

Source: Berkeley Rice, "Performance Review: The Job Nobody Likes," *Psychology Today*, September 1985, 30–36.

rated.‡ Despite these potential pitfalls, somewhat more than half of all large organizations use graphic rating scales in their performance-appraisal systems.[15]

Rankings

Although used with less frequency than rating scales, ranking techniques offer a useful format for appraising employee performance. An **alternating ranking technique** requires that an appraiser first write down the name of the best performer in the work unit. Next, she writes down the name of the poorest performer in the unit. Then, she writes the name of the second best performer,

‡ Perhaps better than anyone, college students are familiar with all four kinds of rating errors. Halo errors sometimes occur when an instructor's grade for a student's term paper is based more on the student's performance on objective exams and daily attendance in class than on the quality of the paper. Some instructors assign grades according to a normal curve (central tendency error), while others are very generous (leniency error) or very stingy (harshness error) in assigning high grades.

■ **Figure 8.2**

Illustration of the Paired Comparison Ranking Technique

	Bill	Pete	Jackie	Julie	Mario
Bill					
Pete	Pete				
Jackie	Jackie	Pete			
Julie	Julie	Julie	Julie		
Mario	Mario	Pete	Mario	Julie	

followed by the second poorest performer, and so on. A major advantage of this simple exercise is that it forces the appraiser to "sort out" the appraisees, since everyone cannot receive the same evaluation. By spreading out the employees on a performance dimension, it is easier to make decisions about who should receive merit raises or be considered for other rewards or sanctions.

A variation on this ranking technique is the **paired comparison**, which requires the evaluator to think of each employee in conjunction with all other employees before making a judgment. Often, a paired comparison involves the creation of a matrix to aid the evaluator. Figure 8.2 shows such a matrix for a work group of five subordinates. In the cells of the matrix, the evaluator enters the name of the appraisee who is judged superior in a one-on-one comparison with each of the other subordinates. A simple tally of the number of times a person "wins" a comparison provides a summary of the relative standing of each subordinate. From the results of this tally, it is clear that Bill is the poorest performer (having won no comparisons), while Julie is the best performer (having won all comparisons). A major advantage of a paired comparison approach is its requirement that each subordinate be consciously considered in the ranking process. No individual can be accidentally overlooked by an evaluator who has to consider all subordinates simultaneously. Also, middle-range performers, who may be difficult to distinguish among as a subgroup, must be deliberately considered against one another.

A serious potential shortcoming of the paired comparison technique is that more and more comparisons must be made as a work group increases in size. When there are five subordinates, only 10 comparisons need be made. But with 20 subordinates, 190 comparisons become necessary.§

Yet another ranking format is the **forced distribution**. Currently popular at Exxon, this technique requires that the evaluator assign specified percentages of employees to each of several classifications.[16] For example, he may be required to assign 10 percent of the employees to each of the categories *excel-*

---

§ A simple equation can be used to determine the number of comparisons to be made: $n(n-1)/2$, where n is the number of employees. Therefore, with 7 employees, the number of comparisons is $7(6)/2 = 21$.

lent and *unacceptable,* 20 percent to each of the categories *above average* and *poor,* and 40 percent to the category *average.* This approach also forces the evaluator to sort out his subordinates. But while avoiding some errors, such as leniency and harshness, it may introduce another: an imposed distribution that is unjustifiable. For example, a normal performance distribution may be imposed, which would assume that most performance falls in the average range. Such an assumption may be unwarranted because entire units can be expected to differ in terms of performance. Some units may be composed of mostly superior performers, while others may contain many poor performers.

One possible problem with any ranking technique is that the results may be difficult to share with subordinates who receive low rankings. Employees tend to have a difficult time accepting the assessment that they are below average (although, by definition, half of the employees in any group must be considered below average).**

Behaviorally Anchored Rating Scales

In recent years, there have been several attempts to develop performance rating scales that are more closely tied to actual employee behavior. **Behaviorally anchored rating scales (BARS)** use examples of employee behavior as anchors for performance dimensions.[17] †† When carefully constructed, BARS are potentially very accurate devices for appraising employee performance.

The creation of a BARS system involves several steps. First, statements that describe competent, average, and incompetent behavior are gathered from employees and supervisors. Supervisors then categorize the statements in terms of performance dimensions, such as interpersonal skills, technical know-how, and so on, and discard those statements that are ambiguous or not classifiable. A group of judges (made up of supervisors from other units or specialized job analysts) are then asked to rate each incident on a seven-point scale in terms of whether the incident represents outstanding (7), average (4), or poor (1) performance. Specific incidents are then selected to serve as anchors or benchmarks on the final scale, with the average of the judges' ratings of an incident used as the numerical index for that anchor. Figure 8.3 shows an example of a BARS for the performance dimension of motivation.

BARS have several distinct advantages as tools for appraising performance. Because the scales are phrased in job-relevant terminology, they are more meaningful to raters than scales that attempt to assess traits. Also, the initial involvement of raters (and sometimes ratees) in the creation of the scales helps to persuade the participants of the relevance and importance of the appraisal process. In addition, the behavioral emphasis of BARS can help the rater to identify a worker's specific strengths and weaknesses, which can then be discussed at a performance feedback session.

***

** One can extend this simple relative assessment notion of "average" to generate some surprising statements. For example, consider that one-half of all medical doctors graduated from medical school in the bottom half of their class!

†† Behaviorally anchored rating scales (BARS) are called behavioral expectation scales (BES) by some authors.[18]

■ **Figure 8.3**

Example of a Behaviorally Anchored Rating Scale

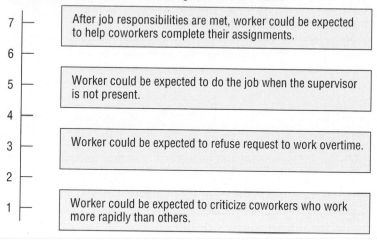

Motivation—the Desire and Willingness to Work Hard

7 — After job responsibilities are met, worker could be expected to help coworkers complete their assignments.

6 —

5 — Worker could be expected to do the job when the supervisor is not present.

4 —

3 — Worker could be expected to refuse request to work overtime.

2 —

1 — Worker could be expected to criticize coworkers who work more rapidly than others.

A practical problem that sometimes arises with BARS is that a rater may have difficulty seeing any similarity between the extremely specific behavioral anchors and a subordinate's performance. In such instances, raters are likely to rely more on their expectations than on their observations. A second problem is that BARS are relatively time consuming and expensive to construct. Because they are tailored for specific jobs and because job requirements tend to change over time, BARS cannot necessarily be used across jobs or over a long period for the same job.

Behavioral Observation Scales

Another behavioral approach to appraising employee performance has been developed by Gary Latham and Kenneth Wexley.[19] Their **behavioral observation scales (BOS)** are developed using a critical incident technique (like that for BARS) in which jobholders and supervisors generate examples of performance behaviors that characterize an entire job. Any behavioral statements judged too rare to be observed ("Has the smell of liquor on his breath" is one example Latham and Wexley cite) are then excluded from the final product.

BOS differ from BARS in that BOS require the evaluator to indicate the *frequency* with which a worker exhibits a specific behavior, whereas BARS ask the evaluator to define superior versus inferior performance. Also, with BOS the focus is on the frequency with which a ratee is observed engaging in the specific behaviors, whereas with BARS the ratee is judged on having displayed a particular behavior during a specific rating period.

Figure 8.4 shows several statements from a BOS that was designed for a department store salesclerk. Note that these items focus on specific performance-related actions. As such, they are very close in content to the kinds of

■   Figure 8.4

Example of a BOS for a Salesclerk

1. Stops talking to another salesclerk as soon as a customer approaches him/her.
   Almost Never   1   2   3   4   5   Almost Always
2. Closes a sale by saying "thank you" to the customer.
   Almost Never   1   2   3   4   5   Almost Always
3. Comes to work without wearing company uniform.
   Almost Never   1   2   3   4   5   Almost Always

statements that are included in job descriptions based on job analyses. Thus, BOS can greatly enhance performance feedback sessions by helping to focus the discussion on specific behaviors instead of personal feelings and emotions.

In order to help the rater interpret the numerical values of BOS items, Latham and Wexley suggest that the following guidelines be used:

Assign a Numerical Rating of	If the Behavior Is	Observed % of the Time
1		0–64
2		65–74
3		75–84
4		85–94
5		95–100

A rater thus selects a numerical value that corresponds to the percentage of the time that the employee displayed the behavior.

Because BOS are a fairly recent innovation, there is relatively little evidence on their limitations.[20] However, in comparing BOS with BARS in terms of reducing rater bias and errors, Bernardin found that BOS were as good as BARS, and Bernardin, Alvares, and Cranny found that they were better.[21]

Management-by-Objectives

In Chapter 7, we considered management-by-objectives (MBO) as a means of *motivating* individual performance. But MBO can also be used in *evaluating* individual performance. Recall from our earlier discussion that the essential elements of an MBO program are (1) the supervisor and each subordinate meet to establish specific goals and the means to attain them, (2) the supervisor aids the subordinates in their efforts to reach the established goals, and (3) the supervisor and each subordinate meet at a later prespecified time to review the extent of goal attainment. The third element in this process, the review and appraisal of goal attainment, represents a performance appraisal exercise. The deliberate tying of organizational rewards to goal attainment can also have a powerful impact on enhancing performance.

Despite their virtues, MBO programs are not without potential pitfalls. For example, they generate additional paperwork and time-consuming meetings — two things that most workers prefer to avoid. In some instances, when rewards (such as merit pay) are tied to goal attainment, subordinates may try to set easy goals and resist taking responsibility for their failure to attain goals. Also, the focus of MBO on attaining specific goals may lead to greater success in some areas while sacrificing accomplishment in other areas that are not being explicitly measured. For example, a sales manager may actively seek to increase her number of new clients because a goal has been set on this dimension. As a result of focusing so much effort and time on acquiring new clients, however, she may pay less attention to maintaining the satisfaction of former, more established clients — something that was not explicitly included in the MBO goals statement. The net result of some MBO programs may be success on certain emphasized (and usually quantifiable) performance dimensions, at the sacrifice of performance on unemphasized, and often less easily quantifiable, dimensions.

Assessment Centers

Perhaps the most elaborate method of appraising managerial ability is through an assessment center. An **assessment center** is a site where appraisals of individual managerial skills are conducted over a period of several days. The appraisal includes interviews, testing, simulations, peer appraisals, and appraisals by experts who observe candidates during their stay at the center. Strictly speaking, assessment centers are designed to appraise individuals' *current* managerial ability as opposed to their *past performance*. The estimate of present ability is then frequently used in forecasting whether an individual is suitable for promotion to a higher-level management position.

Before their adoption by American industry during the 1950s, live-in centers where candidates were appraised by observing their performance in simulations and games were used by the German, British, and United States military during World War II.‡‡ As part of their remilitarization during the 1930s, the German High Command devised a live-in situational testing scheme for assessing military officers. Their assessment focused on whether the officers possessed a "practical disposition." To document this disposition, hidden cameras recorded candidates' facial expressions while they engaged in stress-inducing tasks, such as pulling an expanding-spring exerciser that sent out increasing levels of electric current as it was pulled. Although less interested in stress tolerance, the British and Americans created assessment centers in the 1940s to close an emerging "assessment center gap" with the Germans. The American assessment centers were largely used by the Office of Strategic Service (the forerunner of the CIA) for selecting army volunteers to serve as spies. The OSS model for assessment centers became the foundation for later centers in American organizations, such as AT&T, SOHIO, and IBM.

A typical schedule of events at an assessment center (then and now) might include a lengthy interview covering personal and work history, a battery of mental ability and personality tests, participation in a leaderless group

‡‡ The original creation of situational assessment, however, is credited to Imperial China, circa 220 B.C.[22]

discussion or a formal debate (in which participants are asked to discuss a controversial topic while a group of assessors records each individual's reactions and mannerisms), role playing in front of an audience, and peer appraisals.

In recent years, it has become very common to include an *in-basket exercise* — a simulation in which a participant is asked to go through a stack of papers (consisting of memos, production reports, letters, and the like) that are allegedly taken from a manager's basket of incoming mail. During a one- or two-hour period, the participant must decide how to handle each document contained in the in-basket. For example, in response to a certain memo, a participant may decide to send a letter, schedule a meeting with subordinates, or do nothing at all. The participant's responses are then scored by trained judges in accordance with fairly elaborate grading schemes. In essence, an in-basket exercise simulates the daily activities of most managers. As a simulation, it can help to identify individuals who have the judgment necessary to make high-quality decisions.[23]

One might conjecture that some people could "fake their way" through a three-day assessment. Such an occurrence would be highly unlikely because it would be difficult to maintain a facade for such an extended period. During the course of the experience, observers also keep fairly constant watch on the participants. For example, at athletic events and social functions (such as cocktail parties in the evening), the observers mentally take notes on the conduct of participants. And if a participant clearly displays a tendency to "fake it," this becomes another bit of evidence that will be "grist for the mill" in the final appraisal.

Based on their observations, the assessment center's staff prepares a report on each participant's suitability for promotion. The report is usually fairly detailed and describes the observed strengths and weaknesses of the individual.

A number of studies have been conducted to determine whether the reports generated by assessment center personnel can predict an individual's later success as a manager.[24] By and large, the results suggest that assessment centers can successfully predict later job performance, job progress in terms of pay, and job potential. Several especially well-designed studies, in which the reports from the assessment center were withheld from the candidate's supervisor in order to eliminate the possibility of a self-fulfilling prophecy (see Chapter 7), also concluded that assessment centers can identify individuals who possess key management abilities.

Assessment centers are not without shortcomings, however. The cost of sending a single employee to an assessment center can vary from $600 to as much as $1,000. In addition, the work-group dynamics may change after an individual has been sent to an assessment center. Coworkers may label such a person a "fast-tracker." This can either lead to serious resentment or help guarantee the individual's later success due to a self-fulfilling prophecy.[25]

Another potential drawback is that the center's observers may not be sufficiently familiar with a specific organization or with the positions within an organization to provide useful forecasts of success. Instead, the observers may rely on stereotypes or thumbnail sketches of the jobs for which candidates are being appraised. To avoid such problems, an organization may employ its own managers to serve as observers. These managers, who are usually one or two levels above the candidates, are then trained to administer the exercises and serve as observers. The use of upper-level managers as observers also helps to "sell" the results of the assessment center to the people who will be most interested in the outcome.

The Feedback Interview

No matter what instrument or appraisal method is used, the results must be constructively conveyed to the subordinate in order to produce the desired effects on performance.[26] Most researchers agree that knowledge of appraisal results can enhance employee performance and that the best forum for providing such information is the **feedback interview**. Although the goal of such a session is to establish a give-and-take atmosphere that will encourage corrective changes, the more frequent outcome is emotional tension and defensiveness. Managers invariably report that performance feedback interviews make them very uncomfortable.[27] Subordinates likewise find the experience disagreeable because they frequently disagree with their superiors' appraisals.[28] The tendency to reject superiors' suggestions stems from the fact that most employees view their performance as above average. For example, Carrol and Schneier asked 249 managers to rate themselves as below average, average, or above average on a number of performance dimensions.[29] The mean response across all dimensions was that 67 percent viewed themselves as above-average performers! Furthermore, the person giving the feedback may not have sufficient credibility or power to be effective.[30] An evaluator must be viewed as credible before an appraisee will respect and accept feedback. And if the evaluator also has power (that is, the ability to reward and punish), the appraisee is even more likely to accept his or her comments. When the appraiser lacks credibility or power, the employee is likely to look for other sources of feedback about performance, such as coworkers, himself or herself, subordinates, or the job itself. If the other sources disagree with the evaluator, the employee may adopt their views as a way of protecting his or her self-esteem. Because of these obstacles, many organizations, such as GTE, provide training programs for supervisors on how to conduct a feedback interview.[31]

Conducting a Feedback Interview

When conducting a performance feedback interview, an evaluator can take a number of steps to enhance the process's likelihood of success.§§

Preparation   To be effective in conveying his or her point of view, the evaluator must be able to support comments with facts. Thus, it is important for the evaluator to prepare carefully for the interview. This entails gathering and reviewing all available records of the candidate's performance. For example,

§§ Many of the techniques discussed in this section were originally summarized in a review of the literature by Burke, Weitzel, and Weir.[32]

the evaluator should examine the candidate's record on a variety of dimensions, such as absenteeism, quantity and quality of output, tardiness, and the like, to get a total picture of the individual's performance and to note specific instances that call for comment. Most good evaluators also prepare an outline of the points that they intend to cover, which enables them to stay on track during the interview.

Out of fairness, the employee should be given advance notice of the meeting and information about its primary purpose, that is, whether it will pertain to merit raises, personal development, performance goal setting, or another area. This will give the employee time to prepare his or her thoughts and comments.

As an opening to the interview itself, many appraisers like to ask employees to comment on their own performance. For example, the evaluator may begin by saying, "Tell me how you view your own progress and problems in your job." Such an opening invites the employee's participation, which is a highly desired reaction, since the more subordinates are permitted to express their opinions during a feedback interview, the more satisfied they are likely to be with the appraisal experience.[33]

Phrasing Comments   When providing explicit (and especially critical) appraisal information to a subordinate, an effective evaluator will focus on problems and avoid personalities. For example, the evaluator will not make comments about personal traits, such as, "You don't strike me as a very ambitious person," but rather will keep the feedback fairly specific and behaviorally based. Thus, instead of saying, "You're tardy too often," the evaluator will say: "You've been late for the start of your shift eight times during the past six months. Since we expect an employee to be late no more than once a month, can you suggest some ways that you might be able to achieve this standard in the coming months?" And in place of "You need to improve the quality of your work," an effective evaluator will say: "During the past year, our quality-assurance crew has had to reject 22 percent of the output from your machine. The average reject rate for all other operators is only 2 percent. How can we reduce your reject rate to make it closer to the average?"

Sometimes, an appraiser has strong feelings about a subordinate's personal characteristics and behaviors. For example, he or she may not like the way an employee dresses or talks. If personal characteristics are relevant to the job — as dress and speech are for salesclerks, repairers who visit customers in their homes, and many other workers — they can be legitimately discussed during a feedback interview. But if attire and other personal habits are not job relevant, it is best for the appraiser to try to develop greater tolerance for human diversity.

When it is impossible to avoid criticizing an individual, an effective evaluator will state his or her criticisms without hostility and clearly explain why the action or inaction cannot be continued. For example, the evaluator will point out the consequences of poor performance for people both inside and outside the organization. After voicing criticism, the evaluator should carefully and with an open mind listen to any explanations that the subordinate may offer. Following a complete discussion, the two should work out a series of steps for remedying the problem and set a follow-up date for appraising the progress toward change.

The Sandwich Approach In a feedback interview, the identification of good performance is as important as the correction of substandard performance. In light of this, some performance appraisal specialists suggest that the evaluator highlight the positive points of an employee's performance early in the interview. The evaluator can then lead the discussion to the negative aspects of performance and, finally, close the conversation with several additional positive points. This positive-negative-positive sequence is called the **sandwich approach** to providing feedback. Many appraisers find themselves using this technique almost instinctively. Perhaps this is due to a natural tendency to try to minimize defensiveness by starting out with upbeat comments and to maintain good working relations by ending on a positive note. Critics, however, contend that the sandwich technique may actually blunt the intended purpose of a critical evaluation. The use of positive statements at the beginning and end of the session may mask the intended message of the need for improvement. At present, there is no evidence on the sandwich technique's effectiveness in enhancing the communication of feedback or in changing subsequent performance.

Limiting Criticism If criticism will be a major focus of a feedback session, the evaluator should limit the comments to one or two problem areas to avoid overwhelming the employee and to decrease the potential for defensiveness and conflict. Under even the best circumstances, most people have a very low tolerance for criticism and, when it is given in heavy doses (even if well packaged and presented as a problem-solving exercise), many people find criticism impossible to accept.

Closing the Interview As the feedback interview draws to a close, it is useful to rephrase the agreed-upon steps for improving performance. For example, the supervisor might say, "Let's review our agreement. Next Thursday, you'll talk with Bud about getting his department to respond more quickly to our requests for materials. Then I'll speak with Bud's supervisor the following week if there's no change in their response to our needs."

In closing the session, the appraiser should offer his or her assistance to the subordinate. This offer should be explicit and genuine. By offering to help the subordinate (especially by removing obstacles), a supervisor can minimize his or her role as judge and enhance the subordinate's perception of the supervisor as counselor or coach.

Finally, a supervisor should not wait for a company-mandated appraisal session to provide feedback to subordinates. Daily informal feedback about an employee's positive and negative performance will actually aid in making formal appraisals more effective. Informal appraisals let employees know that the supervisor understands and is concerned with their performance. As a comparison, consider that most sports figures work with their coaches daily

OB Focus

Firing Practices

How employers handle firing has become more important than ever in light of court verdicts holding that some firings have breached employment contracts. According to California lawyer H. Bradley Jones, "Wrongful discharge is . . . even more dangerous than medical malpractice, since few insurance companies sell insurance coverage to protect employers against wrongful discharge lawsuits."

Some companies have hired business consultants or law firms to help them set up programs to avoid wrongful discharge lawsuits. However, Chicago lawyer Paul Cherner counsels against extreme actions. Among the precautions Cherner recommends is to institute a formal system for performance evaluation.

Such a system is the first step in handling firing fairly. If an employee is performing poorly, even just after having been hired, the supervisor should tell him or her that performance is not up to par. The supervisor should set goals for improved performance and help the employee succeed. If the employee doesn't improve, the supervisor should repeat this procedure. If the employee still doesn't improve, he or she should be given a set time in which to meet certain clear standards and told that failure to improve will result in termination. This procedure lets the employee know where he or she stands throughout employment with the company.

If firing is still necessary, the supervisor should start by gathering information. If the

personnel department has overlooked anything — e.g., the employee's pension will vest in two more months, his wife has been in the hospital — it is better to find out before letting the ax fall.

At the termination meeting, the supervisor should be businesslike but sympathetic and should get to the point immediately. Then the supervisor should review the termination benefits the company is offering. Sometimes a company will hire an outplacement specialist to help the employee find the next job. When this is the case, the supervisor should have the employee see the outplacement specialist right away. The employee will recover best when able to start reconstructing his or her career immediately.

Sources: Jill Andresky, "Fear of Firing," *Forbes*, December 2, 1985, 90; Walter Kiechek III, "How to Fire Someone," *Fortune*, March 31, 1986, 166–167.

rather than waiting until contract negotiation time to discuss performance enhancement.

Legal Aspects of Performance Appraisal

Performance appraisal systems form the basis for many important personnel decisions. Promotions, salary raises and cuts, layoffs, and demotions are based on the outcomes of such systems. Given the significant consequences of performance appraisals and the possibility of bias entering into the evaluation process, a number of government regulations have been created to safeguard the groups of employees (especially women and minorities) who are most likely to be victimized by such bias.[34] These government regulations, which include the Equal Pay Act of 1963, the Civil Rights Act of 1964, the Age Discrimination in Employment Act of 1967, and the Vocational Rehabilitation Act of 1973, require that performance be documented in accordance with certain standards when making personnel-related decisions. The Civil Rights Act of 1964 even created a separate federal agency (the Equal Employment Opportunity Commission) to oversee employers' compliance with a set of uniform guidelines for protecting employees' rights:[35] (cf Federal Register, 1978).*** When employees have charged their employers with discriminatory practices in appraisal (as well as initial hiring) systems, the courts have frequently ruled in favor of the employees when one or more specific shortcomings have been identified.

Adverse Impact

A primary issue in discrimination suits is whether the company's actions have an **adverse impact** on a legally protected group. For example, an employer may be accused of having a policy (either formal or informal) that prevents members of a protected group from being promoted. To determine if the allegation is true, the employer's record for promoting individuals from the protected group would be compared with percentages for the same group in the population at large. For example, a construction firm in a large metropolitan area may have only 2 percent of its supervisory positions held by blacks. If data (usually taken from Department of Labor surveys of labor pool availability) suggest that 15 percent is a more reasonable expected proportion, the employer may be liable for discriminatory practices in promoting or hiring or both.

One of the more common checks for adverse impact is to compare a company's rejection rates of protected and nonprotected group members, a process known as applying the **four-fifths rule.** According to this rule, adverse impact exists if a protected group's selection rate for employment decisions (i.e., hiring, promotion, and so on) is less than four-fifths, or 80 percent, of the selection rate of the nonprotected group. For example, a said company's promotion rate is 40 percent for males and 10 percent for females. Given that 10 percent is less than four-fifths of 40 percent ($.8 \times 40 = 32$ percent), adverse impact may exist for female employees. Of course, the four-fifths rule is simply a rule of thumb and, as such, is usually interpreted as merely suggesting discrimination. Other evidence, such as how recently female employees have been hired for certain positions and the company's overall record in providing equal employment opportunities, would have to be considered in determining whether an employer is guilty of discrimination.

Interestingly, an employer can still use appraisal systems that have adverse impact as long as the systems are shown to be valid, that is, as long as they are highly relevant to the job and accurately predict subsequent performance. Also, an appraisal system does not have to be validated if there is no initial evidence of discriminatory impact.††† Of course, it requires a serious commitment from an organization to establish that its employment practices are job relevant and predictively useful. In essence, federal (and many state)

*** Strictly speaking, the Civil Rights Act prohibits discrimination only on the basis of sex, race, religion, color, or national origin. Discrimination on the basis of age or physical disability is covered by separate legislation, but enforcement is overseen by the Equal Employment Opportunity Commission.

††† It can be said that an appraisal system may even be fairly stupid (such as feeling for lumps on a person's head) as long as it is stupid fairly (i.e., it does not reject a larger percentage of protected group members as compared with other candidates).

regulations simply require that employers subscribe to sound principles derived from the behavioral side of management. To ignore these principles leaves an employer vulnerable to charges of discrimination.

Penalties

The penalties for being found guilty of discrimination can be substantial (running into the millions of dollars). They may include back pay settlements to all members of a protected group who were excluded from promotion or transfer opportunities, the forced promotion and training of members of the aggrieved group, fines, court costs, the loss of federal contracts, and/or the hiring of a compliance officer to monitor subsequent employment practices to ensure cooperation with the imposed goals for promotions and hiring.

Legally Defensible Appraisal Systems

To avoid such problems, an employer should know what attributes make a performance appraisal system legally defensible. In a review of this issue, Klasson, Thompson, and Lubben identified a number of critical features.[36] First of all, an ideal appraisal system would be formal and standardized. It would, therefore, be done in accordance with a written policy, and all appraisees would be treated alike, regardless of sex, race, and so on. The appraisal system would be based on a thorough job analysis that would lead to clear standards and fixed measures of performance. Subjective evaluations by a single supervisor would be only one component of an appraisal process that included input from the appraisee and performance-based data. In addition, the appraisers would be given training in how to rate employees. In the present litigious atmosphere, it is essential that every decision to promote, transfer, or terminate an employee on any basis other than seniority be documented with substantial evidence.‡‡‡

The court case of *Rowe v. General Motors* helps to identify many of the shortcomings that still exist in today's performance appraisal systems. In this case, the recommendations of supervisors (all of whom were white) were based on vague and subjective standards. These recommendations led to a lack of promotions for black employees and, consequently, discriminatory treatment. The court's ruling that discrimination existed was based on five points:

1. The supervisor's recommendations were the critical factor in the promotion process.

2. Supervisors were not instructed on the qualifications needed for promotion.

---

‡‡‡ For further information on discriminatory issues, the interested reader should consult Arvey.[37] Several important court decisions have served to direct legal thinking in the area of employer appraisal: *Griggs v. Duke Power Co.*, 3 FEP Cases 175 (1972); *Moody v. Albermarle Paper Co.*, 10 FEP Cases 1181 (1975); *Rogers v. International Paper Co.*, 10 FEP Cases 404 (1975); *Rowe v. General Motors Corp.*, 4 FEP Cases 445 (1972); *Brito v. Zia Co.*, 5 FEP Cases 1207 (1973); *Wade v. Mississippi Cooperative Extension Service*, 372 F. Supp. 126, 7 FEP 282 (1974); *James v. Stockham Values and Fittings*, 15 FEP 827 (1977); *Watson v. Fort Worth Bank and Trust*, 108 S. Ct. 2777, 2790-91 (1988); *Wards Cove Packing Company v. Atonio*, 109 S. Ct. 3115 (1989).

3.   The standards were subjective and vague.

4.   Employees were not given notification of opportunities for promotion.

5.   The appraisal system had no safeguards against discriminatory practices.

In light of these potential shortcomings, it is worth considering how some of the performance appraisal techniques discussed in this chapter measure up to regulations against discriminatory treatment.

Latham and Wexley contend that both BARS and BOS satisfy the requirements of federal legislation in two ways: they allow employees to participate in the identification of a job's critical elements and they focus on actual job behaviors rather than on subjective traits.[38]

The possibility that assessment centers may have adverse impact on women and minorities has been closely studied. In their study of nearly 5,000 women who were assessed during the late 1960s and early 1970s, Moses and Boehm found that the same factors that predicted success for male managers (such as leadership, decision-making ability, and organizing skills) also predicted success for female managers.[39] In another study, Huck reported that assessment centers were as valid for females and blacks as they were for males and whites.[40]

Other performance appraisal devices, such as graphic rating scales and rankings, although not inherently biased, are frequently regarded with suspicion by the courts if they are not clearly derived from an analysis of a job's content. Management-by-objectives systems have not been seriously studied from the standpoint of discrimination against protected groups. It is likely that MBO and other goal-setting systems are fairly defensible, however, and that they minimize disparate treatment if they are properly established and employed in accordance with an appropriate and consistent philosophy.

Summary

1. List reasons for appraising performance.
The basic goal of performance appraisal is to maintain or improve employee effectiveness. Other objectives are to help supervisors decide on relative compensation; to help in evaluating subordinates' suitability for training and development; to help in making appropriate job changes; to open communication between supervisors and subordinates; and to provide subordinates with feedback about their performance.

2. Describe different timetables for performance appraisals.
Annual reviews on a common review date help organizations set budgets that incorporate raises based on the reviews. Annual reviews based on the anniversary of an employee's hiring spread evaluation throughout the year, so that supervisors avoid the burden of appraising everyone at once. Appraisals at naturally occurring events fulfill the need for feedback, as after a probationary period or completion of a major project.

3. Discuss the relative merits of performance appraisal by the immediate supervisor, the employee being appraised, peers or coworkers, subordinates, and people outside the work unit.

Table 8.1 shows advantages and disadvantages of appraisals by these different sources.

4. Describe the process of job analysis.

Job analysis states precisely the activities a job comprises. An observer examines all available data on a given job, including information gathered from interviews with those doing the job and with their supervisor. The observer then writes a job description describing the actual behaviors that are central to the conduct of the job.

5. Explain why performance appraisal cannot be totally objective.

Prior expectations influence even the perception of objective events. The supervisor's beliefs about the employee's ability influence his or her observations of the employee's performance. Also, performance includes many behaviors, some of which can be difficult to measure.

6. List methods of performance appraisal.

Performance appraisal methods include graphic rating scales; rankings, including the alternating ranking technique, paired comparison approach, and forced distribution; behaviorally anchored rating scales (BARS); behavioral observation scales (BOS); management-by-objectives; and assessment centers.

7. Describe sources of tension in feedback interviews.

Tension can arise because subordinates frequently disagree with the supervisor's appraisal of their performance. Also, the evaluator may not have enough credibility or power for the feedback to be effective.

8. List the elements of a successful feedback interview.

The elements of a successful feedback interview are preparation; comments that focus on problems, not personalities; a positive-negative-positive sequence of comments (the sandwich approach); placing a limit on the amount of criticism; and closing the interview on a positive note and with an offer of assistance.

9. Describe how courts evaluate whether a company's actions have had an adverse impact on a group.

The courts review the employer's record for promoting individuals from the group and compare this to percentages for the group in the population at large. Another way is to compare a company's rejection rates of protected and non-protected group members.

10. Describe the characteristics of a legally defensible appraisal system.

A legally defensible appraisal system should be valid; formal and standardized; based on a thorough job analysis leading to clear standards of performance; based on input from the supervisor, employee, and performance-based data; and given by supervisors trained in how to use the system. Promotions, transfers, and terminations should be documented.

Key Terms

Job description

Graphic rating scale

Halo error

Central tendency error

Leniency error

Harshness error

Alternating ranking technique

Paired comparison

Forced distribution

Behaviorally anchored rating scales
   (BARS)

Behavioral observation scales (BOS)

Assessment center

Feedback interview

Sandwich approach

Adverse impact

Four-fifths rule

Review and Discussion Questions

1.   How do companies benefit from performance appraisal systems?

2.   Should performance appraisals take place every day? Explain your
     answer.

3.   How can self-appraisal be used as part of the process of performance
     appraisal? Do organizations generally use self-appraisal as the basis for
     a promotion or a raise?

4.   Which of the following are appropriate components of a job descrip-
     tion? Explain your answers.
     a.   Types reports accurately and neatly.
     b.   Is courteous to customers.
     c.   Performs accounting tasks.
     d.   Maintains weekly production log.

5.   Describe the advantages and disadvantages of the following appraisal
     techniques: graphic rating scales, ranking, behaviorally anchored rat-
     ing scales, behavioral observation scales, management-by-objectives,
     and assessment centers.

6.   Carol Skinner is about to give a feedback interview for the first time.
     Remembering that she has often felt tense when being appraised by
     her own supervisor, Carol wants to understand why feedback inter-
     views can be so uncomfortable. What reasons can you give her? How
     can she make the meeting go more smoothly?

7.   Don Direct, manager of the housewares department of Big Buys de-
     partment store, is not the most tactful supervisor. Salespeople often
     storm out of his office following their annual feedback interview. In
     fact, a few employees have even quit during a feedback interview.
     Following are comments Don has made to employees; suggest a more
     appropriate alternative for each:
     a.   "You're too sloppy."
     b.   "You don't seem very ambitious."
     c.   "I don't like your tone of voice."

8.   When Beatrice Bean evaluates the lab technicians in the microbiology
     lab she supervises, she likes to discuss all the negative points first, to

get them over with. What do you think of this approach? Can you
suggest a better alternative?

9. How can an organization set up a performance appraisal system that
    will reduce its vulnerability to charges of discrimination?

10. Evaluate the concept of adverse impact. Is it beneficial to companies?
    To employees?

■ Critical Incident

Is an Improvement Needed?

Omicron Photo Processing Co. is a fairly large organization that processes film from many different retail outlets, such as drugstores, discount
stores, and so on. They have over 60 employees and use a graphic rating scale
to assess worker performance.

Last week the personnel director called you with a concern about the
performance appraisal system. The staff of the personnel department believe
that the present system does not provide the information needed to improve
job performance and allows the raters to permit personal bias to enter the
picture. There is also concern about the inadequacy of information to develop
and/or improve needed training programs.

When representatives of the department met with the various supervisors
and managers to voice these concerns, the supervisors claimed that there are no
problems with the present system and that they know who the better performers are. They were also concerned that any other system would place more
demands on their time.

The staff in personnel would like to adopt a Behaviorally Anchored
Rating Scale (BARS) system. They believe such a system would provide more
reliable and valid information than the present system.

The personnel director would like to demonstrate the advantages of a
BARS system to the supervisors. He would like your advice on the following
questions:

1. What are the advantages and disadvantages of a BARS system as com-
    pared with the graphic rating scale?

2. Would a BARS system be more reliable and valid than the present
    system? Why?

3. Briefly, design a demonstration to show that a BARS system would be
    more effective than the present system.

Source: Written by Bruce Kemelgor, University of Louisville; used by permission.

■ Experiential Exercise

Designing Behaviorally Anchored Rating Scales

The text material emphasizes the many advantages that Behaviorally
Anchored Rating Scales (BARS) have over the typical trait-oriented appraisal

instrument. First, BARS are job oriented. They focus specifically on what employees do, not on vague personality traits, such as loyalty, initiative, or creativity. Second, BARS enable the employee to understand why a particular rating was given. Feedback to the employee is job related. BARS also make it easy for the supervisor to tell the employee what he or she must do to improve the ratings. Finally, BARS are a quantitative technique that generates a total point rating for each employee. Thus, BARS scores can be easily tied to personnel decisions involving compensation, training, or promotion.

This activity asks you to work with several of your classmates to create a BARS for the position of college instructor.

1. As a member of the entire class, you should participate in generating a list of 5 to 10 job dimensions for the position of college instructor. Such dimensions might include "classroom presentation skills" or "being well prepared for class."

2. Your instructor will divide the class into several groups of 5 to 7 students. Each group will select one of the job dimensions. Using the job dimension (e.g., "use of examples in class"), develop a list of 10 to 15 specific incidents that represent both effective and ineffective behavior.

3. Each group member independently should rate each of the behavioral incidents according to the following scale:
    10 = Excellent performance
     8 = Good performance
     6 = Moderately good performance
     4 = Moderately poor performance
     2 = Poor performance
     0 = Very poor performance

4. As a group, examine the incidents for high rater agreement. You should discard those incidents where there is wide variance among the ratings. For those incidents that will be used, compute an average rating.

5. Prepare the BARS for your particular job dimension. A model scale is provided. (This sample scale is one of many job dimensions for the position of salesperson.) Use the average rating given each incident to place them in an appropriate order.

Client Relationship

Works hard to establish client rapport. Respects every client and appreciates opportunities.	**10** This person has the highest regard for all clients. Looks at even the smallest client as V.I.P. Clients are constantly made to feel important and respected. Constant appreciation for client's business.
	—8— This person is appreciative for his/her clients and the client knows it. A good working relationship between this person and his/her clients. Clients show a dependency on this person.
	—6— This person grooms clients and gleans from the top. Desires to work only with the best and only with a number of clients that can be handled properly. Does not object to passing prospect names to other sales personnel.
Clients regarded as sources of money. Does not work to establish relationship.	This person works with any client who can be approached. Looks for the income vs. developing a continuous business relationship. Not necessarily the right person to represent the company's best interests.
	—4— This person is primarily an order taker. Good manners, but may never see the client. The client forms an opinion of the company from communicating with this person.
	—2— This person accepts clients as a means to receiving an income. This person is never close to the client. A company-client relationship does not exist.
Lacks respect for clients and possibly self in this position. Very marginal contribution.	This person gives the employer short days. Fabricates daily reports. Frequently turns clients off. Company growth is marginal.

6. Your instructor may choose to use one of many options to present the results to the entire class. Using the BARS instrument that you have developed, discuss the following questions:

   a. What do you perceive to be the relative advantages of BARS versus the instructor evaluation form that is presently being used at your institution?

   b. How could the *process* of constructing BARS be helpful to both instructors and students?

Source: Written by Bruce Kemelgor, University of Louisville; used by permission.

Notes

1. R.I. Lazer and W.S. Wikstrom, *Appraising Managerial Performance: Current Practices and Future Direction.* Conference Board Report No. 723 (New York: The Conference Board, Inc., 1977), 26.

2. R.W. Beatty, C.E. Schneier, and J.R. Beatty, "An Empirical Investigation of Perceptions of Rater Behavior, Frequency, and Rater Behavior Change Using Behavioral Expectation Scales," *Personnel Psychology* 33 (1977): 647–658; G.L. Thornton, "Psychometric Properties of Self-Appraisals of Job Performance," *Personnel Psychology* 33 (1980): 236–271.

3. K.S. Teel, "Self-Appraisal Revisited," *Personnel Journal* 57 (1978): 364–367.

4. F.J. Landy and J.L. Farr, "Performance

Rating," *Psychological Bulletin* 87 (1980): 72–107.

5. A.K. Korman, "The Prediction of Managerial Performance: A Review," *Personnel Psychology* 21 (1968): 295–322.

6. M.J. Kavanaugh, A.C. MacKinney, and L. Wolins, "Issues in Managerial Performance: Multi-trait, Multi-method Analyses of Ratings," *Psychological Bulletin* 75 (1971): 34–49; E.E. Lawler III, "The Multitrait–Multirater Approach to Measuring Managerial Job Performance," *Journal of Applied Psychology* 51 (1967): 369–381.

7. K.N. Wexley, "Roles of Performance Appraisal in Organizations," in *Organizational Behavior,* ed. S. Kerr (Columbus, Ohio: Grid Publishing Co., 1979).

8. A.S. DeNisi and J.L. Mitchell, "An Analysis of Peer Ratings as Predictors and Criterion Measures and a Proposed New Application," *Academy of Management Review* 3 (1978): 369–374.

9. J.E. DeJung and J. Kaplan, "Some Differential Effects of Race of Rater and Ratee on Early Peer Ratings of Combat Attitude," *Journal of Applied Psychology* 46 (1962): 370–374; N. Schmitt and M. Lappin, "Race and Sex as Determinants of the Mean and Variance of Performance Ratings," *Journal of Applied Psychology* 65 (1980): 428–435.

10. G. Graen, "Role-Making Processes Within Complex Organizations," in *Handbook of Industrial and Organizational Psychology,* ed. M.D. Dunnette (Chicago: Rand McNally, 1976), 1201–1245.

11. P.W. Maloney and J.R. Hinrichs, "A New Tool for Supervisory Self-Development," *Personnel* 36 (1959): 46–53; G. Latham, C.H. Fay, and L.M. Saari, "The Development of Behavioral Observation Scales for Appraising the Performance of Foremen," *Personnel Psychology* 32 (1979): 299–311.

12. E.J. McCormick, *Job Analysis: Methods and Applications* (New York: AMACOM, 1979).

13. C.E. Schneier and W.E. Busse, "The Impact of Sex and Time in Grade on Management Ratings in the Public Sector: Prospects for the Civil Service Reform Act," *Proceedings, Academy of Management National Meetings,* Detroit, 1980; Schmitt and Lappin, "Race and Sex as Determinants"; E. Pulakos, L. White, S. Oppler, and W. Borman, "Examination of Race and Sex Effects on Performance Ratings," *Journal of Applied Psychology* 74 (1989): 770–780.

14. G.A. Brugholi, J.E. Campion, and J.A. Basen, "Racial Bias in the Use of Work Samples for Personnel Selection," *Journal of Applied Psychology* 64 (1979): 119–123.

15. C. W. Downs and P. Moscinski, "A Survey of Appraisal Processes and Training in Large Corporations" (paper presented at the Annual Meeting of the Academy of Management, 1979).

16. R. Levering, M. Moskowitz, and M. Katz, *The 100 Best Companies to Work for in America* (Reading, Mass.: Addison-Wesley, 1984).

17. P.C. Smith and L.M. Kendall, "Retranslation of Expectations: An Approach to the Construction of Unambiguous Anchors for Ratings Scales," *Journal of Applied Psychology* 48 (1963): 149–155; M. Piotrowski, J. Barnes-Farrell, and F. Esrig, "Behaviorally Anchored Bias," *Journal of Applied Psychology* 74 (1989): 823–826.

18. G.P. Latham and K.N. Wexley, *Increasing Productivity through Performance Appraisal* (Reading, Mass.: Addison-Wesley, 1981).

19. Ibid.

20. R.S. Atkin and E.J. Conlon, "Behaviorally Anchored Rating Scales: Some Theoretical Issues," *Academy of Management Review* 3 (1978): 119–128.

21. H.J. Bernardin, "Behavioral Expectation Scales versus Summated Rating Scales: A Fairer Comparison," *Journal of Applied Psychology* 62 (1977): 422–427; H.J. Bernardin, K.M. Alvares, and C.J. Cranny, "A Recomparison of Behavioral Expectation Scales to Summated Scales," *Journal of Applied Psychology* 61 (1976): 564–570.

22. P.H. Dubois, *A History of Psychological Testing* (Boston: Allyn & Bacon, 1970); M.L. Bowan, "Testing Individual Differences in Ancient China," *American Psychologist* 44 (1989): 576–578.

23. A. Howard, "An Assessment of Assessment Centers," *Academy of Management Journal* 17 (1974): 115–134.

24. J.L. Moses, "Assessment Center Performance and Management Progress," *Studies in Personnel Psychology* 4 (1972): 7–12; B.M. Cohen, J.L. Moses, and W.C. Byham, "The Validity of Assessment Centers," *Journal of Industrial and Organizational Psychology* 10 (1973): 1–43; J.R. Hinrichs, "An Eight-Year Follow-up of a Management Assessment Center," *Journal of Applied Psychology* 63 (1978): 596–601; B. Gaugler and G. Thornton, "Number of Assessment Center Dimensions as a Determinant of Assessed Accuracy," *Journal of Applied Psychology* 74 (1989): 611–618.

25. D.E. Lupton, "Assessing the Assessment Center — A Theory Y Approach," *Personnel* 50 (1973): 15–22.

26. M. Erez, "Feedback: A Necessary Condition for the Goal-Setting Performance Relationship," *Journal of Applied Psychology* 62 (1977): 624–627.

27. Thornton, "Psychometric Properties of Self-Appraisals."

28. H.G. Heneman II, "Comparisons of Self and Superior Ratings of Managerial Performance," *Journal of Applied Psychology* 59 (1974): 638–642.

29. S.J. Carrol and C.E. Schneier, *Performance Appraisal and Review Systems* (Glenview, Ill.: Scott, Foresman, 1982), 165.

30. D.R. Ilgen, C.D. Fisher, and M.S. Taylor, "Consequences of Individual Feedback on Behavior in Organizations," *Journal of Applied Psychology* 64 (1979): 349–371.

31. "Training Managers to Rate Their Employees," *Business Week*, March 17, 1980, 178.

32. R.J. Burke, W. Weitzel, and T. Weir, "Characteristics of Effective Employee Performance Review and Development Interviews: Replication and Extension," *Personnel Psychology* 31 (1978): 903–919.

33. M.M. Greller, "Subordinate Participation and Reaction to the Appraisal Interview," *Journal of Applied Psychology* 60 (1975): 544–549; W.F. Nemeroff and K.N. Wexley, "Relationships Between Performance Appraisal Interview Outcomes by Supervisors and Subordinates" (paper presented at the Annual Meeting of the Academy of Management, Orlando, Florida, 1977); K.N. Wexley, J.P. Singh, and G.A. Yukl, "Subordinate Personality as a Moderator of the Effects of Participation in Three Types of Appraisal Interviews," *Journal of Applied Psychology* 58 (1973): 54–59; C.M. Giannantonio, "The Effect of Recruiter Friendliness, Verifiable Job Attributes, and Nonverifiable Job Attributes on Reactions to the Employment Interview" (Ph.D. diss., University of Maryland, College Park, 1988).

34. V.E. Schein, "Relationships between Sex Role Stereotypes and Requisite Management Characteristics among Female Managers," *Journal of Applied Psychology* 60 (1975): 340; K.M. Bartol and D.A. Butterfield, "Sex Effects in Evaluating Leaders," *Journal of Applied Psychology* 61 (1976): 446–454; H.A. Brown and D.L. Ford, "An Exploratory Analysis of Discrimination in the Employment of Black MBA Graduates," *Journal of Applied Psychology* 62 (1977): 50–56; J.R. Terborg, "Women in Management: A Research Review," *Journal of Applied Psychology* 62 (1977): 647–664; B. Rosen and T.H. Jerdee, "Too Old or Not Too Old?" *Harvard Business Review* 55 (1977): 97–106.

35. Federal Register, *Adoption by Four Agencies of Uniform Guidelines on Employee Selection Procedures*, vol. 43, no. 166, Friday, August 25, 1978, 38295–38309.

36. C.R. Klasson, D.E. Thompson, and G.L. Lubben, "How Defensible Is Your Performance Appraisal System?" *Personnel Administrator* 25 (1980): 77–83.

37. R.D. Arvey, *Fairness in Selecting Employees* (Reading, Mass.: Addison-Wesley, 1978).

38. Latham and Wexley, "Increasing Productivity through Performance Appraisal."

39. J.L. Moses and V. Boehm, "Relationship of Assessment Center Performance to Management Progress of Women," *Journal of Applied Psychology* 60 (1975): 527–529.

40. J.R. Huck, "Assessment Centers: A Review of the External and Internal Validities," *Personnel Psychology* 26 (1973): 196–212.

CHAPTER 9

> Charlatanism is to some degree indispensable to effective leadership.
>
> — Eric Hoffer

> Nice guys finish last.
>
> — Leo Durocher

> Contrary to the cliché, genuinely nice guys most often finish first, or very near it.
>
> — Malcolm Forbes

Learning Objectives

After studying this chapter, you should be able to:

1. *Define and distinguish power, authority, influence, and politics.*

2. *Identify and describe three primary influence processes.*

3. *List and define five bases of power.*

4. *Describe some differences between formal and informal power.*

5. *Distinguish the kinds of power organizations use, name a type of organization corresponding to each type of power, and describe the nature of member involvement in an organization that uses that type of power.*

6. *Describe the cycle of approaches that supervisors use to influence subordinates.*

7. *Identify several political tactics, including devious political tactics and political blunders.*

8. *Explain several techniques for coping with organizational politics.*

9. *Support an argument that pressures to conform are powerful.*

10. *Cite evidence that the predisposition to obey authority is strong.*

Power and Influence

■ Ways to Wield Power

When the boss wants to get something done, he or she has several ways to induce subordinates to act. The boss can threaten them with punishments, offer them a reward, rely on the authority of his or her position, demonstrate superior expertise, or hope to be obeyed because subordinates admire or are impressed by him or her. The tactic a particular leader uses is that person's choice.

How are today's business leaders wielding power? "My predecessor was more imperial, and I tend to be more collegial," says Charles Corry, chief executive officer at USX. At Colgate-Palmolive, CEO Reuben Mark says, "You consolidate and build power by empowering others."

These two executives seem to reflect the prevailing view. In a recent survey of chief executives by *Fortune* magazine, most executives report that they are sharing power more than they used to and more than their predecessor did.

Representative of this view is Ralph Stayer, CEO of Johnsonville Foods of Sheboygan, Wisconsin. Says Stayer, "Real power is getting people committed. Real power comes from giving it up to others who are in a better position to do things than you are. Control is an illusion. The only control you can possibly have comes when people are controlling themselves."

At Johnsonville Foods, this view translates into a company where employees take an active role. Goals are set as far down in the hierarchy as possible, so that top managers can devote their time to choosing which goals should receive priority funding. Is this kind of approach practical? In a six-year period, Johnsonville has doubled its return on assets, and sales have grown twice as fast as the company's payroll.

Business school professors and consultants concur with the CEOs' view. They maintain that today's work force resists being led in a militaristic fashion. Rather, workers respond best to a leader who sets a strategic direction, gets them to agree, gives them money and authority, and then allows them freedom to do the job on their own. According to Raymond E. Miles, dean of the University of California's business school, "The raw use of power doesn't have the acceptance it did 25 years ago. People aren't willing to put up with it."

While today's CEOs are more willing to share authority, they do not believe that they have less power than before. The very act of delegating carries the power to choose and develop the people to whom authority is to be delegated. Often this choice involves the old-fashioned power mechanism of firing the people who don't fit the new style of operating.

This chapter investigates the role of power within organizations. It begins by exploring what power is and what its sources are. Then the chapter turns to types of power and methods of influence used in organizations. The chapter also discusses organizational politics, conformity, and obedience.

Source: Thomas A. Stewart, "New Ways to Exercise Power," *Fortune*, November 6, 1989, 52–54+.

At one time or another, all of us have resisted attempts to be controlled or influenced by others. Likewise, each of us has attempted to control or influence those around us. Control — by others and of others — lies at the very heart of organizational relationships. This give-and-take among people is responsible for much of what is actually accomplished in a work unit, as well as for a fair amount of social friction.

Distinguishing Power and Influence

Power is an essential feature of a manager's role. Without some degree of power, a manager would find it very difficult to direct the efforts of subordinates. Thus, power underlies a manager's effectiveness. Subordinates also possess forms and degrees of power. For example, subordinates can control the work flow or withhold support from their manager. Therefore, to some extent, each member of an organization possesses power.

Because power is intangible, it is very difficult to define clearly and precisely. Also, our language has several similar terms that we tend to confuse with power, such as authority and influence. In the interest of clarity, we shall define **power** as the ability to change the behavior of others. It is the ability to cause others to perform actions that they might not otherwise perform.[1]

Power is not always legitimate. Therefore, we speak of **authority** as the *right* to try to change or direct others. Authority includes the notion of legitimacy. It is the right to influence others in the pursuit of common goals that are agreed upon by various parties. Power, in contrast, does not always pursue common goals and may, at times, be clearly directed to pursuing only a single individual's goals.

Another term, **influence**, is also frequently used when discussing the notion of power. Influence tends to be subtler, broader, and more general than power. Although both influence and power can be defined as the ability to change the behavior of others, power embodies the ability to do so with regularity and ease. Influence is weaker and less reliable than power. Also, power rests on a number of specific sources or foundations, which will be examined in a subsequent section of this chapter. Influence relies on particular tactics and often employs face-to-face interactions. Thus, the exercise of influence tends to be a more subtle process than the exercise of power.

Interpersonal Influence Processes

In a classic article, Kelman distinguished among three primary reasons for an individual to yield to another person's attempt to be directive.[2] If an employee accepts a manager's influence attempt because he believes he will be rewarded or avoid being punished, his response is one of **compliance.** For example, an employee may skip lunch in order to finish typing a report for his supervisor. He may actually hope to receive an expression of appreciation from his supervisor or he may merely wish to avoid the hard feelings that will result if the report is not finished on time. The employee's behavior is strictly motivated by concern with rewards and punishments. Supervisors who strive for consistent compliance must (1) be certain that they can in fact deliver rewards or punishments and (2) be in a position to frequently monitor their subordinates' behavior.

A second influence process, **identification,** occurs when one person follows another's direction because of a desire to establish or maintain a personally satisfying relationship. When a subordinate admires his manager, seeks his approval, and perhaps tries to imitate him, we infer that the subordinate has a strong desire to identify with the manager. One example of this process occurs when a junior executive who greatly admires the CEO of her organization espouses the CEO's philosophy and beliefs when addressing the employees in her own work unit.

In both compliance and identification, the performance of an action in itself is not necessarily personally satisfying. Rather, the action may be due to a desire for specific outcomes (compliance) or an attraction to the source of influence (identification).

Sometimes employees' actions stem from a third reason: the belief that the behavior is congruent with their value systems. **Internalization** occurs when an employee accepts an influence attempt because he or she believes that the resulting behavior is correct and appropriate. For instance, assume that a high-level executive announces that the organization is participating in a United Way fund-raising campaign. Some of her managers may actively encourage subordinates to contribute to the fund because they strongly believe in the goals of United Way. These managers are not motivated by threats or rewards or admiration for their superior but rather by a personal commitment to a set of values.

The Five Bases of Power

Who gets what, when, and how are important concerns for every member of an organization. People at all levels are interested in and affected by the acquisition and distribution of rewards and resources. Of course, power plays a central role in such allocation processes. To explain how power operates, we will first examine the five distinct sources of power proposed by John French and Bertram Raven: reward power, coercive power, legitimate power, referent power, and expert power.[3]

Reward Power **Reward power** is the ability to determine who will receive particular rewards. As long as the rewards are valued, a person who is able to distribute or withhold them can enjoy strong power over others' behavior. Granting promotions, giving raises, and conferring preferred job assignments are some typical rewards most managers can control. Unfortunately, this is not always the case. For example, when a work force is unionized, salary increases and job assignments are based more on seniority and the specifics of a labor contract than on the judgment of a manager or supervisor. As noted in our discussion of motivation (Chapter 6), the relationship between performance and rewards should always be clear. When a manager lacks the ability to administer both extrinsic and intrinsic rewards, it becomes extremely difficult to direct subordinates' behavior. Reward power gives a manager a distinct advantage in obtaining desired ends from his or her work group.

Coercive Power   If reward power can be termed "the carrot," then coercive power is "the stick." **Coercive power** stems from the capacity to produce fear in others. The threat of punishment can be a strong means of invoking compliance. The most obvious examples of punishments are demotions, salary cuts, suspension, removal of such perquisites as a company car or an expense account, and dismissal. However, coercive power can also be more subtle. For example, criticism and the denial of emotional support and friendship may also be effective forms of coercion.

The application of coercive power requires good social judgment. In some instances, a manager is actually expected to be coercive — as when a subordinate is extremely unproductive or interferes with the productivity of others. In such a situation, other employees and managers will rightly expect the supervisor to take firm action.

On the other hand, a manager must be careful when applying coercive power. If he or she is too heavy-handed and indiscriminately inflicts punishment on all employees, morale and productivity are likely to suffer. Such a manager may find that the unit's turnover rate is very high as people seek employment elsewhere. In addition, injured employees may retaliate by sabotaging the unit's operations or withholding useful suggestions for improving the unit's performance.

Despite its potentially negative effects, coercive power underlies much of the routine compliance that occurs in organizations. Decisions to arrive at work on time, meet deadlines, and so forth are often largely due to fear of being fired, ridiculed, or reprimanded. Rightly or wrongly, coercive power is frequently used in most organizations.

Legitimate Power   **Legitimate power** stems from the willingness of others to accept an individual's direction. They feel an obligation to follow the individual's lead and submit to his authority. There are two sources of legitimate power. The first is social conditioning: from early childhood, people are conditioned to accept the direction of authority figures. They learn that teachers and crossing guards, as well as foremen and managers, have the right to lead or direct others. The second source of legitimate power is designation: a person can gain power by being designated an authority figure by someone who already possesses legitimate authority. For example, the president of a company may assign a vice-president the authority to make important decisions on the company's behalf. The president thus gives the vice-president legitimate power to act as his representative and exercise authority accordingly.

Legitimate power can be effective only if it is accepted by the people it is intended to control. If the people withdraw their support from the system that is the basis of power, the power ceases to exist. Such withdrawals of support occur in revolutions, when ruling classes and their social systems are overthrown, and in riots, when a spontaneous but limited rebellion is made against authority.

Referent Power   People with attractive personalities or other special qualities possess a form of power. Their appearance, poise, interpersonal style, or values can inspire admiration and cause others to identify with them. The resulting ability to influence behavior is called **referent power.** It is often easy to identify an individual who possesses such power. For example, most people would agree that successful politicians, athletes, and entertainers — such as George Bush, Joe Montana, and Bill Cosby — have this attribute. However, it is extremely difficult to define exactly what gives these people their charisma. Usually, vigor and the appearance of success play important roles. But other characteristics that contribute to referent power can be very difficult to pinpoint (consider, for example, that Adolf Hitler was judged to be charismatic in the eyes of his countrymen).

Referent power derives from people's desire to identify with the qualities of an attractive individual. Advertising that uses a celebrity to endorse a product is based on referent power, since the sponsor hopes that the audience will buy the product in an attempt to imitate the celebrity's behavior and attitudes.*

Expert Power   Individuals with **expert power** are able to direct others because they are perceived as knowledgeable or talented in a given area. Most of us readily seek and follow the advice of experts, such as our family physician or athletic coach. So too are we likely to follow the directions of a coworker who is seen as having expertise in our field of work. This form of power is usually limited to a fairly narrow and specific realm, however, and does not spread to other areas of social interaction.

Most subordinates presume that their superiors possess expert power in the form of understanding all jobs in the work unit. Generally, greater levels of experience and job-relevant knowledge do give a manager an edge in expertise. However, in highly technical job settings, it may happen that some subordinates have more expert knowledge about certain aspects of their jobs than do their managers. In fact, some managers may be highly dependent on the technical expertise of their subordinates in order to successfully manage their work units. In such a situation, expert power can lead to an atypical reversal of the usual manager–subordinate relationship.

Interplay among the Power Bases

A manager can possess each of the five sources of power to varying degrees, and his or her use of one power base can affect the strength of another. For example, a person can gain greater legitimacy by being promoted to a higher-

---

* This logic parallels the notions of balance theory (see Chapter 4).

level position. Of course, a position of greater legitimate power usually entails more opportunities to use rewards and coercion. The exercise of coercion, however, could reduce the manager's referent power because, as discussed in Chapter 5, coercion tends to produce immediate compliance but may have negative side effects.

Above all, the manager should bear in mind that the tendency to use power can lead to greater effectiveness, while the failure to use power can have the opposite effect. Managers who exercise power with some frequency can be counted on to continue such behavior in future settings and are, therefore, given greater deference by subordinates. More passive managers may have difficulty if they suddenly decide to use their power because their subordinates will have become accustomed to their lack of assertiveness.

Distinctions can be drawn among the five power bases. Expert and referent power bases are more informal in nature, while legitimate, reward, and coercive power bases are more formal. The informal power bases have a greater capacity to affect overall employee satisfaction and performance. The formal power bases, in contrast, have potentially greater impact on immediate behavior. Although formal power can elicit a quick response from an employee, it will not necessarily produce agreement and commitment. For example, a worker may comply with a manager's orders but still resent having been coerced.

Many centuries ago, the Italian philosopher Machiavelli contended that people who have formal power tend to remain in their positions of authority longer than people who rely on informal power. This observation makes some sense in that the informal bases of power can be more easily eroded, since they depend on people's perceptions. For example, a manager may lose his expertise due to changes in technology or his appeal may diminish following a series of unpopular actions or personnel changes. While expert power can be regained through technical training, there are no surefire ways of increasing referent power.

In general, informal power resides in the personal characteristics of the manager, whereas formal power resides in the position itself. It can be forcefully argued, however, that all sources of power can really be reduced to a single category: control over reinforcers. As shown in Chapter 5, the most effective way to control others' behavior is to control when and how they receive reinforcement.

An Organizational Analysis of Power

In his analysis of how complex organizations attempt to direct the behavior of their members, Etzioni identified three kinds of organizational power.[4] One type of organizational power can be characterized as coercive. Such organizations try to extract compliance from members through threats and punishment. Examples of coercive organizations include prisons, some mental institutions, and divisions within the military (such as boot camp).

An Inside Look
Unexpected Influence

Richard F. Wright, vice-president of research and development for Mead Imaging, found out that a manager who has much power has to watch out. That power may be influencing people to act in unintended ways.

Clearly, Wright had become a leader. He had adopted the practice of walking around the laboratory area to find out first-hand what subordinates were doing and to discuss issues with them. As his staff grew, Wright decided that his appearances could be interfering with the development of future leaders within his group, so he started spending more time in the office.

Within two weeks, staff members began asking him where he had been and whether something was wrong. Wright returned to his practice of visiting the labs.

In light of the importance Wright's staff placed on his active involvement, it should come as no surprise to learn that subordinates valued his opinions. In fact, employees sometimes gave his opinions the weight of a decree. Wright's authority as manager led to misunderstandings when this happened.

For example, he once disagreed with the focus of an experiment. Because staff members took Wright's word as law, they went along with his opinion. As it turned out, he was wrong, and the department spent extra time doing the experiment first Wright's way and then the way they had originally planned.

In research, a manager relies heavily on the expertise of the technical staff. This means that Wright not only has to exert power himself, but also has to make sure that his subordinates know that they have the power to express their opinions. Wright concluded, "The manager has a heavy responsibility, therefore, to manage his words as well as his group."

Source: Sharon Nelton, "Walking a Fine Line," *Nation's Business*, vol. 74, April 1986, 17, 20.

Most business organizations, of course, do not rely on coercion, but instead offer contingent incentives: if employees follow directives, they can expect to be rewarded. Such organizations are said to use **utilitarian power** because of their emphasis on the utility of conforming to directives.

A third set of organizations rely on **normative power**. In this type of organization, members accept directives because of their sense of affiliation with the organization and its espoused values. Professional associations (such as the American Dental Association) and religious organizations typically use normative power to influence their members.

All three types of power can be useful in obtaining people's cooperation in organizations. However, the relative effectiveness of each approach depends on the organizational members' orientation or involvement. Etzioni contends that members' involvement can be broadly categorized as alienative, calculative, or moral. Members with **alienative involvement** have hostile, rejecting, and extremely negative attitudes. Members with **calculative involvement** are rational and oriented toward maximizing personal gain. And members with **moral involvement** are committed to the socially beneficial features of their organizations.

According to Etzioni, the three types of organizational power can be matched with the three types of involvement. According to this logic, only one type of power is most appropriate for each type of member involvement.

■ **Figure 9.1**

Etzioni's Model of Power and Involvement

Types of Power

	Coercive	Utilitarian	Normative
Alienative	X		
Calculative		X	
Moral			X

Types of Involvement

The cells on the primary diagonal of the matrix (denoted by X) represent match-ups of types of power and involvement.

Attempts to use types of power that are inappropriate for the type of involvement can reduce effectiveness. Figure 9.1 illustrates Etzioni's model of power and involvement.

Tying It All Together

Sussmann and Vecchio formally compared the three models of power and influence put forth by French and Raven, Kelman, and Etzioni.[5] A good deal of similarity was identified among all three views. For example, French and Raven's concepts of reward and coercive power have a strong similarity to Kelman's notions of compliance. Referent power, in turn, is allied to Kelman's notion of identification, and legitimate and expert power overlap to a great extent with the process of internalization. Both Etzioni and Kelman identify three forms of power (or influence), but while Etzioni focuses on the organizational level of analysis, Kelman focuses on the interpersonal level. Table 9.1 summarizes the comparison of the three views.

 Table 9.1

A Comparison of Three Views of Power and Influence

Interpersonal Influence Process (Kelman)	Power Bases (French and Raven)	Organizational Power (Etzioni)
Internalization	Legitimate Power Expert Power	Normative
Identification	Referent Power	Normative
Compliance (reward-based)	Reward Power	Utilitarian
Compliance (punishment-based)	Coercive Power	Coercive

In a sense, the multiple forms of power identified correspond to the need-level views of Maslow and others (Chapter 6). The correspondence lies in the recognition that there are several levels of motivation or forms of influence. One level is fairly rudimentary: reward and punishment. A higher level is more social in nature: referent or identification. And the highest level is fairly psychological in nature: internalization or legitimacy.

A Social Influence View of Supervisor Behavior

Sussmann and Vecchio also proposed that a supervisor's attempts to exert influence follow a cycle in which he or she tries one of three approaches to influence a subordinate in accordance with the three levels of needs and the three forms of power.[6] This view suggests that a supervisor (or evaluator) will attempt to use compliance, identification, or internalization to influence an individual. Respectively, he or she may try threats, appeals to a subordinate's sense of organizational membership or affiliation, or appeals to his value system.

Such attempts will succeed or fail to the extent that the individual is disposed to accept incentives or threats, identity-related appeals, or value-related appeals. For certain types of subordinates, a particular type of disposition may be more prevalent, as is suggested by Etzioni's notion of involvement. Acceptance of the supervisor's influence attempt leads to behavioral intentions on the part of the subordinate to act in the desired direction. The actual behavior of the subordinate is then compared to the standards that are held in the mind of the supervisor. If the influence attempt is judged to have failed, the supervisor will likely try another attempt, but perhaps with a different type of influence (for example, appealing on a different level). This model suggests that supervisors need to be sensitive to differences in subordinates' preferences for inducement schemes. It is possible that supervisors who are aware of and make use of subordinate preferences for inducements are relatively more effective than other supervisors.

Politics: The Facts of Organizational Life

The terms *politics* and *power* are sometimes used interchangeably. Though they are related, they are nonetheless distinct notions. Pfeffer defines **organizational politics** as "those activities taken within organizations to acquire, develop, and use power and other resources to obtain one's preferred outcomes in a situation in which there is uncertainty or [disagreement] about choices."[7] In a sense, the study of organizational politics constitutes the study of power in action. It may also be said that politics involves the playing out of power and influence.

The word *politics* has a somewhat negative connotation. It suggests that someone is attempting to use means or to gain ends that are not sanctioned by the organization. Actually, political behavior, as we've defined it, is quite neutral. Similarly, power is not inherently negative. Whether a person views power and politics as unsavory topics depends on a number of considerations, most important perhaps being where the individual stands on a specific issue in a given situation. Nonetheless, most managers are reluctant to admit to the political character of their own work settings.

A further point is that all members of an organization may exhibit political behavior. In our previous discussion of power, we took a fairly formal and traditional approach to the topic of influence. Thus, we looked at power from the perspective of a supervisor or manager who directs others. Yet, in the area of politics, everyone is a player. Subordinates, as well as their managers, can engage in the give-and-take of organizational politics.†

Political Tactics

Several authors have identified a variety of political tactics used by employees at virtually all levels.[8] In this section, we will examine a number of these activities.

Ingratiation   This tactic involves giving compliments or doing favors for superiors or coworkers. Most people have a difficult time rejecting the positive advances of others. Ingratiation usually works as a tactic insofar as the target often feels positive toward the source even if the ingratiation attempt is fairly blatant and transparent.

In the behavioral sciences, the notion of "social reciprocity" has been offered to help explain the process of ingratiation. In social reciprocity, there is a feeling of a social obligation to repay the positive actions of others with similar actions. For example, if someone pays you a compliment, there is a strong expectation that you should respond with a compliment of your own. If you fail to do so, you may be judged as being rude. Similarly, ingratiation involves giving positive strokes to a person with the expectation that he or she will feel obligated to return them in some form.

Forming Coalitions and Networks   Another political tactic consists of befriending important people. These people may not be in positions of any obvious political value. However, their jobs may provide them with information that could be useful to have. Some people find that forming friendships with people in upper-level management can help them gain access to important information. They may also find that by being on good terms with their boss's secretary, they can sometimes gain inside information and easier access to the boss.

Impression Management   A simple tactic that virtually everyone uses from time to time is the management of their outward appearance and style. Generally, most organizations prefer a particular image that consists of being loyal, attentive, honest, neatly groomed, sociable, and so forth. By deliberately trying to exhibit this preferred image, an individual can make a positive impression on influential members of the organization.

---

† Nonetheless, it is widely believed that political behavior is far less common and less intense among employees in lower-level positions than among employees in higher-level positions.

Information Management   A further tactic consists of managing the information that is shared with others. The nature, as well as the timing, of information given out can have strong effects on others' conduct. Releasing good or bad news when it is likely to have its fullest impact can greatly promote one person's self-interest or defeat the hopes of others. Similarly, an individual can ask for information (such as sales data or a production report) when it is most likely to make things appear particularly good or bad. People who play the information management game are not likely to lie or spread misinformation, however, because their future credibility would be jeopardized. Instead, they rely on the carefully planned release of valid information to obtain their ends.

Promote the Opposition   It may sound strange, but one way to eliminate opposition is to aid political rivals. For example, it is possible to eliminate a political rival by helping that person become so successful that he or she is transferred to a desirable position someplace else in the organization. Recommending a rival for a new assignment or even a promotion within another division of the organization can make one's own work life easier.

Pursue Line Responsibility   Within virtually every organization, some positions are more closely tied to the primary mission of the organization; these jobs are called line positions. They are at the very heart of the organization. People who occupy support positions are said to be in staff positions. Examples of line positions include engineering, manufacturing, and sales in a customer-oriented firm. People in departments such as public relations, market research, and personnel are usually in staff positions. While staff people may come to wield great power within their own territories, it is the line people who usually "call the shots" on major issues. Line people not only make the more important decisions within the organization, they are also more likely to be promoted to top-level executive positions. In many organizations, there is a preferred department of origin and career path for top-level managers. These are usually line positions. Therefore, one way to gain influence within an organization is to be assigned initially to, or be transferred to, a line position. It will often provide more visibility, influence, and upward mobility.

Devious Political Tactics

Some political tactics are quite honest in nature. For example, accumulating seniority, providing copies of your accomplishments to your boss, and hitching your wagon to yourself are all respectable means for gaining influence.‡ Some other tactics, however, are difficult to defend on moral grounds. In the interest of self-defense, it is worth examining several of these devious political tactics.[9]

Take No Prisoners   Sometimes it is necessary to do something unpopular or distasteful, such as demote or transfer someone or announce pay cuts. During corporate takeovers, many unpopular actions may be necessary. As a result,

---

‡ Pure and simple performance remains an essential ingredient of a successful career in virtually all fields of endeavor.

political enemies are likely to be made. One tactic for dealing with this potential problem is to ruthlessly eliminate *all* individuals who may resent your past actions by having them fired or transferred.

Divide and Conquer   This tactic involves creating a feud among two or more people so that they will be continually off balance and thus unable to mount an attack against you. This is a very old idea that is still practiced in some work settings. An unscrupulous individual who employs this tactic usually encourages bickering between possible rivals by spreading rumors or promoting competition between subordinates or factions. This is a risky tactic, however, as the opponents may eventually compare notes and conclude that someone else is really responsible for creating and maintaining their bad feelings.

Exclude the Opposition   Another devious tactic involves keeping rivals away from important meetings and social occasions. This can be done simply by scheduling important affairs when the opposition is out of town (on vacation or a business trip) or attending another meeting. With the opposition absent, it is possible to influence decision making or to take credit for a rival's efforts.

Political Blunders

While certain tactics can promote desired ends, others can be costly political mistakes. Among the most common are violating the chain of command, losing your cool, saying no to top management, upstaging your supervisor, and challenging cherished beliefs. These activities constitute serious political blunders or mistakes.

Violating Chain of Command   Occasionally, a person will feel that it is his duty to see his boss's boss, either to complain about his treatment at the hands of his own boss or to serve as an informant. A person may even feel that such an "end run" is justified because he is fervently convinced of the rightness of his position. However, going over the boss's head is often a very strong organizational taboo. Generally, it is expected that an employee will ask the boss's permission before seeing his superior on any matter.

Losing Your Cool   Throwing temper tantrums and acting aggressively toward others are often seen as acceptable and sometimes effective tactics in settings such as sports events. But in office settings, these tactics do not work well at all. Fist pounding and snide remarks usually earn a person a reputation for being hard to deal with, a label that can be extremely difficult to overcome. One devious twist on this tactic is to goad a person who tends to be acerbic and aggressive into displaying these tendencies at the wrong times. In this way, such a person's peers help him or her to commit political suicide.

Saying No to Top Management   One of the surest ways to stop your own career progress is to reject a request from top-level management. Instead of feeling fortunate to be selected for an assignment, some individuals believe that they are overburdened and that they are being "dumped on," or that they can afford to defy top management because they are indispensable. This represents poor judgment on two counts: First, people in the lower ranks of an organization are rarely indispensable. Second, if workers are overburdened, they should explain the situation to the manager and try to arrange for additional help.

Upstaging Your Supervisor   Generally speaking, one should avoid publicly criticizing others. For example, it is not considered appropriate for a supervisor to criticize a subordinate in public view. However, the reverse is also true. A subordinate should refrain from implicitly criticizing the boss by upstaging him or her. Upstaging often takes the form of bragging about one's own accomplishments or claiming credit for a unit's success.

Challenging Cherished Beliefs   In many firms, there are a number of cherished beliefs about the nature of the organization, and it is generally considered "poor form" to criticize or challenge such folklore within earshot of company loyalists. Examples of such fond beliefs include "This organization is the best in its field," "Our founder was (or is) an outstanding individual," and "People who leave our organization are people that we are better off without." To be sure, all people are entitled to their own opinions, but it can be politically foolish to engage in an open debate about the truth of certain widely held beliefs.

Coping with Organizational Politics

Political gamesmanship, when carried to the extreme, has many dysfunctional effects: morale is weakened, victors and victims are created, and energy and time are spent on planning attacks and counterattacks instead of on productivity. Thus, combating politics must be part of a manager's job.

Set an Example   When a manager plays political games, such as distorting the facts or manipulating people, he or she conveys to subordinates a message that such conduct is acceptable. A manager can create a climate either tolerant or intolerant of dirty tricks. Clearly, a department is better served by a manager who provides a positive role model by encouraging truthfulness and the even-handed treatment of others.

Give Clear Job Assignments   Politics seem to be more prevalent when overall purposes are unclear and it is difficult to assess the performance of individual employees.§ One way to counter political activities is to give well-defined, discrete work assignments. When expectations are clear and subordinates understand how they will be assessed, game playing becomes less necessary as a device for gaining personal recognition.

Eliminate Coalitions and Cliques   Coalitions and cliques that are detrimental to unit performance can often be reduced in influence or eliminated. While

§ The attributes of an open-ended purpose and difficulty in measuring individual performance are especially relevant to academic departments.

dismissal and transfer are two possible solutions, individuals may also be rotated through different job assignments. Job rotation encourages an employee's perception of the larger enterprise and helps to counter an us–them view of other departments.

Confront Game Players   Even in a climate of trust and openness, individuals may make suggestive comments or offer information that has an ulterior motive. A good response in such a situation is simply to ask, "Why are you telling me this about Sam?" or "Why don't you and I go see Sam's boss about this right now? I think you should tell her what you've just told me." Another useful response is to offer to discuss questionable information in a public forum. A manager may say, for example, "I think I understand your concerns on this issue. Let's bring it up for discussion at our next department meeting." Using a public forum to discuss and choose a course of action is an excellent defense to most dubious suggestions. As a rule, a manager should not get involved in any scheme that he or she is unwilling to have discussed in public. Knowing that all suggestions are subject to open discussion invariably discourages people who hope to engage a manager in political games.

Machiavellianism

Niccolò Machiavelli (Figure 9.2), an Italian philosopher and statesman (1469–1527), was one of the earliest writers on the topic of political behavior. In his works, Machiavelli examined political effectiveness without regard for ethics or morality. Because of his uncompromising view of political reality, Machiavelli has sometimes been called the ultimate pragmatist. In recent years, his name has come to be synonymous with the use of political treachery and maneuvering. Thus, to say that someone is Machiavellian is a serious insult.**

Christie and Geis have tried to assess the extent to which an individual's personal style is Machiavellian in nature.[10] To do so, they converted certain basic tenets of Machiavelli's writings into an attitude scale that can be used to measure the extent to which an individual agrees with Machiavelli's views. The statements of the Machiavellian scale (or **Mach Scale** for short) focus on several factors. Chief among them are (1) the use of manipulative interpersonal tactics ("It is wise to flatter important people" and "Never tell anyone the real reason you did something unless it is useful to do so") and (2) an unfavorable view of human nature ("Generally speaking, people won't work hard unless they are forced to do so" and "Anyone who completely trusts anyone else is asking for trouble").

A good deal is known about people who score high in agreement with Machiavelli's views.[11] Generally, they are able to control social interactions and effectively manipulate others. They are also especially effective in using

** Other world cultures have also had their own version of Niccolò Machiavelli. About 300 B.C., both Lord Shang of China and Koutilya, a prime minister in the south of India, wrote much the same philosophy as Machiavelli. All three writers shared several common themes: humankind is basically weak, fallible, and gullible; therefore, a rational person takes advantage of situations and protects himself or herself from the implicit untrustworthiness of others.

Figure 9.2

Niccolò Machiavelli: The Father of Modern Politics

Source: Historical Pictures Service, Inc.

their skills in face-to-face settings. A series of studies among college students found that highly Machiavellian students were more likely to be involved in medicine as a career and were more critical of their fellow students.[12] They also admitted to having strong feelings of hostility. In one contrived study, when students were induced to cheat and then accused of doing so, highly Machiavellian individuals looked their accuser in the eye and denied cheating longer than did less Machiavellian individuals.

In general, Machiavellian individuals are thought to be socially domineering and manipulative, and they are assumed to engage in political behavior more often than other organizational participants.

Consequences of Using Influence Tactics

Research on attempts to influence others has begun to focus on the specific techniques people use at work. After conversations with employees, David Kipnis and Stuart Schmidt developed a questionnaire for measuring six tactics for influencing others.[13] These tactics include:

1. Reason: relies on using data, logic, and discussion
2. Friendliness: interest, goodwill, and esteem are demonstrated to create a favorable impression
3. Coalition formation: other people in the organization are mobilized to support requests
4. Bargaining: relies on negotiation and exchanging favors
5. Assertiveness: relies on directness and forcefulness in communication
6. Appeal to higher authority: the influence of those higher in the organization is invoked to back up a request.

From responses to their questionnaire, Kipnis and Schmidt grouped employees into four influence styles:

1. Shotguns: people who refuse to take "no" for an answer and who use all of the above tactics to achieve their ends
2. Tacticians: people who try to influence others through reason and logic
3. Ingratiators: people who rely on ingratiation and flattery
4. Bystanders: people who watch the action rather than attempting to influence it.[14]

Comparisons of performance evaluations for the four types of employees revealed that people who assertively attempted to influence their supervisors (Shotguns) were viewed less favorably. Both male and female Shotguns received equally low evaluations from their supervisors. Male supervisors tended to give the highest ratings to male Tacticians, who relied on reason and logic. Women who received the highest ratings were likely to be Ingratiators and Bystanders. In responding to these findings, male supervisors explained that both male Tacticians and female Ingratiators were seen as deferential and thoughtful.

Salary was also found to be associated with influence style. In a comparison of the income of 108 male CEOs, Tacticians earned the most ($73,240), followed by Bystanders ($60,270), Shotguns ($56,480), and Ingratiators ($52,700). Based on both evaluations and income, it seems that Tacticians are valued more than their peers who use other styles. Also, Shotgun-style individuals reported more job tension and personal stress than their counterparts.

Kipnis and Schmidt argue, from these and other findings, that books and training programs that are designed to "put people in charge" (in essence, teach a Shotgun style) are questionable. They contend that people should not be taught to be overly assertive as the best tactic for achieving their desires. Instead, training programs should emphasize less vigorous influence styles that rely on reason and logic.[15]

The Ethics of Organizational Politics

Figure 9.3 presents a model for incorporating ethical considerations into deciding whether to act in a political manner. This model, proposed by Gerald Cavanagh, Dennis Moberg, and Manuel Velasquez, provides guidance on

■ Figure 9.3

A Decision Tree for Incorporating Ethics into Political Behavior Decisions

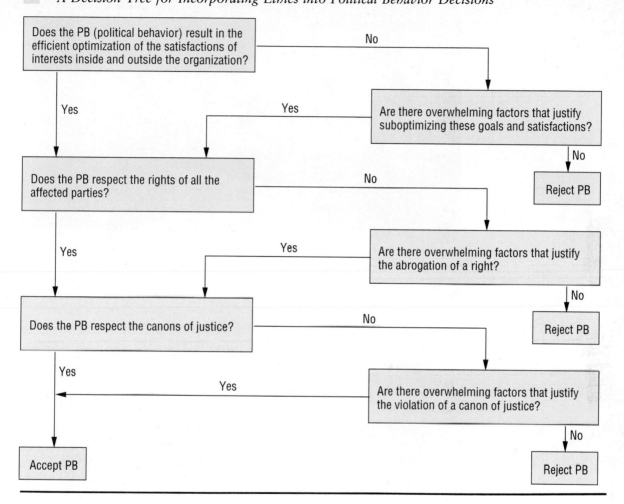

whether a political behavior (PB), or course of action, should be followed in a particular situation.[16] From their perspective, a political behavior is ethical and appropriate only if (1) the behavior respects the rights of all affected parties and (2) the behavior respects the canons of justice — a self-evidently correct judgment of what is equitable and fair. In essence, the model encourages the adoption of nonpolitical behaviors (where such alternatives exist), and the rejection of behaviors that interfere with the canons of justice.

     To illustrate their model, Cavanagh and his associates suggest a case in which two research scientists, Sam and Bill, are in competition in a new-product development lab. Each has prepared a proposal to win a significant cash award for the best new-product idea. Blind reviews of the proposals by other scientists indicate that both are equally meritorious. Sam inquires period-

■ Figure 9.4

Set-Up of the Asch Experiment in Conformity

The experimenter is at the right, and the unsuspecting subject is seated sixth from the left. All other "subjects" are actually in league with the experimenter.

Source: William Vandivert/Scientific American.

ically about the outcome of the bidding process, while Bill wages an open campaign in support of his proposal. Specifically, Bill seizes every opportunity to point out the relative advantages of his proposal to individuals who may have some impact on the final decision. He does this after freely admitting his intention to Sam and others. His campaign of informal pressure is effective and his proposal is funded, while Sam's is not.

Using the decision tree, we first ask whether the outcome, in terms of the broad interests of society and the company, will be optimal. Since both proposals were judged to be equivalent in the blind reviews, we must answer yes to the first question. The second question focuses on whether Bill's behavior respected the rights of Sam. Because Bill told Sam he intended to campaign actively for his proposal, Bill cannot be accused of deceit. Also, Sam's inaction may be viewed as implied consent. The third question highlights the suspect nature of Bill's actions in pointing out irrelevant differences between the proposals. Given the equivalent merit of the proposals, other considerations (for example, which writer was most qualified to implement the proposal, or other evidence of past performance) should have been incorporated in the funding decision.

Responding to Social Influence: Conformity

When a person changes behavior or beliefs in response to real or imagined pressure from others, we say that he or she seeks **conformity**. The word *change* is important in this definition because it suggests that the individual deviated from an earlier position or preference.

■ **Figure 9.5**

A Set of Lines Used in the Asch Experiment in Conformity

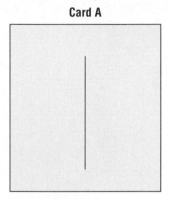
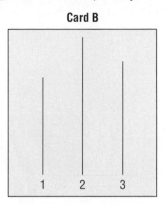

In organizations, social pressures to conform can be very powerful. An individual who dares to deviate from the preferred line of conduct or belief runs the risk of being ostracized or treated with hostility. "To get along, go along" is an old saying in organizational parlance that summarizes much of what we learn in school and in organizational settings about how to survive.

The power of social pressure to conform was illustrated in a series of now-famous studies by Solomon Asch (Figure 9.4).[17] In one experiment, college students were asked to indicate which of three lines on card B was the same size as the line on card A (Figure 9.5). This task was repeated with the identical-sized line being in the first, second, or third position in various trials. Invariably, the students were able to identify the appropriate line. At a later session, a student who had not taken the test before was placed in a group with seven to nine other subjects and asked to identify the identical line. In this instance, the other subjects were confederates of the experimenter and had been trained to give wrong, but uniform, answers to the task. By contrivance, the new subject was asked to respond after nearly all the other subjects had given the same erroneous answer. The critical question was whether the new subject would answer honestly or be induced by group pressure to deliberately give a wrong answer. In 32 percent of the judgments made on the critical trials, the subjects went along with the unanimous opinion of the group. However, some subjects resisted the group pressure throughout the study.

In a subsequent study using the same method, it was found that having another subject (also a confederate) present who defied the group and consistently gave the correct response greatly strengthened the new subject's resistance to the group's pressure.

These results illustrate that behavior can be influenced by the pressures of others. People will even reject relatively clear objective data if others are predisposed to reject it. With more ambiguous and subjective data, such as social information, the power of group pressure is likely to be stronger. When the

■ **Figure 9.6**

A "Learner" in the Milgram Studies on Obedience to Authority

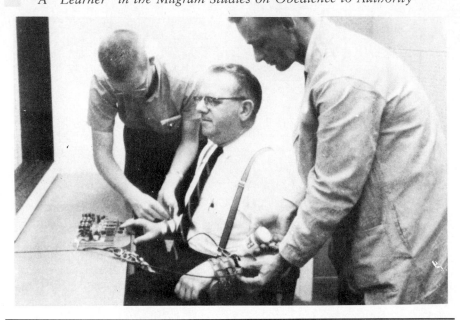

desire to be liked by others is very strong or when continuing group involvement is likely — as is the case in the workplace — the power of pressure to conform becomes even greater.

Responding to Authority: Obedience

For managers to meet their goals, they must rely on their subordinates to obey their directions. Obedience to authority is a strongly ingrained predisposition for most people. Without this predisposition, society would not be able to function. Usually, the depth of our predisposition to obey orders can only be guessed at. Occasionally, we hear of instances of blind obedience to authority, as in the war-crime trials of Adolf Eichmann and Lieutenant William Calley, but we tend to discount such cases as extreme and unusual.

In the early 1960s, Stanley Milgram of Yale University conducted a series of studies to examine the extent to which people would obey, even if the demands of authority violated their moral responsibilities.[18] As part of this research, 40 adult males from a wide variety of occupations were paid to serve as subjects in a learning experiment. Each subject was told that he was participating in a study of the effects of punishment on learning. The subject was then asked to help another adult (actually the researcher's confederate) learn a lengthy list of word pairs by using electric shock as a penalty for each incorrect answer.

The subject (teacher) met with the alleged learner and then watched as the learner was strapped into an apparatus that looked like an electric chair (Figure 9.6). The experimenter then took the subject into the next room and showed him how to communicate with the learner through an intercom system

■   **Figure 9.7**

The Experimental Set-Up in the Milgram Studies

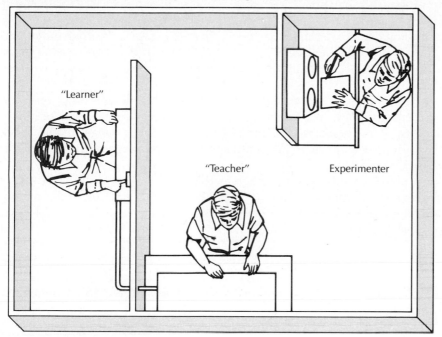

When the "learner" makes an error, the experimenter prods the "teacher" to deliver a painful electric shock.

Source: *Psychology*, 3/e by Spencer A. Rathus, p. 657. Copyright © 1987 by Holt, Rinehart and Winston, Inc., reprinted by permission of the publisher.

(Figure 9.7). The experimenter also explained how to administer the punishment for any errors the learner might make in responding to stimulus words in the list of word pairs. The shock generator contained 30 switches, one for each of 30 different voltage levels ranging from 15 to 450 volts. The switches were also labeled in terms of the increasing strength of the voltage: slight shock, moderate shock, strong shock, very strong shock, intense shock, extreme intensity shock, danger: severe shock, and XXX.

After reading the list of word pairs to the learner, the teacher was to begin quizzing the learner. For each incorrect response, the teacher was to administer an electric shock, and for each additional incorrect response, the teacher was to apply the next higher voltage level on the generator.

The trials passed uneventfully until the learner began to make numerous mistakes. Then, in short order, the teacher found himself administering fairly high levels of voltage to the learner. At that point, the learner would begin to protest, saying that he wanted to drop out of the experiment because his heart was bothering him and the pain of the shocks was too much for him. If the teacher hesitated, the experimenter would encourage him to proceed, saying, for example, "Please go on" or "It is essential that you continue." If the teacher refused to proceed after four verbal encouragements, the experiment was discontinued.

As the voltage levels increased, the confederate (in accord with the experiment's protocol) would voice even stronger objections: he would pound on the wall and, at one point, scream loudly. Beyond a certain voltage level, the learner would no longer answer any of the teacher's questions, giving the impression that he was injured or dead. When this silence occurred, the experimenter would tell the teacher to treat the learner's failure to respond as an incorrect response, to administer the punishment, and to continue on with the next word pair.

Given these conditions, you would probably assume that very few subjects would obey the experimenter. But the actual results revealed that a majority of the subjects administered the maximum voltage on the shock generator and continued their participation in the experiment despite the learner's objections.

Table 9.2 displays the point at which each of the 40 subjects broke off his participation. As the table shows, 26 out of 40, or 65 percent, of the participants administered the maximum level of electric shock. We should note, however, that although most subjects gave the maximum level of shock to the learner, they did not enjoy doing so. Typically, the subjects displayed strong signs of nervous tension, such as nail biting, trembling, and groaning. Many of them also laughed nervously whenever the learner protested or pleaded. However, the constraints of the situation compelled the subjects to continue their participation.††

The high level of obedience displayed by Milgram's subjects suggests that the predisposition to follow authority is very strong. In this case, the experimenter relied on his expertise and legitimacy to give the subject orders. Despite the fact that all subjects received their pay in advance and participated voluntarily, most felt a strong desire to avoid disobeying authority, even in light of the suffering they inflicted on another person.

These results suggest that society may be too successful at socializing its members to obey authority. When people take on roles that prescribe obedience (such as those of research subject, student, soldier, or employee), the sense of responsibility for the outcomes of their own conduct is likely to be diminished. The evidence from Milgram's work implies that human conscience cannot be relied on to step in and halt activities that are injurious to others. It can be inferred that organizational members generally will carry out orders given by those in authority, regardless of the content or consequences of the actions. This suggests that forms of socialization that emphasize personal responsibility to others may be lacking in our society.

Milgram's findings have raised a number of questions. One of the more intriguing is whether there are cultural differences in the predisposition to obey authority. For example, considering the Holocaust — the persecution and extermination of European Jews by Nazi Germany — one might hypothesize that the level of obedience would be higher in Germany than in other countries. To test this notion, the conditions of Milgram's original study were

†† When each subject completed the experiment, he met with the learner and discovered that in fact no shocks had been given. The true purpose of the study was then explained to each subject.

▪ Table 9.2

Voltage Levels Where Subjects Break Off Their Participation

Voltage Level	Number of Subjects Stopping
Slight Shock	
15	0
30	0
45	0
60	0
Moderate Shock	
75	0
90	0
105	0
120	0
Strong Shock	
135	0
150	0
165	0
180	0
Very Strong Shock	
195	0
210	0
225	0
240	0
Intense Shock	
255	0
270	0
285	0
300*	5
Extreme Intensity Shock	
315	4
330	2
345	1
360	1
Danger: Severe Shock	
375	1
390	0
405	0
420	0
XXX	
435	0
450	26

* At 300 volts, the learner no longer responded to the teacher.

OB Focus

Obeying Unethical Orders

When an organization's leaders are pursuing legitimate goals, obedience is a necessary ingredient in the organization's smooth functioning. But if a leader's orders are unethical, obedience can do great damage. For Regina Company, an unethical CEO and obedient subordinates brought about the bankruptcy of the organization.

That CEO was Donald D. Sheelen, who launched his business career as a stockbroker with Bache and Co. after he earned his MBA. He joined Regina in 1980, eventually becoming the vacuum cleaner company's marketing chief. Sheelen's colleagues were impressed by his good ideas backed by an intense drive to succeed. He added new products and boosted the company's profits. Four years after he joined the company, Sheelen was named its chief executive officer. In the following years, the company reported tremendous earnings growth.

But the numbers being reported masked some growing problems.

To support Sheelen's eagerness to boost sales, the company was skipping testing procedures on new products. By the spring of 1987, Regina was being swamped by returned merchandise. In one quarter alone, customers returned more than 40,000 of the company's Housekeeper vacuum cleaners, 16 percent of sales.

To keep the company's stock price high, Sheelen in December 1987 ordered his chief financial officer, Vincent P. Golden, to not record the returned products. Golden initially protested that this would be unethical accounting, but he gave in and had his staff alter the company's computer systems to make the change. His reason for obeying, he reported later through his lawyer, was to protect his job.

Now that he had Golden's cooperation, Sheelen was able to build on the initial deceit. He told Golden to juggle the books to show $180 million in sales, and earnings per share of $1.20. Golden managed to do this by adjusting the way the company reported sales, by understating

expenses, and by generating about 200 phony invoices.

Sheelen's final deceit again involved the company's products. In a meeting with Wall Street analysts (whom Sheelen hoped would recommend Regina's stock), Sheelen demonstrated the purported superiority of the Housekeeper vacuum cleaner by showing how well it cleaned up the corn flakes he sprinkled on the carpet. Unknown to the analysts, engineers had rigged the demonstration model to have greater suction than the machines actually being sold to customers.

But even with the support of his subordinates, Sheelen could not maintain the deceit indefinitely. In the fall of 1988, he reported the company's troubles and resigned his post. After pleading guilty to mail and securities fraud, he was sentenced to a year in a prison work center and fined $25,000. Golden also pleaded guilty, and received half of the same sentence. The following year, Regina began reorganizing under Chapter 11 of the bankruptcy code.

Source: John A. Byrne, "How Don Sheelen Made a Mess That Regina Couldn't Clean Up," *Business Week*, February 12, 1990, 46–47.

recreated in several different countries: England, Canada, Jordan, and West Germany. The results yielded essentially similar findings, suggesting that the level of obedience to authority in the Milgram condition is fairly constant across different societies.[19] By inference, the atrocities that occurred in Nazi Germany could happen elsewhere in the world.‡‡

In addition, the level of obedience in the Milgram study may have been near the "baseline" for injurious behavior. The victim (learner) in Milgram's

‡‡ Such mass atrocities have in fact happened again — witness Cambodia, Uganda, Mao's China, and Stalin's Russia.

original study was an innocent 47-year-old man. If the victim had been someone whom the subject disliked for any number of possible reasons (race, religion, or politics) or had the subject possessed a strong commitment to the
purpose of the study in which he was involved, or expected to be continually
involved with persons in the study, the level of obedience might well have been
much higher.

Since the time of Milgram's studies, greater concern has arisen over
research ethics and specifically the need to protect subjects from traumatic
experiences. Because of these concerns about the rights of subjects, it has
become exceedingly difficult to obtain peer approval to conduct and publish
similar research. Therefore, something of a moratorium exists on conducting
studies such as Milgram's that may involve unpleasant experiences for the
subject. As a result, it cannot be determined whether the present level of
obedience among Americans is lower than in the past. Some national experiences, such as the Watergate scandal and the Vietnam War protests, have
certainly made it more socially acceptable to oppose authority. It is probably
safe to say that it is now somewhat more difficult to extract conformity in a
variety of settings (including work, school, and government) than it has been in
the past.

In summary, Milgram's research suggests that people placed in a conflict
situation pitting moral values against authority will tend to follow the dictates
of authority. Perhaps the most sobering aspect of this discovery lies in how
little real power an authority figure needs in order to succeed in directing
others. Of course, opportunities for the abuse of authority also occur in business organizations. Because of this reality, it is essential that managers recognize the magnitude of their power over others and act in accordance with the
responsibility that such power entails.

Summary

1. Define and distinguish power, authority, influence, and politics.
Power is the ability to change the behavior of others; it may be legitimate or
illegitimate, used to attain common goals or personal gain. Authority is the
legitimate use of power in the pursuit of common goals. Influence is also
defined as the ability to change other people's behavior, but in subtler, more
specific, and less reliable ways. Politics constitutes the actions taken to obtain,
develop, and use power.

2. Identify and describe three primary influence processes.
Kelman identified three reasons a person yields to another's influence: compliance, identification, and internalization. Compliance entails yielding to influence in the hope of receiving a reward or avoiding a punishment. Identification
arises out of the desire to establish or maintain a satisfying relationship with
the person exercising the influence. With internalization, the person being
influenced believes the behavior is correct and appropriate.

3. List and define five bases of power.
According to French and Raven, five bases of power are reward power, coer-

cive power, legitimate power, referent power, and expert power. Reward power is the ability to determine who will receive particular rewards. Coercive power is the ability to punish or produce fear in others. Legitimate power arises from willingness to accept an individual's direction because of social conditioning or designation. Referent power is the ability to influence others because of one's attractiveness or ability to inspire. Expert power is the power that arises from being perceived as knowledgeable or talented in some area.

4. Describe some differences between formal and informal power.
Managers with informal power — expert and referent power — have greater capacity to affect the satisfaction and performance of employees, whereas formal power — legitimate, reward, and coercive power — potentially has more impact on immediate behavior. Formal power will not necessarily produce agreement and commitment. Informal power bases are more easily eroded and can be harder to control. In general, informal power resides in the manager's personal characteristics, while formal power resides in the position itself.

5. Distinguish the kinds of power organizations use, name a type of organization corresponding to each type of power, and describe the nature of member involvement in an organization that uses that type of power.
According to Etzioni, organizations attempt to direct the behavior of their members with three kinds of power: coercive, utilitarian, and normative. Coercive power is used by prisons, some mental institutions, and divisions within the military. Members of these organizations are characterized by alienative involvement. Most businesses rely on utilitarian power and characteristically have members with calculative involvement. Organizations that rely on normative power include professional associations and religious organizations. The involvement of their members is moral in nature.

6. Describe the cycle of approaches that supervisors use to influence subordinates.
According to Sussmann and Vecchio, supervisors' attempts to influence a subordinate follow a cycle in which the supervisor tries using compliance (by threatening), identification (by appealing to the subordinate's sense of membership), or internalization (by appealing to the subordinate's values). If one influence attempt fails, the supervisor then tries a different type of influence.

7. Identify several political tactics, including devious political tactics and political blunders.
Political tactics include ingratiation, forming coalitions and networks, impression management, information management, promoting the opposition, and pursuing line responsibility. Political tactics considered devious include eliminating all enemies, creating a feud between potential rivals, and excluding the opposition. Common political blunders are violating the organization's chain of command, losing one's cool, rejecting a request from top management, upstaging one's boss, and challenging cherished beliefs of the organization.

8. Explain several techniques for coping with organizational politics.

A manager can create a positive climate for subordinates by setting an example of truthfulness and even-handed treatment. A manager can make expectations for performance clear by giving well-defined, discrete work assignments. Coalitions and cliques that interfere with group performance can be eliminated through dismissal, transfer, or job rotation. Managers can bring game playing into the open by confronting the players or offering to discuss the situation in a public forum.

9. Support an argument that pressures to conform are powerful.

In a series of studies by Solomon Asch, many subjects rejected even clear objective data in order to conform to the group's consensus. With more subjective or ambiguous data, the power of group pressure is likely to be even greater. It is also likely to be greater for group members who probably will be involved on a continuing basis and who have a strong desire to be liked by the group.

10. Cite evidence that the predisposition to obey authority is strong.

In a study conducted by Stanley Milgram, subjects obeyed the authority of the researcher, even though the researcher's authority was limited and the subjects were aware that they were severely hurting an innocent person. This research suggests that the predisposition to follow authority is very strong and that when people take on roles that prescribe obedience, their sense of responsibility for the outcome of their conduct is diminished.

Key Terms

Power	Expert power
Authority	Utilitarian power
Influence	Normative power
Compliance	Alienative involvement
Identification	Calculative involvement
Internalization	Moral involvement
Reward power	Organizational politics
Coercive power	Mach Scale
Legitimate power	Conformity
Referent power	

Review and Discussion Questions

1. Dan Williams, vice-president of research and development, is so charming that his colleagues invariably take his side in meetings. As a result, the R&D budget has grown 10 percent every year since 1983. Does Dan have power? Authority? Explain your answers.

2. Bernice Wilson supervises production workers in a small widget assembly factory. She believes that the best way to use her influence is to use rewards and punishments to achieve compliance with company rules. Although Bernice prefers to spend hot summer days in her air-conditioned office, she goes out into the plant at the end of each day

to ask questions and find out who should be rewarded and who punished. What is Bernice forgetting?

3. According to French and Raven, what are the five bases of power? Give an example of each.

4. Should a manager exercise power frequently, or would the manager's power have more impact if he or she saved it for unusual occasions? Explain your answer.

5. Why might people with formal power tend to remain in their positions of authority longer than those who rely on informal power?

6. Sue Blue, sales manager for Acme Hospital Supply, notices that sales are slipping in New Mexico and flies down to visit the New Mexico sales rep, Jean Green. Sue tells Jean, "The hospitals in this state really need our supplies to save patients' lives. Because the hospitals do such important work, you really should try harder." The next month, Sue is disappointed to find that sales in New Mexico have not improved. Based on Etzioni's model of power, offer Sue a possible explanation for her failure to influence Jean.

7. French and Raven, Kelman, and Etzioni describe three models of power and influence. How can these models be reconciled?

8. When Todd McCrae was a teller, nothing motivated him like the fear of being fired. Now that the bank has put him in charge of the tellers, Todd intends to motivate them all in the way that worked for him. After all, he knows first-hand that it works. Do you agree with Todd? Why or why not?

9. Why might ingratiation be a successful political tactic even when the person is using it blatantly?

10. What is a line position? In what ways might it be advantageous to hold a line position in an organization?

11. Name two characteristics that would lead you to consider a person "Machiavellian." Would you expect such a person to engage in political behavior relatively frequently or relatively infrequently?

12. Stanley Milgram's research suggests that people obey authority figures even when they question whether their own behavior is ethical. Do you think the results of his research apply to the people in your community today? Why or why not? Is this good or bad for your community?

Critical Incident

Warner Memorial Hospital

Warner Memorial Hospital is located in a moderate-sized community, approximately 45 miles from a major metropolitan area. It is a 240-bed facility that employs about 300 people. During the past year, there have been wide fluctuations in the patient census. The chief negotiator for the Allied Health Workers Union, Betty Gordon, was visibly concerned about the new labor contract negotiations that were to begin in two days. She was afraid that the union would be asked to agree to wage and benefit concessions. Remembering the last contract negotiations, which resulted in a 41-day strike, did little to ease her concern. At those negotiations three years ago, few of the more critical issues separating labor and management were really settled.

The head of labor relations for the hospital, Bill Lenox, was also thinking about the upcoming negotiations. He recalled the last contract negotiations and some of the unrealistic demands that were presented by the union. Given that this was a healthcare service and delivery organization, Bill was convinced that the workers, especially the nurses and technicians, would be better off without the union.

The union holds a very strong position at Warner Memorial. Most of the eligible workers belong, which affects all aspects of hospital operations. The hospital could not easily replace these employees during a strike. Betty firmly believes that the union members are seeking improvements in wages and benefits. She is not convinced that management wishes to reach an equitable contract agreement. The union members also believe that if management really wanted to attract more patients, they would be investing in newer equipment and initiating a marketing program.

Bill and his staff have been spending weeks getting ready for the negotiations. They have pages of data in support of the need for concessions or at least a wage freeze. Bill is convinced that the union will adamantly oppose any request for concessions and that volatile, emotional arguments are inevitable. The hospital is not in a position to grant meaningful increases in wages and benefits and can ill afford a strike. Perhaps some patients as well as workers would be lost forever to the hospital's market-intensive competitors in a nearby city, 45 miles north.

Questions

1. What bases of power are evident in this case for Betty? For Bill?

2. What political tactics or games can be identified in this case?

3. What do you predict is likely to happen? What do you propose as a possible solution?

Source: Written by Bruce Kemelgor, University of Louisville; used by permission.

Experiential Exercise

Who Has Power?

In organizational settings, there are usually five types of power: legitimate, reward, coercive, referent, and expert. An individual may have one or more of these kinds of power; also, the person who possesses power is not necessarily considered a manager or leader.

This exercise examines power across several sets of individuals or occupations. For example, set 1 considers the power your professor, as the focal person, has over a student, the significant other. Thus, you should check which kind of power the professor has over students. But also in set 1, you should consider another possibility; that is, in the reverse sense, what power might the student as the focal person possess over the professor as the significant other? Complete the table for the eight sets, indicating on the first line the power of the focal person over the significant other and on the second line the power of the significant other over the focal person.

Questions

1. On balance, which person — the focal person or the significant other — has the most power? Make this judgment for each set.

2. Indicate, for each set, which of the five types of power is the most significant.

3. Can you identify instances in which a power base is equally divided between the focal person and the significant other? If so, can you explain why this occurs?

Set	Focal Person	Significant Other	Power				
			Legitimate	Reward	Coercive	Referent	Expert
1	Professor Student	Student Professor					
2	Manager — grocery store Cashier/checker	Cashier/checker Manager — grocery store					
3	President of the U.S. U.S. citizens	U.S. citizens President of the U.S.					
4	Secretary Executive	Executive Secretary					
5	Audit supervisor, IRS Agents for IRS	Agents for IRS Audit supervisor, IRS					
6	Mentor Mentee	Mentee Mentor					
7	University president Deans	Deans University president					
8	Car salesperson Customer	Customer Car salesperson					

Source: Griffin, Ricky W. and Thomas C. Head, *Practicing Management*, Second Edition. Copyright © 1987 by Houghton Mifflin Company. Used with permission.

Notes

1. D.C. McClelland, *Power: The Inner Experience* (New York: Irvington, 1975); D.C. McClelland, "Power is the Great Motivation," *Harvard Business Review* 54 (1976): 100–110.

2. H.C Kelman, "Processes of Opinion Change," *Public Opinion Quarterly* 25 (1961): 57–78.

3. J.R.P. French, Jr., and B.H. Raven, "The Bases of Social Power," in *Studies in Social Power,* ed. D. Cartwright (Ann Arbor: University of Michigan, Institute for Social Research, 1959); T. Hinkin and C. Schriesheim, "Development and Application of New Scales to Measure the French and Raven Bases of Social Power," *Journal of Applied Psychology* 74 (1989): 561–567.

4. A. Etzioni, *A Comparative Analysis of Complex Organizations,* rev. ed. (New York: Free Press, 1975); R. Mayer, "Understanding Employee Motivation through Organizational Commitment" (Ph.D. diss., Purdue University, 1989).

5. M. Sussmann and R.P. Vecchio, "A Social Influence Interpretation of Worker Motivation," *Academy of Management Review* 7 (1982): 177–186; R.P. Vecchio and M. Sussmann, "Preference for Forms of Supervisory Social Influence," *Journal of Organizational Behavior* 10 (1989): 135–143.

6. Ibid.

7. J. Pfeffer, *Power in Organizations* (Boston: Pitman Publishing Co., 1981).

8. R.W. Allen, D.L. Madison, L.W. Porter et al., "Organizational Politics: Tactics and Characteristics of Its Actors," *California Management Review* 12 (Fall 1979): 77–83; A.J. DuBrin, *Winning at Office Politics* (New York: Ballantine, 1978); R.H. Miles, *Macro Organizational Behavior* (Santa Monica, Calif.: Goodyear, 1980), 174–175; Pfeffer, *Power in Organizations.*

9. DuBrin, *Winning at Office Politics.*

10. R. Christie and F.L. Geis, eds., *Studies in Machiavellianism* (New York: Academic Press, 1970).

11. G.R. Gemmil and W.J. Heisler, "Machiavellianism as a Factor in Managerial Job Strain, Job Satisfaction and Upward Mobility," *Academy of Management Journal* 15 (1972): 53–67.

12. R.V. Exline, J. Thibaut, C.O. Hickey et al., "Visual Interaction in Relation to Machiavellianism and an Unethical Act," in *Studies in Machiavellianism,* ed. R. Christie and F.L. Geis (New York: Academic Press, 1970), 53–75; D. Kipnis and S.M. Schmidt, *Profiles of Organizational Influence Strategies* (San Diego: University Associates, 1982); S.M. Schmidt and D. Kipnis, "The Perils of Persistence," *Psychology Today,* November 1987, 32–34; D. Kipnis, *The Powerholders* (Chicago: University of Chicago Press, 1976); P. Block, *The Empowered Manager* (San Francisco: Jossey-Bass, 1988).

13. Kipnis and Schmidt, *Profiles of Organizational Influence Strategies.*

14. Schmidt and Kipnis, "The Perils of Persistence."

15. Kipnis, *The Powerholders;* Block, *The Empowered Manager.*

16. G.F. Cavanagh, D.J. Moberg, and M. Velasquez, "The Ethics of Organizational Politics," *Academy of Management Review* 6 (1981): 363–374.

17. S.E. Asch, "Effects of Group Pressure upon the Modification and Distortion of Judgments," in *Groups, Leadership and Men,* ed. H. Guetzkow (Pittsburgh: Carnegie Press, 1951); S.E. Asch, "Studies of Independence and Conformity: A Minority of One against a Unanimous Majority," *Psychological Monographs* 70, whole no. 416 (1956); S.E. Asch, "Effects of Group Pressure upon Modification and Distortion of Judgments," in *Readings in Social Psychology,* 3d ed., ed. E.E. Maccoby, T.M. Newcomb, and E.L. Hartley (New York: Holt, Rinehart, 1958), 174–183.

18. S. Milgram, "Behavioral Study of Obedience," *Journal of Abnormal and Social Psychology* 67 (1963): 371–378.

19. S. Milgram, *Obedience to Authority* (New York: Harper, 1974); M.E. Shanah and K.A. Yahya, "A Behavioral Study of Obedience in Children," *Journal of Personality and Social Psychology* 35 (1977): 530–536.

Nearly all men can stand adversity, but if you want to test a man's character, give him power.

— Abe Lincoln

The people are the most important element, the land and grain are the next, the ruler is least important.

— Meng-Tse
Chinese Philosopher

By working faithfully 8 hours a day, you may eventually get to be a boss and work 12 hours a day.

— Robert Frost

Learning Objectives

After studying this chapter, you should be able to:

1. *Define leadership.*

2. *List some attributes that are associated with leadership.*

3. *Describe ways in which leader behavior is related to employee attitudes and performance.*

4. *Identify the factors underlying situational favorableness and explain how they influence a leader's effectiveness.*

5. *Explain how leaders can clarify paths to goals to motivate employees.*

6. *Describe the components of subordinate maturity and the relevance of subordinate maturity to leadership style.*

7. *Describe the decision-making styles of the Vroom–Yetton model and explain how to use a decision tree to select the appropriate style.*

8. *Describe a way to evaluate leadership style taking into account managers' views of different employees.*

9. *Identify similarities and differences among the major leadership models.*

10. *Define leadership substitute and leadership neutralizer and give examples of each.*

Leadership

■ Creating Peak Performance

What makes a manager a peak performer? Knowing the characteristics of top performers might make it possible to find — or train — leaders. It's no wonder that many researchers have attempted to identify these characteristics.

Charles A. Garfield, president of the Performance Sciences Institute in Berkeley, California, used interviews to arrive at these ten common traits of top-performing managers:

1. They have foresight and the ability to do effective strategic planning. This makes them less prone to be consumed with achieving short-term gain at the expense of long-term goals.

2. They decide in advance on their needs for staffing, equipment, finances, and other resources.

3. They refuse to become entrapped on a plateau for long; instead, they strive toward ever-higher levels of accomplishment.

4. They have a superior ability to take creative risks. They often assess their risk taking by envisioning the worst possible outcome and then deciding what they would do if this worst case should occur.

5. They demonstrate high levels of self-confidence and self-worth. They treat failure and rejection as only temporary setbacks and heed only criticism that is constructive.

6. They need responsibility and control. They are unafraid of taking action and rarely feel victimized by circumstances. They generate new ways to solve old problems.

7. They mentally rehearse key situations. Envisioning the process and the desired outcome imprints success on their minds.

8. They tend to work for the art and passion of it, not for the praise of others.

9. They concentrate on solving problems, not assigning blame. They use feedback for self-correction. As a result, subordinates act and take risks.

10. They assume ownership of their ideas and products.

Can managers like this be developed, or do people have to be born like the managers described here? Garfield says these qualities can be learned. A management training program can help a manager through these stages in the development of a peak-performing manager:

- *Initiation* — The manager learns to identify him or herself with the role of manager.

- *Fear of success* — The manager may begin to perform so well that he or she actually becomes afraid of doing well, fearing that success will lead to too much additional responsibility.

- *Team building* — The manager becomes fully committed to the management position, but suddenly has difficulty generating new leaders and forming a team. The manager may have trouble delegating at this stage.
- *Affiliation* — The manager realizes that while his or her productivity depends on the work of others, he or she alone is responsible for managerial performance. At this stage, the manager develops upward and downward relationships.
- *Elevation to seniority* — The manager is selected for a position in senior management.

By helping managers to develop as leaders, companies obtain people who are able not only to manage the work, but also to inspire their subordinates.

This chapter explores the important role of leadership. It discusses different ways to evaluate what makes a leader and suggests some characteristics of effective leaders. The chapter also considers situations in which the traits of good leadership may vary or even take second place to other considerations.

Source: Charles A. Garfield, "Peak Performance for Managers," *Sky,* July 1985, pp. 18+.

What makes a manager an effective leader? What personal attributes distinguish effective leaders from ineffective leaders? And what situational factors can help a person be more effective as a leader? These are the questions asked by both managers and the people who study organizational behavior. In an effort to answer these questions, managers have at times helped researchers by serving as subjects in studies of leadership. The results of both empirical and conceptual investigations of leadership have produced an enormous body of knowledge.

In the most recent edition of the *Handbook of Leadership,* a fairly complete compendium of research on the topic, Bernard M. Bass identified nearly 5,000 studies and treatises dealing with the behavioral aspects of leadership.[1] Trying to make sense of such a mass of information is no simple task. Nonetheless, certain themes and consistencies can be identified. In this chapter, we will begin by examining the nature of leadership and its defining characteristics. We will then consider a variety of approaches to understanding the leadership puzzle, each of which offers unique insights into the leadership process.

The Nature of Leadership

Although many different definitions have been offered for leadership, most definitions contain certain common elements. A distillation of these elements suggests that **leadership** can be defined as a process through which a person tries to get organizational members to do something that the person desires. This definition overlaps, to a great extent, with the way in which we defined influence in the previous chapter. Therefore, leadership must be viewed as an influence process.

Typically, we think of leadership as being associated with the role of manager. However, *leader* and *manager* are not equivalent terms. Someone may be an outstanding manager without in fact being a work group's leader. While the group's manager performs planning, organizing, and controlling activities, the real leader may actually be one of the subordinates. So, too, a work group's nominal head may be a great leader, while requiring that others handle the functional duties of planning, organizing, and controlling for the unit.

Leadership thus implies something more than mere supervisory responsibility or formal authority. It consists of influence that extends beyond the usual influence that accompanies legitimacy as a supervisor. Therefore, it can be said that leadership is the *incremental influence,* or additional influence, that a person has beyond his or her formal authority. Incremental influence can exist to varying degrees in every member of a work group. As a result, it is not uncommon to find situations in which a subordinate who lacks formal authority actually possesses substantial incremental influence. We would call such an individual an **informal leader**. Informal leaders are often invaluable to their groups because they can aid coworkers in a number of different ways. For example, an informal leader may possess technical expertise that even the formal leader lacks. Or an informal leader may have special social skills (such as the ability to make people feel good about themselves or their accomplishments) that can maintain or improve group morale.

The presence of an informal leader (or leaders) may sound like a distinct plus for a manager. However, this is not always the case. Occasionally, an informal leader's values may not coincide with those of the formal leader. Sometimes the informal leader may encourage his peers to be less productive or more demanding in order to extract greater rewards from the formal leader. In so doing, an informal leader may become a political opponent. Clearly, the presence of an informal leader is not inherently a good or bad thing. The ultimate value of an informal leader depends on whether he or she supports or opposes the goals of the organization.

Thus, the differences between leadership and headship can be quite distinct, and leadership may exist on both formal and informal levels. While it might not be technically correct to use the terms *leader* and *manager* interchangeably, we will do so throughout the remainder of this chapter, because most views on the topic of leadership refer primarily to formal leaders, or managers, and do not maintain the distinction between leadership and headship.

What Do Managers Actually Do?

Before examining the major studies of leadership, it is instructive to consider what managers do during a typical day. By considering what managers actually do, we can develop an appreciation of what such jobs are like.

Studies of actual on-the-job behavior reveal that most managers perform a large number of brief, highly varied, and fragmented activities. The results of these studies, which are usually obtained through direct observation or by having a manager maintain a daily log of activities, suggest that the popular notion of the harried executive is fairly accurate. One such study found that on only nine occasions during a 4-week period did a manager remain uninterrupted for a 30-minute or longer stretch of time.[2] In another study, it was found that CEOs averaged over 50 written and verbal contacts per day, with half of these activities taking less than 9 minutes and only one-tenth taking more than an hour.[3] Other researchers also have argued that most of a manager's time is devoted to face-to-face or telephone communications. The recurring nature of the problems tackled by a manager over a period of time is difficult to describe succinctly. However, one colorful summarization suggested by Marples is that "the manager's job can usefully be pictured as a stranded rope made up of fibers of different lengths — where length represents time — each fiber coming to the surface one or more times in observable 'episodes' and each representing a single issue."[4]

Given the nonroutine nature of managerial work, it is reasonable to ask where managers find time to communicate with their people on a personal level or to attempt to motivate them. Often, there is truly little time for such activities. More typically, managers are involved in "putting out fires" and managing problems than in developing the human resources within their work units.

Approaches to Leadership

The Trait Approach

Prior to the 1950s, researchers sought to understand leadership by comparing leaders with followers and effective leaders with ineffective leaders. This search for features of leaders, or leader traits, was prompted by a belief that leaders somehow possessed distinguishing traits that set them apart from other people. The logic of this approach is very simple and straightforward: To understand what makes some individuals more effective as leaders, merely measure such people on a large number of psychological, social, and physical attributes and note how they differ from most others.

As the research progressed (mostly during the 1930s and 1940s), the number of traits of suspected importance began to grow. Moreover, the results became increasingly mixed and did not follow a clear pattern. Finally, in 1948, Ralph Stogdill published a review of the trait researchers' findings that was so devastating that it seriously curtailed the amount of trait research that would subsequently be conducted.[5]

By and large, the trait studies did not show any simple pattern of traits that was both strongly and consistently related to leadership.[6] At first glance, this seems surprising. Based on personal experience and observations, we might expect to find consistent differences between effective and ineffective leaders. However, if we consider a large number of effective leaders, we reach a different conclusion. For example, observations and experience may lead one to believe that effective leaders are likely to be outgoing and socially assertive. Yet, there have been outstanding leaders who were relatively shy and withdrawn, such as Abraham Lincoln and Mahatma Gandhi.

The search for leader traits, however, was not a total failure. Several traits do appear to be very modestly but inconsistently associated with leadership. Chief among these traits is intelligence. It appears that people who hold leadership positions tend to be somewhat more intelligent. On the other hand, there is good reason to believe that highly intelligent people are not likely to attain or maintain leadership in many settings.[7] According to this line of reasoning, individuals who are much brighter than their potential followers may have difficulty in communicating and relating to them.* In essence, there may be an optimal level of intelligence for a leader in a given situation.

Although intelligence has been shown to correlate only modestly with leadership, recent work by Fred Fiedler and his associates suggests that under special circumstances, leader intelligence and other cognitive attributes can be highly correlated with effectiveness.[8] In particular, Fiedler found that in situations combining a leader's ability to be directive and a stress-free environment, intelligence can be used to predict work-unit performance with a fairly high degree of accuracy. Called **cognitive resource theory**, this view argues that directive leaders who are intelligent and possess relevant job experience will be more effective if they are in stress-free settings with subordinates that are supportive. This fairly straightforward perspective of what makes for effective leadership is, in fact, the logic that underlies much of the hiring of managers. That is to say, when selecting supervisors, it is common to search for experienced managers possessing a fair degree of intelligence plus social skills that can be used to build supportiveness and reduce interpersonal stress.

Several other traits have also been linked to successful leaders. For example, Stogdill has argued that leaders can be characterized by task persistence, self-confidence, tolerance of interpersonal stress, and the ability to influence others' behavior.[9] And one somewhat surprising finding is a low but positive correlation between leadership status and height, which suggests that taller individuals have something of an advantage in gaining leadership positions. This may reflect a desire on the part of many people to "look up" to their leaders.

Table 10.1 lists the traits and skills that have been frequently linked to effective leaders.[10] However, the usefulness of these traits as predictors of effectiveness depends to a large extent on the specific situation. One conclusion that can be drawn from the modest findings of the trait approach is that the assumption that "leaders are born, not made" is not at all defensible. It appears that effective leadership depends less on the leader's predispositions than on how well the leader can adapt to the unique needs of different situations.

The Behavioral Approach

As interest in the trait approach to leadership declined, researchers focused their attention on leaders' actions rather than on their attributes. These studies of leader behavior tried to identify specific styles of leader conduct and attempted to discover whether leader behavior was associated with employee attitudes and performance.

One of the earliest studies of leader behavior addressed the question of whether a democratic style of leadership is more effective than an authoritar-

---

* This argument is sometimes raised in political commentary to explain why the candidates for the presidency of the United States are usually not terribly intellectual (i.e., a majority of the voting populace would have a difficult time identifying with an intellectual president).

■　**Table 10.1**

*Attributes Found Most Frequently to be Characteristic
of Successful Leaders**

Traits	Physical Factors	Skills
Adaptable to situations	**Activity level**	**Intelligent**
Alert to social environment	Appearance	Conceptually skilled
Ambitious and achievement oriented	Height	Creative
Assertive	Weight	Diplomatic and tactful
Cooperative		Fluent in speaking
Decisive		**Knowledgeable about group task**
Dependable		
Dominant (desire to influence others)		Organized (administrative ability)
Persistent		Persuasive
Self-confident		Socially skilled
Tolerant of stress		
Willing to assume responsibility		

* Boldface attributes have the greatest association with leadership.

Source: G. Yukl, *Leadership in Organizations,* 1981, p. 70. Prentice-Hall Publishing Co., Englewood Cliffs, N.J.

ian or a laissez-faire style. To compare these styles of leadership in a controlled situation, Lewin, Lippett, and White randomly assigned 10-year-old boys to one of three groups involved in hobby activities after school hours.[11] In these groups, the boys did such things as make toy boats and papier-maché masks. Each group was under the direction of an adult who behaved in either a democratic, an authoritarian, or a laissez-faire style.

In the authoritarian condition, the adult leader assigned specific tasks to each individual, decided what was to be done without consulting the boys, assigned work partners, was subjective in his praise, and remained aloof from the group's activities. In contrast, the democratic leader allowed the group to decide who was to perform which task, permitted the boys to pick their own work partners, gave specific feedback on how to improve craftsmanship, and tried to be an involved member of the group. The laissez-faire leader was very detached from the group's activities. He gave the group members complete freedom to do what they wished and provided information only when he was specifically asked.

The boys' reactions were greatly influenced by the style of leadership to which they were subjected. Boys in the democratically led group were more satisfied and displayed less aggression toward one another than did boys in the autocratically led group. While there was a slight tendency for the boys in the authoritarian setting to produce more items, judges rated the quality of output to be highest in the democratically led group. Another interesting finding from this study was that boys in the autocratically led group tended to stop working and engage in horseplay whenever the leader left the room.

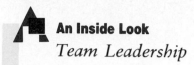

An Inside Look
Team Leadership

How is being a boss like coaching a sports team? There's a lot more to the job than calling the plays. Like a winning coach, a skillful manager is master of strategy and tactics, inspirational leader, authority figure, mother hen, and even occasionally a father confessor.

Briefly, being a leader in an organization means being a thoroughly competent person who sets the organization's goals and is able to express them to subordinates. This means recognizing that people want guidance from their leaders. Movie director George Cukor tried thinking of himself as a fellow collaborator rather than as a boss. However, he concluded that it is "reassuring for people to feel they have a boss, someone who knows the answers and has charted the course."

Although the manager should chart the course, the next step is to let employees get on with the job. People want freedom in carrying out their work. The manager's job is to manage work, not to do it all. The manager should accept workers' imperfections; with guidance and follow-up, they will do increasingly accurate work.

Other tips for would-be leaders: Employees are inspired by a manager who recognizes their accomplishments publicly. In particular, managers should communicate subordinates' accomplishments upward. The manager should also be sure to communicate his or her plans up and down the ranks. Problems often stem from a lack of communication. To keep communications open, managers must be willing to hear bad news as well as good. Managers should listen to criticism; they can also respond by logically presenting their own side of the story.

Leadership seems to come naturally to some managers, but it is in fact a difficult, demanding role. Managers should not despair, however, because leadership skills can be polished with experience. Throughout their careers, managers encounter sources for learning leadership knowledge, skills, and style.

Source: "Be a Better Boss," *Changing Times*, November 1985, pp. 101–104.

It is possible to argue, however, that an autocratic style of leadership may not always be inappropriate. Sometimes a situation may call for urgent action, and in these cases an autocratic style of leadership may be best.[12] In addition, most people are familiar with autocratic leadership and therefore have less difficulty adopting that style. Furthermore, in some situations, subordinates may actually prefer an autocratic style. For example, a group of truckers may have difficulty respecting a truck dispatcher who tries to be participative rather than authoritarian in decision making.[13]

Other researchers have examined leadership styles in terms of task orientation versus employee orientation. **Task orientation** refers to the extent to which a leader shows concern for getting the job accomplished and helps to steer the group to meet its goals, while **employee orientation** reflects the extent to which a leader displays concern for the feelings and welfare of subordinates and uses warmth and friendliness to enhance the social atmosphere within the group.

Ohio State Leadership Studies   Although many researchers have studied these dimensions of leadership, one group of researchers at Ohio State University

Figure 10.1

The Ohio State Leadership Dimensions

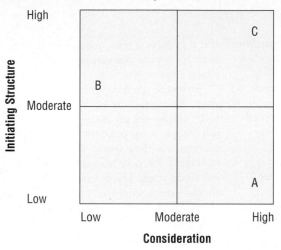

came to be noted for their efforts. These researchers proposed that consideration and initiating structure are two primary dimensions of leadership that parallel the styles of task and employee orientations. **Initiating structure** is the extent to which a leader defines and structures the work that he and his subordinates perform, with an eye toward successful task accomplishment. **Consideration** is defined as the extent to which the leader has job relationships that rely on mutual trust, respect for subordinates, and sensitivity to subordinates' feelings.

These two dimensions of leader behavior are assumed to be independent of each other, so that a leader may possess either a high or a low predisposition toward each dimension. The combination of the two dimensions for an individual suggests that several different types of managers can be identified (Figure 10.1). Manager A in Figure 10.1 would be described as highly considerate of his subordinates, while lacking a concern for employee production. Manager B, on the other hand, lacks concern for the feelings of his employees but is moderately concerned with unit output. Manager C is apparently devoted to maximizing both production and employee well-being. This third case exemplifies what some see as an ideal style, in that it combines the best of both dimensions.

Research on the Ohio State dimensions of consideration and initiating structure has generated some interesting findings. Questionnaires completed by both subordinates and leaders (Table 10.2 provides a sample of the questions) showed that high consideration was related to lower rates of grievance filings and lower turnover. However, beyond a certain point, increases in supervisory considerateness did not appear to decrease turnover and grievances further. In addition, the study found that highly considerate leaders could structure work more without risking an increase in grievances and that supervisors can, to some extent, compensate for displaying a high degree of

■   **Table 10.2**

*Sample Questions from a Questionnaire Used in Ohio State
Research on Leader Behavior*

**How Frequently Does Your Leader Do Each of the Following?
Never, Seldom, Occasionally, Often, or Always?**

Structure	Consideration
Lets work unit members know what is expected of them	Is friendly and approachable
Decides what shall be done and how it should be done	Puts suggestions made by the work unit into operation
Maintains definite standards for performance	Does little things to make it pleasant to be a member of the work unit

Source: R.M. Stogdill, 1963, *Manual for Leader Behavior Description Questionnaire — form XII.* Columbus, Ohio, Ohio State University Bureau of Business Research.

structure if they increase their considerateness. In contrast, supervisors who are low on considerateness cannot eliminate their negative impact by being less concerned with the creation of structure. Low considerateness apparently has a strong and persistent negative effect on relations with subordinates.[14] In addition, other research has rather consistently found that low considerateness is associated with employee dissatisfaction with supervisors.[15]

Although early results suggested that the combination of high consideration and high initiating structure constitutes the most successful managerial style, other studies have not corroborated this finding.[16] Recently, researchers have attempted to state the conditions under which consideration and structure are related to employee satisfaction and performance.[17] Their efforts suggest that many variables can affect the relationship between leader style and subordinate reactions. Table 10.3 lists a number of important subordinate, supervisor, and task variables that can have a moderating influence.

■   **Table 10.3**

*Variables Found to Moderate the Relationship Between
Leader Behavior and Outcome*

Subordinate Characteristics	Supervisor Characteristics	Task Characteristics
Expertise	Influence with superiors	Time urgency
Experience		Physical danger
Competence	Attitude similarity with superior	External stress
Knowledge of job	Similarity of behavior with higher management	Autonomy
Job level		Job scope
Expectations concerning the leader		Ambiguity
		Importance of task
		Meaningfulness of task
		Tolerable error rate

Source: Adapted from F. Landy and D. Trumbo, *Psychology of Work Behavior,* Homewood, Ill.: Dorsey, 1980.

■ Figure 10.2

The Managerial Grid

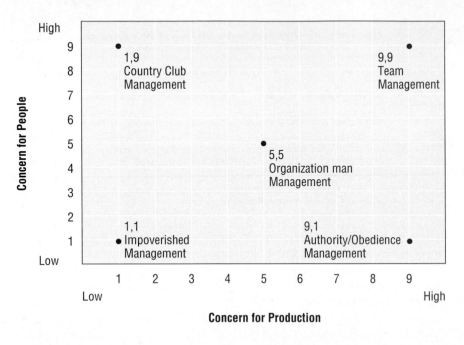

Source: R. Blake and J. Mouton, 1978, *The New Managerial Grid,* Houston: Gulf Publishing Co., p. 11.

The Managerial Grid   Practicing managers have found the Ohio State dimensions of leadership to be an appealing concept. In fact, Robert Blake and Jane Mouton have adapted the Ohio State approach to a managerial training program that explains leadership styles in the context of a grid.[18] In their Managerial Grid, the various combinations of a concern for people and a concern for production define five major leadership styles (Figure 10.2) as follows:

1. *Authority/obedience management,* or a 9,1 style, emphasizes efficiency in operations that results from arranging work conditions in such a way that human elements can only interfere to a small degree.

2. *Country-club management,* or a 1,9 style, involves thoughtful attention to the needs of people, because such satisfying relationships are expected to lead to a comfortable, friendly organizational atmosphere.

3. *Laissez-faire or impoverished management,* or a 1,1 style, is characterized by minimal effort to get the required work done and sustain organization membership.

4. *Organization man management,* or a 5,5 style, is concerned with balancing the necessity to get the work out while maintaining morale at a satisfactory level. The goal is adequate performance.

5. *Team management,* or a 9,9 style, relies on interdependence through a common stake in the organization's purpose. This interdependence leads to relationships based on trust and respect, and work accomplishment from committed employees.

The Managerial Grid model assumes that there is one best or most effective style of management — the team management, or 9,9, style. Managers who emphasize both concern for people and productivity are presumed to be more successful. As mentioned earlier, however, the evidence for a single best style of management is not convincing.†

Contingency Approaches

The behavioral approach to leadership styles was fairly popular into the mid-1960s, at which time there was a growing recognition that leadership could not be explained solely in terms of leader behavior, and that features of the context in which leadership occurred (e.g., subordinate and task attributes) also needed to be examined in order to gain a more complete and accurate understanding of leadership. In this section, we will examine several leadership models that consider situational attributes.

Fiedler's Contingency Model   Fred Fiedler was one of the earliest proponents of a leadership model that explicitly incorporated situational features. The underlying assumption of his **contingency model of leadership effectiveness** is that group performance is a function of the combination of a leader's style and several relevant features of the situation.[20]

Within the model, leadership style and the situation are defined with a high degree of precision. Leadership style is assessed with a semantic differential type of attitude scale (see Chapter 4) that measures esteem for the **least preferred coworker, or LPC.** The scale asks that a person describe the coworker, past or present, with whom he or she has had the most difficulty working. Sample items from the scale are:

Pleasant :_____:_____:_____:_____:_____:_____:_____:_____: Unpleasant
       8   7   6   5   4   3   2   1

Helpful :_____:_____:_____:_____:_____:_____:_____:_____: Frustrating
       8   7   6   5   4   3   2   1

Warm   :_____:_____:_____:_____:_____:_____:_____:_____: Cold
       8   7   6   5   4   3   2   1

A person who completes the LPC scale by giving relatively lenient responses receives a fairly high total score, while a person who gives harsh marks will obtain a relatively low score. Fiedler infers that people who attain high LPC scores are motivated to achieve positive social relations in their work groups. People with low LPC scores are judged to be less relationship oriented and more satisfied by task accomplishment. In short, high-LPC individuals are more relationship motivated, while low-LPC types are more task motivated.

---

† In response to such evidence, however, Blake and Mouton offer conceptual rather than empirical arguments as to why the 9,9 style *should* work when conditions are favorable.[19]

OB Focus

Seeking the Best Leadership Style

Blake and Mouton's Managerial Grid has intuitive appeal: People want to be liked and respected, so it is not surprising that many managers would consider the ideal leadership style to be one that enhances morale as well as productivity. As a case in point, consider Walter Riley, the chief executive of G.O.D. Inc. (for Guaranteed Overnight Delivery), a Kearney, New Jersey-based trucking company.

In 1980, when Riley took over the company, then known as Siegle's Express, his leadership style might have been characterized as a 9,1 style. Riley was consumed with making the company grow, and he admits he gave little thought to whether employees were happy. By finding a niche — guaranteeing overnight delivery to a regional marketplace — Riley soon began to accomplish his goals. G.O.D. became one of the fastest-growing small businesses in the country, and Riley planned that the company would continue to grow at 25 percent a year until sales had risen from an initial $400,000 to $200 million a year.

To motivate employees to achieve such growth, Riley devised a variety of incentive packages. The most basic was a profit-sharing plan, in which employees received a share of profits tied to ratings of their performance. To speed up dock workers, he began paying for the amount of freight moved, and he paid the drivers bonuses tied to the number of pickups and deliveries they completed. The sales staff received bonuses for meeting goals based on gross revenue and new business.

Riley assumed that money would keep the workers happy and productive. "I never looked at the internal processes of the company," he says, "because I never thought they were significant." If people were unhappy, they could quit; if they were unproductive, they would be fired. Responding to this attitude, each worker cared only about his or her own bonuses. Dock workers moved freight fast but not carefully, and goods were damaged. One salesperson earned $7,000 in bonuses in just six weeks — not by selling but by spending time combing through the shipper's list to find even the smallest credits. Workers resisted helping each other if it would cut into their own earnings. According to Karen Crawford, the company's vice-president of sales and marketing, "I was managing a group of individuals. There was no common thread except that they were all motivated by their incentives."

Eventually, Riley had to confront the costs of his leadership style. Not only were employees pulling in different directions but turnover was high. And his managers could not pretend that they trusted him. He decided to change. Explains Riley, "I like trucking, but what I really like is people. I had a vision of a place where people found a lot of compelling reasons to be the best they could be."

Riley brought his top executives together to work as a team, and they hashed out a mission statement for the company. He reduced the emphasis on incentive systems and focused more on teamwork, encouraging managers to do whatever was necessary to keep employees happy. Turnover has fallen. And although profit growth has slowed, Riley is happier with his team management style.

Source: Joshua Hyatt, "Growing Up as a CEO," *Inc.,* July 1989, pp. 60–64+.

Clearly, Fiedler's LPC notion borrows heavily from the behavioral approach to leadership.

Actual work situations are multifaceted. To describe them, Fiedler proposed a single, broad definition of a critical situational dimension (favorableness) and several specific underlying attributes that define this larger dimension. According to his model, situations differ in terms of how favorable they

■ Figure 10.3

Fiedler's Contingency Model

	Most Favorable							Least Favorable
Leader–Member Relations	Good	Good	Good	Good	Poor	Poor	Poor	Poor
Task Structure	Strd.	Strd.	Unstrd.	Unstrd.	Strd.	Strd.	Unstrd.	Unstrd.
Position Power	Strong	Weak	Strong	Weak	Strong	Weak	Strong	Weak
Octant	1	2	3	4	5	6	7	8

are for a leader. **Situational favorableness,** therefore, is a broad notion of how easy or difficult a setting might seem to be for a manager.

Three factors are believed to underlie situational favorableness. In order of relative importance, they are (1) leader–member relations, (2) task structure, and (3) position power.

Leader–member relations reflect the extent to which a leader is accepted and generates positive emotional reactions from his subordinates. A situation in which leader–member relations are relatively good is potentially much easier to manage than a situation in which such relations are strained.

Task structure is the degree to which the job at hand can be clearly specified. Such structure is evident in rules, job descriptions, and policies. When tasks are relatively structured, there is little ambiguity about how they should be approached. In addition, goals are clear, performance measures are understood, and multiple solutions or approaches to a problem are unlikely to exist. With low task structure, the opposite holds true.

Position power is the extent to which a leader has recourse to formal sanctions. That is, can a leader control the fate of subordinates by offering rewards or threatening punishment? Other things being equal, situations in which a leader has position power are considered easier to manage than situations in which such power is lacking.

If we combine these three situational attributes, we obtain eight possible combinations, or octants, representing a range of situations (Figure 10.3). Situations to the left side of this arrangement are highly favorable (that is, they possess attributes that should make it easy to lead), while situations to the right side are highly unfavorable (possessing attributes that make it difficult to lead).

To illustrate these situations, consider octant 1. This is a situation in which all lights are "green." The subordinates and leader get along, the task is clearly structured so that all know what they should be doing, and the leader can fall back on his position power if need be. Such a situation might be enjoyed by a foreman in a nonunionized manufacturing setting who is admired by his subordinates. Octant 8, in contrast, has many obstacles to group perfor-

Figure 10.4

Summary of Fiedler's Original Findings

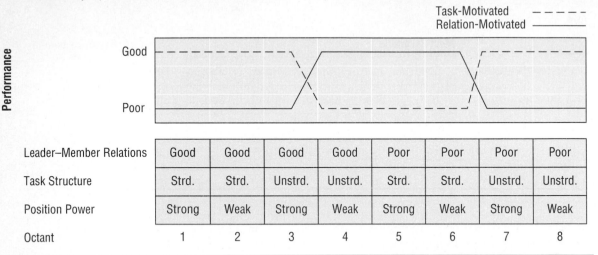

Leader–Member Relations	Good	Good	Good	Good	Poor	Poor	Poor	Poor
Task Structure	Strd.	Strd.	Unstrd.	Unstrd.	Strd.	Strd.	Unstrd.	Unstrd.
Position Power	Strong	Weak	Strong	Weak	Strong	Weak	Strong	Weak
Octant	1	2	3	4	5	6	7	8

Note: Although Figure 10.4 illustrates the essential points of the contingency model, it is not, strictly speaking, accurate in that average levels of performance are not compared between octants, only within octants. Also, there is good reason to believe that average performance levels decline as one moves toward more unfavorable situations simply because the settings become more difficult to manage.[21]

Source: *Leadership and Effective Management* by F.E. Fiedler and M.M. Chemers, 1974, Scott, Foresman & Company.

mance. Here, the leader and the group's members have poor interpersonal relations, the task in which they are engaged is ambiguous, and the leader lacks any real base of power to reward or coerce. Such a situation might arise when an unpopular individual is asked to chair an ad hoc committee to prepare a report on how to ensure the quality of work life in the 21st century. In this situation, all lights are "red."

Fiedler applied his contingency model to a large variety of work groups (service station crews, basketball teams, laboratory groups, bomber crews, and others). The results of this data gathering suggested that high-LPC (interpersonally oriented) leaders were more effective than low-LPC (task-oriented) leaders only in certain octants. Low-LPC leaders were found to be more effective in the remaining octants. Generally, low-LPC leaders were determined to be more effective than high-LPC leaders in extremely favorable and unfavorable situations, while high-LPC leaders were relatively more effective in octants of moderate favorability. Figure 10.4 summarizes Fiedler's original findings.

An important question remains: *Why* should high-LPC leaders be more effective in moderately favorable situations, while low-LPC leaders are more effective in the remaining situations? Presently, there is no satisfactory answer to this question. Even Fiedler admits that the model is still largely a "black box" in that no one has a fully satisfying explanation as to why the observed relationships should be as they were reported.[22] Perhaps the most popular explanation is still the original one offered by Fiedler when he first proposed the model. At the time, he contended that leaders who are task-oriented will be successful in favorable situations because they will emphasize task accomplishment in a situation that merely requires persistence. So, too, in extremely difficult situations (octants 7 and 8) what is needed is firm, task-oriented leadership. In these unfavorable situations, if anything at all is going to be accomplished, the leader must have a strong desire to see results. Interpersonally-oriented leaders, however, may have an advantage in settings that emit "mixed" signals. In these situations, such leaders can apply their social skills to overcoming the more manageable obstacles to performance.

Because the model was induced from empirical findings on group performance, other explanations can be offered for the pretzel-shaped relationship portrayed in Figure 10.4. One currently popular alternative interpretation is that the findings reflect a "matching" of leader complexity with situational complexity. This line of reasoning holds that high-LPC individuals are cognitively complex: they are able to perceive people and events in shades of gray, rather than in simple black-and-white terms. This is reflected by their tendency to give some positive ratings in addition to negative ratings to their least preferred coworker. Low-LPC leaders, on the other hand, may be more cognitively simple in that they judge people and objects in a fairly simplistic fashion (good-bad, black-white) without seeing or accepting complexities and nuances. So, too, we can conceptualize situations as being relatively simple versus complex. Simple situations would be those in which the major attributes are largely congruent — that is, all good or all bad. Examples of such simple situations would be the highly favorable and highly unfavorable octants of the contingency model. Complex situations are those in which the signals are mixed, as in the middle octants.

According to this complexity interpretation, cognitively complex people are better as leaders in relatively complex settings, while cognitively simple people do better as leaders in relatively simple settings. As yet, no one has offered any evidence that clearly refutes a complexity-matching interpretation of Fiedler's original findings.

Critics point out that the lack of a strong explanation for the dynamics of the model means that the model is still little more than a "black box." Because the model relies exclusively on a single method of measuring leadership style (LPC), the model may be viewed as being method-bound (see Chapter 6).

Also, Fiedler's initial results were gathered from a large survey of a variety of work groups. Because of the possibility that these early results may reflect chance, it is necessary that other researchers replicate Fiedler's findings with a different set of work groups. Such efforts have generated very mixed results, so that considerable controversy still surrounds the validity of the contingency model.[23]

Implications of the Contingency Model Perhaps the most basic conclusion to be drawn from Fiedler's model is that a leader who is effective in one situation may be ineffective in another. Managers need to recognize this fact and under-stand the limitations that a situation may place on them.

Fiedler suggests that leaders should attempt to engineer facets of their work setting in order to enhance their personal effectiveness rather than try to change their leadership style.[24] He contends that personal style is fairly difficult to change, even for an individual who strongly desires to do so. Therefore, it can sometimes be easier to change the situational attributes to fit one's own style. This may mean deliberately trying to change the situational favorable-ness by enhancing relations with subordinates, changing the amount of struc-ture in a task, or gaining more formal power with the goal of achieving a more conducive work setting based on personal leadership style.

Path–Goal Theory   Martin Evans[25] and Robert House[26] have proposed an-other perspective on how leaders can be effective. Their **path–goal theory** suggests that leaders can affect the satisfaction, motivation, and performance of group members in several ways. A primary means is by making rewards contingent on the accomplishment of performance *goals*. In addition, a leader can aid group members in obtaining valued rewards by clarifying the *paths* to these performance goals and by removing obstacles to performance.

In order to accomplish these ends, a leader may be required to adopt different styles of leadership behavior as the situation dictates. House has identified four distinct types of leader behavior:

1. **Directive leadership** involves giving specific guidance to subordinates and asking them to follow standard rules. It is similar to the high-structure/low-consideration style in the Ohio State scheme.

2. **Supportive leadership** includes being friendly to subordinates and sen-sitive to their needs. It is similar to the low-structure/high-consider-ation style.

3. **Participative leadership** involves sharing information with subordinates and consulting with them before making decisions. It is much like the high-structure/high-consideration style.

4. **Achievement-oriented leadership** entails setting challenging goals and emphasizing excellence while simultaneously showing confidence that subordinates will perform well. It is not really equivalent to any of the Ohio State styles of management.

House contends that all four styles can be, and often are, used by a single leader in varying situations.

A number of propositions have been generated from path–goal theory regarding the impact of certain leader behaviors on subordinate performance and satisfaction. Chief among these are:

▪   In ambiguous situations, subordinates will be more satisfied with lead-ers who exhibit directive behavior. This satisfaction results from the subordinates' appreciation of the supervisor's help in increasing the probability of their obtaining a desired reward. In situations with greater task or goal clarity, such directive behavior will be of less value to subordinates.

- In stressful environments, supportive leader behavior will serve to ameliorate subordinate dissatisfaction.

- Leaders who possess influence with their own superiors (upward influence) can enhance unit performance and satisfaction. With upward influence, a leader is better able to help subordinates be successful and receive appropriate rewards.

Thus far, there has been little research on path–goal theory. Available evidence suggests that when subordinates are involved with ambiguous tasks, directive leadership can increase satisfaction and motivation. With fairly unambiguous tasks, however, directive leadership can decrease satisfaction and motivation.[27] Also, supportive leader behavior typically is associated with increased subordinate satisfaction. When subordinates are employed on tasks that are inherently distasteful or frustrating, supportive leader behavior can enhance subordinate satisfaction.[28] Although path–goal theory remains as yet largely untested, its greatest theoretical strength seems to lie in its integration of leader behavior and such ideas, contained in expectancy theory (Chapter 6), as providing contingent, valued rewards for performance.

The Hersey–Blanchard Situational Theory   Of the various contingency approaches to leadership, the **Hersey–Blanchard situational theory** has been the least researched.[29] Yet it is widely used in management training programs. The theory is closely based on the leadership styles generated by the Ohio State model. The unique contribution of the model lies in its emphasis on matching a particular leadership style to the "maturity" of the followers.

Subordinate maturity is defined as the capacity to set high but attainable goals, the willingness to take on responsibility, and the possession of relevant education and/or experience. Maturity is judged in relation to a given task. Therefore, a particular subordinate may be quite mature in relation to one task and immature in relation to another. Subordinate maturity contains two components: **job maturity,** or technical knowledge and task-relevant skills, and **psychological maturity,** or feelings of self-confidence and the willingness and ability to accept responsibility. A subordinate who is highly mature possesses both technical competence and self-confidence for a given task. A subordinate who is low on maturity for a task lacks both ability and confidence. Although Hersey and Blanchard acknowledge other variables as potentially important (for example, time pressures), they focus primarily on follower maturity as the critical situational attribute.

The central thesis of their model is that as follower maturity increases, a leader should rely more on relationship-oriented behavior and less on task-oriented behavior. Beyond a certain point on this maturity dimension, however, the leader should rely less on both task-oriented and relationship-oriented behaviors. This pattern is depicted in Figure 10.5. With subordinates who are highly immature (situation M1), the leader should emphasize task-oriented behavior and be very directive and autocratic. In essence, this is a style of leadership that involves *telling* subordinates what to do. For situation M2, subordinates who are still on the somewhat low side of maturity, a leader should focus on being more relationship-oriented. Such a leader works on

■ Figure 10.5

The Hersey-Blanchard Situational Model

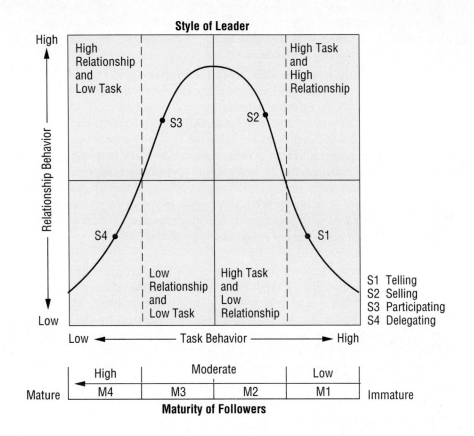

Source: P. Hersey and K. Blanchard, *Management of Organizational Behavior,* 1982, Englewood Cliffs, N.J.: Prentice-Hall, p. 152.

selling his or her ideas to the subordinates. Subordinates who are somewhat high in maturity (M3) will also need a fair degree of support and considerate treatment. The appropriate style in this case is one of *participating* with subordinates. Lastly, subordinates who are highly mature (M4) are self-motivated and can be trusted to rely on their own self-direction. In fact, highly mature employees may actually expect to be given a great deal of autonomy. The preferred style of leadership with such subordinates is one of *delegating*.

Hersey and Blanchard offered their theory with little empirical evidence of its validity. Available research suggests that their model may only be partially correct in that less experienced (i.e., less mature) subordinates may be somewhat more responsive to greater direction. Furthermore, the theoretical aspects of the model have recently been criticized for not giving a coherent or precise rationale for the proposed relationships.[30] Nonetheless, this model possesses an intuitive appeal that makes it an attractive instructional device for practicing managers. It also emphasizes the need for flexible, adaptable leader behaviors. But until more evidence is available, it is impossible to claim that the Hersey–Blanchard model is superior to other perspectives.

The Vroom–Yetton Leadership Model Victor Vroom and Philip Yetton developed a very promising model that deals with one specific facet of leadership: how to select a leadership style for making a decision.[31] The **Vroom–Yetton model** suggests that there are five decision-making styles, ranging from highly autocratic to highly participative. In order of increasing participation, the five styles are:

- *Autocratic I (AI)* — A manager solves a problem using the information that is already available.

- *Autocratic II (AII)* — A manager obtains additional information from subordinates and then decides by himself.

- *Consultative I (CI)* — A manager shares the problem with subordinates on an individual basis and their ideas and suggestions are obtained. Again, the manager chooses a solution to the problem at hand.

- *Consultative II (CII)* — A manager shares the problem with subordinates as a group. The final decision may or may not reflect subordinate input.

- *Group II (GII)* — A manager meets with subordinates as a group. However, the manager acts as a chairperson who focuses and directs discussion but does not impose his or her will on the group. True subordinate participation, in a democratic sense, is sought.

Which of these five styles is most appropriate for a given situation depends on a number of important considerations. In total, Vroom and Yetton identify seven questions that must be answered to determine the appropriate style. These underlying contingencies (or decision rules) focus on such issues as whether sufficient information is available to make a good decision and whether subordinates can be trusted to approach the problem from a perspective that is congruent with organizational goals. The seven questions can be arranged in a sequential fashion that permits us to follow a logical path in matching a single, preferred leader style to a given situation.

Figure 10.6 shows the decision tree that Vroom and Yetton devised for selecting a best or appropriate style. The seven decision rules are listed across the top of the model. For each question, a manager is to provide a yes or no response. At the end of each branch in the tree is a designated style, denoted by AI, AII, CI, CII, or GII.

To see how a manager would use the decision tree, imagine a case in which a manager must deal with an order typist who is not typing enough purchase orders each day (the answer to question A is yes). If the manager has a clear understanding of why the typist is a poor performer (B = yes), if the subordinate must accept the manager's decision in order for the solution to work (D = yes), and if the manager is also certain that his decision will be

■ **Figure 10.6**

The Vroom–Yetton Model

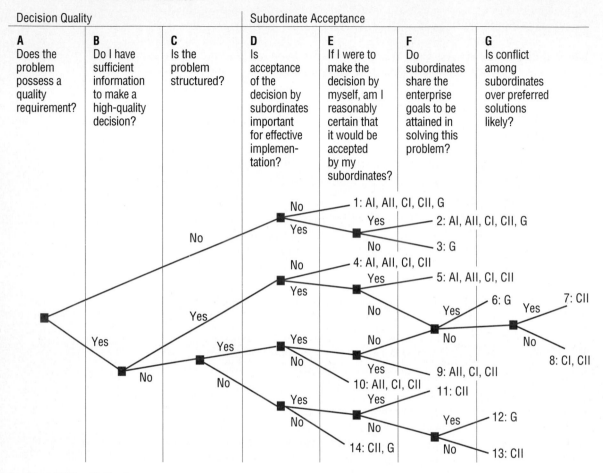

Decision Quality			Subordinate Acceptance			
A Does the problem possess a quality requirement?	**B** Do I have sufficient information to make a high-quality decision?	**C** Is the problem structured?	**D** Is acceptance of the decision by subordinates important for effective implementation?	**E** If I were to make the decision by myself, am I reasonably certain that it would be accepted by my subordinates?	**F** Do subordinates share the enterprise goals to be attained in solving this problem?	**G** Is conflict among subordinates over preferred solutions likely?

1: AI, AII, CI, CII, G
2: AI, AII, CI, CII, G
3: G
4: AI, AII, CI, CII
5: AI, AII, CI, CII
6: G
7: CII
8: CI, CII
9: AII, CI, CII
10: AII, CI, CII
11: CII
12: G
13: CII
14: CII, G

Decision-Making Methods
 AI = Autocratic decision without subordinates' input
AII = Autocratic decision using information gathered from subordinates
 CI = Consultative decision with problem discussed individually with each subordinate
CII = Consultative decision with problem discussed with subordinates as a group
 G = Group decision
Note: The numbers 1–14 denote Problem Types.

Source: Reprinted from *Leadership and Decision Making*, by Victor H. Vroom and Philip W. Yetton, pp. 41–42, by permission of the University of Pittsburgh Press. © 1973 by University of Pittsburgh Press.

accepted by the subordinate (E = yes), then the manager should take a nonparticipative approach to dealing with the problem (AI).

As another example, consider a manager who is contemplating the introduction of flexible work schedules (Chapter 7). For such a decision to be successfully implemented, it is worthwhile to consider what the Vroom–Yetton model suggests. In this situation, one solution is likely to be more rational than another (A = yes), but the manager does not know the extent of individual preferences and job-related obstacles (B = no). The problem is relatively unstructured (C = no), while acceptance by subordinates is quite critical to implementation (D = yes). As the manager cannot be reasonably certain that an imposed solution will be accepted by subordinates (E = no), the final choice of style depends on whether subordinates are judged to share the organization's goals. If the manager believes that the subordinates share the organization's goals, then a highly participative approach is in order (GII). Otherwise, a less participative strategy (CII) is appropriate.

The Vroom–Yetton model provides a useful device for diagnosing a situation. It prescribes a specific type of behavior for a leader who is confronted with a specific problem. As such, it is much more precise and somewhat more practical than the other models we have examined.

Further studies have tended to support the validity of the Vroom–Yetton model. Work by the original researchers as well as by independent investigators indicates that the model closely describes the actual decision process of most managers.[32] Also, the model is widely used by organizations that specialize in managerial training (e.g., Kepner Tregoe).[33]

Recently, Vroom and Jago have attempted to address several shortcomings of the model.[34] For example, it can be very difficult to always answer the seven decision rules with a simple yes or no response. Often, a manager has only a sense of what is likely to occur. In such cases, the manager may be able to give probability estimates but not simple, firm answers. To address this and other problems, Vroom and Jago have made a number of modifications, such as permitting probabilistic responses. As a result, the model is evolving into a very complex and unwieldy set of mathematical equations. Nonetheless, managers who are not particularly interested in precise mathematical advice, perhaps because they lack the time or a computer program to work out the equations, will probably continue to use the decision tree presented in Figure 10.6 as a quick guide to selecting a leadership style.

Graen's Vertical Dyad Linkage Model A further perspective on the leadership process is provided by the **vertical dyad linkage model** (sometimes termed the leader–member exchange model[35]) of leadership proposed by George Graen and his associates.[36] In some respects, this model is similar to the other approaches we have considered in that it focuses on the influence of subordinates on leader behavior and the topic of subordinate participation in decision making. In all other ways, however, the model is unique.

Graen and his associates contend that much of the past theorizing on the leadership process presumes the existence of an average leadership style that a manager exhibits toward all members of a work group. But careful consideration reveals that leaders do not typically display a uniform style of leadership or set of behaviors toward all group members. Instead, they behave somewhat differently toward each subordinate. The model contends that each *linkage,* or relationship, that exists between the leader and a subordinate is likely to differ in quality. Thus, the same supervisor may have poor interpersonal relations with some subordinates and fairly open and trusting relations with others. In each work unit, these pairs of relations, or *dyads,* can be judged in terms of whether an individual is relatively "in" or "out" with the supervisor. Members of the in-group (or, more correctly, in-subgroup) are invited to share in decision making and are given added responsibility. Members of the out-group, however, are supervised within the narrow terms of their formal employment contract. In essence, an in-group member is elevated to the unofficial role of "trusted assistant," while an out-group member is assigned the role of "hired hand." In-group members, in many respects, enjoy the benefits of enriched jobs with many opportunities to participate in decision making. Out-group members are not given these opportunities. Further, it is hypothesized that in-group members will display greater job satisfaction, superior performance, higher commitment, and lower turnover.

How people come to be members of the in-group or the out-group is not as yet fully understood. Preliminary evidence suggests, however, that the leader's initial impression of an employee's competency plays an important role. Certainly, leaders and in-group members strongly believe that competency is the distinguishing characteristic between in-group members and out-group members. Out-group members, however, are just as firmly convinced that ingratiation, favoritism, and politics are more important than competency in the selection of in-group members. In fact, interpersonal attraction probably does play some role in the selection process. However, it is likely that perceived competence plays a much larger and complementary role in most instances.

The existence of in-groups and out-groups is easy to demonstrate. In the original studies on the vertical dyad linkage (VDL) model, employees and their superiors were asked to identify who in each unit was relatively more or less trusted by the superior. Generally, people had little difficulty identifying such a hierarchy. Overall, the membership status of a particular individual (in versus out) is understood by all group members, especially the individual in question.

The original and validating studies on the VDL model generally have provided support for the model's central hypotheses, which are that in-group members are more satisfied and are judged to be superior performers. That in-group and out-group status may be related to employee turnover, however, has received far less consistent support.[37] An additional finding is that in-group members tend to see job-related problems in much the same way as their superiors. Graen and Schiemann observed that in-group members' reports of job problems correlated more closely with their superior's perceptions than did the reports of out-group members.[38]

As is usually the case, the model and its supporting research can be criticized on several counts.[39] For example, in a review of VDL research, John

Miner noted that the research had relied on ratings of subordinate performance rather than on objective measures of performance, that all tests of the model had been made by its developer, and that the model's principles may be limited to white-collar employees.[40] Yet a subsequent study that addressed many of the shortcomings identified by Miner found good support for the model's major hypotheses.[41]

In summary, it seems that leaders do distinguish among their subordinates by inviting some to join an inner cadre, while excluding others. Initial impressions of the competency of subordinates can lead to categorization as in- or out-group members, which may affect their subsequent performance and promotion or turnover.

Transformational and Charismatic Leadership   During the 1980s, leadership researchers began to focus attention on the topics of leader charisma and the revitalization of organizational global competitiveness. Charisma is a Greek word that refers to a divinely inspired gift (for example, being able to perform miracles or predict the future). In the area of leadership, it refers to a type of social influence based on follower perceptions of the leader rather than on the leader's formal authority. **Charismatic leadership** is closest in meaning to the notion of referent power (see Chapter 9). **Transformational leadership** is a broader concept than charisma, and implies reshaping entire strategies of an organization. Nonetheless, both terms overlap to a great extent in that they highlight the influence of a leader's personal attributes and follower trust and willingness to take direction. Two prominent theorists in the area of leadership, Bernard Bass and Robert House, have proposed theories of transformational and charismatic leadership.[42] These theories underscore the importance of vision, intellectual stimulation, and individualized consideration in leadership, and the major role that leadership can have during times of crisis. However, the research base in this area is not as well established as in other areas of leadership. Therefore, practical applications of the features of transformational and charismatic leadership cannot as yet be offered.

A Comparison of the Major Leadership Models

The major models of leadership have many similarities and differences, as summarized in Table 10.4. The similarities include a general focus on leader behaviors as being primarily oriented toward either task accomplishment or social supportiveness. Although the models categorize leadership style in somewhat different ways, all models generally recognize that leaders differ in their behavior and that leader behavior can make a difference in unit outcomes. Other similarities among the models include their frequent attempt to predict performance as an index of effectiveness and their expectation that satisfaction and turnover will be influenced by various leadership principles. The models differ greatly in terms of situational variables; however, the Ohio State/Blake–Mouton perspective mostly ignores the impact of situational features, whereas Fiedler's contingency model attempts to define and measure them precisely.

■ **Table 10.4**

Comparison of Major Leadership Models

Model	Leader Behaviors	Situational Variables	Outcomes/Criteria
Cognitive Resource Theory	Intelligence Directive Relevant job experience	Stress Subordinate supportiveness	Performance
Ohio State/Blake–Mouton	Initiating structure Consideration	None	Satisfaction Performance Grievances Turnover
Fiedler's Contingency Model	Task oriented (low LPC) Relationship oriented (high LPC)	Leader–member relations Task structure Position power	Performance
Path–Goal Theory	Directive Supportive Participative Achievement oriented	Task structure Subordinate characteristics	Satisfaction Motivation Performance
Hersey–Blanchard	Concern for people Concern for task	Subordinate maturity	Effectiveness
Vroom–Yetton	Autocratic Participative	Decision quality Decision acceptance	Quality of decision Acceptance of decision by subordinates
Vertical Dyad Linkage	Differential treatment of subordinates	Subordinate competence Subordinate loyalty	Satisfaction Performance
Transformational Leadership	Leader's personality	Subordinate trust and willingness to follow	Turnover Effectiveness

The amount and quality of evidence supporting each model also differ considerably. For some models, such as Hersey–Blanchard, very little evidence is available. Other models, including Fiedler's contingency and the Ohio State models, have generated a great deal of research. Nonetheless, the results of such research have also been varied. For Fiedler's Contingency model, the results have been mixed, but for the Ohio State scheme, consideration has frequently been found to correlate with subordinate reports of satisfaction. Also, the vertical dyad linkage model has had good success in predicting subordinate satisfaction and performance, but only mixed success in predicting turnover.

A manager's choice of a particular leadership model as a guide to personal conduct depends on his or her goals and on the specific situation. An initial issue is whether the individual hopes to maximize a given outcome, such as satisfaction or performance. Some models, such as Fiedler's Contingency model, are silent on the dimension of satisfaction, and therefore might be eliminated from competition. The next step is to examine the situational variables identified by the models to determine if they are pertinent to the actual work setting. Such an exercise can provide insights into which model is most appropriate to a given manager in a specific situation.

■ **Table 10.5**

*Substitutes and Neutralizers for Supportive and
Instrumental Leadership*

Factor	Supportive Leadership	Instrumental Leadership
Subordinate Characteristics		
1. Experience, ability, training		Substitute
2. "Professional" orientation	Substitute	Substitute
3. Indifference toward organizational rewards	Neutralizer	Neutralizer
Task Characteristics		
1. Structured, routine task		Substitute
2. Task feedback		Substitute
3. Intrinsically satisfying task	Substitute	
Organizational Characteristics		
1. Cohesive work group	Substitute	Substitute
2. Leader lacks position power	Neutralizer	Neutralizer
3. Formalization of goals and plans		Substitute
4. Rigid rules and procedures		Neutralizer
5. Physical distance between leader and subordinates	Neutralizer	Neutralizer

Note: Supportive and instrumental leadership are analogous to leader consideration and leader structuring.
Source: G. Yukl, *Leadership in Organizations*, Englewood Cliffs, N.J.: Prentice-Hall, 1981.

Substitutes for Leadership

Steven Kerr and John Jermier have suggested, somewhat controversially, that leader behavior may sometimes be unnecessary or superfluous because factors in the situation offer sufficient aid to subordinates.[43] Such factors might include subordinate ability, training, or experience. The notion that leaders may not play a crucial role in all settings can help to explain why some work groups do quite well despite the presence of a poor leader. In other words, there can be situations in which leadership is unimportant or redundant.

Kerr and Jermier have suggested two types of variables to account for cases in which leadership may be unimportant or redundant: leadership substitutes and leadership neutralizers. The presence of a **leadership substitute** will make leadership redundant or unnecessary, while the presence of a **leadership neutralizer** prevents a leader from taking action in some fashion. Table 10.5 lists some possible leadership substitutes and neutralizers for two styles of leader behavior.

The essence of Kerr and Jermier's proposal is that leadership is only one factor in successful work-group performance. The notions of substitutes and neutralizers help us to keep a proper perspective on the role of leadership in work groups. While leadership can be critical to unit performance, certain preconditions are necessary. In addition, the idea of leadership substitutes and neutralizers helps to account for the largely mixed results of research on most leadership theories. Studies of leadership that ignore the effect of neutralizers and substitutes may fail to uncover hypothesized relationships because the particular leadership process is irrelevant rather than because the theory is invalid.

Summary

1. Define leadership.

Leadership is a process through which a person tries to get organizational members to do something the person desires. The leader's influence extends beyond supervisory responsibility and formal authority.

2. List some attributes that are associated with leadership.

Table 10.1 shows attributes that have been associated with successful leaders. Those having the strongest association are the desire to influence others, self-confidence, activity level, intelligence, and knowledge of the group's task.

3. Describe ways in which leader behavior is related to employee attitudes and performance.

A democratic leadership style may lead to greater employee satisfaction and higher-quality output. Autocratic leadership may lead to a greater quantity of output, accompanied by decreased quality and employee satisfaction. Up to a point, high consideration for the employee may be related to employee satisfaction, and low consideration may lead to employee dissatisfaction. Both the Ohio State and the Managerial Grid models presume that the most successful managers emphasize concern for both people and productivity.

4. Identify the factors underlying situational favorableness and explain how they influence a leader's effectiveness.

A favorable situation exists when leader–member relations are good, task structure (the degree to which the job can be clearly specified) is high, and the leader's position power (the extent to which the leader has recourse to formal sanctions) is high. Interpersonally oriented leaders are more effective in moderately favorable situations, whereas task-oriented leaders are more effective in situations that are extremely favorable or unfavorable.

5. Explain how leaders can clarify paths to goals to motivate employees.

Path–goal theory suggests that leaders can affect satisfaction, motivation, and performance by basing rewards on the accomplishment of performance goals and by clarifying the paths to these goals and removing obstacles to performance. Depending on the situation, the leader does this by choosing one of four types of leader behavior: directive leadership, supportive leadership, participative leadership, or achievement-oriented leadership.

6. Describe the components of subordinate maturity and the relevance of subordinate maturity to leadership style.

Subordinate maturity consists of job maturity (technical knowledge and task-relevant skills) and psychological maturity (feelings of self-confidence and self-respect). The Hersey–Blanchard theory proposes that the leader should change his or her style to match the employee's level of maturity.

7. Describe the decision-making styles of the Vroom–Yetton model and explain how to use a decision tree to select the appropriate style.

A manager can solve a problem by (1) using already available information; (2) obtaining additional information from subordinates and then making an individual decision; (3) sharing the problem with subordinates individually, obtaining their ideas, and making an individual decision; (4) sharing the problem with subordinates as a group and possibly using subordinates' ideas in reaching a solution; or (5) meeting with subordinates as a group, focusing and directing discussion, but not imposing his or her will. To use a decision tree in a particular situation, the manager answers the questions from left to right, moving along a branch of the tree. At the end of each branch is the style designated appropriate for the particular decision.

8. Describe a way to evaluate leadership style taking into account managers' views of different employees.

In the vertical dyad linkage model, employees are members of an in-group or an out-group in the eyes of the manager. In-group members are invited to share in decision making and are given added responsibility, whereas out-group members are supervised within the narrow terms of their employment contract.

9. Identify similarities and differences among the major leadership models.

The leadership models generally focus on leader behaviors as being primarily oriented to either accomplishing tasks or providing social support. They all recognize that leaders behave differently, and that leader behavior can influence unit outcomes. The models frequently see performance as an index of effectiveness and expect that leadership principles will affect employee satisfaction and turnover. However, the models differ greatly in their consideration of situational variables.

10. Define leadership substitute and leadership neutralizer and give examples of each.

A leadership substitute is a factor that makes leadership redundant or unnecessary; one example would be an extremely cohesive work group. A leadership neutralizer is a factor that prevents a leader from being effective; one such factor would be subordinates who are indifferent to organizational rewards. Other examples of each factor are shown in Table 10.5.

Key Terms

Leadership
Informal leader
Cognitive resource theory
Task orientation
Employee orientation
Initiating structure
Consideration
Contingency model of leadership
   effectiveness

Path–goal theory
Directive leadership
Supportive leadership
Participative leadership
Achievement-oriented leadership
Hersey–Blanchard situational theory
Subordinate maturity
Job maturity
Psychological maturity

Least preferred coworker (LPC)	Vroom–Yetton model
Situational favorableness	Vertical dyad linkage model
Leader–member relations	Charismatic leadership
Task structure	Transformational leadership
Position power	Leadership substitute
	Leadership neutralizer

Review and Discussion Questions

1. Contrast the roles of leader and manager. Is the manager of a group always its leader?

2. What are some attributes of an effective leader? Are these traits clearly related to successful leadership? Can a person without these attributes be a leader?

3. Explain the terms *consideration* and *initiating structure*. What is typically considered the optimal combination of these characteristics? Is this conclusion well founded?

4. What is a high-LPC leader? Why might a high-LPC leader be most effective in moderately favorable work situations?

5. Martha Muffin has just been appointed to chair a committee set up to explore future markets for the company's products (special-purpose gaskets). Although the committee will consist of people from several departments, Martha is dismayed to learn that she is unpopular with most committee members because of a record-keeping procedure she instituted recently. Martha has just read about Fiedler's contingency model, from which she learned that a task-motivated leader would be most effective in this unfavorable situation. Martha sees herself as socially motivated, however, and she wonders how she can change her leadership style. What do you suggest?

6. Describe the types of leader behavior identified in path–goal theory. Which approach works best in ambiguous situations?

7. Hersey and Blanchard suggest that a leader's style should change as subordinates develop job maturity. How should the leader's style change? What are some shortcomings of this approach to leadership?

8. Use the decision tree shown in Figure 10.6 to choose a leadership style appropriate for each of the following situations. Besides giving the name of the decision style, describe how it works.
   a. John Apple notes that Sam Slow, one of the programmers in his group, has not been meeting the deadlines for his portion of the database system John's department is developing. John has also noticed that Sam regularly starts the day late and spends more time on the phone with his girlfriend than on the computer. John wants to inspire Sam to work harder, but he thinks Sam will doubt his assessment that Sam isn't trying hard enough. In the meantime, the other programmers in the office wish Sam would

do better, because everyone will get a bonus if the group finishes its project ahead of schedule.

b. Irma Bloom, production manager at Marvelous Metal Castings, Inc., shares the workers' concern over the recent increase in accidents. No one is quite certain why the accident rate has risen, but the consensus is that some changes should be made. Because Irma has 20 years' experience in the plant, she is confident that workers will respect her ideas for improving safety.

9. According to the vertical dyad linkage model of leadership, leaders do not treat all subordinates in the same way. How does treatment differ? Is this fair? Explain your answer.

10. What does the existence of leadership substitutes and leadership neutralizers tell us about the role of leadership?

Critical Incident

Hal's Halo

Hal Baines has been employed by IFP Financial Services Corporation for more than ten years. Two years ago he was promoted to unit supervisor. Hal has always been a very loyal employee and has worked hard to follow and support the company's policies and procedures. In talking with any of Hal's superiors, one gets the impression that he is well liked and viewed as an asset to the organization.

Because employee dissatisfaction has become more pronounced in Hal's unit, you have been asked to assess the situation. In private talks with his employees, you discover that they think Hal is consumed with the desire to please upper-level management. They don't feel he "goes to bat" for the unit. For example, at each of the past two budget hearings, their department has received little or no increase. Also, whenever new ideas or suggestions from one of the employees are given to Hal to pass on, nothing ever comes of them. This has resulted in frustration and a general feeling of being unappreciated. Finally, whenever a request is made of Hal's department, regardless of whatever else is being done, Hal always promises to get it done immediately. This has meant additional work and long hours without compensation or recognition for many employees.

As the consultant, how would you address the following questions?

1. In terms of the leadership theories discussed in this chapter, how would you portray Hal's leadership style?

2. If you met with Hal right now, what advice or suggestions would you offer to alter his style of leadership?

3. Do you think a leadership skills training program would be helpful to Hal? If so, what should it consist of?

Source: Written by Bruce Kemelgor.

Experiential Exercise

Leadership Style Profile*

According to situational leadership theory, there is no one best way to influence people. Most of the research on leadership indicates that leader behavior is a combination of task and relationship orientations. Task behavior is the extent to which a leader provides direction. Telling people what to do and/or setting goals for them and defining their roles is indicative of a task orientation. Providing support, being open, and being a good communicator are some of the behaviors of a relationship-oriented leader.

One's leadership style is, therefore, a combination of task and relationship behaviors. This exercise is designed to provide you with a profile of your leadership style.

Assume you are involved in each of the following 12 situations. Read each item and then circle the letter of the alternative that would most closely describe your behavior in the situations presented.

Situation 1. The employees in your program appear to be having serious problems getting the job done. Their performance has been going downhill rapidly. They have not responded to your efforts to be friendly or to your expressions of concern for their welfare.

a.   Re-establish the need for following program procedures and meeting the expectations for task accomplishment.

b.   Be sure that staff members know you are available for discussion, but don't pressure them.

c.   Talk with your employees and then set performance goals.

d.   Wait and see what happens.

Situation 2. During the past few months, the quality of work done by staff members has been increasing. Record keeping is accurate and up-to-date. You have made sure that all staff members are aware of your performance expectations.

a.   Stay uninvolved.

b.   Continue to emphasize the importance of completing tasks and meeting deadlines.

c.   Be supportive and provide clear feedback. Continue to make sure that staff members are aware of performance expectations.

d.   Make every effort to let staff members feel important and involved in the decision-making process.

Situation 3. Performance and interpersonal relations among your staff have been good. You have normally left them alone. However, a new situation has

---

* This exercise is adapted from the Managerial Skills Profile, Federal Government Publication 79-141 P. It is based, in part, on Hersey and Blanchard's "Leader Effectiveness and Adaptability Description," University Associates, San Diego.

developed, and it appears that the staff members are unable to solve the problem themselves.

a. Bring the group together and work as a team to solve the problem.

b. Continue to leave them alone to work it out.

c. Act quickly and firmly to identify the problem and establish procedures to correct it.

d. Encourage the staff to work on the problem, letting them know you are available as a resource and for discussion if they need you.

Situation 4. You are considering a major change in your program. Your staff has a fine record of accomplishment and a strong commitment to excellence. They are supportive of the need for change and have been involved in the planning.

a. Continue to involve the staff in the planning, but you direct the change.

b. Announce the changes and then implement them with close supervision.

c. Allow the group to be involved in developing the change, but don't push the process.

d. Let the staff manage the change process.

Situation 5. You are aware that staff performance has been going down during the last several months. They need continual reminding to get tasks done on time and seem unconcerned about meeting objectives. In the past, redefining procedures and role expectations has helped.

a. Allow your staff to set their own direction.

b. Get suggestions from the staff, but see that the objectives are met.

c. Redefine goals and expectations and supervise carefully.

d. Allow the staff to be involved in setting goals, but don't pressure them.

Situation 6. You have just been appointed director of a program that had been running smoothly under the previous director. She had the reputation of running a tight ship. You want to maintain the quality of the program and the service delivery, but you would like to begin humanizing the environment.

a. Do nothing at the present time.

b. Continue with the administrative pattern set by the previous director, monitoring the staff and emphasizing the importance of task accomplishment.

c. Get the staff involved in decision making and planning, but continue to see that objectives are met and quality is maintained.

d. Reach out to staff members to let them feel important and involved.

Situation 7. You are considering expanding your unit's responsibilities. Your staff members have made suggestions about the proposed change and are enthusiastic. They operate effectively on a day-to-day basis and have shown themselves willing to assume responsibility.

a. Outline the changes and monitor carefully.

b. Reach consensus with the staff on the proposed changes and allow the staff members to organize the implementation.

c. Solicit input from the staff on proposed changes, but maintain control of the implementation.

d. Let the staff handle it.

Situation 8. Staff members have been working well. Interpersonal relations and morale are good. The quality of service delivery is excellent. You are somewhat uncomfortable with your apparent lack of direction of the group.

a. Be careful not to hurt your relationship with the staff by becoming too directive.

b. Take steps to assure that staff members are working in a well-defined manner.

c. Leave the staff alone to work as they have been.

d. Discuss the situation with the staff and then initiate the necessary changes.

Situation 9. You have been appointed to replace the chairman of a task force that is long overdue in making requested recommendations for certification requirements. The group is not clear on its goal. Attendance at meetings has been poor. Frequently, the meetings are more social than task oriented. Potentially, they have the knowledge and experience to complete the task.

a. Let the group members work out their problems.

b. Solicit recommendations from the group, but see that the objectives are met.

c. Redefine and clarify the goals, tasks, and expectations, and carefully supervise progress toward task completion.

d. Allow group involvement in setting goals, but don't push.

Situation 10. Your employees are usually able to take responsibility. However, they are not responding well to your recent redefinition of performance standards.

a. Supervise carefully to assure that standards are met.

b. Solicit input from the staff on performance standards. Incorporate their suggestions and monitor their progress toward meeting the standards.

c. Allow staff involvement in the redefinition of performance standards, but don't push.

d. Avoid confrontation. Apply no pressure and see what happens.

Situation 11. You have been promoted to the position of manager. The previous manager appeared to be uninvolved in the affairs of the staff. They have adequately handled their tasks and responsibilities. Their morale is high.

a. Become active in directing the staff toward working in a clearly defined manner.

b. Involve your staff in decision making and consistently reinforce good contributions.

c. Discuss past performance with your staff and then examine the need for new procedures.

d. Continue to leave the staff alone.

Situation 12. You have recently become aware of some internal difficulties on your staff. They had been working well together for the past year. The staff has an excellent record of accomplishment and staff members have consistently met their performance goals. All are well qualified for their roles in the program.

a. Allow your staff members to deal with the new problem themselves.

b. Tell the staff how you propose to deal with the situation and discuss the necessity for these procedures.

c. Make yourself available for discussion, but don't jeopardize your relationship with the staff by forcing the issue.

d. Act quickly and firmly to nip the problem in the bud.

Scoring

1. Circle the letter you chose for each situation in both the charts below, labeled Flexibility and Effectiveness. For example, if you answered alternative C for situation 1, circle the C in row 1 of the Flexibility chart and the C in row 1 of the Effectiveness chart.

Flexibility				
	S1	S2	S3	S4
1	A	C	B	D
2	B	C	D	A
3	C	A	D	B
4	B	A	C	D
5	C	B	D	A
6	B	C	D	A
7	A	C	B	D
8	B	D	A	C
9	C	B	D	A
10	A	B	C	D
11	A	C	B	D
12	D	B	C	A

Situation Number

Effectiveness				
−2	−1	+1	+2	
D	B	C	A	1
A	B	D	C	2
C	B	A	D	3
B	A	C	D	4
A	D	B	C	5
A	D	B	C	6
A	C	D	B	7
B	D	A	C	8
A	D	B	C	9
A	D	C	B	10
A	C	D	B	11
D	B	C	A	12

Situation Number

☐ ☐ ☐ ☐
S1 S2 S3 S4

☐ ☐ ☐ ☐
× × × ×
−2 −1 1 2
‖ ‖ ‖ ‖
☐ + ☐ + ☐ + ☐ = ☐
                    Total

2.   Add the total number of letters you circled in each column of the Flexibility chart and enter these totals in the boxes labeled S1, S2, S3, and S4.

3.   Still focusing on the Flexibility chart, place the total of each column in the corresponding quadrant of the style matrix shown below. That is, the S1 score goes in the Style 1 box (high task, low relationship), the S2 score goes in Style 2 (high task, high relationship), the S3 score goes in the Style 3 box, and the S4 score goes in the Style 4 box.

Style 3	Style 2
High Relationship Low Task	High Task High Relationship
Style 4	**Style 1**
Low Relationship Low Task	High Task Low Relationship

4. Add the total number of letters you circled in each column of the Effectiveness chart and enter these totals in the boxes below each column.

5. Multiply each number in the boxes by the number directly under it (be sure to indicate + or − as appropriate). Put the answer in the next box below that.

6. Add the four numbers and enter the total in the box labeled Total. Again, be sure to include the + or − sign.

7. On the Effectiveness scale below find the number in the Total box and mark it with an arrow.

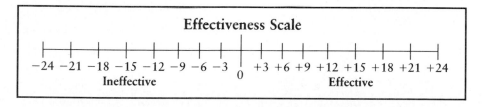

Effectiveness Scale

−24 −21 −18 −15 −12 −9 −6 −3   0   +3 +6 +9 +12 +15 +18 +21 +24

Ineffective   Effective

8. What does your style matrix tell you? How balanced are your scores? Do you have one predominant quadrant (this is not uncommon)? Do you have the potential flexibility to use all four leadership behaviors?

9. In terms of Effectiveness, how well did you do? The most appropriate behavior in each situation is indicated in the +2 column of the Effectiveness chart. You may want to go back to each situation and attempt to discover why that leadership behavior was best.

Your instructor may choose to discuss the results and implications of this exercise for leadership effectiveness.

Notes

1. B.M. Bass, *Stogdill's Handbook of Leadership* (New York: Free Press, 1981).
2. R. Stewart, *Managers and Their Jobs: A Study of the Similarities and Differences in the Ways Managers Spend Their Time* (London: Macmillan, 1967).
3. H. Mintzberg, "The Manager's Job: Folklore and Fact," *Harvard Business Review* 53 (July–August 1975): 49–61; H. Mintzberg, *The Nature of Managerial Work* (New York: Harper & Row, 1973).
4. D.L. Marples, "Studies of Managers — A Fresh Start," *Journal of Management Studies* 4 (1967): 282–299.
5. R.M. Stogdill, "Personal Factors Associated with Leadership: A Survey of the Literature," *Journal of Psychology* 25 (1948): 35–71.
6. R.M. Stogdill, *Handbook of Leadership* (Glencoe, Ill.: Free Press, 1975); Bass, *Stogdill's Handbook of Leadership*.
7. E. Ghiselli, *Exploration in Managerial Talent* (Santa Monica, Calif.: Goodyear, 1971).
8. F.E. Fiedler and J.E. Garcia, *New Approaches to Effective Leadership* (New York: John Wiley and Sons, 1987); F.E. Fiedler, "The Contribution of Cognitive Resources and Behavior to Leadership Performance" (paper presented at Annual Meeting of the Academy of Management, Boston, Mass., 1984); F.E. Fiedler and A.F. Leister, "Leader Intelligence and Task Performance: A Test of a Multiple Screen Model," *Organizational Behavior and Human Performance* 20 (1977): 1–14; J. Blades, "The Influence of Intelligence, Task Ability, and Motivation on Group Performance" (Ph.D. diss., University of Washington, 1976); R.P. Vecchio, "Cognitive Resource Theory: Successor to the 'Black Box' Model of Leadership," *Contemporary Psychology* 33 (1988): 1030–1032; R.P. Vecchio, "A Theoretical and Empirical Examination of Cognitive Resource Theory," *Journal of Applied Psychology* 75 (1990): 141–147.
9. Stogdill, *Handbook of Leadership*.
10. G. Yukl, *Leadership in Organizations* (Englewood Cliffs, N.J.: Prentice-Hall, 1981).
11. K. Lewin, R. Lippitt, and R.K. White, "Patterns of Aggressive Behavior in Experimentally Created Social Climates," *Journal of Social Psychology* 10 (1939): 271–301.
12. B. Bass, *Leadership, Psychology, and Organizational Behavior* (New York: Harper & Row, 1960); C. Gibb, "Leadership," in *The Handbook of Social Psychology*, 2d ed., ed. G. Lindzey and E. Aronson, vol 4 of 5 (Reading, Mass.: Addison-Wesley, 1969), 4:205–282.
13. V.H. Vroom and F.C. Mann, "Leader Authoritarianism and Employee Attitudes," *Personnel Psychology* 13 (1960): 125–140.
14. E.A. Fleishman and E.F. Harris, "Patterns of Leadership Behavior Related to Employee Grievance and Turnover," *Personnel Psychology* 15 (1962): 43–56.
15. Stogdill, *Handbook of Leadership*; Yukl, *Leadership in Organizations*.
16. L.L. Larson, J.G. Hunt, and R. Osburn, "The Great Hi–Hi Leader Behavior Myth: A Lesson from Occam's Razor," *Academy of Management Journal* 19 (1976): 628–641.
17. S. Kerr, C.A. Schriesheim, C.J. Murphy et al., "Toward a Contingency Theory of Leadership Based upon the Consideration and Initiating Structure Literature," *Organizational Behavior and Human Performance* 12 (1974): 62–82; Stogdill, *Handbook of Leadership*; Yukl, *Leadership in Organizations*.
18. R.R. Blake and J.S. Mouton, *The New Managerial Grid* (Houston: Gulf Publishing Co., 1978).
19. R.R. Blake and J.S. Mouton, "A Comparative Analysis of Situationalism and 9,9 Management by Principle," *Organizational Dynamics* 24 (Spring 1982): 21.
20. F.E. Fiedler, *A Theory of Leadership Effectiveness* (New York: McGraw-Hill, 1967).
21. R.P. Vecchio, "An Empirical Investigation of the Validity of Fielder's Model of Leadership Effectiveness," *Organizational Behavior and Human Performance* 19 (1977): 180–206.
22. Fiedler, "The Contribution of Cognitive Resources."
23. R.P. Vecchio, "Cognitive Resource Theory"; Vecchio, "A Theoretical and Empirical Examination"; Vecchio, "An Empirical Investigation of the Validity of Fiedler's Model"; M.J. Strube and J.E. Garcia, "A Meta-analytic Investigation of Fiedler's Contingency Model of Leadership Effectiveness," *Psychological Bulletin* 90 (1981): 307–321; R.P. Vecchio, "Assessing the Validity of Fiedler's Contingency Model of Leadership Effectiveness: A Closer Look at Strube and Garcia (1981)," *Psychological Bulletin* 93 (1983): 404–408; M.J. Strube and J.E. Garcia, "On the Proper Interpretation of Empirical Findings: Strube and Garcia (1981) Revisited," *Psychological Bulletin* 93 (1983): 600–603.
24. F.E. Fiedler, "The Leadership Game: Matching the Man to the Situation," *Organizational Dynamics* 4 (1976): 6–16.

25. M.G. Evans, "The Effects of Supervisory Behavior on the Path–Goal Relationship," *Organizational Behavior and Human Performance* 5 (1970): 277–298; M.G. Evans, "Extensions of a Path–Goal Theory of Motivation," *Journal of Applied Psychology* 59 (1974): 172–178.

26. R.J. House, "A Path–Goal Theory of Leader Effectiveness," *Administrative Science Quarterly* 16 (1971): 321–338.

27. A.D. Szilagyi and H.P. Sims, "An Exploration of the Path–Goal Theory of Leadership in a Health-Care Environment," *Academy of Management Journal* 17 (1974): 622–634; C.A. Schriesheim and A.S. DeNisi, "Task Dimensions as Moderators of the Effects of Instrumental Leadership: A Two-Sample Replicated Test of Path–Goal Leadership Theory," *Journal of Applied Psychology* 66 (1981): 589–597.

28. R.J. House and G. Dessler, "The Path–Goal Theory of Leadership: Some Post Hoc and A Priori Tests," in *Contingency Approaches to Leadership,* ed. J.G. Hunt and L.L. Larson (Carbondale, Ill.: Southern Illinois University Press, 1974); H.K. Downey, J.E. Sheridan, and J.W. Slocum, "Analysis of Relationships among Leader Behavior, Subordinate Job Performance, and Satisfaction: A Path–Goal Approach," *Academy of Management Journal* 18 (1975): 253–262.

29. P. Hersey and K.H. Blanchard, *Management of Organizational Behavior,* 3d ed. (Englewood Cliffs, N.J.: Prentice-Hall, 1977).

30. C.L. Graeff, "The Situational Leadership Theory: A Critical Review," *Academy of Management Review* 7 (1983): 285–291; Yukl, *Leadership in Organizations;* R.P. Vecchio, "Situational Leadership Theory: An Examination of a Prescriptive Theory," *Journal of Applied Psychology* 72 (1987): 444–451.

31. V.H. Vroom and P.W. Yetton, *Leadership and Decision Making* (Pittsburgh: University of Pittsburgh Press, 1973).

32. V.H. Vroom, "Leadership Revisited," in *Man and Work in Society,* ed. E.L. Case and F.G. Zimmer (New York: Van Nostrand Reinhold, 1975); V.H. Vroom and A.G. Jago, "On the Validity of the Vroom–Yetton Model," *Journal of Applied Psychology* 63 (1978): 151–162; R.H. Field, "A Test of the Vroom–Yetton Normative Model of Leadership," *Journal of Applied Psychology* 67 (1982): 523–532; W.C. Wedley and R.H. Field, "The Vroom–Yetton Model: Are Feasible Set Choices Due to Chance?" *Academy of Management Proceedings* (1982): 146–150.

33. B. Smith, "The TELOS Program and the Vroom–Yetton Model," in J.G. Hunt and L. Larson, eds., *Crosscurrents in Leadership* (Cardondale, Ill.: Southern Illinois University Press, 1979): 39–40.

34. V.H. Vroom and A.G. Jago, "Leadership and Decision Making: A Revised Normative Model" (paper presented at Annual Meeting of the Academy of Management, Boston, Mass., 1984).

35. R.M. Dienesch and R.C. Liden, "Leader–Member Exchange Model of Leadership: A Critique and Further Developments," *Academy of Management Review* 11 (1986): 118–134; D. Duchon, S. Green, and T. Tabor, "Vertical Dyad Linkage," *Journal of Applied Psychology* 71 (1986): 56–60.

36. F. Danserau, G. Graen, and W.J. Haga, "A Vertical Dyad Linkage Approach to Leadership within Formal Organizations: A Cognitudinal Investigation of the Role-Making Process," *Organizational Behavior and Human Performance* 15 (1975): 46–78; G. Graen and J.F. Cashman, "A Role-Making Model of Leadership in Formal Organizations: A Developmental Approach," in *Leadership Frontiers,* ed. J.G. Hunt and L.L. Larson (Kent, Ohio: Kent State University Press, 1975): 143–165: R.C. Liden and G. Graen, "Generalizability of the Vertical Dyad Linkage Model of Leadership," *Academy of Management Journal* 23 (1980): 451–465; R.P. Vecchio, "Are You IN or OUT with Your Boss?" *Business Horizons* 29 (1987): 76–78; R.P. Vecchio, "A Dyadic Interpretation of the Contingency Model of Leadership Effectiveness," *Academy of Management Journal* 22 (1979): 590–600.

37. J. Miner, *Theories of Organizational Behavior* (Hinsdale, Ill.: The Dryden Press, 1980); R.P. Vecchio, "Predicting Employee Turnover from Leader–Member Exchange," *Academy of Management Journal* 28 (1985): 478–485; G. Ferris, "Role of Leadership in the Employee Withdrawal Process: A Constructive Replication," *Journal of Applied Psychology* 70 (1985): 777–781.

38. G. Graen and W. Schiemann, "Leader–Member Agreement: A Vertical Dyad Linkage Approach," *Journal of Applied Psychology* 63 (1978): 206–212.

39. R. Katerberg and P.W. Hom, "Effects of Within-Group and Between-Groups Variation in Leadership," *Journal of Applied Psychology* 66 (1981): 218–223; R.P. Vecchio, "A Further Test of Leadership Effects Due to Between-Group Variation and Within-Group Variation," *Journal of Applied Psychology* 67 (1982):

200–208; R.P. Vecchio, R.W. Griffeth, and P.W. Hom, "The Predictive Utility of the Vertical Dyad Linkage Approach," *Journal of Social Psychology* 126 (1987): 617–625.

40. Miner, *Theories of Organizational Behavior.*

41. R.P. Vecchio and B.C. Gobdel, "The Vertical Dyad Linkage Model of Leadership: Problems and Prospects," *Organizational Behavior and Human Performance* 34 (1984): 5–20.

42. R.J. House, "A 1976 Theory of Charismatic Leadership," in J.G. Hunt and L.L. Larsen, eds., *Leadership: The Cutting Edge* (Carbondale, Ill.: Southern Illinois University Press, 1977); B.M. Bass, *Leadership and Performance Beyond Expectations* (New York: Free Press, 1985); J.M. Howell and B.J. Arolio, "Transformational versus Transactional Leaders: How They Impact Innovation, Risk-Taking, Organizational Structure and Performance" (paper presented at Annual Meeting of the Academy of Management, Washington, D.C., 1989).

43. S. Kerr and J.M. Jermier, "Substitutes for Leadership: Their Meaning and Measurement," *Organizational Behavior and Human Performance* 22 (1978): 375–403; S. Kerr, "Substitutes for Leadership: Some Implications for Organization Design," *Organization and Administrative Sciences* 8 (1977): 135.

When it is
necessary to make
a decision,
sometimes it is
necessary to not
make a decision.

— Lord Falkland

It isn't what you
know that counts,
it's what you think
of in time.

— Anonymous

Originality is the art
of remembering
what you hear but
forgetting where
you heard it.

**— Not sure who
said this**

Learning Objectives

After studying this chapter, you should be able to:

1. *Describe the types of decisions managers make.*

2. *List the steps of a highly rational decision-making process.*

3. *Describe some constraints on the decision-making process.*

4. *Identify obstacles to effective decision making.*

5. *Define groupthink and list its symptoms.*

6. *Describe techniques to improve decision making.*

7. *Identify characteristics of creative organization members.*

8. *Describe the steps in the creative process.*

9. *Identify ways that groups and individuals can enhance creativity.*

10. *List ways organizations can establish a climate that encourages creativity.*

Decision Making

■ Who Decides?

At Semco, Brazil's largest manufacturer of marine and food-processing machinery, president Ricardo Semler believes in treating his 800 employees "like responsible adults." In his view, this includes letting them make the decisions.

The company's policy of democratic decision making means that employees collectively make decisions that in most companies would be the province of the executives. For example, when the company's marine division needed a larger plant, Semco first hired real estate agents to find a location, but they found nothing. The company then asked the employees for help; over the first weekend they found three nearby factories for sale. The division shut down for a day, and all the workers went out to inspect the three buildings. Then the workers voted on which plant they wanted.

As it turned out, the plant that won the vote was not a plant that management wanted. However, the company went along with the decision on the assumption that letting the workers participate in the decision would enhance motivation and morale. In fact, once the workers were in the new plant, the division's productivity, in dollars per year per employee, shot up from $14,200 in 1984 to $37,500 in 1988.

The logic of letting employees make their own decisions extends to day-to-day concerns, such as what to wear, when to report to work, and whether to fly first-class. The company abolished its dress code and its rules about travel expenses. About the travel policy, Semler says, "If we can't trust people with our money and their judgment, we . . . shouldn't be sending them overseas to do business in our name."

Semco has also eliminated time clocks, relying instead on the employees' maturity and their desire to benefit from the company's policy of paying regular bonuses of 23 percent of profits. The flextime policy worked out even better than expected, with no abuses or production interruptions. Quite the contrary: In one work area, a man wanted to start at 7:00 A.M., but he couldn't get the parts he needed until 8:00, when the forklift operator showed up. The employees discussed the problem and resolved it by having everyone in that work area learn to operate a forklift. The union didn't object, because the idea came from the workers.

This responsibility for decision making commits the employees to carrying out their decisions. For example, factory workers set their own schedule, so they are committed to fulfilling their plans. One group decided to make 220 meat slicers during a month. When the end of that month came, the slicers were ready except for the motors; the supplier still hadn't sent them. Two employees drove to the supplier and arranged to have the motors delivered at the end of that day, the 31st. The motors arrived, and the whole work force stayed overnight, fin-

341

ishing the meat slicers at 4:45 the next morning.

Of course, good decision making requires informed decision makers. So that workers understand the impact of their decisions, Semco trains all of them to read financial reports, then provides them with a monthly balance sheet, profit-and-loss state-ment, and cash-flow statement for their division.

Even with such training, many company executives would be reluctant to delegate so much decision-making authority. How-ever, no matter who makes the decisions in an organization, cer-tain pitfalls can impede the selec-tion of the best option. This chap-ter discusses how an organization's members make decisions and ways to improve decision making. It also describes obstacles to avoid in the decision-making process. The chapter con-cludes by considering creativity, which can enhance the quality of decisions.

Source: Ricardo Semler, "Managing without Managers," *Harvard Business Review,* September–October 1989, pp. 76–84.

It can be reasonably argued that decision making is the most central activity of management, that it is the very essence of a manager's job. The nature of a manager's decisions, of course, is quite varied. They can range from such major issues as deciding whether to create a new product line to such seem-ingly minor issues as deciding where to take a client to lunch. In a given day, a manager will make a great number of decisions. The quality of these decisions can have a powerful impact on unit performance and, perhaps ultimately, on the performance of the entire organization.

Types of Organizational Decisions

Before considering the major models of decision making, let us first examine the variety of decisions a manager may make. Two useful classifications focus on whether decisions are (1) personal versus organizational and (2) pro-grammed versus nonprogrammed.

Personal versus Organizational Decisions

Every day we engage in **personal decision making.** Such decisions directly affect ourselves rather than others. For example, each of us decides what clothes to wear on a given day and whether to ride our bike, take a bus, or drive a car to work. Although personal decisions are often fairly trivial, they can sometimes be quite important. Selecting a college or a field in which to major, as well as applying for a particular job, are personal decisions that can have profound effects on the course of a person's life.

In contrast, **organizational decision making** involves decisions that per-tain to the problems and practices of a given organization. Like personal decisions, some organizational decisions can be fairly trivial, such as deciding which brand of typewriter ribbon to order. But others may have a major impact on the organization, such as choosing an advertising campaign or deciding whether to acquire a competing firm. The essential distinction be-tween personal and organizational decision making lies in the object of the process. Personal decision making focuses on the actions and life of an individ-

■ Figure 11.1

Types of Decisions

	Personal	**Organizational**
Programmed	Daily Routines Habits	Standard Operating Procedures Rulebooks and Manuals
Nonprogrammed	Job Choice Career Selection	Strategic Planning Issues Crisis Management

ual, while organizational decision making focuses on the practices and perfor-mance of an organization.

Programmed versus Nonprogrammed Decisions

Another useful way of distinguishing among decisions has been proposed by Herbert Simon, who contends that decisions can be characterized in terms of whether they are fairly routine and well-structured or novel and poorly struc-tured.[1] Well-structured decisions are termed **programmed decisions,** while poorly structured decisions are termed **nonprogrammed decisions.**

A good example of a programmed decision is when a clerk checks the on-hand inventory against a pre-established minimum standard. If the on-hand inventory falls below that standard, he knows that it is time to order more stock.

With decisions that are unique and nonroutine, taking a preprogrammed approach becomes difficult. For example, the leaders of a nation may have trouble deciding how much to spend on military armaments for national de-fense, because of the uniqueness of political relations with neighboring coun-tries and the difficulty of predicting the intentions of other world leaders. Not surprisingly, such nonprogrammed decision making may rely more on an indi-vidual's intuition and experience in similar situations.

By combining these two types of decisions (personal versus organiza-tional and programmed versus nonprogrammed), we can create four classes or varieties of decisions (Figure 11.1). Personal programmed decisions involve simple, repetitive personal matters. Most people devote very little time to such decisions and tend to rely on established habits or simple decision rules. For example, an employee may usually park her car in the same spot in a parking lot, but on days that it rains, she may park in a different spot.

Personal nonprogrammed decisions arise during rare but significant events in an individual's personal life. For example, choosing which company to work for or whom to marry are personal decisions that people make only rarely. While some personal nonprogrammed decisions can be directly job-related, as when a person decides to quit one firm in hopes of finding a better position with another, others that are not so obviously job-related can also affect workplace behavior. For example, a person's choice of a marriage partner may mean having to relocate to be near him or her.

Organizational programmed decisions are typically handled according to established guidelines, rules, or procedures. Many simple problem situations can be dealt with by merely referring to a manual or rulebook that outlines the appropriate solution. In most organizations, it is lower-level personnel who are responsible for handling organizational preprogrammed decisions. For example, a worker may be responsible for monitoring a control panel that provides information on the temperature and pressure within a vat. If the readings indicate that these values are outside of a predetermined range, the worker is instructed to adjust the necessary mechanisms in order to maintain control of the process.

Organizational nonprogrammed decisions pertain to rare and unique situations that have potentially significant impact on the organization. Major planning issues and problems are often the topic of such decision making. How to acquire capital, whether to sell off unprofitable corporate divisions, and whether to launch a new product line are examples of organizational nonprogrammed decision issues. Because of the critical nature of such decisions for the very well-being of the organization, they are more typically handled by high-level personnel. Organizational nonprogrammed decision making affords the greatest opportunities for creativity.

Classical Decision Theory

The traditional approach to understanding decision making, often called **classical decision theory,** assumes that decision making is, and should be, a highly rational process. The classical theory of decision making is often referred to as the **rational-economic model** because of the model's presumption that decision makers are rational and its strong ties to the classical economic view of behavior. The process can be described in terms of a sequence of steps that a decision maker should follow in order to enhance the probability of attaining a desired goal. Figure 11.2 illustrates the proposed steps in classical decision theory.[2]

As the figure shows, a situation must exist that triggers the decision-making process. A set of circumstances leads the decision maker to recognize the existence of the problem or opportunity that demands action. Recognition is an essential early step in decision making because unless a person believes a problem or opportunity exists, the decision-making process will not occur. Following recognition, the decision maker defines the nature of the situation. This definition leads to the generation of alternative approaches to coping with the situation. The manner in which the situation is defined will dictate the nature and variety of alternatives. The next steps in the process entail gathering information about each alternative (such as its relative cost and likelihood of success) and evaluating its desirability by weighting and combining the obtained information. From this evaluation, a single best course of action will emerge. This course of action is the one that will be implemented and subse-

Figure 11.2

Steps in the Decision-Making Process: The Classical View

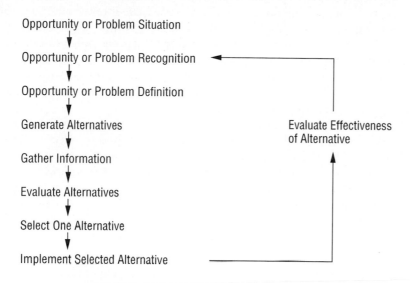

---

quently evaluated in terms of its effectiveness in eliminating the problem or taking advantage of the opportunity. By monitoring the effectiveness of the solution, the decision maker can judge the extent to which it was appropriate and determine whether further action can or should be taken. It may be that the problem or opportunity will need to be redefined in light of the results. In essence, this step in the model provides feedback about how well the decision-making process was carried out.

The classical view is in fact popular with many scholars.* It does a fairly good job of describing how a decision *should* be made; in particular, the view points to the features managers should focus on when trying to improve the caliber of the decision-making process. Yet, the classical view is largely inaccurate as a description of *how* managers typically make decisions. Furthermore, its prescriptions for making better decisions are often in error.

One major set of deficiencies in the classical approach lies in its assumptions that all alternatives will be considered, that the consequences of each alternative will be considered, that accurate information is available at no cost, and that decision makers are totally rational beings.

In reality, a manager rarely considers all possible alternatives, since there often are too many to list. Additionally, many alternatives may not even occur to the decision maker. The assumption that the consequences of each alternative are considered is similarly impractical. In many circumstances, it may be

---

* Most economists subscribe to the classical view of decision making.

impossible to estimate all the consequences. But even when full consideration is possible, examining all alternatives may require too much time and effort.

Rarely, if ever, is a manager's information perfectly accurate. More typically, the available information is often dated (because it takes time to gather, distill, and digest information) and only partially relevant to the question at hand (because information is often gathered for purposes other than a manager's specific needs). Also, information is not a free good. The cost of generating or purchasing needed data adds another constraint to the decision-making process. As a consequence, a manager is often forced to make decisions based on incomplete or insufficient information.

Furthermore, studies show that decision makers do not have the mental ability needed to store and process all of the data required to select the single best alternative. Available evidence suggests that people are simply not capable of performing the cognitive calculus that the classical view requires.[3]

Finally, there are a number of real-world constraints on a manager's decision making. For example, a manager may not have sufficient time to devote to making a decision. Despite a decision's importance, the need for prompt action may rule out a formal analysis of the situation.

A Behavioral Theory of Decision Making

Given the shortcomings of the rational-economic model, an alternative perspective has emerged that provides a more descriptive view of managerial behavior. This approach is termed a **behavioral theory of decision making,** also sometimes called the **administrative model.**[4] Figure 11.3 illustrates the essential steps in the administrative model of decision making.

The administrative model explicitly acknowledges the real-world limitations on managers' decision making. Specifically, it holds that decision makers must work within conditions that provide a **bounded rationality.** The concept of bounded rationality means that managers are restricted in their decision-making processes and must, therefore, settle for something short of an ideal or optimal solution. Bounded rationality recognizes that (1) all possible alternatives and their associated consequences cannot be generated, (2) both the available information and the definition of the situation are likely to be incomplete and inadequate to some degree, and (3) the final decision may be based on criteria other than simple optimization or outcome maximization.†

Due to the personal and situational limitations on managerial decision making, managers tend to make decisions that are "good enough" for the situation at hand. When managers seek solutions that are "good enough" rather than "ideal," they **satisfice** rather than **maximize.** When maximizing, a manager attempts to find the best or optimal solution. In contrast, when

† It is interesting to consider what an organization would be like if it were staffed with totally rational beings. In point of fact, it is because organizations are not staffed with collections of individuals like Mr. Spock (*Star Trek*'s science officer) that organizations pose many intriguing problems for the field of organizational behavior (in addition to making organizational life much more exciting).

■ Figure 11.3

Steps in the Decision-Making Process: The Administrative View

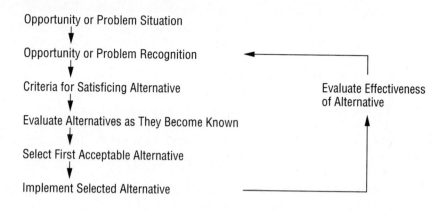

satisficing, a decision maker considers each alternative until one arises that is reasonably acceptable. Such an alternative meets all necessary requirements for a solution, but may not be the very best choice. March and Simon have provided a very useful illustration of the essential difference between satisficing and maximizing: Maximizing (or optimizing) is analogous to searching through a haystack for the sharpest needle to be found, whereas satisficing is much like searching through a haystack until a needle can be found that is sharp enough to sew with.[5]

Also included in the administrative model is the notion of **bounded discretion,** which suggests that optimal solutions are sometimes not feasible courses of action because they are ethically improper. In some circumstances, the best or optimal solution may actually involve morally questionable behavior. A retailer, for example, may reason that one way out of a difficult financial situation is to set his store on fire in order to collect the insurance. Or a food processor may have the option of significantly reducing product quality (perhaps by decreasing the amount of meat and increasing the proportion of filler in a hamburger patty) as a means of lowering costs and thereby raising profits. Most managers (but, of course, not all) prefer to avoid such unethical behavior. Therefore, bounded discretion represents a further constraint on the decision-making process.

In addition, Simon and others contend that managers often follow rules of thumb, or **heuristics,** when making decisions.[6] Because of the volume, variety, and complexity of business decisions, managers frequently use simplified decision rules to achieve satisficing solutions. For example, a heuristic for some investors is that if a stock drops 10 percent or more below its purchase price, they will decide to sell. These investors use this heuristic with great consistency and regardless of other circumstances to avoid holding on to a potentially disastrous, but previously attractive, stock.

The administrative model provides an interesting comparison to the rational-economic model. The two differ, most fundamentally, in their approaches to how decisions *should be* and *are* made. Each is successful in its own domain: The rational-economic model provides a useful summary of how decisions *should be made,* while the administrative model gives a good description of how decisions typically *are made.*

The Influence of Judgmental Strategies

Recently, researchers have come to recognize that decision makers frequently go beyond the information they are given when making inferences. Daniel Kahneman and Amos Tversky have identified two judgmental strategies (sometimes termed judgmental heuristics) on which people frequently rely.[7] The strategies, unfortunately, oftentimes mislead people into making erroneous inferences.

The first judgmental strategy, termed the **availability heuristic,** reflects the influence of the relative availability of objects or events (i.e., their accessibility via memory, perception, or imagination). Occasionally, the availability heuristic can be misleading. Consider a pollster who asks adults in the United States to estimate the current level of national unemployment. It is likely that a bias will be reflected in these estimates such that unemployed individuals will tend to overestimate the rate of unemployment, while employed individuals will underestimate it. Many people would not recall newspaper or television accounts of estimates of unemployment or attempt to compensate for their possible bias by deliberately considering the impact of their own experiences on their beliefs.

The second judgmental strategy proposed by Kahneman and Tversky, termed the **representativeness heuristic,** involves the application of one's sense of resemblance between objects or events. In applying this heuristic, a person assesses the extent to which an object or event possesses features that would enable them to categorize the object or event appropriately. As an illustration of this tendency, consider the following question: I have a friend who is a professor. He likes to write poetry, is rather shy, and is small in stature. Which of the following is his field of expertise: (a) Chinese studies or (b) psychology?

If you are inclined to answer "Chinese studies," you have been seduced by the representativeness heuristic. That is to say, you judged the personality profile to be a better fit for the stereotype of a sinologist than a psychologist. However, the odds are that any person is more likely to know psychologists, and psychologists are far more numerous than sinologists. In light of this more critical base-rate information, the better answer (from a statistical standpoint) would be "psychology."

Numerous decision-making tasks, of course, rely on accurate estimation and categorization. Therefore, both the availability heuristic and the representativeness heuristic are important tools in drawing inferences. While they often may lead us to correct inferences, they have the potential to lead to erroneous judgments as well. It should also be understood that Kahneman and Tversky's notions of availability and representativeness are not, strictly speaking, heuristics, in the sense of being explicit and invariant devices or formulae for making decisions. Rather, they represent automatic and nonconscious processes that are frequently involved in judgment and decision-making processes.

Obstacles to Effective Decision Making

A number of potential obstacles to effective decision making have been identified. In this section, we will examine three of the most common: escalation of commitment, groupthink, and the willingness of groups to take risks.

Escalation of Commitment

Barry Staw has suggested that people are sometimes unwilling to change a course of action despite unequivocal evidence showing that their decision was incorrect.[8] In essence, a person may decide to "stay the course" because he or she has already invested substantial time, effort, and/or money in the existing situation. All the more remarkable is the tendency of people to invest still more resources in a course of action that appears doomed to failure. As examples of escalating commitment, Staw cites the following:

> Imagine a person who has purchased a stock at $50 a share. Yet, when the stock drops in price to $20, he buys more shares at the lower price. When the price drops still further, the individual must decide whether to buy more, sell out, or hold on to what he has purchased.
>
> Consider a person who spends several years working toward an academic degree in a field which offers minimal job prospects (for example, in the humanities). Yet, the person invests still more time and money in completing the degree (rather than changing fields). Ultimately, the person is faced with the choice of being unemployed, underemployed (that is, working in a job which is below his capabilities), or starting over in another field or career path.
>
> During the early phase of U.S. involvement in the Vietnam War, the Undersecretary of State (George Ball) wrote to President Johnson: "The decision you face now is crucial. Once large numbers of U.S. troops are committed to direct combat, they will begin to take heavy casualties in a war they are ill-equipped to fight in a noncooperative, if not downright hostile, countryside. Once we suffer large casualties, we will have started a well-nigh irreversible process. Our involvement will be so great that we cannot — without national humiliation — stop short of achieving our complete objectives. Of the two possibilities, I think humiliation would be more likely than the achievement of our objectives." (Memo dated July 1, 1965.)[9]

We have all seen situations in which people stay committed to a specific course of action despite negative feedback. By committing additional resources to a losing strategy, they in essence throw good money after bad. There are several explanations of this phenomenon. One is that people pursue a course of action *in spite of* negative feedback largely *because of* negative feedback. This argument suggests that people value tenacity, or stick-to-it-iveness. They feel that a "damn the torpedoes, full speed ahead" stance has a certain social value. Because people generally admire those who stick to their principles, a decision maker may adopt a persistent approach in response to perceived social pressure. A second explanation suggests that people will forsake a more rational approach to difficult decision situations out of concern for establishing consistency.

To test the notion that social norms explain managerial consistency, Staw and Ross used practicing managers, college business majors, and other undergraduate students as subjects in a study.[10] Each subject was presented with a case study summary of a manager's behavior. The case portrayed the manager as being either consistent or experimenting (less consistent) in following a course of action. In addition, the manager's behavior was described as ultimately leading to either success or failure. In the consistency condition, the manager adhered to a single course of action despite a series of negative results. In the experimenting condition, the manager initially tried one course of action, then shifted to a second and a third course when negative results were obtained.

The subjects responded most favorably to the managers who followed a consistent course of action and were successful in the end. In addition, the hypothetical manager who persisted to an ultimately successful outcome was judged more highly than would be predicted from the separate effects of the variables of consistency and outcome success. In essence, Staw and Ross found a form of "hero effect" in which a manager who remained committed despite two setbacks *and* succeeded in the end was regarded quite positively. Furthermore, the researchers found that the subjects' reactions to consistency varied across groups of raters. Practicing managers showed the strongest appreciation, followed by college business majors and then other undergraduates. This suggests that consistency is viewed as important to effective management and that this perception may be acquired through participation in business roles.‡

Escalation of commitment is most likely to occur in certain predictable settings. Among these are situations in which a person feels a strong sense of personal responsibility, as when selecting a career or setting a policy with which the individual will be publicly associated. To counter the escalation tendency, Staw suggests employing outside advisers who do not feel personal responsibility for previous losses or gains.[13] It may also be wise to rotate decision-making responsibility across managers if there is a history of losses due to the tendency to escalate commitment.

Groupthink

Irving Janis has identified a fascinating phenomenon that can lead groups to commit serious errors in decision making. In describing this situation, which he called **groupthink,** Janis proposed that highly cohesive working groups (that is, groups whose members enjoy a high degree of interpersonal attraction) are in danger of taking a distorted view of situations that confront them.[14]§ As a

---

‡ Research on the escalation of commitment phenomenon has been criticized for not yet employing decision-making situations in which the continued commitment of resources is explicitly inadvisable on economic grounds.[11] Also, the perception of escalation may largely be a mental construction that is made after the fact.[12]

§ Janis selected the term *groupthink* to label this phenomenon because it had Orwellian overtones (cf. *newspeak* in George Orwell's novel *1984*).

result, the group's decision-making processes may be slanted toward seeking *consensus* rather than exploring alternative courses of action. Because dissent and critical analysis are not encouraged in discussion sessions, the group may select a course of action that ignores potential dangers and pitfalls.

Janis has provided a number of illustrations of groupthink, including the Watergate cover-up by the Nixon administration, the escalation of U.S. military involvement in Vietnam, the failure of the Roosevelt administration to prepare for the Japanese raid on Pearl Harbor, and — perhaps the most clear-cut example — the Bay of Pigs incident during the presidency of John Kennedy (the incident in which President Kennedy and his top advisers unanimously decided to adopt a CIA proposal to invade Cuba and overthrow Fidel Castro). None of Kennedy's advisers voiced opposition to the proposal. The operation was spearheaded by 1,400 Cuban exiles who were given air and naval support by the U.S. military and the CIA. The invasion, which occurred at the Bay of Pigs on the south coast of Cuba, was a total failure within a few days of the invasion, with a majority of the invaders being taken prisoner by the Cuban army.**

In retrospect, Kennedy and his advisers appear to have been victims of groupthink. Their decision to proceed with the invasion was based on a certain amount of wishful thinking in that the plan relied heavily on a popular uprising by the Cuban people in support of the invaders. Kennedy and his advisers assumed that the invasion would be a simple operation that could not fail and would quickly lead to Castro's overthrow. They also gave no advance consideration to the possible adverse consequences of a failed invasion — the most significant of which were the anger of normally friendly Latin American and European countries and the growth of closer military ties between the Soviet Union and Cuba. Later, Castro's concern for defense led to the installation of Soviet-built nuclear missiles in Cuba, within 90 miles of the United States. This defensive move precipitated a further problem for the Kennedy administration — the Cuban Missile Crisis.

Following the Bay of Pigs invasion, the confidence of Kennedy and his top advisers (such men as Robert McNamara, Robert Kennedy, Dean Rusk, and Arthur Schlesinger, Jr.) was deeply shaken as they came to realize their own tendencies toward self-deception. In writing about the decision process, Schlesinger observed that

> *Had one advisor opposed the adventure, I believe Kennedy would have canceled it. No one spoke against it. . . Our meetings took place in a curious atmosphere of assumed consensus. . . In the months after the Bay of Pigs, I bitterly reproached myself for having kept so silent . . . though my feelings of guilt were tempered by the knowledge that a course of objection would have accomplished little save to gain me a name as a nuisance. I can only explain . . . that one's impulse to blow the whistle on this nonsense was simply undone by the circumstances of the discussion (Janis, 1972, pp. 39–40).*

** To the credit of Kennedy and his policy advisers, they recognized the mistakes they made during the Bay of Pigs invasion and tried to compensate by having open and frank discussions when coping with the Cuban Missile Crisis.

Janis has proposed eight main symptoms or signs of groupthink:

1. *An illusion of invulnerability.* Group members may develop a sense of powerfulness that leads them to ignore obvious danger signals. They may take extreme risks as a result of being overly optimistic.

2. *Rationalization.* The members may discredit or ignore evidence that contradicts the group's consensus. Sources of disagreeable information may be attacked, or elaborate rationalizations may be offered to explain away the information.

3. *An assumption of morality.* Group members may view themselves as highly ethical and above reproach. The views of outsiders are then defined as intrinsically immoral or evil. Adopting a stance of self-righteousness makes it easier for the group to follow a course of action that is morally questionable because the members view themselves as pursuing a higher morality.

4. *Negative stereotyping.* Groups that suffer from groupthink may come to view opponents and people outside the group in simple negative stereotypic terms. By casting outsiders in negative terms, the group makes them easier to ignore because their opposition is to be expected.

5. *Pressure to conform.* The expression of dissent is suppressed by the group's members. Persons who voice objections or express doubts may be ostracized or expelled.

6. *Self-censorship.* Each member of the group may carefully monitor his or her own thoughts and suppress personal objectives, in essence withholding dissent.

7. *An illusion of unanimity.* As a result of self-censorship, no reservations are expressed. The consequence of this lack of dissent is the apparent unanimous endorsement of proposals.

8. *Mindguards.* Certain individuals in the group may take it upon themselves to serve as mindguards, guarding a manager's thoughts in the same way a bodyguard protects a leader's personal safety. These mindguards will act against sources of information or dissenters by deflecting them or their objections.

As this discussion of groupthink suggests, the existence of an apparently admirable condition — group cohesion — can have detrimental effects on the quality of decision making. Janis suggests that several steps be taken if a highly cohesive decision-making body is disposed to groupthink. Specifically, group members should be encouraged to voice criticisms, doubts, and objections. To promote open debate, managers should avoid stating their preferred positions during the early stages of group discussion. It may also be valuable for the group to invite outside experts to sit in on their sessions occasionally and offer suggestions.

Another tactic for countering groupthink is to assign several group members to teams that will investigate the advisability of alternative courses of action. After gathering evidence in support of an assigned position, the teams can present their arguments and participate in a directed debate. Such a con-

An Inside Look

Stirring Up Good Decisions

Some antagonism can be good for an organization's decision makers. Professor Charles R. Schwenk recommends that businesses use devil's advocates to help managers make the right decisions. A devil's advocate can be used in a basic approach or in techniques called *multiple advocacy* and *dialectical inquiry*.

In the basic approach, one person or a group of people take the role of devil's advocate and criticize a proposal. The devil's advocate researches the proposal beforehand. Then he or she points out weaknesses, inconsistencies, and problems that may cause the proposed plan or project to fail. Managers can then make their decision with confidence that they have heard all sides of the argument.

Multiple advocacy involves using several devil's advocates from every dissenting faction. Dozens of different opinions may come to the surface with multiple advocacy. Therefore, it is important one person have the role of "custodian of unpopular views." That person makes sure sufficient time is devoted to discussing each issue.

With dialectical inquiry, decision makers are divided into subgroups on the basis of their personalities and problem-solving orientations. The subgroups develop alternatives to the recommended strategy, focusing on the assumptions used to arrive at the recommendation. It is important to question assumptions, because top executives view the company

differently than lower-level managers. Because subgroup members have different backgrounds and come from different departments, management gets a variety of opinions on proposals and their underlying assumptions. This technique has been used with success at Eastman Kodak as part of its strategic marketing decision making.

Devil's advocacy works best with unique problems that are difficult to solve. For devil's advocacy to work in an organization, the person making the decision must be willing to listen to other points of view. Also, the devil's advocate should be an objective observer, not a person who is already committed to a proposal.

Source: Walecia Konrad, "Want Better Decisions? Stir Up a Little Conflict," *Working Woman*, November 1985, pp. 28–31; R. Kilmann, K. Thomas, D. Slevin, R. Nath, and S. Jerrel, eds., *Producing Useful Knowledge for Organizations* (New York: Praeger, 1983), 147–166.

frontation of alternative points of view can lead to new insights on the issues underlying a decision-making situation.

A somewhat related technique is to appoint a group member to serve as a devil's advocate at each group meeting.†† This person's responsibilities would include actively criticizing the proposals (and the implicit assumptions) raised by all group members.

Another suggested technique is the scheduling of a **last-chance meeting** at which all group members are encouraged to raise any nagging doubts or hesitations they may have.

Last, and perhaps most important, a manager can help to overcome groupthink through a willingness to accept criticism. Setting an example of openness to criticism, as opposed to resentment or fear of subordinates' objections, can help to promote serious discussion of the pros and cons of alternative courses of action.

†† The procedure of appointing a "devil's advocate" originated with a Catholic church practice of assigning someone the role of arguing against the canonization of a candidate for sainthood.

Risk Taking within Groups

Imagine that you are a manager who must make a decision that entails a fair amount of risk — for example, deciding whether to expand your production facilities into a politically unstable country in Latin America. The risks are great in that your entire investment could be lost if the country is taken over by extremists who intend to nationalize all industry. However, the potential profits will be substantial if the country does not experience a revolution. Would you make the final decision on such an investment by yourself or would you turn it over to a committee?

Most people would argue that committee decisions tend to be conservative and that individuals, in comparison, are not constrained by the dynamics of debate or the doubts that might be raised within a committee. Boldness and initiative are more typically associated with individuals than with committees.‡‡

James Stoner, while a graduate student at MIT, was one of the first people to investigate whether groups are more cautious than individuals in decision making that involves risky propositions.[15] In his research, he devised a series of cases involving the propensity (or willingness) to take risks. The cases dealt with such diverse topics as (1) choosing between a secure though modest-paying job with one employer versus taking a high-paying job with a newly founded but financially less sound firm in a highly competitive field, and (2) choosing between calling a football play that would likely result in a tie versus calling a play that is riskier but could result in a victory.

In his research, Stoner found that individuals tended to take a less risky route, while groups favored riskier actions. When the individuals were placed in a group setting, they shifted their endorsement to a riskier position. This phenomenon, in which a group endorses a riskier position than would its individual members, is called the **risky shift.**

A number of explanations have been offered to account for the risky shift. One of the more popular is the concept of **diffusion of responsibility.** This line of reasoning holds that when individuals are in groups, they may feel less personal responsibility for the consequences of their actions. The diffusion of responsibility concept has also been used to account for the failure of an individual to come to the aid of an injured person if a large number of people are nearby. Thus, a mugging victim who is lying on the floor of a subway station is less likely to receive aid as the size of the crowd increases. Similarly, group decision making may sometimes reflect this sense of personal anonymity in endorsing a course of action. From studies of incidents similar to the subway station mugging, researchers have inferred that risky shifts can even occur in the absence of group discussion.[16]

Although the shift toward endorsing risk within groups has been found in a variety of settings,[17] there have been occasions where groups opted for the more cautious alternative action. For example, in one study, groups of house-wives and students were asked whether a married couple should abort a preg-

‡‡ As an illustration of the belief that committees tend to be conservative, consider the old saying that "A camel is a horse that was designed by a committee."

nancy when future complications in the pregnancy could endanger the life of the mother. In this decision scenario, groups endorsed a more cautious course (abortion) than did the members acting alone.[18] In another study, groups were again more cautious than individuals in recommending that a couple not go ahead with their plan to be married when the couple expressed disagreement on a number of issues.[19] The tendency of groups to move in a more conservative direction than would individuals is called the **cautious shift.**

Clearly, the risky shift and the cautious shift are contradictory in their predictions of how groups will behave when faced with a decision that involves an element of risk. A close examination of the studies that have identified both risky and cautious shifts suggests that the prior inclination of the group's members (that is, when they make their premeeting judgment of their preferences) is an important factor in determining whether a shift will occur in a cautious or a risky direction. If the premeeting inclination is toward caution, the group's decision tends to go to the extreme of the cautious direction. If the premeeting inclination is toward risk, however, the group's decision is likely to go toward the risky extreme.

The tendency of groups to move toward extremes has been termed **group polarization.**[20] This phenomenon is most probably the result of several factors. First, the premeeting inclinations of the group's members encourage a certain bias during discussions that leads the group to explore and endorse arguments and information that support the members' initial positions. Throughout discussions, the group's members will voice, and thereby encourage, additional rationales for being either conservative or risky, depending on their original bias.

Group polarization can also be explained by the tendency of groups to make decisions that endorse dominant cultural values. The content of the decision then becomes an important issue in predicting whether a cautious or a risky shift will occur. For business- and career-related decisions, the dominant cultural value favors risk taking. Within our culture, taking chances in competitive arenas is greatly admired and seen as an often necessary step in attaining success. Other topics, such as weighing the value of a mother's life versus the life of an unborn child, are traditionally decided more conservatively. Thus, a group would probably favor preserving the mother's life rather than the child's. In general, group members try to endorse the prevalent social view on the appropriateness of risk versus conservatism in a given situation. Nonetheless, the observed instances of groups endorsing risk appear to outnumber the instances of groups endorsing caution.

Techniques for Improving Decision Making

Individual versus Group Decision Making

In the previous discussion of individual versus group decision making, it was noted that groups tend to endorse extreme positions when confronted with decisions involving an element of risk. In situations where risk is not great or where achieving a high-quality solution is the primary goal, the question of the relative advantages of group versus individual decision making can be raised.

A good deal of research has been devoted to the issue of whether solutions generated by decision-making groups are superior, inferior, or equal to the solutions generated by individuals working alone on the same problem.

Studies of individual versus group decision making have typically relied on one of two approaches: (1) individuals initially work alone on a problem and subsequently work on similar problems in groups (and vice versa), or (2) some individuals work alone on several problems, while other individuals simultaneously work in groups on the same problems. The problems studied ranged from simple puzzles to complex reasoning tasks. Performance has frequently been measured in terms of quality of solution, time required to reach a solution, and sheer number of problems solved.

Despite variations in their designs and samples, these studies overall have yielded quite similar results. By and large, research that has pitted individuals against groups has shown that groups will outperform individuals working in isolation. That is, the group's solutions to problems are typically of higher quality than the average of the individuals' solutions. One interesting additional finding is that the best solitary worker may often outperform the group. But in general, and for a variety of tasks, groups can be expected to outperform the vast majority of individuals who work alone.

Precisely why groups have an advantage over individuals has also been the subject of much research. One self-evident explanation is that groups can pool information and abilities. By pooling these resources, the group gains access to a collection of knowledge that is greater than any single individual's. This knowledge enables the group to reject obviously incorrect approaches and provides a check on the possibility of committing errors.

Being in a group also tends to motivate and inspire group members. The stimulation of being in a social setting can enhance an individual's level of contribution. In addition, there are social rewards for making a significant contribution to a group's efforts. For example, praise, admiration, and feeling valuable to the group can be strong incentives for an individual to exert greater effort.

Finally, depending on the situation, it may be possible to divide a group's general assignment into smaller, more manageable tasks that can then be delegated to individual group members. Thus, groups have the potential for employing division of labor.

Despite these advantages, potential problems may arise. As we noted earlier, highly cohesive groups sometimes encourage a restricted view of alternatives (groupthink). Groups may also polarize toward extreme points of view if an appreciable element of risk is involved (risky and cautious shifts). Although it has not been formally studied yet, it is possible that groups may be successful in exerting social pressure on a manager to escalate commitment to a losing course of action because of the manager's desire to appear consistent in the eyes of the group's members.

In addition to these potential disadvantages, group decision making has other likely drawbacks. For example, group decision making tends to be much more costly than individual decision making. Given the time and energy that meetings can consume, it is usually best to reserve group decision making for

OB Focus

Letting Workers Decide Their Fate

For Jack Stack, the chief executive officer of Springfield Remanufacturing Corporation, hiring someone carries a responsibility for that person. In his words, "We took great pride in the fact that when we brought someone in here, we were putting food on somebody's table." Therefore, job security is for Stack a major goal and one with ethical implications.

In 1987 Springfield's major customer, General Motors, cut back its orders by 5,000 engines, representing 20 percent of Springfield's business of remanufacturing automotive diesel engines. Financial projections showed Stack that this cutback was equivalent to 100 workers' jobs. The decision facing Stack was an agonizing one: Could the company avoid layoffs and still survive?

Management spent many hours looking for ways to cut nonpersonnel costs. But the numbers kept showing 100 too many people to cover overhead. As Stack began to doubt whether he could make a decision he could live with, it occurred to him that people should be able to make the decisions affecting their lives. He decided to try group decision making.

At each company site, Stack called a meeting of the employees and asked them what they wanted to do. He provided them with the best information he could, painting a bleak picture of the company's prospects. To keep everyone, he explained, the company would have to generate approximately 50,000 worker-hours of new business. And if that didn't work, the company might have to lay off 200 people instead of 100.

The response from the workers was nearly unanimous. They wanted to try to keep all the employees and build the business.

The decision was difficult to implement, but the workers' commitment made it achievable. The company took any job it could get and sold in any market that would buy its products. To produce the new products well, employees had to put in many extra hours of planning and testing.

Stack was amazed by the results of all that effort. Despite the loss of $8 million in business from GM, the company's overall sales actually increased $2 million over the year before. Instead of laying off workers, the company had to hire another 100 to meet the demand. Less tangible but also important, the workers and Stack feel proud of the decision they made and executed.

Source: Jack Stack, "Crisis Management by Committee," *Inc.*, May 1988, p. 26.

more important decisions that require high-quality solutions. Group discussions can also give rise to hostility and conflict. This is especially likely when group members have divergent and strongly held opinions on alternative courses of action. In addition, decision making in groups tends to be influenced by the relative status of group members. Thus, when a group member who possesses relatively little status offers an objectively good suggestion, it may be rejected. But if the same suggestion is offered by a group member with high status, the likelihood of its being adopted is greatly increased.[21]

As Table 11.1 illustrates, there are many advantages and disadvantages to entrusting decision making to groups rather than to individuals. Before choosing a format for decision making, a manager should examine the points outlined in the table to determine if any specific conditions strongly advise for or against the use of groups.

■ **Table 11.1**

Advantages and Disadvantages of Group Decision Making

Advantages	Disadvantages
Pooling of information and resources	Groupthink
Social arousal of participants	Endorsement of extreme positions
Social rewards for participation	Escalation of commitment
Division of labor	Greater cost in time and energy
Higher-quality solutions	Split positions can generate conflict
	Status biases in member involvement

The Nominal Group Technique

One approach that attempts to capitalize on the positive feature of group decision making, while avoiding many of the potential pitfalls, is the **nominal group technique (NGT)**. In this technique, seven to ten individuals are brought together to participate in a structured exercise that includes the following steps:

1. The members silently and independently record their ideas about how to tackle a problem.

2. In turn, each member presents one of his or her ideas to the group. As each idea is offered, it is summarized and recorded on a chalkboard or wall chart, without discussion of its merits.

3. A discussion is held in which all ideas are clarified and evaluated.

4. Individuals silently and independently vote on each idea. This voting may involve a rating of the proposals or a rank ordering. The group's decision is then derived by pooling the votes or rankings into a single preferred alternative.[22] Table 11.2 shows the results from a typical NGT session.

The nominal group technique is a quite popular means of reaching a group decision because it avoids many of the potential problems of group decision making outlined in Table 11.1. For example, a decision can be reached in a reasonable amount of time without being greatly influenced by the leader's preferred position. Also, the technique can be used effectively in a variety of organizations (for example, General Electric, ARA Services, government agencies, and universities have employed the technique). Perhaps the strongest drawback of NGT is its high degree of structure. As a result, the group may tend to limit its discussion to a single and often highly focused issue.

The Delphi Technique

Another technique for capitalizing on a group's resources while avoiding several possible disadvantages of relying on group decision-making processes was developed by the Rand Corporation.[23] This approach, called the **Delphi tech-**

■ **Table 11.2**

Results of an NGT Session

Nominal Grouping Technique Form

Group Name: *Industrial Engineering Department*
Date: *January 27, 19—*   Facilitator: *D. Scott Sink*
Number of Group Members: *14*   Number of Objectives to be Ranked: *8*

Problem: Identify specific objectives the Industrial Engineering Department should strive to accomplish during the next year.

Objectives (Ranked in Preference)	Votes Received (Most Important = 8)	Total (Number of Votes/ Total Vote Score)
1. Faculty development	8-8-8-8-8-8-8-7-6-5-4-4-1	13/83
2. Graduate student recruitment	8-7-7-7-5-5-5-4-3	9/51
3. Industry relations	8-8-7-6-6-4-4-3-2-2	10/50
4. Faculty support	7-7-7-6-6-3-3	7/39
5. Intradepartment communication	7-6-5-2-2-2-1	7/25
6. Working paper series	8-6-4-3-1	5/22
7. Ph.D. program development	6-4-4-2-1-1	6/18
8. Course content coordination	4-3-3-3-2-1	6/16
9. National conference attendance	5-5-5-1	4/16
10. Co-op program	8-3-2-2	4/15
11. Interdisciplinary research	7-6-1	3/14
12. Graduate student support	7-4-3	3/14
13. Timely information on funding opportunities	6-5-3	3/14
14. Beginning and ending course evaluations	6-5-3	3/14
15. Manufacturing institute	5-4-2	3/11
16. Faculty performance indices	7-3	2/10
17. Material handling/plant layout course	6-4	2/10

Note: Forty-one objectives were identified; 33 received votes; the top 17 are listed above.

Source: Adapted from D. Scott Sink, "Using the Nominal Group Technique Effectively," *National Productivity Review* 2 (Spring 1983): 181.

nique, is similar to NGT in several respects, but also differs significantly in that the decision makers never actually meet. The steps in the Delphi technique are:

1.   Select a group of individuals who possess expertise in a given problem area, for example, forecasting social trends or technical breakthroughs.

2.   Survey the experts for their opinions via a mailed questionnaire.

3.   Analyze and distill the experts' responses.

4.   Mail the summarized results of the survey to the experts and request that they respond once again to a questionnaire. If one expert's opinion differs sharply from the rest, he or she may be asked to provide a rationale. This rationale could then be forwarded to the other participants.

5.   After this process is repeated several times, the experts usually achieve

a consensus. If not, the responses can be pooled to determine a most preferred view.

The Delphi technique has a number of advantages and disadvantages. Its greatest advantage is that it avoids many of the biases and obstacles associated with interacting groups (that is, groups where the members meet face-to-face). It has also been shown to generate fairly useful information and high-quality solutions.[24] A strong disadvantage stems from the amount of time it takes to complete the entire Delphi process — rarely less than several weeks, and often as long as five months. Clearly, urgent problems cannot be solved in this manner. Finally, like NGT, the Delphi technique follows a highly structured format. As a result, it does not offer much flexibility if conditions change. And, obviously, since respondents never meet face-to-face, social interaction and free dialogue are lost.

In an interesting comparison of three approaches to group decision making — interacting groups, NGT, and Delphi technique — Van de Ven and Delbecq gave an identical problem to 60 different seven-person groups.[25] Twenty of the groups tackled the problem in an interacting format, while the remaining groups were assigned to either NGT or Delphi approaches. In terms of effectiveness, the NGT groups were somewhat more productive, followed in turn by the Delphi and interacting groups. Members of NGT groups also reported higher satisfaction than did members of the other groups. These results suggest that the presence and increased involvement of others can sometimes diminish the quality of decision making.

Bootstrapping

Bootstrapping (sometimes called expert systems) is a device for improving both individual and group decision making. It is derived from the efforts of decision scientists to understand how managers and other decision makers actually formulate alternatives and make choices. To an observer, it often seems that decision makers do not follow a clear or consistent set of decision rules when making judgments. However, by recording the actual decision-making process in a group or having a solitary manager "think out loud" as he or she makes a decision, it is possible to uncover the information that was used, the relative weight that was assigned to each piece of information, and the decision rule that was employed. By examining enough decision-making episodes, it is possible to capture the process that is actually being used. Under scrutiny, an apparently haphazard and unpredictable decision-making process often turns out to be quite reasonable and understandable. A flowchart based on the results constitutes a model of the decision-making process that can be employed as an aid in making subsequent decisions. Research suggests that such a flowchart can be used to make consistently high-quality decisions.

Thus, by explicitly stating a poorly understood set of rules, a decision maker can improve the effectiveness of later decisions. He or she can then consistently follow an established set of principles, whereas previously the decision-making process followed the implicit logic in an inconsistent fashion. The procedure of analyzing an individual's or group's decision-making process and employing the resultant model is termed *bootstrapping*. The term *bootstrapping* is based on the notion that a decision maker starts with nothing more than apparent intuition and "lifts himself by his own bootstraps" to arrive at a formal decision model.[26]§§

Creativity and Decision Making

Many problems, especially nonprogrammed decisions that are broad in scope and consequences, require creative solutions. Given the competitive nature of business, it can be argued that those firms that can generate creative strategies for coping with decisions may enjoy an important competitive edge.

Creativity can enter the decision-making process at any step. The way in which a problem situation is defined, the generation of alternatives, the perception of opportunities, and the actual implementation of a solution can all be enhanced by creative perspectives.

In this section, we will discuss several aspects of creativity. Initially, we will consider the characteristics of creative individuals and how individual creativity can be measured. Then we will examine the steps in the creative process and some methods for enhancing creativity.

Characteristics of Creative Individuals

People vary in the extent to which they are creative. Although one widely held belief is that highly creative individuals are the products of peculiar childhoods, the available evidence does not support such a view.

Although the results are not highly consistent, some studies have found that in the United States, creativity is greater in females than males after about age 10.[27] In India, however, boys have been found to be more consistently creative than girls.[28] These results suggest that cultural differences in emphasizing the appropriateness of being creative can be important.

The impact of age on creativity has also been heavily researched, with more conclusive results. A study of professionals in a variety of fields, including both the arts and the sciences, found that most individuals tended to be most creative between the ages of 30 and 40.[29] The peak period of creative productivity, however, seems to vary somewhat by discipline. In the field of music and other arts, creative accomplishment peaks during the period from age 35 to 39, while in the sciences the peak creativity period appears to be from age 30 to 34. It should be pointed out, of course, that people can still make creative contributions later in life (that is, they may continue to take out patents or compose symphonies). However, the frequency of creative productivity tends to decrease for most people as they age.

---

§§ Following a discussion of decision-making techniques, it must be noted that effective decision making is not equivalent to effective decision implementation. Simply being able to decide on the best course of action does not ensure a particular outcome. Decision implementation is actually the concern of much of the field of OB in that effective implementation involves influencing others, managing group meetings, and building consensus.

In terms of personality, creative individuals typically have a wide range of interests, value independence, and enjoy aesthetic impressions.[30] In analyzing creative executives, Raudsepp concluded that some of their more salient characteristics include:

- A willingness to give up immediate gain to reach long-range goals
- A great amount of energy
- An irritation with the status quo
- Perseverance
- A pursuit of hobbies and specialized interests
- A belief that fantasy and daydreaming are not a waste of time[31]

Other studies of creative individuals have offered further insights. One study found that highly creative engineers did not identify as strongly with their employing organization as did their less creative coworkers.[32] In addition, highly creative people are more likely to change jobs frequently, although the precise reasons for this higher turnover are not yet understood.[33]

Measuring Individual Creativity

Especially in occupations related to research and development, advertising, and mass media, individual creativity is an important resource. To optimize the creative resources of their employees, managers must understand how to measure individual creativity.

One simple device for assessing the creative potential of employees is to observe their actions in situations that call for creative responses. For example, a manager may give an employee a challenging assignment, such as designing the cover of a newsletter, and then carefully monitor both the employee's problem-solving process and the final product. A more direct approach is to administer a paper-and-pencil test of creativity. Organizations that are strongly interested in creativity are more likely to use standardized creativity tests or devise their own. For example, the AC Spark Plug Division of General Motors has developed its own test of creativity for engineers and supervisors.[34]

Numerous tests of creativity are available. Although they appear to identify the general ability to be creative, they may not be particularly relevant to a given occupation. To illustrate this point, consider these sample items from some typical tests of creativity:

- Write a four-word sentence in which each word starts with the following letters: K. . . U. . . Y. . . I. . .
- In the next 30 seconds, name fluids that will burn.
- During the next 60 seconds, write words beginning with the letter J.

Another test asks a person to envision the consequences of various situations. For example:

- In a two-minute period, write down as many answers as you can to the question "What would happen if people no longer needed or wanted to sleep?"

Steps in the Creative Process

Most students of the creative process divide it into five stages:[35]

1. *Opportunity or problem recognition.* In this phase, an individual becomes aware of the existence of a problem or opportunity that needs attention. For example, an employee may remark, "There must be a better way of doing this."

2. *Immersion.* At this stage, the individual collects and recalls information that is relevant to the situation. He or she also generates hypotheses without appraising their value, for example, "I think I recall reading somewhere that some firms use a different set of procedures."

3. *Incubation.* At this point, the information simmers in the person's subconscious. The individual does not appear to be actively focusing on the problem, yet is subconsciously rearranging the available information into new patterns.

4. *Insight.* While a person is engaged in an unrelated activity, an integrative idea will come to mind — for example, "A new reporting system that keeps both departments simultaneously apprised of our needs should do the trick!" Many people report that at this stage it is usually a good idea to jot down the creative insight, as it may quickly be forgotten.

5. *Verification.* Finally, the individual tests out the solution by logic or actual experimentation. At this point, tenacity may be critical, because other people often resist innovative ideas or quickly reject them as impractical.

Although this list of steps suggests that the creative process follows a certain order, creative insight does not happen in such an orderly or neat fashion. For example, incubation may occur during verification. Furthermore, the process is often repetitive because initial ideas may be unsatisfactory and require further revision.

Methods of Enhancing Creativity

Several methods are suggested for enhancing or "freeing up" individual creativity. Studies show that attempts to improve creative ability through training techniques are frequently successful. In fact, one review of 40 studies in the area of increasing creativity found that 90 percent of such efforts succeeded.[36]

We have already considered two of the more popular ways of maximizing group output: the nominal group technique and the Delphi technique. In the area of creativity enhancement, both of these techniques have applicability.

Brainstorming may also be used to train individuals to be more creative and to tackle complex problems. In a brainstorming session, a group of people are encouraged to exchange ideas freely in an atmosphere that is nonjudgmental and noncritical. When presented with a problem, group members try to generate as many ideas or solutions as they can. At this point, the quality of the ideas is not important. Instead, sheer quantity is emphasized. Outlandish ideas are especially encouraged because they may serve as springboards to useful solutions. Later, the recorded proposals are refined and evaluated.

A study of the effectiveness of having individuals brainstorm in isolation versus in groups found that individuals in isolation produce more and better ideas than do an equivalent number of people in groups.[37] These results suggest that the presence of others, despite any possible instructions of group leaders to the contrary, inhibits personal creativity and reduces the range of ideas that are generated.

Another technique in the creativity arsenal is called **grid analysis.** In this technique, ideas or materials of possible relevance to a problem are listed on the sides of a two-dimensional grid. Then each possible combination of ideas is created and examined for its usefulness as a solution. For example, a marketing firm may be interested in promoting alternative uses for its current products. To uncover such novel uses, they may list their products on a horizontal dimension and target audiences or other products that they do not manufacture on the vertical axis. The resulting combinations may suggest new markets for their products, or the possible conversion of their equipment or goods to the manufacture of other products.

Andrew DuBrin has suggested a number of techniques that individuals can use to increase their creativity.[38] Although these techniques do not offer formal guidance for solving specific problems, they can be valuable aids to personal development.

Don't Be Afraid to Try and Fail   Many people find it intimidating that a large proportion of their attempts at creativity are likely to fail. In fact, it is the *absolute number* of successful new ideas that counts and not the *percentage*. Roger Von Oech summarizes this point by saying, "We learn by trial and error, not by trial and rightness."[39]

Let Your Playful Side Come Out   One way to get into a creative state of mind is to think humorously. Approaching a problem with humor can generate novel perspectives and insights.

Identify Your Creative Time Period   Some people have a specific time of day when they are most likely to be creative. By recognizing this and scheduling work sessions accordingly, they can capitalize on peak periods. Some people find they are most creative while exercising or traveling. Others feel most creative shortly after a rest. Most people, however, report that one of their most creative periods occurs just before falling asleep.

Borrow Ideas   Studying ideas already in use in related fields can suggest new approaches to one's work problems. Reading books, magazines, and newspapers and contacting people who have related interests may give rise to ideas that, if appropriately modified, can be converted into workable solutions.

Maintain an Idea Notebook   Because many novel ideas are generated and lost in the course of daily activities, a notebook can be a practical means of recording flashes of insight for future reference. Some executives keep a separate "idea file" for storing bits of information that are useful in themselves or that may serve as the basis for other useful ideas.

Establishing a Climate for Creativity

As the previous discussion suggests, creativity must be encouraged if it is to flourish. The proper environment is crucial to fostering creative thought. For example, an organization that shows intolerance of change and a lack of trust in its employees can greatly inhibit creativity. On the other hand, the following factors encourage creativity within an organization:

1. Tolerance of risk taking and failure

2. Open channels of communication within the organization and with the outside environment

3. Tolerance for a variety of personality types

4. Freedom for employees to interact and set goals (that is, individual autonomy)

5. Rewards for being creative

6. Use of creativity-enhancing techniques, such as suggestion boxes and brainstorming

Managers can play a crucial role in the establishment of a climate for creativity by expressing an openness to ideas, encouraging different approaches to problem solving, and allocating rewards for creative efforts.

Summary

1. Describe the types of decisions managers make.
Personal programmed decisions involve simple, repetitive personal matters. Personal nonprogrammed decisions arise during rare but significant events in an individual's personal life. Organizational programmed decisions pertain to relatively simple problem situations in an organization and are handled according to established guidelines or procedures. Organizational nonprogrammed decisions pertain to rare and unique situations that have a potentially significant impact on the organization.

2. List the steps of a highly rational decision-making process.
The steps are as follows: When an existing situation triggers the decision-making process, recognize the existence of a problem or opportunity that demands action. Define the nature of the situation. Generate alternative ways to cope with the situation. Gather information about each alternative and evaluate its desirability. From this evaluation, arrive at a single best course of action. Implement this alternative. Evaluate the decision's effectiveness.

3. Describe some constraints on the decision-making process.
Constraints on the decision-making process include inability to generate all possible alternatives and their associated consequences, unavailability of accurate information, ethical restrictions on otherwise optimal solutions, and managers' tendency to use heuristics and to satisfice (consider alternative actions only until a reasonably acceptable one is found).

4. Identify obstacles to effective decision making.
Obstacles to effective decision making include escalation of commitment,

groupthink, and the tendency of groups to endorse extreme positions when confronted with decisions involving an element of risk.

5. Define groupthink and list its symptoms.
Groupthink is the tendency of highly cohesive groups to take a distorted view of situations. Symptoms of groupthink include an illusion of invulnerability, rationalization, an assumption of morality, negative stereotyping of outsiders, pressure to conform, self-censorship, an illusion of unanimity, and the presence of mindguards (who deflect critics and criticisms).

6. Describe techniques to improve decision making.
Weigh the advantages and disadvantages of group versus individual decision making when choosing a format for making a decision. To take advantage of the positive features of group decision making, use the nominal group technique or the Delphi technique. Bootstrapping — the procedure of analyzing an individual's decision-making process and using the resulting model — is a technique for improving both individual and group decision making.

7. Identify characteristics of creative organization members.
Characteristics of creative people include willingness to forgo immediate gain in favor of long-term goals, high energy, irritation with the status quo, perseverance, pursuit of hobbies and specialized interests, belief that fantasy and daydreaming are not a waste of time, relatively weak identification with their employing organization, and greater likelihood of changing jobs.

8. Describe the steps in the creative process.
The first step is opportunity or problem recognition, during which an individual becomes aware that a problem or opportunity needs attention. Next comes immersion, during which the individual collects and recalls relevant information and generates hypotheses. Next is the incubation stage, when the individual subconsciously rearranges the available information. In the insight stage, while a person is engaged in an unrelated activity, an integrative idea will come into his or her consciousness. Finally, in the verification stage, the individual tests the solution with logic or experimentation.

9. Identify ways that groups and individuals can enhance creativity.
Groups can improve creativity with brainstorming and grid analysis. People can enhance their own creativity by being unafraid of failure, permitting playfulness, identifying creative time periods in each day, borrowing ideas, and maintaining an idea notebook.

10. List ways organizations can establish a climate that encourages creativity.
Organizations can encourage creativity by tolerating risk taking and failure, opening communication channels, tolerating various personality types, giving employees autonomy, rewarding creativity, and using techniques such as brainstorming that enhance creativity.

Key Terms

Personal decision making
Organizational decision making
Programmed decision
Nonprogrammed decision
Classical decision theory
Rational-economic model
Behavioral theory of decision
  making
Administrative model
Bounded rationality
Satisfice
Maximize
Bounded discretion
Heuristics

Availability heuristic
Representativeness heuristic
Groupthink
Last-chance meeting
Risky shift
Diffusion of responsibility
Cautious shift
Group polarization
Nominal group technique (NGT)
Delphi technique
Bootstrapping
Brainstorming
Grid analysis

Review and Discussion Questions

1. Give an example of each of the following kinds of decisions:
   a. Personal programmed decision
   b. Personal nonprogrammed decision
   c. Organizational programmed decision
   d. Organizational nonprogrammed decision

2. The classical view of decision making describes how a decision *should* be made. In what ways does it fall short in describing how managers actually make decisions? List the steps a typical manager takes in making a decision.

3. In what type of situation is a manager's commitment to a policy likely to intensify, even if the policy is leading to failure? How can an organization counter this tendency?

4. At its staff meeting, the accounting department is discussing the likelihood that the company's recent performance will look bad in a soon-to-be-published financial report. Several members of the department are advocating that numbers in the company's books be changed to look more favorable. These employees argue that they can make the changes in a way that no one will be able to detect and that changing a few numbers is a small matter next to the important goal of keeping the company alive so that hundreds of workers can keep their jobs. It appears that other employees are afraid to argue against this view. Lynette Hayes, manager of the accounting department, is concerned that the department may succumb to groupthink. What are some ways she can prevent this?

5. What causes some groups to adopt a riskier position than individuals would? Why do groups tend to make decisions at the extremes?

6. What are the advantages of making decisions in a group? What are the disadvantages?

7. Daniel Beach is executive vice-president of marketing for Trustworthy Savings and Loan Association. He is concerned that consumer interest in individual retirement accounts has been lagging and wants to develop other ways to build interest in saving at Trustworthy. Daniel's plan is to meet with key managers next Thursday to explore possibilities and to begin implementing an idea within the following month. Because he wants to avoid some of the pitfalls of group decision making, Daniel wants to use either the nominal group technique or the Delphi technique. What is involved in each of these approaches to decision making? Which approach do you recommend? Why?

8. Amanda Crisp wants to hire creative people to work in her advertising agency. How can she identify such people?

9. Amanda has hired a staff of people she thinks are creative. How can she help them to work creatively as a group? What advice can she give them as individuals?

10. How does creativity improve the quality of decision making? What would an organization be like if all its employees were highly creative? In some situations, might creativity be seen as an undesirable trait?

Critical Incident
The Root of All Evil

The Ajax Toy Corporation is a medium-sized firm located in southern Michigan. The firm designs and manufactures toys and games. The wage and salary program of the company operates on a low profile basis; that is, no information on salary ranges in regard to grade classification is given to employees and they are not given minimum, medium, or maximum pay ranges attainable in their present job levels. When employees are formally evaluated each year, a merit increase, when given, is usually a small percentage increase, with management retaining any information as to how much money is available for merit increases. When management was asked by employees why merit increases and salaries were handled in this manner, the standard answer was, "It is company policy that this information cannot be given to employees. Only staff personnel have knowledge of this information."

The employees of the Research and Development Department for new products are due for a performance appraisal. Their current minimum and maximum level of wages is from $25,000 to $44,000 per year. These salaries are average for the industry. Last year, the company's conservative wage and salary policies resulted in two of the best people in the department being pirated by Ajax's largest competitor . . . hurting the performance of the Research and Development Department this year. Pirating of employees in other departments has also been a problem for the past two years.

A new director of Research and Development has recently been hired and management has charged her with proposing recommendations to reduce the pirating of people from her department, while also conducting the department's individual performance appraisals and merit distribution. The manager of Human Resources will later review her ideas against the present system to determine what changes, if any, they may wish to make.

Additional information about the Research and Development Department and its employees is as follows:

Roger Ballard: 60 years of age; 20 years experience with Ajax; has not designed any new products during the past year, but works well with others to develop their ideas. Current salary: $44,000 (top of his salary range).

John Connelly: 45 years of age; 10 years with Ajax; is seldom late for work, but doesn't work well with others in the department; was a very good friend of the previous manager; has designed only one new product this year. Current salary: $39,000.

David Browing: 32 years of age; 4 years with Ajax; has designed two new products this year, one of which has been completed; past evaluations have shown him as an average performer, but this year his work has been very good. Current salary: $31,000.

Karen Harding: 24 years of age; was hired 10 months ago to replace one of the pirated employees; has designed two new products which have been completed and are doing very well; has ideas for three more new products; is currently working on these three new ideas with help from Roger; has not received a raise since joining Ajax. Current salary: $25,000.

The director of Research and Development was confidentially informed by the company that she has $12,000 to distribute for use as merit increases. Her recommendation of distribution of the merit dollars requires your approval. As Human Resources manager, you have just received the following merit increase recommendations from the director of Research and Development:

1. Roger Ballard . . . $2,000
2. John Connelly . . . $1,000
3. David Browing . . . $4,750
4. Karen Harding . . . $4,250

Questions

1. As Human Resources manager would you agree with the distribution of the merit money among the four employees?

2. Defend and explain your decision.

From Jack L. Simonetti, *Experiential Exercises and Cases for Human Resource Management* (New York: Allyn & Bacon, 1987).

Experiential Exercise
How Creative Are You?

In recent years, several tests have been developed to measure creative abilities and behavior. While certainly useful, they do not adequately tap the complex network of behaviors — the particular personality traits, attitudes, motivations, values, interests, and other variables — that predispose a person to think creatively.

To arrive at assessment measures that would cover a broader range of creative attributes, one organization developed an inventory type of test. A partial version of this instrument is featured below.

After each statement, indicate with a letter the degree or extent with which you agree or disagree:

A = Strongly agree
B = Agree
C = In between or don't know
D = Disagree
E = Strongly disagree

Mark your answers as accurately and frankly as possible. Try not to "second guess" how a creative person might respond to each statement.

1. I always work with a great deal of certainty that I'm following the correct procedures for solving a particular problem.   _____

2. It would be a waste of time for me to ask questions if I had no hope of obtaining answers.   _____

3. I feel that a logical step-by-step method is best for solving problems.   _____

4. I occasionally voice opinions in groups that seem to turn some people off.   _____

5. I spend a great deal of time thinking about what others think of me.   _____

6. I feel that I may have a special contribution to give to the world.   _____

7. It is more important for me to do what I believe to be right than to try to win the approval of others.   _____

8. People who seem unsure and uncertain about things lose my respect.   _____

9. I am able to stick with difficult problems over extended periods of time.   _____

10. On occasion I get overly enthusiastic about things.   _____

11. I often get my best ideas when doing nothing in particular.   _____

12. I rely on intuitive hunches and the feeling of "rightness" or "wrongness" when moving toward the solution of a problem.   _____

13. When problem solving, I work faster when analyzing the problem and slower when synthesizing the information I've gathered. _____

14. I like hobbies which involve collecting things. _____

15. Daydreaming has provided the impetus for many of my more important projects. _____

16. If I had to choose from two occupations other than the one I now have, I would rather be a physician than an explorer. _____

17. I can get along more easily with people if they belong to about the same social and business class as myself. _____

18. I have a high degree of aesthetic sensitivity. _____

19. Intuitive hunches are unreliable guides in problem solving. _____

20. I am much more interested in coming up with new ideas than I am in trying to sell them to others. _____

21. I tend to avoid situations in which I might feel inferior. _____

22. In evaluating information, the source of it is more important to me than the content. _____

23. I like people who follow the rule "business before pleasure." _____

24. One's own self-respect is much more important than the respect of others. _____

25. I feel that people who strive for perfection are unwise. _____

26. I like work in which I must influence others. _____

27. It is important for me to have a place for everything and everything in its place. _____

28. People who are willing to entertain "crackpot" ideas are impractical. _____

29. I rather enjoy fooling around with new ideas, even if there is no practical payoff. _____

30. When a certain approach to a problem doesn't work, I can quickly reorient my thinking. _____

31. I don't like to ask questions that show ignorance. _____

32. I am able to more easily change my interests to pursue a job or career than I can change a job to pursue my interests. _____

33. Inability to solve a problem is frequently due to asking the wrong questions. _____

34. I can frequently anticipate the solution to my problems. _____

35. It is a waste of time to analyze one's failures. _____

36. Only fuzzy thinkers resort to metaphors and analogies. _____

37. At times I have so enjoyed the ingenuity of a crook that I hoped he or she would go scot-free. _____

38. I frequently begin work on a problem which I can only dimly sense and not yet express. _____

39. I frequently tend to forget things, such as names of people, streets, highways, small towns, etc. _____

40. I feel that hard work is the basic factor in success. _____

41. To be regarded as a good team member is important to me. _____

42. I know how to keep my inner impulses in check. _____

43. I am a thoroughly dependable and responsible person. _____

44. I resent things being uncertain and unpredictable. _____

45. I prefer to work with others in a team effort rather than solo. _____

46. The trouble with many people is that they take things too seriously. _____

47. I am frequently haunted by my problems and cannot let go of them. _____

48. I can easily give up immediate gain or comfort to reach the goals I have set. _____

49. If I were a college professor, I would rather teach factual courses than those involving theory. _____

50. I'm attracted to the mystery of life. _____

Scoring Instructions. To compute your percentage score, circle the value assigned to your answer for each question, as indicated below, and then add up all the values.

	Strongly Agree A	Agree B	In-between or Don't Know C	Disagree D	Strongly Disagree E
1.	−2	−1	0	+1	+2
2.	−2	−1	0	+1	+2
3.	−2	−1	0	+1	+2
4.	+2	+1	0	−1	−2
5.	−2	−1	0	+1	+2
6.	+2	+1	0	−1	−2
7.	+2	+1	0	−1	−2
8.	−2	−1	0	+1	+2
9.	+2	+1	0	−1	−2
10.	+2	+1	0	−1	−2
11.	+2	+1	0	−1	−2
12.	+2	+1	0	−1	−2
13.	−2	−1	0	+1	+2
14.	−2	−1	0	+1	+2
15.	+2	+1	0	−1	−2
16.	−2	−1	0	+1	+2
17.	−2	−1	0	+1	+2
18.	+2	+1	0	−1	−2
19.	−2	−1	0	+1	+2
20.	+2	+1	0	−1	−2

	Strongly Agree A	Agree B	In-between or Don't Know C	Disagree D	Strongly Disagree E
21.	−2	−1	0	+1	+2
22.	−2	−1	0	+1	+2
23.	−2	−1	0	+1	+2
24.	+2	+1	0	−1	−2
25.	−2	−1	0	+1	+2
26.	−2	−1	0	+1	+2
27.	−2	−1	0	+1	+2
28.	−2	−1	0	+1	+2
29.	+2	+1	0	−1	−2
30.	+2	+1	0	−1	−2
31.	−2	−1	0	+1	+2
32.	−2	−1	0	+1	+2
33.	+2	+1	0	−1	−2
34.	+2	+1	0	−1	−2
35.	−2	−1	0	+1	+2
36.	−2	−1	0	+1	+2
37.	+2	+1	0	−1	−2
38.	+2	+1	0	−1	−2
39.	+2	+1	0	−1	−2
40.	+2	+1	0	−1	−2
41.	−2	−1	0	+1	+2
42.	−2	−1	0	+1	+2
43.	−2	−1	0	+1	+2
44.	−2	−1	0	+1	+2
45.	−2	−1	0	+1	+2
46.	+2	+1	0	−1	−2
47.	+2	+1	0	−1	−2
48.	+2	+1	0	−1	−2
49.	−2	−1	0	+1	+2
50.	+2	+1	0	−1	−2

Very creative	80 to 100
Above average	60 to 79
Average	40 to 59
Below average	20 to 39
Noncreative	−100 to 19

Source: E. Raudsepp, *Personnel Journal,* April 1979. Further information about this text is available from Princeton Creative Research, Inc., P.O. Box 122, Princeton, NJ 08542.

Notes

1. H.A. Simon, *The New Science of Managerial Decision Making,* 2d ed. (Englewood Cliffs, N.J.: Prentice-Hall, 1977).

2. A. Elbing, *Behavioral Decisions in Organizations,* 2d ed. (Glenview, Ill.: Scott, Foresman, 1978).

3. H.A. Simon, *Administrative Behavior,* 3d ed. (New York: Free Press, 1976); K.R. MacCrimmon and R.N. Taylor, "Decision Making and Problem Solving," in *Handbook of Industrial and Organizational Psychology,* ed. M.D. Dunnette (Chicago: Rand-McNally, 1976).

4. H.A. Simon, *Models of Man* (New York: Wiley, 1957).

5. J.G. March and H.A. Simon, *Organizations* (New York: Wiley, 1958).

6. Simon, *Models of Man*.

7. D. Kahneman and A. Tversky, "Subjective Probability: A Judgment of Representativeness," *Cognitive Psychology* 3 (1972): 430–454; D. Kahneman and A. Tversky, "On the Psychology of Prediction," *Psychological Review* 80 (1973): 237–251; A. Tversky and D. Kahneman, "Judgment Under Uncertainty: Heuristics and Biases," *Science* 185 (1974): 1124–1131; A. Tversky, "Features of Similarity," *Psychological Review* 84 (1977): 327–352; D. Kahneman and A. Tversky, "Intuitive Prediction: Biases and Corrective Procedures," *Management Science* 62 (1980): 250–257.

8. B.M. Staw, "The Escalation of Commitment to a Course of Action," *Academy of Management Review* 6 (1981): 577–587.

9. Ibid., 577.

10. B.M. Staw and J. Ross, "Commitment in an Experimenting Society: An Experiment on the Attribution of Leadership from Administrative Scenarios," *Journal of Applied Psychology* 65 (1980): 249–260.

11. C.F. Northcraft and G. Wolf, "Dollars, Sense, and Sunk Costs: A Life Cycle Model of Resource Allocation Decisions," *Academy of Management Review* 9 (1984): 225–234.

12. M.G. Bowen, "The Escalation Phenomenon Reconsidered: Decision Dilemmas or Decision Errors?" *Academy of Management Review* 12 (1987): 52–66; S. Goltz, "A Reinforcement Theory View of the Escalation Phenomenon" (paper presented at the University of Notre Dame, 1987); M. Bowen, S. Goltz, and R. Vecchio, "Learning and Contextual Influences on Escalation in Decision Making" (paper presented at Midwest Academy of Management Meeting, 1989); E. Conlon and J. Parks, "Information Requests in the Context of Escalation," *Journal of Applied Psychology* 72 (1989): 344–350.

13. Staw, "The Escalation of Commitment."

14. I.L. Janis, *Victims of Groupthink* (Boston: Houghton-Mifflin, 1972); G. Whyte, "Groupthink Reconsidered," *Academy of Management Review* 14 (1989): 45–56.

15. J.A.F. Stoner, "A Comparison of Individual and Group Decisions Involving Risk" (master's thesis, Sloan School of Management, MIT, 1961).

16. A.F. Teger and D.G. Pruitt, "Components of Group Risk Taking," *Journal of Experimental Social Psychology* 3 (1967): 189–205.

17. N. Kogan and M.A. Wallach, "Group Risk Taking as a Function of Members' Anxiety and Defensiveness," *Journal of Personality* 35 (1967): 50–63.

18. J.A.F. Stoner, "Risky and Cautious Shifts in Group Decisions: The Influence of Widely Held Values," *Journal of Experimental Social Psychology* 4 (1968): 442–459.

19. N. Kogan and M.A. Wallach, *Risk Taking: A Study of Cognition and Personality* (New York: Holt, Rinehart and Winston, 1964).

20. D.G. Myers and H. Lamm, "The Group Polarization Phenomenon," *Psychological Bulletin* 83 (1976): 602–627.

21. M.E. Shaw, *Group Dynamics,* 3d ed. (New York: McGraw-Hill, 1981).

22. A.H. Van de Ven and A.L. Delbecq, "The Effectiveness of Nominal, Delphi, and Interacting Group Decision-Making Processes," *Academy of Management Journal* 17 (1974): 605–621.

23. N. Dalkey, *The Delphi Method: An Experimental Study of Group Opinions* (Santa Monica, Calif.: The Rand Corporation, 1969).

24. A.L. Delbecq, A.H. Van de Ven, and D.H. Gustafson, *Group Techniques for Program Planning* (Glenview, Ill.: Scott, Foresman, 1975).

25. Van de Ven and Delbecq, "The Effectiveness of Nominal, Delphi, and Interacting Group Processes."

26. R.M. Dawes, "A Case Study of Graduate Admissions: Applications of Three Principles of Human Decision Making," *American Psychologist* 26 (1971): 180–188; J.S. Wiggins, *Personality and Prediction: Principles of Personality Assessment* (Reading, Mass.: Addison-Wesley, 1973).

27. E.P. Torrance and N.C. Aliotti, "Sex Differences in Levels of Performance and Test–Retest Reliability on the Torrance Tests of Creative Thinking Ability," *Journal of Creative Behavior* 3 (1969): 52–57.

28. Ibid.

29. H.C. Lehman, *Age and Achievement* (Princeton, N.J.: Princeton University Press, 1953).

30. D.W. MacKinnon, "Assessing Creative Persons," *Journal of Creative Behavior* 1 (1967): 303–304.

31. E. Raudsepp, "Are You a Creative Manager?" *Management Review* 58 (1978): 15–16.

32. T. Rotondi, "Organizational Identification: Issues and Implications," *Organizational Behavior and Human Performance* 13 (1975): 95–109.

33. E.P. Torrance, "Is Bias against Job

Changing Bias Against Giftedness?" *Gifted Child Quarterly* 15 (1971): 244–248.

34. R.M. Guion, *Personnel Testing* (New York: McGraw-Hill, 1965).

35. J.F. Mee, "The Creative Thinking Process," *Indiana Business Review* 3 (1956): 4–9; F.D. Randall, "Stimulate Your Executives to Think Creatively," *Harvard Business Review* (July–August 1955): 121–128.

36. S.J. Parnes and E.A. Brunelle, "The Literature of Creativity, Part I," *Journal of Creative Behavior* 1 (1967): 52–109; D.J. Treffinger and J.C. Gowan, "An Updated Representative List of Methods and Educational Programs for Stimulating Creativity," *Journal of Creative Behavior* 5 (1971): 127–139.

37. D.W. Taylor, R.C. Berry, and C.H. Black, "Does Group Participation When Using Brainstorming Techniques Facilitate or Inhibit Creative Thinking?" *Administrative Science Quarterly* 3 (1958): 23–47.

38. A.J. DuBrin, *Contemporary Applied Management* (Plano, Texas: Business Publications, Inc., 1985).

39. R. Von Oech, *A Whack on the Side of the Head: How to Unlock Your Mind for Innovation* (New York: Warner Books, 1984).

A committee is a
group that keeps
minutes but
squanders hours.

— *Anonymous*

To get along — go
along.

— *Sam Rayburn*

Learning Objectives

After studying this chapter, you should be able to:

1. *Contrast formal and informal groups and open and closed groups.*

2. *List some reasons people join groups.*

3. *Describe influences on the degree to which people are attracted to one another.*

4. *Describe stages of group formation and development.*

5. *List some important group properties that affect performance.*

6. *List factors that induce and sustain cohesiveness in a group.*

7. *Describe types of groups commonly used in modern organizations.*

8. *Discuss ways to improve the effectiveness of meetings.*

Group Dynamics

■ Family Ties

Psychologist Jacqueline Hornor Plumez says that, for many, the corporation has become like a family. In modern times, being part of a group at work fills a void. Today half of all Americans move every five years, and half of all marriages end in divorce. For many of those who are desperately looking for something or someone to belong to, the only alternative is the corporation. Their major source of emotional gratification comes from the workplace. Bosses become like parents, and coworkers like siblings.

Individuals can benefit from this kind of relationship with their employer. The employee gets an instant circle of friends and instant camaraderie. A channel for positive feedback and a support system are in place immediately. For people who find casual friendships easier than intimacy, the constructed relationships at work are easy to manage. The relationships are close, although less so than in a real family.

A good relationship with peers is one of the best benefits a job can offer. This is especially true in today's society, where job pressures, frequent relocations, and constant change make it difficult to maintain friendships. A person's corporate "siblings" share the same anxieties and pleasures. In the words of Plumez, "They know the politics behind that unfriendly memo; they instantly understand what the new assignment means."

Of course, problems can arise. People can replay with their bosses the unresolved problems they have with their parents. For example, a subordinate who as a child felt abandoned or afraid of abandonment by a parent might try overly hard to be very good and please the boss, no matter how belittling that boss might be. Or an employee with an unresolved need for a loving parent might idealize a boss, even a cruel one. Such an employee might stay in a frustrating situation, continually trying to please the boss,

even though the boss is eroding the employee's self-esteem.

What makes these problems particularly tricky is that it is much harder to be objective about negative feedback coming from a person who represents a parent. Thus, employees might tend to internalize criticism, whether or not it is justified. Seeing the company as the family also can make it harder to leave a bad situation. The sense of attachment is even stronger if the company is prestigious.

Just as workers replay parent–child relationships with their bosses, they also replay sibling relationships with their coworkers. Relations akin to sibling rivalries can develop. For example, a woman who has an unresolved rivalry with her brother might play it out by getting into a desperate fight with a man on the job. Even if she wins, she doesn't feel any better — she just finds another "brother" to struggle with.

Comparing the dynamics of

group relationships to those of families gives some indication of just how complicated groups can be. This chapter takes a look at the nature of groups. It discusses why people join groups and what they are attracted to in group members. The stages of group formation and development and the ways a group's characteristics can affect its performance are also covered. The chapter concludes with a discussion of specific kinds of groups that are commonly found in organizations.

Source: Rosemary L. Bray, "Heart at Work," *Savvy*, November 1985, pp. 60–62 +.

Managers spend a sizable proportion of their day working in groups and dealing with groups. As a member of a work group and as a representative of a firm who interacts with various groups both inside and outside the organization, a manager must understand the dynamics of groups.

Groups constitute an essential part of organizations that can strongly influence the total level of accomplishment. They can also satisfy the social needs of their members. Thus, it is fair to say that groups have the potential to satisfy the needs of both individuals and organizations. The extent to which these needs are met, and the processes by which they can be met, are the concerns of this chapter. We will examine the nature of groups, the reasons for joining groups, group formation and development, the major variables that affect group performance, and the various kinds of groups that are typically found in modern organizations. Managers who understand the basic principles of group dynamics often find it easier to direct the efforts of a group in a desired direction.

The Nature of Groups

People are social animals — they seek the company of others both to satisfy social needs and to pool resources for improved effectiveness. The presence of others can satisfy a great variety of needs. Hence, people participate in groups. For our purposes, we can define a **group** as two or more people who interact with each other, share certain common beliefs, and view themselves as being members of a group. At a minimum, to be considered a group, at least two people must deal with one another on a continuing basis. Before they interact with each other, they are likely to share common beliefs that impel them to band together. Over time, other shared values may emerge and be solidified. As a consequence of continuing interaction and awareness of shared beliefs, the individuals will come to see themselves as belonging to a distinct entity — the group.

Formal versus Informal Groups

In organizations, people are frequently assigned to work groups. These teams, which are essentially task oriented, are classified as **formal groups.** For example, employees are typically assigned to departments or work crews. A committee is another example of a formal group. It can be said that every organizational member must belong to at least one formal organizational group — that

■ **Figure 12.1**

A Linking Pin View of Group Membership

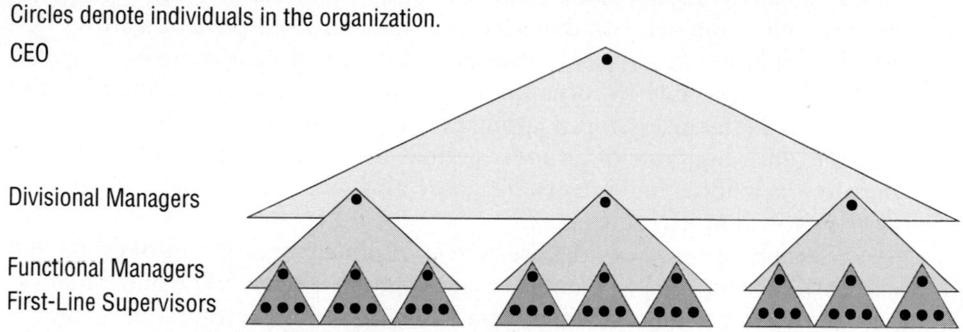

Circles denote individuals in the organization.

CEO

Divisional Managers

Functional Managers
First-Line Supervisors

is, every employee must have at least one formal role. Some organizational members may hold two or more formal group memberships (for example, by being on several different committees). Such multiple members can serve as "linking pins" within the organization who can enhance integration by sharing information across groups and passing on directives to lower levels.[1] Figure 12.1 shows how managers who belong to several groups may serve as linking pins.

Informal groups arise from social interaction among organizational members. Membership in such groups is voluntary and more heavily based on interpersonal attraction. Sometimes the activities or goals of an informal group are attractive to prospective members. For example, department softball and bowling teams are informal groups whose activities attract interested individuals. Not all informal groups, however, have a specific set of activities. Often, they are simply composed of coworkers who share common concerns. For example, a department head may informally meet with other managers to share information (or rumors) about an impending merger.

Informal groups are not inherently good or bad for an organization. When the informal group's goals are congruent with the organization's — such as when both seek to maximize customer satisfaction and produce a high-quality product — then all is well and good. In other instances, however, an informal group may oppose the organization's goals, as when employees decide to restrict daily output. In fact, informal groups are often sources of resistance to organizational change. They sometimes oppose approaches to job redesign and organizational restructuring. Because of the status and personal satisfaction they derive from their affiliation, members of informal groups can be counted on to resist attempts to disrupt or disband their social arrangement.

Open versus Closed Groups

Groups in organizational settings can also be classified in terms of whether they are open or closed.[2] An **open group** frequently changes its membership, with people constantly moving in and out of the group. In contrast, a **closed group** has a relatively stable membership. In addition, most closed groups have well-established status relationships among their members, whereas open groups tend to fluctuate on dimensions of individual power and status. Open groups are also more subject to disruption because of their changing membership and are less able to focus on long-term issues because of their relative instability. Nonetheless, open groups have certain relative advantages. For example, their high rate of turnover permits the infusion of "new blood," and therefore new ideas and talents. They are also more adaptable to changes in their surrounding circumstances.

Certain types of activities are better performed by each type of group. For example, for long-range planning, a closed group is likely to be more effective because it has a stronger commitment to dealing with the future. For developing new ideas or new products, an open group is likely to be more effective because of its more fluid and change-oriented atmosphere. Closed groups possess a stronger historical perspective, while open groups are more tolerant of developing and implementing new perspectives.

Reasons for Joining Groups

By and large, people join groups for two reasons: to accomplish a task or goal and to satisfy their social needs. These two reasons are not perfectly distinct, however, because many group activities satisfy both task and social needs. In fact, a review of the various needs that were considered in Chapter 6 — such as those in Maslow's hierarchy — would reveal that to some extent, nearly all needs can be satisfied by joining a group.

Security and Protection　Group membership can give an individual a sense of security and a real degree of protection. Being one member of a large organization can generate feelings of insecurity and anxiety, but belonging to a small group can reduce such fears by providing a sense of unity with others. During times of stress, such as when an organization is changing direction or leadership, belonging to a stable and supportive work unit can reduce individual anxieties.

By virtue of sheer numbers, groups afford a degree of protection that an individual might not otherwise enjoy. This principle is embodied in the union movement, which attempts to give members a sense of protection through highly organized collective strength.

Affiliation　An individual's need for affiliation and emotional support can be directly satisfied by membership in a group. Acceptance by others is an important social need. Feeling accepted by others at work can help to enhance one's feeling of self-worth.

Esteem and Identity　Groups also provide opportunities for an individual to feel important. They can give a person status and provide opportunities for praise and recognition. Many work-related achievements may not be appreciated or understood by people unfamiliar with the nature of the job. But in joining a group that does understand the job (either within organizations or through professional associations), people gain opportunities to receive recognition and esteem for their accomplishments.

Membership in a group also helps people to define who they are in the social scheme of things. Seeing oneself as a salesperson, an economist, or a teamster helps foster a feeling of identification with a larger purpose. Through membership in a work group, a person gains a formal title and a sense of purpose.

Task Accomplishment   A primary reason that groups are created is to facilitate task accomplishment. A group can often accomplish more through joint effort than can an equal number of individuals working separately. In fact, many goals are attainable only through cooperative group effort. By sharing ideas, pooling resources, and providing feedback to members, a group can be an effective mechanism for attaining otherwise difficult goals.*

Interpersonal Attraction

People sometimes join and remain in groups because of interpersonal attraction. Three key determinants of interpersonal attraction are physical distance, psychological distance, and similarity.

Physical and Psychological Distance

Having an opportunity to interact is an important determinant of attraction to others, especially for informal groups. Generally, people who are physically closer to one another develop closer relationships than those who are farther apart. This principle of proximity has been found to hold not only in work settings but also in relationships among neighbors.[3]

In addition to actual physical distance, psychological distance is also important. Figure 12.2 shows how two sets of offices can be arranged either to facilitate social interaction or to discourage it. The top office arrangement (A) encourages social interaction by providing common access to elevators and a shared secretarial-reception area. The lower office layout (B) discourages interaction by offering two avenues of entry and exit that discourage overlapping traffic patterns. People on each side of the layout would tend to use only the nearer elevator. In addition, the placement of the office doors does not encourage eye contact as people enter and leave their work spaces. Although the physical distance separating the office workers in both layouts is not great, the psychological distance is greatly augmented in layout B because of the impact that the physical arrangements will have on social relations. As a result, the office workers in layout B would *feel* farther apart than those in layout A.

* It has been suggested that early in the history of humankind, it was recognized that members benefited from cooperative effort. For example, members of a primitive tribe would work together in relays to wear out a game animal that the tribe would then share as a meal. No individual alone could defeat the animal, but together it was easy (and even something of a sport).

■ **Figure 12.2**

Two Office Layouts

A is designed to encourage social interaction, while B is arranged to discourage it.

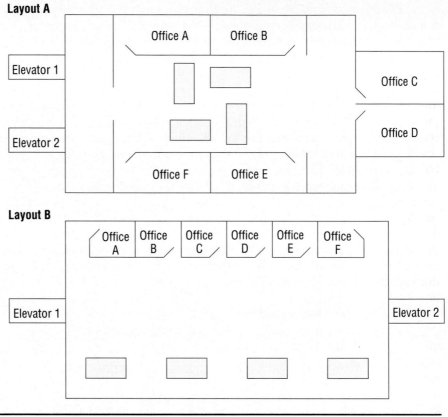

Source: H.J. Reitz, *Behavior in Organizations* (New York: Irwin, 1981).

Therefore, managers can consciously structure work settings, depending on whether the goal is to create camaraderie and group spirit or to reduce informal contacts.

Similarity

There has been a fair amount of debate on the issue of whether "opposites attract" or "birds of a feather flock together." That is, do people who are dissimilar in terms of sex, race, income, age, religion, and the like find each other's company more satisfying than people who are highly similar on these dimensions? Although much of the research on this topic points to the potential for both processes, attraction among similar people appears to be somewhat more common and more easily produced in formal studies.[4]

One particularly powerful and reliable finding in this area deals with similarity of attitudes. The proportion of similar attitudes that two people have in common (that is, whether they share a small, moderate, or high percentage of similar attitudes) appears to be a very strong determinant of interpersonal attraction. The greater the proportion, the greater the degree of attraction.[5] In fact, this finding has been found with such a high degree of reliability that it is sometimes termed the **law of attraction.**†

Although the notions of "opposites attract" and "birds of a feather flock together" may seem contradictory, one does not necessarily exclude the other. Most social scientists agree that individuals who possess similar *attitudes* and complementary *needs* and *abilities* will be highly attracted to one another. People often find each other's needs and abilities highly attractive because, by joining forces, they can achieve a form of need-completion or personal fulfillment. For example, in a successful business partnership, two partners may share common goals and values, yet one of them will be skilled at managing the financial aspects of their enterprise, while the other excels at marketing, public relations, and innovation.

In their **social exchange theory,** Thibaut and Kelley define *rewards* as any satisfaction that is derived from a relationship.[6] Financial investments (such as time and energy) as well as social problems (such as embarrassment and conflict) that are associated with a relationship are considered *costs*. According to this theory, a person is continuously monitoring rewards, costs, and the difference between rewards and costs — or *outcomes*. If rewards exceed costs, so that a person greatly benefits from a relationship, we would expect the relationship to continue. But if costs greatly exceed rewards, we would perhaps intuitively expect the relationship to cease.

Actually, the theory suggests much more than the notion of "rewards minus costs." Thibaut and Kelley propose that a person will judge the outcomes of a relationship against two standards: a comparison level (CL) and a comparison level of alternatives (CL_{alt}). The **comparison level** is the magnitude of outcomes that the individual expects as a result of past experiences and knowledge of similar relationships. Knowing that others in similar jobs are treated in much the same way (for example, given the same title or equivalent respect) will be an important determinant of a worker's satisfaction with how he or she is treated. Therefore, whether an employee's outcomes (rewards minus costs) exceed, equal, or fall short of the CL will determine the degree of satisfaction with a relationship.

While the comparison of outcomes to CL determines satisfaction, it does not solely or directly determine the length of the relationship. According to this theory, an individual's desire to remain in or leave a relationship will depend largely on what alternative relationships are available. The highest level of outcomes that an individual could hope to attain from another relationship is termed the **comparison level of alternatives** (CL_{alt}). If a person is in a dissatisfying relationship but it is the best available relationship at that time, he or she is likely to remain in that relationship until a better opportunity arises.

---

† Most social scientists believe that these and other findings in the area of social attraction can be explained in terms of reinforcement or reward principles, that is, we like those who reaffirm our beliefs and are likely to reward us for holding a particular point of view.

■ **Table 12.1**

Predictions for Satisfaction and Longevity of Relationships

	Outcomes exceed CL_{alt}	Outcomes below CL_{alt}
Outcomes exceed CL	Satisfied and stable relationship	Satisfied but uncommitted to the relationship
Outcomes below CL	Dissatisfied but continuing relationship	Dissatisfied and uncommitted to the relationship

Table 12.1 summarizes the predictions of social exchange theory for the various combinations of outcomes in relation to CL and CL_{alt}. These predictions are for the issues of employee satisfaction and employee propensity to remain in or leave a relationship.

Stages in Group Development

Groups are not static, but change and develop over time. Tuckman has offered a popular view of the four stages through which groups pass as they develop.[7]

In the earliest stage of a group's development, members are concerned with testing each other's reactions to determine which actions are acceptable and unacceptable. In addition, the members depend on each other for cues about what is expected in the way of contribution and personal conduct. Problems associated with starting a group (for example, scheduling, finding a location, and obtaining resources) are also a significant part of this stage. Tuckman calls this initial stage **forming.**

The second stage, **storming,** involves intragroup conflict. Hostility and disagreement arise as the group's members wrestle with how power and status will be divided. Members may resist the formation of a group structure and ignore the desires of the group's leader.

During the third stage, **norming,** feelings of cohesiveness develop. New standards and roles are adopted and opinions about task accomplishment are freely voiced. The members' attraction to the group is strengthened, and job satisfaction grows as the level of cohesiveness increases. Cooperation and a sense of shared responsibility are primary themes of this stage.

In the final stage, **performing,** the group has established a flexible network of relationships that aids task accomplishment. Internal hostility is at a low point as the group directs its energies toward the successful performance of valued tasks.

Of course, not every group goes through these four stages in a fixed sequence. For more formal groups, for example, in which the division of power may be less subject to debate, storming may be virtually eliminated. Also, as a group experiences change, it may return to an earlier stage. For example, if an

Figure 12.3

Stages of Group Formation and Development

Stages	Concerns
Forming	Testing and Dependency
Storming	Division of Power
Norming	Rule Making
Performing	Accomplishing Goals

established group receives a new leader, it may temporarily give up performing and return to storming or norming. Figure 12.3 outlines Tuckman's sequence of group development.

Impact of Group Properties on Performance

The Mere Presence of Others

Perhaps the most fundamental feature of groups is the presence of other people. Some interesting research has focused on the effects of the mere presence of others on an individual's task performance. In these studies, an individual is asked to perform a task without interacting with others who are present. Results of such studies indicate that having others nearby tends to facilitate performance on relatively simple and well-rehearsed tasks.[8] However, for fairly complex tasks, the presence of others can have a detrimental effect. The positive effect of others being present is called the **social facilitation effect**, while the detrimental effect is termed the **social inhibition effect**.

You may have noticed such effects greatly magnified if you have ever been asked to perform in front of an audience. If your assigned task was relatively simple, such as giving your name or reciting other well-rehearsed information, you probably had little difficulty. But if you were asked to solve a problem that you had never encountered before, you probably did poorly.‡ The implications of this line of research are fairly direct: for tasks that are simple and repetitive, the presence of coworkers can have positive effects, while for complex and novel tasks, working in isolation is preferable.

Size

Group size has detectable effects on group performance. In larger groups, the potential impact and contribution of each individual are somewhat dimin-

‡ One of the more intriguing aspects of the social facilitation effect has been the pervasiveness of the phenomenon across species. It appears that even cockroaches and chickens demonstrate a social facilitation effect with well-rehearsed behaviors when in the presence of other members of their species!

ished, but the total resources of the group are increased. Administering a larger group also creates unique problems for managers.

Although most organizations settle on groups of five to seven persons to handle most problem-solving tasks, some organizations employ much larger "spans of control" for simple tasks. Hard evidence about an ideal size for groups is sparse, yet several conclusions seem possible.

First, members appear to become more tolerant of authoritarian and directive leadership as group size increases. Apparently, group members recognize and concede the administrative difficulties that can arise in a larger work unit. In addition, as unit size increases, it becomes more difficult for a handful of subordinates to be influential, and members may feel inhibited about participating in group activities.

Second, larger groups are more likely to have formalized rules and set procedures for dealing with problems. Despite this greater formality, larger groups require more time to reach decisions than smaller groups. Additionally, subgroups are more likely to emerge as group size increases. Problems may arise when subgroups are not committed to the full group's formal goals and prefer instead to pursue the more selfish interests of a few members.

Third, in a review of research on group size, Steers suggests that job satisfaction is lower in larger groups.[9] This probably occurs because people receive less personal attention and fewer opportunities to participate. It is also likely that employees in smaller work units feel that their presence is more crucial to the group and therefore are inclined to be more involved. For blue-collar workers, absenteeism and turnover also increase in larger work units. Cohesion and communication diminish with increased group size, making a job inherently less attractive and lessening the worker's desire to attend. In white-collar jobs, on the other hand, employees may have other sources of satisfaction to draw on.

Fourth, as group size increases, productivity reaches a point of diminishing returns because of the rising difficulties of coordination and member involvement. This may be a primary reason that five-member groups are so popular. Groups of five have several advantages. The group size is not intimidating, so that a member who disagrees with the majority is less inclined to remain silent. Having an odd number of members means that a tie or split decision can be avoided when voting. Members of such a group also have less difficulty in shifting roles within the group.[10]

Research has uncovered one other interesting problem that tends to arise in larger groups: members may engage in **social loafing.** In an early study of this phenomenon, Ringelmann, a German psychologist, had workers pull as hard as they could on a rope. Each subject performed this task first alone and then with others in groups of varying sizes while a meter measured the strength of each pull. Although the total amount of force tended to increase as the size of the work group increased, the amount of effort exerted by each person actually decreased. In other words, the average productivity per group member decreased as the size of the work group increased. Latane, Williams, and Harkins, who later replicated Ringlemann's finding, have argued that such social loafing occurs because each individual feels that the needed effort will be

An Inside Look
Group Illusions

E.F. Hutton was in trouble when a check-kiting scheme at the company was uncovered. It worked like this: Say a branch of the company had $70,000 on deposit in a small midwestern bank. The Hutton branch would wire a $1 million cash transfer from the account. The bank wouldn't want to lose Hutton's business, so it would advance the money. The next day, Hutton would replace it. Hutton had the use of $1 million of the bank's money for a day.

Such oversights happen from time to time in business banking, but Hutton was overdrawing its accounts by millions of dollars a day. The interest the company earned on this money became a major source of revenue. When the Justice Department investigated Hutton, the company was cited on 2,000 counts of mail

and wire fraud, received a $2 million fine, and was required to set up a multimillion-dollar fund to reimburse banks for the interest payments they lost on their funds.

How could Hutton's management have let such a practice go on? A common group dynamic was apparently at work. The group, in this case Hutton personnel, erected barriers against information or ideas that might be upsetting. People at Hutton did not want to think about the practice being unethical or illegal. As this example shows, group resistance to unfavorable information can be costly.

A similar group dynamic was at work at a battery assembly plant in the South. This company had set up self-managed work groups to eliminate red tape and let workers manage themselves.

The groups consisted of workers doing similar tasks, say, in a maintenance group or a quality control group.

At one meeting, the group responsible for quality control reviewed a production team's complaint that quality control inspections were taking too long. While the quality control team did their tests, production lines were shut down, and the production people who were idled resented the inconvenience. Was the quality control group willing to accept the idea that they might have to adapt or improve their performance? No. They quickly concluded that the production workers were unreasonable and didn't understand how long the tests take. The group dropped the matter without taking the complaint seriously or searching for a solution.

Source: Daniel Goleman, "Following the Leader," *Science '85*, October 1985, pp. 18, 20.

shared by the group's members and that he or she can count on others to take up any necessary slack.[11] The social loafing phenomenon suggests that under some circumstances, a group's effort may actually be less than the expected sum of individual contributions.§

Composition

How well a group performs a task depends in large part on the task-relevant resources of its members. The diversity versus redundancy of members' traits and abilities, then, is an important factor in explaining group performance. Groups composed of highly similar individuals who hold common beliefs and have much the same abilities are likely to view a task from a single perspective.

§ This line of reasoning is very similar to the concept of *diffusion of responsibility* considered in Chapter 11.

Such solidarity can be productive, but it may also mean that members will lack a critical ingredient for unraveling certain kinds of problems. As we saw in our discussion of individual versus group problem solving (Chapter 11), one of a group's greatest assets in comparison to individuals acting alone is the likelihood of achieving higher-quality solutions. Carrying this logic a step further, we can reasonably expect that diversified groups tend to do better on many problem-solving tasks than do homogeneous groups of highly similar individuals.[12]

The diverse abilities and experiences of the members of a heterogeneous group offer an advantage for generating innovative solutions, provided the skills and experiences are *relevant* to the task. Thus, merely adding more people to a problem-solving group to broaden the pool of skills and experience will not guarantee a better job. Attention must be paid to the relevance of the members' attributes and the mix of these attributes within the group. Additionally, the more *competent* members of a work group must also be the most *influential* members. As noted by Maier, if the people who are the least informed are the most influential group members, the quality of the decision will be diminished.[13]

One interesting finding about group composition is that members are more socially conforming in mixed-sex groups than in same-sex groups.[14] This suggests that members of mixed-sex groups focus more on interpersonal relations and therefore conform more than members of same-sex groups. Members of same-sex groups tend to be more concerned with accomplishing the task at hand.**

Roles

Every member of a group has a differentiated set of activities to perform. The set of expected behaviors relating to an individual's position within a group is called a role. Although the term **role** seems familiar enough (we can each easily define the roles of schoolteachers, managers, students, and others), it can be viewed in several different ways.

A person's **expected role** is the formal role that is defined in a job description or manual. This role may be conveyed through both a written job description and the signals that other members of a work unit send as they teach newcomers how to perform their jobs. An individual's expected role, however, may differ from his or her perceived role. A **perceived role** is the set of activities that an individual believes he or she is expected to perform. The perceived role may or may not greatly overlap with the expected role that originates with other members of the organization. Finally, an **enacted role** is a person's actual conduct in his or her position. It is more likely to reflect the individual's perceived role than the expected role.

Figure 12.4 illustrates how individuals receive information about their role and adjust their behavior accordingly. As this figure suggests, the process

---

** Although this finding suggests that managers should segregate the sexes or mix them depending on whether task accomplishment or social conformity is a major goal, it is difficult to defend any contention that espouses segregating the sexes within work settings.

■ Figure 12.4

A Representation of a Role Episode

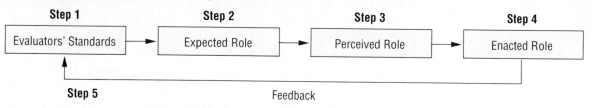

generally begins with the standards that are held by evaluators, such as managers, supervisors, peers, and subordinates. These standards or expectations are then communicated to the individual. Because communication is often imprecise, the expected (or sent) role may not be identical to the perceived (or received) role. Furthermore, due to constraints on actual behavior, the enacted role may not closely resemble the expected role or the perceived role. The enacted role is observed by the evaluators, who then compare it to the standards they have set. This feedback then completes a single **role episode.** If the individual's behavior does not come sufficiently close to the standards, another role episode may be initiated.

It should be noted that steps 1 and 2 of a role episode involve the group members who surround the individual, while steps 3 and 4 involve the thoughts and actions of the individual alone. Also, steps 1 and 3 are mental and perceptual in nature, while steps 2 and 4 involve actions and the transmittal of information.

As the figure suggests, many things can go wrong in a role episode. Sometimes the evaluators do not send consistent signals. For example, your superior may assign you a task, while his superior, in turn, may later tell you that you should not perform that duty, perhaps because it is not your responsibility or not included in your job description. Different groups sometimes send different signals, as when a supervisor's subordinates indicate that they would like less pressure for production, while her superiors simultaneously insist on higher levels of output. Differing signals from evaluating groups and individuals result in **role conflict.** On occasion, the messages that evaluators send are not clear, or they give incomplete information, which leads to **role ambiguity.** At each step in the role episode depicted in Figure 12.4, poor communication and other obstacles may interfere with the process.

Although role conflict and role ambiguity seem to be undesirable, there are some indications that in modest amounts and under the right conditions, they may actually have positive effects.[15] In fact, a work setting that is totally devoid of conflict and ambiguity can be dull and uninspiring. Thus, in order to avoid stagnation and encourage innovation, managers should perhaps seek to create a productive level of conflict and ambiguity. This novel proposal will be considered in greater detail in Chapter 13.

Gross has compiled a list of the roles that employees most commonly assume in a work group.[16] Although Gross's categories do not fit into a workable model of role episodes, they do provide an insightful view of the dominant ways in which individual group members tend to behave:

- *Task-oriented Employees:* Those who can be counted on to "get the job done" and "deliver the goods."
- *People-oriented Employees:* Those who are the Good Samaritans and social leaders.
- *Nay-sayers:* Those who oppose most proposals, have thick skins, and find fault with nearly everything.
- *Yea-sayers:* Those who counter the nay-sayers and help to circumvent the opposition.
- *Regulars:* Those who are "in," accept the group's values, and are accepted by the group.
- *Deviants:* Those who depart from the group's values—the mavericks.
- *Isolates:* The "lone wolves" who depart further from the group than the deviants.
- *Newcomers:* Those who know little and need to be taken care of by others, people who are expected to be "seen but not heard."
- *Old-Timers:* Those who have been around a long time and "know the ropes."
- *Climbers:* Those who are expected to get ahead, often on the basis of potential rather than ability.
- *Cosmopolitans:* Those who view themselves as members of a larger professional or cultural community.
- *Locals:* Those who are firmly rooted in the organization and the local community.

Status

Status is the social ranking or social worth accorded an individual because of the position he or she occupies in a group. Although we typically speak of status as a single notion, it is in fact made up of numerous factors, such as salary, title, seniority, and power. However, a difference on only one of these dimensions is often sufficient to confer status. For example, a group of tool-and-die makers may all have equivalent job titles, but the oldest member of the department, due to his seniority, may enjoy higher status and, as a result, greater deference. Of course, status must exist in the eyes of those who confer it. If the other tool-and-die makers in the work unit do not respect seniority, then the oldest individual will not in fact enjoy high status (although he may still feel that he deserves it).

While status is often conferred on the basis of achievement, personal characteristics, and the ability to administer rewards, it is perhaps most frequently associated with formal authority. Symbols of status, such as titles and perquisites, are designed to communicate difference and distinction, and serve several purposes.[17] Status symbols *provide stability* to the social order, which helps to reduce uncertainty about the appropriateness of conduct and role expectations. In addition, they can *provide incentives* for people to strive for superior performance. Finally, status symbols *provide a sense of identification* by giving individuals information about group membership and reminding them of the group's values.

If all attributes of a high-status individual are greater than those of low-status individuals, the high-status individual is said to be congruent on all dimensions of status. For example, if the highest-level executive is also the oldest, most expert, most experienced, best educated, and best paid member of that organization, then he is similar, or congruent, on all aspects of status. If, however, that executive holds the highest level on all attributes except pay (i.e., if another member of the organization were highest paid but lacked equal standing on the other dimensions), the executive would experience **status incongruence.**

Status incongruence can have an unsettling effect on group relations. In progressive organizations, people are more likely to be promoted for personal achievement than for length of service. In such organizations, status incongruence can be prevalent as younger, talented managers are promoted over their more senior colleagues. A situation in which a subordinate is substantially older than his or her superiors can be uncomfortable for both an older person and a fast-track manager. As a consequence, some amount of jealousy and hostility can be expected in group situations involving status incongruence.††

Status differences may also have undue influence on group decision making. In a well-known study by Torrance, bomber crews were assigned a task that could not be easily completed.[18] After struggling with the task for some time, the men took a break during which one member of each crew (either the pilot or the tail gunner) was given a clue to the problem's solution. In crews where the clue was planted with the pilot, the suggestion was frequently adopted. But in crews where the tail gunner offered the new approach, the suggestion was adopted much more rarely. Pilots and tail gunners differ sharply on a number of status-related dimensions: pilots are older, more highly educated, hold higher military rank, have greater responsibility, and have more flying time than tail gunners. Thus, it is safe to conclude that the crews showed a bias toward favoring high-status individuals rather than objectively assessing the quality of the proposal.

Norms

Norms are rules of conduct that are established to maintain the behavioral consistency of group members. They may be written (as in a code of professional ethics) or unwritten. Deviation from norms is frequently punished by ostracism and verbal attacks. Other more formal sanctions may also be used, as when an unethical lawyer is disbarred. As we saw in the Bank Wiring Room Study in Chapter 1, work-group norms can be a powerful determinant of output.[19]

†† In order to appreciate how uncomfortable a person can be in situations involving status incongruence, imagine taking a high-level math course that is taught by a professor who is 17 years old.

Norms have two primary purposes: (1) they give members a useful frame of reference for explaining and comprehending their group, and (2) they identify appropriate and inappropriate conduct. In addition, norms ensure that group members will focus their efforts in a common direction. This uniformity of purpose improves the group's chances of attaining its goals. J.R. Hackman has identified five major characteristics of norms:[20]

1. *They represent the structural characteristics of the group.* Group norms are analogous to individual personalities in that they reveal the underlying processes that regulate behavior.

2. *They apply strictly to behavior and not to private thoughts and feelings.* Private acceptance of group norms is not necessary. What really matters is public compliance.

3. *They are developed only for behaviors that are judged to be important by the majority of group members.*

4. *Although they usually develop slowly, norms can be developed rapidly if the need arises.*

5. *Not all norms apply to all members.* High-status individuals may be exempted from certain norms, but new group members may be expected to comply closely with all norms. Often it is expected that distasteful tasks will be handled by initiates.

As is true of many social phenomena in isolation, group norms are not either good or bad. Their value to an organization depends on whether they are directed to enhancing, rather than restricting, productivity. If norms lead a work group to produce a high-quality product or to be the best in its industry, they are highly desirable. But norms that encourage workers to reduce productivity are clearly undesirable because they undercut management's goals.

As a manager, you may find yourself enforcing group norms when they are congruent with your own goals or opposing them when they are incongruent. Alvin Zander has developed a set of guidelines for achieving both ends.[21] If you wish to enforce group norms, these guidelines should be followed:

1. Show a group member that the difference between the group's wishes and his wishes is not great, and that there is little need to resist group pressures.

2. Develop methods for rewarding employees who conform to group standards, such as bonuses, honor rolls, public recognition, and trophies.

3. Help members to understand how their contributions help the group accomplish its purposes.

4. Give participants a say in establishing standards, since standards are more closely followed by those who set them.

5. Make it known that members who do not conform to the group's standards will be removed from the team (while also helping anyone who is removed to overcome the resulting guilt and loss of self-esteem).

If the work group's standards are in opposition to your own, the following guidelines should be employed:

1. Recognize like-minded members and ally yourself with them.

2. Try to establish joint opposition with like-minded members by discussing your views and plans with them.

3. Do not give up legitimate professional preferences in order to prevent disharmony.

4. Hold out against social pressures by concealing from others what you do or think.

5. Attempt to publicize the value of cooperation and resultant rewards.

Cohesiveness

Cohesiveness is the extent to which members are attracted to a group and desire to remain in it.[22] Cohesiveness is sometimes described as the sum of all forces acting on individuals to remain in the group. As the term implies, cohesiveness pertains to how group members "stick together." Listed below are the factors that induce and sustain cohesiveness in groups and the effects of cohesiveness on group members and the organization.

Factors That Induce and Sustain Group Cohesiveness

1. *Similarity of attitudes and goals.* As mentioned in the discussion of interpersonal attraction, when group members have similar attitudes, they find each other's company pleasurable. So, too, individual members will be attracted to a group whose goals and ambitions are similar to their own.

2. *Threats.* The presence of external threats can help to increase group cohesion in that sharing a mutual fate can lead to greater awareness of interdependence. Competition from sources outside the group can also enhance cohesiveness, whereas competition among group members will tend to decrease cohesion.

3. *Unit size.* Smaller groups tend to be more cohesive than larger groups because smaller groups offer greater opportunities to interact with all members. Since diversity (and therefore dissimilarity of attitudes and values) tends to increase with group size, larger groups are likely to be less cohesive. In addition, in large units, the need for more rigid work rules and procedures reduces the informal nature of relations and communication among group members.

4. *Reward systems.* Cohesiveness can also be enhanced by offering rewards on a group, rather than an individual, basis. Group incentives, such as bonuses based on team performance, encourage a perception of a common fate and enhance cooperation. In contrast, reward schemes that encourage competition among group members—such as a winner-take-all bonus system for the single best performer in a unit—tend to diminish group cohesiveness.

5. *Work unit assignments.* The deliberate composition of work units based on interpersonal attraction, similarity of values, and common goals can facilitate cohesion. In a classic study, Van Zelst assigned carpenters and bricklayers to teams based on a prior secret balloting of preferred workmates.[23] The work teams that were formed on the basis of personal preferences had higher levels of job satisfaction than did the randomly assigned work units that served as a control group.

6. *Isolation.* Generally, groups that are isolated from others are more likely to be cohesive. Groups in isolation come to view themselves as unique and different. Isolation also helps to foster group members' sense of a common fate and need for defense against outside threats.

The Effects of Cohesiveness

1. *Satisfaction.* Members of highly cohesive groups are generally much more satisfied than members of less cohesive groups. This is, of course, to be expected, since the very definition of group cohesion implies a strong attraction among group members.

2. *Communication.* Communication among group members is significantly greater in highly cohesive groups than in less cohesive groups. Because members of cohesive groups are likely to share common values and goals and to find their own company satisfying, they are inclined to greater communicativeness. This communication in turn tends to foster greater personal revelation and depth of understanding, which cements positive social relations.

3. *Hostility.* Hostile and aggressive acts are more frequent in highly cohesive groups, but such hostility is usually directed toward people who are not members of the group.[24] Cohesion apparently creates a sense of superiority among group members, which can result in hostility toward, and rejection of, outsiders.

4. *Productivity.* Studies of the relationship between group cohesion and productivity have yielded highly mixed results.[25] Some researchers have found cohesive groups to be very productive, while others have found that highly cohesive groups are not as productive as less cohesive groups. Still other researchers have reported no relationship between productivity and group cohesion. It appears that a primary determinant of the effect of cohesion on productivity is whether the group's goals are congruent with those of the organization. If the goals of a cohesive group include high performance, then high performance can be reasonably expected. Conversely, if a highly cohesive group values reduced productivity, then a relatively low level of productivity can be expected. In short, cohesive groups are more likely to attain their goals than are less cohesive groups. In a study of 228 small work groups in a manufacturing setting, Seashore found that cohesive groups also tended to be less variable in their performance regardless of their absolute level of output.[26] This occurred because cohesive groups tend to emphasize compliance with work norms. Whether its

norms endorse high or low productivity, a group will probably produce within its own relatively narrow but prescribed range of output.

5. *Resistance to change.* Although it is less well documented, social scientists generally believe that highly cohesive groups are more resistant to change than are less cohesive groups. Changes that disrupt the status quo threaten a group's networks and social supports and are, therefore, likely to be resisted. Attempts at job redesign that ignore the existing social relations among employees run a greater risk of failing.[27]

Use of Groups in Organizations

Modern organizations rely on groups to perform many activities. In this section, we will examine several of the more frequently used kinds of groups: task forces and committees, boards and commissions, and quality circles.

Task Forces and Committees

As we have suggested before (Chapter 11), under the proper circumstances, groups can outperform individuals.‡‡ Two formal embodiments of an organization's desire to have a task handled by a group are the task force and the committee. Task forces are usually formed to handle a fairly specific problem. They exist as long as necessary to deal with the problem, and then they are dissolved. Problems that span several organizational units or departments usually require the creation of special task forces. Representatives from each unit are assigned to the task force based on the relevance of their expertise and training.

Committees, or standing committees, are typically designed to operate over a long period of time in order to handle a continuing need or problem. Examples of standing committees include ethics committees, college curriculum review committees, and executive decision-making committees.

Boards and Commissions

Boards typically comprise individuals who are elected or appointed to manage an institution. For example, the stockholders of a corporation will select a board of directors to manage company operations. Communities elect school board members to select principals and determine educational policies. Board members are usually more concerned with the desires of constituencies outside of an organization than are members of task forces and standing committees.

Commissions resemble boards in that members of commissions also possess decision-making authority for larger organizational issues. However, they are usually appointed by government officials rather than elected. Examples of commissions include the Federal Trade Commission and the Securities and Exchange Commission.

---

‡‡ Of course, it can be argued that a committee will never be able to create the equivalent of a Rembrandt painting.

These various forms of groups have several common advantages and disadvantages. Dale suggests that the advantages of such groups include:

1. Better quality decisions
2. Enhanced likelihood of implementation
3. Improved coordination
4. Controlled training for managers
5. Dispersion of power to reduce the potential for abuse

   The disadvantages of relying on groups include:

1. Premature agreements and mediocre compromises (for example, the groupthink phenomenon)
2. Domination by the group leader
3. Diffusion of responsibility
4. Wasting of time and money[28]

Increasing the Effectiveness of Meetings

Managers devote a substantial proportion of their day to meetings. By one estimate, meetings can consume as much as two-thirds of a typical workday.[29] It has also been estimated that up to one-half of the time spent in meetings is actually wasted. Because of these considerations, techniques for enhancing the effectiveness of meetings need to be considered. Peter Turla and Kathleen Hawkins suggest that:

1. The group's goals should be defined in advance to reduce discussion of that topic.
2. The group's authority should be specified in advance so that members know whether they are to investigate, advise, or recommend.
3. The size and composition of the group should be based on the feasibility of a given number of members and the need for various kinds of expertise.
4. An agenda and supporting material should be distributed to the members in advance of each meeting.
5. Meetings should start and stop on time. When an ending time is announced at the outset, members can better budget the time allotted to presentations and discussions.[30]

   Group leaders also need to understand how to manage a meeting. Anthony Jay has offered the following seven rules for leading a meeting:

1. Control the garrulous.
2. Draw out the silent.
3. Protect the weak.
4. Encourage the clash of ideas.
5. Watch out for the suggestion-squashing reflex.
6. Come to the most senior people last.
7. Close on a note of achievement.[31]

Figure 12.5

A Model of the Quality Circle Process

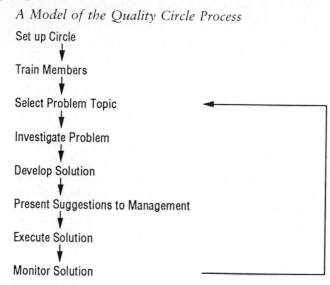

Set up Circle

Train Members

Select Problem Topic

Investigate Problem

Develop Solution

Present Suggestions to Management

Execute Solution

Monitor Solution

Quality Circles

In recent years, quality circles have begun to appear in a growing number of firms in the United States. **Quality circles** are employee committees of eight to ten workers who meet once a week (usually on company time) to discuss production and problems with product quality. Although the notion of quality circles originated in the United States, it took root in Japan after World War II (after being introduced in Japan by American consultants). Recently, the use of quality circles has been reintroduced to the United States, partly due to a fascination with Japan's business success.

In a quality circle program (1) membership is voluntary (employees must not be coerced into participating), (2) circle members are trained in problem-solving techniques, (3) members develop solutions to problems that they submit to management through formal presentations, and (4) members monitor the outcome of their solutions. Figure 12.5 presents a model of the quality circle process.

It has been estimated that from 12 to 25 percent of the Japanese work force participates in quality circles.[32] While the proportion of the United States work force that participates in quality circles is still relatively small, it has been growing rapidly since the late 1970s. Most of this growth has been in the manufacturing sector, and the firms that have implemented quality circles have experienced impressive success. For example, at Honeywell, a high-technology electronics firm, several hundred quality circles are in use and, in addition to improving productivity, they have reduced absenteeism. Other large U.S. companies that have successfully introduced quality circles include American Airlines, General Motors, Ford Motor Company, Hughes Aircraft, International Harvester, Texas Instruments, Westinghouse, and Northop. Many smaller

OB Focus

Teamwork in a Global Marketplace

Today, the word *teamwork* is used to refer to a variety of forms of employee involvement, of which quality circles are the oldest and most widely used format in the United States. Besides quality circles, companies have tried using special-purpose teams, which carry the quality-circle approach a step further, involving workers in higher-level decisions, such as designing new technology and meeting with suppliers and customers. An even higher level of worker participation comes from self-managing teams that produce an entire product instead of individual components, with workers rotating among many jobs and making managerial decisions, such as scheduling employees and ordering materials.

Quality circles first became popular in the United States in the 1970s, based on the success of this technique in Japanese companies. According to a 1987 survey of 476 large companies by the U.S. General Accounting Office, 70 percent had instituted the use of quality circles for at least some of the work force.

Since the mid-1980s, U.S. companies have begun moving to forms of teamwork that more closely reflect the American rather than the Japanese culture. In American-style teamwork, employees not only have a voice in shop-floor operations, they also take on such traditionally managerial duties as scheduling work and vacations, ordering materials, and hiring new team members. Also, in American companies, union officials often demand a role as consultants or participants in plantwide decisions such as production scheduling, capital expenditures, and the introduction of new technology. With these shifts, special-purpose teams and self-managing teams became more popular beginning in the 1980s.

In contrast, in Japan, teamwork is not designed to give workers more autonomy. Rather, quality circles are designed simply to help them identify problems in the production line so that the company does not produce defective goods. The U.S. approach seems to parallel more closely the approach taken in. Sweden, where at two Volvo plants teams of workers assemble large units of car, or even an entire car, with little supervision.

These changes help American industry meet the need to manufacture more customized products in a global marketplace. When work practices are flexible and workers know how to perform a variety of tasks, they can quickly change over to new models and products. At a General Electric plant in Salisbury, North Carolina, for example, teamwork enables employees to change product models a dozen times a day, which has increased productivity by 250 percent.

Source: John Hoerr, "The Payoff from Teamwork," *Business Week*, July 10, 1989, pp. 56–62.

firms have experimented with quality circles, too, as have such service-oriented institutions as hospitals and YMCAs.

Although all quality circles share certain common elements, programs may vary on a number of features. While there is very little hard evidence to indicate exactly which details are critical to a quality circle's effectiveness, Blair, Cohen, and Hurwitz have suggested that certain traits are characteristic of successful programs.[33] Chief among these is *commitment by top-level management* to the program. If top management does not fully endorse and support a circle program, its lack of enthusiasm will be detected and duplicated by others. As a result, the circle program will probably not receive the serious support it needs from lower-level supervisors. Second, successful programs are more likely to have *group facilitators*—usually senior workers rather than supervisors—*who have been specially trained* in both group relations and problem-solving strategies. Third, members of circles must be assured that they *will not lose their jobs or have their responsibilities reduced as a result of their suggestions*. Fourth, *recognition must be given* to individuals and circles for suggesting workable solutions to operational problems. At Northop, for example, a quality circle is awarded 10 percent of any dollar savings that result from its suggestions. Such monetary rewards are uncommon, however, as most organizations prefer to rely on psychological rewards to motivate participation.

Advocates of quality circles are quick to point out the approach's relatively low cost and logical reliance on front-line workers to suggest improvements in operations. When employees are the source of suggested improvements, they are more likely to accept changes because they feel a sense of ownership and responsibility. In addition, workers, managers, stockholders, and the public generally take a very positive view of the quality circle concept.

The quality circle concept is not without its critics, however. Some critics question the real cost effectiveness of quality circles. They contend that since employees are not performing their normal duties while they meet in circles (most circles meet on company time) and since most circle suggestions generate only minor savings, it is difficult to prove that the savings gained from the groups' suggested improvements justify the time lost from work. Union representatives in particular have had mixed reactions to the quality circle concept. For example, leaders of the United Auto Workers are favorably inclined toward quality circles as long as the programs do not produce layoffs or increase the work pace. They look less favorably on the fact that most circles are not compensated for generating cost-saving solutions.

In addition, the motives of people who volunteer for quality circles are not fully understood. Some people who volunteer for the program may do so in order to get away from the assembly line and gain a sanctioned work break. Others may join merely to voice their frustrations and complain about their jobs rather than to offer constructive suggestions. Only recently has research focused on the attributes of quality circle volunteers. The results suggest that circle participants are likely to be more highly educated, younger, in jobs of greater responsibility, and more satisfied with their jobs than are employees who show no interest in membership.[34]

Because they are by definition voluntary, it is not possible to study circles in a rigorous scientific fashion.§§ Some quality circle improvements may be due to nothing more than a Hawthorne effect (see Chapter 1). An additional concern relates to the longevity of quality circle programs. One review reported that nearly 75 percent of the initially successful circle programs in the United States were no longer operating after only a few years.[35] Continuing interest in and support for circles may be difficult to sustain in many organizations. It is also possible that some of the attractiveness that has surrounded

§§ Random assignment of employees to conditions is not possible (see Chapter 2) because it violates the voluntary nature of a quality circle.

quality circles may be wearing off as firms recognize the limitations of the programs.

Even in Japan (where 76 percent of manufacturing employees are involved in quality circles, versus 27 percent in the United States), disenchantment has been reported.[36] For example, roughly one-third of Toyota's employees feel that circle participation is a "burden."[37] At Mitsubishi Chemical Industries, some employees report a sense of obligation to attend quality circles and a concomitant feeling of monotony during meetings.[38] It appears that in order to rekindle enthusiasm and overcome apathy, well-established quality circle programs must find new ways of challenging and rewarding circle members.

Summary

1. Contrast formal and informal groups and open and closed groups.
Formal groups are task-oriented groups to which people are assigned; informal groups arise from voluntary social interaction among members of the organization. Open groups frequently change their membership; closed groups have a relatively stable membership.

2. List some reasons people join groups.
People join groups for security and protection, for affiliation and emotional support, for esteem and a sense of identity, and to accomplish tasks.

3. Describe influences on the degree to which people are attracted to one another.
The less the distance between people, the greater their interpersonal attraction. Distance can be either physical or psychological. People with similar attitudes or complementary needs and abilities feel greater attraction.

4. Describe stages of group formation and development.
A popular view is that groups pass through four stages as they develop: (1) forming, during which group members look to each other for clues about what actions are acceptable and expected; (2) storming, a stage of intragroup conflict during which power and status are allocated; (3) norming, the development of feelings of cohesiveness; and (4) performing, the accomplishment of valued tasks.

5. List some important group properties that affect performance.
Performance is affected by the mere presence of others, the size and composition of the group, the roles and status of group members, the norms of the group, and the degree of cohesiveness of the group.

6. List factors that induce and sustain cohesiveness in a group.
These factors include similarity of attitudes and goals, the presence of external threats, small group size, reward systems based on group performance, work unit assignments based on personal preferences, and isolation from other groups.

7. Describe types of groups commonly used in modern organizations.

Typically occurring groups are task forces, usually formed to handle a fairly specific problem; committees, typically designed to operate over a long period of time; boards, which comprise individuals elected or appointed to manage an institution; commissions, which comprise individuals who have decision-making authority and were appointed by government officials; and quality circles, employee committees that discuss production and quality-maintenance issues.

8. Discuss ways to improve the effectiveness of meetings.
Some specific procedures are defining goals and specifying authority in advance; selecting the size and composition of the group based on feasibility and needs; distributing the agenda in advance; starting and stopping the meeting on time; controlling talkative participants and drawing out quiet ones; protecting weak participants; encouraging conflicting ideas; avoiding dismissing suggestions prematurely; coming to the most senior person last; and closing on a note of achievement.

Key Terms

Group	Social inhibition effect
Formal group	Social loafing
Informal group	Role
Open group	Expected role
Closed group	Perceived role
Law of attraction	Enacted role
Social exchange theory	Role episode
Comparison level	Role conflict
Comparison level of alternatives	Role ambiguity
Forming	Status
Storming	Status incongruence
Norming	Norms
Performing	Cohesiveness
Social facilitation effect	Quality circle

Review and Discussion Questions

1. Give an example of a formal and an informal group. What characteristics of open and closed groups can help a manager choose between them for a given task?

2. When Betty Lee started her new job with Acme Auto Insurance, one of the other claims adjusters invited her to join a group of people who always eat together in the cafeteria. Within weeks, Betty found she prefers to have lunch with these people every day. What are some possible explanations for Betty's desire to be part of a group?

3. In terms of forming groups, do opposites attract?

4. Sam Samson is in charge of the new committee to recommend activities for next year's orientation program for first-year students. It seems

to him that most of the first meeting was spent in bickering and game playing, and the second meeting is going even worse. Sometimes when Sam tries to call the meeting back to order, everyone ignores him. Sam wonders whether he should quit or ask for a new group of committee members. What information about group development might encourage Sam?

5. Would a bagger in a grocery store likely perform the job better working alone or in the presence of others? What about the executive who is planning marketing strategy for the grocery store chain?

6. Marlene Megabyte wants all the systems analysts in her division to be top performers, so she goes to great lengths to be sure that they experience no conflict or ambiguity about what they are supposed to be doing. In general, what causes of role conflict and role ambiguity should Marlene be aware of? Is she correct about the benefits of eliminating conflict and ambiguity?

7. What are some sources of status? What benefits do status symbols provide? How does status influence groups?

8. Generally, a manager is expected to enforce the organization's norms. However, managers sometimes find themselves in situations where the group makes a decision that does not mesh with the manager's personal norms. For example, imagine that you are the sales manager in a company that has decided to continue manufacturing a product when tests do not clearly indicate it is safe. What might you do? Assume that you can't leave the organization immediately.

9. Over lunch, the six researchers at A-1 Pharmaceuticals usually discuss the latest research and the likelihood that A-1 will make further cutbacks in the research department. The researchers doubt that any other employees really appreciate the importance of their work; at company functions, talk seems to focus only on sales and production. Probably no one else understands enough about microbiology to follow a conversation about research anyway. Would you say this group of researchers is cohesive? What are some advantages and disadvantages of this degree of cohesiveness (or lack of it)?

10. What are some advantages of using groups rather than individuals to make decisions? What are some disadvantages?

11. Marv Marvelous assembled a group of people to review the company's sales goals and evaluate whether they should be revised. To make sure that all ideas would be considered, he invited two people from every department, for a total of 16 people. The meeting was scheduled for 2:00 P.M. At 2:15, Marv said, "Well, everyone is here except one, so we might as well get started. Please pass around these copies of the agenda I prepared for you." Then Marv turned to the most senior vice-president in attendance, Sid Senior, and asked him, "Perhaps you would start us off by suggesting some guidelines for evaluating the

sales figures." Suggest some ways in which Marv could have made this meeting more effective.

12. What is a quality circle? How do quality circle programs work? What kinds of programs are most likely to succeed?

Critical Incident
A Difficult Task Force

As chair of a task force on in-process materials handling, Jim had scheduled an initial meeting for 10:00 A.M. A month earlier, quality assurance at the large manufacturing company where Jim works had noticed that a significant number of parts were scratched when they arrived at the assembly room. A fact-finding committee (of which Jim was a member) had determined that the problem was caused by rough handling of the parts as they were moved around the plant. The committee's solution was to transport the parts in special divider trays. Representatives of the departments involved in the processing and transportation of the parts — including process engineering, plant transportation, industrial engineering, product design, and quality assurance — had been appointed to a task force responsible for designing the trays. The members, most of whom had been with the company for a decade or more, were chosen for their expertise and familiarity with these parts and their manufacture. All had agreed to work on the project, but they had not been asked what they thought of the fact-finding committee's report.

When the task force members arrived, Jim started the meeting by reviewing the history of the problem and the activities of the fact-finding committee. He stressed that the task force was to come up with a design concept for the special divider trays. He then opened the meeting for comments and suggestions.

Bob, from industrial engineering, spoke first. "In my opinion the solution to the problem is to make sure the workers are more careful in handling the parts, rather than in designing some new contraption to get in the way." Mary, from product design, agreed. She urged the committee to recommend that new handling procedures be written and enforced. Jim interrupted the discussion: "The earlier fact-finding committee already decided, with the approval of top management, that new divider trays will be designed and used." He knew that the earlier committee had considered new handling procedures with better enforcement but had rejected this solution because of the extent of the damage and the very expensive parts involved. He told the task force this and reminded them that the purpose of this committee was to design the new dividers, not to question the fact-finding committee's solution.

The task force members then began discussing the design of the dividers. But the discussion always returned to the issue of handling procedures and enforcement. Finally, George, from plant transportation, spoke up: "I think we ought to do what Mary suggested earlier. It makes no sense to me to design dividers when written procedures will solve the problem." The other members nodded their heads in agreement. Jim again reminded them of the task force's purpose and said a new recommendation would not be well received by top management. Nevertheless, the group insisted that Jim write a memo to the vice-president of manufacturing with the recommendation. The meeting adjourned at 10:45 A.M.

Jim started to write the memo, but he knew that it would anger several of his supervisors. He hoped that he would not be held responsible for the actions of the task force, even though he was its chair. He sat wondering what had gone wrong and what he could have done to prevent it.

Questions

1. Which characteristics of group behavior discussed in the chapter can be identified in this case?

2. If you were in Jim's position, what would you have done differently?

3. If you were in Jim's position, what would you do now?

Source: G. Moorhead and R. Griffin, *Organizational Behavior*, 2d ed. (New York: Houghton Mifflin, 1989), p. 286.

Experiential Exercise

Participating in and Observing Group Processes

This exercise is designed to provide the experience of either participating in or observing a task group.

The group is comprised of seven members who have been appointed to the personnel committee. This committee has been asked to select a manager for the department that provides administrative services to other departments. Before the committee can begin interviewing candidates, it must develop a list of the personal and professional qualifications the manager needs. The list will be used as the selection criteria.

Step 1   Select seven members of the class to serve on the committee.

Step 2   Those not on the committee should be grouped as follows:

a. At least one person, and preferably two people, should be assigned to each committee member as an Individual Role Observer. These observers will use Observation Guide B.

b. The remaining class members should become Group Process Observers. They will use Observation Guide A.

Step 3   The committee should rank the items on the following list in order of importance as criteria to be used in selecting the department head. The observers should follow the instructions given with their Guide.

Selection Criteria

_____ Strong institutional loyalty	_____ Stable personality
_____ Ability to give clear instructions	_____ High intelligence
_____ Ability to discipline subordinates	_____ Ability to grasp the overall picture
_____ Ability to make decisions under pressure	_____ Ability to get along well with people
_____ Ability to communicate	_____ Familiarity with office procedures
	_____ Professional achievement
	_____ Ability to develop subordinates

Step 4   When the selection criteria have been prioritized, the Group Observers should provide feedback to the committee members. Once this information has been shared, the Individual Observers should share their data or information.

Step 5   Based on what was shared and observed, the entire class should discuss how the committee might improve its performance.

A. Group Process Observation Guide

Instructions: Observe the group behavior in the following dimensions. Prepare notes for feedback.

Group Behaviors	Description	Impact
Group Goal: Are group goals clearly defined?		
Decision Procedure: Is the decision procedure clearly defined?		
Communication Network: What kind of communication network is used? Is it appropriate?		
Decision Making: What kind of decision process is used? Is it appropriate?		
Group Norm: Observe the degrees of cohesiveness, compatibility, and conformity.		
Group Composition: What kind of group is it?		

Other Behavior: Are there any other behaviors that influence the group process?

B. Individual Role Observation Guide

Instructions: Observe one committee member. Tabulate (or note) behaviors that he or she exhibits as the group works.

Initiating Ideas: Initiates or clarifies ideas and issues.	**Confusing Issues:** Confuses others by bringing up irrelevant issues or by jumping to other issues.
Managing Conflicts: Explores, clarifies, and resolves conflicts and differences.	**Mismanaging Conflicts:** Avoids or suppresses conflicts, or creates "win-or-lose" situations.
Influencing Others: Appeases, reasons with, or persuades others.	**Forcing Others:** Gives orders or forces others to agree.
Supporting Others: Reinforces or helps others to express their opinions.	**Rejecting Others:** Deflates or antagonizes others.
Listening Attentively: Listens and responds to others' ideas and opinions.	**Showing Indifference:** Does not listen or brushes off others.
Showing Empathy: Shows the ability to see things from other people's viewpoints.	**Self-serving Behavior:** Exhibits behavior that advances one's own interests, especially at the expense of others.
Exhibiting Positive Nonverbal Behaviors: Pays attention to others, maintains eye contact, composure, and other signs.	**Exhibiting Negative Nonverbal Behaviors:** Tense facial expression, yawning, little eye contact, and other behaviors.

Source: Excerpt from *Organizational Behavior* by Kae H. Chung and Leon C. Megginson, pp. 241–244. Copyright © 1981 by Kae H. Chung and Leon C. Megginson. Reprinted by permission of HarperCollins Publishers Inc.

Notes

1. R. Likert, *New Patterns in Management* (New York: McGraw-Hill, 1961).
2. R.C. Ziller, "Toward a Theory of Open and Closed Groups," *Psychological Bulletin* 64 (1965): 164–182.
3. W.H. Whyte, Jr., *The Organization Man* (New York: Simon & Schuster, 1956).
4. H.J. Lott and B.E. Lott, "Group Cohesiveness as Interpersonal Attraction: A Review of Relationships with Antecedent and Consequent Variables," *Psychological Bulletin* 64 (1965): 259–302.
5. D. Bryne and G.L. Clore, "A Reinforcement Model of Evaluative Responses," *Personality: An International Journal* 1 (1970): 103–128; D. Bryne, *The Attraction Paradigm* (New York: Academic Press, 1971).
6. J.W. Thibaut and H.H. Kelly, *The Social Psychology of Groups* (New York: Wiley, 1959).
7. B.W. Tuckman, "Developmental Sequence in Small Groups," *Psychological Bulletin* 63 (1965): 384–399.
8. R.B. Zajonc, "Social Facilitation," *Science* 149 (1965): 269–274.
9. R.M. Steers, *An Introduction to Organizational Behavior* (Glenview, Ill.: Scott, Foresman, 1984).
10. P.A. Hare, *Handbook of Small Group Research* (New York: Free Press, 1962).
11. B. Latane, K. Williams, and S. Harkins, "Many Hands Make Light the Work: The Causes and Consequences of Social Loafing," *Journal of Personality and Social Psychology* 37 (1979): 822–832.
12. M.E. Shaw, *Group Dynamics,* 3d ed. (New York: McGraw-Hill, 1981).
13. N.R.F. Maier, *Problem Solving and Creativity in Individuals and Groups* (Belmont, Calif.: Brooks-Cole, 1970).
14. H.T. Reitan and M.E. Shaw, "Group Membership, Sex-Composition of the Group, and Conformity Behavior," *Journal of Social Psychology* 64 (1964): 45–51.
15. S.P. Robbins, *Managing Organizational Conflict* (Englewood Cliffs, N.J.: Prentice-Hall, 1974).
16. B.M. Gross, *Organizations and Their Managing* (New York: Free Press, 1968), 242–248.
17. W.G. Scott, *Organization Theory* (Homewood, Ill.: Irwin, 1967).
18. E.P. Torrance, "Some Consequences of Power Differences on Decision Making in Permanent and Temporary Three-Man

Groups," *Research Studies, Washington State College* 22 (1954): 130–140.

19. F. Roethlisberger and W.J. Dickson, *Management and the Worker* (Cambridge, Mass.: Harvard University Press, 1939).

20. J.R. Hackman, "Group Influences on Individuals," in *Handbook of Industrial and Organizational Psychology,* ed. M.D. Dunnette (Chicago: Rand McNally, 1976), 1455–1525.

21. A. Zander, *Making Groups Effective* (San Francisco: Jossey-Bass, 1983), 55–56.

22. Shaw, *Group Dynamics.*

23. R.H. Van Zelst, "Validation of a Sociometric Regrouping Procedure," *Journal of Abnormal and Social Psychology* 47 (1952): 299–301.

24. L. Berkowitz and J.A. Green, "The Stimulus Qualities of the Scapegoat," *Journal of Abnormal and Social Psychology* 64 (1962): 293–301; K.L. Dion, "Cohesiveness as a Determinant of Ingroup–Outgroup Bias," *Journal of Personality and Social Psychology* 28 (1973): 163–171.

25. R.M. Stogdill, "Group Productivity, Drive, and Cohesiveness," *Organizational Behavior and Human Performance* 8 (1972): 26–43.

26. S.E. Seashore, *Group Cohesiveness in the Industrial Work Group* (Ann Arbor: University of Michigan Press, 1954).

27. E. Trist and K. Bamforth, "Some Social and Psychological Consequences of the Long-Wall Method of Goal-Setting," *Human Relations* 4 (1951): 1–38.

28. E. Dale, *Organizations* (New York: American Management Association, 1967).

29. P.A. Turla and K.L. Hawkins, "Meaningful Meetings," *Success,* June 1983, 40.

30. Ibid.

31. A. Jay, "How to Run a Meeting," *Harvard Business Review* 54 (1976): 43–57.

32. R. Cole, *Work, Mobility and Participation: A Comparative Study of American and Japanese Industry* (Berkeley: University of California Press, 1980); E. Yeager, "Quality Circles — a Tool for the '80's," *Training and Development Journal* (August 1980): 60–62.

33. J.D. Blair, S.L. Cohen, and J.V. Hurwitz, "Quality Circles: Practical Considerations for Public Managers," *Public Productivity Review* 10 (March 1982): 14.

34. R.P. Vecchio, "Employee Attributes and Interest in Quality Circles," *Proceedings of the Southeast Regional Meeting of the American Institute for Decision Sciences,* 1985, 106–108; S.A. Zahra, W.J. Lundstrom, and D.R. Latham, "An Empirical Investigation into the Dynamics of Volunteerism for Quality Circle Participants" (paper presented at Southern Management Association, 1983); M. Marks, "The Question of Quality Circles," *Psychology Today* 20 (1986): 36–46; M. Marks, P. Miruis, E. Hackett, and J. Grady, "Employee Participation in a Quality Circle Program: Impact on Quality of Work Life, Productivity, and Absenteeism," *Journal of Applied Psychology* 71 (1986): 61–69; J. Brockner and T. Hess, "Self-Esteem and Task Performance in Quality Circles," *Academy of Management Journal* 29 (1986): 617–622.

35. Blair, Cohen, and Hurwitz, "Quality Circles: Practical Considerations."

36. J. Lincoln, M. Hanada, and K. McBride, "Organizational Structures in Japanese and U.S. Manufacturing," *Administrative Science Quarterly* 31 (1986): 338–364.

37. R. Cole, "Made in Japan — Quality Control Circles," *Across the Board* 16 (1979): 72–78.

38. T. Wada and R.P. Vecchio, "Quality Circles at Mitsubishi," *Quality Circles Journal* 7 (1984): 33–34.

Let us never
negotiate out of
fear; but let us
never fear to
negotiate.

— *John F. Kennedy*

If compromise
continues, the
revolution will
disappear.

— *Lenin*

Learning Objectives

After studying this chapter, you should be able to:

1. *Define conflict.*

2. *Contrast competition and conflict.*

3. *Explain how the understanding of conflict has changed.*

4. *List some sources of conflict.*

5. *Describe strategies for managing conflict in an organization.*

6. *List ways a manager can induce desirable conflict.*

Conflict Management

■ Conflict at the Top

The early years of Wang Laboratories were an entrepreneurial success story. The company was founded in 1951 by An Wang, who, six years after arriving in America from Shanghai, earned a Ph.D. in applied physics from Harvard and patented an invention for magnetic-core memory, a system for storing data on computers. Thanks to Wang's technical genius, the company grew rapidly beginning in 1965, primarily on the basis of three products: the first programmable desktop calculator, Wang's innovative word processing system, and the VS minicomputer.

But by 1989 the company was facing financial disaster. It was operating at a loss, and banks were threatening to cut off credit. Underlying these problems, conflict over the leadership of Wang Labs was pulling the company apart at a time when it desperately needed to be united to introduce innovations.

The focus of the conflict involved who would succeed An Wang as the company's chief executive. In the Chinese tradition, An Wang had for years been grooming his eldest son, Frederick A. Wang, to assume the post. At the same time, two other men played a dominant role in the company. Harold Koplow, one of the company's best technicians, collaborated with An Wang nearly every day and was unafraid to challenge his ideas. John F. Cunningham led the company's sales force and provided the politically sensitive perspective badly needed in a company headed by a man whose first love was the technical arena.

Koplow and Cunningham became widely perceived in the company as An Wang's "surrogate sons." Thus, when Fred Wang joined the company in 1972, upon graduating from Brown University and completing a management program at Harvard, his presence offended many who had been moving up in the company's ranks. "You wonder if Fred could ever have succeeded in such a hostile atmosphere," says a Wang senior executive. "It was death by a thousand cuts."

The younger Wang started out writing computer code for the VS minicomputer. As long as his position was outside the R&D-based power structure, his presence was widely tolerated. However, in 1980 An Wang put his 30-year-old son in charge of research and development. Unlike his father, who settled disputes and turf battles through the force of the respect he commanded, Fred Wang tended to be more conciliatory. Unfortunately, the compromises he devised tended to satisfy no one and led to the perception he was in over his head.

Fred Wang's conflict with Koplow came to a head in 1981, when Koplow felt it was imperative to develop a new word processing system using microcomputer workstations, the hardware of choice for big business. Koplow wanted to head a new team to develop this product. However, existing divisions vied for responsibility over the new product, and Fred Wang settled the dispute by splitting the project, assigning one aspect to the word processor group and the other to the minicomputer group. Furious at the decision, Koplow quit.

Two years later, Cunningham lost a power struggle involving the younger Wang. An Wang told Cunningham he was going to change his title so he could name Fred Wang president. Disappointed and angry, Cunningham, too, left Wang Labs.

The result was a void in leadership. Koplow and Cunningham had been the only executives who felt able to challenge An Wang's ideas; Fred Wang tended to defer to his father out of old-fashioned deference. The company made a series of poor business decisions that led to its financial difficulties, and in 1989 Fred Wang announced his resignation as president.

As this story illustrates, conflict, when poorly managed, can disrupt an organization. This chapter explores what conflict is and how it has been viewed over the years. The chapter also identifies sources of conflict and strategies for managing it.

Source: Daniel Cohen, "The Fall of the House of Wang," *Business Month*, February 1990, pp. 23–25+.

Conflict may well be an inevitable product of organizational life. Although most of us think of conflict as a negative experience to be avoided, it actually has the potential to produce positive organizational outcomes if properly managed. To increase understanding of how conflict can affect performance, we will examine the nature and origins of this phenomenon and some techniques for managing it.

Conflict

Conflict is the process that results when one person (or a group of people) perceives that another person or group is frustrating, or about to frustrate, an important concern.[1] Conflict involves incompatible differences between parties that result in interference or opposition.

It is important to distinguish between conflict and competition. Conflict is directed against another party, whereas competition is directed toward obtaining a desired goal without interference from another party. For example, competition may exist between two salespeople who vie for an annual performance award, but conflict (that is, incompatible differences) may not exist so long as the two do not interfere with or oppose each other. Students also compete for grades, yet they are not usually placed in a competitive system that induces conflict. To be sure, *intense competition* can sometimes lead to conflict. But conflict can result without the existence of competition.

If two parties can both gain from their competitive efforts, then competition is less likely to lead to conflict. For example, if two faculty members are trying to obtain a promotion, the efforts of one person need not block the other's success. In such a case, the promotion of both individuals is possible and, therefore, direct conflict is not likely to arise. In essence, the difference between competition and conflict lies in whether actions are taken to interfere with another's goal attainment. This difference suggests that eliminating opportunities for interference is a useful management tactic for preventing the escalation of competition into conflict.

Changing Views of Conflict

How social scientists and managers view the topic of conflict has changed over the years.[2] Until the mid-1940s, it was popular to consider conflict as harmful and unnecessary. The existence of conflict was regarded as a sign that something was wrong and required correction. According to this *traditional view*, conflict serves no useful purpose because it distracts managers' attention and saps energy and resources. Thus, conflict should be avoided. In addition, conflict was seen as the result of poor management and the efforts of troublemakers. Through proper management techniques and the removal of troublemakers, conflict could be eliminated and optimal performance could be achieved.

In recent years, management scholars have shifted their view of conflict. Today, conflict is seen as inevitable in every organization and oftentimes necessary to ensure high performance. That conflict can be harmful in some instances is not denied, but emphasis is placed on recognizing that some forms of conflict can be useful in achieving desired goals. According to this perspective, conflict can encourage a search for new tactics and strategies, and help overcome stagnation and complacency. Conflict as a device for directing effort is, therefore, sometimes a desirable state. The focus of this *contemporary view* is on the successful management of conflict rather than its total elimination.

The successful management of conflict involves both sustaining a target level of conflict and selecting a conflict-reduction strategy. In addition, managers may purposely create conflict. In situations that call for creativity and when frank discussions of alternatives are needed (as when resisting a tendency toward groupthink), the stimulation of conflict is advisable.

In itself, conflict is neither desirable nor undesirable. It is only in terms of its effects on performance that the value of conflict can be judged. Figure 13.1 illustrates this notion, which suggests that an optimal level of conflict exists for any given situation. Carried to a high extreme, conflict can lead to chaos and disorder. In contrast, an extremely low level of conflict can result in complacency and poor performance due to lack of innovation.

Identifying the optimal level of conflict for a specific situation is not a simple matter. It requires a good understanding of the individuals involved and the nature of their assignments. Also, a manager needs a degree of creativity to determine strategies and tactics for reducing or, if necessary, increasing the level of conflict. Furthermore, simply increasing conflict when it appears necessary is not in itself sufficient: for conflict to foster creativity, it must be channeled and directed. Maintaining conflict at an optimal, or "Goldilocks," point is also a difficult managerial challenge.* In the succeeding sections of this chapter, we will consider techniques for reducing as well as for intentionally stimulating conflict.

---

* The Goldilocks point is the point on a curve where the conditions are "just right."

■ Figure 13.1

*Contemporary View of the Relationship between
Conflict and Performance*

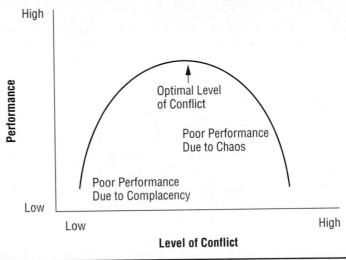

Sources of Conflict

Conflict can spring from a variety of sources. Robbins suggests that these sources can be grouped into three general categories: communication, structural, and personal behavior factors.[3]

Communication Factors

Managers typically attribute a sizable proportion of the conflicts that arise in organizations to poor communication. If we define true communication as creating a mental picture in the mind of a receiver in exactly the same detail as intended by the sender, then true or perfect communication is certainly rare. Given this inherent imperfection, there are many opportunities for misunderstanding to develop in the communication process. To be sure, conflict stemming from such unsuccessful communication is not the same as conflict based on substantive differences, yet it can still have powerful effects.

Incorrect, distorted, or ambiguous information can create hostility. For example, a manager may fail to communicate clearly to his subordinates regarding who will be responsible for performing a distasteful task while he is away on vacation. Upon his return, he may find that his subordinates are "at each other's throats" and that the task remains to be done.

Structural Factors

Size   In a review of studies examining the relationship of conflict to organizational size, Robbins found fairly consistent evidence suggesting that conflict is greater in larger organizations. It is likely that increases in size are associated with less goal clarity, greater formality, increased specialization, more supervisory levels, and increased opportunities for information to become distorted as it passes through more levels.

Staff Heterogeneity   It appears that differences among staff members in terms of authority, longevity, and values may also be sources of conflict. Differences among staff members, however, can also have beneficial effects on performance. As we discussed in Chapter 10, problem-solving groups comprised of relatively diverse individuals have an advantage over homogeneously composed groups. The diversity that exists in heterogeneous groups can serve to bring in different ideas and perhaps create challenges among members that foster superior achievement.

Participation   One might expect that greater subordinate participation (for example, in decision making) would reduce conflict. From a human relations perspective, one might even argue that inviting subordinates to participate can satisfy a possible drive to be fully involved. Research on this topic, however, has shown that just the opposite is true: when subordinate participation is greater, levels of conflict tend to be higher. This somewhat unexpected result may occur because increased participation leads to greater awareness of individual differences. Also, simply participating in decision making does not ensure that an individual's point of view will prevail, since a subordinate can be involved in decision making but lack the authority to have his or her preferences put into action. However, as mentioned earlier, the increased conflict associated with greater participation is not necessarily undesirable. If the results of subordinate participation, and the subsequent conflict, enhance the overall performance of a work unit, then the existence of conflict can be productive.

Line–Staff Distinctions   In surveys of managers, one of the most frequently mentioned sources of conflict is the distinction between line and staff units within organizations. Line units perform jobs that are directly related to core activities of the organization. In a manufacturing setting, the production department would be a line unit, while in a customer-oriented setting, the marketing or sales department might be considered line. Staff units perform jobs that support the line function. Examples of staff departments include research and development, public relations, personnel, and marketing research.

Conflict occurs between many line and staff divisions because of the functions they perform, their differing goals, and the values and backgrounds of their members. Line divisions are generally more operations oriented, while staff divisions are more removed from central operating activities. Line personnel are often very loyal to their firm, while staff personnel tend to be (and feel that it is their duty to be) critical of company practices. In fact, staff people frequently identify more strongly with a professional group or discipline than with the organization in which they are employed. For example, personnel officers and marketing researchers may belong to national associations that give them a sense of professional identification. Thus, a staff person may see herself primarily as a public relations specialist who happens to be working at Inland Steel, while a line person's strongest identification is likely to be with his employer. Lastly, the two groups' time horizons often differ — staff people more typically think in terms of long-range issues, while line people are more involved with short-term or day-to-day concerns. Given these differences in orientation, it is not too surprising that line and staff personnel experience a fair degree of conflict.

Reward Systems   If one party obtains rewards at the expense of another party, conflict can be easily generated. This form of conflict can arise among individuals and groups, as well as among entire organizations. How mutually exclusive reward systems operate is not always obvious. For example, staff people are generally rewarded for being innovative and identifying the need for change. By suggesting and attempting to induce change, they are able to demonstrate their usefulness to the larger organization. On the other hand, most line people strongly prefer to avoid change because for them, it is both disruptive and inconvenient. In fact, line people are generally rewarded for productivity that results from uninterrupted activity.

Resource Interdependence   Typically, groups must compete for the resources of their organization. With a growing supply of money and other resources, such as space, equipment, and materials, conflicts may not arise. However, such bountifulness is not the norm for organizations. As a result, conflict and the resulting lack of coordination and cooperation between divisions exist.

Power   The distribution of power within an organization can also be a source of conflict. If a group feels that it possesses far less power than it should, or if it believes that an excessive amount of power is held by another group, it is likely to challenge the existing order. If departments are ostensibly equal when in fact they hold differing amounts of power, serious discontent can arise. For example, in many companies, staff people must continually justify their need to exist, be understanding of problems in line departments, and make constant efforts to get along with the line personnel. Similar expectations do not exist for line personnel, however, because the line usually wields greater authority than the staff.[4] Such asymmetry of power distribution can add further tension to an already difficult situation.

Personal Behavior Factors

Another source of conflict lies in differences among individuals. Some people's values or perceptions of situations are particularly likely to generate conflict with others. For example, a manager may highly value the idea that all employees must "pay their dues." His argument might be that he spent much of his early career in an unglamorous lower-level position and that others would benefit from a similar experience. Of course, the imposition of this value on ambitious young subordinates could create serious conflict. Similarly, if a manager tends to perceive people in a certain way (for example, if he is quick to infer laziness or incompetence from only limited evidence), his responses to certain situations can be a source for conflict. In addition, some people simply enjoy being argumentative and combative. For such individuals, whose personal style is especially conflict-prone, life is a continuing series of escalating hostilities and battles.

Studies show that conflict-prone individuals are likely to possess certain traits. For example, highly authoritarian individuals are prone to antagonize their coworkers by escalating otherwise trivial differences. Also, individuals with low self-esteem may more readily feel threatened by others and therefore overreact. Both authoritarianism and low self-esteem can predispose people to feel the need to "defend their turf" against (objectively) trivial threats.[5]

Levels of Conflict

Conflict can be examined at several different levels. Conflict that exists within an individual is termed **intrapersonal,** while conflict between two people is termed **interpersonal.**† Conflict between groups is labeled **intergroup.** In this section, we will examine specific aspects of intrapersonal, interpersonal, and intergroup conflict.

Intrapersonal Conflict

A common form of intrapersonal conflict in everyday life involves choices between mutually exclusive goals. Selecting one option in many instances eliminates any other alternative. Several other types of intrapersonal goal conflict can be identified, depending on the nature of the choices.

Approach–Approach Conflict   **Approach–approach conflict** arises when an individual must choose between two attractive alternatives. For example, an employer faces an approach–approach conflict when she must choose between two highly qualified applicants for a single position. Similarly, a job seeker must cope with an approach–approach conflict when deciding which of two outstanding but equally appealing job offers to accept. Approach–approach conflicts pose a problem for only a brief period of time, that is, of course, if they are not immobilizing. If we model such a situation in terms of the strength of each motive to approach a desired goal, as in Figure 13.2A, we can see that a person should initially be caught between the two alternatives (position X in the graph). However, even slight movement in the direction of one of the choices is enough to break the deadlock and lead to the selection of that particular option.

One interesting aspect of approach–approach conflicts is the change that occurs in the individual's attitude toward the rejected option. Often, he or she regrets not having selected that alternative, as when a person buys one of two different cars and afterwards feels that he made a poor decision. Frequently, a person will then try to reduce this sense of regret by rationalizing that the

---

† Similarly, conflict within an organization can be labeled *intraorganizational*, while conflict between organizations can be labeled *interorganizational*.

An Inside Look
An Ethical Dilemma

Intrapersonal conflict often arises in ethical decisions. In many cases, an ethical choice clashes with some sort of immediate gain to the decision maker, such as money or a boss's approval.

Such was the ethical dilemma faced by Mark Morze in his experience with ZZZZ Best Company, a business with a notorious history. Barry Minkow, a Californian in his late teens, started the carpet-cleaning company in the garage of his parents' home and, over the next several years, through a series of scams and ever-growing loans, built it into a company valued at $200 million. Along the way, Minkow recruited a variety of people to work with him. One of them was Mark Morze.

When he met Minkow, Morze was operating a small bookkeeping business, preparing tax returns for about 100 clients. Initially, Morze was amazed by the lack of paperwork documenting ZZZZ Best's business, but he pieced together what he could, establishing a semblance of financial record keeping.

His first major ethical conflict arose in 1986, when Minkow was scrambling to get a $400,000 loan from a California company called California Factors and Finance to repay a previous lender. Minkow told Cal Factor the loan was to cover a big restoration job in Arroyo Grande, California. Unfortunately for Minkow, Cal Factor would not lend the money without seeing the job site — which didn't actually exist.

Minkow solicited Morze's help. "So what's the problem?" Morze replied, suggesting that Minkow let Cal Factor see the job site. When Minkow explained that there was no job site, that he had made it up, Morze was in a bind. He knew that the company needed another loan to survive. On a more personal level, ZZZZ Best owed him at least $50,000.

Deciding that a little deception wouldn't do too much damage, Morze rented a car and drove to Arroyo Grande. What he saw was discouraging. He was supposed to document the restoration of an eight-story building, but nothing in the sleepy little town stood over three stories tall. Undeterred, Morze bought a Polaroid camera, selected a two-story building, then lay on his back, seeking an angle that would disguise the true size of the building.

This deception was only the beginning of Morze's involvement in the ZZZZ Best scams. In planning to raise money by taking his company public, Minkow learned that the company would need three years' worth of audited statements. However, such documentation did not exist, and what did often painted an unflattering picture. Again, he turned to Morze, who developed an intricate system of photocopying checks, invoices, bank statements, and tax returns, then cutting and pasting the numbers on them to show ZZZZ Best's status in a more favorable light. Morze knew that he was taking a risk, but he liked to gamble, and he was tantalized by the big money that could result from a public stock offering.

Of course, a business cannot prosper on borrowing alone, and the ZZZZ Best scam eventually began to unravel. In January 1989, Morze was sentenced to eight years in prison and five years' probation, and he was ordered to make restitution in an unspecified amount.

Source: Joe Domanick, *Faking It in America: Barry Minkow and the Great ZZZZ Best Scam* (Chicago: Contemporary Books, 1989).

chosen option is inherently better or by actively trying to avoid information that would suggest that the choice was not superior.‡

Avoidance–Avoidance Conflict   **Avoidance–avoidance conflict** involves a choice between two equally unattractive options. For example, a person may

‡ This postdecision regret can be understood in terms of the theory of cognitive dissonance (see Chapter 4).[6]

■ Figure 13.2

Models of Motive Strength in Three Types of Intrapersonal Conflict

**A. Approach–Approach
   Conflict**

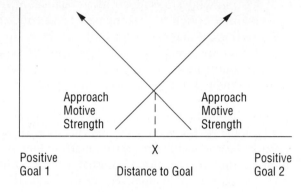

**B. Avoidance–Avoidance
   Conflict**

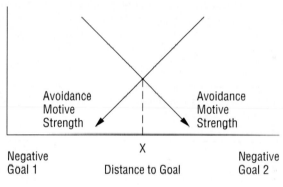

**C. Approach–Avoidance
   Conflict**

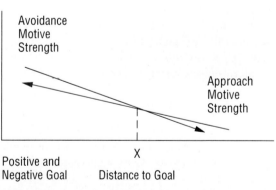

have a physical disorder that is very uncomfortable, such as ulcers. Yet the person may have a strong fear of going to the hospital for surgery. The net result is that the person is caught between the two options. Faced with an avoidance–avoidance conflict, most people will vacillate between the two options, without resolution of the conflict (point X in Figure 13.2B). However, if one of two motives becomes stronger, the conflict can be resolved. Thus, if the ulcer sufferer's discomfort becomes unbearable, his motive to avoid pain may override his motive to avoid surgery and the conflict will be resolved.

People who are trapped in avoidance–avoidance situations sometimes have another option for dealing with their conflict — leaving the situation. In some settings, it may not be possible, however, to quit one's job or leave one's family for other reasons. As this discussion suggests, avoidance–avoidance conflict is difficult to resolve as the conflict places the person in a situation of trying to maintain distance between opposing outcomes.

Approach–Avoidance Conflict   In an **approach–avoidance conflict,** the individual must decide whether to approach or avoid a single goal that has both positive (attractive) and negative (unattractive) qualities. This is not an uncommon circumstance in organizational settings, where many goals have mixed outcomes for an individual. For example, such a conflict could arise when a student considers choosing a college major that offers a greater guarantee of employment on graduation but involves uninteresting course work, or when an employee is offered a promotion to an otherwise attractive position that involves reporting to a person who is difficult to work for. If the motive to avoid the goal is stronger than the motive to approach it, the person will be caught where the strengths of the motives are roughly equal (point X in Figure 13.2C). As the person moves toward or away from the goal, the relatively stronger motive takes over and brings the person back to a point where he vacillates.

The resolution of an approach–avoidance conflict requires the strengthening of one motive over the other. Then it is possible for the person to reach the goal. This can be accomplished if the goal is made more attractive or if the individual does more rationalizing to overcome the conflict. Although the person might thereby reach the goal, the strength of the avoidance motive would still be high and the person would remain highly anxious. Lowering the strength of the motive to avoid the goal is, therefore, also important in finding a tolerable resolution to the conflict.

Interpersonal Conflict

Researchers have used a number of contrived situations in laboratory settings to determine which factors influence the tendencies to compete or cooperate when conflict exists. One such contrived conflict scenario is called the Prisoner's Dilemma:

> Two suspected criminals are taken into custody and separated. The district attorney is certain that they are guilty of a specific crime, but he does not have adequate evidence to convict them at a trial. He points out to each prisoner that each has two alternatives: to confess to the crime the police are sure they have done or not to confess. If they both do not confess, then the district attorney will book them on some very minor, trumped-up charge. . . ; if they both confess, they will be prosecuted, [and] he will recommend [a rather severe] sentence; but if one confesses and the other does not, then the confessor will receive rather lenient treatment for turning state's evidence whereas the latter will get the "book" slapped at him.[7]

Figure 13.3

Outcomes of Choices Available in a Prisoner's Dilemma Scenario

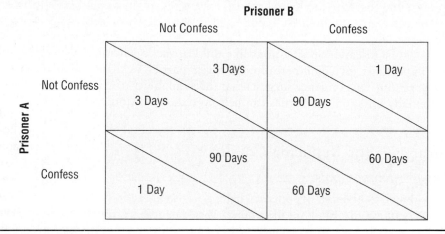

This situation is designed to create mixed motives for the prisoners. If each chooses what is best for him personally and ignores the other's circumstances, he will decide not to confess. However, if one prisoner does not confess and the other does, the holdout will suffer severely (by receiving a longer sentence). The best option for both prisoners, therefore, is to resist the divide-and-conquer strategy of the attorney and stick to their pleas of innocence. Of course, the question is whether they can really trust their partner in crime not to confess. Figure 13.3 shows the outcomes of the various choices for each prisoner. The outcome for each individual depends on the actions of the other participant.§

In role-playing studies using college students as subjects and substituting monetary rewards and penalties for threatened jail sentences, it has been found that the tendency of the participants to compete versus cooperate with each other can be influenced by a variety of forces. Chief among these is the penalty–reward structure for cooperating and competing. By altering the rewards and penalties for various actions, it is possible to induce more or fewer choices of competition or cooperation.

As a real-world illustration of how the size of penalties and rewards can influence the choice of a competitive strategy, consider the payoff matrix for the United States and the Soviet Union with respect to the use of nuclear weapons. If both countries attack each other, the magnitude of total annihilation is enormous (this is analogous to the values in the lower right-hand cell of Figure 13.3 being the electric chair). If one country tries to preemptively (or sneak) attack the other with confidence that the other will strive to be cooperative, the attacker may gain a clear advantage. However, the retaliatory capabil-

§ In actuality, the practice of separating suspected criminals and offering these alternatives is effective in extracting confessions.

ity of the attacked country cannot be ruled out. Therefore, each finds it to its advantage to avoid taking the competitive option of "pushing the button" because the costs are too high. In short, excessive penalties can force a form of cooperativeness (or at least reduce aggression) between otherwise contentious parties.

Other research on situations like the Prisoner's Dilemma also points to the importance of communication between parties as a means of inducing cooperation. This evidence suggests that the availability of "hot lines" between potentially antagonistic parties can help to reduce tension and conflict.

Strategies for Reducing Conflict

Superordinate Goals

Providing higher-level, or superordinate, goals to antagonistic parties can help to avert or reduce the level of conflict. When people share a common superordinate goal, they must cooperate to achieve a degree of success or avoid disaster.

In a demonstration of the conflict-reducing power of superordinate goals, Sherif conducted a field experiment with groups of 12-year-old boys attending neighboring summer camps.[8] Initially, he established two independent groups of boys who were unaware of the other group's existence. These boys engaged in the usual summer fun and developed norms of behavior within their groups. Sherif then created a degree of conflict by informing both groups that the other camp would be using certain equipment, such as canoes, and that as a result, they would be unable to engage in that activity. (In essence, he created win-lose situations for the groups.) As a result, the two groups came to resent each other strongly.

As the situation approached open warfare, Sherif experimented with several techniques to induce harmony between the camps. Initially, Sherif tried to give each group some favorable information about the other. This effort failed because the boys' negative impressions led them to reject the information. Next, Sherif had the boys eat their meals and attend movies together. This also failed to work, since hostility (such as name calling) erupted when the camp members were near each other. Then Sherif asked the group leaders to negotiate and share favorable information about their groups that could later be conveyed to their respective camps. Once again, the strategy failed because the leaders feared being "dethroned" by their constituents if they were seen to be too friendly to the out-group.

Finally, Sherif attempted to create superordinate goals for the camps by staging situations in which both groups needed to participate in order to benefit their members. These planned situations involved a breakdown of the camps' food truck (boys from *both* camps were needed to push the truck in order to get it started), a disruption of the camps' water supply, and a cooperative effort to obtain funds to rent a desired film.

Because of the need to meet a common threat, the boys of the two camps eventually adopted friendly and cooperative behaviors. For example, near the end of their stays, when one group had excess funds, it used them to purchase refreshments for both camps, rather than solely for its own members.

The implementation of this strategy in organizational settings has not proved to be easy. Robbins reports that in the early 1970s, General Motors attempted to use superordinate goals to unite management and labor in a battle against the threat of foreign competition.[9] The Chevrolet Vega, GM's intended answer to imported subcompacts, was to be manufactured in new production facilities in Lordstown, Ohio. Despite management's efforts to unite workers with managers through an attitude-change campaign focusing on the need to counter the foreign threat, a strike and open violence occurred not long after the plant opened. This experience suggests that a superordinate approach may need to be highly credible if it is to be effective.[10]

Structural Approaches

A number of options exist for managers who wish to reduce conflict via structural change. One technique is to transfer conflict-prone individuals to other units. Of course, this apparently simple approach cannot always be used, since some employees are nearly indispensable to their unit's performance. In some instances, it is the recognition of their value to the unit that gives such individuals the confidence to engage in battles over what they see as important issues.

One way to overcome line–staff conflict is to appoint one person to serve as moderator (and mediator) at line–staff meetings. This person tries to manage the interaction between the two factions to ensure that the relations between the two groups remain constructive. For example, before a meeting takes place, an effective moderator may try to help both groups better understand the nature of their counterparts so that they will be more tolerant of each other. To ensure that the meeting goes smoothly, the moderator may also encourage both sides to "do their homework" and prepare for questions that may arise and encourage staff people to consult with line people as they develop their proposals.

The moderator is expected to serve as a buffer between the units and encourage understanding by both sides. However, because higher management often selects a moderator from among the line people, staff people may question that person's real loyalty and biases. Being the moderator of such conflict, therefore, can pose a serious challenge for anyone asked to serve in such a role. Furthermore, what little evidence is available on the effectiveness of moderators suggests that many organizational members perceive them as having only limited positive impact on line–staff relations.[11]

Conflict management methods can be customized to match specific situations. A common technique is to create an appeals procedure (for example, a grievance system or arbitration) that provides a higher authority for resolving conflicts and a set of specific steps to follow when filing an appeal. One major shortcoming of an appeals procedure, however, is that the losing party often has difficulty in accepting the verdict. Although obliged to go along with the decision in theory, the person may feel compelled to "even the score" at a later

■ **Table 13.1**

Five Conflict-Handling Styles

Conflict-Handling Style	Related Term	Proverb
Forcing	Competing Conflictful Moving against the other	Put your foot down where you mean to stand
Collaborating	Problem solving Integrating Confronting	Come let us reason together
Compromising	Splitting the difference Sharing Horse-trading	You have to give some to get some
Avoiding	Moving away from the other Withdrawing Losing–leaving	Let sleeping dogs lie
Accommodating	Yielding–losing Friendly–helping Moving toward the other	It is better to give than to receive

Source: K.W. Thomas, "Organizational Conflict," in *Organizational Behavior,* edited by S. Kerr (Columbus, Ohio: Grid, 1979).

time by a subtle but vengeful action or inaction. Thus, for an appeals process to succeed, the losing party must be helped to maintain self-esteem and further efforts must be made to bring the two parties closer together.

Styles of Conflict Management

Managers differ in their ways of dealing with conflict. Ken Thomas has suggested five major styles of conflict management that managers can adopt: forcing, collaborating, compromising, avoiding, and accommodating.[12] Table 13.1 summarizes the characteristics of these styles.

Forcing   In addition to defining the five basic styles of conflict management, Thomas has suggested a two-dimensional framework for comparing them (Figure 13.4). According to this framework, the **forcing** style attempts to overwhelm an opponent with formal authority, threats, or the use of power. Its underlying features are assertiveness and uncooperativeness.

Collaborating   The **collaborating** style represents a combination of assertiveness and cooperativeness. Collaborating involves an attempt to satisfy the concerns of both sides through honest discussion. Creative approaches to conflict reduction — for example, the sharing of resources — may actually lead to both parties' being materially better off. For this style to be successful, trust and openness are required of all participants.

Accommodating   An **accommodating** style combines unassertiveness and cooperativeness. At its simplest level, this style may merely involve giving in to

Figure 13.4

A Two-Dimensional Model of Conflict Behavior

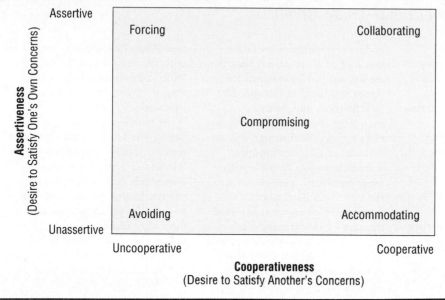

Source: K.W. Thomas, "Organizational Conflict," in *Organizational Behavior*, S. Kerr, ed. (Columbus, Ohio: Grid, 1979), p. 156.

another's wishes. Accommodating behavior may be motivated by a desire to be altruistic or prosocial, but sometimes no other approach is feasible for someone in a truly weak position.

Avoiding   The combination of unassertiveness and uncooperativeness leads to an **avoiding** style, in which a person implies that he or she will either improve a difficult situation or attempt to appear neutral. In some cases, it may not be possible to adopt a truly neutral position, but a manager may nonetheless prefer to avoid the situation. Although a manager who avoids difficult issues is likely to be resented by his subordinates, this strategy may be effective under certain circumstances. For example, a manager may initially stay out of a disagreement to avoid escalating the conflict during a particular phase of its development. Later, when she judges the time is right, she may take a more active role in finding a productive solution.

Experienced managers also recognize that action is not always necessary because some problems dissipate over time or are resolved by other organizational processes. For example, an intense conflict between two subordinates may seem to require intervention by their manager. But if the manager knows that one of the individuals will soon be transferred to another department or promoted to another position, it may be advisable to ignore the situation and let the impending changes resolve the difficulty.

OB Focus

Settling International Trade Conflicts

The governmental official charged with negotiating the terms of international trade is the U.S. Trade Representative. Under President George Bush, that person is Carla A. Hills. Hills spelled out her style of conflict management vividly when she said she hopes to bring down trade barriers "with a handshake wherever possible" and with "a crowbar where necessary." In sum, she adopts a highly assertive style that emphasizes forcing and, perhaps to a lesser degree, collaborating. For example, while some government officials are reluctant to use trade sanctions against countries found guilty of unfair trade practices, Hills finds them a convenient method for winning concessions.

In 1989, the European Community (EC) issued a preliminary directive requiring that half of all television time in the EC nations be reserved for shows produced in Europe. The directive was designed to encourage local programming. In Hills's view, the directive was an early move to make European nations less open to trade with other countries. And, she added, the step "was particularly reprehensible because it involved the area of thought and free expression, which Americans hold dear." It was also a move that upset U.S. television producers, who had a lucrative business syndicating shows in Europe.

Hills responded by battling the move fiercely. As a result, the EC modified the proposed regulations to take the form of a recommendation. However, she also generated some hard feelings.

Said Alain Le Diberder, an official with the French Culture Ministry, "She talks about goods, we talk about culture. She is a Stalinist of free trade."

In Hills's negotiations with Japan, she has been attempting to remove Japan's entrenched trade barriers. The Japanese only reluctantly agreed to talks, then offered few significant concessions. In fact, the Japanese negotiators have also adopted a forcing style, responding to U.S. demands by criticizing U.S. problems, such as the budget deficit and low savings rate, that support the nation's trade deficit. Hills has responded with attempts at collaborating: "After all," she says, "we are asking them to do what's best for them, for their consumers." However, the Japanese so far remain unconvinced.

Source: Paul Magnusson, "Carla Hills, Trade Warrior," *Business Week*, January 22, 1990, pp. 50–55.

Compromising   The fifth style, **compromising,** involves intermediate amounts of assertiveness and cooperativeness and strives for partial satisfaction of both parties' desires by seeking a middle ground. To succeed at compromising, both parties must be willing to give up something.

Although people may be tempted to consider some styles of conflict management more effective than others (for example, collaborating versus avoiding), there is good reason to believe that each style works best in certain situations. Through a survey of chief executives, Thomas has attempted to identify the most effective match-ups of style and situation (Table 13.2).

Intergroup Conflict

Conflict between groups can result from a variety of causes. Competition for resources, differences in goals, and interpersonal conflict can serve as the basis for conflict among groups or departments. Line and staff conflict, discussed earlier in this chapter, is a prime example of intergroup conflict. The management of conflict between groups or departments can be achieved through a variety of strategies.[13] Table 13.3 lists specific techniques for managing intergroup conflict.

■ **Table 13.2**

Uses of Five Styles of Conflict Handling

Conflict-handling Styles	Appropriate Situations
Competing	1. When quick, decisive action is vital, e.g., emergencies.
	2. On important issues where unpopular actions need implementing, e.g., cost-cutting, enforcing unpopular rules, discipline.
	3. On issues vital to company welfare when you know you're right.
	4. Against people who take advantage of noncompetitive behavior.
Collaborating	1. To find an integrative solution when both sets of concerns are too important to be compromised.
	2. When your objective is to learn.
	3. To merge insights from people with different perspectives.
	4. To gain commitment by incorporating concerns into a consensus.
	5. To work through feelings that have interfered with a relationship.
Compromising	1. When goals are important but not worth the effort or potential disruption of more assertive modes.
	2. When opponents with equal power are committed to mutually exclusive goals.
	3. To achieve temporary settlements to complex issues.
	4. To arrive at expedient solutions under time pressure.
	5. As a backup when collaboration or competition is unsuccessful.
Avoiding	1. When an issue is trivial, or more important issues are pressing.
	2. When you perceive no chance of satisfying your concerns.
	3. When potential disruption outweighs the benefits of resolution.
	4. To let people cool down and regain perspective.
	5. When gathering information supersedes immediate decision.
	6. When others can resolve the conflict more effectively.
	7. When issues seem tangential or symptomatic of other issues.
Accommodating	1. When you find you are wrong — to allow a better position to be heard, to learn, and to show your reasonableness.
	2. When issues are more important to others than to you — to satisfy others and maintain cooperation.
	3. To build social credits for later issues.
	4. To minimize loss when you are outmatched and losing.
	5. When harmony and stability are especially important.
	6. To allow subordinates to develop by learning from mistakes.

Source: K.W. Thomas, "Toward Multi-Dimensional Values in Teaching: The Example of Conflict Behaviors," *Academy of Management Review* 2 (1977): 484–490.

Rules and Procedures A fairly direct approach to managing intergroup conflict is the establishment of rules and procedures. This approach is likely to work best if the rules and procedures are set up before conflict arises. However, as a way of sorting out and managing differences even after conflict has emerged, it is still a potentially useful technique. As an example, consider two departments that need to use a specific piece of equipment that can only accommodate one user at a time. To manage the potential conflict in this situation, certain times of day or certain days of the week can be reserved for each department to have exclusive use of the equipment. Rules and procedures often help to avert conflict or defuse tense situations by reducing the amount of contact between groups.

■ Table 13.3

Techniques for Managing Intergroup Conflict
Rules and Procedures
Higher Authority
Boundary-spanning Positions
Teams
Integrating Departments

Appeal to Higher Authority   In circumstances where rules and procedures are not easily established, a higher authority may be relied on to decide how to best manage the needs of groups. For example, a supervisor may be assigned to make decisions about how each group will have its desires satisfied, with an eye toward satisfying the larger needs of the organization rather than just those of the immediate groups. This technique can also have drawbacks. For instance, group members may try to befriend the supervisor in an attempt to receive unwarranted, additional consideration in scheduling decisions. Also, the supervisor may find that continually trying to manage the interests of these groups is very time-consuming and detracts from time needed to perform other supervisory duties.

Boundary-spanning Positions   When the coordination of the efforts and interests of departments becomes increasingly continuous and complex, it is sometimes desirable to assign a person on a full-time basis to manage relations between departments. Such a person's job entails spanning the boundaries, or crossing the divisional lines, between groups. In essence, a **boundary-spanning position** is one that requires a person to serve as a liaison, or communications link, between groups. Liaison, or boundary-spanning, positions can increase the frequency of contact between groups (through meetings and communiqués). Increased contact between groups can facilitate coordination and, ideally, foster cooperation. On the downside, employees who serve as go-betweens within organizations experience a good deal of job-related conflict and ambiguity concerning their actual role in the organization. This may, in part, account for the finding that boundary-spanners report somewhat lower job satisfaction.[14]

Teams   Teams are collections of employees who are assigned to manage intergroup relations. Teams may be created to manage long-term, continuous intergroup relations, or they may be established to examine a specific problem on a short-term basis. The primary purpose of teams is to tackle recurring problems resulting from intergroup conflict and to develop remedies for managing the conflict. Typically, such teams comprise employees who hold membership in the competing groups. However, the team members usually have a functional specialty that justifies their membership on the team. Such teams work best, of course, when the members take a problem-solving approach to the task and set aside competitive or antagonistic feelings toward members of the opposing group.

Integrating Departments   At the extreme, groups may require extensive coordination of efforts. Simultaneously, conflict may exist. As an ultimate form of response to such a situation, an organization can create an integrating department. An integrating department actually has few members. It might consist of a head and a few staff members who possess expertise in the specialties associated with the other departments. The **integrating department** is a formal and permanent mechanism with a goal of integrating the efforts of the departments of interest. Initially, an integrating department may not be taken seriously by contesting departments. However, it can be given greater formal authority by providing the head with influence in decision making that affects the affairs, and especially the budgets, of the other departments.

Stimulating Conflict

At the outset of this chapter, we suggested that there is an optimal level of conflict for any situation. While the optimal level may sometimes be zero, in most cases a modest level of conflict actually encourages involvement and innovation. This indicates that some situations may in fact benefit from the creation of conflict. According to Robbins, some signs that a manager needs to stimulate conflict include an unusually low rate of employee turnover, a shortage of new ideas, strong resistance to change, and the belief that cooperativeness (the principle trait of a "yes-man") is more important than personal competence.[15]

Among the specific techniques that Robbins offers for inducing conflict are:

1.   *Appointing managers who are open to change.* In some units, a highly authoritarian manager will tend to suppress opposing viewpoints. The resulting lethargy can be overcome to some extent by the appropriate selection and placement of change-oriented managers.

2.   *Encouraging competition.* The use of individual and group incentives to performance, such as pay increases, bonuses, and recognition, tends to enhance competition. And competition, if managed properly, can result in creative conflict.

3.   *Restructuring the work unit.* Changing members of work teams, rotating personnel, and altering lines of communication can do much to shake up an organization. Restructuring can also create new jobs to be filled by outsiders whose values and styles will contrast with the prevailing but lethargic set of norms.

Summary

1. Define conflict.

Conflict is the process that results when a person or group perceives that another person or group is frustrating, or about to frustrate, an important concern.

2. Contrast competition and conflict.

Conflict is directed against another party, whereas competition is directed toward obtaining a desired goal without interference from another party. The difference lies in whether one party takes actions to interfere with another's efforts to attain a goal.

3. Explain how the understanding of conflict has changed.

Until the mid-1940s, the popular view was that conflict is harmful and unnecessary. Today, conflict is considered to be inevitable in every organization and often necessary to ensure high performance, although conflict can sometimes be harmful. The value of conflict depends on how the conflict affects performance.

4. List some sources of conflict.

Conflict can arise from poor communication, increased size of the organization, staff heterogeneity, greater subordinate participation, differences between line and staff personnel, mutually exclusive reward systems, competition for limited resources, unequal distribution of power, and differences among individuals.

5. Describe strategies for managing conflict in an organization.

The manager can provide superordinate goals to antagonistic parties, so that they will cooperate to achieve the common goal. The manager can transfer conflict-prone individuals to other units, or institute an appeals procedure.

6. List ways a manager can induce desirable conflict.

The manager can appoint managers who are open to change, encourage competition, and restructure the work unit to change lines of communication or to create new positions.

Key Terms

Conflict	Forcing
Intrapersonal conflict	Collaborating
Interpersonal conflict	Accommodating
Intergroup conflict	Avoiding
Approach–approach conflict	Compromising
Avoidance–avoidance conflict	Boundary-spanning position
Approach–avoidance conflict	Integrating department

Review and Discussion Questions

1. What is the difference between conflict and competition? What insights does this difference give you into how a manager can prevent competition from escalating into conflict?

2. What are some advantages of conflict? What consequences can result from extremely high or low levels of conflict? How can managers maintain an optimal level of conflict?

3. Orville Snorr has found that his subordinates frequently misinterpret his policy memos, surprising him with their dissatisfaction. Furthermore, his procedural memos often confuse his subordinates. When Orville is out of town — and hence unable to explain what he has written — arguments erupt and little work gets accomplished. Orville realizes he has a communication problem and decides that everyone will be happier if they develop policies and procedures jointly in staff meetings. To Orville's surprise, however, he finds that much of the arguing has moved into the meetings. Inviting subordinates to participate in decision making doesn't seem to have helped the conflict at all. Suggest a reason why conflict still exists. Should Orville try to reduce or eliminate the conflict? Why or why not?

4. What are some sources of conflict between line and staff employees? What can be done to manage this conflict?

5. What traits typically characterize a person who is prone to conflicts?

6. An intrapersonal conflict can be an approach–approach conflict, an approach–avoidance conflict, or an avoidance–avoidance conflict. Describe these three kinds of conflicts and give an example of each.

7. The text describes the balance of power between the United States and the Soviet Union as an example of the "prisoner's dilemma." What is your opinion of this arrangement as a way to control conflict between the two nations? Would some of the other strategies for managing conflict discussed in this chapter be more suitable, or do those strategies apply only to business organizations? Explain.

8. Alice Chalmers is considering whether to redecorate the restaurant in her hotel. Ted Quince argues vehemently for redecoration, saying it would boost business dramatically. He came to the meeting armed with sketches of how the refurbished restaurant would look. Rosalie Bean brought graphs and statistics. She begins earnestly explaining the costs of renovation, making clear her view that spending money on the restaurant will soon drive the hotel into bankruptcy. Ted looks wounded and exclaims that he wouldn't support an idea that would lead to bankruptcy and that clearly Rosalie is exaggerating. Soon the two are trading barbed remarks. Alice breaks in and says, "Leave your information with me. I'll consider what you've said, and we'll talk more later." Is Alice justified in avoiding the conflict between Ted and Rosalie? Why or why not?

Critical Incident

A Manager's Nightmare

Wearever Tire has operated in Happyville, New York, for forty-five years. Well known for its superior human relations policies and competitive benefits, Wearever has enjoyed good labor–management relations and has offered what is virtually lifetime employment to several generations of local families. The company has a reputation for being environmentally concerned, and for providing strong community support.

Today, Wearever faces a serious threat. It has just learned that a "bread and butter" account will cut its orders this year due to foreign competition. Bob Stone, Industrial Division manager, has been advised that he must reduce his staff by 20%. A thorough plan drafted by the human resource department details his options. Some of the necessary labor cost reduction will come from attrition, that is, from normal levels of turnover and forecasted retirements. The bulk, however, will have to come from "forced" reductions, via either early retirements or layoffs.

For those who will be laid off and are too young to retire, Wearever will offer a lump-sum service bonus intended to offset the emotional and financial costs of the layoff, and will offer each laid-off employee the opportunity to utilize outplacement services. The range of outplacement services provided will include career counselling, interviewing skills and job search training techniques, and clerical support for transmission of telephone messages, résumé preparation, cover letter generation, etc. The placement firm also makes physical facilities available to clients, including desks, telephones, and conference areas.

To encourage early retirement among those close to retirement age, Wearever will offer a "5-5-4" package. Under this arrangement, employees will be given the opportunity to retire five years before normal retirement age; they may add five years to their length of service with the firm (thus increasing their retirement pay); and they get four weeks of pay for every year that they have been employed with the firm as a one-time, lump-sum bonus.

Bob dreads informing the staff at large of the cuts. A company-wide assembly will be held at 2:00 to announce the details of the plans, but he wants to forewarn them, so he will call everyone into his office after lunch. He has already drafted a sketch in his mind of who will likely consider the 5-5-4 option. He knows that their decisions will not be easy ones to make. They will be enticed by the offer, yet he would like to make sure that they are acting out of prudent self-interest, and not because the offer is too good to pass up. He also has an idea whom he will target to be laid off. Some of the unfortunate few are his best employees, yet their positions can no longer be protected, and there's no place left in the organization for them to move to.

Questions

1.   Why might employees in their late fifties face approach-avoidance conflict in their decision regarding early retirement?

2.   Corporate downsizing causes considerable conflict among both workers who are laid off and among remaining employees not laid off.
     a. What has Wearever done to mitigate the conflicts for employees targeted for layoff?
     b. List three possible forms of conflict that a remaining Wearever employee might perceive.

c. What can Wearever do for the remaining employees at Wearever to reduce the conflicts that they might perceive?

Source: Susan Stites Doe, State University of New York at Buffalo.

Experiential Exercise
How Well Do You Manage Conflict?

Step 1 Listed below are 15 pairs of statements people use to describe why they behave the way they do in conflict situations. Allocate 3 points between the two alternative statements in each pair. Base your point allocation on your assessment of each alternative's relative importance to you as a means of handling conflict.

Allocate the points between the first and second statement as follows:

(a) __3__   (a) __2__   (a) __1__   (a) __0__

    or   or   or

(b) __0__   (b) __1__   (b) __2__   (b) __3__

There can be no tied allocations and each pair's numbers must add up to 3.

1. I am apt to give up something in order to get something. (a) ____

   I am usually quite firm in pursuing my goals. (b) ____

2. I usually work to soothe the other person's feelings to preserve our relationship. (c) ____

   I try to get all of our concerns immediately out into the open. (d) ____

3. I usually try to get the other person's help in working out a solution. (e) ____

   I try to avoid taking a position that is likely to create a controversy. (f) ____

4. I try to do what is necessary to avoid tensions. (g) ____

   I sometimes give up my own wishes for the desires of the other person. (h) ____

5. I usually press to get my points across. (i) ____

   I usually let the other person have some of their wishes if they allow me to have some of mine. (j) ____

6. I am usually quite firm in pursuing my goals. (k) ____

   I usually try to get the other person's help in working out a solution. (l) ____

7. I am apt to give up something in order to get something. (m) ____

   I try to avoid taking a position that would create a controversy. (n) ____

8. I usually work to soothe the other person's feelings to preserve our relationship. (o) _____

   I usually let the other person have some of their wishes if they let me have some of mine. (p) _____

9. I usually press to get my points across. (q) _____

   I sometimes give up my own wishes for the desires of the other person. (r) _____

10. I am apt to give up something in order to get something. (s) _____

    I try to get all of our concerns immediately out in the open. (t) _____

11. I try to do what is necessary to avoid tensions. (u) _____

    I usually let the other person have some of their wishes if they let me have some of mine. (v) _____

12. I usually work to soothe the other person's feelings to preserve our relationship. (w) _____

    I am usually quite firm in pursuing my goals. (x) _____

13. I try to avoid taking positions that would create a controversy. (y) _____

    I usually press to get my points across. (z) _____

14. I usually try to get the other person's help in working out a solution. (aa) _____

    I sometimes give up my own wishes for the desires of the other person. (bb) _____

15. I try to get all of our concerns immediately out in the open. (cc) _____

    I try to do what is necessary to avoid tensions. (dd) _____

Step 2   Score the survey by entering the score you have given to each of the statements and then total the scores for each column.

I	II	III	IV	V
(a) _____	(b) _____	(c) _____	(d) _____	(f) _____
(j) _____	(i) _____	(h) _____	(e) _____	(g) _____
(m) _____	(k) _____	(o) _____	(l) _____	(n) _____
(p) _____	(q) _____	(r) _____	(t) _____	(u) _____
(s) _____	(x) _____	(w) _____	(aa) _____	(y) _____
(v) _____	(z) _____	(bb) _____	(cc) _____	(dd) _____
═══	═══	═══	═══	═══

These scores reflect your perception of your use of various conflict-handling styles. Your highest total suggests a preferred style; however, we all have the potential to apply various conflict-management approaches depending on the situation. The various styles are labeled I, compromising; II, forcing; III, accommodating; IV, collaborating; and V, avoiding.

The following steps are optional and may be used at the discretion of your instructor.

Step 3 Read the following brief incident, then join others in your class to discuss this situation and propose a plan of action to resolve it.

> *Seville Electronics manufactures various computer components to be used in a variety of industrial and military applications. All parts must be produced according to exacting standards.*
>
> *Stuart Van Ault was hired recently as vice-president of production. Last week he toured the plant and was stopped by one of the production supervisors. This supervisor was visibly upset and shouted, "I'm glad you're here. We can't get anything done with the quality of materials we have to work with and the people personnel sends us!" Stuart was taken aback by this outburst. He asked the supervisor to visit him after work to discuss these problems.*
>
> *When they met, the supervisor explained that they were having to send more and more materials back to their suppliers because they didn't meet Seville's exacting quality standards. He felt that these standards were unrealistic and that quality control was messing up. The supervisor also complained about the lack of skilled, reliable help. Both absenteeism and turnover were running above industry norms. Finally, he pointed out that various production runs were halted in favor of some other components that, according to the sales department, had to be run immediately.*

Step 4 Each group will be asked to report its plan of action. Select one member of your group to act as spokesperson. Be as specific as possible in describing what you would do and why. Look for the implications of these plans for conflict management.

Source: Written by Bruce Kemelgor, University of Louisville.

Notes

1. K.W. Thomas, "Organizational Conflict," in *Organizational Behavior,* S. Kerr, ed. (Columbus, Ohio: Grid, 1979).
2. S.P. Robbins, *Managing Organizational Conflict* (Englewood Cliffs, N.J.: Prentice-Hall, 1974).
3. Ibid.
4. M. Dalton, *Men Who Manage* (New York: John Wiley & Sons, 1959).
5. J.M. Rabbie and F. Bekkers, "Threatened Leadership and Intergroup Competition," *European Journal of Social Psychology* 8 (1978): 19–20.
6. L. Festinger, *Theory of Cognitive Dissonance* (Evanston, Ill.: Free Press, 1957).
7. R.D. Luce and H. Raiffa, *Games and Decisions* (New York: Wiley, 1957), p. 95.
8. M. Sherif, *In Common Predicament: Social Psychology of Intragroup Conflict and Cooperation* (Boston: Houghton Mifflin, 1966).
9. Robbins, *Managing Organizational Conflict.*
10. J. Lowell, "GMAD: Lowdown at Lordstown," *Ward's Auto World,* April 1972, 29.
11. L.A. Allen, "The Line–Staff Relationship," *Management Record* 17 (1955): 346–349; E.C. Schleh, "Using Central Staff to Boost Line Initiative," *Management Review* 65 (1976): 17–23.
12. Thomas, "Organizational Conflict."
13. J.W. Galbraith, *Designing Complex Organizations* (Reading, Mass.: Addison-Wesley, 1973).
14. R.T. Keller and W.E. Holland, "Boundary-spanning Activity and Research and Development Management: A Comparative Study," *IEEE Transactions and Engineering Management* (1975): 130–133.
15. Robbins, *Managing Organizational Conflict.*

CHAPTER 14

The fast track in business: B.B.A., M.B.A., C.E.O. . . . D.O.A.

— Jim Fisk and Robert Barron

If my doctor told me I had only 6 months to live, I wouldn't brood, I'd type a little faster.

— Isaac Asimov

Learning Objectives

After studying this chapter, you should be able to:

1. *Define stress.*

2. *Explain various views of job-related stress.*

3. *Identify personal causes of stress.*

4. *List organizational causes of stress.*

5. *Describe typical reactions to stress.*

6. *List ways of managing stress.*

7. *Explain the concept of a wellness program.*

Stress

■ The High Cost of Stress

A high-level executive at a midwestern company was prospering until the changes began. First, his company promoted him to a position with twice his former work load. Then his child, who has an incurable disease, became seriously ill.

At that point, the executive felt overwhelmed. "It's like you're a live wire with no insulation," he explained. "The slightest little nudge, and you spark. . . . Even when the phone rings, it irritates you. You don't eat right or sleep well." During a single week, the executive told off three of his superiors, including the company's chief executive officer, in public. At that point, he was demoted and threatened with firing. Fortunately, his colleagues told top management about the child's illness, saving his job.

Most stories are less dramatic, but stress affects employees at all levels, especially in these days of corporate mergers, restructuring, and cutbacks. Baby boomers may be at relatively greater risk of

suffering the effects of stress because they are more mobile, less religious, marry later, and have fewer children than other people. This means they have fewer support systems that can help people cope.

Stress generally accompanies change, but its effects are especially noticeable when a crisis hits. For example, when the stock market plunged in October 1987, a recession began on Wall Street. Within weeks of the crash, 15,000 people were laid off (with layoffs and shrinking bonuses continuing two years later). The following spring, brokers, traders, and analysts at the major Wall Street firms were complaining of chronic insomnia, irritability, tension, and worry.

Similarly, when Baxter Travenol Laboratories merged with American Hospital Supply Corporation in 1985, managers from both companies were required to reapply for jobs in the merged organization. This process was more than a formality; 4,000

jobs were eliminated. Reports Anthony J. Rucci, "Anecdotally, I can guarantee that the degree of alcohol, drug, and child abuse went up."

Some people respond to stress by coming down with minor illnesses; others turn to alcohol and drugs. When stress goes untreated, it also can lead to such serious illnesses as depression and anxiety.

Why should organizations be concerned about this problem? One reason is that stress is expensive. According to estimates, businesses spend $150 billion annually on stress-related problems and mental illness by bearing such costs as lost productivity, health insurance, and disability claims.

In response, over 90 percent of the nation's largest companies have instituted a form of employee assistance or wellness program designed to counteract stress. Unfortunately, such programs rarely address the company-based sources of stress. For example, a

California employee-assistance manager notes that the companies that encourage stress management may be the same ones that "set unrealistic deadlines for their employees or put them in work overload for long periods of time with no relief."

Clearly, managing stress is an organizational challenge that has yet to be overcome. This chapter examines what stress is, what causes it, and how people in the workplace feel and behave when they are under stress. The chapter concludes with ideas for coping with stress.

Sources: Sana Siwolop, "The Crippling Ills That Stress Can Trigger," *Business Week,* April 18, 1988, pp. 77–78; Emily T. Smith, "Stress: The Test Americans Are Failing," *Business Week,* April 18, 1988, pp. 74–76.

From our daily experiences, we all know that conflict-filled situations produce feelings of physical and psychological discomfort. When a person is confronted with a situation that poses a threat (as when extreme conflict arises), the form of physiological and emotional arousal he or she experiences is termed **stress**. Prolonged exposure to stressful situations is believed to produce serious dysfunctional influences that can affect job performance. In this chapter, we will examine the principal causes of stress, reactions to stress, and techniques for coping with stress.

Views of Job-related Stress

As early as 1700, Bernardino Rammazini (the father of occupational medicine) had described in detail how certain diseases were associated with different types of work.[1] Presaging current ecological views, he advocated prevention rather than simple treatment of occupational illness. In the early 1900s, psychologist Hugo Munsterberg studied the effects of fatigue in various occupations.[2] Based on his findings, he recommended the institution of rest periods to improve morale, reduce fatigue, and thereby raise productivity. More recently, Dr. Hans Selye identified three distinct stages of a person's response to stress: alarm, resistance, and exhaustion.[3] These three stages define a **General Adaptation Syndrome** associated with stress.

In the alarm stage of the stress response, muscles tense, respiration rate increases, and blood pressure and heart rate increase. Following this stage, a person experiences anxiety, anger, and fatigue. These responses indicate that the person is resisting stress. During this resistance stage, the person may make poor decisions or experience illnesses. Because a person cannot sustain this resistance indefinitely, exhaustion occurs (see Figure 14.1). During this exhaustion stage, the individual develops such stress-induced illnesses as headaches and ulcers. Also, the capacity to respond to other work-related demands is greatly reduced. Although a person may be able to respond effectively to a threat during one of the earlier stages in this reaction, being unable to cope with a threat in the later stages can have serious detrimental effects for the individual. Selye's view suggests that all people go through the same pattern of response and that all people can tolerate only so much stress before a serious, debilitating condition of exhaustion occurs.

■   **Figure 14.1**

The General Adaptation Syndrome

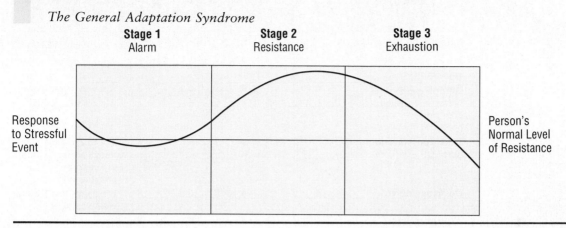

The three-stage response to stress described above is sometimes termed the "fight or flight" response. It is an automatic form of response to threat that once served our species well when our primary concerns were finding food and protection from wild animals. In ancient times, the powerful stress reaction was an aid in quickly responding by either fighting or swiftly fleeing from a predator. In the modern world, however, persistent forms of stress (for example, unresolved social problems) have a powerful effect on the nervous system of an individual without achieving resolution. Consider the lingering discomfort that results when an employee is harshly reprimanded by his or her supervisor. In such a situation, neither fighting with one's boss nor fleeing from the situation is an appropriate response. Nonetheless, the employee's physiological response prepares him or her to take some form of action when none may be possible. In essence, our physiological response to stress is no longer correct for many situations we currently face.

Despite the drawbacks of stress, its complete or near absence may be less than ideal for performance.[4] In situations where stress is low or absent, employees may not be sufficiently aroused or involved in their tasks. Instead, to maximize performance, low levels of stress are preferable because, in moderate amounts, stress can stimulate individuals to work harder and accomplish more. A certain amount of stress may thus be beneficial. Stress that has positive effects should be termed *eustress* (the prefix *eu*- is Greek for "good"). Eustress occurs when pressure for performance helps a person to achieve. When stress levels rise too high, however, employee performance is impaired. Extreme stress can leave workers feeling emotionally incapacitated, at least in the short run, and sap their energies and drive. The relationship between stress and employee performance follows the curve depicted in Figure 13.1 of the previous chapter.

Two experts in the area of job stress, John Ivancevich and Michael Matteson of the University of Houston, have outlined the major causes of stress as well as reactions to it.[5] In the two sections that follow, we will

■ **Table 14.1**

Self-Test for Type A or Type B Personality

To determine your personality type, circle the number that best represents your own behavior.

Am casual about appointments	1	2	3	4	5	6	7	8	Am never late
Am not competitive	1	2	3	4	5	6	7	8	Am very competitive
Never feel rushed, even under pressure	1	2	3	4	5	6	7	8	Always feel rushed
Take things one at a time	1	2	3	4	5	6	7	8	Try to do many things at once, think about what I am going to do next
Do things slowly	1	2	3	4	5	6	7	8	Do things fast (eating, walking, etc.)
Express feelings	1	2	3	4	5	6	7	8	"Sit" on feelings
Have many interests	1	2	3	4	5	6	7	8	Have few interests outside work

Total points _____ multiplied by 3 = _____ Final Score

Final Score	Personality Type
120 or more	A+
106 to 119	A
100 to 105	A−
90 to 99	B+
Below 90	B

Source: Adapted from R. W. Bortner, "A Short Rating Scale as a Potential Measure of Patterns of Behavior," *Journal of Chronic Diseases* 22 (1966): 87–91.

consider their summary of the major causes and consequences of stress. Following these sections, we will consider techniques for coping with stress.

Causes of Stress

Personal Factors

Type A Personality   Some people are more stress-prone than others. Especially susceptible are individuals who display a cluster of traits known as **type A personality.** Type As tend to be impatient, competitive individuals who feel that they are constantly under time pressure. They also tend to be aggressive, try to accomplish several things at the same time, and have difficulty relaxing. In contrast, individuals with the **type B personality** are relatively more mild-mannered, in less of a hurry, and far less competitive.[6]

In recent years, researchers have used personality tests to assess whether managers are type A or type B personalities. A simple example of one such test is presented in Table 14.1. When type A and type B managers were studied in terms of certain physical disorders, some interesting results arose. For example, Rosenman and Friedman found that type A men were twice as prone to heart disease and fatal heart attacks as type B individuals.[7] Of 133 coronary heart disease patients, Jenkins found that 94 were classifiable as type A person-alities.[8]

The same traits that predispose type A individuals to certain physical disorders also appear to predispose them to certain types of work. For exam-ple, 60 percent of a sample of managers could be clearly identified as type A while only 12 percent were clearly classifiable as type B.[9] Surprisingly, the characteristics that seem most helpful to type A individuals in their rise through managerial ranks (such as persistence, fanatic observance of dead-lines, and the like) do not aid them in their performance as top-level managers. Rather, it appears that type B individuals have better performance records in top management positions. The relaxed and patient attitude of type B individ-uals appears to give them a better perspective on running large organizations. This evidence may seem to suggest that once people reach the top of their professions they should abandon type A behaviors and switch to type B. How-ever, the tendency to display type A traits is fairly well engrained in such individuals, and they find it very hard to adopt the type B behavior.

Changes in One's Life   Another personal factor that can produce stress is both the magnitude and the frequency of changes in an individual's life. For example, a major change such as getting fired or the death of a spouse can have a strong impact on a person's health. The frequent occurrence of many less dramatic changes over a short period of time can also have a negative effect. In studying this phenomenon, Holmes and Rahe compiled a list of life changes that are especially stressful and devised a weighting system that reflects the relative severity of each event (Table 14.2).[10] If a person experiences the equiv-alent of more than 150 points of stressfulness in one year, there appears to be a better than 50 percent chance that he or she will suffer a serious physical disorder during the following year. The chance of illness increases to 80 per-cent for scores that exceed 300.

Organizational Factors

Responsibility for Others   Alan McLean, a medical researcher, has reviewed a variety of studies suggesting that having responsibility, in general, can lead to greater stress.[11] Beyond that, having responsibility for *other people,* rather than responsibility for the other features of an enterprise, can be highly stress-ful.* For managers who deal with people, the stress associated with recogniz-ing the impact of their actions on others' lives is more immediate and real than it is for managers who deal with things and ideas.

* In an experiment sometimes called the "executive monkey" study, two rhesus monkeys were strapped into electrified chairs. Five seconds after the illumination of a red warning light, both monkeys received mild electric shocks. After learning that the light served as a warning of the impending shock, an arm of one of the monkeys was released so that he could reach a lever, which would prevent both monkeys from being shocked. After a time, the monkey that had the opportu-nity to reach the lever came to control the occurrence of the shock reliably. The monkey with the responsibility (the "executive monkey") had to remain constantly vigilant. When the experiment was over, researchers examined the intestinal tracts of both monkeys. The "executive monkey" had begun to develop ulcers, while the companion monkey had not experienced intestinal distress.

■ Table 14.2

Relative Weights of Life Changes

Life Event	Scale Value
Death of spouse	100
Divorce	73
Marital separation	65
Jail term	63
Death of a close family member	63
Major personal injury or illness	53
Marriage	50
Fired from work	47
Marital reconciliation	45
Retirement	45
Major change in health of family member	44
Pregnancy	40
Sex difficulties	39
Gain of a new family member	39
Business readjustment	39
Change in financial state	38
Death of a close friend	37
Change to a different line of work	36
Change in number of arguments with spouse	35
Mortgage or loan for major purchase (home, etc.)	31
Foreclosure of mortgage or loan	30
Change in responsibilities at work	29
Son or daughter leaving home	29
Trouble with in-laws	29
Outstanding personal achievement	28
Spouse begins or stops work	26
Begin or end school	26
Change in living conditions	25
Revision of personal habits	24
Trouble with boss	23
Change in work hours or conditions	20
Change in residence	20
Change in schools	20
Change in recreation	19
Change in church activities	19
Change in social activities	18
Mortgage or loan for lesser purchase (car, etc.)	17
Change in sleeping habits	16
Change in number of family get-togethers	15
Change in eating habits	15
Vacation	13
Christmas	12
Minor violations of the law	11

Source: T.H. Holmes and L.O. Rahe, "Scaling of Life Change: Composition of Direct and Indirect Methods," *Journal of Psychosomatic Research* 15 (1971).

■   **Table 14.3**

High-stress versus Low-stress Jobs

High-stress Jobs	Low-stress Jobs
Construction laborer	Craft workers
Secretary	Stock handlers
Inspector	College professors
Office manager	Heavy equipment operators
Foreman	
Waitress/Waiter	

Working Conditions   The work environment also plays a role in determining the amount of stress an employee experiences. Certain occupations are noted for the high levels of stress they entail. As you might imagine, it is truly difficult to prove conclusively that one occupation is more stressful than another. Nonetheless, in one fairly direct attempt to study the possible link of occupation to illness, the health records of over 22,000 employees in the state of Tennessee were examined for stress-related disorders. The results of comparisons for over 100 occupations revealed the existence of significant differences (see Table 14.3).[12] Stress was found to be generally greater in such jobs as construction laborer, secretary, inspector, office manager, foreman, waitress/waiter, mine operative, air traffic controller, and clinical lab technician. In contrast, stress was relatively low for craft workers, stock handlers, college professors, and heavy equipment operators. In addition, the researchers found that occupational status level was not significantly related to stress-related disorders, that is, both white-collar *and* blue-collar employees and skilled *and* unskilled workers showed high and low incidences of disorders.

Other research has linked the repetitive and "dehumanizing" work environment created by assembly lines to health-related disorders. One study of 4,000 industrial workers reported that employees in companies using assembly-line technology were more likely to show evidence of early coronary heart disease than were employees involved in other work technologies. Piecework systems have similarly been implicated. Piecework systems generally lead to higher productivity than do other pay systems, but the toll on the employee can be questioned. For example, the number of accidents is also higher under piece-rate systems than under salaried systems.[13]

The absence of intrinsically enjoyable and rewarding work is associated with feelings of stress, as is being overloaded. For example, a correlation has been found between tax deadlines and illness for accountants.[14]

Role Conflict   **Role conflict** occurs when two or more sets of demands are made on an employee so that compliance with one set of demands makes it more difficult to comply with another.[15] In essence, an employee is expected to perform contradictory, or conflicting, activities. For example, a supervisor may

An Inside Look

Entrepreneurial Couples: Double the Stress

Starting a business is a stress-provoking way to make a living. The hours are long, the responsibility tremendous, the future uncertain. But some couples are willing to risk the even greater stress of starting a business together.

While mom-and-pop stores have been around for years, the pattern is extending to more complex enterprises as women increasingly move into management and professional careers. These couples risk bringing the tension of the workplace home *and* bringing the tensions of home to the workplace. They must sort out their roles; the way responsibility is shared in a marriage may not work out as well in a business that requires more of a hierarchy of responsibility. As a result of such stresses, working together can destroy both the marriage and the business.

Still, some entrepreneurial couples are finding success and happiness. One strategy is to make sure the roles at work are clearly defined and based on talents rather than gender stereotypes. Susan and Michael Morgan, for example, founded Softview Inc., a computer software concern. Susan served as chief executive while her husband focused on software design. "I was the one better suited to running the company," she explains. "Mike's the shy type. He's more comfortable designing the product and explaining it to me." When Susan wanted to focus on developing and marketing a new product, the Morgans hired an outsider to serve as chief executive.

Similarly, when William Carrico and Judith Estrin started Network Computing Devices, they agreed, in Carrico's words, that "there had to be a CEO and that was me." Estrin agrees that the arrangement is optimal because her husband has more experience. Besides, she adds, "If a couple's ever going to work together, they have to decide who's boss early."

Couples may also look for other ways to minimize stress. For example, they may choose not to emphasize rapid growth, thereby avoiding the intense commitment to work that such a strategy requires. John McClelland and Linda Seaverson decided to develop MTEC Photoacoustics, their high-tech instrument company, gradually. That strategy allows them to balance research with growth, to manage the company themselves, and to spend time with their two young children. As the children get older, McClelland and Seaverson intend to plan for more ambitious expansion.

Source: Udayan Gupta, "And Business Makes Three: Couples Working Together," *The Wall Street Journal*, February 26, 1990, p. B2.

find that his superior expects increased productivity from his department, while his subordinates expect his support in finding ways to reduce their daily quota. Likewise, a college faculty member may find that she is expected to devote significant amounts of time to preparing and delivering lectures, while at the same time she is expected to publish in highly competitive scholarly journals. If possible, one may resolve the conflict by devoting more time and energy to the most pressing demand in a given situation (for instance, by preparing a lecture as the time for a class approaches). It is well established that employee job satisfaction decreases as role conflict increases.[16] In addition, role conflict has been found to be connected with heart disease, high blood pressure, elevated cholesterol, and obesity.[17] Furthermore, abilities to make high-quality decisions and to be creative are likely to be impaired in situations containing a high degree of role conflict.

Role Ambiguity   **Role ambiguity** refers to the absence of clarity regarding how to perform one's job. Ambiguity or uncertainty may surround knowing what goals to set and how to best achieve them, and determining one's level of accomplishment. Initially, all newly hired employees experience some degree of role ambiguity when they are assigned to their tasks. However, some jobs are consistently more lacking in clarity concerning how to perform them. For example, managerial jobs generally lack a specific, well-defined set of activities that are to be routinely carried out. Project team managers are also likely to experience greater degrees of uncertainty, especially in the early stages of work.

Role ambiguity is closely associated with a variety of negative consequences. As with role conflict, decreased job satisfaction is thought to be a result of increased role ambiguity. In addition, lower levels of self-confidence, decreased satisfaction with life in general, and increased expression of intentions to quit have been found to be correlated with role ambiguity.[18]

Role Overload   In addition to conflict and ambiguity, role processes can play a part as a source of stress in yet a third fashion: role overload. **Role overload** occurs when too many activities are expected of an employee, given the time available and the ability level of the employee. Indications of role overload include working in excess of sixty hours a week, holding down two jobs, and foregoing vacations. Being in a situation where one lacks the necessary time to perform required tasks has been found to be a possible cause of increased blood cholesterol levels.[19] Furthermore, overload has been found to be related to job dissatisfaction, lower self-esteem, increased heart rate, and increased cigarette consumption.[20]

Shift Work   Approximately 20 percent of the U.S. work force is involved in rotating (afternoon and evening) work schedules as opposed to fixed daytime work schedules.[21] Certain services must be available twenty-four hours a day, and hence require shifts. Firefighters, police officers, medical and military personnel, and utility operators, for example, must work in shifts around the clock. Because of the unpopularity of afternoon and evening shifts, many employers find it necessary to rotate staff through shifts.

Shift rotation, understandably, has an adverse influence on sleeping patterns and on opportunities for normal social activities. However, the range of adverse consequences of shift work is substantial. Table 14.4 lists a number of these problems.[22]

Reactions to Stress

Physical Problems

As suggested above, a high level of stress has been associated with a host of physical disorders, including heart disease, arthritis, ulcers, high blood pressure, and high levels of cholesterol.[23] There is also some suspicion that stress may be linked to cancer.[24]

■ **Table 14.4**

Stress Symptoms Associated with Shift Work

Fatigue
Difficulty obtaining sleep
Disturbances in appetite, digestion, and elimination
Increased divorce rate
Increased incidence of sexual problems
Reduced involvement in social and religious organizations
Reduced contact with friends
Lowered productivity
Increased accidents
Reduced commitment to the organization

While it is impossible to quantify the personal cost of serious physical ailments for an individual, it is possible to estimate the cost of such problems for an organization. For example, Ivancevich and Matteson have created a worksheet for estimating the yearly costs associated with replacing employees lost to heart disease.[25] For a company that employs 4,000 people, the estimates would be:

1.	Number of employees	4,000
2.	Men in age range 45 to 65 (0.25 × line 1)	1,000
3.	Estimated deaths due to heart disease per year (0.006 × line 2)	6
4.	Estimated premature retirement due to heart problems per year (0.003 × line 2)	3
5.	Company's annual personnel losses due to heart disorders (sum of lines 3 and 4)	9
6.	Annual replacement cost: the average cost of hiring and training replacements for experienced employees (line 5 × $4,300)	$38,700

As these figures suggest, heart disease can be a significant cost to an organization, and the absolute number of employees who are likely to die eventually of heart disease is not trivial. Furthermore, the additional costs of hospitalization coverage, lost wages, and lost performance are not included in the above estimate.

To be sure, a single organization cannot assume full responsibility for all employee deaths due to heart disease. In addition to work-related stress, many other factors play a role in the development of heart disease, including heredity, diet, and general state of well-being.

Alcoholism and Drug Abuse

The National Institute on Alcohol Abuse and Alcoholism estimates that between 6 and 10 percent of all employees are alcoholics. Although drug usage is not as widespread as alcohol abuse, it is nonetheless a serious problem. Both alcohol and drug abuse are linked to higher levels of stress among employees. In addition to threatening their own well-being, employees who attend work while under the influence of alcohol or drugs pose a serious threat to the well-being of their coworkers because they are more prone to on-the-job accidents.

Absenteeism, Turnover, and Dissatisfaction

Research reviews by Porter and Steers, Steers and Rhodes, and Mobley and colleagues have generally pointed to a relationship between stress and increases in such withdrawal behaviors as absenteeism and turnover.[26] A correlation has also been found between dissatisfaction and work-related stress.[27] Because these studies of stress as a predictor of turnover, absenteeism, and dissatisfaction have all been correlational in nature, it is difficult to state conclusively what factors are responsible for the relationship (see Chapter 2).

Mass Psychogenic Illness

Perhaps one of the strangest suspected responses to the experience of stress is the occurrence of **mass psychogenic illness.** One report of such an instance stated that 30 workers in an electronics assembly facility complained for two weeks of headaches, sleepiness, nausea, and dizziness. Another report involved 27 women in an aluminum furniture assembly plant. Although no chemicals were used in the assembly process, these women reported symptoms of dizziness, lightheadedness, dry mouth, and a bad taste in the mouth after smelling a strange odor. Other employees stated that they had seen a "blue mist" in one section of the plant. As word spread, a near panic among the 300-plus employees resulted in a temporary shutdown of the plant. Despite these problems, an analysis of air samples yielded no evidence of toxic chemicals or other agents. When the plant reopened a few days later, 27 employees (19 of whom were not involved in the initial hysteria) reported similar symptoms.

In a third reported incident, 35 employees in a frozen-fish packing plant complained of headaches, dizziness, and difficulty in breathing shortly after their shift began. A few years earlier, a carbon monoxide leak in the plant had affected several employees, yet the recent symptoms were not those of carbon monoxide exposure. Furthermore, a detecting–recording device showed that the level of carbon monoxide in the air where the employees complained was well below the level necessary to create ill effects.[28]

In the Middle Ages, such outbreaks might have been labeled "demon possessions."† Much later they were termed "assembly-line hysteria" or "epidemic hysteria," and today, such events are called "mass psychogenic reactions." Occupational health professionals are beginning to examine possible causes, and chief among the suspects is work-related stress. Further investigations have suggested that the actual incidence of mass psychogenic illness may be much greater than reported in the medical literature.[29] The number of such outbreaks may be expected to increase as work-related stress combines with

---

† And a few people would probably have been burned at the stake in order to remove the demons and get on with the business at hand.

■ Table 14.5

The Burnout Checklist

	Mostly True	Mostly False
1. I feel tired more frequently than I used to.	_____	_____
2. I snap at people too often.	_____	_____
3. Trying to help other people often seems hopeless.	_____	_____
4. I seem to be working harder but accomplishing less.	_____	_____
5. I get down on myself too often.	_____	_____
6. My job is beginning to depress me.	_____	_____
7. I often feel I'm headed nowhere.	_____	_____
8. I've reached (or am fast reaching) a dead end in my job.	_____	_____
9. I've lost a lot of my zip lately.	_____	_____
10. It's hard for me to laugh at a joke about myself.	_____	_____
11. I'm not really physically ill, but I have a lot of aches and pains.	_____	_____
12. Lately I've kind of withdrawn from friends and family.	_____	_____
13. My enthusiasm for life is on the wane.	_____	_____
14. I'm running out of things to say to people.	_____	_____
15. My temper is much shorter than it used to be.	_____	_____
16. My job makes me feel sad.	_____	_____

Interpretation: The more of these questions you can honestly answer mostly true, the more likely it is that you are experiencing burnout. If you answered twelve or more of these statements mostly true, it is likely you are experiencing burnout or another form of mental depression. If so, discuss these feelings with a physical or mental health professional.

Source: A.J. DuBrin, *Contemporary Applied Management*, Plano, Texas; Business Publications, 1982; p. 243. Reprinted with permission. The checklist is based in part on the questionnaire printed on the dust jacket of *Burn Out* by Freudenberger.

greater employee awareness of and sensitivity to issues of toxic chemical exposure and environmental protection.

Burnout — A Companion Problem

Like stress, **burnout** is a reaction to prolonged and energy-depleting difficulties. Its primary symptoms include feeling drained or used up. It typically affects people who are highly conscientious and work in the helping professions, such as police officers, schoolteachers, social workers, and nurses. At some point, such employees may come to feel that they are not receiving the rewards that they expected for their efforts to help others. Their frustration leads to feelings of apathy and failure, which may result in physical symptoms such as high blood pressure and ulcers, and mental symptoms such as depression and irritability. In many respects, burnout and stress are highly similar reactions. A checklist for assessing burnout is presented in Table 14.5.

Coping With Stress

Helping a person maintain the level of stress that is best for him or her is the goal of various stress management techniques. By and large, the techniques we will consider focus primarily on the reduction rather than the increase of stress.

Flight or Fight

Flight and fight are two reactions that can serve as a primary means of successful coping. *Flight,* or leaving a distressing situation, is a perfectly reasonable response to stress if an avenue of flight is available. For example, some individuals try their hand at supervising others and find that they simply do not like it. This is not to say that they cannot handle the job, but rather that they prefer other types of assignments or activities. For such individuals, the recognition of this personal preference is an important and useful insight that can help them cope with the stress that may accompany supervisory responsibilities.

Fight, or confronting a threat or stressor, can also be an effective response. The desire to confront a threat may actually be the best way to bring about a change that will reduce the level of stress. For example, the urge to fight may lead an employee to confront her superior on an issue that has been bothering her for some time. The confrontation may then lead to a workable resolution.‡

Exercise

Physical exercise, including participation in sports, enables a person to develop resistance to the detrimental effects of stress. Exercise can both improve health and reduce fatigue. Fatigue plays a key role in stress-producing situations because people who are feeling fatigued are more apt to overreact to frustration. Therefore, tolerance for frustration can be increased by being in better physical health. Regular exercise is also thought to be of value in reducing the likelihood of coronary diseases. Some large organizations, such as Tenneco, Weyerhauser, Johns-Manville, and Exxon, provide a gymnasium at company headquarters to promote employee fitness.

Social Support

One means of resisting stress is to have a strong network of social supports. Studies indicate that the availability of sympathetic others (especially co-workers) can help a person deal with job-related stress.[30] The reassurance derived from knowing that others can be called on to help when needed can be invaluable.

Job Redesign

Jobs can be redesigned to minimize the creation of stress. One approach to job redesign that seeks to reduce assembly-line pressures and the dull, repetitive aspects of such work is job enrichment. As discussed in Chapter 7, one way in which job enrichment makes a task more attractive is by giving greater autonomy (usually self-pacing) to the individual worker. Such autonomy is critical to alleviating feelings of pressure and the resultant stress. Two other common ways of reducing stress are to provide employees with opportunities to participate in decision making and to improve communication, both of which can reduce workers' feelings of helplessness and dependence.

‡ Of course, it might also lead to her dismissal.

Relaxation Techniques

Relaxation techniques such as progressive relaxation, yoga, and Transcendental Meditation rely on the idea that relaxation of the major voluntary muscles reduces anxiety levels. The goal of these techniques is to achieve a state of physiological and psychological rest, and evidence suggests that such improvements can in fact result.[31] Although some corporations (such as New York Telephone Company and Metropolitan Life Insurance) are beginning to explore the sponsored use of relaxation techniques for their managers,[32] evidence of the effectiveness of these techniques within organizational settings is not yet available.

Developing a New Philosophy of Life

One technique for coping with stress is to develop a philosophy of life that incorporates a more tolerant and broader view of life (versus the "looking out for number one" perspective). In order to achieve a new perspective, some individuals turn to philosophical exercises for enlightenment and understanding. Some approaches to achieving a greater acceptance of oneself and others rely on Eastern thought (such as Taoist or Buddhist philosophy) for insights not found in Western thought.[33]

Siu, a consultant in the field of strategy and decision critique, has offered a set of guidelines that exemplify this approach to seeking contemplative insights. He has designed the following list of proverbs to guide the "journeyman-executive" who wishes to become a "philosopher-executive."[34]

Five proverbs for planning are

1. The bird hunting the locust is unaware of the hawk hunting him.
2. The mouse with but one hole is easily taken.
3. In shallow waters, shrimps make fools of dragons.
4. Do not try to catch two frogs with one hand.
5. Give the bird room to fly.

Four proverbs for operations are

1. Do not insult the crocodile until you have crossed the river.
2. It is better to struggle with a sick jackass than carry the wood yourself.
3. Do not throw stone at mouse and break precious vase.
4. It is not the last blow of the ax that fells the tree.

Such time-proven proverbs are intended to provide a challenging and provocative stimulus to rethinking one's view of stressful situations. As suggested by McLean, a consideration of one's job circumstances from a slightly altered perspective can help to restore a sense of balance.[35]

Time Management: A Practical Approach to Reducing Stress

One especially useful strategy for coping with job-related stress is effective **time management.** An inability to manage time can result in overcommitment, a lack of planning, and missed deadlines. Strictly speaking, one does not manage time as such, in that time moves at its own rate and is not subject to any effort to manipulate it. In truth, effective time management is really effective self-management. Time-management specialists have developed a number of useful techniques for gaining control over one's work life and, thereby, one's sanity.[36]

Time Log   The first step in trying to manage one's time is to develop a time log, or inventory. By jotting down the events that occur in a typical day with the time required for each activity, it is possible to learn where one's time is being spent. The results of a time log (which might be reviewed at the end of a week) can offer surprising insights. For example, some executives are amazed to find that a large percentage of each day is devoted to dealing with interruptions and pointless socializing. The results of such an inventory can help pinpoint sources of time wastage and thus help focus attention on using time more effectively.

Structuring Time   One can gain greater control over one's life by structuring the day so that time wasters are blocked or eliminated. For example, not being accessible by phone or to visitors for an hour or two in the morning provides a block of uninterrupted time during which mail can be read or writing can be done. Similarly, all visits can be arranged between 2:00 and 4:00 in the afternoon. Meetings can be strategically set one-half hour or an hour before lunch or quitting time to ensure that the participants will help complete the meeting on time.

Just Say No   Sometimes an employee is victimized by a desire to be accommodating to everyone. In such instances, others learn that their requests are seldom refused by such an employee and may take advantage of his or her good nature. For such individuals, an important step in gaining control of their lives is to learn how to say no to requests for their time and energy. Refusing the requests of others requires some delicacy, and should be done politely but firmly. For people who are already heavily committed to their primary job duties, taking on the added responsibility of managing the office baseball team and the fund-raising drive will largely provide needless stress.

Make a List   One of the most useful techniques for managing time is to prepare a list of "things to do." Interviews with highly effective managers reveal that they invariably maintain a planning list of activities that aids their memories and focuses their attention and energy. A planning list contains such items as phone calls that must be returned, correspondence that must be prepared, meetings that need to be scheduled, and projects that must be monitored. In addition, the items on the list should be prioritized. The most critical items are labeled "category A," while the next most critical items are labeled "category B," and so on. Then, category A items are handled first, category B items are tackled if time permits, and lower-category items are put off until even later. In maintaining a "to-do" list, it is important to keep the list current, to never give in to the temptation to clean up the "small" or "easy" items first,

OB Focus

Rubbing Stress Away

SNI Companies of Flourtown, Pennsylvania, which provides nurses and consultants to the health care industry, can't afford to build a gym for an employee wellness program. Instead, the company has Harris Fishkin.

Fishkin has the unusual role of full-time corporate masseur at SNI. Every week or every other week, each of SNI's 60 Flourtown employees receives Fishkin's standard 15-minute massage of the back, head, and neck. Employees sit in a small, darkened room, leaning forward on a specially designed chair and listening to New Age music. Fishkin also travels to the Albert Einstein Medical Center in Philadelphia once a week to give massages to SNI's eight critical-care nurses there.

This stress-reduction benefit, known as on-site massage (OSM),

became known to the corporate world when David Palmer, who devised OSM, introduced it to Apple Computer in the early 1980s. Now OSM is available to at least some workers at over 30 companies, including American Airlines, AT&T, H. J. Heinz Company, and Pillsbury. The number of OSM practitioners has grown from about 100 since the technique's introduction to over 3,000.

The practice might catch on even faster, except that some managers view massage as having a dubious connotation associated with X-rated massage parlors. In fact, OSM is intended to be strictly therapeutic and involves no undressing or oils. Advocates of the technique claim that it increases blood circulation, stimulates the lymphatic system, calms the autonomic nervous system, reduces lactic acid in the

muscles (allowing them to stay relaxed), and boosts productivity and morale. Lynn Fauerbach, an employee of SNI, credits her weekly massages with putting an end to severe headaches.

Some preliminary data, while only suggestive, support the idea that massage is an effective stress-reduction technique. A dozen nurses at two Philadelphia-area hospitals took a standardized stress test and then received a series of six massages. When they retook the stress test, 10 of the nurses (83 percent) scored lower on stress. Eleven of the nurses received another six massages; afterward, ten of them (90 percent) showed even less stress as measured by the test.

If further evidence supports the benefits of OSM, perhaps regular back rubs will eventually become part of the daily work routine.

Source: Sandy Bauers, "There's the Rub: Masseurs Tackle Stress on Job," *Chicago Tribune*, February 19, 1990, sec. 4, p. 3.

and to scrutinize the list for items that can be reasonably delegated to subordinates.

Wellness Programs

Following a discussion of work-related stress, it is fitting to recognize the growth of the "wellness" movement in the United States and Canada. The movement represents a proactive rather than reactive approach to the issue of health management. Prevention, the core notion of the wellness movement, has gained recognition as a wise investment as employers are faced with the burden of the rising cost of health care. In essence, it is more prudent to promote employee health, or wellness, than to cope with illness. **Wellness programs** involve educating employees on health-risk factors (e.g., smoking, obesity, poor nutrition), providing physical exams (e.g., blood pressure checks), and offering plans for assisting employees in reducing health risks. The variety of existing wellness programs is quite broad. Some organizations simply distribute literature to employees regarding health-related topics, while others provide on-site exercise equipment and uniforms.

Control Data Corporation's "Staywell Program" provides an outstanding example of a wellness program. The program, which is available to employees and their spouses at many company locations throughout the United States, includes medical screening, health education, and activities designed to change life-styles. The medical screening includes a physical exam, blood sampling, a blood pressure check, and a "computerized health-risk profile." Participants may also attend one-hour health-awareness courses that cover such topics as drug abuse and cancer detection. Programs designed to change life-styles focus on such issues as nutrition, obesity, hypertension, and smoking. In these programs, ongoing employee support groups are formed.

The Control Data wellness program has been credited for significant reductions in health-care costs due to decreased smoking and hypertension, and increased exercise. Absenteeism and time lost due to illness have also been reduced. Other corporations that have introduced wellness programs (such as Prudential Insurance, Johnson and Johnson, Campbell Soup, Tenneco, and Blue Cross–Blue Shield) have reported significant reductions in sickness rates and absenteeism, and improved job performance and work-related attitudes.[37]

Summary

1. Define stress.

Stress is the extreme physiological and emotional arousal a person experiences when confronted with a threatening situation.

2. Explain various views of job-related stress.

Hans Selye has proposed three stages that characterize a person's response to stress: alarm, resistance, and exhaustion. These stages constitute the General Adaptation Syndrome. Another view holds that a certain degree of stress may be beneficial in that it may increase achievement.

3. Identify personal causes of stress.

A major personal cause of stress is the possession of a type A personality. People with such a personality tend to be impatient and competitive. Another major personal cause of stress is change in one's life (e.g., death of a spouse or loss of a job).

4. List organizational causes of stress.

Organizational influences include having responsibility for others, being involved in shift work, and working in a stress-inducing occupation or dehumanizing work environment. Role conflict, role ambiguity, and role overload also contribute to the experience of stress.

5. Describe typical reactions to stress.

High levels of stress are associated with physical disorders, including heart disease, arthritis, ulcers, high blood pressure, high levels of cholesterol, and, possibly, cancer. Stress is linked to poor job performance, abuse of alcohol and other drugs, absenteeism, job turnover, worker dissatisfaction, mass psychogenic illness, and burnout.

6. List ways of managing stress.
People can manage stress by weighing the merits of fighting or fleeing a particular situation. Physical exercise and a strong network of social supports help people resist stress. Managers can redesign jobs to minimize the creation of stress. People can reduce stress by using time-management and relaxation techniques, and by developing a more tolerant and broader philosophy of life.

7. Explain the concept of a wellness program.
A wellness program focuses on the prevention of illness. Such programs educate employees about health-related issues, provide physical exams, and assist employees in reducing health risks.

Key Terms

Stress   Role overload
General Adaptation Syndrome   Mass psychogenic illness
Type A personality   Burnout
Type B personality   Time management
Role conflict   Wellness program
Role ambiguity

Review and Discussion Questions

1. What are type A personality characteristics? Do people with such personality types usually perform best as top-level managers?

2. What are some working conditions that are associated with stress among employees?

3. Lance Lucky marries the woman of his dreams. She is not only beautiful but also a successful cardiologist. With her income, they will easily be able to travel and live more comfortably than Lance ever imagined he would. They buy a comfortable house, taking out a $95,000 mortgage. Shortly after they move in, Lance receives a phone call; he has just been named "Realtor of the Year" in his community. He is ecstatic; it seems as though everything is going right. But when he goes to his doctor for a checkup, he learns that his blood pressure and cholesterol levels are both high. "I think it's stress," the doctor tells him. Lance is shocked at the diagnosis. How can Lance be suffering from stress when his life is going so well? Suggest ways he can cope with the stress.

4. What are the major techniques associated with time management? How do they help to reduce job-related stress?

5. Distinguish among role conflict, role ambiguity, and role overload.

6. Bill says that he gets nervous every time he has to make a presentation, and that he experiences "butterflies in the stomach" from the stress. Clayton tells Bill not to worry, that a certain amount of stress is

actually good for him. "The trick," he says, "is to get your butterflies to fly in formation." Can Clayton be correct in stating that stress can be beneficial?

7. Len is impatient and highly competitive, while Mel is very relaxed and easygoing. Assuming that Len and Mel typify the type A and type B personalities, what might they be like to work with as coworkers? As bosses?

8. Jobs can be characterized in terms of how stressful they are. Compare the high-stress jobs of office manager, waitress/waiter, and secretary with the low-stress jobs of stock handlers and college professors. What specific aspects of these jobs are responsible for creating differing degrees of stress?

9. What stress symptoms are associated with shift work? How might some of these symptoms be ameliorated?

■ **Critical Incident**

No Response from Monitor 23

Loudspeaker: IGNITION MINUS 45 MINUTES.

Paul Keller tripped the sequence switches at control monitor 23 in accordance with the countdown instruction book just to his left. All hydraulic systems were functioning normally in the second stage of the spacecraft booster at checkpoint I minus 45. Keller automatically snapped his master control switch to GREEN and knew that his electronic impulse along with hundreds of others from similar consoles within the Cape Kennedy complex signaled continuation of the countdown.

It used to be an incredible challenge, fantastically interesting work at the very fringe of knowledge about the universe. Keller recalled his first day in Brevard County, Florida, with his wife and young daughter. How happy they were that day. Here was the future, the good life . . . forever. And Keller was going to be part of that fantastic, utopian future.

Loudspeaker: IGNITION MINUS 35 MINUTES.

Keller panicked! His mind had wandered momentarily, and he lost his place in the countdown instructions. Seconds later, he found the correct place and tripped the proper sequence of switches for checkpoint I minus 35. No problem. Keller snapped the master control to GREEN and wiped his brow. He knew he was late reporting and would hear about it later.

Loudspeaker: IGNITION MINUS 30 MINUTES.

Keller completed the reporting sequence for checkpoint I minus 30 and took one long last drag on his cigarette. Utopia? Hell! It was one big rat race and getting bigger all the time. Keller recalled how he once naively felt that his problems with Naomi would disappear after they left Minneapolis and came to the Cape with the space program. Now, 10,000 arguments later, Keller knew there was no escape.

> *Only one can of beer left, Naomi? One stinking lousy can of beer, cold lunchmeat, and potato salad? Leftovers after 12 hours of mental exhaustion?*
>
> *Oh, shut up, Paul! I'm so sick of you playing Mr. Important. You get leftovers because I never know when you're coming home . . . your daughter hardly knows you . . . and you treat us like nobodies . . . incidental to your great Space Program.*
>
> *Don't knock it, Naomi. That job is plenty important to me, to the Team, and it gets you everything you've ever wanted . . . more! Between this house and the boat, we're up to our ears in debt.*
>
> *Now don't try to pin our money problems on me. You're the one who has to have all the same goodies as the scientists earning twice your salary. Face it, Paul. You're just a button-pushing technician regardless of how fancy a title they give you.*

Loudspeaker: IGNITION MINUS 25 MINUTES.

A red light blinked ominously indicating a potential hydraulic fluid leak in subsystem seven of stage two. Keller felt his heartbeat and pulse rate increase. Rule 1 . . . report malfunction immediately and stop the count. Keller punched POTENTIAL ABORT on the master control.

Loudspeaker: THE COUNT IS STOPPED AT IGNITION MINUS 24 MINUTES 17 SECONDS.

Keller fumbled with the countdown instructions. Any POTENTIAL ABORT required a cross-check to separate an actual malfunction from sporadic signal error. Keller began to perspire nervously as he initiated standard cross-check procedures.

"Monitor 23, this is Control. Have you got an actual abort, Paul?" The voice in the headset was cool, but impatient. "Decision required in 30 seconds."

"I know, I know," Keller mumbled, "I'm cross-checking right now."

Cross-check one proved inconclusive. Keller automatically followed detailed instructions for cross-check two.

"Do you need help, Keller?" asked the voice in the headset.

"No, I'm O.K."

"Decision required," demanded the voice in the headset. "Dependent systems must be deactivated in 15 seconds."

Keller read and reread the console data. It looked like a sporadic error signal.

"Decision required," demanded the voice in the headset.

"Continue count," blurted Keller at last. "Subsystem seven fully operational." Keller slumped back in his chair.

Loudspeaker: THE COUNT IS RESUMED AT IGNITION MINUS 24 MINUTES 17 SECONDS.

Keller knew that within an hour after lift-off, Barksdale would call him in for a personal conference. "What's wrong lately, Paul?" he would say. "Is there anything I can help with? You seem so tense lately." But he wouldn't really want to listen. Barksdale was the kind of person who read weakness into any personal problems and demanded that they be purged from one's mind.

More likely Barksdale would demand that Keller make endless practice runs on cross-check procedures while he stood nearby . . . watching and noting any errors . . . while the pressure grew and grew.

Loudspeaker: IGNITION MINUS 20 MINUTES.

The monitor lights at console 23 blinked routinely.

"Keller," said the voice in the earphone. "Report, please."

"Control, this is Wallace at monitor 24. I don't believe Keller is feeling well. Better send someone to cover fast!"

Loudspeaker: THE COUNT IS STOPPED AT 19 MINUTES 33 SECONDS.

"This is Control, Wallace. Assistance has been dispatched and the count is on temporary hold. What seems to be wrong with Keller?"

"Control, this is Wallace, I don't know. His eyes are open and fixed on the monitor, but he won't respond to my questions. It could be a seizure or . . . a stroke."

Questions

1. Is there any way of avoiding the more serious manifestations (as with Paul Keller) of pressure on the job? Explain.

2. Are there any early warning signs given by employees under stress? If so, what are they?

3. What is the proper role of the supervisor here? Should he attempt counseling?

Source: Adapted with permission from Robert D. Joyce, *Encounters in Organizational Behavior*, pp. 168–172. Copyright 1972, Pergamon Press PLC.

Experiential Exercise
Health Risk Appraisal

The Health Risk Appraisal form was developed by the Department of Health and Welfare of the Canadian government. Their initial testing program indicated that approximately one person out of every three who completed the form would modify some unhealthy aspects of his or her life-style for at least a while. Figuring the potential payoff was worth it, the government mailed out over 3 million copies of the questionnaire to Canadians who were on social security. Subsequent checking indicated that initial projections of the number of recipients altering their behavior was correct. Perhaps you will be among the one-third.

Choose from the three answers for each question the one answer that most nearly applies to you. Note that a few items have only two alternatives.

Exercise

_____ 1. Physical effort expended during the workday: mostly?
   (a)   heavy labor, walking, or housework
   (b)   —
   (c)   deskwork

_____ 2. Participation in physical activities — skiing, golf, swimming, etc., or lawn mowing, gardening, etc.?
   (a)   daily
   (b)   weekly
   (c)   seldom

_____ 3. Participation in vigorous exercise program?
   (a)   three times weekly
   (b)   weekly
   (c)   seldom

_____ 4. Average miles walked or jogged per day?
   (a)   one or more
   (b)   less than one
   (c)   none

_____ 5. Flights of stairs climbed per day?
   (a)   more than 10
   (b)   10 or fewer
   (c)   —

Nutrition

_____ 6. Are you overweight?
   (a)   no
   (b)   5 to 19 lbs
   (c)   20 or more lbs.

_____ 7. Do you eat a wide variety of foods, something from each of the following five food groups: (1) meat, fish, poultry, dried legumes, eggs, or nuts; (2) milk or milk products; (3) bread or cereals; (4) fruits; (5) vegetables?
   (a)   each day
   (b)   three times weekly
   (c)   —

Alcohol

_____ 8. Average number of bottles (12 oz.) of beer per week?
  (a) 0 to 7
  (b) 8 to 15
  (c) 16 or more

_____ 9. Average number of hard liquor (1½ oz.) drinks per week?
  (a) 0 to 7
  (b) 8 to 15
  (c) 16 or more

_____ 10. Average number of glasses (5 oz.) of wine or cider per week?
  (a) 0 to 7
  (b) 8 to 15
  (c) 16 or more

_____ 11. Total number of drinks per week including beer, liquor, or wine?
  (a) 0 to 7
  (b) 8 to 15
  (c) 16 or more

Drugs

_____ 12. Do you take drugs illegally?
  (a) no
  (b) —
  (c) yes

_____ 13. Do you consume alcoholic beverages together with certain drugs (tranquilizers, barbiturates, illegal drugs)?
  (a) no
  (b) —
  (c) yes

_____ 14. Do you use painkillers improperly or excessively?
  (a) no
  (b) —
  (c) yes

Tobacco

_____ 15. Cigarettes smoked per day?
  (a) none
  (b) less than 10
  (c) 10 or more

_____ 16. Cigars smoked per day?
  (a) none
  (b) less than 5
  (c) 5 or more

_____ 17. Pipe tobacco pouches per week?
       (a)   none
       (b)   1
       (c)   2 or more

Personal Health

_____ 18. Do you experience periods of depression?
       (a)   seldom
       (b)   occasionally
       (c)   frequently

_____ 19. Does anxiety interfere with your daily activities?
       (a)   seldom
       (b)   occasionally
       (c)   frequently

_____ 20. Do you get enough satisfying sleep?
       (a)   yes
       (b)   no
       (c)   —

_____ 21. Are you aware of the causes and dangers of VD?
       (a)   yes
       (b)   no
       (c)   —

_____ 22. Breast self-examination? (if not applicable, do not score)
       (a)   monthly
       (b)   occasionally
       (c)   —

Road and Water Safety

_____ 23. Mileage per year as driver or passenger?
       (a)   less than 10,000
       (b)   10,000 or more
       (c)   —

_____ 24. Do you often exceed the speed limit?
       (a)   no
       (b)   by 10 mph
       (c)   by 20 mph or more

_____ 25. Do you wear a seat belt?
       (a)   always
       (b)   occasionally
       (c)   never

_____ 26. Do you drive a motorcycle, moped, or snowmobile?
       (a)   no
       (b)   yes
       (c)   —

_____ 27.   If yes to the above, do you always wear a regulation safety hel-
met?
(a)   yes
(b)   —
(c)   no

_____ 28.   Do you ever drive under the influence of alcohol?
(a)   never
(b)   —
(c)   occasionally

_____ 29.   Do you ever drive when your ability may be affected by drugs?
(a)   never
(b)   —
(c)   occasionally

_____ 30.   Are you aware of water safety rules?
(a)   yes
(b)   no
(c)   —

_____ 31.   If you participate in water sports or boating, do you wear a life
jacket?
(a)   yes
(b)   no
(c)   —

General

_____ 32.   Average time watching TV per day (in hours)?
(a)   0 to 1
(b)   1 to 4
(c)   4 or more

_____ 33.   Are you familiar with first-aid procedures?
(a)   yes
(b)   no
(c)   —

_____ 34.   Do you ever smoke in bed?
(a)   no
(b)   occasionally
(c)   regularly

_____ 35.   Do you always make use of equipment provided for your safety
at work?
(a)   yes
(b)   occasionally
(c)   no

To Score: Give yourself 1 point for each *a* answer; 3 points for each *b* answer;
5 points for each *c* answer. *Total Score:* _____

- A total score of 35–45 is *excellent*. You have a commendable life-style based on sensible habits and a lively awareness of personal health.

- A total score of 45–55 is *good*. With some minor change, you can develop an excellent life-style.

- A total score of 56–65 is *risky*. You are taking unnecessary risks with your health. Several of your habits should be changed if potential health problems are to be avoided.

- A total score of 66 and over is *hazardous*. Either you have little personal awareness of good health habits or you are choosing to ignore them. This is a danger zone.

Source: Dept. of Health and Welfare of Canada as found in J.M. Ivancevich, M.T. Matteson, *Organizational Behavior and Management*, 2d ed. (Homewood, Ill.: BPI/Irwin, 1990), p. 250.

Notes

1. B. Ramazzini, *De Morbis Artificum Diatriba* (1713), trans. under the auspices of the New York Academy of Medicine (New York: Hafnor Press, 1964).

2. H. Munsterberg, *Psychology and Industrial Efficiency* (New York: Houghton Mifflin, 1913).

3. H. Selye, *The Stress of Life* (New York: McGraw-Hill, 1976).

4. W.E. Scott, "Activation Theory and Task Design," *Organizational Behavior and Human Performance* (1966): 13–30.

5. M.T. Matteson and J.M. Ivancevich, *Controlling Work Stress* (San Francisco: Jossey-Bass, 1987).

6. M. Friedman and R. Rosenman, *Type A Behavior and Your Heart* (New York: Knopf, 1974).

7. R. Rosenman and M. Friedman, "The Central Nervous System and Coronary Heart Disease," *Hospital Practice* 6 (1971): 87–97.

8. C.D. Jenkins, "Psychologic and Social Precursors of Coronary Disease," *New England Journal of Medicine* 284 (1971): 244–255.

9. J.H. Howard, D.A. Cunningham, and P.A. Rechnitzer, "Health Patterns Associated with Type A Behavior: A Managerial Population," *Journal of Human Stress* 2 (1976): 24–31.

10. T.H. Holmes and R.H. Rahe, "Social Readjustment Rating Scale," *Journal of Psychosomatic Research* 11 (1967): 213–218.

11. A.A. McLean, *Work Stress* (Reading, Mass.: Addison-Wesley, 1979); J.V. Brady, "Ulcers in Executive Monkeys," *Scientific American* 199 (1958): 89–95.

12. M.M. Smith, M. Colligan, R.W. Horning et al., *Occupational Comparison of Stress-Related Disease Incidence* (Cincinnati: National Institute for Occupational Safety and Health, 1978).

13. McLean, *Work Stress*, p. 80.

14. Ibid., p. 82.

15. R.L. Kahn et al., *Organizational Stress* (New York: Wiley, 1964).

16. Ibid.

17. J. Cassel, "Psychosocial Processes and Stress: Theoretical Formulation," *International Journal of Health Services* 4 (1974): 471–482; W.H. Hendrix, N.K. Ovalle, and R.G. Troxler, "Behavioral and Physiological Consequences of Stress and Its Antecedent Factors," *Journal of Applied Psychology* 70 (1985): 188–201; W.H. Hendrix, "Factors Predictive of Stress, Organizational Effectiveness and Coronary Heart Disease Potential," *Aviation, Space, and Environmental Medicine* (July 1985): 654–659; J. Martocchio and A. O'Leary, "Sex Differences in Occupational Stress," *Journal of Applied Psychology* 74 (1989): 495–501.

18. B.L. Margolis, W.M. Kroes, and R.P. Quinn, "Job Stress: An Unlisted Occupational Hazard," *Journal of Occupational Medicine* 16 (1974): 659–661.

19. Friedman and Rosenman, *Type A Behavior and Your Heart*.

20. J.R.P. French and R.D. Caplan, "Organizational Stress and Individual Stress," in A.J. Marrow, ed., *Failure of Success* (New York: AMACOM, 1972).

21. C.M. Winget, L. Hughes, and J. La Don, "Physiological Effects of Rotational Work Shifting: A Review," *Journal of Occupational Medicine* 20 (1978): 204–210.

22. A. Brief, R.S. Schuler, and M. Van Sell, *Managing Job Stress* (Boston: Little, Brown & Co., 1981).

23. T.G. Cummings and C.L. Cooper, "A Cybernetic Framework for Studying

Occupational Stress," *Human Relations* (1979): 395–418.

24. K. Bammer and B.H. Newberry, eds., *Stress and Cancer* (Toronto: Hogrefe, 1982).

25. J.M. Ivancevich and M.T. Matteson, *Stress and Work* (Glenview, Ill.: Scott, Foresman, 1980).

26. L.W. Porter and R.M. Steers, "Organizational, Work, and Personal Factors in Employee Turnover and Absenteeism," *Psychological Bulletin* 80 (1973): 151–176; R.M. Steers and S.R. Rhodes, "Major Influences on Employee Attendance: A Process Model," *Journal of Applied Psychology* 63 (1978): 391–407; W.H. Mobley, R.W. Griffeth, H.H. Hand, et al., "Review and Conceptual Analysis of the Employee Turnover Process," *Psychological Bulletin* 86 (1979): 493–522.

27. A. Kornhauser, *Mental Health of the Industrial Worker* (New York: Wiley, 1965).

28. Smith et al., *Occupational Comparison of Stress-Related Disease Incidence.*

29. B. Cohen, M. Colligan, W. Wester et al., "An Investigation of Job Satisfaction Factors in an Incident of Mass Psychogenic Illness at the Workplace," *Organizational Health Nursing* 26 (1978): 10–16.

30. McLean, *Work Stress.*

31. R.K. Wallace and H. Benson, "The Physiology of Meditation," *Scientific American* (1972): 84–90; T. Schultz, "What Science Is Discovering about the Potential Benefits of Meditation," *Today's Health,* April 1972, 34–37.

32. A.J. DuBrin, *Fundamentals of Organizational Behavior* (New York: Pergamon Press, 1978), p. 142.

33. R.G. Siu, "Work and Serenity," *Occupational Mental Health* 1 (1971): 5–6; R.G. Siu, "The Tao of Organization Management," in *Reducing Occupational Stress,* ed. A. McLean, DHEW-NIOSH Publication no. 78-140 (National Institute for Occupational Safety and Health).

34. Siu, "The Tao of Organization Management," pp. 143–144.

35. McLean, *Work Stress,* p. 108.

36. A. Lakien, *How to Gain Control of Your Time and Your Life* (New York: Peter Wyden, 1973); R.A. MacKenzie, *The Time Trap* (New York: McGraw-Hill, 1972).

37. R. Kreitner, "Personal Wellness: It's Just Good Business," *Business Horizons* (1982), p. 28; D. Gebhardt and C. Crump, "Employee Fitness and Wellness Programs in the Workplace," *American Psychologist* 45 (1990): 262–272.

Yvon Chouinard founded Chouinard Equipment in 1957 to market a small line of rock climbing equipment he manufactured in his backyard using an $800 forging die. He sold the products from the back of his van. During the early days, Chouinard made ends meet by working as a private detective for Howard Hughes.

In 1965, eight years after making his first prototypes, Chouinard opened a retail store to market his products in a small tin building behind a slaughterhouse in Ventura, California. Today the company's headquarters stands on that same site, and the original store has grown into a division of five stores under a holding company named Lost Arrow, Inc. Lost Arrow includes the corporation's retail arm, Great Pacific Iron Works, Patagonia, the clothing division, and Chouinard Equipment, the mountaineering equipment firm. It generated estimated sales revenues in 1989 of $76 million. The company has remained in private hands, despite numerous purchase offers.

Chouinard's values and his unique leadership style and business approach have played strong roles in shaping the culture of Patagonia. "You don't have to be in the Rotary Club or lunch with bankers to be a success," he says. "You take risks, use common sense and you make good products." He has been labeled an "anti-marketer" and an effortless success, but such labels deceive. Chouinard has ingrained in his employees a focus on producing the finest quality outdoor gear available.

Employees must understand and share the Patagonia mission because the company's owner is not present to direct activities for seven months of the year. Though Chouinard spends some of this time in business travel, he spends most of it having fun. The business's location in Ventura near one of the finest surfing beaches in California is no accident. Chouinard actively participates in 20 sports, including fly fishing, kayaking,

alpine skiing, sailing, and surfing. Several personal business goals guide his activities:

1. Make money
2. Give money away
3. Be creative
4. Maintain pride
5. No hassles
6. "Pfun"

Chouinard realizes that someone has to manage Patagonia, he just doesn't want to be the one to do it. He works to duck the day-to-day burden by delegating authority. He has developed systems to make this leadership style work.

First, the firm hires the right people. Each of Lost Arrow's approximately 400 employees is hired with one basic question in mind, "Would I want to have dinner with this person?" If not, the candidate probably wouldn't fit in at Patagonia. Chouinard says, "We try to get the most intelligent people we can . . . but in the end, you really end up with fairly average people. The secret is to try to get average people to do above average work." He tries to accomplish this by giving each employee a sense of responsibility, keeping the direct result of the work visible, and showcasing its effect on the rest of the organization.

Another product of Chouinard's leadership approach is the 5–15 report, completed each week by virtually every Patagonia employee. This report must, by definition, take no longer than 15 minutes to prepare, and no more than 5 minutes to read. It focuses on three things: a summary of the employee's accomplishments for the week, an evaluation of the department's morale, and a single idea for improving the company, either within the employee's department, or company-wide.

Completed 5–15s travel up the organization chart to supervisors and managers, who likewise compile and pass along their own 5–15s. The sequence stops at the top with Chouinard, who receives approximately two dozen reports from Ventura each week, wherever in the world he happens to be, indicating the climates at all levels of Patagonia. The reports may signal the need for job redesign or expansion of responsibilities to remedy revealed boredom or undermotivation. Department managers sometimes share ideas from 5–15s. In addition, the reports foster creativity, employee participation in decision making, and enhanced communications.

Yvon Chouinard takes a long-term view of his company. He wants employees to view it as their company, too, to be happy and fulfilled. He estimates that each time an employee leaves the company, it costs him an average of $50,000 to find and train a replacement. To avoid this, he pays careful attention to benefits. For example, he offers flextime scheduling, recognizes outstanding performance via a formal recognition program, and allows employees to use vacation time in one-hour increments to surf or attend a kindergarten graduation ceremony, for example.

Besides offering its employees all the standard benefits, and then some, Patagonia maintains above average compensation levels ranging from $6 an hour to $50,000 to $60,000 annually for middle managers. "You get out of benefits what you put into them," says Chouinard. The company also subsidizes employees' wilderness adventures and sells them clothing at 10 percent below wholesale cost.

Of the many benefits, one of the most important is the excellent on-premise child care facility, Great Pacific Child Development Center. This center further emphasizes Patagonia's family-like concern for its employees, helping to integrate children's daily activities with their parents' workplace into an everyday environment, relieving anxiety and frustration for both. This also brings work satisfaction and productivity increases, creating a total and mutual benefit. Each staff member at the center meets or exceeds all qualifications required by the State of California, and the center maintains a staff-child ratio that allows individualized care and an enhanced learning environment for the children.

Patagonia also provides an excellent cafeteria facility for its employees that specializes in healthful and nutritious foods. Rather than going out to lunch at a cost of an hour and a half or so of work time, most employees dine in the cafeteria. Many take their meals back to their offices.

Questions

1. Blake and Mouton developed a training program that explains leadership styles by comparing leaders' concern for people against their concern for production. Where does Chouinard fit on the managerial grid? Explain your answer.

2. What types of rewards does Chouinard use to enhance employee performance? What evidence can you cite that these rewards are effective?

3. In terms of group dynamics, why might someone want to work at Patagonia? That is, why would someone want to join the Patagonia group?

4. In terms of the French and Ravens bases of power, what *informal* bases of power does Chouinard have in relation to employees? In relation to customers?

5. How would you typify Chouinard's personality and his ability to handle stress?

Sources: "The Man Is the Message," *Forbes,* April 17, 1989, p. 148; "Patagonia's Rugged Wear Leads the Pack," by Gary Strauss, *USA TODAY,* January 11, 1989; *Growing a Business,* by Paul Hawken (Fireside, 1988); "Patagonia Finds Keeping Workers Happy Keeps Them Around," *News Chronicle,* Thousand Oaks, Calif., April 23, 1989, p. 30.

Case

Ethical Decision Making: Morton Thiokol and the Space Shuttle Challenger Disaster

On January 28, 1986, the space shuttle *Challenger* lifted off on the 25th mission of NASA's shuttle program. Its voyage ended tragically with an explosion just 73 seconds into flight. All seven crew members perished. The shock of the tragedy humbled a once-proud agency. It brought months of investigations as a presidential commission searched for the cause.

In its final report, issued June 10, 1986, the commission identified the immediate, technical reason for the disaster as a failed seal of O-rings in the right Solid Rocket Booster field joint due to the freezing temperatures preceding lift-off. The commission singled out the "flawed decision-making process" that led to the launch as a "contributing cause of the accident."

Multiple warnings, some dating back years and others voiced just hours before the fateful launch, were communicated all the way up to the highest levels of NASA. Morton Thiokol Inc. (MTI), the makers of the booster, had initially recommended against the launch during a telephone conference call between MTI and NASA officials the evening before the launch. The MTI engineers and managers were stunned when their unanimous recommendation was challenged by NASA middle-level managers Larry Mulloy and George Hardy. After a half-hour break in the teleconference, the MTI people returned to announce that they had reconsidered their position and had concluded that it was safe to fly.

How could this have happened? As former Morton Thiokol engineer and seal expert Roger Boisjoly pointed out, "We could have stopped it. We had initially stopped it. And then the decision was made to go forward anyways."

Disaster by Design

The origins of the *Challenger* disaster may ultimately be traced back to the day NASA selected Morton Thiokol to build the Solid Rocket Boosters, which would propel the shuttle into space. On November 29, 1973, Thiokol won the contract over three competitors, despite earning the lowest rank in engineering design. The main reason: NASA was then drastically cutting costs to live within its shrinking post-Apollo budget. Thiokol's bid represented a sizeable cost advantage.

During seven years of development and testing, NASA engineers at Marshall Space Center found the design of the O-ring joints to be "completely unacceptable." In spite of these objections, the joints were certified for flight, and the space shuttle *Columbia* lifted off for the first time on April 12, 1981. By mid-1985, after 19 missions, NASA headquarters acknowledged the increasing erosion problems in the O-ring joints, yet continued to fly, referring to the erosion as "an allowable risk."

NASA had become a victim of its own gung-ho, can-do philosophy. The agency had promoted the still-experimental Space Transport System as an operational space truck, and was pushing for 15 launches in 1986, and 24 a year by 1990. Such a goal was ambitious when contrasted with the 1985 high of 9 missions, but far short of the 60 missions a year originally envisioned by NASA.

Headquarters had underestimated the fragility of the complex system and overestimated its own capability for resolving problems without disrupting its flight schedule. During the summer and fall of 1985, concern over the dangers posed by the faulty boosters was escalating both within NASA and at Morton Thiokol.

On July 31, 1985, Roger Boisjoly, a rocket engineer at MTI and its top expert on the Solid Rocket Motor seals, wrote a memo to his Vice President of Engineering, Bob Lund, cautioning that, "The mistakenly accepted position on the joint problem was to fly without fear of failure" and modify the joint within the limits of the flight schedule. He warned that failure to address the problem would result in "a catastrophe of the highest order—loss of human life." He concluded, "It is my honest and very real fear that if we do not take immediate action to dedicate a team to solve the problem, with the field joint having the number one priority, then we stand in jeopardy of losing a flight along with all the launch pad facilities."

On August 19, 1985, Al McDonald of Morton Thiokol briefed NASA headquarters on the O-ring joint erosion problem. The presidential commission concluded that the briefing was "sufficiently detailed to require corrective action prior to the next flight," and that no correction was made because "meeting flight schedules and cutting cost were given a higher priority than flight safety."

On January 21, 1986, one week before the launch of the *Challenger,* NASA announced it would seek bids for a "second source" to supply shuttle boosters. The contract was worth over $1 billion to Morton Thiokol.

The Teleconference

On Monday, January 27, 1986, the lift-off of *Challenger* Flight 51-L was scrubbed for a fourth time. Following right on the heels of the most delayed flight in shuttle history, it was a disappointing setback for NASA. Perhaps even more significantly, that mission was to showcase President Reagan's "Teacher-in-Space" program by carrying the spritely, effervescent Christa McAuliffe as a crew member. Further, the president was scheduled to deliver his annual State of the Union Address the following evening.

The temperature for launch time the next morning was projected to be 23 degrees, with overnight lows forecast in the teens. Marshall Space Flight Center's Stan Reinartz and Larry Mulloy, the Level III third and fourth ranking shuttle launch officials (see Figure 1), were at Cape Kennedy for the launch along with Thiokol's Al McDonald. They asked MTI to assess the effects of the cold snap. In the afternoon, Thiokol's Bob Lund, recalling that the seals nearly burned through at 53 degrees on the January 1985 flight of the *Discovery,* echoed the recommendations of Boisjoly and the rest of his engineering team, informing Reinartz and Mulloy that, "It looks to me like 53 degrees is about it. I don't want to fly outside of our experience base." Thiokol was asked to fax its data to the Marshall Space Flight Center in Huntsville, Alabama, and the Kennedy Space Center in Florida for a full teleconference review to begin at 8:45 p.m.

During the teleconference, Boisjoly and his

Final Teleconference between Thiokol–Marshall–Kennedy Key Participants (January 27, 1986)

	Marshall Space Flight Center (NASA)	**Morton Thiokol, Inc.**
	George Hardy, Deputy Dir., Science and Engineering John Miller, SRM Technical Asst. Ben Powers, Propulsion Engineer (and 11 others)	**Management** Jerry Mason, Senior VP Joe Kilminster, VP, Space Boosters Bob Lund, VP, Engineering **Engineers** Roger Boisjoly, SRM Seal Expert Arnie Thompson, SRM Cases Expert Brian Russell, SRM Ignition Expert (and 8 others)
Kennedy Space Center	Stanley Reinartz, Manager, Shuttle Project Larry Mulloy, Manager, SRM Project	Allan McDonald, Dir., SRM Project, MTI

Telecon, 8:45 to 11:00 p.m. Includes Thiokol off-link caucus (10:30 to 11:00 p.m.).

■ **Figure 1**

The NASA Launch Chain of Command

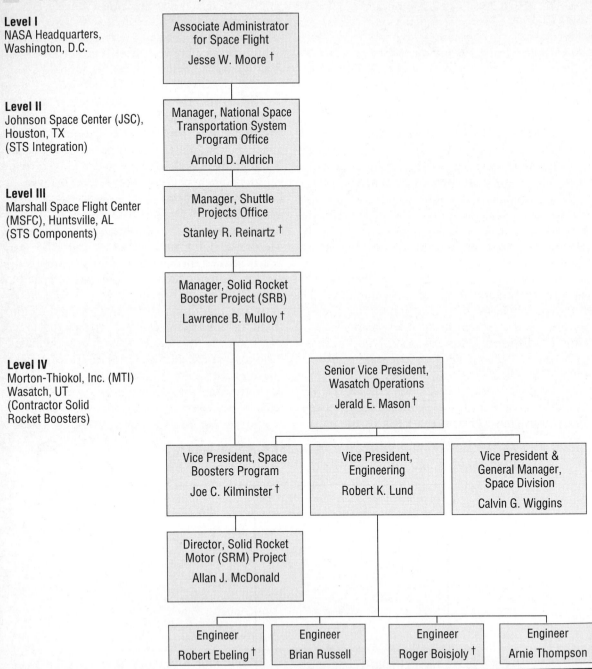

Level I
NASA Headquarters,
Washington, D.C.

Associate Administrator
for Space Flight

Jesse W. Moore [†]

Level II
Johnson Space Center (JSC),
Houston, TX
(STS Integration)

Manager, National Space
Transportation System
Program Office

Arnold D. Aldrich

Level III
Marshall Space Flight Center
(MSFC), Huntsville, AL
(STS Components)

Manager, Shuttle
Projects Office

Stanley R. Reinartz [†]

Manager, Solid Rocket
Booster Project (SRB)

Lawrence B. Mulloy [†]

Level IV
Morton-Thiokol, Inc. (MTI)
Wasatch, UT
(Contractor Solid
Rocket Boosters)

Senior Vice President,
Wasatch Operations

Jerald E. Mason [†]

Vice President, Space
Boosters Program

Joe C. Kilminster [†]

Vice President,
Engineering

Robert K. Lund

Vice President &
General Manager,
Space Division

Calvin G. Wiggins

Director, Solid Rocket
Motor (SRM) Project

Allan J. McDonald

Engineer

Robert Ebeling [†]

Engineer

Brian Russell

Engineer

Roger Boisjoly [†]

Engineer

Arnie Thompson

† = No longer with the organization.

colleagues presented data suggesting, though not conclusively proving, that the joints would fail at such a cold temperature. Specifically, the data indicated that

1. The temperature would be about 25 degrees colder than any previous shuttle launch.

2. Colder temperatures would make the rubber O-rings harder and less resilient.

3. Harder O-rings would take longer to seal.

4. If the primary O-ring did not seat, the secondary seal might not be able to pressurize in time, although the effect was impossible to precisely quantify.

5. Therefore, the prudent choice was to stay within the experience base and simply wait until the temperature reached at least 53 degrees.

The unanimous recommendation of the Thiokol engineers and management, including Senior Vice President Jerry Mason, and Vice Presidents Joe Kilminster, Calvin Wiggins, and Bob Lund, was not to launch. Accustomed to NASA's safety-first philosophy, the MTI participants were caught completely off-guard when Larry Mulloy sharply challenged their recommendations, telling them their data were "inconclusive" and didn't "hang together." "My God, Thiokol," he said, "When do you expect us to launch? Next April? The eve of a launch is a hell of a time to be generating new Launch Commit Criteria!" George Hardy at Marshall added that he was "appalled" at Thiokol's recommendation but said he would not launch over a contractor's objection.

It was the first time in the history of space flight that a contractor's no-launch recommendation had been challenged. Thiokol was placed in the position of proving that a launch would be unsafe (i.e., that the joint would fail), when their entire history with NASA had been to establish why a launch was safe. Nearly to a man, the Thiokol participants would later testify to the significance of this reversal of philosophy.

The managers at MTI temporarily left the teleconference to discuss the NASA challenge. When

asked by Stan Reinartz to respond to Mulloy's comments, Joe Kilminster instead requested, and was granted, a five-minute break in the telecon so that Thiokol could caucas and reassess its data. As the caucus began, Jerry Mason turned to his three vice presidents and softly announced, "We have to make a management decision." Engineers Arnie Thompson and Roger Boisjoly, fearful of an impending reversal, argued with the managers and urged them to stand by their original decision. Although they knew the launch would be unsafe, they were unable to prove absolutely that the joint would not work. They backed away when it was clear that the managers had no intention of listening to them. Thompson testified that he could not understand "why we just couldn't wait another day."

Bob Lund was the sole holdout among the four senior managers, but after 25 minutes he capitulated when Mason asked him to "Take off your engineering hat and put on your management hat." A vote was taken of the four senior managers, who then agreed unanimously to launch.

At 11:00 p.m. Thiokol went back to the teleconference and Kilminster announced their reversal to Stan Reinartz, who promptly accepted the new recommendation. When questioned by the commission about his willingness to accept the decision so hastily, Reinartz testified, "Mr. Chairman, when I asked very clearly and very deliberately on the telecon, while all parties were involved, I asked if there were any disagreements . . . and there was no comment, no objection or anything raised at that time."

Larry Mulloy testified that, "I did not discuss with Mr. Aldrich the conversations that we had just completed with Morton Thiokol [because] at that time, and I still consider today, that was a Level III [Marshall] issue. . . . There was no violation of Launch Commit Criteria. There was no waiver required, in my judgement, at that time and still today. . . . It was clearly a Level III issue that had been resolved." Stan Reinartz, who was in the reporting channel to Aldrich and Moore, claims he said nothing of the initial recommendation because he concluded: (1) there was no Launch Commit Criteria violation, (2) there was no Level II requirement violation that required that the information be passed upward, (3) there was, in the end, no disagreement concerning the Thiokol launch recommendation from anyone at Level III, and (4) Thiokol and Marshall had "fully and openly examined the concern and satisfactorily dispositioned that concern."

On January 28, 1986, at 11:38 a.m., *Challenger* lifted off on its final voyage from launch pad 39-B. The overnight lows of 8 degrees at the O-ring joint hopelessly compromised the effectiveness of the seals, as predicted by the Thiokol engineers. The seals were vaporized at ignition and only a fragile seal, formed by the products of combustion, kept *Challenger* from blowing up on the pad. Roger Boisjoly and the other engineers who participated in the teleconference at Thiokol breathed a collective sigh of relief, believing they were home free. Sixty seconds later, the fragile seal shattered and hot gases roared through the joint like a giant blow torch directed against the external fuel tank. At T+73 seconds, the orbiter broke up. Pilot Michael Smith's last recorded words are, "Uh-Oh." The astronauts survived the breakup, but perished when their flight deck slammed into the Atlantic Ocean at a speed of over 200 m.p.h.

It could—and should—have been prevented.

Questions

1. The presidential commission concluded that the *Challenger* decision-making process was "seriously flawed." If that is the case, who is responsible for the "flaw"? From what you have read and seen, who among the following is *most* to blame for the *Challenger* disaster?
    a. NASA senior management (Levels I and II: e.g., Moore, Aldrich)?
    b. NASA middle-level management (e.g., Level III personnel at Marshall Space Flight Center: Reinartz, Mulloy)?
    c. Morton Thiokol senior management (e.g., Mason, Lund, Kilminster, Wiggins)?

2. Was the decision-making process an example of groupthink? Explain.

3. a. Assume that Thiokol had held firm and recommended against the launch. From what you can infer from the case, what do you think would have been the result? Explore all facets and ramifications (for NASA, Thiokol, particular individuals, etc.).
    b. Assuming the decision had been to delay the launch, how could you prove that delaying it was the right thing to do? How would you be able to know you did the right thing?

4. "To the extent that the Presidential Commission faulted the decision-making process that led up to the launch of the *Challenger* and the death of its seven crew members, it was essentially handing down an indictment of the standard operating procedure which characterizes most of our large-scale organizations." Do you agree or disagree? Explain.

5. Was the decision-making process more reflective of the classical or administrative model of decision making?

IV

Organizational Structure and Processes

■ **Chapter 15**
Communication

■ **Chapter 16**
Organizational Design

■ **Chapter 17**
Environmental Forces

■ **Chapter 18**
Cultural Influences

■ **Chapter 19**
*Managing Organizational Change
and Development*

CHAPTER 15

Learning Objectives

After studying this chapter, you should be able to:

1. List the steps in the communication process and name some obstacles to communication.

2. Identify common forms of communication in organizations.

3. Explain how a group's pattern of communication affects its performance.

4. Describe the nature of downward, upward, and horizontal communication.

5. Identify roles a person fills in an organization's communication network.

6. Describe how the concepts of transactional analysis aid in understanding the messages an organization's members send.

7. Identify basic dimensions of nonverbal communication.

8. Describe individual barriers to communication.

9. Describe organizational barriers to communication.

10. List techniques for improving organizational communication.

Communication

■ Listen to Me!

After years of working for big restaurant chains, Keith Dunn and two partners formed their own restaurant, which they named McGuffey's. The three men were determined to avoid mistreating their employees, as Dunn felt he had been when he worked for the chains. In contrast, they were determined to make workers feel appreciated.

To do this, they instituted a two-week training program for new employees, gave them a meal after every shift, allowed them the freedom to give away appetizers and desserts, and provided a week's paid vacation each year. The employees responded by working hard and developing a sense of camaraderie. Sales at the first McGuffey's boomed, so the partners opened a second restaurant, then a third.

As the business grew, Dunn and his partners became overloaded with responsibility. They no longer had time for greeting, talking to, or orienting their workers. Said one partner, "You get pulled in so many directions that you just lose touch." Instead, as sales lagged, the partners responded by adding fringe benefits and trying out a variety of incentive programs.

Employees grew resentful as they found it increasingly difficult to communicate with the top. The service they provided often reflected their attitude. Concerned about the restaurants' suffering performance, Dunn sent employees a questionnaire asking them to rate the owners' performance on a scale of one to ten. Dunn had hoped for reassurance, but he was to be disappointed. One questionnaire, then another, rated him a zero. Other employees gave him a one or a two.

At first Dunn was furious: Weren't the employees grateful about all the benefits they were receiving? Eventually, however, he conceded that the evidence of dissatisfaction was overwhelming. He began to make more efforts to listen to his workers.

Dunn created an associate board, a group consisting of two cooks, two servers, and a bartender from each restaurant. This group met with the owners once a month to serve as a sounding board. Initially Dunn made the mistake of also inviting the restaurant managers, who at times retaliated when their staff members complained at meetings of the associate board. Dunn uninvited the managers.

He also instituted employee focus groups, at which employees would meet with an owner. Each employee was to participate in such a focus group at least once every six months.

As Dunn began listening, employee morale picked up. Turnover fell from an embarrassing 220 percent to only 60 percent — about one-fourth the average for the restaurant industry. "You feel like you're a person here," explains Geri O'Brien, a hostess at the Charlotte, North Carolina, McGuffey's.

Listening is an essential part of the process of communicating. This chapter discusses the way communication works and some of the forces that can interfere with effective communication. The chapter concludes with ideas for improving communication in organizations.

Source: Joshua Hyatt, "The Odyssey of an 'Excellent' Man," *Inc.*, February 1989, pp. 63–69.

A Model of the Communication Process

In Chapter 13, we defined true **communication** as the creation of a mental image in the mind of a receiver in exactly the same detail as intended by the sender. There are also many other definitions of communication. For example, Baskin and Aronoff define communication as the "exchange of messages between persons for the purpose of constructing common meanings."[1] Both of these definitions suggest a view of communication that is interpersonal, involving the use of verbal and nonverbal signs and symbols to create understanding.

True, or accurate, communication is often difficult to achieve because it requires a complex sequence of steps: idea generation, encoding, transmitting via various channels, receiving, decoding, understanding, and responding. As the diagram in Figure 15.1 suggests, potential obstacles to successful communication exist at every step. These obstacles, which can be described as noise, barriers, and filters, have the potential to disrupt or alter the communication process.

To illustrate the communication process, consider the example of an inventory control clerk who determines that the supply of labels needed for packaging a product is running low. The *generation of the idea* that labels must be ordered results in the clerk's *encoding* a message consisting of symbols that will convey the desired information. In this case, the clerk's encoded message is a typewritten form that is sent to the purchasing agent. Encoded messages may also be simple verbal instructions. The encoded message is then *transmitted* via one or more channels. For example, a memo might be transmitted by interoffice mail and a verbal instruction could be delivered personally or over the phone. In addition, several channels may be used simultaneously, as when a person verbally makes a statement and uses appropriate gestures and facial expressions to emphasize its meaning.

Receiving the message involves attending to and actually perceiving a written, spoken, or otherwise transmitted message. Reception is then followed by *decoding,* which involves deciphering the message. The receiver's personality, prior experience, and intellect may intervene at this stage. *Understanding* results from the decoding process. However, understanding is often imperfect. To the extent that the decoded message matches the encoded message, we can say that understanding has been achieved.

Figure 15.1

A View of the Interpersonal Communication Process

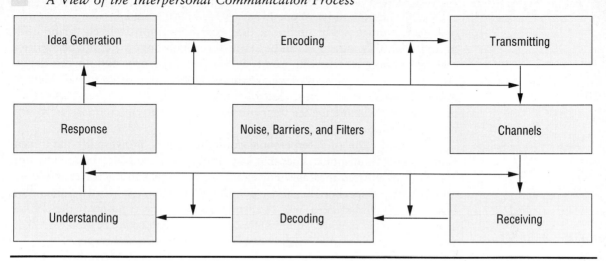

The final step in this cyclical process is the receiver's *response* to the communicative effort. This response may take the form of action or inaction. In our example, the purchasing agent may act by ordering more labels, or she may tell the clerk that labels will no longer be needed because of a change in the packaging process. This response, or action, serves as a form of feedback to the initiator of the process and determines the nature of any subsequent efforts at communication.

Because communication involves so many steps, numerous factors can intervene to confound the process. For example, the encoded message may not accurately correspond to the intended message because of the sender's poor choice of words, or the response may not accurately reflect the intent of the receiver as a result of forces outside of the receiver's control.

As this discussion implies, continually successful communication can be difficult to achieve. This fact contributes to the widespread belief that poor communication is responsible for many problems within organizations and that many larger problems would be resolved if only people tried to improve their communication skills. However, Gary Johns has pointed out that although communication may be at the root of many problems, it is possible to overestimate its role.[2] He contends, for example, that *more* communication is not necessarily *better* communication. Furthermore, difficulties in communication may really be the symptom or outcome of another problem, rather than the cause of the target problem.

To keep the proper perspective, it is crucial to recognize that communication is a social process that includes both perception and influence. The accurate conveyance and reception of a message, plus the impact that the message has on the receiver, are equally important in explaining the phenomenon of communication.

Types of Communication

In organizations, there are several common forms of interpersonal communication. By far, the most frequently used form is the spoken word, since it is usually the quickest. In addition, oral communication is likely to be quite accurate because messages can be clarified through ongoing dialogue. Written communication is also important within organizations. Employees devote large portions of their workdays to expressing ideas in written form.* Memos, letters, reports, order forms, electronic mail, and the like can serve as permanent records, which enhance their precision and clarity in comparison to oral communication.

A third form of interpersonal communication, **nonverbal communication,** consists of unspoken cues that a communicator sends in conjunction with a spoken or written message. For example, through hand gestures, nodding, and posture, a speaker can underscore his or her spoken words. Sometimes, however, nonverbal cues may seem to contradict the content of the spoken word, as when a speaker smiles while announcing bad news. In such instances, sorting out the intended content can be a challenge for the receiver.

Nonverbal communication may also take the form of symbols. For example, the uniform a person wears or the specific form on which a message is written can convey additional information to the receiver. The topic of nonverbal communication will be examined more closely later in this chapter.

Communication Networks

The formal structure of relationships in an organization can affect various aspects of the communication process. Research on the impact of structure on communication has focused on how different kinds of **networks,** or patterns of relationships, influence communication. Of special interest has been the effect of a network's degree of centralization on the communication process. Figure 15.2 illustrates the amount of centralization in five different types of five-person communication networks that have been closely studied. The **centralized networks** are characterized by their members' differing abilities to obtain and pass on information. Note that in each centralized network, information must flow through a pivotal or *central* person (indicated by an X in Figure 15.2). In contrast, in a **decentralized network**, each member has an equal opportunity to participate in the communication process.

The formal study of networks has relied on the creation of experimental conditions in which subjects are placed in cubicles and permitted to communicate only with prespecified members of their group. From such studies, several sets of fairly reliable results have emerged.[4]

Generally, members of decentralized networks report greater satisfaction, while the more centralized a structure is, the lower the satisfaction of its members. Wheel networks generate the lowest satisfaction ratings, while com-

---

* In a review of the literature on managerial communication, O'Reilly and Pondy concluded that managers generally overestimate the amount of time they spend reading and writing, and tend to underestimate the amount of time they spend talking.[3]

■ **Figure 15.2**

Five Basic Types of Group Communication Networks

Each circle represents a person and an X indicates the most central position.

Centralized

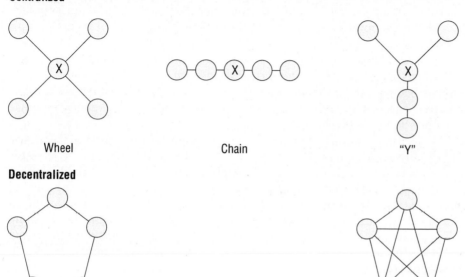

Wheel   Chain   "Y"

Decentralized

Circle   Completely
                                              Connected

pletely connected networks produce the highest ratings. Apparently, the more group members must depend on others for information and decision making, the less they enjoy their participation.

The networks also differ in their effectiveness in handling various kinds of problems. For relatively simple and routine tasks, when the goal is to finish a task quickly and make few mistakes, centralized networks are more efficient. But for complex tasks that require the sharing of information, decentralized networks have a relative advantage.

The nature of the task has also been found to influence the formation of a communication pattern. In one study, Faucheux and MacKenzie initially placed subjects in completely connected networks and assigned them several simple problems to solve.[5] Next, they asked the subjects to tackle a set of relatively complex tasks. When the groups worked on the simple tasks, they tended to adopt a centralized structure, converting into a wheel. However, as the tasks became more complex, the persons occupying the more central role felt that the demands on them were too great, and the groups reverted to their original, more decentralized structure.

The appearance of a single leader tends to occur more frequently in centralized networks due to the existence of a hub, or pivotal position. The greater availability of information to the hub occupant, plus the relative dependency of others on him for information and decision making, leads to the emergence of the hub occupant as a leader. By being such a critical link in the network, the person in the hub position comes to dominate group accomplishment. Furthermore, this person is typically the most satisfied of the group's members.

Centralized networks are also more prone to information overload. Members who occupy the more central positions experience greater requirements being placed on them to be effective. In a decentralized network, information and, ultimately, decision making are shared. As a result, no single position is easily overloaded.

The implications of the results of communication network research are fairly direct. Communication patterns should be established to best serve the dual purposes of enhancing task accomplishment and group satisfaction. The nature of the task to be performed, to a large extent, dictates the appropriate network, but attention must also be paid to the social consequences of an assigned network or pattern of relationships. Below a certain level, group dissatisfaction can have serious negative effects, including lack of commitment to decisions and increased turnover. Therefore, when selecting a communication structure for a work group, a manager should consider both member morale and the goals of the task.

The Direction of Communication

In an organization, messages may travel in several directions: downward, upward, and laterally (horizontally).

Downward Communication

Downward communication travels from the upper levels of an organization to the lower levels. Traditionally, such downward flows of communication occur one step at a time, with no intermediate levels excluded. The primary kinds of messages that travel downward in organizations include job instructions and directives, explanations of tasks and their relationship to other tasks, feedback on individual performance, statements of organizational policies and practices, and statements of mission designed to indoctrinate the members with established goals.[6] Information sent downward often becomes condensed or distorted as it passes through various levels. Therefore, the originator of a downward message should check whether it was accurately received at its intended destination.

Another problem with downward communication is that its recipients tend to interpret it as a sign of dissatisfaction in the upper levels of the organization. This common perception reflects the belief that if upper management takes the time to send a memo, they must have detected an exception to the norm that needs correction.

An Inside Look

Westinghouse's High-Tech Network

At Westinghouse, an advanced computer system enables employees at all levels to communicate through what amounts to decentralized networks. Members of various departments and diverse operations can link into the network to send and receive information throughout the world.

For example, on a Saturday morning, the company's president, Paul Lego, can turn on his home computer and find out how the company is doing in Taiwan, where it is still nighttime. After evaluating the data, he can send it to marketing managers in, say, Texas. Such electronic message sending gives the company a competitive edge in the global marketplace by speeding communications without regard to time zone or distance.

Altogether, the Westinghouse Information Network, as it is called, links more than 600 locations in Europe, Asia, and the Americas. Every day it is used by more than 90,000 people. The

system is an integrated network, which means that it carries voice as well as data transmissions. It provides information for making decisions, selling products, and satisfying customers.

A basic feature of the information network is an electronic mail system, which almost any Westinghouse employee can use to send a message to or receive a message from another employee. The transmitting employee merely enters the message into the computer; the receiving employee can view it on his or her own computer screen when convenient. What is more unusual, employees can tie their home phones into this network, and traveling managers can connect into it with laptop computers or check their messages through voice mail. Not only can the system carry voice messages, it can transmit technical drawings.

Executives also benefit from using the system's videoconferencing technology to hold meetings at which each

participant can remain in his or her own office. Higher-quality images and easier-to-use equipment make this technology more desirable than it once was. Besides making life easier for executives, it saves the company money on travel expenses.

Another aspect of the system that is important for internal communications is its EDGE advanced negotiations system. As salespeople carry out complex negotiations, they may need to draw on the knowledge of those responsible for pricing, manufacturing, and delivering the product. The EDGE system includes a database that contains information about each product. Any of the responsible employees can tap into the database, so information can move swiftly among the people who need it. According to Jack Froggatt, manager of information systems for Westinghouse Distribution and Control, this system has "cut the salesperson's negotiation time by 80 percent."

Source: William R. Ruffin, "Wired for Speed," *Business Month*, January 1990, pp. 56–58.

Upward Communication

Upward communication travels from the lower levels of an organization to the upper levels. The most common kinds of information that flow upward in an organization include suggestions for improving work procedures, information on progress and goal attainment, requests for assistance, and individual reactions to work and nonwork issues.[7]

A number of obstacles may deter upward communication. For example, many employees feel that they will be rebuked if they speak up to their superiors, and employees who hope to obtain promotions and other rewards are less likely to be outspoken.[8] In addition, like downward communication, upward communication is subject to condensation and distortion.

Upward and downward communication are not simply reverse processes, however. Differences in authority between levels can alter the accuracy, frequency, and effect of these two forms of communication. For instance, lower-level employees are expected to react quickly to communications from above, and high-level employees have the authority to monitor their reactions and issue follow-up orders. On the other hand, higher-level employees are not formally obligated to respond quickly, if at all, to communications from subordinates. In fact, an upper-level employee who is highly responsive to communications from below risks giving the appearance of "letting the tail wag the dog." Furthermore, a lower-level employee is not normally expected to remind his superiors of previous messages or to monitor their final reaction to a message. Thus, employees who occupy lower-level positions receive less feedback about the impact of their upward communications than do higher-level employees about their downward communications.

Horizontal Communication

Horizontal communication consists of messages sent between employees who occupy the same level within an organization. Examples include communication between members of different departments or between coworkers in a single department. Because employees are grouped into departments, or sometimes work in relative isolation from others who occupy parallel positions, there is typically little opportunity for horizontal communication. Yet, coordination of actions sometimes necessitates that employees communicate quickly without going through the process of sending messages up the organizational hierarchy and then down the appropriate branch.

Some years ago, Henri Fayol suggested that a formal communication channel, or gangplank, should sometimes be laid between units to facilitate cooperation.[9] Figure 15.3 provides an example of how Fayol's gangplank would work. In this situation, units may communicate directly only if they share a linkage, as indicated by the solid lines. If unlinked units wish to communicate, they must send their messages through higher levels of the organization until a shared link is reached. For example, if unit 3 wanted to communicate with unit 11, it would have to route its message up to unit 6, which would then pass the message back down again. To increase speed and accuracy, Fayol would advocate opening a new channel of communication directly between units 3 and 11, as shown by the dotted line.

Communication Roles

The specific functions a person serves in an organization's communication network may comprise his or her **communication role.** Rogers and Rogers have identified four roles that organizational members may play: gatekeeper, liaison, isolate, and cosmopolite.[10]

Gatekeepers

A **gatekeeper** is an individual who passes information to others or controls messages. Common examples of gatekeepers are secretaries and assistants to upper-level managers. A gatekeeper who has the ability to control the sub-

Figure 15.3

An Illustration of Fayol's Gangplank

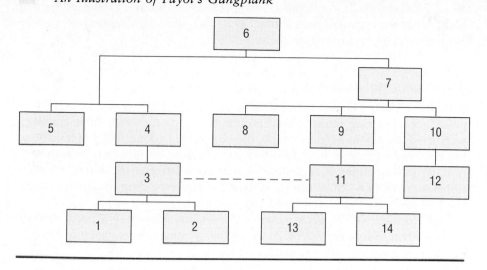

stance and/or the timing of the information that is given to a decision maker can actually influence the final decision.[11] Because the risk of information overload is greater at high organizational levels, top-level managers come to rely heavily on gatekeepers to condense and edit incoming messages. As a result of this greater trust, gatekeepers tend to have increasing influence at higher levels in an organization.

Liaisons

An individual who serves as a communication link between groups, but is not a member of either group, is a **liaison**. This person serves as a bridge between groups that need to exchange messages. The gatekeeping function is implicit, to a degree, in the liaison role. Firms that use liaisons to link departments are relatively more effective than firms that do not.[12]

Isolates

An **isolate** is someone who has very little or no contact with other members of the organization. Certain jobs, such as night guard and messenger, are characterized by a lack of sustained contact with others in an organization. Yet some people whose jobs offer more opportunities for contact may still remain uninformed. They may consciously choose not to socialize with coworkers or participate in grapevines. Feelings of alienation tend to be associated with such social isolation. Evidence suggests that isolates are somewhat younger, less educated, less satisfied, and poorer performers.[13]

Cosmopolites

A **cosmopolite** is a person whose communication network frequently extends into the organization's external environment. By definition, cosmopolites have a greater interest in national, rather than local, affairs and tend to have stronger professional affiliations. They are also more likely to change jobs than are other employees. Like liaisons, cosmopolites can serve a gatekeeping function in that the organization's contact with and information from the outside world must be passed through them.

Transactional Analysis

Eric Berne[14] and Thomas Harris[15] have popularized a simple and useful approach to analyzing interpersonal communication. Although their concepts were used initially in psychotherapy, they have been adopted by organizations for teaching employees how to overcome obstacles to effective communication. By relying on terms and concepts that are relatively jargon-free, **transactional analysis (TA)** constitutes a system for understanding the intended and implied messages that people send to each other.

According to TA, each person's personality has three aspects, or ego states: Parent, Adult, and Child. At any given moment, a person acts out of one of these states more than the others.

The Child

The *child ego state* is characterized by immaturity, dependency, and impulsiveness — traits that derive from childhood experiences. Thus, an employee who has an emotional outburst or behaves in a similarly immature manner would be acting out of the child ego state.

The Adult

The *adult ego state* is characterized by rational thinking and mature behavior. The experiences of adolescence and adulthood serve as the basis for learning how to behave in a goal-oriented and logical style. This ego state focuses largely on logic and information. In an organizational setting, an employee operates in the adult ego state when he or she gathers facts, generates alternatives, and weighs choices when making logically defensible decisions.

The Parent

The *parent ego state* is characterized by authoritarianism and self-righteousness. Sometimes this state may be nurturing, while at other times it may be domineering and controlling. In essence, this state is based on opinions rather than emotions or logic. Supervisors and others act out of a parent ego state when they talk down to employees or adopt a superior but nurturing stance.

These three ego states closely mirror the ego states of id, ego, and superego proposed by Sigmund Freud. However, one major difference between the TA ego states and Freud's is that the TA system examines the social interplay between the changing ego states of different people.

When the communication between two people is predictable (for example, if a person acting out of a child ego state is dealing with a person acting out of a parent ego state, the relationship is predictable), it is considered a **comple-**

mentary transaction. A supervisor/parent may demand, "Why haven't you turned in your monthly report to me? Can't you handle even the simplest assignments?" To this, the employee/child may respond, "Get off my back. Do you think all I have to do is work on your dumb report?" Other complementary transactions can include child–child, parent–parent, and adult–adult.

Parent–child interactions, although unhealthy for most situations, are believed to be fairly common in organizations because of the formal authority differences that exist between members. Often, the interactions between parent and child ego states appear to be positive. For example, a subordinate may request help on a project in a very submissive and dependent manner, and his superior will agree to help, but will do so in a very superior and paternal fashion. Interactions between two people acting out of their adult ego states are the ideal for organizational settings because, in most business contexts, the logical, problem-solving approach is generally most appropriate. For instance, a superior may ask a subordinate, "Do you have the most recent sales figures?" This adult question would be best answered with an adult answer, such as, "They're not quite ready yet. But as soon as I have them compiled, I will prepare a copy for you."

Noncomplementary transactions occur when an unexpected ego state appears in response to a sender's attempted communication. For example, a manager/adult may say, "Do you have the most recent sales figures?" If, in place of a complementary adult ego state response, this question is met with a child ego state response, such as, "You're not my department head. I'll get a copy of the figures to you when I get around to it," then the transaction is not likely to continue. Noncomplementary transactions cause much of the interpersonal hostility and conflict that occur among organizational members.

Two additional concepts are important to the TA framework: strokes and games. **Strokes** are positive reactions from others, including praise, recognition, and signs of affection. Everyone needs to be stroked. In early childhood, this need demands actual physical contact and stroking from others, but as we grow, the stroking we need becomes more psychological.†

Strokes form the basis of social **game playing**. The giving and getting of strokes motivates much of the social interplay of people in organizations. Most of these games are designed to have winners and losers, with the net outcome for the organization being negative because so much time and emotional energy are taken up by such activities.

Based on TA concepts, Fred Luthans and Mark Martinko have identified several common organizational games:

- *Poor Me*. The employee portrays himself or herself to the boss as being helpless, thereby avoiding criticism for poor performance and gaining sympathy.

- *Yes, But*. A boss invites participation from subordinates but shoots down each new idea or suggestion by saying "Yes, but . . . " and states reasons why the idea will not work.

† The notion of strokes can be understood as a simple way of describing the concept of reinforcement (see Chapter 5).

- *Hero*. A boss creates situations that employees cannot handle without coming to him or her for help, thereby demonstrating the supervisor's superiority and maintaining the subordinates' dependency.
- *Prosecutor*. Based on details in company regulations or a union contract, an employee creates situations that will force the boss to act in a seemingly arbitrary manner. Then the employee files a grievance or otherwise tries to embarrass the boss.[16]

Transactional analysis is not without its critics, especially since there is not much empirical evidence of TA's validity.[17] Yet the appeal of the approach is very strong, primarily because we know from self-observation that our own thought processes do seem to change from parent to child to adult states across situations and that game playing in organizations unquestionably exists.

Nonverbal Communication

As mentioned at the outset of this chapter, two people can exchange information without the use of words. Through nonverbal communication, people use facial expressions, gestures, manner of dress, and the larger social context to convey silent messages. In popular terms, this type of communication is sometimes referred to as "body language." However, despite the suggestion of several best-selling books on this topic, there is not yet — nor is there likely to be — a "magical way to know employees' or customers' thoughts without having to ask them."[18] There is no precise key for translating nonverbal signals into consistently reliable messages. For example, while a clenched fist may indicate anger, many individuals also clench their fists when they are nervous.

Dimensions of Nonverbal Communication

Despite these limitations, it is possible to attribute limited meaning to certain general patterns of behavior in many situations. According to Albert Mehrabian, nonverbal communication can be understood in terms of several fairly basic dimensions.[19]

Immediacy   Nonverbal signals may be interpreted in terms of their **immediacy**. Generally, people approach other people and objects that they like and desire, and withdraw from those that they evaluate negatively. This simple concept explains much of the hidden meaning in nonverbal messages. For example, we lean toward someone or ask more questions if we find them interesting or attractive, and we pull away or lean back (or even push our chair back) if we prefer to avoid involvement. When we wish to end a conversation, we often make abbreviated walking-away motions, for example, making little circles as we gradually walk farther away. Such motions are intended to convey the message that we are getting ready to leave (a message that may not be accepted, although it is usually understood, by the other person). Similarly, giving a very firm and long handshake to a person conveys a message of desired immediacy. Too prolonged a handshake, however, can make another person extremely nervous and uncomfortable, especially at a first meeting.

OB Focus

Comic Communication

Malcolm Kushner, a former lawyer who has a master's degree in communications, is a humor consultant. Says Kushner, "Humor is a serious communications tool." He adds that humor "can gain attention, create rapport, and make ideas more memorable. If it's used properly, it can also relieve tension, defuse hostility, and motivate an audience."

Michael Burger is another humor consultant. In a typical presentation, a company's chief executive introduces Burger to the employees and explains that the keynote speech for the meeting will be made by a highly qualified expert brought in to overhaul the company. Burger, the "expert," then lambastes individual managers with a heavy dose of sarcasm and winds up with an obvious comedy routine. Burger coats the chief executive's genuine concerns with humor, getting the message across without the need for a critical lecture from the company head and the gloom that would result.

Robert Orben conducts seminars and publishes a weekly newsletter to help executives perk up their speeches. Orben views humor as a bonding device. He explains, "If you're a leader, you're viewed from a distance by the average person. When you are giving a speech, you are on stage. You don't want this emotional separation from people. Telling them a joke says, 'I understand your problems, and I am with you.'"

Some basic guidelines apply to business people who want to use humor to get a message across:

- Keep the humor relevant to your message and audience.
- Be brief and conversational.
- Be self-effacing. Distinguish between taking your message seriously and taking yourself seriously.

Used appropriately, humor can be a useful tool for communicating. Says Michael Burger, "If you get people in a relaxed mood, they're much more receptive."

Source: "Getting Down to Funny Business," *Nation's Business,* November 1985, pp. 44+.

Total attraction toward another person can be understood in terms of the combined effects of the actual spoken words, the vocal expression of the message, and the facial expressions accompanying the message. Spoken words are the actual words in the message and their meaning is self-evident. Vocal expression involves the intonation and inflection in a spoken message.‡ Facial expressions refer to the clearly nonverbal aspects of the message. Mehrabian and Wiener have provided evidence suggesting that the total feeling or reaction one has to another's communication can be understood in accordance with the following approximate equation:[20]

Total feeling = 7% verbal feeling + 38% vocal feeling + 55% facial feeling

Notice that facial expressions are far more important than verbal content in explaining how people react to a message. Therefore, it is not *what* is said but *how* it is said (i.e., facial feeling plus vocal expression) that largely determines meaning. In short, whether the boss is smiling or grimacing when he says

‡ Consider how changing the accent in the following sentence can dramatically alter the meaning:
   The auditor will be HERE Tuesday.
   The AUDITOR will be here Tuesday.
   The auditor will be here TUESDAY.

you're one of the most unusual employees he's ever known makes all the difference!

Power   A second dimension that enters into the interpretation of nonverbal communication is **power**.[21] Generally, the relative status of individuals can be inferred from how they relate to each other nonverbally. A person of higher status can assume a relaxed posture in the presence of others, but a person of lower status is expected to display a more tense body posture when superiors are present. Asymmetric postures, such as putting your feet on your desk or leaning your head on your arm, are considered acceptable for people of high status but are unacceptable when in the presence of people of higher status. The posture of people of lower status is expected to resemble the military posture of "attention." It has been suggested that the relatively more symmetric body postures of women reflect a lower-status position in society.[22]

Many of the above points can be used to explain why people dislike dealing with strangers. The uneasiness that commonly arises from dealing with strangers grows partly out of concern over how the other person will react to us. One study suggests that if a person wants to be liked by others, including strangers, it helps simply to smile more and be more positive in new situations.[23] People differ greatly in their predisposition to be positive or negative when meeting others. Such differences are significant because this predisposition tends to shade the quality of the relationships that later develop. Young people first entering the job market often fail to take advantage of nonverbal ways of conveying interest and positive emotion during job interviews. Many people who might otherwise by very good employees are not hired because they unwittingly convey negativism and dislike to an interviewer by avoiding eye contact and displaying "withdrawing" gestures (as a result of nervousness and self-consciousness). In essence, the greatest need of the "nonverbally handicapped" is an awareness of their own style and the impact that it has on those around them.

Proxemics

In his notion of **proxemics**, Edward Hall, an anthropologist, contends that physical space serves an important purpose in communication.[24] People tend to stand at a predictable distance from each other in accordance with the specific roles they occupy. For example, we tend to stand farther away from strangers than from people with whom we are intimate. When we find ourselves thrust together with strangers, as in elevators or on subway trains, we try very hard to avoid giving nonverbal signals that could be interpreted as inappropriate. For example, we do not smile or gaze for very long at a stranger when riding an elevator. If caught staring at someone, we are expected to smile (to show no mean intent) and then to avert our gaze (preferably to watching the elevator's floor indicator or our shoes).

Hall suggests that in the United States there are definable **personal space zones**:

1. *Intimate zone (0 to 2 feet).* To be this close, we must have an intimate association with the other person or be socially domineering.

2. *Personal zone (2 to 4 feet).* Within this zone, we should be fairly well acquainted with the other individual.

3. *Social zone (4 to 12 feet).* In this zone, we are at least minimally acquainted with the other person and have a definite purpose for seeking to communicate. Most behavior in the business world occurs in this zone.

4. *Public zone (beyond 12 feet).* When people are more than 12 feet away, we treat them as if they did not exist. We may look at others from this distance, provided our gaze does not develop into a stare.[25]

Related to the notion of personal space is the concept of **territory.** Unlike personal space, which each of us carries with us, territory is assigned to a specific physical location. In terms of territory, there are many interesting analogies between human behavior in organizational settings and animal behavior. For example, more dominant animals have larger territories than less dominant animals.[26] Dominant animals visit the turf of lesser animals, but lesser animals do not visit the territories of their superiors. If a lesser animal does approach the territory of a dominant animal or the animal itself, it shows signs of nervousness and submission. Similarly, in organizational settings, employees of higher status have larger offices than employees of lower status; supervisors intrude on the work space of employees, but employees do not intrude on the work space of supervisors; and if an employee wants to enter a superior's office, he will usually stand at the doorway and ask, "Are you busy?"

In one of his classic works on behavior in work settings, William F. Whyte studied the relations of kitchen workers and other restaurant employees.[27] In the process, he noted that the kitchen workers had a proprietary attitude (akin to a sense of territory) toward the kitchen area itself. If other employees entered the kitchen area, the routine pattern of social interaction was disrupted. Lower-status "invaders" were often openly blocked from entering, while higher-status invaders (who could not be blocked) were tolerated until their departure.

Spatial Arrangements

The arrangement of furniture, such as desks and chairs, affects the frequency and nature of interpersonal communication. Osmond has suggested that the areas that drive people away from each other should be termed **sociofugal,** while those that bring people together should be termed **sociopetal.**[28] In his studies of hospital waiting areas, he found that arranging furniture around the perimeter of a room was one of the surest ways to decrease social interaction.§

Baskin and Aronoff, however, report that simply restructuring the workplace to minimize social communication may not necessarily increase productivity.[30] As an example, they cite the case of a young manager who attempted to increase worker productivity by decreasing the amount of time workers devoted to social interaction. To accomplish this, he rearranged the workers'

§ Intriguingly, the arrangement of furniture in college dormitory lounges tends to be similar to that of dayrooms in mental hospitals.[29]

equipment to make it difficult for them to speak to each other while they were at their posts. Although the amount of social communication on the job did decrease, so did the level of output.

Time

Although this form of nonverbal communication is more subtle in nature, status can be conveyed by the use of time. The way in which a request is phrased ("As soon as possible . . ." or "At your convenience . . .") implies how urgent the request is and how it should be approached. Arriving late for a social occasion, such as a business meeting or a dinner, may convey any number of different messages, including carelessness, lack of interest, and lack of ambition. Yet, the late arrival of a person of high status invariably reaffirms their relative social superiority. Their tardiness implies that they have a very busy schedule and that others will understand and forgive them. The same generosity does not extend to individuals of low status who are late. People who arrive 15 or so minutes *early* for an event are typically regarded as low in status and also as relatively lacking in sociability.[31]

Individual Barriers to Communication

Differences in Status

As we have seen throughout this text, status strongly influences people's behavior in organizations. Their willingness to listen to and react to an attempt at communication differs in response to the status of the communicator. Generally, employees are more responsive to, and even solicitous of, communication from people of equal or higher status. Moreover, managers report that they tend to find it more valuable and personally satisfying to communicate with superiors than with subordinates.[32] Given this bias, upward communication is often understandably less effective and less likely to elicit change.

Another barrier related to status is the attempt to convey superiority by using jargon to exclude the uninitiated rather than to clarify a point. Individuals in academia or the professions sometimes use complex phrases to achieve this purpose. To illustrate the silliness of this tendency, Haney has created a "Buzz Phrase Generator" for producing verbose and impressive-sounding but nonsensical phrases.[33] To use the Generator, simply pick any three-digit number from the columns below. For example, the number 262 produces the

A	B	C
0. integrated	0. management	0. options
1. total	1. organizational	1. flexibility
2. systematized	2. monitored	2. capability
3. parallel	3. reciprocal	3. mobility
4. functional	4. digital	4. programming
5. responsive	5. logic	5. concept
6. optical	6. transitional	6. time-phase
7. synchronized	7. incremental	7. projection
8. compatible	8. third-generation	8. hardware
9. balanced	9. policy	9. contingency

impressive-sounding but ridiculous phrase "systematized transitional capability."

The Credibility of the Source

As noted in the discussion of attitude change (Chapter 4), the source of a communication can greatly influence whether the receiver accepts or rejects the message. For communication to be effective, its source should be credible. And a source who combines power and attractiveness with credibility is likely to be an especially effective communicator.

Perceptual Biases

According to an old saying, people tend to hear what they want to hear. To be sure, this phenomenon is as common in organizations as it is in society in general. Employees may "tune out" what they do not wish to recognize, which is a form of selective perception keyed to their dominant needs and interests. When people are confronted with information that they find unsettling or distasteful, they are also likely to ignore it. This process is partly responsible for the failure of employees to accept critical comments during performance appraisal interviews (see Chapter 8).

Organizational Barriers to Communication

Information Overload

When an abundance of information is directed to a single position within an organization, decoding and interpreting the messages can become overwhelming. The primary result of such **information overload** is diminished effectiveness. In designing information channels, it is important to consider the amount and complexity of information that can be reasonably handled by one person. In addition, the amount of time it takes to examine and reach an understanding of messages must be taken into account. Two effective ways of eliminating information overload are to encourage employees to screen their messages and to encourage senders to condense their messages and send only essential information.

Time Pressures

The need to take quick action in response to a problem may require that information be sent out or requested on short notice. Such urgency can lead to superficiality and poor timing of communication. For example, data may not be detailed enough or they may arrive too late for employees to act on them. For communication to be effective, it must arrive at an appropriate time, as well as be accurate and complete.

Organizational Climate

The larger social system within an organization can be a barrier to effective communication. If the climate is one of openness and trust, then incomplete or controversial communications are more likely to be interpreted favorably. But when distrust is the norm, messages may be harshly scrutinized for "hidden meanings," and even good news may be greeted with suspicion and ridicule.

Informal Communication

Up to this point, we have focused on formal communication in organizational settings, but most organizations also have numerous pathways of informal communication. Since employees are generally free to exchange information with one another as part of their jobs, little can or should be done to directly control or eliminate such informal communication. While informal networks may serve useful functions by cutting red tape and leading to greater loyalty through positive social relations, they may also give birth to pathways called **grapevines.**** While organizational theorists generally regard grapevines as inevitable outgrowths of organizational structure,[35] most managers believe they have a negative impact on organizational functioning.

Because they are flexible and personal, grapevines may be one of the most rapid communication systems that exist in most organizations. In one outstanding example of the speed of grapevines, Davis found that nearly half the managers in an organization knew within only 13 hours that another manager's wife had given birth to a baby (the birth had occurred at 11:00 P.M.).[36] The remarkable speed of grapevines can be attributed to the fact that their messages are oral rather than written. Moreover, people enjoy passing on timely information because it makes them appear in touch and well informed, and there is social value attached to bringing surprising news to others.

Davis also suggests that grapevine members differ in behavior.[37] Some behave as "gossips," nonselectively communicating with everyone they meet, while others are more selective about whom they give information to. Most grapevines are made up of clusters of close associates, but when information reaches an occasional "gossip," its rate of spread is greatly increased.

Studies of grapevine behavior have yielded interesting results. One study of the accuracy of 30 rumors dealing with such topics as pay raises, profit sharing, promotions, and transfers found that 16 of the rumors were untrue, 9 were accurate, and 5 were only partly correct.[38] Other studies, however, have indicated that the accuracy of grapevines is usually quite high, especially when the information is noncontroversial.[39] With controversial information, the grapevine can be greatly in error. In light of these findings, it is perhaps not too surprising that a large proportion of employees view grapevines as their central source of information about events within their organizations.[40]

Of the varieties of information that are passed through grapevines, rumors are of special interest. **Rumors** are unverified beliefs that are transmitted from one person to another. Because rumors can harm both individuals and the organization itself, managers must consider how to control and eliminate rumor mills. For example, in one widespread rumor based on a misinterpreta-

---

** The term *grapevine* is believed to have originated during the Civil War, when telegraph lines were sometimes strung from tree to tree, resembling grapevines. Because of their jerry-rigged nature, these telegraph systems often generated ambiguous and garbled messages. Hence, distorted messages were said to "come from the grapevine."[34]

tion of its corporate logo, which showed a moon and stars, Procter and Gamble was accused of promoting satanism. The company was finally forced to discontinue its use of the emblem. In another case, McDonald's was rumored to be selling hamburgers that contained worms, which forced the company to mount an advertising campaign emphasizing the purity and nutritiousness of its product. These rumors involve customer (rather than employee) perceptions, and show the potential harm that rumors can do to customer relations and possibly sales.

To cope with rumors, DuBrin suggests the following techniques:

1. Try to wait them out. Some rumors dissipate over time and do little actual harm.

2. If waiting does not work, publicly refute the rumor. Refuting and even ridiculing a rumor in public negates its "news value." This approach may also lead people to distrust those who later attempt to pass the rumor along.

3. Feed valid information into the grapevine to counteract the undesired message.[41]

This last point suggests a possible positive feature of grapevines. Managers can use grapevines to serve organizational purposes by "leaking" positive information to grapevine members. For example, through the grapevine, a manager may be able to influence employees' reactions to proposed changes in work procedures.

Improving Organizational Communication

Effective communication of all kinds is crucial to the success of every organization. Chung and Megginson have outlined a number of suggestions for improving the effectiveness of organizational communication.[42]

1. *Use appropriate language.* Words, gestures, and symbols should be appropriate to the receiver's level of understanding.

2. *Practice empathic communication.* The receiver's frame of reference (i.e., assumptions and attitudes) should be understood by the communicator.

3. *Encourage feedback.* Two-way communications can improve the communication process. Through feedback, a communicator can check whether a message has been accurately received.

4. *Develop a climate of trust.* Communication is enhanced if the participants have a trusting relationship. Gaining and maintaining the trust of others requires continual effort and the willingness to engage in honest and frank dialogue. At Tandem Computers headquarters, management and employees have regular Friday beer parties to exchange information and ensure that everyone is abreast of what is happening in the company.

5. *Use appropriate media.* Not all forms of organizational communication are equally appropriate for all purposes. Rather, the form of com-

munication should match the situation. Oral communication is best for discussing employee problems, such as tardiness and poor performance. Written communication is best in matters that require future action, but it is too slow for issues that call for quick action, and too impersonal for discussing employee problems. A combination of oral communication followed by written communication is best for conveying information that requires quick action, job-specific directions, and procedural changes.

6. *Encourage effective listening.* Listening habits can also be improved. Among the techniques that encourage more effective listening are the avoidance of evaluative judgments, listening to the total meaning of the sender's message, and offering responsive feedback (sometimes called *active listening*) about the listener's degree of understanding. Active listening, which involves restating the speaker's remarks and reflecting on them, conveys the message that the listener is interested in the speaker as a person, and feels that what is being said is important.

7. *Ensure that formal communication efforts are in unison with overall corporate strategy.* At Allstate Insurance Company, a Communication Board (consisting of top management and communication professionals) meets regularly to review public relations efforts as well as internal communication programs involving employees to ensure that the messages being sent are "in synch" with the corporation's overall strategy.[43]

Summary

1. List the steps in the communication process and name some obstacles to communication.
The steps in the communication process are generation of an idea, encoding, transmitting, receiving, decoding, understanding, and responding. Obstacles to communication are noise, barriers, and filters.

2. Identify common forms of communication in organizations.
Common forms of communication in organizations are oral communication, written communication, and nonverbal communication.

3. Explain how a group's pattern of communication affects its performance.
The more group members must depend on others for information and decision making, the less satisfied they are. Centralized communication networks are most effective for quickly and accurately accomplishing simple and routine tasks. Decentralized networks are preferable for complex tasks that require the sharing of information. Centralized networks more often have a single leader. Members of centralized networks are more prone to information overload.

4. Describe the nature of downward, upward, and horizontal communication.

Downward communication travels from the upper to the lower levels of an organization, ideally one step at a time. Upward communication travels from a lower level to upper levels of an organization. Horizontal communication travels between employees who occupy the same level of an organization. Often such communication is informal.

5. Identify roles a person fills in an organization's communication network.

Communication roles consist of gatekeepers, liaisons, isolates, and cosmopolites. Gatekeepers pass information to others or control messages. Liaisons serve as communication links between groups but are not members of those groups. Isolates have little or no contact with other members of the organization. Cosmopolites have communication networks that extend into the organization's external environment.

6. Describe how the concepts of transactional analysis aid in understanding the messages an organization's members send.

In each personality, there are three ego states: (1) parent (authoritarian and self-righteous); (2) adult (rational and mature); and (3) child (immature, dependent, and impulsive). One of these states dominates a person's behavior in any given situation. Complementary transactions (communication that is predictable) can involve parent and child, child and child, parent and parent, or adult and adult. Noncomplementary transactions occur when the receiver of a message reacts with an unexpected ego state. In organizations, adult–adult transactions are generally the most appropriate.

7. Identify basic dimensions of nonverbal communication.

Nonverbal signals may be interpreted in terms of their immediacy (the degree to which people approach or withdraw from others) and the relative status or power of the people in the transaction.

8. Describe individual barriers to communication.

Differences in status inhibit the effectiveness of upward communication. A source that lacks credibility communicates less effectively. Perceptual biases also interfere with communication; specifically, people may tune out messages that are unsettling or distasteful.

9. Describe organizational barriers to communication.

Organizational barriers include information overload (too much information directed to a single position), time pressures, and an organizational climate of distrust.

10. List techniques for improving organizational communication.

Techniques for improving communication in organizations are: using appropriate language; practicing empathic communication; encouraging feedback; developing a climate of trust; using appropriate media; encouraging effective listening; and ensuring that efforts are in unison with overall corporate strategy.

Key Terms

Communication	Complementary transaction
Nonverbal communication	Noncomplementary transaction
Networks	Strokes
Centralized networks	Game playing
Decentralized networks	Immediacy
Downward communication	Power
Upward communication	Proxemics
Horizontal communication	Personal space zones
Communication role	Territory
Gatekeeper	Sociofugal areas
Liaison	Sociopetal areas
Isolate	Information overload
Cosmopolite	Grapevine
Transactional analysis (TA)	Rumors

Review and Discussion Questions

1. What are the steps in the communication process? Identify those steps in the following example: Bob observes on his computer screen that Ace Carpentry has ordered 200 8-foot two-by-fours from the lumberyard where he works. He prepares an invoice and mails it to Ace Carpentry. At Ace, Judy opens the invoice and writes a check to the lumberyard.

2. What are the characteristics of a centralized communication network? In what situations would a manager want communication to be centralized?

3. What are some potential problems with upward and downward communication? How can managers alleviate these problems?

4. Art director Natasha Blue stopped by the drafting tables to see how work was progressing. "Is that sketch ready for the Morrison Trucking account?" she asked Dennis Green.

    "No, it's not," cried Dennis, "but it's not my fault! People keep coming in here and interrupting me. I can't help it if people keep bothering me."

    "Well, tell them to leave," replied Natasha briskly. "I want that sketch on my desk before you leave here tonight."

    When Natasha had left, Dennis turned to Emily White. "Did you hear that?" he asked. "She's always on my case about something. She just doesn't like me."

    How can Emily explain this transaction to Dennis? What can Dennis do to improve his relationship with his supervisor?

5. How do people interpret the nonverbal messages of immediacy and power?

6. The recipient of a spoken message bases his or her total reaction on

the actual words, the speaker's vocal expression, and the speaker's facial expression. Which has the most influence on the recipient's reaction? Which has the least influence? What implications does this have for writing a business letter?

7. Identify the barriers to communication in each of the following situations.

   a. The sales manager sends the vice-president, to whom he reports, a memo describing ways to increase sales. A month later, he still hasn't heard anything.

   b. The new programmer in the company — a recent college graduate — unsuccessfully tries to explain to her colleagues why the system they are developing won't work as effectively as her idea. The department has been developing the system for two years.

8. What are some organizational barriers to communication? How can managers eliminate or reduce these problems?

9. What are some advantages and disadvantages of communications through the grapevine? How can managers cope with rumors?

10. Review the suggestions for improving organizational communication listed at the end of this chapter. Which of these suggestions has your instructor adopted in teaching this course? Which of these suggestions would make the information in this course easier to understand? Which suggestions can you put into practice in your everyday communications?

Critical Incident

A Failure to Communicate

Jeff Williams, M.D., is head of surgery at a major urban hospital. Most of his time is spent in administrative duties such as handling budgets, coordinating facility use, working with staff and resident surgeons, meeting with hospital administrators, serving on hospital committees, and handling complaints.

Dr. Williams relies a great deal on his administrative assistant, Jackie Jones, to handle many of the day-to-day matters. Jackie has worked at the hospital for 12 years, the last 3 in surgery. Dr. Williams has been head of surgery for 6 months. Because of his position and the nature of surgery, Dr. Williams often works nontraditional hours. He therefore leaves work for Jackie on her desk with brief instructions.

Jackie arrived at work Thursday morning to find a small stack of papers with an accompanying note that read, "Please complete these as soon as possible." Among the papers were a request for transfer and some items concerning the budget. Jackie felt that these were the most important items so she addressed them first. After carefully checking them, she passed them on to a secretary for typing.

It was almost 4:00 and Jackie was preparing to leave. Dr. Williams hurried into her work area and asked for the budget information. Jackie explained that it was being typed and that they would have it sometime the next morning. Dr. Williams became rather agitated because he had a 7:00 A.M. breakfast meeting and needed that information immediately.

Jackie rushed over to the secretary, only to discover that she had not even started typing the budget proposal. Jackie felt there was no other recourse but to type it herself. She returned to her work area to find Dr. Williams waiting. "The budget isn't ready," she explained, "so I'm going to stay and prepare it myself." Dr. Williams was glad to hear that Jackie would have it ready, but he also was concerned that she did not have it available already.

Jackie became rather assertive and said, "Ready now? Nothing in your note said you needed it by this afternoon." Dr. Williams picked up his instruction sheet and said, "It reads, right here, that they should be done as soon as possible."

Questions

1. What went wrong in the communication process?
2. Which person was in error in terms of failing to communicate?
3. How could this situation have been prevented?

Source: Written by Bruce Kemelgor, University of Louisville.

Experiential Exercise

Are You Really Listening?

Listening is probably one of the most important skills anyone can develop. It is used in all interpersonal verbal transactions and is essential for understanding to occur between sender and receiver. Effective listening is more than simply receiving a message, however. Effective listening involves active participation in helping a speaker be understood. Thus, someone who has actively listened has an understanding of both what was said and what was meant.

The skill of active listening involves using responses that do not offer advice or opinion. The response simply captures the listener's understanding of what the speaker is saying and why. This opens up the communication process so that the speaker knows that the listener actually *heard* what was said. A more meaningful conversation, free of initial judgmental roadblocks, can then ensue.

Step 1 Below are some statements that were made by employees to their manager. Read each statement and select the response that best represents active listening by placing an X next to it.

1. Each day brings new problems. You solve one and here comes another. . . . What's the use?
   _____ a.   I'm surprised to hear you say that.
   _____ b.   That's the way it is. There's no use getting upset over it.
   _____ c.   I know it's frustrating and sometimes discouraging to run into problem after problem.
   _____ d.   Give me an example so I know what you're referring to.

2. At our meeting yesterday, I was counting on you for some support. All you did was sit there and you never said anything!
   _____ a.   I was expecting you to ask for my opinion.
   _____ b.   You're evidently upset with the way I handled things at the meeting.
   _____ c.   Hey, I said some things on your behalf. You must not have heard me.
   _____ d.   I had my reasons for being quiet.

3. I don't know when I'm going to get that report done. I'm already swamped with work.
   _____ a.   See if you can get someone to help you.
   _____ b.   All of us have been in that situation, believe me.
   _____ c.   What do you mean swamped?
   _____ d.   You sound concerned about your workload.

4. I've been scheduled to be out of town again on Friday. This is the third weekend in a row that's been messed up!
   _____ a.   Why don't you talk with someone higher up and get it changed?
   _____ b.   Going on the road must be a burden to you.
   _____ c.   Everyone has to be on the road — it's part of the job.
   _____ d.   I'm sure this is the last trip you'll have to make for a while.

5. It seems like other people are always getting the easy jobs. How come I always get the hard ones?
   _____ a.   You feel I'm picking on you and that I'm being unfair in assigning work.
   _____ b.   What evidence do you have for saying that?
   _____ c.   If you'd look at the work schedule, you'd see that everyone has hard and easy jobs.
   _____ d.   What about that job I gave you yesterday?

6. When I first joined this company, I thought there would be plenty of chances to move up. Here I am, four years later, still doing the same thing.
   _____ a.   Let's talk about some of the things you could do to be promoted.
   _____ b.   Maybe you just haven't worked hard enough.
   _____ c.   Don't worry, I'm sure your chance will come soon.
   _____ d.   Getting ahead must be important to you. You sound disappointed.

7. Performance evaluations are here again. I wish I could just give all my people good ratings — it sure would be easier.

_____ a.   I know, but that's not possible.

_____ b.   We all feel that way. Don't get upset over it.

_____ c.   Performance evaluations seem to bother you.

_____ d.   Just do the best you can.

8. It's the same old thing day in and day out. Any child could do this job!

_____ a.   Your work is evidently getting you down and making you feel useless.

_____ b.   I always thought you liked your job.

_____ c.   What good is complaining going to do?

_____ d.   If you've got some ideas on improving your job, I'll be happy to listen.

9. I really appreciate getting the promotion. I just hope I can do the job.

_____ a.   Don't worry. I'm sure you'll get better as you get more experience.

_____ b.   What makes you think you can't do the job?

_____ c.   Don't worry. Most people have those same feelings.

_____ d.   I'm sure you can do it, or you wouldn't have been promoted.

10. I'm tired. That last sale really wore me out. I don't think I can handle another customer.

_____ a.   Sure you can. Just rest a few minutes and you'll be fine.

_____ b.   What have you been doing that's gotten you so tired?

_____ c.   You sound like you're exhausted.

_____ d.   We all get feeling that way; don't worry about it.

Step 2   Your instructor has information about the appropriate responses. You can verify your answers with this data.

Notes

1. O.W. Baskin and C.E. Aronoff, *Interpersonal Communication in Organizations* (Glenview, Ill.: Scott, Foresman, 1980), 4.

2. G. Johns, *Organizational Behavior: Understanding Life at Work* (Glenview, Ill.: Scott, Foresman, 1983).

3. C.A. O'Reilly and L.R. Pondy, "Organizational Communication," in *Organizational Behavior*, ed. S. Kerr (Columbus, Ohio: Grid, 1979), 119–150.

4. A. Bavelas and D. Barrett, "An Experimental Approach to Organization Communication," *Personnel* 27 (1951): 366–371; H.J. Leavitt, "Some Effects of Certain Communication Patterns on Group Performance," *Journal of Abnormal and Social Psychology* 46 (1951): 38–52; M.E. Shaw, *Group Dynamics: The Psychology of Small Group Behavior* (New York: McGraw-Hill, 1976).

5. C. Faucheux and K. MacKenzie, "Task Dependency and Organizational Centrality: Its Behavioral Consequences," *Journal of Experimental Sociology and Psychology* 2 (1966): 361–375.

6. B.L. Hawkins and P. Preston, *Managerial Communication* (Santa Monica, Calif.: Goodyear, 1981).

7. L.W. Rue and L. Byars, *Communication in Organizations* (Homewood, Ill.: Irwin, 1980).

8. A. Vogel, "Why Don't Employees Speak Up?" *Personnel Administration* 12 (1967): 19–23.

9. H. Fayol, *General and Industrial Management*, trans. Constance Storrs (London: Pitman, 1949).

10. E.M. Rogers and R.A. Rogers, *Communication in Organizations* (New York: Free Press, 1976).

11. A. Pettigrew, "Information Control as a Power Resource," *Sociology* 6 (1972): 187–204.

12. P.H. Lawrence and J.W. Lorsch, *Organization and Environment: Managing Differences and Integration* (Homewood, Ill.: Irwin, 1969).

13. K.H. Roberts and C.A. O'Reilly, "Some Correlates of Communication Roles in Organizations," *Academy of Management Journal* 22 (1979): 42–57.

14. E. Berne, *Games People Play* (New York: Grove Press, 1964).

15. T.A. Harris, *I'm OK — You're OK* (New York: Harper & Row, 1969).

16. F. Luthans and M.J. Martinko, *The Practice of Supervision and Management* (New York: McGraw-Hill, 1979), 386–387.

17. D.D. Bowen and R. Rath, "Transactional Analysis in OD: Applications within the NTL Model," *Academy of Management Review* 3 (1978): 79–89.

18. Baskin and Aronoff, *Interpersonal Communication in Organizations,* 102.

19. A. Mehrabian, "Verbal and Nonverbal Interaction of Strangers in a Waiting Situation," *Journal of Experimental Research in Personality* 5 (1971): 127–138; A. Mehrabian, *Silent Messages* (Belmont, Calif.: Wadsworth, 1971).

20. A. Mehrabian and M. Wiener, "Decoding of Inconsistent Communications," *Journal of Personality and Social Psychology* 6 (1967): 109–114.

21. Ibid.

22. A. Mehrabian, "Significance of Posture and Position in the Communication of Attitude and Status Relationships," *Psychological Bulletin* 71 (1971): 359–372; Mehrabian, "Decoding of Inconsistent Communications."

23. Ibid.

24. E.T. Hall, "A System for the Notation of Proxemic Behavior," *American Anthropologist* 5 (1963): 1003–1026.

25. E.T. Hall, *The Hidden Dimension* (Garden City, N.Y.: Doubleday, 1966).

26. R. Ardrey, *The Territorial Imperative* (New York: Atheneum, 1966).

27. W.F. Whyte, "The Social Structure of the Restaurant," *American Journal of Sociology* 54 (1949): 302–308.

28. H. Osmond, "Function as the Basis of Psychiatric Ward Design," *Mental Hospitals* 8 (1957): 23–32; H. Osmond, "The Relationship Between Architect and Psychiatrist," in *Psychiatric Architecture,* ed. C. Goshen (Washington, D.C.: American Psychiatric Association, 1959).

29. S. Van der Ryn and M. Silverstein, *Dorms at Berkeley: An Environmental Analysis* (Berkeley: Center for Planning and Development Research, 1967).

30. Baskin and Aronoff, *Interpersonal Communication in Organizations.*

31. E.H. Marcus, "Neurolinguistic Programming," *Personnel Journal* 27 (1983): 972.

32. E.E. Lawler, L.W. Porter, and A. Tannenbaum, "Managerial Attitudes Toward Interaction Episodes," *Journal of Applied Psychology* 52 (1968): 432–439.

33. W.V. Haney, *Communication and Interpersonal Relations* (Homewood, Ill.: Irwin, 1979).

34. K.E. Davis, *Human Behavior at Work* (New York: McGraw-Hill, 1977).

35. Ibid.

36. K.E. Davis, "Management Communication and the Grapevine," *Harvard Business Review* 31 (1953): 43–49.

37. Ibid.

38. R. Hershey, "The Grapevine — Here to Stay but not Beyond Control," *Personnel* 20 (1966): 64.

39. E. Walton, "How Efficient Is the Grapevine?" *Personnel* 15 (1961): 45–49; Davis, *Human Behavior at Work*; B. Marting, "A Study of Grapevine Communication Patterns in a Manufacturing Organization" (Ph.D. diss., Arizona State University, 1969); E. Rudolph, "A Study of Informal Communication Patterns Within a Multi-Shift Public Utility Organization Unit" (Ph.D. diss., University of Denver, 1971).

40. W. St. John, "In-House Communication Guidelines," *Personnel Journal* (1981): 877.

41. A.J. DuBrin, *Foundations of Organizational Behavior* (Englewood Cliffs, N.J.: Prentice-Hall, 1984).

42. K.H. Chung and L.C. Megginson, *Organizational Behavior: Developing Managerial Skills* (New York: Harper & Row, 1981), 203–204.

43. D. Craib, "Allstate's Communication Strategy: It's a Tool for Growth," *Communication World,* May 1986, 24–26.

16

Properly organized,
even crime pays.

— *Jim Fisk and
Robert Barron*

Corporation: an
ingenious device for
obtaining individual
profit without
individual
responsibility.

— *Ambrose Bierce*

Learning Objectives

After studying this chapter, you should be able to:

1. *Define decentralization and identify strengths and weaknesses of a decentralized organization.*

2. *Contrast tall and flat organizations.*

3. *Describe unity of command and chain of command.*

4. *Describe the six systems in the behavioral approach to organizational design.*

5. *Describe the relationship between technological and social systems in an organization.*

6. *Describe modern organizational designs.*

7. *Discuss advantages and disadvantages of different organizational designs.*

Organizational Design

■ P&G's Redesign

Procter & Gamble, the corporation known for virtually creating consumer marketing, found that its success required the company to re-create itself. During the mid-1980s, the once phenomenally successful company's profits were beginning to suffer, and leading products such as Crest and Pampers were losing market share. Observers blamed the company's massive size and cumbersome bureaucracy.

Under the leadership of then-CEO John Smale, P&G began to reorganize so that it could respond more quickly to changes in the marketplace. The company started with its sales force. The original system used 11 national sales forces, each selling a single product line such as foods or detergents. This meant that P&G's customers — retail stores — had to meet with different salespeople, all from the same company, but each selling different product lines and using different promotions. The system was awkward for retailers, but P&G was such an important supplier that they put up with the arrangement.

The restructured sales force is based on servicing customers, rather than on pushing products. Under the reorganized system, teams of representatives from finance, distribution, manufacturing, and other functions are assigned to cover the large retailers. The teams move beyond writing up sales to helping these customers improve inventory, distribution, and sales promotion. For example, a team working with Wal-Mart helped that retailer set up a just-in-time inventory system for Pampers and Luvs diapers. When a store's stock of diapers runs low, it transmits an order to a P&G factory via computer; the factory responds by automatically shipping more diapers to the store.

Having reorganized P&G's sales force, Smale turned to the company's celebrated brand management system. At the heart of this system are brand managers, coveted positions responsible for every aspect of a brand, including marketing, advertising, sales, and product development. In the old structure, each brand manager reported to a division head, which meant that each division head had to keep track of the activities of as many as 14 brand managers.

To have a major decision made, a brand manager might have to go through three or four layers of management. One manager reports that he had to wait a year just for approval of a simple change in package design. Furthermore, the brand managers were so focused on a single product that they might use tactics that hurt another P&G product, and no one was able to referee the harmful competition. Says a former employee, "There was a lot of cannibalization. You'd issue coupons at the same time for P&G's liquid and powdered detergents."

Therefore Smale developed an organizational structure called category management. He divided the company into 39 product categories and assigned them to 26 category managers (some have more than one category). Brand managers report to a category manager, who is responsible for the profitability of the entire product line — for example, all laundry detergents, including Tide, Cheer, and Ivory Flakes. This category manager must ensure that decisions are for the benefit of the entire product line. The category management system also speeds up decision making by authorizing the category managers to make decisions involving expenditures of up to $1 million per project.

These changes are designed to reduce the number of layers of management required for decision making. Says Smale, "The creation of these category profit centers was really a continuation of the basic philosophy that small is good, that you bring focus to a specific business when you create a stand-alone operation."

As Procter & Gamble's executives have found, the way an organization is structured is an ongoing concern. Sometimes a structure appropriate for the company's early years must be changed. This chapter describes some characteristics of the designs that organizations adopt. It also discusses advantages and disadvantages of different organizational designs.

Source: Brian Dumaine, "Marketing Rules," *Fortune,* November 6, 1989, pp. 34–36+.

In the previous chapters of this text, we examined concepts that apply to either individuals or small groups of individuals in organizational settings. In this chapter, we will turn our focus to the impact that the organization has on behavior. Thus, while the previous chapters emphasized the micro aspects of organizational behavior, this chapter will look at some macro influences. In this context the terms *micro* and *macro* refer to different levels of analysis or conceptualization. The *micro level* examines conditions and processes from a more individually oriented perspective, while the *macro level* deals with conditions and processes involving organizations and the external environment.*

In this chapter, we will consider initially the major principles of organizing. Next, we will examine the classical, behavioral, and sociotechnical views of organizational design. Then, we will examine some contemporary notions of organizational design.

Principles of Organizing

Organizations can be described in terms of how their component parts are put together and operate. Researchers who study the concepts of organizational structure and function frequently describe organizations in terms of several important dimensions: decentralization versus centralization, tall versus flat structure, unity of command, and chain of command.

Decentralization versus Centralization

Decentralization is the degree to which decision making occurs lower down in an institution. In a more centralized institution, there is relatively less participation by employees in a variety of decisions. Decentralized organizations are characterized by less monitoring or checking on decisions made by employees.

---

* It has been humorously suggested that the micro approach to OB examines employees as if the organization did not matter, while the macro approach to OB examines organizations as if the employees did not matter.

It is especially difficult to measure the extent of decentralization that exists in an organization. To be sure, we cannot rely on the statements of top management regarding the extent of decentralization present in their own corporation, since executives tend to endorse the value of decentralization and to perceive its existence. One particularly useful means of assessing the degree of decentralization is to examine the dollar amount of expenses employees are permitted to incur without prior approval by a superior. Generally, the larger the amount of latitude allowed employees on expenditures, the greater the extent of decentralization that may be inferred. In addition, the variety and magnitude of decisions made outside of the top or central office can provide an index of the degree of decentralization.

Although the concept of decentralization has acquired a positive halo,† it is not reasonable to endorse the notion of decentralization for all organizations and all situations. Most organizational researchers believe that it is best to think in terms of an optimal level of decentralization for any given organization or its divisions. The identification of the specific forces that dictate the optimal level of decentralization has been a focus of much macro-level research.

Robert Duncan has offered a number of possible weaknesses associated with decentralized organizational structures:

1. Because of a lack of integrative and coordinated direction, there is a tendency to focus on current problems and functions, and to ignore opportunities for growth and innovation.

2. Shared resources (such as computer equipment, staff, and lab facilities) may pose problems because of the need to allocate their usage. Similarly, shared functions (such as research and development and purchasing departments) may create coordinating difficulties.

3. Internal disputes and conflicts may arise. These conflicts may not be easily resolved because each department or division operates with relative independence. Also, potential disputes between units are not as likely to be detected, averted, or well managed if the actions of units are not coordinated.[1]

As these points imply, extreme decentralization can lead to a lack of needed integration and coordination. Nonetheless, decentralization is often touted as a beneficial organizational attribute because of its anticipated enhancement of employee motivation, performance, satisfaction, and creativity. According to this popular line of reasoning, the greater level of autonomy that decentralization affords to employees leads to greater employee involvement and commitment. As a consequence, employees' attitudes and performance are enhanced. Many successful organizations have relied heavily on being decentralized. For example, Digital Equipment Corporation, following the philosophy of its founder, Kenneth H. Olsen, achieved significant growth in large part because of a decentralized organization structure that gave each senior man-

---

† One of the earliest "success stories" of the use of decentralization is reported in the Old Testament. In Exodus 18, Moses is reported to have been overburdened by judicial decision making. On the advice of his father-in-law, Jethro, Moses restructured the process so that a system of judges took responsibility for making many minor decisions.

■ **Figure 16.1**

Examples of Tall and Flat Structures

Flat Organization

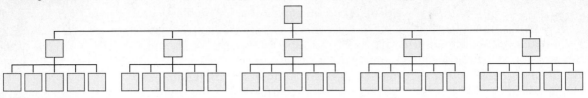

Tall Organization

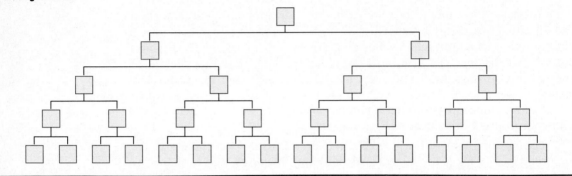

ager substantial responsibility for an individual product line.[2] Evidence in the area of job enrichment (see Chapter 7) generally confirms the positive impact of increasing employees' self-direction and sense of responsibility. Of course, these enrichment studies have not typically attempted the sweeping changes that radical decentralization of an entire organization implies. Hence, the limits of decentralization (that is, the dysfunctional effects due to the lack of integration and coordination of efforts) have not been observed in studies of job enrichment.

Tall versus Flat Structures

Tall structure versus **flat structure** refers to the number of levels of authority and the width (or size) of each level. Tall organizations have more levels, while flat organizations have fewer levels. Figure 16.1 provides examples of both types of organization. Note that the tall organization has five levels of management, while the flat organization has three. Also, both organization structures used in the figure happen to involve the same number of units, 31. Thus, configuration rather than size determines the tallness or flatness of a structure.‡

‡ Noted management consultant, Peter Drucker, recommended (in 1954) that seven layers of administration is the maximum necessary for any organization. More recently, Thomas Peters, another widely read consultant, insisted that five layers is the maximum for a large organization (based partly on the reasoning that five administrative layers are employed by the Catholic church to oversee 900 million members). For less sizable organizations, Peters recommends three administrative layers as the maximum.[3]

OB Focus

Centralized Structure Positions Ford for Changes in Europe

In 1992, trade barriers are coming down in Western Europe. This economic restructuring should bring about a new generation of winners and losers among the companies who do business there. In the auto industry, the changes are expected to bring in more outside manufacturers, especially from Japan. Many companies are likely to establish European subsidiaries, in case the European countries band together to limit imports from outside the European Community.

One company that is expected to be a winner is Ford Motor Company. Ford has production facilities in six European nations, including Spain and Portugal, where labor costs are low. Each of these plants is large enough to serve all of Europe. For example,

Ford's transmission plant in the Bordeaux region of France is the region's largest exporter, surpassing even the wine for which Bordeaux is famous.

What is especially important for Ford's competitive edge is the centralized structure of these operations. Under the coordination of Ford of Europe headquarters, the company routinely ships components and assembled vehicles from one nation to another. This setup parallels Ford's North American operations.

This arrangement is no accident. Back in 1967, when it first appeared that the West European nations were headed toward economic unity, Henry Ford II concluded that the company should function as if there were one European market.

In response, the company consolidated its assembly operations and built giant plants to replace older, smaller facilities. Ford continued to use national sales forces, but placed them under the authority of Ford of Europe.

Even before the European unity of 1992, this arrangement made Ford's European operations profitable when performance in the United States was suffering. But most important for the future, the company has already had practice in manufacturing and distributing its cars on a continental scale. Michael Coleman, an attorney with Baker and McKenzie, a law firm specializing in European trade issues, calls Ford "the archetype of the true European firm."

Source: Michael Arndt, "Ford Is Providing a Model for Conquering New Europe," *Chicago Tribune*, December 11, 1989, sec. 4, pp. 1, 4.

Tall and flat structures also differ in terms of the **span of control** they employ. Span of control refers to the number of employees who report to a single supervisor and thus partially dictates the height of an organization. In the tall organization depicted in Figure 16.1, the span of control is two; in the flat organization, it is five. It can be said that the span of control partially dictates the tallness of the organization. Therefore, the question can be raised, "What is the ideal span of control?" The most widely used logic on this point argues that spans can be larger at lower levels in an organization than at higher levels. Because subordinates in lower-level positions are typically doing much more routine and uniform activities, more subordinates can be effectively supervised at lower levels. In fact, larger spans are often found at lower levels in organizations. However, there is a tendency in many organizations characterized by very large spans (for example, 20 or more subordinates) to employ informal team leaders within a unit. These informal team leaders report to the unit's supervisor. Yet, they may not be officially recognized as a layer of management within the organization. The informal team leader approach allows a supervisor to expand the number of subordinates he can effectively supervise and at the same time not create a cumbersome layer of management.

Generally, a taller organization, with its narrower spans of control, allows for closer control of subordinates in that supervisors have more time to devote to monitoring fewer individuals. Therefore, tall organizations tend to discourage decentralization, while flat organizations are more predisposed to use decentralized decision making.

In terms of overall performance, it has traditionally been assumed that tall organizations are superior to flat organizations. However, research conducted by James Worthy on Sears, Roebuck and Company has challenged this assumption.[4] He observed that those Sears stores utilizing flat structures had relatively better sales, profitability, and employee job satisfaction than stores with taller structures. These results suggest that larger spans of control may produce positive advantages. The precise mechanism by which such gains can be achieved is not clearly understood as yet. However, it is likely that flatter structures possess greater decentralization, and decentralization serves as the driving force for improving employee performance and attitudes.

While flatter structures may have some unanticipated advantages, they also can be the source of disadvantages. When carried to an extreme, "flatness" can be dysfunctional. As an illustration, consider the following case of a small, family-owned construction company. The firm initially did relatively simple repair jobs and modest home improvement projects. Soon business improved, and the founder needed to hire additional workers. These workers had to be supervised in teams, since the several groups were geographically dispersed when working on various projects. Eventually, a full-time accountant was needed to handle the financial side of the enterprise. Then, a sales manager was hired to prepare newspaper and radio ads, to meet with clients, and to close deals. Next, a full-time engineer was employed by the firm to draw up and modify construction plans. As business continued to improve, the owner discovered that it would be better to stock and maintain an inventory of needed materials rather than depend on other sources for his supplies. The creation of the resulting warehouse operation afforded a new opportunity for revenues: people in the area came to his warehouse to purchase home repair and improvement materials (such as nails, siding, and lumber). As a result, the owner set up a successful outlet store as part of the warehouse operation.

At about this time, he came to recognize that running the firm was simply too burdensome for one individual. The structure of the organization was totally flat. All divisions of the enterprise reported to one person, the company's founder. Whenever a decision had to be made (regarding, for example, how much lumber to stock, whether to start a large project, or the hiring of construction workers), the owner felt obliged to make the decision. As a result, employees were continually approaching him with major, and many minor, issues. As his workweeks came to exceed 80 and 90 hours, the company's founder called in a consultant to recommend ways of improving efficiency and helping him to cope with the demands of the job.

The consultant's recommendation was to redesign the organization so that it would be taller. Specifically, he recommended that two managers be

Figure 16.2

Organizational Structures for a Construction Firm

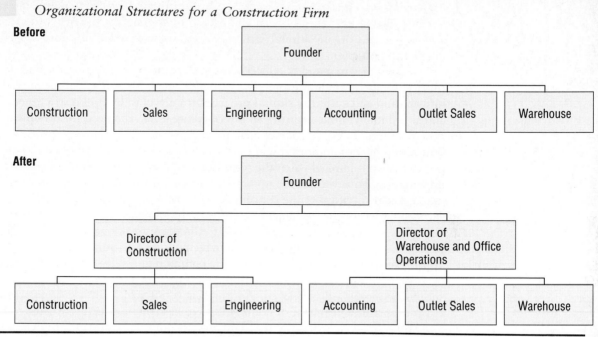

appointed, one to oversee warehouse/office operations and the other to oversee the construction/sales side of the firm. Figure 16.2 illustrates the original and the redesigned organization structures for the firm. As the figure shows, the newer, taller structure affords greater control of each unit because of reduced spans of control. In addition, the founder no longer must coordinate the efforts of a large number of diverse units.

Alternatively, the founder could have tried delegating decision-making authority to the various units (i.e., decentralizing the operations of the firm). Instead, he opted for the taller structure, which helped to increase rather than decrease his control of the firm. Given the high personal financial stakes involved in running a firm, it is not uncommon to find that founders are predisposed to seek greater personal control.

Unity and Chain of Command

Unity of command and chain of command are two further principles of organizing. **Unity of command** means that every subordinate should have one and only one supervisor, that is, each subordinate is accountable to and takes orders from a single supervisor. As you might imagine, this notion is intended to improve performance by reducing potential conflicts and ambiguities that might arise if a subordinate dealt with several superiors. By clearly assigning each subordinate to a specific superior, speed of response to problems and information flow should be optimum.

It has long been assumed that unity of command is a cornerstone of organizational efficiency. However, the notion that unity of command must not be violated has recently been challenged by the matrix system, a modern and innovative organizational structure that we will examine more closely later in this chapter.

Chain of command is concerned with the flow of information and authority within an organization. As a principle, chain of command means that information and authority should proceed from level to level in a strict hierarchical fashion without omitting an intermediate level. The need for downward flow of authority is, of course, easy to understand. The converse process, a bottom-up flow of authority, while still within the logic of chain of command, is generally not implied when the term chain of command is invoked. Flow of information, however, can be upward or downward within the chain of command. What is critical to the concept in terms of information flow is that each succeeding level of management be completely informed.

The suspected advantages of strict adherence to the chain of command principle are that no higher level of management will be uninformed and that appropriate levels are involved in seeking common goals. By following a chain of command approach, coordination of effort and integration of activities should be more easily achieved. Although it is not widely invoked, a further reason for following chain of command involves simple courtesy to superiors and subordinates. Generally, it is best not to omit or "end-run" individuals within the chain of command, since they are likely to learn about it informally and be resentful of not having been informed or involved in the process.

Organizations differ in the extent to which chain of command is strictly followed. In organizations where uniformity of mission and purpose are important (such as in maintaining orthodoxy in a religious organization), chain of command is likely to be more firmly engrained as a practice. Similarly, in organizations where coordination of effort is highly valued, such as the military, chain of command is also closely followed. Less formally structured organizations (such as voluntary associations or social clubs) may have less serious need to follow the chain of command principle strictly.

The Classical Approach to Organizational Design

In the early part of this century, Max Weber, a German sociologist, outlined a systematic view of organizations based on the notion of bureaucracy. Weber suggested that **bureaucracy** was the best administrative form for the rational and efficient pursuit of organizational goals.[5]

According to Weber, a perfect bureaucracy possesses:

1. *Rules and procedures.* Weber believed that a rational approach to managing tasks should be the dominant principle in organizations. In a bureaucracy, standard operating procedures provide greater certainty and aid in coordinating efforts.

2. *The principle of hierarchy.* In Weber's model, positions are arranged hierarchically, with the lower positions controlled and supervised by the higher ones. Such an arrangement helps to maintain control over

■ **Table 16.1**

Potential Pluses and Minuses of Bureaucracy

Pluses	Minuses
Control	Barriers to change
Order	Reduced employee satisfaction
Efficiency	Reduced discretion
Stability	Red tape
Memory	Power seeking
Rule by reason	

the members of the organization and ensures order. In essence, Weber advocated a clear chain of command or hierarchy of authority.

3. *Division of labor and specialization.* Tasks should be broken down and assigned to employees. Each employee should have the expertise needed to master his or her work assignment. The obtainment of such expertise would be aided by making certain that each work assignment is highly specialized. In addition, each employee should be given the authority and resources to perform his or her duties.

4. *Impersonality.* In the idealized bureaucratic system, managers would maintain an air of impersonality toward employees, especially subordinates. This impersonal attitude would help to ensure that rational considerations were the basis for decision making, rather than favoritism or personal prejudice. Maintaining such a formal atmosphere would also make it easier to evaluate employees solely on the basis of actual performance.

5. *Competence.* Technical ability and expertise should be the basis for hiring, job assignments, and promotions. Possession of relevant qualifications and evidence of merit rather than family ties or friendship would determine the receipt of rewards.

6. *Record keeping.* People's memories enable them to recall the outcomes of past dealings with their surroundings and thereby adjust their future conduct in order to obtain advantages. Organizations can, in a sense, possess memories through the maintenance of written records. Such documents enable the organization's members to check on past performance and to record decisions and rules. Written records also aid in the creation of a base of information for training employees to perform specific tasks.

An Assessment of Weber's View

Weber advocated the bureaucratic form as an ideal approach to structuring organizations. Clearly, the widespread presence of bureaucracies throughout our nation and the world attests to the appeal of his principles. Yet the many positive aspects of the bureaucratic form are offset in practice by some negative features, as summarized in Table 16.1.[6]

One major drawback of bureaucracy stems from its *emphasis on authority*. Managers in bureaucratic organizations are often unwilling to surrender their authority and are typically interested in acquiring more power. They may also use their authority to preserve their own territory and eliminate challenges. For example, managers in a bureaucracy frequently resist proposed changes in rules and procedures. As a result, bureaucracies can be characterized as *conservative and inflexible,* characteristics that discourage innovation.

Reliance on rules and the maintenance of an impersonal attitude can lead to other dysfunctions, including the inability to cope with unique cases that do not "fit the mold" and for which the rule book does not dictate a solution. Impersonality can also lead to feelings of *frustration* for people who must work in or with a bureaucracy due to the system's lack of a "soft side" or "human face." In addition, the emphasis on rules and procedures can produce *excessive red tape.* The creation of new rules to cover emerging situations and new contingencies can make the official procedures, delays, and inaction of such systems virtually unbearable.

Highly specialized task assignments can lead to feelings of *alienation* or *estrangement* among employees, and the related lack of challenge and novelty can lead to dissatisfaction and turnover. As discussed in Chapter 7, people generally prefer jobs that are not highly fragmented or specialized. Because competence can be difficult to measure in bureaucratic jobs and because a high degree of specialization enables most workers to master their required tasks in little time, there is also a tendency to *base promotions more on seniority and loyalty* than on competence and merit.

For many of us, the term bureaucracy has a negative connotation. It conjures up a vision of a large unfeeling institution that is frustrating to deal with. Among the organizations that fit this negative stereotype are agencies of the federal government, such as the Internal Revenue Service and the Defense Department, and state and local government agencies, such as boards of education.

But despite the problems they may create, bureaucratic characteristics have also been associated with positive measures of organizational performance. Specifically, it has been found that greater degrees of bureaucracy (when controlling for differences in the size of various organizations) are associated with higher levels of performance. Organizations that try to maintain a more informal structure do less well if they are relatively large. Smaller organizations of less than roughly 2,000 members tend to have better performance records when they are less bureaucratic.[7] Figure 16.3 portrays this relationship.

Richard Daft suggests that certain organizational attributes dictate that bureaucratic characteristics be avoided.[8] For example, smaller organizations should try to maintain informality by reducing rules and red tape, and they should use face-to-face interactions as the basis of supervision.[9] Professionals do not respond well to bureaucracies either. As a result of their training and the prevailing norms in their fields, researchers, technical specialists, consultants, and the like prefer freedom from rules and procedures. Finally, organizations that are experiencing a high rate of environmental change need to be

■ Figure 16.3

*Relationship between Size of Organization,
Bureaucracy, and Performance*

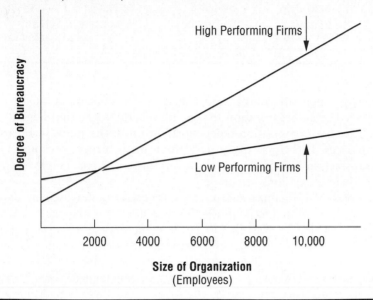

Source: Adapted from John Child, "Managerial and Organizational Factors Associated with Company Performance, Part II. A Contingency Analysis," *Journal of Management Studies* 12 (1975): 12–27.

more free flowing and flexible. A bureaucracy would be too slow moving for organizations that need to adapt frequently or quickly to meet constant changes in customer needs or innovations in technology.

In summary, bureaucracy offers many advantages for improving organizational performance. These benefits can be best realized in larger organizations that function in relatively stable environments and employ workers who are tolerant of the limitations of bureaucracy.§

The Behavioral Approach to Organizational Design

Given the speed of technological change, an increasing rate of innovation, and growing demands by a more highly educated work force, many scholars suggest that the classical view of organizations will become outdated. In response to the resulting frustration, bureaucracies will begin to fade away and will be replaced by more creative forms of organization. Rensis Likert, a proponent of a behavioral alternative to the bureaucratic approach, has proposed a multilevel classification of organizations (Figure 16.4).[11]

Each of the systems can be characterized in terms of a number of attributes. A System O organization is a permissive type of organization character-

§ Resistance to bureaucracy may also stem from individual differences in the ability to adjust to the characteristics of bureaucracy. People who react to bureaucracy with strong suspicion due to their own immaturity may be termed *bureauotics;* those who suffer from "bureausis" rarely rise very far in an organization's hierarchy.[10]

System 0 Permissive	**System 1** Exploitive Authoritative	**System 2** Benevolent Authoritative	**System 3** Consultative	**System 4** Participative	**System 4T** Total Participation

ized by large spans of control and substantial confusion. It might best be characterized as an organization that is in an early, formative stage.

A System 1 organization relies mostly on fear and punishment to motivate employees. Distrust is likely to be high in such organizations, and employee satisfaction low. Because authoritarianism prevails, employees are not consulted before decisions are made.

In a System 2 organization, rewards are used to motivate employees and employees are permitted to comment on directives, but managers still control the decision-making process. Employees may have some freedom in how they conduct their jobs, yet their relations with superiors are guarded and cautious.

In a System 3 organization, subordinates are more readily consulted; however, major decisions are still made by upper management. Threats are avoided as a means of motivating employees, and there is a degree of trust between managers and subordinates. Employee performance and satisfaction are expected to be higher in this system than in Systems 1 and 2.

System 4 is viewed by Likert as an ideal state toward which managers should try to move their organizations. Trust is extremely high among System 4 members, and a variety of economic, ego, and social factors are used as incentives. Communication moves not only downward but also upward and horizontally. Most critically, decision making occurs at all levels and involves all members equally. In a sense, System 4 approaches a democratic, or highly participative, form in that the input of employees is fully incorporated in the decision-making process. As a consequence of these positive attributes, Likert predicted that both employee performance and satisfaction would be greatest in a System 4 organization.

System 4T is a somewhat idealized type of organization in which authority is based on intragroup relationships and overlapping group memberships instead of on a hierarchy. The *T* stands for *total* participation, and implies stable and strong working relationships among members.[12] Performance and employee satisfaction should be maximal in this type of organization.

Research on the accuracy of Likert's model is sparse. In a review of the available evidence, Miner suggests that the model may work best at the level of the work group, since it is largely stated in terms of work group processes.[13] Furthermore, the accuracy of the model probably depends on particular circumstances.[14] However, the model is not sufficiently specific to help a manager identify the appropriate circumstances in advance.

Although Likert's view has value as a guide to consultants who wish to bring about organizational change, one of its underlying premises is difficult to

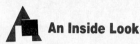

An Inside Look

Restructuring for Customer Service

Likert probably would have approved of the changes instituted in the organizational structure of United Technologies Corporation by Robert F. Daniell, the company's chief executive. In an effort to get managers and workers to assume greater responsibility for satisfying customers, Daniell has been transforming the company from what was in effect a System 1 (exploitative authoritative) organization to more of a System 4 (participative) organization.

The changes are especially apparent at UTC's subsidiary, Pratt & Whitney Company, which makes jet engines. There, in the two years since the restructuring began, orders have ballooned eightfold.

In the past, autocratic management and an overly intricate bureaucracy left employees with little power to get things done. For example, if the Pratt & Whitney workers making an airplane want to mount an engine a fraction of a millimeter closer to the wing than the blueprint specifies, a good engineer could normally look at the blueprint and decide whether the change would work. But under the old company structure, such a change would have to be approved by nine departments as well as a committee that met only once a week.

Under Daniell's leadership, the company whittled away much of this paperwork. Now a design engineer can make such a decision after obtaining three signatures. Consequently, average response time for approving changes has plummeted from 82 days to 10, and the backlog of requests has shrunk from 1,900 to less than 100.

Employee participation in decision making extends to the company's service representatives in the field. In the past, approval for warranty replacements costing millions of dollars had to come from company headquarters, which could take weeks. Airframe makers that used parts from Pratt & Whitney had to shut down their assembly lines as often as 40 times a month waiting for parts from the company. Under the restructuring, field reps were given authority to authorize replacements on the spot. Now the company causes only an average of two work stoppages a month.

Source: Todd Vogel, "Where 1990s-style Management Is Already Hard at Work," *Business Week*, October 23, 1989, pp. 92–94+.

accept. Likert assumed that a single, best solution exists for all settings, an assumption that also underlies Weber's advocacy of the bureaucratic form. As a result, both Weber's and Likert's approaches can be viewed as being somewhat simplistic.

The Sociotechnical Systems Approach

Eric Trist and his associates at the Tavistock Institute in Great Britain are well known for conducting a series of studies that led to a new, insightful approach to understanding organizational functioning.[15] These studies, which focused on the coal-mining industry in Great Britain, examined the interaction of technological systems and social systems. At the beginning of their studies, coal mining was performed by a time-honored method known as shortwall mining. This method involved groups of two to eight miners working as teams to extract coal. In addition to being paid as teams for their output, the groups selected their own members and rotated the various and numerous tasks associated with mining a small section (or seam) of coal. Because of the dangers of working with explosives in dark, confined areas seldom more than 3 feet high, the men came to develop strong emotional ties with group members. These social relations below ground were closely mirrored in social relations above ground as well.

As technology advanced, newly developed mining equipment dictated a radically different approach to coal mining. In this new longwall method, the miners were reorganized into large shifts of specialized workers. During the first shift of the day, all of the miners performed the same operation: cutting into the coal wall. The second shift was responsible for shoveling coal into a new type of conveyor. The miners on the third shift worked exclusively at advancing the face of the wall, enlarging gateways, and building roof supports (relatively low-prestige tasks).

In addition, the miners on each shift were spread out along the face of the coal wall at such distances that they could not easily communicate with one another. Similarly, the single supervisor of an entire shift group, consisting of 40 to 50 miners, was not able to monitor the activities of each miner because of the manner in which the men were dispersed.

Although the longwall method had promised to raise productivity, a norm of low productivity emerged. With reduced variety and challenge, the miners found the redesigned work to be unpleasant. They preferred to operate autonomously and to perform *all* of the tasks rather than to be solely performing the tasks of cutting, shoveling, or filling.

While the Tavistock researchers eventually helped to ameliorate the negative consequences of the longwall method, the message was clear: a technological change that appears quite rational from a purely engineering perspective can disrupt the existing social system so as to reduce greatly the anticipated benefits of the new technology. Of more fundamental importance is the insight gained by the Tavistock researchers on the interplay of technical and social systems. This notion of a **sociotechnical system** arose, therefore, from a consideration that any production-oriented organization involves both a technological system (equipment, task, and process design) and a social system (working relations). While the technological system places demands on the social organization, the social organization has properties of its own, quite independent of the technology, that have an impact on the technological system. Attempts to change the technological and/or social system must be mindful of the relationship between the two systems.

The sociotechnical approach has much to suggest to job redesign (see Chapter 7). In fact, the approach has been employed in numerous job redesign efforts. Some of the better publicized redesign efforts have been attempted at General Foods, Rushton Mining, and General Motors. At the Kalmar plant of Volvo, automobile assembly procedures were radically altered from traditional methods in light of an approach that was sensitive to the interface of social and technological systems. By and large, the results of these efforts have netted reduced turnover, absenteeism, and accident rates and superior product quality and efficiency.[16]

In contrast to the behavioral and classical approaches, the sociotechnical approach does not espouse a simplistic view of organizational processes. How-

■ Figure 16.5

Example of the Functional Form of Organization

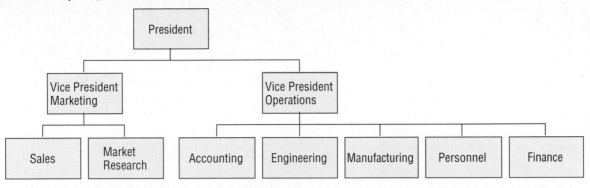

ever, despite its relative sophistication, the sociotechnical perspective is currently overshadowed by a more recently developed approach, the contingency view of organizational design.

A Look at Some Modern Organization Designs

Far and away, the most prevalent organization designs in use today are of three varieties: functional, product, and a hybrid of functional and product. Each of the three varieties offers advantages for coping with various contingencies. However, each form also has potential weaknesses.

Functional Form

Organizations designed along functional lines group personnel and activities according to the resources that are essential to the production process. The contributions of the resulting functional departments aid in the total organizational mission. Figure 16.5 provides an organization chart for a hypothetical firm with a functional design.

A **functional form** is especially appropriate when the most important needs of an organization are collaboration and expertise within a defined set of operations, when the environment is stable, and when only one or a few products are produced. However, the functional form suffers from several weaknesses. It tends to be slow to respond to changes in the organization's environment. It may also result in less innovation and a restricted view of and allegiance to the organization's broader goals. The functional form may also have difficulty in coordinating activities among departments. The measurement of the contribution of each department is also problematic as the end product is a composite result of production, personnel, engineering, design, and marketing efforts. Last, the distinct advantage of the functional form (i.e., greater coordination) may become a disadvantage as the organization becomes larger and more complex.

Figure 16.6

Example of a Product Form of Organization

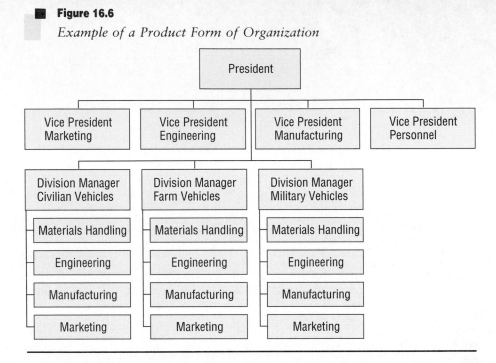

Product Form

An organization that selects a **product form** groups personnel and activities according to organizational output. Each product line is provided with its own production, marketing, and development resources as part of the structuring. The primary goals of a product structure are coordination within product lines and attention to customer desires. Figure 16.6 provides an organizational chart for a hypothetical firm with a product design.

A product form of organization is better suited to adapt to changes in the organization's environment and is especially appropriate for organizations that produce many diverse products or are highly consumer oriented. At the same time, a product form organization may lead to tremendous losses in economies of scale, redundancy of effort, and little cooperation across product lines. Sharing of competencies and technical advantages is also limited. Internal competition may arise as well. Although competition can be healthy up to a point, the structure of the organization may propel the initial competition into a full-blown power struggle.

Hybrid Form

As a consequence of either form's limitations, few firms use a pure functional or product structure. More typically, large modern organizations combine the advantages of both functional and product forms into a **hybrid form.** Some functions may be highly specialized and located at corporate headquarters,

■ **Figure 16.7**

Example of a Hybrid Organization Structure

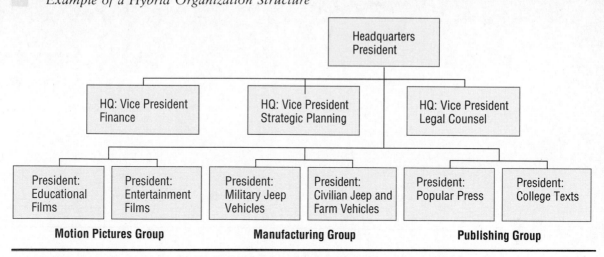

while other product or market units may be self-contained and located else-where. By striving for a balance between functional and product forms, an organization can have the best of both worlds. Hybrids typically provide prod-uct groups with the functional support they need within a product line, while also trying to maintain functional departments for activities that are required by all divisions of the organization. Figure 16.7 presents a sample organization chart of a hybrid organization involved in three distinct product areas.

Of course, an organization's structure is rarely static. More commonly, structure changes and evolves over time as top-level managers attempt to better adapt their firm to the changing features of its surroundings.

Matrix Design   In some unique situations, a refined balance between func-tional and product structures is required to give recognition to both functional and product-related issues. When continuous interchange between product and function is necessary, a matrix organizational design may be warranted. In a **matrix design,** the functional and product managers enjoy equal authority. Personnel are required to report to managers from both the functional and product divisions. In essence, a matrix design involves a dual hierarchy.

To illustrate more precisely what is meant by a matrix system, consider Figure 16.8. In this organization, a top-level manager oversees one manager whose responsibilities are functional and one manager whose responsibilities are product related. These two managers, in turn, oversee the single employee whose work relates to both their areas. Thus, in violation of the principle of unity of command, the employee is involved in a two-boss system.

Carrying this illustration a step further to include an entire management group, we could create the matrix design shown in Figure 16.9. At each inter-

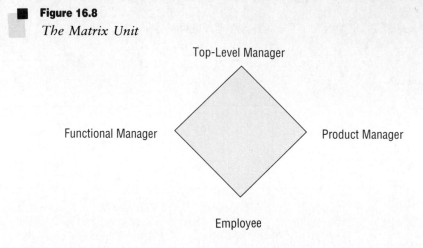

■ **Figure 16.8**
The Matrix Unit

Top-Level Manager

Functional Manager   Product Manager

Employee

section of the lines of authority and responsibility for the product and functional divisions, project groups would exist. As this figure suggests, personnel and resources would be grouped together to tackle product-specific problems.

In theory, everyone in an organization could be in the web of a matrix. However, most organizations that employ a matrix design limit its use to management-level personnel and maintain a traditional pyramid-shaped structure for the remainder of the firm.[17] Figure 16.10 illustrates such a configuration.

On the negative side, matrix systems can create significant frustration and confusion, especially for the employee who reports to two superiors. In addition, employees who are not adequately trained in how to adapt to a matrix system may persist in behaving as if they were in a more traditional top-down, one-boss situation. Finally, the use of a matrix design is very time-consuming. Frequent meetings and conflict-resolution sessions are likely to be necessary, and communications must often be duplicated for the benefit of both superiors. Performance evaluation may also become complicated because in appraising a single subordinate, the potentially conflicting views of two superiors must be resolved. In short, many of the problems that one would expect from violating the principle of unity of command will occur in a matrix system if people do not cooperate in resolving conflicts over the sharing of power and resources. A collaborative and collegial spirit is therefore necessary if a matrix form of organization is to succeed.

Matrix designs are used in manufacturing, service, professional, and non-profit organizations. Although matrix systems were first used in the 1960s,[18] their use did not spread until the 1970s and 1980s. Davis and Lawrence characterize this phenomenon as something of a "quiet revolution" that began largely in the aerospace industry and whose end is not yet in sight.[19]

Matrix systems are extremely flexible in their use of both human and material resources, and they can aid in coordinating responses to the dual

■ **Figure 16.9**

Example of a Matrix Organization

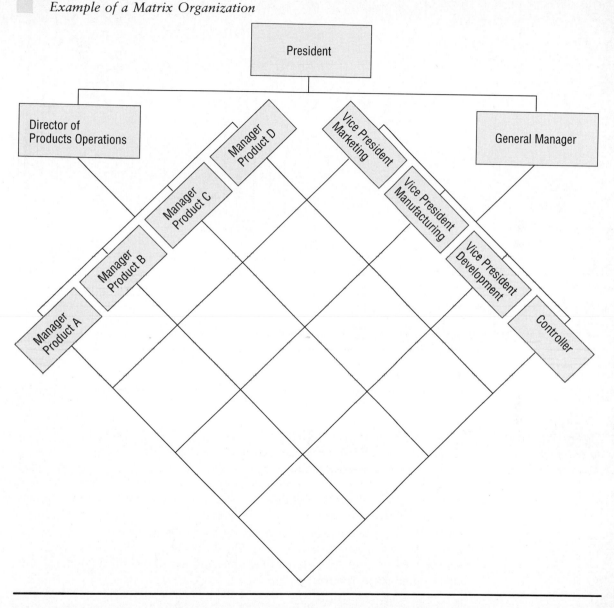

difficulties created by customer- and production-related pressures.** Given their flexibility, matrix designs are especially appropriate for organizations that exist in unstable environments, for example, groups that are growing rapidly due to increasing rates of change in technology and consumer preferences.

** Given the continual reshuffling of human and material resources, a good way of describing the dynamics of matrix design is with the three-dimensional analogy of a Rubik's cube.

Figure 16.10

A Combination Matrix and Pyramid Structure

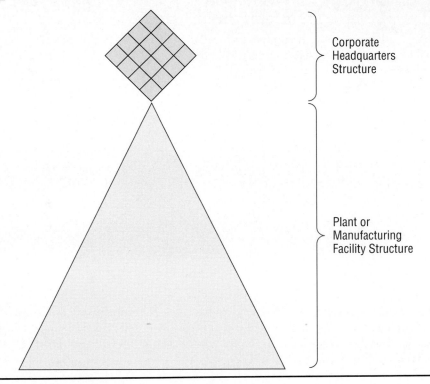

Corporate
Headquarters
Structure

Plant or
Manufacturing
Facility Structure

Summary

1. Define decentralization and identify strengths and weaknesses of a decentralized organization.
Decentralization is the degree to which decision making occurs lower down in an organization. A strength of decentralization is that it can enhance employee motivation, performance, satisfaction, creativity, involvement, and commitment. Weaknesses include a tendency to focus on immediate problems and ignore opportunities for future growth, difficulties in allocating shared resources and coordinating shared functions, and internal conflicts that are difficult to detect and resolve.

2. Contrast tall and flat organizations.
Tall organizations have more levels and narrower spans of control than flat organizations. Generally, tall organizations allow for closer control of subordinates. Tall organizations tend to discourage decentralization, while flat organizations are more likely to be decentralized.

3. Describe unity of command and chain of command.
Unity of command is the idea that every subordinate should have only one supervisor. Chain of command maintains that information and authority proceed from level to level in a hierarchical fashion without omitting any level.

4. Describe the six systems in the behavioral approach
to organizational design.

An organization in an early, formative stage may be characterized as permissive, with large spans of control and much confusion (System 0). An exploit-
ative-authoritative organization (System 1) relies on fear and punishment to
motivate employees. Decision makers do not consult employees. A benevolent-
authoritative organization (System 2) uses rewards to motivate employees.
Employees may comment on directives, but managers still make the decisions.
In a consultative organization (System 3), managers consult subordinates more
readily and avoid using threats, but upper management still makes the major
decisions. In a participative organization (System 4), decision making occurs at
all levels and involves all members equally. Trust is extremely high, and incentives include economic, ego, and social rewards. An idealized form of organization (System 4T) is based on intragroup relationships and overlapping group
memberships.

5. Describe the relationship between technological and social
systems in an organization.

The technological system (equipment, task, and process design) interacts with
the social system (working relations), each influencing the nature of the other.

6. Describe modern organizational designs.

The functional form of organization groups personnel and activities according
to the resources that are essential to the production process. The product form
groups personnel and activities according to organizational outputs. The hybrid form often combines functional and product forms. A matrix system is a
hybrid design involving a dual hierarchy.

7. Discuss advantages and disadvantages of different
organizational designs.

A functional design is useful when collaboration and expertise are needed and
the environment is stable. However, a functional design is slow to respond to
environmental changes and is less likely to foster innovation. A product design
offers greater attention to customer needs and is better suited to respond to
environmental changes. A product design, however, incorporates redundancy
of effort. A hybrid design strives to balance the functional and product designs.
A hybrid design can be highly flexible and can coordinate responses to cus-
tomer- and production-related pressures, plus offer a greater degree of responsiveness to environmental change. A hybrid design may create problems for
evaluating employee performance as well as generate confusion.

Key Terms

Decentralization	Bureaucracy
Tall structure	Sociotechnical system
Flat structure	Functional form
Span of control	Product form
Unity of command	Hybrid form
Chain of command	Matrix design

Review and Discussion Questions

1. What is decentralization? What are some benefits and drawbacks of decentralization in an organization?

2. What is a tall organization? Do tall organizations have more units than flat organizations? Does a manager have closer control in a tall organization or a flat one?

3. Susan Floyd reports to two supervisors, each of whom wants his assignments done first. Susan finds that when she tries to please both of them, she winds up satisfying neither. She decides to take matters into her own hands and sends a memo to the person her two supervisors report to, asking this manager to resolve the conflict. In this situation, which two principles of organizing are violated? Explain these principles.

4. Max Weber described a bureaucracy as an ideal form of organization. What are the characteristics of such an organization? Do most organizations actually match this description? What kinds of organizations benefit most from a bureaucratic structure?

5. Phil McGreevy is in charge of planning operations for the refrigerator assembly plant his company is redesigning. Phil and his team have planned for the necessary equipment, and they have studied the assembly process and divided it into the tasks to be done. In planning the refrigerator assembly system, what else should Phil consider? Why?

6. CJS Financial Accountants emphasizes rules and procedures and respects hierarchy. The company is seeking to hire someone to do routine bookkeeping tasks. One candidate, Linda Burns, has indicated that she is looking for a job that involves challenge, responsibility, and opportunity for growth. Another candidate, George Ronstadt, seemed mainly interested in the salary. Both candidates are qualified; which is most likely to be satisfied? Explain your choice.

7. At General Products, Inc., one vice-president is responsible for all aspects of producing and selling breakfast cereal, another has responsibility for frozen pizzas, and a third has responsibility for hosiery. What form of organization does General Products have? What are some advantages and disadvantages of this kind of organization?

8. What is a matrix design? What are some advantages and disadvantages of this type of organizational design?

9. 2K Company manufactures and distributes floppy disks and cassette tapes. Because of changes in technology and the marketplace, the company frequently encounters customer- and production-related pressures. 2K's management has decided that reorganizing the company into a matrix system will help it remain competitive. For employees to adapt to the matrix system, what kinds of skills will they need to learn? Do you think employees could learn these skills well enough for a matrix system to work? How practical is a matrix system?

Critical Incident

A Structural Straightjacket at Wild Wear

Wild Wear, Inc., makes clothes, raingear, and sleeping bags for hikers and other outdoor enthusiasts. The company began when Myrtle Kelly began sewing pile jackets that her husband Ray sold on college campuses. It now employs almost 500 people organized into traditional divisions such as marketing, manufacturing, and research and development.

Not so long ago, it became apparent that although Wild Wear's balance sheet appeared healthy, the company was stagnant. Everyone seemed to work hard, and the company's products seldom flopped, yet Wild Wear seemed to have developed a "me-too" posture, bringing new products to market a season or a full year after competitors.

The Kellys, who still run the company, pored over performance appraisals looking for the weak points that might be holding the company back. But it seemed that the personnel department had been doing its work. R&D was coming up with a respectable number of new products, the manufacturing facility was modern and efficient, and the marketing tactics often won praise from customers.

Baffled, the Kellys called a meeting of middle-level managers, hoping they could provide some answers that they had missed. They were shocked when they noticed that the managers were introducing themselves as they came in and sat down. People who had been working in the same company for years had never even met! The meeting began with this observation, and for ninety minutes the Kellys sat back and listened to the problems their managers raised.

It became clear that, in the attempt to grow from a family operation into a company, the Kellys had assumed that the two needed to be very different. When they started out, the two of them handled all aspects of the business. Ray would hear from a customer that backpackers really needed a certain product, would pass the idea on to Myrtle and order the materials she needed, and within a few weeks would offer the product to the same—now delighted—customer. As the company grew, the Kellys began to worry about their lack of formal business training and hired professionals to run each division and set up appropriate rules and procedures.

What they had created, the middle managers informed them, was a number of very efficient, productive divisions that might as well have been separate companies. The R&D people might come up with a new breathable fabric for raingear only to find that production had just begun making a new rainwear line out of the old fabric and that marketing was turning all its attention to selling the big inventory of sleeping bags. Each division did the best it could with the information it had, but that information was very incomplete. Products progressed linearly from one division to the next, but it always seemed as though an idea that had been ahead of its time did not yield a product until the time had passed.

To remedy the problem, the Kellys decided to call in a management consultant to create more of a matrix structure for Wild Wear. While they were waiting for the consultant's solutions, they began holding weekly "Horizon" meetings. The group of middle managers would get together every Monday and discuss what they saw on their horizon. After less than a month of such meetings, the excitement generated seemed to promise better things for Wild Wear, as the managers stretched to expand their own horizons and to help others bring their ideas to light.

Questions

1. What would be the ideal organizational design for a company like Wild Wear?

2. What does Wild Wear's experience say about the need for periodic corporate restructuring?

Experiential Exercise
City of Brookside Redesign

Step 1   Review the organizational structure of the City of Brookside shown in Figure 1.

Step 2   Answer the following questions individually, in small groups, or with the entire class (your instructor will select the appropriate format):

1. Describe the organization's existing structure: its division of labor and coordinating mechanisms.

2. How do the following factors influence structure?
    a. goals
    b. environment
    c. technology
    d. work force
    e. size
    f. age

3. How does the organization's structure fit with the factors above?

4. Is the current design appropriate? Is it likely to be effective?

5. What changes should be made?

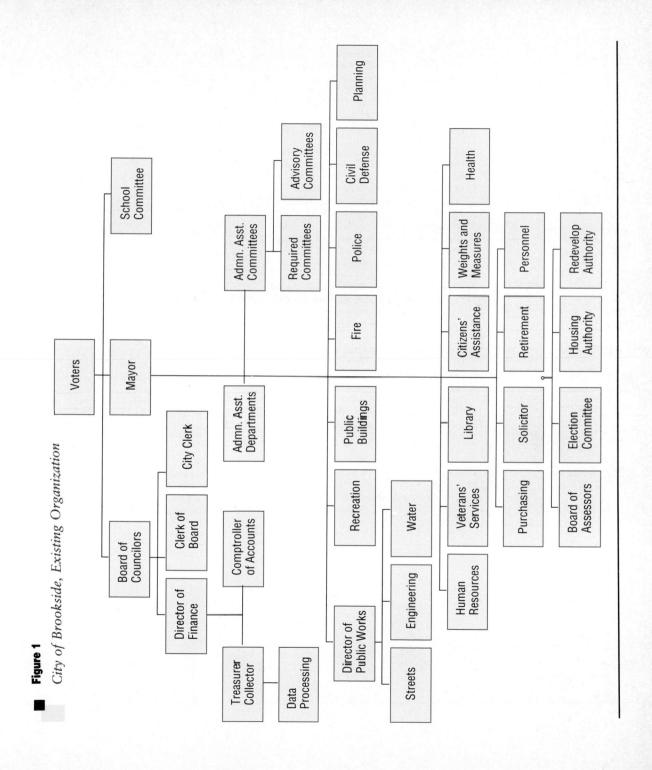

■ Figure 1

City of Brookside, Existing Organization

Notes

1. R. Duncan, "What is the Right Organization Structure?" *Organizational Dynamics* 33 (1979): 66.
2. P. Petre, "America's Most Successful Entrepreneur," *Fortune*, October 27, 1986, 24–32.
3. T. Peters, *Thriving on Chaos* (New York: Harper & Row, 1987), 430.
4. J.C. Worthy, "Organizational Structure and Employee Morale," *American Sociological Review* 15 (1950): 169–179.
5. M. Weber, *The Theory of Social and Economic Organizations,* trans. A. Henderson and T. Parsons (New York: Free Press, 1947).
6. P.M. Blau, *On the Nature of Organizations* (New York: Wiley, 1974); V.A. Thompson, *Modern Organization* (New York: Knopf, 1961).
7. J. Child, "Managerial and Organizational Factors Associated with Company Performance, Part II. A Contingency Analysis," *Journal of Management Studies* 12 (1975): 12–27.
8. R.L. Daft, *Organizational Theory and Design* (New York: West, 1983).
9. Child, "Managerial and Organizational Factors Associated with Company Performance."
10. Thompson, *Modern Organization.*
11. R. Likert, *The Human Organization: Its Management and Value* (New York: McGraw-Hill, 1967).
12. R. Likert and J.G. Likert, *New Ways of Managing Conflict* (New York: McGraw-Hill, 1976).
13. J.B. Miner, *Theories of Organizational Structure and Process* (Hinsdale, Ill.: Dryden Press, 1982), p. 52.
14. J.B. Miner, "Limited Domain Theories of Organizational Energy," in *Middle Range Theory and the Study of Organizations,* ed. C.C. Pinder and L.F. Moore (Boston: Maritimes Nijhoff, 1980), 273–286.
15. E.L. Trist and K.W. Bamforth, "Some Social and Psychological Consequences of the Longwall Method of Goal Setting," *Human Relations* 4 (1951): 1–38.
16. D.S. Cohen, "The Quality-of-Worklife Movement," *Training HRD* 30 (January 1979): 24.
17. S.M. Davis and P.R. Lawrence, *Matrix* (Reading, Mass.: Addison-Wesley, 1977); W.F. Joyce, "Matrix Organization: A Social Experiment," *Academy of Management Journal* 29 (1986): 536–561.
18. C. Argyris, "Today's Problems with Tomorrow's Organizations," *Journal of Management Studies* 32 (1967): 31–55; J.F. Mee, "Ideational Items: Matrix Organization," *Business Horizons* 7 (1964): 70–72.
19. Davis and Lawrence, *Matrix,* 9.

17

Learning Objectives

After studying this chapter, you should be able to:

1. *Identify three dimensions that describe an organization's external environment.*

2. *Explain how the environment influences which organizations will succeed and which will fail.*

3. *Explain how organizations handle their dependency on their environment.*

4. *Describe two strategies organizations can use for managing the environment.*

5. *Identify an organization's structural dimensions and contextual dimensions.*

6. *Explain when differentiation is likely to characterize an organization.*

7. *Describe how an organization's structure complements its technology.*

8. *Explain how strategy and structure may be related.*

Environmental Forces

■ Coping with Peace

As Soviet bloc nations adopt new freedoms and plan for military reductions, many observers are predicting that the result in the United States will be a "peace economy." Various forces are pushing for more or less reduction in military spending, and the long-term results of whatever changes ensue will be unknown for years to come.

Some defense experts have predicted a decline in military spending from about 6 percent of the U.S. gross national product at the end of the 1980s to around 4 percent by the late 1990s — the lowest level since the military demobilization that followed World War II. Such spending cuts could reduce the federal government's borrowing needs, thereby reducing interest rates and inflation.

Many organizations besides the government would be affected by such changes. For example, defense contractors might have to lay off workers. Housing contractors, in contrast, could find their business booming if interest rates fall.

Businesses can plan for such changes by forecasting their possible effects. One forecast compared the results of either cutting defense spending by 5 percent a year for four years beginning in 1991, then holding expenditures steady, or else making more modest reductions in defense spending.

According to this forecast, lower defense spending would ultimately lead to greater economic growth and greater business investment in plants and equipment. Lower interest rates would make U.S. businesses more competitive in the international arena. Housing starts would rise, leading to 500,000 more housing units by the year 2000 under a peace economy. Demand for autos and consumer appliances also would be strengthened. The government might spend some money saved on defense to do much-needed work on roads, bridges, and airports, which could be a boost for construction firms.

However, some businesses would be losers, notably those producing electronic components, aircraft, and communications equipment. These industries sell a large share of their products to the military. Particular regions of the country also could suffer, because large shares of Pentagon contracts are concentrated in businesses located in a few metropolitan areas.

If these projections are correct, the peace economy is a case in point of how businesses can be dramatically affected by external events, such as changes in government policy or even in other nations' governments. Fortunately, organizations are not helpless to manage such change and uncertainty.

Besides forecasting what the environment will be like, organizations can prepare themselves to adapt to change. For example, some defense contractors are diversifying into other areas of business. Rockwell International Corporation cut the share of its sales attributable to defense work from 50 percent in 1986 to less than 30 percent in 1989. According to Donald R. Beall, the company's chief executive officer, Rockwell began planning in 1985 for the B-1 bomber program to end in 1988. The company also acquired nondefense businesses and began emphasizing nondefense electronics, computerized manufacturing, and civilian space work.

Government policies and spending are among the many dimensions of an organization's external environment. This chapter explores what constitutes this environment and how the external environment influences the performance of organizations. It also describes how organizations manage the external environment in ways that are compatible with the organization's structure.

Source: Karen Pennar and Michael J. Mandel, "The Peace Economy," *Business Week,* December 11, 1989, pp. 50–55.

As we have seen throughout this text, employees' attitudes and behaviors are influenced by the immediate circumstances in their work units, such as their tasks, intragroup relations, and rules and policies. The circumstances that define these subenvironments within the work unit are, in turn, determined by diverse facets of the larger organizational structure.

In Chapter 16, we focused on the influence of the organization's structure, and we emphasized that effective management requires an understanding of how larger structural issues affect individuals. In this chapter, we will examine dimensions of external environments and strategies for actually managing the external environment, with the ultimate goal of controlling the resulting structures and the subenvironments within these structures. Then we will examine the relationship of organizational structure to environment and strategy.

Dimensions of External Environments

An organization exists within a particular external environment that is composed of all the various factors (such as the government, legal system, labor pool, suppliers, customers, and state of existing technology) that can affect the organization's functioning. In analogous fashion to a living organism, an organization is influenced by and influences its surroundings. Similarly, the organization is highly dependent on environmental features and must quickly adapt to changes in the environment if it is to survive.

The number of features that constitute an organization's external environment is considerable. However, organizational researchers have attempted to reduce these features to a few critical dimensions. Chief among these schemes for analyzing external environments are those developed by James D. Thompson[1] and Robert Duncan.[2] These theorists have suggested three important dimensions for understanding environments: simplicity–complexity, static–dynamic, and environmental uncertainty.

Simplicity–Complexity

Environments can be characterized in terms of their intricacy and relative diversity. A simple environment contains few factors that impact on the organization and tends to be relatively unvaried. In contrast, a complex environment contains many more elements of importance and is more diverse. As an illustration of a simple environment, consider the environment faced by a manufacturer of washboards at the turn of the century. In such a setting, the technology was relatively simple, and the market was unchanging. In comparison, consider a present-day drug manufacturer. The number of products produced is highly varied, and the customers are quite different (for example, hospitals, doctors, and over-the-counter drugstores). The manufacture, marketing, and distribution of drugs is also highly complex. In addition, there are government regulations covering the preparation and distribution of drugs.

Static–Dynamic

A second important dimension of environments is the degree of stability or dynamism that characterizes the organization's surroundings. Environments can be said to differ in terms of the rate at which change is occurring; hence, they can be said to differ in terms of predictability. In our example of the washboard manufacturer, we can say that the surrounding environment was relatively static during the beginning of this century. (Washboards were widely used until washing machines became available and affordable later in the century.) Today's drug manufacturer functions in a highly dynamic and changing environment. New drugs are continually being developed and tested. There are continuing changes in the packaging of drugs in response to customer concerns over possible product tampering. In addition, the drug industry is responsive (quickly adapts) to innovations in the drug-manufacturing process.

Environmental Uncertainty

The degree of uncertainty that characterizes the environment is intricately related to the descriptive dimensions of simplicity–complexity and static–dynamic. According to Duncan, environmental uncertainty is a consequence of the inability to assign probabilities to environmental factors with a high degree of confidence, and a lack of information concerning both the factors that are important to decision making and the costs associated with poor decision making.[3] Duncan has proposed a model to help explain the relationship of uncertainty to the dimensions of simplicity–complexity and static–dynamic (see Figure 17.1). In his model, high degrees of uncertainty are associated with complex–dynamic environments, while low degrees of uncertainty are associated with simple–static environments. Moderate degrees of uncertainty are associated with the combinations of complex–static and simple–dynamic.

Studies of Duncan's model have yielded results that are generally supportive.[4] In addition, results suggest that the static–dynamic dimension may be of greater importance in determining the level of perceived environmental uncertainty.

The Population Ecology Perspective

In recent years, organizational theorists have proposed a new view of how organizations relate to their environments.[5] According to the **population ecol-**

■ **Figure 17.1**

Duncan's Model of Environmental Uncertainty

Environments with

	Low Perceived Uncertainty	Moderately Low Perceived Uncertainty
Static	1. A small number of similar factors in the environment	1. A large number of dissimilar factors in the environment
	2. Factors are unchanging	2. Factors are unchanging

versus

	Moderately High Perceived Uncertainty	High Perceived Uncertainty
Dynamic	1. A small number of similar factors in the environment	1. A large number of dissimilar factors in the environment
	2. Factors are constantly changing	2. Factors are constantly changing

(Left axis label: Environments That Are)

Source: R. Duncan, "The Characteristics of Organizational Environments and Perceived Environmental Uncertainty," *Administrative Science Quarterly* 17 (1972): p. 320.

ogy perspective, organizations seek to find a niche in a highly competitive surrounding so that they will be able to survive. In this view, a niche is defined as a combination of environmental resources and needs that are capable of sustaining the organization. Initially, a niche may be fairly small. But as the organization grows, it may expand the size of its niche. The population ecology perspective borrows heavily from the notions of natural selection in biology. In both views, entities are seen as competing for survival in a difficult, sometimes predatory, and crowded environment.*

In order to maintain one's existence, an entity must possess an appropriate **organizational form.** The appropriate organizational form represents a configuration of goals, human resources, products, and technology that will be acceptable to the environment. If an element of the form is inappropriate (for example, the technology is out of date, or the products are not in demand), then the organization risks being rejected by the environment. As is also true of life in the jungle, the population ecology perspective holds that chance, random forces, and continual change are important elements in determining survival and demise.

The population ecology view suggests that there are three stages in the change process: variation, selection, and retention. **Variation** is analogous to the concept of genetic mutation in the theory of evolution. Organizations with

---

* Interestingly, the mortality rates of the young of many species and of young organizations are very high.

■ Figure 17.2

Stages in the Population Ecology View of Organizations

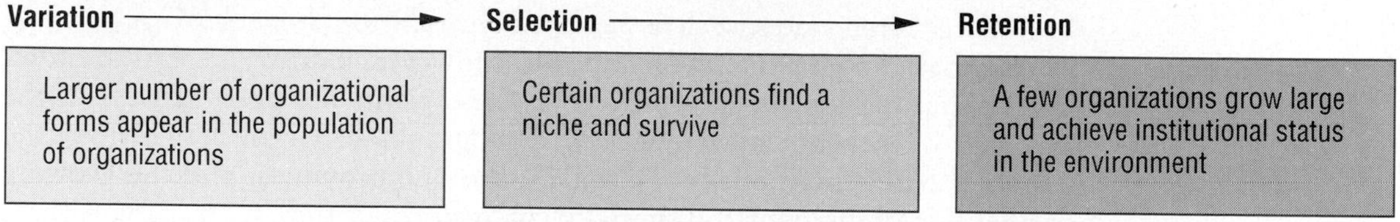

Variation ⟶ Selection ⟶ Retention

| Larger number of organizational forms appear in the population of organizations | Certain organizations find a niche and survive | A few organizations grow large and achieve institutional status in the environment |

Source: R. L. Daft, *Organization Theory and Design* (St. Paul, Minn.: West Publishing, 1983), p. 521.

unique attributes are continually being born. Often, these new organizations are deliberately designed to cope with a particular set of environmental constraints. If the new organization possesses adaptive variations, it will likely be successful. Those organizations that do not possess the needed organizational form will fail. Failure may be due to the organization's lack of skilled personnel, lack of sufficient capital, or chance factors (such as a takeover by another company). Consequently, a process of **selection** occurs. Over a long period, only a few organizations (out of the large number founded every year) can be expected to survive and be reasonably prosperous. **Retention** refers to the institutionalization of certain adaptive organizational forms. As long as the organization's outputs are sought or endorsed by the larger society, the organization will be a critical component of the society. Examples of institutionalized organizational forms include state governments, educational institutions, and automobile manufacturers. In the long term, even these established institutionalized forms may disappear. The key determinants of the longevity of institutionalized organizational forms are the extent of change in the environment and the organization's ability to adapt to such change. Figure 17.2 illustrates the process of change as proposed by the population ecology perspective.

As an example, consider the process of change related to the roadside hamburger stand. In the past, independently owned and operated hamburger stands served an important societal need. As the public became more mobile, roadside dining became a more frequent activity for the average citizen. Over time, chains of franchised hamburger stands (McDonald's, Burger King, Wendy's) came to dominate the roadways by offering the customer a standardized product along with the convenience of fast service and drive-through windows.

At present, the original, independently owned hamburger stands must hold second place (in terms of appeal and sales) to the large institutionalized forms of fast-food restaurants. The clientele of the nonfranchised restaurants are now more likely to be repeat customers who live in the surrounding neighborhood than the traveling public. In this example, we see how the small, independent organizations are gradually being selected out of the environment. With time, it is, of course, possible that the current domination of fast-food restaurants will end. For this to occur: (a) the chains must be supplanted by a new (as yet unforeseen) organizational form that is superior in some fashion, (b) the desires of the public will have to change (for example, the public must lose its desire to eat beef, or its desire to eat out must be greatly diminished), and (c) the fast-food chains must fail to respond (or be incapable of responding) to the challenge.

Large retail stores, such as Sears, Roebuck, Montgomery Ward, and J.C. Penney, have long held a leadership role. However, industry experts are forecasting that the long-term prospects of these giants are poor because of the high cost of their operations, shifting demographics that are fragmenting the customer base (traditionally the middle-class homeowner), and the growing competition of discount and specialty chain stores. If they are to survive these challenges, the retail leaders will have to make changes in order to adapt to a new environment.

The population ecology view is particularly useful as a device for explaining organizational change, especially in terms of innovations in organizational design. The evolutionary perspective offered by the notions of variation, selection, and retention help to account for the emergence of new organizational structures, new products, and organizational failures.

The Resource Dependence Model

Jeffrey Pfeffer and Gerald Salancik have proposed yet another view of how organizations relate to their environments.[6] In their **resource dependence model,** they contend that organizations are highly dependent on their external environments for raw resources and markets. The success of any organization is, therefore, a function of the extent to which the organization can manage its environment. Because organizations are vulnerable to their environments, they must take action to reduce or eliminate their dependency. One approach to this dependency is to purchase or control those forces that can exert influence. For example, a manufacturer who relies heavily on certain raw materials may try to purchase the operations of various suppliers. This represents an attempt to reach out and change the environment (see the next section of this chapter). Also, an organization may attempt an internal change in order to deal with its vulnerability. These internal changes include increases in structural complexity and the creation of boundary-spanning roles.

Increases in organizational complexity reflect the complexity of the external environment. For example, marketing departments are created and specialized in order to identify new markets and understand customer desires and needs. Legal departments interface with federal and state agencies in order to protect the firm from legal constraints. Purchasing agents focus on identifying suppliers and new sources of raw materials. As the complexity of the external environment increases, the complexity of the organization's structure will likely increase in order for the organization to more effectively cope with its surroundings.

An organization needs to have effective relationships with the major elements of its environment. To achieve this end, **boundary-spanning positions** are often created. Boundary spanners seek to understand the external environment and to represent the organization to various constituencies. Examples of boundary-spanning roles include positions in public relations, marketing research, college recruiting, and purchasing. However, the boundary-spanning function is not solely the province of specialized positions. Many employees whose jobs are primarily directed toward performing duties within the organization may occasionally engage in boundary-spanning activities. For example, someone in the finance department may call a friend who works for a supplier in order to learn more about the operations of the supplier, or someone in accounting may meet with a job candidate for a position in another department in order to persuade the candidate to join the organization.

Managing the External Environment

Daft has suggested that it is possible to change the external environment via two major strategies.[7] The first consists of establishing favorable linkages with critical elements in the external environment. The second involves controlling the environmental domain. Each of these strategies can be accomplished through several different methods.

Establishing Favorable Linkages

To improve relations, linkages (or associations) can be set up with elements of the external environment. One useful way of establishing a linkage is to acquire another organization through a merger. Mergers can eliminate dependence on an external factor by gaining control over it. For example, uncertainty about a supplier's ability to deliver sufficient quantities of materials on time can be reduced by acquiring the supplier and thereby guaranteeing preferential treatment. When one firm acquires another with the goal of controlling forces that affect its production process, it is termed **vertical integration.** Examples of vertical integration include an automobile manufacturer that acquires an auto radio and battery producer and a food processor that purchases a poultry farm.

Hiring practices can also help to establish favorable linkages. In one approach, a firm may decide to recruit executives from other firms with which it wishes to have good relations. Thus, a defense contractor may hire retired military officers from the Department of Defense to join its contract-negotiating division. Another approach is to select board members who represent various constituencies, such as customers, suppliers, or community interest groups. Membership on a board of directors provides these individuals with an appreciation of, and a continuing interest in, the performance of the firm. A similar tactic involves placing board members of another corporation on your own board. This tactic creates **interlocking directorates.** As a result of sharing board memberships, the individuals experience a sense of common interests.

Last, a firm can attempt to establish favorable linkages by investing in advertising and public relations. Such efforts attempt to enhance the firm's image in the eyes of customers and the public and, as a result, influence the way in which these groups relate to the firm.

Controlling Environmental Domains

Daft also suggests various means by which an organization can attempt to control the domains in which it operates. One direct approach is simply to buy

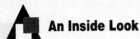

An Inside Look

Management Style in a Changing Environment

For many people, feminism has changed expectations about male behavior. This in turn has led some male managers to reconsider their management style. Experts are recommending that the most effective managerial style may include some skills that have been considered feminine: listening attentively, trying to consider people's feelings, and deriving satisfaction from the accomplishments of others.

Companies are beginning to accommodate some of these environmental changes affecting their male managers. For example, many organizations have had to learn greater tolerance for executives who resist relocation. To some extent, companies may also be more interested in finding managers who have skills considered feminine as well as masculine — a sort of androgynous management style.

Organizations often seem less willing to accommodate managers' desires to be more actively involved with their families. While one survey showed that of 384 large corporations, 114 offered paternity leave, over 40 percent of those 114 companies said they didn't consider any amount of time off to be reasonable. These companies simply offered the benefit as a way to avoid lawsuits. The standard is for managers to give the organization priority over the family. Says one corporate lawyer, "I live in a fair amount of pain day-to-day, because I'm not living up to my own standards for how I should be caring for my children."

Corporate executives receive many rewards, but the expectation that they give most of their energy to the corporation is only one of the costs of those rewards. The executive is expected to sacrifice his or her right to personal thought and expression. He or she is expected to avoid doing anything to express dissent with the organization's decisions, purposes, or activities. While the executive makes many speeches, he or she speaks for the company, not self. The message that results is cautious, not exciting.

Corporate executives may also be sacrificing the opportunity to be creative. Few if any of today's top-level managers will ever make a personal contribution in the arts or politics. In the past, however, such an opportunity was the purpose of attaining wealth.

Source: John Kenneth Galbraith, "Corporate Man," *New York Times Magazine,* January 22, 1984, p. 39; Walter Kiechel III, "Is a New Male Manager Emerging?" *Fortune,* February 3, 1986, pp. 135–136.

or sell a product line. This involves seeking or avoiding different suppliers, competitors, government regulations, customer groups, and so on.

A second device consists of joining with other similar organizations that have common goals and interests. For example, coal mine operators may join forces to form a trade association, with the aim of lobbying for their interests. The goals of such associations include encouraging regulators to pass or rescind laws that promote or restrict an industry's well-being.

The Contingency View of Organizational Design

Today, scholars of organizational design generally subscribe to a view that organizations are **open systems.** As an open system, an organization must deal with its environment by obtaining and consuming resources, and exporting finished goods or services. Organizations do not exist in a vacuum nor can they operate independently from their environment; that is, they cannot function as **closed systems.**

OB Focus

McDonald's in Moscow

Managing the external environment is a tricky business when the environment is as complex as the Soviet Union. For example, when McDonald's opened the first of 20 outlets in Moscow, the company had to comply with labor laws requiring it to organize a work collective for its staff. McDonald's also had to contend with central planning, getting the business included in the system to ensure it would be allocated enough sugar and flour, both of which are in short supply.

Despite these obstacles, the Moscow enterprise — a joint venture between McDonald's Restaurants of Canada Ltd. and Moscow city authorities — has developed a number of ways to manage the environment by establishing favorable linkages. For example, the restaurant has a small laundry room where the uniforms of its 630 employees are washed in West German machines and ironed by hand. According to Roy Ellis, a personnel specialist with McDonald's, this approach enables the restaurant to "ensure our standards."

A major concern is ingredients. The Soviet agricultural system is notorious for its uncertain supply and less-than-ideal quality. To overcome these shortcomings, McDonald's has taken control of many aspects of producing and supplying food. The company built a $40 million food-processing plant on the outskirts of Moscow, where several hundred employees test, clean, chop, and freeze potatoes, meat, buns, onions, pickles, and lettuce. McDonald's even had the right types of seeds shipped to the Soviet Union and helped plant them on local farms.

Another risk of the Soviet environment involves distribution in the form of competition from the black market. In the case of such potentially desirable goods as hamburgers, the company risks having people buy its product in bulk and sell it at a premium outside the restaurants. To combat this risk, the company has limited customers to 10 Big Macs each.

Finally, a company can establish favorable linkages with customers through publicity. That linkage was certainly operating when McDonald's opened its first Moscow restaurant in what *The Wall Street Journal* termed "a blaze of publicity." Even though a Big Mac, french fries, and a soft drink cost the equivalent of an average worker's pay for four hours, customers were willing to stand in line as long as two hours to get into the 700-seat restaurant on Pushkin Square.

Sources: Francis X. Clines, "Russian Milkshakes and Human Kindness," *New York Times,* February 1, 1990; Peter Gumbel, "Muscovites Queue Up at American Icon," *The Wall Street Journal,* February 1, 1990, p. A12.

Given this view of organizations as open systems, it is useful to consider how an organization's internal characteristics are influenced by the larger features of the environment and the entire organization itself. These internal characteristics, called **structural dimensions,** include such features as specialization, hierarchy of authority, decentralization, and complexity. Characteristics of the entire organization and its environment, called **contextual dimensions,** include size, technology, and external constituents such as customers, suppliers, competitors, and the government. The goal of the contingency view is to explain how differences in the contextual and structural dimensions are related. As the term *contingency* implies, this approach does not seek simple universal principles that can be used for every situation, but instead seeks to explain how one attribute or characteristic depends upon another. In the search for contingencies, several landmark studies have been conducted.

Table 17.1

Features of Mechanistic and Organic Organizational Forms

Mechanistic	Organic
Specialized tasks	Employee contributions to a common task
Hierarchy of authority	Less adherence to formal authority and control
Hierarchical communication	Network communication
Centralized knowledge and control	Decentralized knowledge and control
Insistence on loyalty and obedience to the organization	Loyalty and commitment given to the project or group
High degree of formality	High degree of flexibility and discretion

Burns and Stalker's Mechanistic and Organic Systems

In a study of 20 firms in England, Burns and Stalker examined the relationships between external environments and the nature of internal organizational structure.[8] Relying on unstructured observations and interviews (a relatively anthropological research approach), they attempted to characterize the manner in which internal management operations were structured and the rate of change in the external environment. Their results indicated that firms in relatively stable or unchanging environments tend to have more highly structured and formal management operations. They termed such organizations **mechanistic** because of their emphasis on rules, procedures, and dominance by a hierarchy of authority. In contrast, firms in more unstable environments tend to have a free-flowing, decentralized, and more adaptive internal organization that they called **organic**. Table 17.1 summarizes the major differences between mechanistic and organic organizations.

Central to Burns and Stalker's contribution to the area of organizational design is the notion that these two extreme forms of organizational systems are most appropriate for different environments: organic systems are more capable of adapting to change, while mechanistic systems are appropriate to relatively static settings.† For example, a computer software company must survive in a dynamic, rapidly changing environment characterized by constant technical innovations, so it needs a more organic form of organization. At the other extreme, a synthetic fabric firm operates in a relatively predictable and stable environment, so it would probably have a more mechanistic form of organization.

Extending Burns and Stalker's Model   More recently, Porter, Lawler, and Hackman proposed a model that attempts to relate the mechanistic-organic dimension of organizations to the added dimensions of job type and individual

† It should be noted that Burns and Stalker's research did not actually prove that effectiveness is greater when organic systems exist within unstable environments, and so on, but merely that an organic system was associated with environmental change. Nonetheless, the implication is straightforward: mechanistic organizations are presumed to be limited in their adaptability as a result of their rigidity.

preference.[9] Their model proposes that *congruency* — that is, an appropriate matching of these three dimensions — should result in improved employee attitudes. Individuals who seek challenge and responsibility in their jobs should prefer relatively complex or enriched jobs, and a complex job is more congruent with an organic, rather than a mechanistic, organization. Therefore, the combination of employee higher-order growth need strength with a complex or enriched job in an organic setting should produce greater employee satisfaction because all three factors are congruent.‡ When any or all of the three factors (individual needs, job type, and system structure) are incongruent, employee attitudes will be less positive.

Vecchio and Keon further refined the model based on the frequent finding that employees typically find complex jobs more satisfying than fairly simple jobs.[10] Using this finding and a set of rules for weighting congruence/incongruence, they proposed the following rank ordering of employee satisfaction in conjunction with congruence among individual needs, job design, and system structure.

Most Congruent	System Structure	Job Design	Growth Need Strength
1	Organic	Complex	High
2	Mechanistic	Complex	High
3	Organic	Complex	Low
4	Mechanistic	Complex	Low
5	Mechanistic	Simple	Low
6	Organic	Simple	Low
7	Mechanistic	Simple	High
8	Organic	Simple	High
Least Congruent			

Tests of the predicted rank orderings with satisfaction data obtained in a variety of organizations largely confirmed the accuracy of these predictions: employees in relatively congruent combinations tend to be more satisfied than employees in less congruent combinations.

Lawrence and Lorsch's Contingency Research

The importance of environmental attributes in determining the effectiveness of organizational systems is also underscored by studies conducted by Lawrence and Lorsch.[11] In their research, they examined the environments of firms in three diverse industries: plastics, food, and containers. Based on interviews with managers in these firms, they found it useful to describe environments in terms of turbulence (or change) and uncertainty versus stability and certainty. Next, they examined the subenvironments faced by three divisions within each of the firms: production, marketing, and research and development. Environmental uncertainty was found to vary for each division, with uncertainty being greatest in R&D departments, followed in order by marketing and produc-

‡ For explanations of higher-order growth need strength and job enrichment, see Chapter 7.

Table 17.2

Differences in Goals and Orientations among Departments

	Departments		
Characteristic	Production	Marketing	R&D
Time Horizon	Short	Short	Long
Goals	Efficient production	Customer satisfaction	New developments
Formality	High	High	Low

tion. The key finding of Lawrence and Lorsch's research was that the nature of structuring within these divisions varied in accordance with environmental uncertainty. Production departments tended to have the highest degree of structure, followed by marketing and, last, R&D. Each department could also be characterized in terms of primary goals and orientations. Table 17.2 summarizes these differences.

Lawrence and Lorsch also examined how units within organizations are related. In the process, they found that organizations differ in terms of integration and differentiation. **Integration** refers to a state of collaboration among departments that seek to achieve unity of effort.[12] It concerns the quality of interdepartmental relations. **Differentiation** is reflected in the degree of specialization of labor and the psychological orientation of managers within departments. When department managers feel psychologically distant from managers in other departments, differentiation is greater.

Lawrence and Lorsch observed that differentiation among departments tended to be greater in organizations that operated in more complex and changing environments. Furthermore, these firms also needed more mechanisms designed to achieve integration among units. The plastics firms, for example, were most differentiated and thus needed to establish more mechanisms for coordinating efforts, such as liaison officers who facilitate communication among departments. In the least turbulent environment, that of the container firms, differentiation among departments was low, as was the number of mechanisms needed to integrate the departments.

Woodward's Studies of Technology

Another contextual variable of suspected importance in the structure of organizations is **technology,** the tools, techniques, and knowledge used to transform raw resources into finished goods. Some of the most important studies of the impact of technology were conducted by Joan Woodward, a British industrial sociologist.[13]

In her studies, which focused on 100 firms in England, Woodward initially set out to determine what structural factors were associated with commercial success. The results, however, did not identify characteristics that were more strongly associated with effectiveness (for example, more bureaucratic organizations were not necessarily more or less successful than less bureau-

■ **Table 17.3**

Major Findings of Woodward's Studies on Technology and Structure

Structural Attribute	Unit Production	Mass Production	Long-Run Process Production
Number of management levels	Low	Moderate	High
Formalization	Low	High	Low
Centralization	Low	High	Low
Verbal communication	High	Low	High
Written communication	Low	High	Low
Overall structure	Organic	Mechanistic	Organic

cratic organizations). In further analyses on these data, Woodward sought to uncover underlying factors that might help to explain the otherwise meaningless patterns in the data. By reclassifying organizations in terms of type of technology, a set of meaningful results began to emerge suggesting that organizational structure should complement technology. Specifically, Woodward classified the firms into one of three categories: unit (or small-batch) production, mass (or large-batch) production, and long-run process production.

Unit production firms manufacture small orders that are custom-made for the purchaser. Made-to-order products such as furniture, electronics, and specialized construction equipment characterize this type of enterprise. **Mass production** firms manufacture standardized articles that do not require much specialized or varied attention. For example, automobile and mobile home manufacturers employ mass production technology. **Long-run process production** requires mechanization of the entire manufacturing operation. From beginning to end, the process is highly controlled, so the quality of the final product can be very easily predicted. Among the users of long-run process production technology are oil refineries, chemical plants, and distilleries.

Based on this classification system, certain patterns of results suggested that structuring within the sampled firms was indeed related to type of technology. For example, the number of management levels increased from unit to long-run process production, that is, as technological complexity increased.

Woodward also observed several complex patterns in her results. For example, the amount of verbal communication tended to be lowest in mass production organizations, whereas the amount of written communication was greatest. In addition, mass production firms tended to be more highly centralized and to employ more formalized procedures than did the other types of firms. Overall, the unit and long-run process production firms were relatively more organic, while the mass production firms were relatively more mechanistic. Table 17.3 summarizes these findings.

Further analyses by Woodward on the financial success of the same firms, as measured by market share, reputation, and the like, showed that successful firms tended to fit the pattern of structural attributes that was most typical for their technology grouping, as outlined in Table 17.3. For example, successful mass production firms tended to have mechanistic structures, while successful unit or long-run process production firms tended to have organic structures. Other studies in the United States[14] and Japan[15] have corroborated Woodward's findings that technology is related to structure and that appropriateness of structure is related to organizational performance.

Thompson's Typology of Technology

One of the most widely cited approaches to classifying technology is that of James D. Thompson.[16] This typology specifies three varieties of technology: long-linked, mediating, and intensive. According to Thompson, all organizations can be classified with this typology.

A **long-linked technology** involves sequential, or serially linked, operations. A clear illustration of this type of technology is provided by an auto assembly plant. Because of the interdependence that results from the sequential nature of the tasks, this variety of technology is not very adaptable to environmental demands for change.

A **mediating technology** joins otherwise effective independent units of an organization or different types of customers. The "joining" is achieved by the use of standard operating procedures. For example, a commercial bank conducts relatively independent transactions (such as lending funds and receiving deposits). By using standard procedures, the bank serves the diverse needs of its clients. The rigidity of a mediating technology, which results from an adherence to procedures, can interfere with attempts to respond to changing demands.

Last, an **intensive technology** uses skills or services to transform an object. The decision about which skill or service to apply is determined by the results of previous efforts to transform the object. An outstanding example of an intensive technology is a hospital. Here, the object of interest is the patient and the skills and services are the staff and the various techniques embodied in specialties. Depending on how a patient responds to a given treatment, he or she will receive another possible form of therapy. This type of organization requires a high degree of coordination and communication, and is generally more responsive to change than other types of technology.

Structure and Strategy

An issue of continuing interest to organizational theorists is the relationship between organizational structure and strategy. Specifically, does one influence the other? Does **strategy** (which we will define as a plan of action formulated by top-level management to better prepare the organization to deal with the future) grow out of an organization's structure? Or does structure largely determine an organization's apparent strategy for dealing with the external environment? Further, is it not possible that both structure and strategy influence each other?

In a widely cited study, Alfred Chandler, Jr., a historian, tackled this issue by conducting an in-depth analysis of several large corporations.[17] Using data gathered from company records and interviews with managers, he concluded that structure, especially decentralization, followed from strategy. However, the chief reasons for this tendency to modify organizational structure differed in each corporation. In the case of Du Pont, a more decentralized structure was created in response to a business strategy of product diversification. Standard Oil of New Jersey came to be more decentralized over time, but in an uncoordinated and gradual fashion. Yet, the trend toward decentralization occurred in response to a deliberate business strategy. Sears, Roebuck and Company likewise went through a process of decentralization in response to a specific strategy. Chandler's research further suggested that restructuring was generally in response to a desire to deal with growth. Although it is intuitively appealing to view strategy and structure as being able to influence each other (such that structure has implications for strategy formulation, and strategy has implications for organizational design), available evidence seems to suggest that the mutual influence view may not be correct.[18]

Summary

1. Identify three dimensions that describe an organization's external environment.
Environments can be relatively simple or complex; they can be static or dynamic; and they possess varying degrees of environmental uncertainty.

2. Explain how the environment influences which organizations will succeed and which will fail.
To maintain its existence, the organization must have an appropriate form, including goals, human resources, products, and technology. Chance, random forces, and continual change are also important elements in determining which organizations survive. Organizations with varying attributes are continually formed, and those that lack the needed organizational form will fail. A few adaptive forms will survive.

3. Explain how organizations handle their dependency on their environment.
Organizations try to manage their environment. They might try to purchase or control influential forces. They might try to make internal changes that will make them less vulnerable. Such changes include increasing structural complexity and creating boundary-spanning roles.

4. Describe two strategies organizations can use for managing the environment.
Organizations can change the external environment by establishing favorable linkages with critical elements in the environment and by controlling the environmental domain. Establishing favorable linkages includes vertical integration, hiring executives from companies the organization wants to link with, recruiting directors from targeted constituencies, creating interlocking directorates, and investing in advertising and public relations. Controlling environ-

mental domains includes buying or selling a product line and joining with similar organizations having common goals or interests.

5. Identify an organization's structural dimensions and contextual dimensions.

Structural dimensions are internal characteristics of the organization, such as specialization, hierarchy of authority, decentralization, and complexity. Contextual dimensions are characteristics of the organization and its surroundings, and include size of the organization, technology, and external constituents (e.g., customers, suppliers, competitors, and the government).

6. Explain when differentiation is likely to characterize an organization.

Differentiation among departments tends to be greatest in organizations that operate in complex and changing environments. These organizations need more mechanisms to achieve cooperation among departments.

7. Describe how an organization's structure complements its technology.

In ascending order of technological complexity, manufacturers can be classified as unit production firms, mass production firms, or long-run process production firms. The number of management levels increases as technological complexity increases. Mass production firms tend to be more mechanistic in structure, while unit and long-run process production firms are relatively organic.

8. Explain how strategy and structure may be related.

Strategy and structure are popularly believed to influence one another. Strategy is believed to have implications for the design of an organization. The design of an organization, in turn, is believed to have implications for how strategy may be formulated. Empirical evidence suggests, however, that structure may be largely influenced by strategy, rather than vice versa.

Key Terms

Population ecology
 perspective
Organizational form
Variation
Selection
Retention
Resource dependence
 model
Boundary-spanning
 positions
Vertical integration
Interlocking directorates
Open system
Closed system
Structural dimensions
Contextual dimensions

Mechanistic organiza-
 tion
Organic organization
Integration
Differentiation
Technology
Unit production
Mass production
Long-run process
 production
Long-linked technology
Mediating technology
Intensive technology
Strategy

Review and Discussion Questions

1.   For each of the following organizations, indicate whether the environment is simple or complex, static or dynamic. Which of these environments would have the most uncertainty?
     a.   A manufacturer of paper clips
     b.   A pharmaceutical company
     c.   A university

2.   How are an organization's efforts to grow and thrive like those of a living organism?

3.   Fertile Earth Enterprises sells seeds and garden tools through catalogs mailed to customers nationwide. What are some ways this company is dependent on its environment? What are some ways in which the company can reduce or eliminate this dependency?

4.   In what ways does technology influence organizational design?

5.   What is an organization's strategy? Does its strategy grow out of its structure or its structure grow out of strategy, or do they influence each other?

6.   The strategic planning committee presents its report to the board of directors of United Board Games. The committee concludes that the environment is changing, but only moderately. Assuming that the directors accept the committee's conclusions, what standards should they set for innovation, control, and development of new ideas?

■ Critical Incident

Environmental Pressures Intensify at Health-Rite

Robert Gore is president and owner of Health-Rite Equipment Co., Inc., a manufacturer of fitness equipment. The company employs 95 people at their facility in Portland, Oregon. Their physical fitness equipment has been selling well, which has resulted in rapid growth in the number of employees as well as revenue.

The rapid growth has been both a blessing and curse for Mr. Gore in that he had always managed the firm much like a family business. Now, however, he has had to create an authority structure, employing six supervisors, or managers. The supervisors in charge of the manufacture and assembly of the various lines of equipment handle production scheduling, inventory control, materials procurement, and quality control. Mr. Gore handles all the financial management and personnel matters. He also keeps track of governmental reports and regulations. One manager is in charge of sales, and another, of new product development.

A recent complaint of discrimination was filed with the EEOC (Equal Employment Opportunity Commission), leading to an official inquiry. The matter is under review. In addition, OSHA (Occupational Safety and Health

Administration) representatives made a surprise visit a few weeks ago and found several deficiencies. Health-Rite has ten more days to be in full compliance.

Because of the growing interest in personal health and fitness, several competitors have emerged in the last year. And although business has continued to be good, the competitive environment has become much more turbulent.

Finally, Mr. Gore has noticed increasing trouble in filling some orders. Some of the problems stem from suppliers either not shipping enough material or delaying shipments entirely. Other problems have been internal — production delays due to scheduling, quality control, and so forth. This has placed tremendous pressure on Mr. Gore, and he has not had time to address all these problems as he should. Recently, he also has had to deal with above-average turnover. Mr. Gore realizes that some changes need to be made, but he is not sure what to do.

Questions

1. What types of environmental forces are pressuring Health-Rite now? What forces could enter the picture in the future?

2. What types of changes would you recommend in terms of Health-Rite's organizational design to address these pressures?

3. Would you recommend any other changes? If so, explain.

Source: Written by Bruce Kemelgor, University of Louisville.

Experiential Exercise

Assessing Some Dimensions of an External Environment

Many factors influence the external environment of an organization. Complex organizations may find that their various divisions or departments are being influenced by so many different forces that the external environmental domain is heterogeneous (complex) rather than homogeneous (simple).

Using the table below and working either alone or as a member of a small group, describe the various factors that can affect the critical dimensions of an external environment.

Step 1　Your instructor may ask you to form groups of four to six people to complete this exercise, or you may be asked to work independently and discuss your results with the entire class.

Step 2　Using your school's basketball or football team, fill in the boxes below to complete an analysis of the key dimensions of the team's external environment. For example, in the recruitment of student athletes, how diverse is the environment that the recruiter and school must deal with? Using some specific examples, fill in the box under Simplicity–Complexity.

Do the same for each of the remaining boxes. Space has been provided if members of the class can identify another significant element.

Dimensions of the External Environment

Elements of the External Environment	Simplicity–Complexity	Static–Dynamic	Uncertainty
Recruiting of student-athletes			
Season and single-event ticket sales			
Marketing and promotion			
Media and public relations (sports information)			
Additional element*			

* Must be agreed upon by the entire class

Step 3   Once the table is complete, answer the following questions:

1.   Were any of the boxes more difficult than others to complete? Why?

2.   Using the information from the chart, what types of strategies might be developed for dealing with these elements?

3.   Is this a helpful way to diagnose the external environment and then plan for ways to deal with it? Why or why not?

Source: Written by Bruce Kemelgor, University of Louisville.

Notes

1. J.D. Thompson, *Organizations in Action* (New York: McGraw-Hill, 1967).
2. R.B. Duncan, "The Characteristics of Organizational Environments and Perceived Environmental Uncertainty," *Administrative Science Quarterly* 17 (1972): 313–327.
3. Ibid.
4. J.B. Miner, *Theories of Organizational Structure and Process* (Hinsdale, Ill.: The Dryden Press, 1982).
5. H.E Aldrich, *Organizations and Environments* (Englewood Cliffs, N.J.: Prentice-Hall, 1979).
6. J. Pfeffer and G. Salancik, *The External Control of Organizations* (New York: Harper & Row, 1978); D. Wholey and J. Brittain, "Organizational Ecology: Findings and Implications," *Academy of Management Review* 11 (1986): 513–533.
7. R.L. Daft, *Organization Theory and Design* (St. Paul, Minn.: West, 1983).
8. T. Burns and G.M. Stalker, *The Management of Innovation* (London: Tavistock, 1961); T. Burns, "Industry in a New Age," *New Society* 31 (1963): 17–20.
9. L.W. Porter, E.E. Lawler, and J.R. Hackman, *Behavior in Organizations* (New York: McGraw-Hill, 1975).
10. R.P. Vecchio and T.L. Keon, "Predicting Employee Satisfaction from Congruency

among Individual Need, Job Design, and System Structure," *Journal of Occupational Behavior* 2 (1981): 283–292.

11. P.R. Lawrence and J.W. Lorsch, *Organization and Environment: Managing Differentiation and Integration* (Homewood, Ill.: Irwin, 1969).

12. Ibid., p. 11.

13. J. Woodward, *Industrial Organization* (London: Oxford University Press, 1965).

14. W.L. Zwerman, *New Perspectives on Organizational Theory* (Westport, Conn.: Greenwood, 1970).

15. R.M. Marsh and H. Mannari, "Technology and Size as Determinants of the Organizational Structure of Japanese Factories," *Administrative Science Quarterly* 26 (1981): 33–56.

16. Thompson, *Organizations in Action.*

17. A.D. Chandler, Jr., *Strategy and Structure* (Garden City, N.J.: Anchor Books, 1966).

18. Miner, *Theories of Organizational Structure and Process.*

18

When I hear the word *culture*, I reach for my revolver.

— *Hanns Johst*

America is the land of opportunity if you're a businessman in Japan.

— *Lawrence J. Peters*

We are very different from the rest of the world. Our only natural resource is the hard work of our people.

— *Japanese executive*

Learning Objectives

After studying this chapter, you should be able to:

1. *Define organizational culture and describe influences on its creation and maintenance.*

2. *Explain how organizational culture may influence strategy.*

3. *Explain the importance of research comparing employees across nations.*

4. *Describe characteristics of typical managers in the United States.*

5. *Contrast Japanese and American management styles.*

6. *Give some examples of the differences in social customs and business practices in other cultures.*

7. *Identify two methods of cross-cultural training.*

Cultural Influences

■ Mistakes Welcome

From the beginning, Minnesota Mining & Manufacturing Company was a place where mistakes happened. The company was founded by five Minnesotans — a doctor, a lawyer, two railroad executives, and a meat-market manager — who bought a parcel of land where they planned to mine corundum, an abrasive used in sandpaper. Only after the company bought machinery, hired workers, and started mining did the five entrepreneurs discover that what they thought was corundum was in fact a worthless mineral.

This big mistake forced 3M Company to innovate its way to survival. First, the company introduced an abrasive cloth used for metal finishing. Then, inventor Francis G. Okie came up with 3M's first big hit: a waterproof sandpaper, which the company dubbed Wetordry. The sandpaper produced a better finish on automobiles and created less dust than conventional sandpapers, so it became the standard product used by the auto industry.

Since then, 3M Company has built on its past to develop an atmosphere that encourages experimentation and innovation throughout the company. This means that, among the employees, stories about massive failure are as legendary as tales of spectacular success. Thus, Okie is as well known for his efforts to promote rubbing one's cheeks with sandpaper as an alternative to shaving as he is for his invention of Wetordry sandpaper.

Fortunately for 3M, many of its innovations meet a need. For example, Scotch tape was invented in 1929 to seal insulation in airtight shipping packages, and eventually grew into a product bringing in three-quarters of a billion dollars annually. Also in the 1920s, 3M inventor Richard G. Drew noticed that painters on automobile assembly lines had difficulty keeping the borders straight on two-tone cars. In response, Drew invented masking tape.

Company policies support the atmosphere of innovation. Divisions are expected to derive 25 percent of sales from products introduced in the preceding 5 years. Researchers, marketers, and managers visit customers to look for new-product ideas. Technological advances made in one division are expected to be shared throughout the company.

The company even provides for workers who have an idea that doesn't seem to fall within the scope of one of the company's divisions. If someone has a product-related idea, that person is allowed to devote 15 percent of his or her time to prove that the idea is workable. The most famous success arising from this policy is Arthur L. Fry's invention of Post-it notes. Fry was looking for a way to keep the bookmark from falling out of his hymnbook. As a result, he developed the light adhesive now applied to the little notes stuck on business reports and refrigerators around the country.

The policies that foster such

innovations are deeply ingrained in 3M's history. William L. McKnight, one of the company's early chief executives, who started as an assistant bookkeeper and worked his way up as a salesperson, is viewed by employees as the spiritual founder of the company. After he became chief executive, McKnight wrote, "If management is intolerant and destructively critical when mistakes are made, I think it kills initiative." Tolerance for mistakes and encouragement of innovation are widely credited for the success of a company whose base products are as mundane as sandpaper and tape.

The strong emphasis on risk-taking and innovation at 3M Company is the basis of a distinctive culture. This chapter discusses in greater detail what constitutes an organization's culture, as well as some ways cultures are created and maintained. The chapter also compares Western culture with the cultures of other parts of the world.

Source: Russell Mitchell, "Masters of Innovation," *Business Week,* April 10, 1989, pp. 58–63.

Every organization exists in an external culture and perpetuates its own internal culture. The study of cultural influences, a topic that is central to the field of anthropology, has existed for some time, but its application to business organizations is a fairly recent phenomenon. In this chapter, we will initially examine cultures within organizations. Then, we will turn our attention to the topic of cultural, or national, differences in employee attitudes and behaviors.

Organizational Culture

Although the notion of organizational culture is currently enjoying much popularity, a precise definition of it is difficult to offer. Edgar Schein suggests that organizational culture has been variously defined as a philosophy that underlies an organization's policy, the rules of the game for getting along, and the feeling or climate conveyed by the physical layout of the organization.[1] Ralph Kilmann proposes that organizational culture is largely a matter of norms.[2] Examples of some organizational norms include: Don't say what the boss doesn't want to hear; Don't be associated with an ugly event; Do cheat on your expense account; Don't criticize the company to outsiders; Don't be a bearer of bad news; and (perhaps the most ironic norm) Don't make norms explicit to anyone who inquires about them.*

Although there is considerable variation in the suggested definitions of organizational culture, it appears that most contain several common elements. Based on these, we can define **organizational culture** as the shared values and norms that exist in an organization and that are taught to incoming employees.† This definition suggests that organizational culture involves common

* Intriguingly, Kilmann reported that more than 90 percent of the norms cited by organizational members are negative in tone and connotation.

† Strictly speaking, the notions of values and norms already exist in the field of organizational behavior. Also, socialization of new members is a topic in itself. Therefore, the concept of organizational culture continues to be a rather fuzzy notion. In addition, organizations are themselves products of a culture, so it is confusing to speak of cultures existing within a cultural artifact. As yet, the debate on the usefulness and meaningfulness of the concept of organizational culture is unresolved.

beliefs and feelings, regularities in behavior, and a historical process for transmitting values and norms. Despite its lack of precision, the concept of organizational culture is coming into wide use in management circles, sometimes as a convenient catch-all explanation for why things happen or do not happen in a particular way in a firm, as in, "It's the way we do things here — it's part of our culture."

Rituals and Stories

Organizational rituals and stories (notions borrowed from cultural anthropology) play key roles in maintaining and building organizational cultures. For example, a number of ceremonial rituals may accompany the appointment of a new chief executive officer, including introductory announcements, banquets, meetings, and speeches. Similarly, the public awarding of a lapel pin can take on powerful meaning if employees believe that such an award symbolizes a significant achievement.

The function and origin of organizational stories or myths are often unclear.[3] Occasionally, a story will convey a theme that embodies the values of the corporation's founder or other major figures. Depending on its goal, its tone may be either positive or negative. For example, a positive story may recount how the president attended a company picnic and displayed great personal warmth toward the spouses and children of the firm's employees. Such a story is meant to convey the underlying concern that the president has for the corporate family. Or a story may retell how all employees in the firm (from the CEO on down) agreed to a 10 percent wage cut during an economically difficult period in order to avoid any layoffs. On a more negative note, a story may be spread of how a former employee was ruthlessly dismissed and his career ruined by being blacklisted for the "crime" of disloyalty. The intent of such a story is, of course, to induce fear and control employees' behavior through intimidation.

The Measurement and Change of Organizational Culture

Before the study of organizational culture can make a substantial contribution to the field of organizational behavior in a scientific sense, it is necessary to have a set of methods for studying organizational culture. Unfortunately, the study of organizational culture presents unique challenges. Schein has observed that achieving an understanding of an organization's culture can be aided by locating a motivated insider within the organization, someone who is capable of deciphering the organization's culture and is motivated to discuss it.[4] Of course, a researcher is highly dependent on an insider's ability to provide reconstructions of events and the beliefs of others. Therefore, the direct observation of important facets of an organizational culture's features may not be possible (short of personal membership in an organization).

In addition to interviewing organizational members and joining the organization, surveys can be used to obtain data on insiders' perceptions of the organization's culture. However, the quality of the responses is likely to be limited because the investigator cannot interact with the respondent to probe issues. Furthermore, the use of the survey method presupposes that the investigator is already familiar enough with the culture to know what questions and issues need to be investigated.

Although surveys, interviews, and partial membership in an organization are all potentially useful for studying organizational culture, Schein and Kilmann advocate the use of group sessions by an investigator in order to check his or her emerging perceptions against actual members' views.[5] Kilmann also proposes that group members be asked to list a set of new norms that would facilitate organizational performance. With such lists, one can begin to discuss the changing of norms and, thereby, the changing of a major element of the organization's culture. Kilmann reports that some of the proposed norms that employees most frequently list include: Treat everyone with respect; Listen to other members' views even if you don't agree with them; Provide recognition to those who suggest new ideas and ways of doing things; and Speak with pride about your organization and department. Such lists of desired norms can serve as a useful starting point for altering an organization's culture. However, the commitment to changing cultural features must of necessity be obtained from top-level administrators if the desired change is to occur and to be maintained.

Increasing the potential to change organizational cultures in desired directions may be the greatest benefit of studying corporate cultures. By creating means for developing desired cultural features, the study of organizational culture can make a significant contribution to the field of organizational behavior.

The Creation and Maintenance of Organizational Culture

Since our research-based knowledge of organizational culture is presently very limited, it is difficult to state, with firm confidence, detailed prescriptions for creating and maintaining organizational cultures. Nonetheless, several observations and cautious suggestions can be made, based on the available understanding of organizational culture. It appears that there are at least four major influences on the origins of organizational culture:[6]

1. The *beliefs and values of the organization's founder* can be a strong influence in the creation of organizational culture. During his or her tenure, these beliefs and values can become embedded in the organization's policies, programs, and informal statements perpetuated by continuing members of the organization (akin to the oral tradition of story telling). For example, James Cash Penney infused his organization with "the Penney idea," consisting of such guiding principles as "Treat everyone as an individual" and "Value loyalty."

2. The *societal norms* of the firm's native or host country can also play a role in determining an organization's culture. That is, the culture of the surrounding society influences the culture of firms existing within it.

3. *Problems of external adaptation and survival* pose challenges for organizations that its members must meet via the creation of organizational culture (that is, norms). For example, the development of strate-

■ Figure 18.1

A Framework for Analyzing Organizational Culture

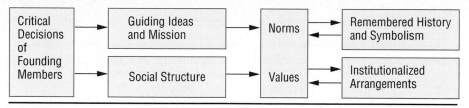

gies and goals and the selection of methods to achieve goals require the creation of norms. At PepsiCo, competition with Coca-Cola has produced an internal atmosphere of extreme competition where careers are made or destroyed by slight fluctuations in market share.

4. *Problems of internal integration* can lead to the formation of organizational culture. For example, setting rules for social relations and the distribution of status, and establishing criteria for group and organizational membership require the development of norms and the acceptance of a set of beliefs.

The maintenance or reinforcement of an organization's culture can be best understood by knowing (1) what managers consider important (what they measure and control); (2) the manner in which top management reacts to crises and critical events; (3) what types of deliberate role modeling are provided by managers; (4) criteria for distributing rewards and status; and (5) criteria for hiring, firing, and promotion.[7] These five elements for understanding the maintenance of organizational culture also provide insights as to how to change an organization's culture. That is, culture may be best changed by altering what managers measure and control, changing the manner in which crises are handled, using different role models for new recruits and altering the socialization/orientation process, establishing different criteria for allocating rewards, and changing the criteria for promotion, hiring, and dismissal.

A Framework for Understanding Organizational Culture

Recently, Smith and Vecchio proposed that the origin, maintenance, and modification of an organization's culture can be understood in terms of the following six central concepts[8] (see Figure 18.1).

Critical Decisions of the Entrepreneur or Founding Members

The founders of an organization, in essence, lay the foundation for the creation of the organization's culture. The vision and aspiration of the founders as well as their values and sense of mission play a critical role in forming norms and values within the organization. Moreover, the founders influence the formation of the organization's culture through such means as key recruiting decisions and critical decisions regarding the firm's market, and through the selection of their successors.

OB Focus

Neurotic Corporations

The research of Professors Manfred F. R. Kets DeVries and Danny Miller has led them to an interesting view of organizational behavior. They have found that the neurotic behavior of a chief executive can lead to dysfunction in the organization. They identify five common pathological types of organization: paranoid, compulsive, histrionic, depressive, and schizoid.

The paranoid organization is suspicious of people and events inside and outside the firm. It emphasizes intelligence, and controls and develops sophisticated ways to gather information in order to identify threats and challenges. Paranoid organizations try to maintain strict control over internal matters by monitoring all facets of their operations. These organizations are reactive, which can interfere with the development of a consistent strategy. These firms often diversify to reduce the risk of relying upon any one market.

The compulsive organization emphasizes ritual; it plans every detail in advance and carries out its activities in a routine, preprogrammed style. Thoroughness and conformity are valued. These organizations are hierarchical and generally have elaborate policies, rules, and procedures. The strategies of compulsive firms reflect their preoccupation with detail and established procedures. Each compulsive organization has a distinctive area of competence and specializes in this area, not in response to the marketplace.

The histrionic organization is hyperactive, impulsive, dramatically venturesome, and dangerously uninhibited. In such an organization, decision makers act only on hunches and impressions, taking on widely diverse projects. Top managers reserve the right to start bold ventures independently; subordinates have limited power.

The depressive organization lacks confidence, is inactive, conservative, and insular, and has an entrenched bureaucracy. The only things that get done are activities that have been made routine. Depressive organizations are well established and serve a single, mature market.

The schizoid organization lacks leadership. Its top executive discourages interaction. Sometimes the second level of executives make up for the leader's lack of involvement, but often they simply fight to fill the leadership vacuum. In such organizations, strategy more often reflects individual goals and internal politics than threats or opportunities concerning the organization as a whole.

Source: "The Neurotic Corporation," *Harper's*, December 1984, pp. 24–25.

Guiding Ideas and Mission

The organization's leaders articulate a small set of guiding ideas. These guiding ideas, or superordinate goals, constitute a statement of purpose, or mission. Typically, they embody a belief in a core idea, such as a commitment to service or a commitment to fostering innovation. Actions that fulfill this commitment come to define the organization's distinctive identity.

Social Structure

The leaders also play a role in creating the organization's social structure. The structure consists of the pattern of interaction among people and groups within the organization. The social structure is a consequence of the leaders' decision on how best to design the organization's structure in light of technical considerations. These task-based issues, in turn, affect the pattern of formal and informal relations that emerges.

Norms and Values

Norms and values are the heart of what is meant by organizational culture. As the framework suggests, norms and values are influenced by the mission and the social structure. **Norms** are expectations for the behavior of the organization's members, while **values** are preferences among activities and outcomes. By participating in common organizational experiences, members develop greater degrees of shared values and norms, which then serve as aids to further communication and decision making. These norms and values also influence remembered history and institutionalized arrangements.

Remembered History and Symbolism

Norms and values can influence the process whereby organizational history is selectively remembered and interpreted. Some events may be exaggerated or distorted, while others may be forgotten. **Symbolism** includes rituals and ceremonies. Symbols communicate values, legitimize practices, and help to socialize members and build loyalty. Remembered history and symbolism thus can influence existing norms and values.

Institutionalized Arrangements

Formal policies, reward systems, and lines of authority and communication exemplify **institutionalized arrangements.** These arrangements constitute an organization's "way of doing business" and can have a powerful influence on the attitudes and behaviors of the organization's members. Institutionalized arrangements (for example, the forms people must complete, the training the organization provides, and the promotion and compensation systems) exert a subtle yet powerful form of control over employee actions. These arrangements are a result of norms and values. However, norms and values are continually influenced by the arrangements as well. Both institutionalized arrangements and the remembered history and symbolism help to perpetuate the organization's culture over time.

Culture and Strategy

Organizational researchers recognize the importance of an organization's culture in shaping the organization's strategy. The manner in which culture and strategy influence each other is thought to be quite complex. Figure 18.2 presents a simplified view of a mutual influence explanation of the relationships among environment, culture, and strategy. In this view, the perception of the organization's environment by the top management (strategy formulating) team is necessarily influenced by initial values and practices of members (that is, the organization's culture). Culture, therefore, plays a filtering role in terms of which facets of the environment are deemed important and deserving of attention. The top management team's strategic response (that is, its effort to respond to the environment or to manage a portion of the environment) will necessarily be influenced by the existing culture. That is to say, the ability of the top management team to respond quickly to a perceived threat will be affected by existing cultural characteristics of the organization.

Figure 18.2

The Reciprocal Influence View of Strategy and Environment as Moderated by Organizational Culture

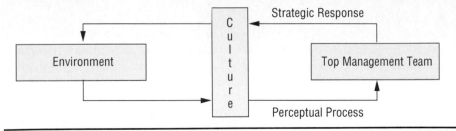

Source: C. G. Smith and R. P. Vecchio, "Elements of Organizational Culture: A Review and Synthesis" (Paper presented at the National Meeting of TIMS/ORSA, New York, 1989).

The model portrayed in Figure 18.2 argues that organizational culture operates as an intervening variable (see Chapter 2) in that it is a useful construct that cannot be perfectly and directly measured. This model also implies that a key element in judging the usefulness of an organizational culture is whether that culture is in proper "alignment" with the requirements of the organization's strategy. For example, if an organization is in a highly dynamic environment and requires rapid response to new forms of competition, the culture needed is one that endorses flexibility and coordination of efforts. To the degree that the existing culture approximates this ideal state, one can say that the organization's culture is in alignment with its strategy. In essence, cultural alignment is potentially an important determinant of an organization's longevity.

Cross-Cultural Research

While the study of organizational culture focuses on the conduct of individuals within organizations, cross-cultural research explores the differences and similarities among members of different cultures. Defining what is meant by the term *culture* at this level of analysis is no less problematic. Most often, national boundaries are used as the basis for defining culture, but this is largely a convention of convenience, since the important dimensions of culture are sometimes difficult to specify.‡ In the realm of organizational behavior, it may be more accurate to say that the concern is with cross-national studies or comparative organizational behavior rather than with cross-cultural issues.

Even if we accept a label devoid of the term *culture,* the results of research comparing employees across different countries are still difficult to interpret. This difficulty stems from a lack of theoretical notions for explaining what culture or nationality is, and an inability to predict the effects of culture or nationality on other variables.[10] In short, it is difficult to make sense out of the results of cross-national studies without a theoretical scheme. We are often left simply with a group of results stating that a group of employees in Country

‡ A strong case can even be made that the term culture could be dropped or avoided in discussing behavioral processes.[9]

■ **Table 18.1**

The Pace of Life in Six Countries

	Accuracy of Bank Clocks	Walking Speed	Post Office Speed
Japan	1	1	1
United States	2	3	2
England	4	2	3
Italy	5	4	6
Taiwan	3	5	4
Indonesia	6	6	5

Source: R. Levine and E. Wolff, "Social Time: The Heartbeat of Culture," *Psychology Today*, March 1985, 28–35.

A did or did not differ from a group of employees in Country B. Why these results occurred and how any differences were brought about are often unexplained.

Despite the difficulties of drawing inferences from the results of cross-national research, investigators have continued to make comparisons across nations. Continuing interest is spurred by the belief that cultural processes possess regularity and meaning that will ultimately become better understood, perhaps after more results are gathered and the patterns are examined to identify underlying principles. Further driving forces in cross-national research are the proliferation of multinational corporations (firms that are based in several different countries) and the growth of international trade. Increased contact between employees from different countries has led to a growing awareness of the need to better understand members of other cultures.

Cultural Differences

Studies of the differences between national groups have uncovered some interesting results. For example, research on the pace of life in various countries suggests that Westerners tend to have fairly precise measures of time and a stronger concern for punctuality than have most other people. Levine and Wolff checked clock accuracy, walking speed, and the average time it took postal clerks to sell stamps in six countries.[11] A rank ordering of their results in terms of fastest to slowest (1 to 6) corroborates anecdotal suggestions that the pace of life differs across countries (Table 18.1).

Other research, based on interviews with roughly 1,000 people in each of five countries, identified strong differences in levels of interpersonal trust. Specifically, it was found that the percentage of respondents who agreed that "most people can be trusted" varied as follows:

United States	55%
England	49%
Mexico	30%
Germany	19%
Italy	7%

■ Table 18.2

National Need for Achievement Levels

Country	National Score
Turkey	3.62
India	2.71
France	2.38
Australia	2.38
Israel	2.33
Canada	2.29
U.S.A.	2.24
West Germany	2.14
U.S.S.R.	2.10
Iraq	1.95
U.K.	1.67
Mexico	1.57
Sweden	1.52
Italy	1.33
Japan	1.29
Switzerland	1.20
Chile	1.19
Poland	.86
Belgium	.43

Source: D.C. McClelland, *The Achieving Society* (Princeton: Van Nostrand, 1961).

Further research on cultural/national differences has focused on the need for achievement (see Chapter 6). In an examination of the themes in the literature of different countries, David McClelland noted the existence of strong differences.[12] Table 18.2 presents a sampling of his results.

In a comparison of the values of 3,600 managers representing 14 countries, Haire, Ghiselli, and Porter observed a number of similarities in dimensions of leadership and attitudes.[13] Other research by George England on the value systems of 2,600 managers in five countries also found many similarities, suggesting that managers often have many common views on business-related activities regardless of national affiliation.[14]

Certain patterns and clusters of results have also been observed in these and similar cross-national studies. Specifically, it has been found that managers from the United States, Canada, Australia, and Britain tend to hold fairly similar attitudes; Japanese and Korean managers tend to have greater agreement on value issues; Central and South Americans tend to agree; and so on. These clusters of responses suggest that although many similarities may exist among managers worldwide, they can also be sorted into clusters based on. similarities that are historical, religious, linguistic, and racial in nature.

Reliable differences between clusters of countries are frequently reported. In the Haire, Ghiselli, and Porter study and other follow-up studies, it has been found that various clusters of countries often differ on attitudes toward sharing information and the belief that individuals have the capacity for leadership

■ **Table 18.3**

Attitudes of 3,600 Managers in 14 Countries*

Countries	Individual's Capacity for Leadership and Initiative	Advisability of Sharing Information and Objectives
Nordic-European countries (Denmark, Germany, Norway, Sweden)	−.24	.04
Developing countries (Argentina, Chile, India)	.21	−.59
Latin-European countries (Belgium, France, Italy, Spain)	−.25	.22
Japan	.39	.04
Anglo-American countries (England, United States)	.45	.36

Source: Adapted from M. Haire, E. E. Ghiselli, and L. W. Porter, *Managerial Thinking* (New York: Wiley, 1965).

* Positive average numbers denote democratic values, while negative average numbers denote values that are more autocratic.

and initiative (Table 18.3).[15] By and large, these results suggest that Anglo-American managers are much more democratic in their orientation, while managers from other countries tend to be more autocratic.

Another attitudinal difference between the United States and other countries can be seen in the extent of gender bias. A failure to appreciate this continuing bias in attitudes toward women in other countries can lead to difficulties for those who hope to conduct business in the international arena. In addition, class consciousness and de facto caste systems are prevalent outside the United States. Even in some European countries, hirings and promotions are still based on social and academic origins rather than on objective merit. Fraternization across management levels and between managers and workers is frowned upon in many countries in the world. However, a limited degree of informal socializing of upper management with the "troops" is regarded quite favorably by most Americans. By and large, Americans object to elitist conduct and class distinctions, while the peoples of many other countries do not hesitate to invoke social rank.[16]

Dimensions of Cultural Differences

One of the most ambitious studies of cultural differences as they relate to organizational issues was undertaken by Geert Hofstede, a Dutch scholar.[17] This research involved data on over 116,000 employees of IBM representing 40 countries. Based on his empirical results and a review of evidence in the field of cultural differences, Hofstede deduced four useful criteria for comparing cultures: power-distance, the avoidance of uncertainty, individualism versus collectivism, and masculinity versus femininity.

Power-distance refers to the degree that the members of a culture accept the unequal distribution of power, and the appropriateness of maintaining distance between people. *Avoidance of uncertainty* is the degree to which

■ **Table 18.4**

Dimensions of Cultural Differences

Power-Distance

Small Power-Distance	**Large Power-Distance**
Inequality among people should be reduced	There should be a degree of inequality, where everyone has a rightful place
Leaders and followers consider each other to be just like themselves	Leaders and followers view one another as being different
Those in power should try to appear less powerful	Those in power should try to appear powerful

Avoidance of Uncertainty

Weak Avoidance	**Strong Avoidance**
There should be few rules	There is a need for written rules
Competition can be used constructively	Competition can unleash aggression and should, therefore, be avoided
Authorities should serve citizens	Citizens lack competence compared to authorities

Individualism versus Collectivism

Individualist	**Collectivist**
"I" consciousness is dominant	"We" consciousness is dominant
People should strive for themselves and only immediate family	People belong to extended families or clans
Emphasis on initiative and leading	Emphasis on belonging and following

Masculinity versus Femininity

Feminine	**Masculine**
Men need not be assertive, but can be nurturing	Men should be assertive and women should be nurturing
Equality of sexes is ideal	Men should dominate in society
People and environment are valued	Wealth and goods are valued

Source: G. Hofstede, *Culture's Consequences* (New York: Sage Publications, 1980) p. 122, 184, 235, 295.

members of a culture are able to cope with ambiguous or anxiety-provoking situations.

Individualism versus collectivism refers to whether the members of a culture endorse a view that people are expected to take care of only their immediate families (individualism) versus a view that people are expected to care for members of an extended family and offer loyalty to groups (collectivism).

Masculinity versus femininity is concerned with whether members of a culture value traits and attributes that are traditionally defined as masculine versus traits and attributes that are more characteristically feminine in nature. Table 18.4 summarizes the defining endpoints of these four dimensions.

In a comparison of managers from the United States with managers from 39 countries on these four dimensions, Hofstede found that the United States ranked 26th (below average) on power-distance, 32nd on avoidance of uncertainty (again, below average), 1st on individualism (that is, highly individualistic), and 13th on masculinity (above average). In their totality, these results suggest that U.S. managers (in the aggregate and relative to managers in other countries) prefer a small power-distance, feel capable of coping with ambiguity, are highly individualistic, and endorse traditionally masculine values.

Japanese Management

Much has been written in recent years about the alleged superiority of **Japanese management** techniques in comparison to the American style of management. The major characteristics of the Japanese approach to management (assuming that it is fair to speak in very general terms of a nation's system of management) have been identified by such writers as Ouchi and Price,[18] Chung and Gray,[19] and Rehder.[20] Contrasting their descriptions with how American firms are structured or tackle similar problems produces some interesting differences.

A major stylistic difference between the two approaches lies in the extent to which consensus is sought when making decisions. Japanese firms involve many more workers in the decision-making process and try to work on a solution until all of those involved are reasonably satisfied. In the United States, decision making is more often an individual manager's prerogative.

A second major difference between the two styles of management lies in their amount of commitment to the worker. Japanese firms sometimes offer the equivalent of lifetime employment to their employees, thereby creating feelings of security and family membership. U.S. firms, in contrast, tend toward a short-term view of employment, releasing employees when the company finds it necessary.

Third, Japanese evaluation and promotion systems are designed to reward seniority more than merit. A consequence of this feature, coupled with a commitment to employment security, is that individuals must wait a long time to rise through management ranks. In the United States, young managers expect that they will rise rapidly within a firm or, if they do not, they will seek employment elsewhere.

Other less frequently cited features of Japanese management include intensive socialization of employees to create greater group cohesiveness, emphasis on quality and productivity, and reliance on an informal approach to controlling the behavior of employees. Figure 18.3 summarizes the six major components most frequently identified with Japanese management. William Ouchi, a professor at UCLA, argues that highly successful U.S firms may be benefiting from the adoption of these six features, which he views as characterizing a unique form of management called **Theory Z**.[21] According to this view, an organization is more likely to be successful to the extent it incorporates the principles of Theory Z.

It is commonly suggested that the features of Theory Z management are responsible for the Japanese economic miracle. While it is true that Japan's *rate* of productivity growth has been greater than that of the United States in past years, it does not follow that Japanese industry is stronger or that the Japanese approach to management is better in any meaningful sense. The fact that differences exist is not in itself sufficient to explain Japan's productivity gains.

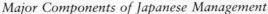

Figure 18.3

Major Components of Japanese Management

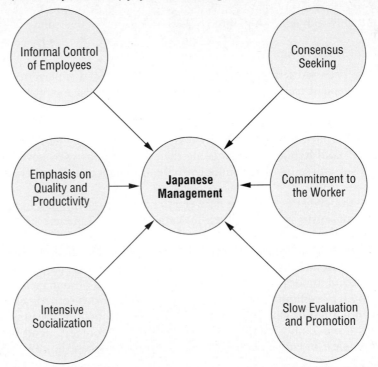

Furthermore, Japan's relative economic advantage is only seen in certain areas, such as steel and iron production. U.S. productivity leads Japan's in the areas of textiles, printing, foods, general machinery production, paper products, and chemicals, to name only a few.

If for the sake of argument we assume that Japanese management practices are superior to American practices, we must then consider whether it is feasible to adopt the Japanese approach in the United States. Many students of Japanese management feel that it is not reasonable to think in terms of transplanting many features of Japanese management.[22] For example, the notions of promoting slowly and rewarding heavily for seniority rather than merit would find little acceptance among U.S. employees. Other features, such as seeking consensus in decision making, may be more workable but may also be unnecessary. That is to say, frequent group meetings to achieve consensus may have evolved in Japan because of the difficulty of relying on written communication in the Japanese language. As a result, oral communication may have come to be preferred for business purposes.[23]§

§ Gutenberg's invention of printing from movable type — a technique not readily adaptable to the enormous number of Japanese written characters — may, therefore, be responsible for the Western emphasis on written business communications.

Finally, many of the vaunted positive features of Japanese management are not common in the country's larger companies. For example, it is estimated that only 30 percent of Japanese workers enjoy the security of a lifetime job guarantee.[24] In addition, there are few opportunities for females to enter management ranks. By and large, these and other shortcomings of Japanese business practices argue against a simple transplanting of Japanese management practices to the United States.[25] In addition, it has been suggested that young Japanese employees are less committed to their work than were their predecessors. One comparison found that only 14 percent of young Japanese were satisfied with the workplace versus 70 percent of their U.S. counterparts. A major source of dissatisfaction seems to be the Japanese practice of assigning employees to jobs without regard for their preferences. A cross-cultural comparison by the Aspen Institute for Humanistic Studies found that Japanese (and British) workers reported the greatest disparity between what they desired in a job and what they actually experienced. Although the touted Japanese commitment to work is not in danger of collapse, these and related findings suggest a growing sense of alienation among Japanese workers.[26]

In closing this discussion of differences among managers in various countries, it should be stated that many students of comparative management believe there is a general set of management practices that can be applied across all cultures. Thus, they contend that management can be practiced in a generic sense. One typically finds the major organizational functions (that is, marketing, production, and finance) existing in firms around the world. In short, the principles of effective management may be said to be fairly universal, or lacking a high degree of uniqueness, for various cultures.[27]

Doing Business Overseas

The increasing globalization of the world economy has produced a growing demand for managers skilled in international business practices. The sophistication required to work effectively with people from other countries takes considerable time to develop. As a first step in learning to relate with people from other cultures, it is useful to consider how we are seen by others. Below are some observations made by visitors to the United States.[28]

- "Americans seem to be in a perpetual hurry. Just watch the way they walk down the street. They never allow themselves the leisure to enjoy life." (India)

- "Americans appear to us rather distant. They are not really as close to other people — even fellow Americans — as Americans overseas tend to portray. It's almost as if an American says, 'I won't let you get too close to me.' It's like building a wall." (Kenya)

- "Once we were out in a rural area in the middle of nowhere and saw an American come to a stop sign. Though he could see in both directions for miles and no traffic was coming, he still stopped!" (Turkey)

- "The tendency in the United States to think that life is only work hits you in the face. Work seems to be the one type of motivation." (Colombia)

- "In the United States, everything has to be talked about and analyzed. Even the littlest thing has to be, 'Why, Why, Why?' I get a headache from such persistent questions." (Indonesia)
- "The American is very explicit; he wants a 'yes' or 'no.' If someone tries to speak figuratively, the American is confused." (Ethiopia)
- "The first time . . . my (American) professor told me, 'I don't know the answer, I will have to look it up,' I was shocked. I asked myself, 'Why is he teaching me?' In my country, a professor would give the wrong answer rather than admit ignorance." (Iran)

Functioning as a manager in another country requires an understanding of the traditions, customs, and business practices of the host country. Although there is little empirical evidence of the precise requirements to be effective in doing business overseas, the collected wisdom of experienced overseas managers does give some insight on what works (and what doesn't) in specific countries.[29]

Latin America   Conducting business in Latin America takes time. Few people rush into business. Although some customs are changing, men and women still congregate into separate groups at social functions (until recently, having a chaperone was still an accepted practice). Latins also stand more closely together than do North Americans when in conversation. Instead of shaking hands, men may embrace. Guests invariably arrive late for functions (although North Americans are expected to be punctual). Several unique traits are the *mañana* concept (meaning a belief in an indefinite future and, therefore, little need to worry about deadlines), *machismo* (an expectation that in business a male will display forcefulness, self-confidence, and leadership with a flourish), and *fatalism* (a resignation to the inevitable, or taking whatever comes, sometimes seen as a heroic posture). As a rule for non-Latins, when in doubt, be formal.

East Asia (Japan, the Chinas, Korea)   Initially, business meetings are devoted to pleasantries — serving tea, engaging in inconsequential chitchat, and developing a relationship. Indirect and vague communication is considered acceptable. Sometimes statements are left unfinished so that the listener can reach the conclusion in his or her own mind. Forcing another to admit failure or impotency is to be avoided. Seniority and elderliness command respect. When confronted with a strange, unexpected, or emotionally powerful situation, East Asians may laugh or smile in a seemingly inappropriate manner (as a function of releasing tension rather than finding the circumstance humorous). In addition, many are convinced that East Asians consciously use slowdown techniques as bargaining ploys in the belief that they can exploit a natural inclination of Westerners to be impatient. Finally, it is very much expected that business cards will have one side printed in English and the other in oriental characters (although the presentation of your business card may not always result in your being offered a business card by the other party).

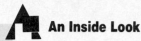

An Inside Look
The Perils of Uninformed Travel

Why should a manager from the United States be worried about fitting in with the business practices and customs of other cultures? Perhaps the following blunders speak for themselves.

On a trip to Malaysia, a businessman was introduced ceremoniously to someone he thought was named Roger. Throughout the important contract negotiations that followed, he referred to this person as "Rog." Only later did he learn that his potential client was a rajah (a title of nobility), not someone named Roger. He might have avoided tremendous embarrassment by learning ahead of time that one of the states in Malaysia is headed by rajahs (the others are controlled by sultans).

Learning about another country's culture ahead of time can prevent inadvertent insults as well as embarrassment. An American executive with an oil company traveled to a Middle Eastern nation to sign a contract.

An hour before the signing ceremony, the executive met for tea with the government official responsible for the contract. The American relaxed by propping his feet on the table, with his soles facing the Arab host. Furious, the official left the room, and the company spent another year in negotiations before the contract was signed. The American executive had not realized that exposing the sole of one's shoe to an Arab is a serious insult.

Some thorough homework might also have prevented the embarrassment experienced by an executive who went to a small Caribbean country to close a sale. He entered the prime minister's conference room and opened his presentation by saying, "Honorable Mr. Tollis and esteemed members of the cabinet." The prime minister suggested that the executive start over. The businessman repeated his opening phrase, to the apparent annoyance of the prime minister, who suggested that he again start over.

A sympathetic cabinet minister took the American aside and whispered, "Mr. Tollis was deposed six months ago. You are now addressing the Honorable Mr. Herbert."

Fortunately for their companies, American managers have begun to realize that successful negotiations depend on knowing their customers as well as their products. American businesspeople in Japan, for example, have learned to navigate that country's practices with regard to patents and distribution. But, notes an official of a major Tokyo trading company, some visitors still refuse the customary cup of green tea offered during a company visit. "Why don't they just take it?" wonders the official. "It's so simple, but refusing can throw off the whole pace of a meeting."

The lesson in this complaint is that seemingly minor details can make or break an important contract or business relationship.

Sources: Ted Holden, "The Delicate Art of Doing Business in Japan," *Business Week*, October 2, 1989, p. 120; Charles F. Valentine, "Blunders Abroad," *Nation's Business*, March 1989, pp. 54, 56.

Soviet Union   Notorious for being protocol conscious, the Soviets expect to do business with only the highest-ranking executives. To Westerners, they appear stiff and dull. When greeting foreigners for the first time, Soviets frequently use the stilted term *gospodin* (citizen). In private, however, Soviets are far more expressive and sociable. Written agreements are essential as informal, quid pro quo understandings may not be honored. Unfortunately, writing a contract can be difficult as there are no Russian equivalents for many Western business terms. Contracts, therefore, must be back-translated (that is, translated from English into Russian and then translated from Russian back into

English to determine if the exact meaning is retained). In a land of chronic shortages and few choices, the Soviets have virtually no advertising experience. The basic sales philosophy can be summarized in the words of a Soviet citizen who was asked how he might go about attracting more customers to stay at his hotel. "Well," he responded, "I would hope that all the other hotels were full."

Middle East   Middle Easterners are known to occasionally prefer to act through trusted third parties rather than deal directly. Personal honor is given a high premium, and the avoidance of shame is very important. Fatalism influences the view of time. A favorite expression is "Burka insha Allah" — "Tommorow if God wills." Compared with people of other societies (especially East Asians), Middle Easterners are far more emotionally expressive. They stand closer together, and eye contact is more intense. Also, occasional bodily contact during conversations (for example, gently tapping another's arm or knee) is not unusual. Guests should avoid discussing politics, religion, and the host's family and personal possessions (commenting on the host's female family members is a taboo, and praising a possession implies the host should offer the item as a gift). A signal that a meeting is concluded is given by the offer of coffee or tea.

Methods of Cross-Cultural Training

Cross-cultural training programs have been created to teach members of one culture ways of interacting effectively in another. Programs vary, with the simplest consisting merely of lectures and readings concerning the host culture. More extensive programs may involve role-playing exercises, simulations, and practice in functioning within the host country itself. In this section, we will examine two techniques used in orientation programs: the Culture Assimilator and simulation.

The Culture Assimilator   The **Culture Assimilator** is a programmed learning exercise designed by social scientists at the University of Illinois under the direction of Harry Triandis.[30] The assimilator is culture-specific — there is a programmed learning exercise for each of a number of countries. The assimilator provides the learner with immediate feedback on his or her response to a hypothetical situation. In addition to simply finding out whether the chosen response is correct, the learner is given an explanation regarding why the response is or is not correct. The following is an example from the Thailand assimilator. The example was developed after a U.S. student reported being bothered by Thai teachers' lack of punctuality. Although Thai students were similarly disturbed, they reported that they would never show these feelings to their professors.

> One day a Thai administrator of middle academic rank kept two of his assistants waiting about an hour for an appointment. The assistants, although very angry, did not show it while they waited. When the administrator walked in, he acted as if he were not late. He offered no apology or explanation. After he was settled in his office, he called his assistants in; they all began working on the business for which the administrator had set the meeting.

> *If the incident is observed exactly as it is reported in this passage, which of the following best describes the chief significance of the behavior of the people involved?*
>
> 1. *The Thai assistants were extremely skillful at concealing their true feelings.*
>
> 2. *In Thailand, subordinates are required to be polite to their superiors, no matter what happens or what their rank may be.*
>
> 3. *Since no one commented on it, the behavior indicated nothing of unusual significance to the Thais.*

The feedback for each choice is as follows:

1. This is not entirely correct, although it is characteristic of Thais to try to appear reserved under any circumstances. If the assistants were skillful at concealing their true feelings, there would be no doubt about their feelings. Also, the reference to the chief significance of the behavior of the people involved may limit the inference to the assistants.

2. This choice is correct. The information in the episode is fully used. This "deference to the boss" may be observed anywhere in the world, but it is likely to be carried to a higher degree in Thailand than in the United States. Certain clues indicate this choice — the assistants concealed their feelings, the administrator failed to apologize, the tardiness was not mentioned, and the appointment was kept.

3. This answer is completely wrong. Although the behavior in the passage does not seem as significant to the Thais as it might to Americans, why was nothing said about the tardiness? And why were the assistants "very angry" although they "did not show it"?

The Culture Assimilator has been studied extensively, perhaps more than any other cross-cultural training method. In general, the data suggest that assimilator training reduces interpersonal and adjustment problems between the trainees and members of the host country.

Simulation   In simulation training, a situation is created through which individuals experience certain elements of behavior they may encounter in another country. Learning is primarily inductive in that participants are expected to draw insight and deeper understanding from the experience. One example is the game "Bafa, Bafa." Bafa, Bafa is a simulation in which participants are assigned membership in one of two artificial cultures, Alpha and Beta. Each group first learns certain customs that characterize its culture (for example, the Alpha culture is warm, friendly, patriarchal, and English-speaking; the Beta do not speak English but are hard workers who seek to maximize points in any game). The two groups are then brought together to play a card game for points, and inevitably experience frustration and hostility in dealing with each other. A post–role-playing debriefing helps participants understand their own and others' negative behavior. Participants are led to realize that fully understanding the subtleties of another culture requires experience. They learn that what is accepted as sensible and reasonable in one culture may seem irrational or unimportant to an outsider, that differences among people are often seen as potentially threatening, and that stereotyping is a fairly natural process.

Summary

1. Define organizational culture and describe influences on its creation and maintenance.

Organizational culture comprises the shared values and norms in an organization that are taught to incoming employees. Influences on the creation of cultures are: the beliefs and values of the organization's founder; societal norms; problems of external adaptation and survival; and problems of internal integration. Maintaining an organizational culture depends on managers' priorities; top management's reactions to critical events; role modeling by managers; criteria for distributing rewards and status; and criteria for hiring, firing, and promotion.

2. Explain how organizational culture may influence strategy.

The perception of an organization's environment by its top management team is affected by, or filtered through, elements of the organization's culture (i.e., the initial values and practices of the founding members). This perception affects the team's strategic response to the environment, and that response, in turn, influences the culture. In essence, culture serves as an intervening variable.

3. Explain the importance of research comparing employees across nations.

The research may reveal patterns that will identify underlying principles about cultural processes. Multinational corporations are proliferating, and international trade is growing. As a result, increased contact among nations has heightened the need for better understanding by members of different cultures.

4. Describe characteristics of typical managers in the United States.

In the aggregate, U.S. managers prefer a small power-distance, feel capable of coping with ambiguity, are highly individualistic, and endorse values traditionally considered masculine.

5. Contrast Japanese and American management styles.

Japanese firms involve many more workers in the decision-making process and try to achieve consensus, while in the United States managers more often make decisions individually. Japanese management places more emphasis on job security, whereas U.S. companies tend to take a more short-term view. Japanese systems tend to reward seniority more than merit; in the United States, young managers expect to rise rapidly within a company or will leave it.

6. Give some examples of the differences in social customs and business practices in other cultures.

In Latin America, there is less attention to punctuality but more physical contact. In East Asia, seniority is given great respect. Soviets tend to be formal in public settings but expressive and sociable in private. Middle Easterners value honor and tend to be emotionally more expressive.

7. Identify two methods of cross-cultural training.
The Culture Assimilator uses a culture-specific programmed learning exercise to explain why people behave differently in different cultures. Simulation training involves role-playing exercises that provide participants with an opportunity to learn more about the values, feelings, and behaviors of members of different cultures.

Key Terms

Organizational culture	Institutionalized arrangements
Norms	Japanese management
Values	Theory Z
Symbolism	Culture Assimilator

Review and Discussion Questions

1. When Don left XYZ Galvanizing, the following story circulated through the grapevine: Don's boss, June, had overheard Don discussing XYZ on the telephone. Don was telling the other party that XYZ was having problems because it was selling products that had been improperly galvanized, and customers were beginning to complain and threaten lawsuits. After June overheard Don, she started reviewing all his outgoing mail and frequently passed by his office in order to keep track of his phone conversations. When the time came for Don's salary review, June told him that he would not be getting a raise. At that time, Don realized that his career at XYZ was over, and he resigned. What norm does this rumor illustrate? How might such a norm have developed?

2. Is research into cross-cultural differences in organizations valid? Consider whether a culture is a meaningful unit for comparison, the benefits of cross-cultural research, and your own opinion of the merits of the findings so far. For example, does the available research supply information that aids our understanding of other people, or does it merely reinforce baseless stereotypes?

3. People discussing management styles often suggest that a Japanese style of management would greatly improve the performance of U.S. companies. What factors characterize a Japanese management style? Should U.S. companies adopt this style?

4. How might one measure the elements of an organization's culture?

5. Describe the major influences on the origins of organizational culture. How might these influences be used deliberately to change an organization's culture?

6. Do academic institutions have different organizational cultures? In what ways might these cultures be said to differ?

7. Maryann is considering applying for an overseas assignment that would take her to a country that values masculinity over femininity. What are some issues she should be prepared to deal with?

8.   You are given an opportunity to work overseas in one of several countries — Mexico, Korea, the Soviet Union, or Egypt. Assuming the assignments are equivalent in all major respects, in which country would you prefer to work? Why?

9.   Several young managers in your unit are about to be assigned overseas. What steps might you take to help them prepare for their new assignments?

Critical Incident
Keeping Things the Same

Metropolitan Hospital was built two years ago and currently has a work force of 235 people. The hospital is small, but because it is new, it is extremely efficient. The board has voted to increase its capacity from 60 beds to 190 beds. By this time next year the hospital will be over three times as large as it is now in terms of both beds and personnel.

The administrator, Clara Hawkins, feels that the major problem with this proposed increase is that the hospital will lose its efficiency. "I want to hire people who are just like our current team of personnel — hard-working, dedicated, talented, and able to interact well with patients. If we triple the number of employees, I don't see how it will be possible to maintain our quality patient care. We are going to lose our family atmosphere. We will be inundated with mediocrity and we'll end up being like every other institution in the local area — large and uncaring!"

The chairman of the board is also concerned about the effect of hiring such a large number of employees. However, he believes that Clara is overreacting. "It can't be that hard to find people who are like our current staff. There must be a lot of people out there who are just as good. What you need to do is develop a plan of action that will allow you to carefully screen those who will fit into your current organizational culture and those who will not. It's not going to be as difficult as you believe. Trust me. Everything will work out just fine."

As a result of the chairman's comments, Clara has decided that the most effective way of dealing with the situation is to develop a plan of action. She intends to meet with her administrative group and determine the best way of screening incoming candidates and then helping those who are hired to become socialized in terms of the hospital's culture. Clara has called a meeting for the day after tomorrow. At that time, she intends to discuss her ideas, get suggestions from her people, and then formulate a plan of action. "We've come too far to lose it all now," she told her administrative staff assistant. "If we keep our wits about us, I think we can continue to keep Metropolitan as the showcase hospital in this region."

Questions

1. What can Clara and her staff do to select the type of entry-level candidates they want? Explain.

2. How can Clara ensure that those who are hired come to accept the core cultural values of the hospital? What steps would you recommend?

3. Could Clara use this same approach if another 200 people were hired a few years from now?

Source: Fred Luthans, "Keeping Things the Same," *Organizational Behavior*, 5/e, p. 73. Copyright 1989 McGraw-Hill, Inc. Used with permission.

Experiential Exercise

Is Your Culture Gap Showing?

This activity is designed to help you better understand the culture at your college or university. There are no good or bad cultures per se. The cultural norms either help or hinder the organization in realizing its goals, mission, and purposes.

Following are several sets of paired statements concerning elements that constitute the college culture. Please work quickly and do not read too much into each statement.

Step 1 Complete the following cultural assessment instrument. Respond to each pair of statements in the following manner:

a. Choose the (A) or (B) item in each pair that is the *actual* norm right now. Mark that norm with an A.

b. Label the (A) or (B) norm that is the *desired* condition with a D. This may be the same or the opposite statement you labeled in part a. Thus, you could have one of the following configurations:

(A) A   (A) D   (A) AD   (A)
(B) D   (B) A   (B)   (B) AD

c. Using the following 7-point scale, indicate the importance of the choice (or issue) to you.
   7: This is a critical issue.
   6: This is very important.
   5: This is moderately important.
   4: This is a neutral issue.
   3: This is moderately unimportant.
   2: This is very unimportant.
   1: This is an extremely unimportant issue.

		Actual/Desired	Importance
1.	(A) The professors go out of their way to help students.	_____	
	(B) The professors just teach their classes.	_____	_____
2.	(A) Channels for expressing student complaints are readily accessible.	_____	
	(B) Few people pay serious attention to student complaints.	_____	_____
3.	(A) Many students here develop a strong sense of responsibility about their roles in contemporary social and political life.	_____	
	(B) The expression of strong personal belief or conviction is pretty rare around here.	_____	_____
4.	(A) Students respect the rules.	_____	
	(B) Students pay little attention to rules.	_____	_____
5.	(A) Most of the professors are very thorough teachers and really probe into the fundamentals of their subjects.	_____	
	(B) Most of the professors just cover the bare facts.	_____	_____
6.	(A) Students are conscientious about taking good care of school property.	_____	
	(B) Students are indifferent to or abuse school property.	_____	_____
7.	(A) Students set high standards of achievement for themselves.	_____	
	(B) Students do just enough to get by.	_____	_____
8.	(A) Many students play an active role in helping new students adjust to campus life.	_____	
	(B) Most students pay little attention to new students.	_____	_____
9.	(A) The administration and faculty make every effort to treat everyone equally.	_____	
	(B) Anyone who knows the right people among the faculty or administration can get a better break here.	_____	_____
10.	(A) The big college events draw a lot of student enthusiasm and support.	_____	
	(B) Major college events are usually greeted with indifference.	_____	_____
11.	(A) Academic advisors are knowledgeable and provide quality advice.	_____	
	(B) The academic advisors provide little useful information.	_____	_____

		Actual/Desired	Importance
12.	(A) Information of concern to students, such as the last date to drop a course, is readily available.	———	
	(B) Information of concern to students is not well publicized.	———	———
13.	(A) The talk among people on campus is warm and friendly.	———	
	(B) People are polite but reserved.	———	———
14.	(A) Many students get involved in clubs and organizations.	———	
	(B) Only a small number of students seem to be involved in organizations.	———	———
15.	(A) Faculty members are available for conferences and meetings.	———	
	(B) Faculty members are rarely available for meetings.	———	———
16.	(A) Students have a high regard for ethics and values.	———	
	(B) Students do not seem interested in what's ethical.	———	———
17.	(A) Most faculty show warmth, interest, and helpfulness toward students.	———	
	(B) Most faculty do not seem to care about the students as people.	———	———
18.	(A) Students have a great deal of freedom and latitude concerning such things as class attendance.	———	
	(B) Students have very few opportunities to express freedom of choice.	———	———
19.	(A) Students respect the value of learning and do their own work.	———	
	(B) Students resort to various forms of cheating to get by.	———	———
20.	(A) Residence halls seem to be congenial, fun places to live.	———	
	(B) Residence hall life is dull and sterile.	———	———
21.	(A) The administration seems to really care about student welfare.	———	
	(B) The administration seems to be indifferent toward students.	———	———
22.	(A) Students help each other with course assignments and projects.	———	
	(B) Students regard classwork as "everyone for himself or herself."	———	———

(continued)

(Continued)	Actual/Desired	Importance

23.   (A) Innovative courses or programs of study are introduced and tried.   _____

       (B) The courses and programs seem to be always the same.   _____   _____

24.   (A) Fraternities and sororities seem to have a major impact on the social atmosphere.   _____

       (B) Fraternities and sororities exist but seem to have little impact on campus.   _____   _____

25.   (A) Students seem to make extensive use of the library as a source of information.   _____

       (B) Students do not seem to make use of the library resources.   _____   _____

26.   (A) It is quite common to find students browsing through the bookstore.   _____

       (B) The bookstore is only a place to buy your texts.   _____   _____

27.   (A) Intramural athletic activities and other forms of recreation (bowling, ping pong) seem to be a significant part of student life.   _____

       (B) Intramurals and other recreational pursuits are not part of the campus scene.   _____   _____

28.   (A) The courses provide students with a basis for improving their social and economic status in life.   _____

       (B) The courses provide students with skills and techniques applicable to a job.   _____   _____

Step 2   To score your answers, look for paired statements in which the A and D labels are associated with different norms. Examples: (A) A, (B) D; or (A) D, (B) A.

Using the table below, record the importance score for *only* those items in which a difference exists between Actual and Desired.

Task	Social	Task	Social
1. _____	3. _____	17. _____	14. _____
2. _____	4. _____	18. _____	16. _____
5. _____	6. _____	21. _____	19. _____
9. _____	7. _____	23. _____	20. _____
11. _____	8. _____	25. _____	22. _____
12. _____	10. _____	26. _____	24. _____
15. _____	13. _____	28. _____	27. _____

Step 3   Either as a class or in small groups, examine the results and look for one or two norms where a major difference exists. If the entire class is involved, try to reach a consensus on the predominant area(s) of concern. If

small groups are used, each group should focus on a particular area of concern. In either case, develop a brief action plan to address what should be done to reduce the culture gaps. Consider the following when developing your plan:

a.   What are the current norms?

b.   What would be some ideal norms?

c.   Establish some new norms.

d.   How can each individual contribute to altering the culture toward the new norms?

Step 4   (For small group situations only) Each small group should be prepared to present its action plan. Comments and discussion are encouraged.

Source: Written by Bruce Kemelgor, University of Louisville.

Notes

1. E.H. Schein, *Organizational Culture and Leadership* (San Francisco: Jossey-Bass, 1985).
2. R.H. Kilmann, "Corporate Culture," *Psychology Today*, April 1985, 62–68.
3. Schein, *Organizational Culture and Leadership*.
4. Ibid.
5. Ibid.; Kilmann, "Corporate Culture."
6. Schein, *Organizational Culture and Leadership*.
7. Ibid.
8. C.G. Smith and R.P. Vecchio, "Elements of Organizational Culture: A Review and Synthesis" (Paper presented at the National Meeting of TIMS/ORSA, New York, 1989).
9. J. Child, "Culture, Contingency and Capitalism in the Cross-National Study of Organizations," *Research in Organizational Behavior* 3 (1981): 303–356.
10. K.H. Roberts, "On Looking At an Elephant: An Evaluation of Cross-Cultural Research Related to Organizations," *Psychological Bulletin* 74 (1970): 327–350; B. Meglino, E. Ravlin, and C. Adkins, "A Work Values Approach to Corporate Culture," *Journal of Applied Psychology* 74 (1989): 424–432.
11. R. Levine and E. Wolff, "Social Time: The Heartbeat of Culture," *Psychology Today*, March 1985, 28–35.
12. D.C. McClelland, *The Achieving Society* (Princeton: Van Nostrand, 1961).
13. M. Haire, E.E. Ghiselli, and L.W. Porter, *Managerial Thinking* (New York: Wiley, 1965).
14. G.W. England, *The Manager and His Values* (Cambridge, Mass.: Ballinger, 1975).
15. Haire, Ghiselli, and Porter, *Managerial Thinking;* R. Griffeth, P. Hom, A. DeNisi et al., "A Multivariate Multinational Comparison of Managerial Attitudes," in *Proceedings of the 40th Annual Meeting of the Academy of Management* (1980): 63–67.
16. R. Vernon and L.T. Wells, *Manager in the International Economy* (Englewood Cliffs, N.J.: Prentice-Hall, 1981).
17. G. Hofstede, *Culture's Consequences* (New York: Sage Publications, 1980).
18. W.G. Ouchi and M. Price, "Hierarchies, Clans and Theory Z: A New Perspective on Organization Development," *Organizational Dynamics* 32 (Autumn 1978): 24–44.
19. K.H. Chung and M.A. Gray, "Can We Adopt the Japanese Methods of Human Resources Management?" *Personnel Administrator* 64 (May 1982): 43–47.
20. R.R. Rehder, "Education and Training: Have the Japanese Beaten Us Again?" *Personnel Journal* 64 (January 1983): 42–47.
21. W.G. Ouchi, *Theory Z: How American Business Can Meet the Japanese Challenge* (Reading, Mass.: Addison-Wesley, 1981).
22. L.S. Dillon, "Adopting Japanese Management: Some Cultural Stumbling Blocks," *Personnel* 32 (July 1983): 77–81.
23. Ibid.
24. Ibid.
25. S. Kamata, *Japan in the Passing Lane* (New York: Pantheon, 1983).
26. L. Smith, "Cracks in the Japanese Work Ethic," *Fortune*, May 14, 1984, 162–168.
27. R.N. Farmer, "International Management," in *Contemporary Management: Issues and Viewpoints,* ed. J.W. McGuire (Englewood Cliffs, N.J.: Prentice-Hall, 1974).

28. N.J. Adler, *International Dimensions of Organizational Behavior* (Boston: Kent, 1985).

29. P.R. Harris and R.T. Moran, *Managing Cultural Differences* (Houston: Gulf, 1987).

30. F. Fiedler, T. Mitchell, and H.C. Triandis, "The Culture Assimilator: An Approach to Cross-Cultural Training," *Journal of Applied Psychology* 55 (1971): 95–102; H.C. Triandis and W.W. Lambert, eds., *Handbook of Cross-Cultural Psychology: Perspectives* (Boston: Allyn and Bacon, 1980).

Learning Objectives

After studying this chapter, you should be able to:

1. Identify external and internal sources of change in an organization.

2. Describe the stages of organizational growth.

3. List causes of organizational decline.

4. Identify factors that lead to an organization's success or failure.

5. Describe the phases in the process of change in an organization.

6. Identify the components of an organization's readiness for change.

7. Describe techniques that organizational design specialists use to help bring about change in organizations.

8. Identify the conditions that enhance the likelihood an OD effort will succeed.

9. Explain how evaluation researchers evaluate OD programs.

10. Evaluate the track record of OD programs.

Managing Organizational Change and Development

■ Life Cycles of an Organization

How is an organization like a human being? They both grow and change, and decline; they both have life cycles. Professor Ichak Adizes describes what corporations are like at each stage of their life cycle.

During the organization's birth and infancy, the founder's personality dominates. Management emphasizes what employees accomplish, not what they think. The company lacks a hierarchy, hiring system, and dress code. Behavior is informal — first names are used, and meetings take place anywhere. Management chases after sales and may overcommit.

During the organization's childhood years, the emphasis continues to be on achievement. The management style is aggressive and entrepreneurial. At this stage, a company rarely has policies, systems, procedures, or budgets. The atmosphere is frantic, fast-paced, and excited, with most employees working overtime. Corporate meetings are held in the president's office, which is cluttered and often shared with a secretary. The company is beginning to develop a vision of its future.

Next, the organization enters its adolescence, characterized by conflict and strife. The company has become too big for its founder to handle, so administrators may come on board. The pace is still fast, but some momentum is lost. Memo forms appear, but most employees still scrawl notes on scraps of paper. Employees are expected to wear suits. Meetings take place in certain offices or over lunch.

In its maturity, the organization's profits and sales are solid and predictable. Employees understand and accept plans and procedures. Long-term goals, including growth from within, are well defined. The company's style is efficient, and there's a sense of security. The new meeting room is a mess, but full of activity. Communications are careful and clear. This stage is usually brief.

When it reaches middle-aged aristocracy, the company no longer focuses on what employees do, but on how they do it. Rituals and networks emerge. Management views itself as having risen above the competition and has lost interest in new ideas. Dress has become formal, and memos are written on forms sporting the company's name. Important meetings take place in the elegant corporate boardroom.

In early bureaucracy, the organization is feeling its age. It feels competition from some new company, but managers turn against one another instead of uniting against the new company. The top priority becomes personal survival. Managerial paranoia is demonstrated in the new company forms, which all come with multiple carbons. Top management looks for a scapegoat, and firings begin.

Senility is the organization's late bureaucracy stage. Managers become pleasant to one another; they agree a lot, but nothing happens. Systems and procedures have ceased being a means to an end —

they themselves are the end. Personal communication is top priority; memos pour out, only to be filed. Outsiders have trouble getting through to anyone. Few people take any responsibility.

What happens next? In private business, the next stage is death, unless management successfully attempts violent contraction and rebirth. If the senile organization is a government agency or a monopoly, it could continue indefinitely on life-support systems.

Happily, there's more to leading an organization than submitting to this life cycle. Managers can help an organization grow and succeed, and watch out for causes of failure. This chapter describes some of what is involved. The first part discusses how organizations change and grow, as well as some causes of success and failure along the way. The second part of the chapter considers specialists who use knowledge of organizations to help them develop.

Source: Barbara Bartocci, "Corporate Passages: How the Company's Life Cycle Affects Your Career," *Working Woman*, August 1984, pp. 88–89.

Organizations are not static, but continuously change in response to a variety of influences coming from both inside and outside the organization. For administrators, the challenge is to anticipate and direct change processes so that organizational performance is enhanced. In this chapter, we will examine what is meant by organizational change and how it occurs. Then, we will consider techniques for managing and evaluating organizational change.

Sources of Change

"The one unchanging principle of life is the principle of change." This old saying contains an important element of truth: Change is an inevitable feature in both the lives of individuals and the lives of organizations. For both people and organizations, some facets of change are slow and nearly imperceptible, while others occur quite rapidly. In addition, the impact of change processes can vary from quite minor to truly substantial. Among the most common and influential forces of organizational change are the emergence of new competitors, innovations in technology, new company leadership, and evolving attitudes toward work.

It is useful to classify the sources of change as either external or internal. *External sources of change* originate in the organization's environment. In addition to competitors and suppliers, the external environment includes customers, the prevailing economic climate, the labor force, and the legal environment. Changes in any of these features of the external environment can have profound positive or negative effects on an organization. The rise and fall of competitors has obvious implications for organizational performance, as does the cooperativeness and competencies of suppliers. If the preferences of customers change as a result of changes in taste, the well-being of a product line can be affected. Recessions, periods of inflation, and upturns or downturns in the local or national economy can have both direct and indirect influences on organizations. The education, talents, and attitudes of potential employees also play an important role in an organization's well-being. Changes in these facets of the labor force can lead to a shortage or a surplus of qualified employees. Last, legislation can produce change. Federal legislation, such as the enforcement of the policies of the Equal Employment Opportunity Commission and the Federal Trade Commission, can alter the procedures an organization traditionally employs in its recruiting and marketing functions.

Internal sources of change exist within the organization itself. Examples of internal pressures for change include shifts in workers' attitudes toward their supervisor or their benefits package, declining productivity, and changes in key personnel, whose goals and values influence large populations of the organization. Changes in attitudes among employees (due to increased age or changes in job responsibility) can result in changes in job satisfaction, attendance behavior, and commitment. Changes in top-level and other key individuals in an organization can alter the internal character of the organization. For example, if an incoming president emphasizes corporate ethics and customer service to his or her staff, those concerns will come to be reflected in the creation of new programs, the restructuring of the organization, and the evolution of a different organizational culture.

Organizational Growth and Decline

Organizational change often follows an evolutionary pattern of gradual growth and decline. The study of organizational change at the macro level of analysis reveals that forms of evolution and revolution occur as organizations grow.

In a popular model of organizational growth, Larry Greiner contends that every organization has an ideal structure that corresponds to its stage in the growth process.[1] For example, large organizations need more formalization of procedures and operations than do small, newly created organizations.

Greiner suggests that a series of stages characterize organizational growth. Each stage has a dominant theme or set of issues, and each new stage is preceded by a period of transition, which may be termed a *growth crisis*. Figure 19.1 depicts Greiner's model of organizational growth.

Growth through Creativity

At its birth, an organization is usually fairly informal and loose in structure. The control and moment-to-moment involvement of the organization's founders are likely to be strong. The creative energies of this founding group will help to carry the organization through its birth process. With the growth of the fledgling organization, the nature and variety of problems change. Personnel problems arise as the size of the work force increases. Also, the organization's founders (whose first love may be closer to innovating and marketing than to management, operations, and personnel) may find themselves ill-equipped to lead their growing firm. This represents a *crisis of leadership*. This crisis can be overcome, most often, by acquiring professional managers to direct the organization.

■ **Figure 19.1**

Greiner's Model of Organizational Growth

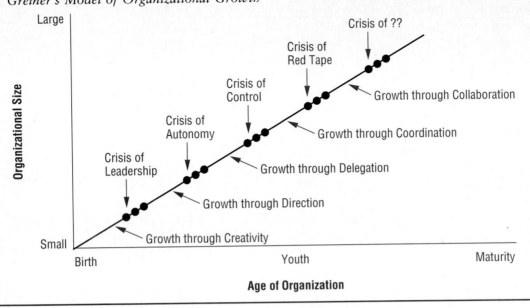

Source: L.E. Greiner, "Evolution and Revolution as Organizations Grow," *Harvard Business Review* 50 (1972):37–46.

Growth through Direction

Following resolution of the crisis of leadership, the organization enters a stage of growth through direction. Formalization is introduced by the professional managers. Greater bureaucratization takes place as departments and programs are established to help manage the organization. One result of this growth of bureaucracy is the creation of specialized divisions. Such specialization can lead to problems because as individuals within each division become increasingly skilled, they may seek greater control of their operations. These efforts at greater self-direction may be resisted by the same upper-level managers who originally introduced the specialization. The resulting tension can produce a *crisis of autonomy*.

Growth through Delegation

The next stage, delegation, follows the successful resolution of the crisis of autonomy. The crisis of autonomy is overcome by delegating greater decision-making power to middle- and lower-level managers, and top management begins to focus on long-range, strategic planning. However, middle- and lower-level managers eventually come to realize that the autonomous divisions sometimes pull in different directions and that performance may suffer due to a lack of control. Thus, the organization faces a *crisis of control*.

Growth through Coordination

The crisis of control can be resolved through increased coordination. For example, linkages may be created between members of different departments to enhance communication. Consultants may be hired to assess the extent of coordination needed and to suggest ways of improving efficiency and reducing redundancy. Project groups and task forces may be created to improve coordination, and matrix design concepts may be introduced. However, one consequence of creating these coordinating mechanisms is a profusion of managerial programs, and the resulting complexity may mean that more time and effort are spent on coordinating systems than on increasing actual productivity. The strangulation caused by such a proliferation of programs creates a *crisis of red tape.*

Continued Growth through Collaboration

Simplification of programs and systems and reliance on self-control and social norms may eventually replace more formal structures as an organization works its way through the red-tape crisis. Larger organizations often will bring in outside consultants to help them in their continued quest for collaboration. The goal of this stage is to teach managers how to cope with the organization's structure without giving in to the impulse to create additional structure.

Just as organizations can be said to go through phases of birth, youth, and maturity, they also go through periods of decline.* David Whetten defines **organizational decline** as a "cutback in the size of an organization's work force, profits, budget, or clients."[2] This degeneration can occur in any industry and in any size organization. Among the organizations that are currently experiencing decline are the United States steel industry, religious orders, and small liberal arts colleges.

Whetten suggests a number of specific factors that can lead to organizational decline. For example, within the organization itself, atrophy may occur. That is to say, the organization may simply become less efficient over time and lose its will to compete. Further problems may be created by self-complacency, loss of competitive drive, and a recalcitrant work force.

An organization may also be in danger of declining if it is in a vulnerable state. Newly created organizations that are not yet fully established are especially vulnerable because they often lack cash reserves and managers who are experienced in handling crises. Economic downturns and vigorous competitors can also undo vulnerable organizations.

Changes in societal values and consumer tastes can lead to a loss of legitimacy and subsequent decline. For example, an organization that manufactures a product that the buying public no longer desires may well decline.

---

* Organizations also experience death, although this topic has not received much serious study. In taking a long-term perspective, it is interesting to note that very few formal organizations have survived since 1500. Among the survivors are the Catholic church, some European guilds, and some universities. Therefore, organizational death is not a rare phenomenon. Somewhat surprisingly, organizations that are dying (that is, being shut down) actually experience an increase in employee productivity, possibly a peculiar form of employee pride.

OB Focus
Ethics in Managing Decline

During the 1980s, the market share of General Motors declined 11 percent, to 34.8 percent of the U.S. market at the end of 1989. Analysts predict that the share held by GM and the other Big Three producers will continue to slide throughout the nineties.

Factors blamed for this decline include high costs, relatively poor quality, and sluggish innovation. For example, GM needs to hire 5 workers a day for each car it builds, compared to 4.4 at Chrysler, 3.4 at Ford, and fewer than 3 at Japanese factories in the United States. With regard to quality, GM has improved from building cars with an average of 7.4 defects to only 1.7 defects per car; however, Japanese automakers have improved their rate of defects from 2.0 to 1.2 per car. And in terms of innovation, U.S. automakers were reportedly taken aback by Japan's innovations at the 1989 Tokyo Motor Show.

One way GM has managed the resulting decline in market share is by cutting back its work force.

During the 1980s, it laid off more than 40,000 white-collar workers (the equivalent of an entire company the size of Chrysler), and it plans to lay off another 25,000 by the mid-1990s. From 1979 to 1989, the company's total automotive employment plummeted 34 percent, from 618,000 workers to 405,000.

Accompanying these cutbacks have been numerous plant closings. Just in the period between January 1987 and February 1990, the company closed five factories. During that same period, GM opened only one new plant in the United States: the Saturn plant in Spring Hill, Tennessee.

Of course, managing change by shutting factories affects more than the organization; it also eliminates the livelihood of many thousands of workers. Is such a response to decline ethical? Are some ways of closing a factory more ethical than others? Are the people responsible for the decline the ones who bear the brunt of such changes?

Such questions were implied in

the recent movie *Roger & Me*, in which filmmaker Michael Moore records his efforts to persuade GM's chairman, Roger B. Smith, to visit Flint, Michigan, a city devastated by GM's plant closings. But while the movie portrays Smith as the villain of a tragedy, the answers to the real-life questions are far less definitive.

One way to seek the answers is to consider the moral responsibilities of a corporation and its leaders, beginning with the responsibility of the board of directors regarding the interests of the shareholders and the responsibility of management regarding what the company produces and how. A company and its managers are also responsible to employees and to the community as a whole. The company should inform workers about management decisions that affect them. The company also has a moral obligation to consider the impact of its actions on its community, which often has made a substantial investment in housing and services for a company's workers.

Sources: Richard T. DeGeorge, *Business Ethics* (New York: Macmillan, 1982), pp. 133–137, 213–221; Susan Duffy, "The Real Villain in *Roger & Me*? Big Business," *Business Week*, January 8, 1990, pp. 42, 44; Paul Ingrassia, "Auto Industry in U.S. Is Sliding Relentlessly into Japanese Hands," *The Wall Street Journal*, February 16, 1990, pp. A1, A6.

An instance of these processes can be found in the reduced purchase of toy guns by parents during a time of war.

Last, organizations may decline because of insufficient external resources. Needed resources may become scarce, or uncertainty about a reliable supply may make it difficult to produce and deliver a finished good. Dependency on suppliers and the suppliers' ability to obtain and deliver resources can threaten the survival of many organizations.

■ **Figure 19.2**

Factors That Lead to Organizational Success and Failure

Source: Adapted from R.L. Daft, *Organization Theory and Design* (St. Paul, Minn.: West, 1983).

Managing decline requires many of the same administrative skills as managing growth. The ability to seek creative solutions, the willingness to innovate, and the tactful management of conflict are necessary skills for managers of all organizations, declining or growing. "Toughing it out," minimizing losses, and making it to the next upswing, however, become management's top priorities during periods of decline.

Critical Determinants of Organizational Success and Failure

The features of organizations that make for success are not always the same ones that lead to failure.[3] Based on reports generated by professional consultants, it is possible to identify the specific factors that contribute most to success and failure. It is also possible to classify these factors as primarily environmental, structural, or management-oriented. Figure 19.2 summarizes this classification system.

Factors That Lead to Success

Although a successful organization need not possess all of the positive attributes shown in Figure 19.2, most successful organizations show more positive than negative attributes. Successful organizations tend to focus on customers and their needs. They invest in ways to improve sales and provide superior service to clients, and they do not forget that their customers and their customers' needs underlie their organization's existence.

Successful organizations also adapt their structures to the needs of their missions. At the department level, controls may be simultaneously loose, in that managers have autonomy, and tight, insofar as specific performance goals may be set. Highly successful organizations often maintain a simple but appropriate structure that employs an adequate number of staff; they avoid empire building and padding with surplus staff. Also, entrepreneurship is encouraged within the divisions of the organization by rewarding successful innovation and encouraging risk taking.

A major management feature that can lead to success is a deliberate bias toward implementing solutions to problems. Management discourages "paralysis through analysis" of alternatives, and, instead, emphasizes satisficing action (see Chapter 11) that ensures goal attainment. Another management feature in successful firms is a commitment to the organization's original arena of expertise. This is called "sticking to one's knitting." It involves staying close to what the organization knows how to do best and not being led down different paths in pursuit of attractive but uncertain alternative product lines.

Successful organizations also tend to stress a single value, such as delivering a quality product, reducing the cost of services to customers, or concern for each customer's unique needs. By emphasizing a single dominant value in their promotional materials and in their training of employees, the organization establishes a useful, distinct reputation for excellence in a specific area.

Finally, managers in successful companies often try to improve performance by achieving the agreement or consensus of employees. Thus, managers and workers may work together to set mutually agreeable performance goals. Employee suggestions are actively sought and a positive work group spirit, which will serve as a basis for enhanced motivation, is encouraged.

Factors That Lead to Failure

Different factors in an organization's environment, structure, and management may lead to its failure.

Among the environmental factors, changes in technology are a major cause of organizational failure. Technological innovations by competitors, as well as innovations that cannot be implemented within the organization itself, can lead to lost business.

Two forms of dependency — dependency on suppliers and dependency on a single customer — can also create problems. Difficulties in obtaining raw materials and financing from other institutions can prove fatal for an organization in a competitive environment. In addition, a customer that realizes that another organization is highly dependent on its business may use its resulting

An Inside Look
Coping with Technological Change

Computers are changing the structure of offices. Managers are discovering that the capabilities and alternatives of new office equipment are requiring them to redefine jobs and reorganize work loads. But how can a manager anticipate what equipment the department will need if the equipment is going to change the requirements of the jobs the equipment is for? Furthermore, how can a manager figure out the best way to manage employees whose work load is changing as a result of office automation? Managing is especially difficult when the manager's own role is changing as well.

The Association of Information Systems Professionals has identified some important points for managers to consider when confronted with the changes that accompany new technology in the office:

■ Remember that an information system blends people, procedures, software applications, development, and hardware — not just a few computers scattered about on desks. The manager must consider all those aspects of the system when planning for it.

■ To increase productivity, the manager must adapt highly structured electronic systems to the less structured flow of activity in the workplace. This is an ongoing process. As the manager becomes more familiar with the technology, he or she can adapt it to the department's needs.

■ If the office is already organized inefficiently, no amount of automation will increase productivity. Office automation merely reinforces strengths or weaknesses. For example, a bottleneck will only get worse when a computer is introduced. The manager should streamline any office inefficiencies while introducing the new technology.

■ Managers are often surprised by some of the dramatic changes office automation brings. For example, information may become available more quickly, requiring the manager to make fast decisions.

■ While the department's employees are learning the new technology, managers need to allot extra time and possibly extra people to handle the inevitable disruptions.

Source: Roxane Farmanfarmaian, "How to Revamp Old Jobs with New Tools," *Savvy*, August 1986.

power to drive down prices or extract greater concessions by threatening to take its business elsewhere.

In terms of structure, inadequate control mechanisms may contribute to failure. For example, an organization may lack devices for sensing when changes occur that need to be corrected. As a result, product quality may suffer or changes in employee or customer satisfaction levels may be ignored.

Management factors may also contribute to failure. Courageous and decisive leadership can inspire an organization to overcome difficult situations or take quick action. In contrast, a tendency to overanalyze data or to take a "wait-and-see" attitude may cause a firm to lose ground to competitors and may exacerbate internal problems. The kinds of expertise that enable a young organization to thrive may become outdated as an organization matures. The need for professional managers to aid, or replace, the founding group may go unrecognized, and the importance of hiring new talent to revitalize the innovative process may be ignored.

As we saw in Chapters 9 and 13, conflict can lead to serious dysfunction if it is not well managed. Conflicting groups often set their own goals for political and personal gain ahead of organizational goals. For this reason, conflict should be managed to ensure that it remains in desired forms and at desired levels. (Recall that a certain level of internal conflict is probably inevitable and even desirable.)

As Figure 19.2 suggests, success and failure factors are not evenly distributed across the three major sources. For example, more environmental factors may contribute to failure than to success. Conversely, more structural factors are potential sources of success than of failure. And an almost equal number of management factors seem to lead to both success and failure. This analysis, albeit simplistic, suggests a useful insight: Environmental factors are more likely to pose potential threats to an organization's well-being, while structural factors are an organization's major means of achieving success or, at least, coping with threats. It almost goes without saying that management-related factors are potential sources of both organizational success and organizational failure.

Organizational Development

Organizational development (OD) is a distinct area within the field of organizational science that focuses on the planned and controlled change of organizations in desired directions. In general, outside consultants rather than organizational members are usually responsible for managing the development process. In essence, OD attempts to change an organization as a totality by changing the organization's structure, technology, people, and/or tasks. Figure 19.3 presents a popular view of OD that emphasizes these four facets of an organization. In reality, any facet of an organization is a legitimate target of OD. In our discussion we will focus primarily on change efforts that are directed at people rather than at tasks, structure, or technology. A popular definition of OD, which we can use for discussing the people side of planned change, has been offered by French and Bell. For these authors, OD is a "long-range effort to improve an organization's problem-solving and renewal process . . . through a more effective . . . management of organization culture . . . with the assistance of a change agent . . . and the use of the theory and technology of applied behavioral science."[4]

Phases in the OD Process

All OD specialists recognize the difficulties inherent in bringing about successful, positive changes. Some years ago, Kurt Lewin, a famous behavioral scientist, argued that the process of change involves three basic phases: unfreezing, changing, refreezing.[5] **Unfreezing** begins to occur when a situation is recognized as being deficient or inadequate in some way. The recognition that employees' attitudes or skills are insufficient, or that rules and procedures generate problems that hinder task completion, may trigger the unfreezing process. Sometimes a crisis must occur before a problem is given the attention it deserves. For example, unsafe working conditions may be allowed to con-

■ **Figure 19.3**

Interdependent Organizational Elements That May Be the Focus of Change in OD

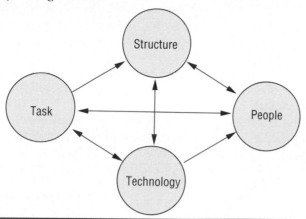

Source: Adapted from Leavitt, 1975.

tinue until a wildcat strike or a life-threatening accident forces management to acknowledge the problem and take action. Unfreezing must occur before OD can succeed because an individual's failure to recognize or accept the existence of a problem can block any desire to change.

The second phase in the process, **changing,** occurs when a new plan or system is implemented in the organization. Such a plan may call for a new recruiting or orientation program, or the introduction of a new accounting system. It may affect the entire organization, as would a total restructuring, or it may focus on only a few key individuals, as would a values-clarification exercise involving the top-level management team.

Refreezing, the third phase in the change process, occurs as the newly created patterns of behavior and techniques become part of ongoing organizational processes. During the refreezing phase, OD specialists usually attempt to appraise the effectiveness of their intervention. If they believe that intervention has failed, they may redirect their efforts to compensate for their program's shortcomings.

Resistance to Change

Attempts at organizational development are often met with resistance. Employees tend to fear change, partly from a desire for security and contentment with the status quo. Consequently, they may be quick to identify shortcomings in a proposed plan for change and use them to their advantage. If their objections are registered but not redressed, they may act to ensure that the identified problems actually do undercut the program for change.

Resistance to change, one of the most serious challenges for an OD specialist, may be overcome in a number of ways. One of the most common techniques is *education,* not in the formal sense but in terms of meeting with groups of employees to address their concerns and explain the planned changes. *Participation* in the development of plans for change is also an effective way of overcoming resistance. In one well-known study, Coch and French observed that resistance to change can be significantly reduced by having the affected employees actually participate in the design of the change effort.[6] Programs for change that are, in a sense, "owned" by the people who are most affected are often more likely to succeed.[7] Another means of overcoming resistance is *negotiation*. When dealing with employees who have taken a stand against change, this means obtaining statements in writing about trade-offs and concessions that both management and employees will make in order to accommodate change.

In practice, strong-arm tactics, despite their questionable ethical merit, are sometimes used. Chief among these methods are outright *coercion,* such as threatening people with dismissal if they resist the planned change, and *manipulation of opinion* through the careful selection and timing of the information released so as to ensure a favorable impact.

Determining Whether an Organization Is Ready for Change

For change efforts to be effective, they must be supported by favorable conditions. Michael Beer has identified the most important factors and expressed them in a rough formula for predicting change:[8]

$$C = (D \times S \times P) > X$$

where

C = change
D = dissatisfaction with the current state of affairs
S = an identifiable and desired end-state
P = a practical plan for achieving the desired end-state
X = cost of change to the organization

As this formula suggests, change is a function of dissatisfaction, a desired goal, a means to obtain the goal, and a reasonable cost. If dissatisfaction with the status quo is very low (or near zero), then the expression in parentheses in the formula will result in a near zero value. As a consequence, these values will be near or less than the cost of implementing the change. If the various pressures for change are greater than the anticipated costs of the change to key individuals and groups, then change should occur.

As this formula suggests, dissatisfaction, the desired end-state, plans for change, and cost must be addressed if change is to occur. For OD specialists, these critical elements must be assessed when determining whether an organization is ready for change.

OD Techniques

Survey Feedback   One of the most widely used sources of information for OD specialists is **survey feedback**. To obtain the information they need, they administer written questionnaires or interview employees. The questions in these surveys typically touch on such topics as satisfaction, leadership, and decision making. The results are summarized and statistically analyzed before they are given back to top-level administrators. Once senior management has examined the results and considered their meaning, the data are fed back to the participants for their consideration and interpretation. In practice, such feedback is often intended to arouse awareness of the need for change. For example, through survey feedback, top management may discover that morale is especially low among members of a particular department, or a group of employees may begin to recognize that they all share a common view of a problem. Following recognition of the need for change, employees' suggestions for designing and implementing change programs are solicited.

Although the OD survey feedback technique may sound similar to the traditional notion of conducting a survey of employees, there are important distinctions between the two approaches.[9] In the traditional approach, data are usually collected only from lower-level employees, but in survey feedback, everyone in the organization is likely to be surveyed. Similarly, in the traditional approach, only top management is likely to see the results, but in the OD variation, everyone in the organization receives feedback at some point. Furthermore, the development of plans to deal with survey results is the prerogative of top management in the traditional approach, but everyone can have input in the survey feedback approach. Because of these essential differences, the survey feedback approach is more likely to achieve productive change.

Team Building   Another OD technique, **team building,** has been widely used by specialists in recent years at such diverse organizations as Trans Australia Airlines, Mead Corporation, and Tandem Computers. The hub of team building is existing work groups, called *family groups,* or newly formed groups of employees brought together for a particular purpose, called *special groups.* The goal in both existing work groups and special groups is to improve performance by tackling problems and obstacles.

In a typical team-building effort, a small group of people is brought together at a retreat-like location removed from their place of employment. By getting away from the workplace, they can avoid interruptions and fully concentrate on problem solving.

At their initial meeting, the work group might examine both "hard" and "soft" data that pertain to productivity problems, such as monthly sales figures and customer satisfaction reports. The purpose of examining these data is to encourage the group to enter the unfreezing phase of the OD process and get them to recognize the need for change. During subsequent meetings, the OD specialist attempts to facilitate the process by encouraging frank and open discussions of various aspects of the problem facing the group. Ultimately, the group will be encouraged to develop a specific plan for attaining a desired end-state. At later meetings, the group will review the success of the plan and develop and implement refinements of its content.

Sensitivity Training   A third technique that has been widely used by OD specialists is **sensitivity training.** Sometimes called T-groups (for training groups), this approach originated in the 1940s at the National Training Laboratory in Bethel, Maine. Over the years, despite some changes in name to *encounter groups* and *laboratory training*, the technique has remained much the same. In a T-group, 8 to 12 individuals are brought together for a series of 2- to 3-hour sessions. The group's trainer does not take an active role in the group's discussions, but instead serves more as a guide or facilitator. The ostensible goal of the sessions is to increase self-awareness and sensitivity to others. To achieve this goal, members are expected to focus on behavior and on giving feedback about their perceptions of one another. Getting to the point at which personal and social learning occurs is sometimes difficult, and, in some cases, group members' reactions may get out of hand. For example, the group may turn on one particular member and severely criticize him or her without reaching a positive reconciliation by the end of the session. Because the group does not have an agenda, some members who are used to working in an ordered and goal-directed social system may become uncomfortable. Often, one member will strive to become group leader to fill the leadership vacuum created by the trainer's refusal to control discussions and behavior. Later, other group members may criticize and resent the individual who attempted to take the leadership role.

For some groups, a state of open and frank discussion is difficult to achieve. This is especially true for groups composed of people who work together in a naturally occurring work unit. To encourage freer discussions, some trainers prefer to work with stranger groups — groups whose members do not know one another — and cousin groups — groups whose members work within the same organization but do not report to one another.

In recent years, T-groups have been declining in popularity due to a variety of factors. One of the chief forces lies in a fear that people "may be taken apart like a clock and not put back together." Team building, with its focus on the enhancement of productivity instead of social skills, has been more widely adopted.

Confrontation Meetings   A further technique for bringing about desired change attempts to manage dysfunctional conflict (see Chapter 13) through **confrontation meetings.** In this approach, conflicting groups are brought together in a structured situation that is designed to enhance cooperation.[10]

Most confrontation meetings follow a predictable sequence. First, the conflicting groups' leaders discuss the need for change with the OD specialist. At this session, the leaders and the consultant draw up a specific plan for meetings between the two groups. Next, each group meets separately to create a list that summarizes their views of the other group's attitudes and behaviors. In addition, they attempt to develop a list of impressions that they believe the other group would devise in describing themselves. Next, at a formal joint meeting, a spokesperson for each group reads aloud his or her group's lists. No discussion or reaction is allowed. The groups then meet again in separate rooms to discuss what they have learned about themselves and the other group. Each also draws up a list of issues that need to be resolved.

At the second joint meeting, all members openly discuss the lists of issues that need resolution and develop a plan of action for reducing conflict and achieving cooperation. At subsequent meetings, groups discuss their progress toward implementing their plans and the removal of further obstacles to improved collaboration.

Quality of Work Life   In many Western industrialized countries, there has been a growing recognition of the importance of simultaneously enhancing both the value of employees' psychological experiences at work and employees' productivity. This philosophy is embodied in the **quality of work life (QWL)** approach to OD.[†] QWL is not a set of specific techniques, but rather an approach that seeks to enhance the total work climate in an organization or its subsystems. QWL programs focus on such issues as conflict reduction, employee satisfaction, and worker participation. In terms of actual techniques, QWL programs often encompass job redesign (Chapter 7), employee involvement in decision making (Chapter 11), redesign of pay systems (Chapter 7), and/or the creation of quality circles (Chapter 12). In essence, QWL represents a desired end-state that emphasizes the importance of providing opportunities for employees to contribute to their jobs as well as to receive more from their jobs.[11] Successful QWL programs have been used in such firms as AT&T, IBM, Texas Instruments, Xerox, and Proctor and Gamble. At present, it appears that QWL programs will continue to enjoy popularity and slow expansion.[12]

Conditions for the Successful Adoption of OD

From numerous successes and failures in implementing OD programs, practitioners have been able to generate a specific list of conditions that help to ensure that an OD effort will succeed. According to French and Bell, among the most important are:

1. Use of an outsider who is trained in the behavioral sciences as a change agent

2. Recognition by top-level management that problems exist

3. Support and involvement in the program by top-level management, work group supervisors, and opinion leaders

4. Early successes in the OD program that suggest that the program is working and thereby encourage further cooperation

5. Respect for the managerial talents of those whose domain of responsibility is being improved

6. Cooperation and involvement on the part of human resource managers

7. Effective coordination and control of the OD program

8. Measurement of outcomes[13]

[†] QWL is often pronounced "quill" by OD specialists.

Evaluating OD Interventions

The evaluation of OD programs poses many problems. If we rely on the opinions of those who have a stake in the program's success, such as the OD consultant and the manager who hired the change agent, some bias can be expected. Because of this and other considerations, people who are knowledgeable in the techniques of **evaluation research** may be called in to provide a more objective assessment of the true merits and impact of an OD intervention.

Evaluation researchers rely on the logic of research design when trying to evaluate a program.[14] In the vernacular of research design, there are three major designs: pre-experimental, experimental, and quasi-experimental.

In a **pre-experimental design,** no control is made of the event or program of interest. One simply takes readings or measures following an OD program. For example, an evaluation researcher may conduct interviews with employees on their impressions of the value of a training program after the employees have completed it. If we diagram this example with the simple notation that O represents the taking of observations and X represents the occurrence of the training program, then we have

$$X \qquad\qquad O$$

$$\xrightarrow{\qquad\qquad}$$
$$\textbf{Time}$$

This diagram is, in essence, an example of a case study. As you may recall (see Chapter 2), a case study merely involves the collection of information and an attempt to relate the information to some prior event(s). Because the researcher exercises no formal control over the event, it is not possible to say whether X had any effect. Many alternative explanations (i.e., events other than X) can be offered to account for whatever values are observed.

A somewhat better pre-experimental evaluation design is the **one-group pretest–post-test design.** In this design, observations are collected both before and after the program is introduced. In our example of studying the effects of a training program, we might survey the program's participants both before and after the introduction of the program.

As a diagram, we would portray this design as

$$O_1 \qquad X \qquad O_2$$

$$\xrightarrow{\qquad\qquad}$$
$$\textbf{Time}$$

Although we might be tempted to draw conclusions about the effects of the program (X) from differences observed at time 1 and 2, we really cannot draw any firm conclusions because several loose ends exist in this design. One problem lies in the fact that other changes in the participants or their jobs may have been occurring at the same time as the training program (e.g., the employees may have received salary increments). These simultaneous changes may be partially or largely responsible for changes observed in the measures of employee attitudes or performance. Also, during pre-testing, the employees may have been sensitized to the fact that they are involved in a study. Almost certainly, when employees are questioned a second time on their impressions, they will likely conclude that they are being studied. Their responses at the second time may, therefore, reflect a willingness to show cooperativeness with the apparent purpose of the surveys or a desire to appear consistent by trying to recall their previous answers. Finally, employees in a given department or work unit may be relatively atypical in terms of abilities and attitudes. In order to counter the problem of uniquely group-related differences, employees should be randomly assigned to one of two work groups where a training program is introduced in one group, and not immediately introduced in the other.

A design that is truly *experimental* and that overcomes many of the above problems is:

Random Assignment	O_1	X	O_2
Random Assignment	O_1		O_2

$$\longrightarrow$$
Time

The above **pretest–post-test control group design** is a true experiment in that at least one formal comparison is being conducted. Because employees are randomly assigned to treatments and a comparable (control) condition is created that does not experience the training program, it is possible to draw cautious conclusions about the effect of X. One remaining potential problem is respondent **reactivity** to being pretested, that is, the problem of an employee responding in a particular fashion simply because he or she is aware of being involved in a study.

A superior experimental research design examines the question of whether pretesting has sensitized the respondents. It can be diagrammed as:

Random Assignment	O_1	X	O_2
Random Assignment	O_1		O_2
Random Assignment		X	O_2
Random Assignment			O_2

$$\longrightarrow$$
Time

The above design is termed a **Solomon four-group design.**[15] In this design, employees are randomly assigned to one of four conditions that are identical except for the introduction of the training program. Because employees are randomly assigned to groups, we can assume that the four groups are roughly identical at the start of the study. By comparing results obtained for the four groups at time 2 (as well as comparisons between time 1 and time 2 where possible), we can draw conclusions about the causal effect of the training program as well as the influence of pretesting on our results.

Although the Solomon four-group design represents perhaps the highest degree of control, it is a very costly design to employ. In many organizations, it is very difficult or impossible to introduce such controls as the creation of a comparison group or random assignment of employees to conditions. In the absence of such controls, a variety of **quasi-experimental designs** is available for studying the effects of OD interventions. These designs have the dual strengths of selecting who is measured and when. To illustrate one example of a quasi-experimental design, consider the following:

$$O_1 \qquad O_2 \qquad O_3 \qquad O_4 \qquad X \qquad O_5 \qquad O_6 \qquad O_7 \qquad O_8$$

$$\longrightarrow$$

Time

This **time-series design** greatly extends the frequency of the pretest and post-test observations around our hypothetical training program. Because no formal comparison group exists, we are attempting to use a single group as its own control. As an illustration, consider a series of monthly performance reports taken before and after the introduction of a training program. In this example, it would be possible to draw a cautious inference concerning the impact of the training program (if we are willing to assume that other processes were not operating at the same time, and so on).

Figure 19.4 shows several possible sets of results we may expect to obtain from a time-series design. Outcome A suggests that the training program had an influence on performance that was of considerable duration. Outcome B also suggests that the program had an influence on performance, but this influence was fairly transitory and faded away over time. In Outcome C, the training program had no discernible impact on performance. Although the results of a time-series design cannot tell us conclusively that the training program had a particular effect on an outcome measure of interest, they can provide some insights that may be useful in deciding whether to continue, expand, or curtail a training program.

In practice, however, much of the evaluation of OD programs is fairly simple and unsophisticated. If key personnel are reasonably satisfied that the OD effort has been positive, based on their personal and subjective impressions, then the effort is labeled a success. Sometimes, simple measures of participants' attitudes are taken before and after the OD effort. If the results show "improvement" over time, then a "success" is declared. Unfortunately, improvement or change on an attitude scale can be due to a variety of factors (in addition to real change).

Terborg, Howard, and Maxwell[16] and Golembiewski and Billingsley[17] have suggested that additional complexities need to be considered. These authors suggest that any of three types of change may underlie differences in perceptual report data gathered before and after an OD effort. If an OD program does in fact produce the observed change, we refer to this type of difference as **alpha change**. However, the change may be due to other processes. In **beta change**, employees change in the way in which they respond to

■ **Figure 19.4**

Possible Results from a Time-Series Design

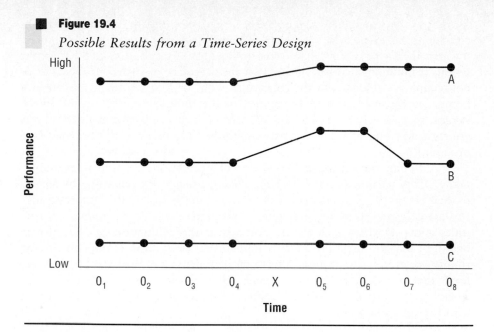

the survey. This occurs when the respondents change their perceptions of the endpoints or ranges of the scales. For example, employees may initially rate their jobs very harshly. After a lecture on job enrichment (as part of a job redesign program) and related topics, they may become more realistic about the possible range of jobs for which they qualify and the constraints on their own job mobility. As a result of this shift in how they view their job (i.e., that it's not too bad, all things considered), they may assign a more favorable rating to their redesigned job. This higher rating is not the result of the job being more meaningfully changed, but rather of a shift in how the employee interprets the scale. A third type of shift in response can result when an employee shifts his or her idea or conceptualization of the construct. This is termed **gamma change.** In our example, this could occur if the employees initially viewed their jobs as merely a means to make a living. Following the OD effort, they may come to see their jobs as having some social value. As a consequence of this shift in perception, they may rate their redesigned job more favorably. Of course, no real change in the way in which the job is performed may have occurred. Also, productivity may not increase because work methods have not improved. Yet, the survey results would give the appearance that meaningful change has occurred. Determining whether alpha, beta, or gamma change processes are at work in a set of results requires substantial effort on the part of an evaluator. Fortunately, sophisticated techniques for uncovering these three sources of change are available.[18]

Finally, it should be mentioned that some OD practitioners believe that the effectiveness of OD efforts should only be evaluated at the level of individual personal satisfaction with the experience. This point of view, although not widely prevalent in the field of OD, views the attempt to measure human attributes as a fundamentally impersonal and mechanistic technique that is counter to OD's mission of helping people to achieve personal fulfillment through their work. To suggest measurement and evaluation of OD efforts reveals (to humanistic proponents) that the advocate of such a proposal does not completely understand the concept of what OD strives for in the area of human development. An OD specialist of the humanistic bent would likely suggest that someone who is a proponent of measuring and evaluating OD efforts is a prime candidate for participating in a humanistically oriented OD program![19]

Although the technical knowledge of evaluation research is available, many OD practitioners opt for a simplified approach to evaluating the results of their efforts. This usually consists of a combination of "soft," impressionistic data collected from key individuals and pretest and post-test data on attitudes and performance. A third approach to the evaluation of OD efforts, based on philosophical grounds, is that formal evaluation is impossible and should not even be attempted. This third view, from a humanistic perspective, holds that it is dehumanizing to attach numbers or measures to individuals. Therefore, in respect for human dignity, feelings (for example) should not be formally quantified.

Does OD Work?

Despite the difficulty of measuring the effects of OD efforts, it is possible to draw some tentative conclusions about the general value of OD in enhancing organizational effectiveness.

In their examination of 35 studies, Porras and Berg sorted the obtained results into outcome variables and process variables.[20] Outcome variables refer to measures of productivity, efficiency, absenteeism, profits, and so on (relatively "hard" measures), while process variables refer to measures of trust, perceptions of leadership, motivation, and decision making (relatively "soft" measures). In addition, they further divided their sample of studies into categories based on whether the OD efforts were directed at groups, organizations, individuals, or leaders. Their analyses of these studies suggested that group outcome variables (e.g., group productivity) were most likely to be enhanced following OD interventions. Individual process variables also showed relatively positive improvement (e.g., individual job satisfaction increased in roughly 40 percent of the OD studies in which it was measured). Table 19.1 summarizes these results in order of positive impact.

A further analysis was made of these studies in terms of the impact of various OD procedures. By and large, Porras and Berg observed that the most common OD techniques, such as team building and survey feedback, were reported to have positive effects, while T-groups were somewhat less effective (Table 19.2).

Porras and Berg also observed that OD efforts that used four or more techniques (the eclectic approach) were likely to produce more meaningful change. This suggests that a multifaceted approach to achieving organizational change is most appropriate. In addition, they noted that interventions lasting

■ **Table 19.1**

Effects of OD Efforts on Outcome and Process Variables

Outcome Variables	Examples	Number of Studies	Average Positive Change
Group	Performance, length of meetings	8	63%
Organization	Profit, return on investment	12	47%
Individual	Performance, satisfaction	14	42%
Leader	Performance	3	—
Total		22	51%

Process Variables	Examples	Number of Studies	Average Positive Change
Individual	Self-awareness, self-actualization	10	62%
Group	Trust, involvement	20	49%
Leader	Openness to influence, interaction facilitation	20	45%
Organization	Leadership, decision making	27	36%
Total		35	46%

Source: Adapted from J.I. Porras and P.O. Berg, "The Impact of Organization Development," *Academy of Management Review* (1978):249–266

at least 6 days had superior results, with maximum benefits being reported when the duration was between 10 and 20 days. This suggests that OD efforts should be neither too brief nor too extended.

Despite the methodological shortcomings of many of the studies that Porras and Berg examined and the tendency of OD specialists to report their results in the most positive light (OD failures are less frequently written up), these results suggest that the efforts are usually effective.‡ As Porras and Berg's analysis suggests, the precise nature of OD's impact will depend on the type of technique, its duration, and the measures chosen to evaluate the intervention.

OD in Perspective

Although Porras and Berg's review points to many positive conclusions, the value of OD as commonly conducted is often questioned by both managers and behavioral scientists. Some of this criticism derives from a healthy skepticism on the part of managers and behavioral scientists. However, other factors can partially account for this criticism.[22]

First of all, OD is not a cure-all for every difficulty an organization may face. Its successful use requires skill and expertise, and it is most applicable to interpersonal problems. When used by nonexperts and applied to inappropriate situations, OD cannot be expected to succeed.

‡ A specific finding that should increase our caution in drawing inferences about the merits of OD is that the more methodologically rigorous a study is, the less likely it is to report that an OD effort has been successful.[21]

Table 19.2

Positive Changes in Association with OD Technique

Percentage Change*

Dominant Technique	Process Variables	Outcome Variables
Eclectic approach	52% (5)	52% (5)
Team building	45% (14)	53% (3)
Survey feedback	48% (4)	53% (3)
T-groups	44% (8)	44% (8)

* Values in parentheses are the number of studies in each classification.
Source: Adapted from Porras and Berg, 1978.

Users may also be disappointed to find that OD often does not live up to its stated ideal as described in articles and texts, but the flaw may be traceable to the users' approach. For example, OD is often performed at the lower levels of an organization, following top management's endorsement. The attitude that OD is a task to be delegated to lower-level managers is likely to minimize the impact of most such programs. Yet high levels of participation, support, and concern for OD efforts from top-level management are fairly rare.

As discussed earlier, resistance to change is a significant obstacle to OD efforts. While resistance on the individual level may be manageable, more difficult challenges arise when resistance stems from the total organizational system and its need to cope with its external environment. The external environment, of course, cannot be meaningfully changed by most OD efforts — and OD efforts are rarely intended to make such changes. Therefore, this larger constraint limits the progress that is possible within the organization.

In addition, organizations may be based on values that can significantly curtail certain forms of change. For example, religiously affiliated organizations typically adhere to specific sets of values, mission statements, and codes of conduct that set limits on what is feasible in the way of change. Thus, the perceived nature of an organization and what it stands for will dictate what changes are deemed permissible by both its members and its constituent groups in the larger society.

It has also been suggested that the chief values espoused by OD specialists — trust, openness, and power sharing — are not appropriate for some organizations. As part of their work, OD practitioners attempt to convert employees to their value system. Then, when the specific OD effort is completed, the employees must function within the larger, as yet unchanged, system of their organization. At this point, OD training may backfire because an employee who attempts to implement a philosophy of openness in a hostile environment may experience frustration and punishment rather than acceptance. In fact, as observed by DuBrin, people who adopt an open sytle of conduct may have problems competing with the more political and devious members of their organization.[23] In some instances, highly valued, competent, and successful employees may come to so fully embrace the values of openness and honesty that they reject their employment setting because it does not support their new-found values. As a result, the organization may actually lose valuable employees due to a shift in personal values induced by an OD effort. The irony, of course, is that the OD effort was intended to help such individuals to perform better rather than to encourage them to leave. In such cases, critics may contend that OD has made the employees less able to cope with the real world.

Bennis has suggested that OD practitioners rely largely on "truth and love" as sources of influence.[24] OD is, of course, more appropriate under conditions of truth and collaboration. But, in practice, OD specialists may sometimes rely on the truth–love model when it is inappropriate, that is, in situations characterized by distrust and conflict. This, then, is the basic dilemma for OD specialists: How can they help people in situations of conflict to realize and affirm the values of trust and collaboration? As further noted by Bennis, the truth–love model is more typically endorsed by wealthy and powerful organizations, such as IBM, AT&T, and Union Carbide. But many "disadvantaged organizations" most in need of OD, such as local governments, smaller firms, and social action groups, are less likely to be involved in OD efforts.

In the future, organizations may need to rely more heavily on the services of OD specialists as they are forced to undergo planned change. This need for managed change will result from a variety of emerging forces. Rapid changes in technology, for example, will require organizations to adjust their structure and processes. Also, the environment for many organizations will become more turbulent and uncertain. Contributing to this pressure will be an increasingly global business environment and a shrinking qualified labor pool (caused by both a "baby bust" and an inability of the American educational system to produce even minimally competent individuals). All of these forces will require organizations to be more flexible and responsive. The ability to effectively implement planned change will be of great importance in the years to come.

Summary

1. Identify external and internal sources of change in an organization.
External sources of change include competitors, suppliers, customers, the prevailing economic climate, the labor force, and the legal environment. Internal sources of change include shifts in workers' attitudes, declining productivity, and changes in key personnel.

2. Describe the stages of organizational growth.
An organization begins with a loose structure and grows through creativity until a crisis of leadership develops. The organization hires professional managers and enters a phase of growth through direction. A more formal structure leads to tension among specialized divisions and a crisis of autonomy. During the next stage, growth through delegation, middle- and lower-level managers receive greater power to make decisions, and a crisis of control arises. In the next stage, growth through collaboration, programs to increase coordination

resolve the crisis of control but create a crisis of red tape. To continue growth through collaboration, the organization simplifies programs and systems.

3. List causes of organizational decline.

Organizations decline as a result of atrophy within the organization, self-complacency, loss of competitive drive, a recalcitrant work force, vulnerability because of low resources or inexperienced management, economic downturns, vigorous competition, changes in societal values, and lack of external resources.

4. Identify factors that lead to an organization's success or failure.

Organizations that succeed emphasize customers and their needs, exercise loose control at the departmental level but tight control over specific goals, have a simple structure, encourage entrepreneurship within the organization, emphasize action, maintain a commitment to original areas of expertise, stress a key value, and seek consensus among employees. Factors leading to failure include technological changes, dependency on suppliers or a single customer, inadequate control mechanisms, hesitancy to make change, lack of expertise, and unmanaged conflict.

5. Describe the phases in the process of change in an organization.

The first phase, unfreezing, begins with recognition that a situation is deficient. The second phase, changing, occurs with implementation of a new plan or system. The third phase, refreezing, occurs as the newly created patterns of behavior and techniques become part of ongoing organizational processes.

6. Identify the components of an organization's readiness for change.

An organization is relatively ready for change if dissatisfaction with the status quo is high, an identifiable and desired solution exists, a practical plan for change exists, and the cost of change is low.

7. Describe techniques that organizational design specialists use to help bring about change in organizations.

OD specialists use feedback from surveys to obtain information and arouse awareness of the need for change. Another technique, team building, uses discussion of problems as a way to improve performance. Sensitivity training attempts to increase self-awareness and sensitivity to others. The goal of confrontation meetings is to manage dysfunctional intergroup conflict. Quality of work life programs use techniques such as job redesign, employee involvement in decision making, redesign of pay systems, and quality circles to enhance the total work climate.

8. Identify the conditions that enhance the likelihood an OD effort will succeed.

Conditions favorable to success include the use of a trained outsider, top-level management recognition that problems exist, leader support of and involvement in the program, early successes in the OD program, respect for the talents of the affected managers, cooperation and involvement from human resources managers, effective coordination and control of the OD program, and measurement of outcomes.

9. Explain how evaluation researchers evaluate OD programs.

Evaluation researchers sometimes use one of three major designs to evaluate a program. In a pre-experimental design, observations are taken either after or before and after implementing an OD program. An experimental design overcomes many of the problems of a pre-experimental design by including a control group that does not experience the OD program. When the controls necessary for experimental research are unavailable, a quasi-experimental design may be desirable.

10. Evaluate the track record of OD programs.

The success of an OD program depends on the type of technique, its duration, and the way the results are measured. Overall, research suggests that OD programs are usually effective. Efforts using four or more techniques and lasting 10 to 20 days are likely to produce more meaningful change.

Key Terms

Organizational decline	Pre-experimental design
Organizational development (OD)	One-group pretest–post-test design
Unfreezing	Pretest–post-test control group
Changing	design
Refreezing	Reactivity
Survey feedback	Solomon four-group design
Team building	Quasi-experimental design
Sensitivity training	Time-series design
Confrontation meetings	Alpha change
Quality of work life (QWL)	Beta change
Evaluation research	Gamma change

Review and Discussion Questions

1. What are some external sources of change in organizations? What are some internal sources?

2. What crises can arise at each stage of an organization's growth? How can the organization overcome each crisis?

3. Are large organizations immune to organizational decline? Why are new organizations particularly vulnerable to decline?

4. Danielle Irons learns that the restaurant next door to her bookstore is for sale. Danielle's bookstore has been very profitable this year, so she thinks it would be a good time to expand, and a restaurant sounds like a fun business to expand into. Danielle goes to see her banker about getting a loan to buy the restaurant. "Ms. Irons," says her banker, "before we discuss your application, I have a word of advice: Stick to your knitting." What does the banker mean? How is this advice relevant to Danielle's business?

5. Futuristic Computing is a new company set up to make special high-speed computers for the U.S. Defense Department. The company had a

relatively easy time getting the government contract because their product is at the cutting edge of computing technology. Futuristic Computing is ready to start production; all key positions have been filled except for the Quality Control Manager. Company executives have been considering applications for this position for the past five months; they hope to be able to select a candidate in a few weeks but don't want to be hasty. Futuristic Computing is vulnerable to some of the factors that can lead to organization failure. Which of these factors should the company's executives be concerned about?

6. What is organizational development (OD)? What are the phases of the OD process?

7. Burt Stilgoe, chief executive officer of Quick & True Appraisal Company, wants to give individual appraisers more autonomy. As soon as Burt announces his plan, some employees at Quick & True begin raising objections to this change. How can Burt overcome this resistance? Which techniques do you recommend and why?

8. Robin Finch is an OD specialist who has contracted with Clean Sweep Incorporated, a janitorial services company that provides cleaning services in most of the city's largest office buildings. Clean Sweep has asked Robin to help the company improve its productivity. Describe some techniques Robin might use. Should she select a single technique, or more than one?

9. What are some advantages and drawbacks of the pre-experimental, experimental, and quasi-experimental research designs?

10. Should the effectiveness of an OD program be measured in terms of changes in employee performance, or in terms of individual personal satisfaction? If the goal of OD is personal fulfillment, who should be responsible for this? Are the values of OD appropriate for all organizations? Explain.

Critical Incident
Staunch Resistance at Metropolitan Police Department

Jerry Spore was disgusted. As commander of the 10th Division of the Metropolitan Police Department (MPD), he had just issued an ultimatum to Deputy Chief Robert Powell. All officers not in compliance with the new uniform standards within two weeks' time would be issued official reprimands that carry time-off-without-pay sanctions. He just couldn't understand what the problem was. "Don't these guys want to move into the 1990s?" he wondered.

It all began two years ago, when a group of city officials responded to complaints from citizens about the Gestapo-like design of MPD officers' uniforms. Until that time, officers still donned the 1940s-style eight-pointed hat. Their other accessories were also traditional in style. Leather Sam Browne belts were worn over leather pants belts. Gun holsters, cuffs, and other equipment pertinent to the job were attached to the Sam Browne belts. City officials perceived citizens' comments to be reflective of the total MPD image, and they prompted Spore to work on improving that image by modifying the uniforms.

Spore took the task seriously. He formed a committee of local citizens and businesspeople to research and evaluate possible uniform modifications. Uniform suppliers called on the committee and encouraged them to adopt coordinated uniforms and accessories designed to maximize utility. The committee's conclusions were that they could get a lot of "bang for their buck" by simply changing key accessories in the uniform. They recommended that the city purchase new Sam Browne belts, new pants belts, and new rounded-top hats for the officers. The committee recommended that the uniforms be introduced in the police academy, and then adopted by the entire force over a period of six months, allowing for ample acquisition and distribution time.

All new recruits, therefore, were issued new belts and hats, as were all experienced officers. The hats were accepted almost without comment, but the belts met with resistance. The outside of the pants belt was Velcro as was the inside of the Sam Browne belt, thus allowing them to be conveniently attached. Belt closures were also Velcro. The belts required less maintenance and were slightly less expensive than the former standard belts.

Officers claimed that the rigid Velcro backing cut the pants loops. They also said that the belts were uncomfortable to wear. Spore observed that the problem probably related more to obesity than to the belt design. The more portly officers were accustomed to wearing their belts low, under their abdomens, and the backing material on the new belts did not cooperate. A few of the older officers also complained that the new belts were dangerous. They argued that each officer placed tools necessary for protection in a slightly different spot on the belts, and that this change could actually cost an officer's life in an emergency situation.

Most officers fresh out of the academy had replaced the issued Velcro-style belts, which they had discarded, with leather versions. Anyone seen with a Velcro belt was labeled as "green," or "nerdy." The change had been completely ignored by the other officers, and apparently Powell had been reprimanded by the now-disbanded committee about the waste of its time and money.

Meanwhile, Powell had been given the task to shape up these guys. Powell sensed that there was a lot more than logic behind the officers' resistance. Powell judged that Spore had made one key mistake in handling this whole uniform business, and that that mistake was affecting the entire change process. He didn't blame the guys for their gripes, but he also knew that his own neck was on the line. Powell was only one year from retirement, and didn't want to blow things now.

Questions

1. What do you think Spore's key mistake was?

2. What were the forces for change behind the uniform issue?

3. Use Kurt Lewin's model of change to recommend an ideal plan for making the change to the new uniform.

Source: Adapted by Susan Stites Doe, State University of New York College at Buffalo. Used with permission from pages 444–446 of ORGANIZATION AND PEOPLE, Fourth Edition by J. B. Ritchie and Paul R. Thompson; Copyright © 1988 by West Publishing Company. All rights reserved.

Experiential Exercise

Introducing a Change — A Role Play

Most changes in organizations go far beyond the technical aspects of doing work; they usually involve alterations that influence the work satisfaction of the employees. In fact, change is often encountered on a personal level by most people. And frequently their reaction to change is one of resistance — not necessarily to the change itself but to what the change represents: the loss of known satisfaction.

As a manager, one might think of a continuum of approaches to introducing change, not unlike the leadership continuum (Chapter 10). At one end is telling/selling, where facts and arguments are presented showing the advantages of the change. In the middle is consultation, where the manager discusses the need for change with subordinates, solicits their ideas, and makes the decision. At the other end is collaboration, where the manager and the subordinates discuss the need for change and reach a consensus on a plan for implementing the change. The nature of the discussion that the manager initiates, plus the valence or attractiveness of what's at stake, will go a long way toward affecting the forces for and against change.

Step 1   This activity is a role-play that concerns a change that must be introduced. The change affects everyone personally. Four volunteers will be selected for the roles. The remaining class members will serve as observers. Your instructor will provide each of the role-players with a description of his or her role (the role descriptions are provided in the *Instructor's Manual*). If you are a role-player, you should *not* let anyone else know the role situation you are in.

Step 2   The remaining class members will receive an observer's form from the instructor. It is very important for this activity that you fulfill your responsibilities as an observer. Having read and interpreted the roles, each role-player should move to the front of the classroom. Four chairs arranged in a semicircle will represent the supervisor's office. On the instructor's signal, the group supervisor should begin the meeting.

Step 3   Once the role-play has resulted in an acceptable outcome, the entire class can reconvene to discuss the observers' responses. The questions posed to the observers explore the dynamics of change in a manner that seeks recognition of the importance of power, influence, communication, motivation, and so forth. This activity will enable you to integrate most of the issues you have learned about in organizational behavior.

Source: Written by Bruce Kemelgor, University of Louisville.

Notes

1. L.E. Greiner, "Evolution and Revolution as Organizations Grow," *Harvard Business Review* 50 (1972): 37–46.
2. D.A. Whetten, "Organizational Decline: A Neglected Topic in Organizational Science," *Academy of Management Review* 5 (1980): 557; E. Stark, "Surviving Organizational Death," *Psychology Today*, June 1989, 17; R. D'Aveni, "The Aftermath of Organizational Decline," *Academy of Management Journal* 32 (1989): 577–605.
3. J. Basaszewski, "Thirteen Ways to Get a Company in Trouble," *Inc.*, September 1981, 97–100; R.L. Daft, *Organization Theory and Design* (St. Paul, Minn.: West, 1983); T.J. Peters, "Putting Excellence into Management," *Business Week*, July 21, 1980, 196–205.
4. W.L. French and C.H. Bell, *Organization Development: Behavioral Science Interventions for Organization Improvement*, 2d ed. (Englewood Cliffs, N.J.: Prentice-Hall, 1978), 14.
5. K. Lewin, *Field Theory in Social Science* (New York: Harper & Row, 1951).
6. L. Coch and J.R.P. French, "Overcoming Resistance to Change," *Human Relations* 1 (1948): 512–532.
7. P.R. Lawrence, "How to Deal with Resistance to Change," *Harvard Business Review* 47 (1969): 115–122.
8. M. Beer, *Organization Change and Development: A Systems View* (Glenview, Ill.: Scott, Foresman, 1980).
9. French and Bell, *Organization Development*.
10. R.R. Blake, H.A. Shepard, and J.S. Mouton, *Managing Intergroup Conflict in Industry* (Houston: Gulf, 1965).
11. S.E. Seashore, "Defining and Measuring the Quality of Work Life," in *The Quality of Working Life*, vol. 1, ed. L.E. David and A. Cherns (New York: Free Press, 1975), 105–118.
12. J.M. Rosow, "Quality of Work Life Issues for the 1980s," in *Work in America*, ed. C. Kerr and J. Rosow (New York: Van Nostrand, 1979), 157–187.
13. French and Bell, *Organization Development*.
14. T.D. Cook and D.T Campbell, *Quasi-experimentation: Design and Analysis Issues for Field Settings* (Chicago: Rand McNally, 1979).
15. R.L. Solomon, "An Extension of Control Group Design," *Psychological Bulletin* 46 (1949): 137–150.
16. J.R. Terborg, G.S. Howard, and S.E. Maxwell, "Evaluating Planned Organizational Change: A Method for Assessing Alpha, Beta, and Gamma Change," *Academy of Management Review* 5 (1980): 109–121.
17. R.T. Golembiewski and K.R. Billingsley, "Measuring Change in OD Panel Designs: A Response to Critics," *Academy of Management Review* 5 (1980): 97–103.
18. Terborg, Howard, and Maxwell, "Evaluating Planned Organizational Change."
19. N.C. Roberts and J.I. Porras, "Progress in Organization Development Research," *Group and Organization Studies* 7 (1982): 91–116.
20. J.I. Porras and P.O. Berg, "The Impact of Organization Development," *Academy of Management Review* 3 (1978): 249–266.
21. D. Terpstra, "Relationship between Methodological Rigor and Reported Outcomes in Organizational Development Evaluation Research," *Journal of Applied Psychology* (1981): 541–542.
22. A.J. DuBrin, *Foundations of Organizational Behavior* (Englewood Cliffs, N.J.: Prentice-Hall, 1984).
23. Ibid., 471.
24. W.G. Bennis, *Organization Development: Its Nature, Origins, and Prospects* (Reading, Mass.: Addison-Wesley, 1969).

Lakeway Resort and Conference Center, located on Lake Travis in Austin, Texas, offers guests 65 miles of shore line, golfing, fishing, boating, parasailing, tennis, hiking/walking trails, a fully equipped Nautilus fitness center, and horseback riding, along with some of the finest conference and meeting facilities in the region. For 25 years, it operated as a local resort serving primarily middle-aged Texans, who returned again and again to its scenic and relaxing environs. During the first 25 years, those loyal patrons provided 87 percent of Lakeway's revenues. The resort was targeted at the needs of middle-aged empty nesters, those with no children living at home, and older parents.

As Austin began to attract a new base of high-tech industry, many middle- to upper-class young families moved into the area. These hard working new professionals had unique needs. They sought vacation spots that provided diverse recreational outlets for themselves and their families. In particular, they required supervised care and entertainment for their children. For themselves, they desired challenge and adventure on vacation.

As the demographics of Austin and its surrounding communities changed, so did opportunities for Lakeway. The strengths of its first quarter century began to lead to declining revenues. Its appeal to middle-aged, local Texans could no longer guarantee its survival.

In 1985, the resort's strategic focus changed dramatically after its owners signed a management agreement with Dolce Corporation. Dolce was pursuing a corporate strategy of placing resort facilities in five different locations around the United States: Florida, Texas, California, Chicago, and New York. Lakeway seemed to fit nicely with this strategy. Dolce stated a mission for Lakeway to become a world-class conference and recreational facility. By 1989, this had changed the mix of Lakeway customers from almost 90 percent Texans to 60 percent.

Lakeway exemplifies a number of organizational behavior principles. First, management communicates strategic decisions to all levels of the organization. Employees share in problem solving and enjoy continuous updates on the financial condition of the company. Also, Dolce rewards employees directly for their commitments to high-quality service to customers. Three separate awards recognize and reward employees who meet and exceed service requirements and who treat guests with unfailing friendliness and helpfulness. Further, the company places employees very carefully within the organization as best suits their personalities. The company is determined to maintain a steady stream of employees to fill its needs throughout the coming decade.

Lakeway's organizational structure is designed to pass information freely downward through the ranks. The resort is managed by the Executive Committee, which takes its direction from Lakeway's private investors. The committee includes the general manager and the department heads of each of the six profit centers, namely, Conferences, Sales and Marketing, Accounting, Food and Beverages, Human Resources, and Engineering. Every Monday, the Executive Committee meets to discuss progress toward goals and solutions to problems. Every Tuesday, all administrative staff members join the committee in a roundtable meeting to air concerns and contribute ideas for problem solving.

Elected employee representatives from each department meet once a month in the Employee Council, along with the general manager and the human resource director. Through these representatives, employees can air any grievances concerning their jobs and propose solutions to problems they raise. The administrative staff realizes that line employees can contribute advice to problem-solving efforts from their operational perspective, and therefore their ideas receive careful attention.

In addition to these sessions, each department holds a monthly staff meeting of all departmental employees. This combination of Executive Committee, Employee Council, and monthly staff meetings links all levels of the organization and joins their efforts toward meeting organizational objectives. Each employee understands management's plans, and each can contribute to the formation of those plans.

Within this network, department managers run their departments as C.E.O.s of their own small companies. The general manager, Lawrence Barbere, believes that this encourages managers' accountability for their actions.

Still, all managers recognize employees as Lakeway's secret ingredient of success. To maintain a consistently superior service for its guests, Lakeway has developed careful selection and development programs to ensure that those who must meet customers' needs are willing and able to do so. The company places employees in positions they will fill most capably on the basis of criteria established in detailed job descriptions. Personality factors determine much about an employee's placement. Outgoing, personable candidates take visible positions that require frequent interaction with resort guests.

Each job description ends with an affirmation of commitment to the company's service goals. The basic message states: We must never forget that we have jobs only because our investors feel we can make a profit by offering a service our guests want to purchase.

Employees' inclusion in company communication loops is not their only form of participation. They also share in the company's profits. After being employed at Lakeway for 90 days, each employee receives a stock certificate that represents a share of the profits collected in the Employee Fund. Funds are distributed at the end of every fiscal year.

Three awards recognize employees' service to customers. The Employee of the Month award, given out by the Executive Committee, brings workers cash, satin Lakeway jackets, and prominent displays of their pictures on a wall plaque at the front desk. The Employee of the Year award brings more cash and recognition from management. The Aggressive Hospitality award, given

by the Employee Council, brings the worker a lapel pin, displays of his or her name on all paychecks for one month, and his or her photo in the Hardware Cafe (the employee dining room) for one year. Despite the cash given with the awards from management, the employee-dispensed award is the most coveted, due in part to the peer recognition it implies.

Many kinds of efforts earn recognition. One employee took a guest's laundry home and did it herself. Another borrowed a VCR from his parents' home so that a guest could conduct a business meeting on schedule. This kind of behavior exemplifies Lakeway's philosophy. This is its competitive edge.

Lakeway's operational philosophy derives from an awareness that only a few resorts can be considered really outstanding. To be recognized as outstanding, a resort has to understand and satisfy guests' needs better than any other resort. The attitude that drives Lakeway toward this goal is what its people call "aggressive hospitality." Employees routinely do whatever it takes to make guests want to return to Lakeway. Extra effort is standard performance.

In order to ensure a steady supply of these excellent workers in the future, Lakeway's management tracks demographic trends and alters its recruitment policies to match the available work force. Increasing high school dropout rates are reducing the labor pool of every service-intensive company in the United States. Substance abuse magnifies this problem. The personnel director at Lakeway already runs a high school work program in which seniors work at Lakeway for school credit. She hopes to expand the company's work with such students.

Lakeway also offers its employees proactive social education. It has provided AIDS awareness information and promotes an active safety program to curtail work-related injuries.

Questions

1. Discuss Lakeway's reward systems. Do they reflect the culture of the organization?

2. What factors have molded the culture at Lakeway? How would you describe its culture?

3. What has Lakeway management done to ensure efficient communication within the organization?

4. Would you characterize Lakeway as an organic or a mechanistic organization, according to Burns and Stalkers' classic models of organizational design?

5. How would Lakeway's policy of active communication, its broad reward systems, and its culture of hospitality change under an autocratic and bureaucratic general manager?

6. Lakeway's personnel director is preparing for the time when employees will be in high demand and short supply. If trends in literacy and dropout rates continue, she may have to do even more to attract and retain qualified personnel. Suggest three creative steps by which she might improve the odds.

Source: Written by Susan Stites Doe, State University of New York College at Buffalo.

Case

Moscow McDonald's Golden Arches: Gateway to the West

Imagine yourself standing in the waiting line to the Pushkin Square McDonald's restaurant in Moscow. First you notice that the line extends over 500 yards, eclipsing the procession of visitors to Lenin's tomb. Perhaps you wonder how Lenin would react to the site of the golden arches within walking distance of the Kremlin. Would he be outraged that a beacon of capitalism and freedom of choice would shine across the globe from the capital of communism? Could he have ever imagined that an icon of free enterprise would transfer innovative agricultural technology, effective management training and development, and philosophies of product quality and customer service to the receptive arms of his comrades? You may also wonder if Ray Kroc, the founder of McDonald's, ever imagined that his golden arches would serve as a gateway in Moscow to western technology and management principles.

As you approach the largest McDonald's in the world, you may wonder if the anxious and hungry Soviets, who wait in line for 45 minutes to spend about one-fourth of a day's pay for a Big Mac, appreciate the significance of this joint venture and the factors that have led to its success.

The January 31, 1990, grand opening of Mc-Donald's in the center of Moscow represents an important milestone for McDonald's Restaurants and for the food service industry in the Soviet Union. The state-of-the-art renovated building, formerly a cafe and a cultural gathering place, seats over 700 people inside the building, has outside seating for 200, and is fully accessible to the handicapped. It employs over 1,000 people, the largest McDonald's crew in the world, and has served over 30,000 people per day. The original plans were to serve between 10,000 and 15,000 customers per day.

The Soviet Union has become the 52nd country to host the world's largest quick-service food restaurant company, and the Russian language is the 28th working language in which the company operates. McDonald's Corporation, based in Oak Brook, Illinois, serves over 22 million people daily in 11,000 restaurants in 52 countries. The Soviet population of over 291 million represents the largest potential market of new customers for McDonald's.

In recent years, responding to Gorbachev's call for *perestroika* (restructuring), a number of joint ventures have been formed with the Soviet Union with varying degrees of success. The McDonald's venture is a success story for Gorbachev's policies and for the McDonald's organization because of several factors: entrepreneurial leadership with a long-term perspective, international cooperation, the transfer of innovative production technology, a focus on quality control and customer service, effective management and employee training, and a commitment to the community.

George A. Cohon, Vice Chairman of Moscow McDonald's and President and Chief Executive Officer of McDonald's Restaurants of Canada, Limited, provided the leadership for the company's successful venture. Much of the success of the venture can be attributed to Cohon's entrepreneurial spirit nurtured by the McDonald's organization. Cohon opened his first McDonald's restaurant in 1968 after leaving his home town of Chicago to move to Canada as the McDonald's licensee for eastern Canada. In 1971, McDonald's restaurants throughout Canada were reorganized under ownership as McDonald's Restaurants of Canada, Limited; Cohon was named president. Under his leadership the organization has grown to become Canada's seventh largest employer with over 600 restaurants across the country. Cohen's personal commitment and energy were irreplaceable during the long period of negotiations on the joint venture with the Soviet Union.

Cohon's Canadian team spent over twelve years negotiating the agreement for McDonald's to enter into the Soviet market. In April 1988 McDonald's Canada completed negotiations for the largest joint venture ever made between a food company and the Soviet Union. This concluded the longest new-territory negotiations by the company since it was founded in 1955. Cohon and his Canadian team spent thousands of hours in Moscow making presentations to hundreds of senior trade officials, staff at various ministries, and countless other groups within the Soviet Union. Despite numerous setbacks and requests for endless submissions and revisions to their proposals, Cohon persisted because many Soviets appeared to genuinely want to establish closer ties with the West. According to Cohon, McDonald's negotiations "outlived three Soviet premiers."

Cohon stated that what ultimately sold the Soviets on McDonald's was the food technology it had to offer. In addition, the company's emphasis on quality, service, cleanliness, and value (QSC&V) convinced the Moscow city officials that McDonald's could work in their city. Vladimir Malyshkov, Chairman of the Board of Moscow McDonald's, stated that McDonald's "created a restaurant experience like no other in the Soviet Union. It demonstrates what can be achieved when people work together."

The historic joint venture contract provides for an initial 20 McDonald's restaurants in Moscow and a state-of-the-art food production and distribution center to supply the restaurants. The first McDonald's accepts only rubles. The next restaurant is scheduled to open at the end of 1990. McDonald's Canada is managing the new venture in partnership with the Food Service Administration of the Moscow City Council in a 51 to 49 percent Soviet-Canadian partnership.

Moscow McDonald's was clearly an international venture. McDonald's personnel from around the world helped prepare for the opening. Dutch agricultural consultants assisted in improving agricultural production. For example, they helped plant and harvest a variety of potatoes needed to make french fries that met McDonald's quality standards. Other international consultants assisted in negotiating contracts with farmers throughout the country to provide quality beef and other food supplies, including onions, lettuce, pickles, milk, flour, and butter. Once the Soviet farmers learned to trust the consultants, they became eager to learn about the new Western production technologies. Working together with Soviet farmers, McDonald's doubled the average potato yield on 60 hectares of land in 1989.

The development of the 10,000-square-meter food production and distribution center, located in the Moscow suburb of Solntsevo, was also an international effort with equipment and furnishings from Austria, Canada, Denmark, Finland, Holland, Italy, Japan, Spain, Sweden, Switzerland, Taiwan, Turkey, the United Kingdom, the United States, West Germany, and Yugoslavia.

The center provides a state-of-the-art food processing environment that meets McDonald's rigid standards.

At full capacity the center will employ over 250 workers from the Soviet Union. Also, at full capacity the meat line will produce 10,000 patties per hour from locally acquired beef. Milk will be delivered in McDonald's refrigerated dairy trucks from a local Soviet farm and will be pasteurized and processed at the center. Flour, yeast, sugar, and shortening from sources in the Soviet Union will be used to produce over 14,000 buns per hour on the center's bakery line. Storage space at the center will hold 3,000 tons of potatoes and the pie line will produce 5,000 apple pies per hour, made from fruit from local farmers.

Training for the McDonald's crew and managers is essential to the customer service that the company provides. According to Bob Hissink, Vice President of Operations, Moscow McDonald's hiring was just the beginning of assembling the largest McDonald's crew in the world. Over 25,000 applications were sorted and 5,000 of the most qualified candidates were interviewed. Finally, the 630 new members of the first Moscow McDonald's team were selected. Initial training sessions were compressed into a four-week period with four or five shifts 12 hours a day. Seasoned McDonald's staff from around the world assisted the Soviet managers with crew training. The new crew of 353 women and 277 men were trained to work in several different capacities at the restaurant and had accumulated over 15,000 hours of skills development. During restaurant operating hours, about 200 crew members at a time will be on duty.

The training requirements were more extensive for McDonald's managers. Four Soviets selected as managers of Moscow McDonald's spent more than nine months in North American training programs that must be completed by any McDonald's manager in the world. The Soviets graduated from the Canadian Institute of Hamburgerology after completing over 1,000 hours of training. Their studies included classroom instruction, equipment maintenance techniques, and on-the-job restaurant management.

Their training also included a two-week, in-depth study program at Hamburger University, McDonald's international training center in Oak Brook, Illinois. With more than 200 other managers from around the world, they completed advanced restaurant operations studies in senior management techniques and operating procedures. The Soviet managers are qualified to manage any McDonald's restaurant in the world.

Another factor contributing to the success of the Moscow McDonald's venture was Cohon's personal and corporate commitment to the community. As the first non-Soviet citizen appointed as North American President and Director of the Soviet Children's Fund, the largest children's charity in the Soviet Union, George Cohon pledged to support the Fund. Advertising revenues from the Soviet broadcast of the 84th Annual Santa Claus parade in Toronto were donated to provide needed medical equipment and treatment for a number of Soviet children. In addition to the proceeds from an international gala celebrating the opening day of the first McDonald's restaurant in Moscow, half of the opening-day sales of the new restaurant were donated to the Soviet Children's Fund.

Other examples of McDonald's commitment to the community included "parents' night," where all the new employees of the Moscow restaurant were invited to bring their families for a meal and tour of the new restaurant. The three-hour event, a tradition wherever a McDonald's opens, helped foster an understanding for the company values among the families of its employees.

In addition, technology transfer provided important long-term benefits to the Soviet citizenry. For example, through the transfer of agricultural technology and equipment, the Soviet potato farm, Kishira, increased its yield by 100 percent. According to the Kishira Chairman, farmers from all over the Soviet Union have requested technical training in production methods to increase their crop yields. Also, since the Soviet machinery lagged 15 to 20 years behind Western technology, new machinery from Holland was used to harvest the potatoes used to make french fries. However, according to a Dutch agricultural consultant, because of the McDonald's venture it may not take the Soviets 20 years to catch up to Western production methods.

According to one Soviet official, the greatest impact of the McDonald's venture is the changes in the attitudes of the Soviet people. According to Vladimir Malyshkov, Chairman of Moscow Mc-Donald's, the joint venture was formed to fill the needs of its citizens, but the Soviets acquired more than they first imagined from their Mc-Donald's partners, including jobs, technology, and management expertise about motivation and organization. The impact on agricultural and production methods has established a foundation for a revolution in the food production system in the Soviet Union and has magnified the vivid imagination and entrepreneurial spirit of the Soviets.

According to Cohon, "McDonald's is a business, but also is a responsible member of the communities it serves. The joint venture with the Soviet Union should help foster cooperation between nations and a better understanding among people. When individuals from around the world work shoulder-to-shoulder, they learn to com-municate, to get along, and to be part of a team. That's what we call burger diplomacy." There is a Soviet expression that says that you must eat many meals with a person before you come to know him. At 30,000 meals per day, it may not take long for the Soviets to come to better understand the West through its corporate ambassador, McDonald's.

Questions

1. What type of multinational corporate strategy did McDonald's choose to enter the Soviet market? What important environmental factors are evident in this case? Discuss.

2. What were the key strategy implementation factors for success of the Moscow McDonald's venture? Explain.

3. How did innovation contribute to the success of the venture? What is the impact of this entrepreneurial venture on the Soviet economy? Discuss.

4. How should Mr. Cohon measure the success of Moscow McDonald's? What factors should be considered when measuring the performance of the venture? Discuss.

References

1. "A Month Later, Moscow McDonald's Is Still Drawing Long and Hungry Lines," *Houston Post*, March 1, 1990.
2. Background information from McDonald's Restaurants of Canada, Ltd.
3. Tannenbaum, Jeffrey A., "Franchisers See a Future in East Bloc," *The Wall Street Journal*, June 5, 1990, B-1.
4. Maney, Kevin, and Diane Rinehart, "McDonald's in Moscow Opens Today," *USA Today*, January 31, 1990, B-1.
5. "McDonald's on the Volga," *Employment Review*, Vol. 3, No. 10, 1990.
6. Moscow McDonald's videotape produced for Dryden Press, 1990.
7. Wates, Oliver, "Crowds Still Gather at Lenin's Tomb but Lineups are Longer at McDonald's," *The London Free Press*, June 9, 1990.

Glossary

Accommodating A style of conflict management involving giving in to another's wishes.

Achievement-oriented leadership In path–goal theory, a leader behavior that entails setting challenging goals while simultaneously showing confidence in the subordinates' abilities.

Administrative model A decision-making model recognizing that bounded rationality limits the making of optimally rational-economic decisions.

Adult ego state In transactional analysis, an ego state characterized by rational thinking and mature behavior.

Adverse impact A primary issue in legal cases charging companies with discriminatory practices: Does an employment practice have a disparate negative effect on the opportunities of a protected class of employees?

Affective component The emotional aspect of an attitude.

Alienative involvement Organizational involvement typified by members' hostile and extremely negative attitudes.

Alpha change A shift in response that is produced by a program itself.

Alternating ranking technique A ranking of employees that entails writing down the name of the best performer, followed by that of the poorest performer, followed by that of the next-best performer, and so on.

Approach–approach conflict A type of intrapersonal conflict arising when an individual must choose between two attractive alternatives.

Approach–avoidance conflict A type of intrapersonal conflict arising when an individual must choose whether to approach or avoid a goal that has both attractive and unattractive qualities.

Archival research A type of OB research using existing information found, for example, in scholarly books and journals, newspapers, and government documents.

Assessment center An evaluation technique using situational exercises conducted over a period of several days in order to identify promotable, high-potential employees.

Attitude An idea charged with emotion that predisposes a set of actions to a specific set of stimuli.

Attribution theory A theory that suggests that we observe the behavior of others and then attribute internal or external causes to it.

Audience factor A factor involved in attitude change that deals with the influence of individual characteristics of the target person.

Authoritarianism The extent to which a person believes that power and status should be concentrated in a leader or class. The stronger the belief, the more the person is said to be authoritarian.

Authority Power based on the legitimate right to try to change others' behavior or tell them what to do.

Availability heuristic A process used when an individual estimates the frequency or probability of an event or class of objects by the ease with which instances can be brought to mind.

Avoidance–avoidance conflict A type of intrapersonal conflict arising when an individual must choose between two equally unattractive alternatives.

Avoiding   A style of conflict management in which a person attempts to adopt a neutral stance.

Balance theory   The idea that individuals try to maintain consistency among their beliefs.

Bank Wiring Room study   One of the Hawthorne studies, revealing ways in which peer pressure can affect individual productivity.

Behavior modification   An approach to motivation that uses the principles of operant conditioning.

Behavioral component   The aspect of an attitude predisposing a set of actions.

Behavioral observation scales (BOS)   Rating scales similar to BARS that measure the frequency with which a ratee engages in specific behaviors.

Behavioral theory of decision making   An approach to decision making that recognizes that bounded rationality limits the making of optimal decisions.

Behaviorally anchored rating scales (BARS)   Rating scales developed by raters and/or ratees in which specific behavioral incidents serve as anchors for each scale.

Beta change   A shift in response that reflects a change in the way an employee responds to the survey.

Bootstrapping   The procedure of analyzing an individual's or group's decision-making process and using the resultant model as an aid in subsequent decisions. The bootstrapping approach is sometimes termed an expert systems approach.

Boundary-spanning position   A position within an organization that represents the organization to various constituencies in the external environment.

Bounded discretion   Limitations imposed on the decision-making process that result from moral and ethical constraints.

Bounded rationality   The assumption that organizational, social, and human limitations lead decision makers to settle on decisions that are "good enough" rather than optimal.

Brainstorming   A technique designed to generate creative solutions to problems by encouraging group members to express their ideas freely in a noncritical atmosphere.

Bureaucracy   An organizational structure proposed by Weber emphasizing rationality and including such features as adherence to formal rules, a hierarchy of authority, specialization, hiring based on qualifications, and promotion based on merit.

Burnout   Physical, emotional, and mental exhaustion resulting from prolonged exposure to stressful situations.

Calculative involvement   Organizational involvement in which members' relationship to the organization is rational and oriented toward maximizing personal gain.

Case study   A type of OB research consisting of an in-depth examination of an organization, usually conducted over an extended time period.

Cautious shift   A tendency for groups to make more conservative decisions than individuals.

Central tendency error   The tendency to rate all ratees around the middle range of a scale.

Central traits   Specific traits of individuals that are more responsible than others in influencing the formation of impressions.

Centralized network   A communication network in which members have unequal opportunities to obtain and pass on information. Information flows through a pivotal or central person.

Chain of command   A concept maintaining that information and authority proceed from level to level in a strict hierarchical fashion.

Changing   The second phase of Lewin's model of change, in which a new plan or system is implemented.

Charisma   Refers to a type of social influence based on follower perceptions of the leader rather than on the leader's formal authority.

Child ego state   In transactional analysis, an ego state characterized by immaturity, dependency, and impulsiveness.

Classical conditioning   An approach to learning in which an unconditioned stimulus is repeatedly paired with a neutral stimulus until the neutral stimulus alone can elicit the same response that was evoked by the unconditioned stimulus. When this occurs, the neutral stimulus is termed a conditioned stimulus and the response, a conditioned response.

Classical decision theory   An approach to decision making that assumes that decision makers are objective, have complete information, and consider all possible alternatives and their consequences before selecting the optimal solution. *See also* Rational–economic model

Closed group   A group in which the membership remains fairly stable.

Closed system   A system that does not interact with its external environment.

Coercive power   Power based on the extent to which an individual or organization has control over punishments. The opposite of reward power.

Cognitive component   The knowing aspect of an attitude.

Cognitive dissonance   Occurs when a person exhibits behavior that is inconsistent with his or her attitudes.

Cognitive resource theory   The view that directive leaders who are intelligent and possess relevant job experience will be more effective if they are in stress-free settings with subordinates who are supportive.

Cognitive style   Mode of gathering and evaluating information. Jung identified four types: sensing, intuiting, thinking, and feeling.

Cohesiveness   The sum of all forces acting on group members to remain a part of the group.

Collaborating   A style of conflict management that attempts to satisfy the concerns of both sides through honest discussion.

Communication   The creation of a mental image in the mind of a receiver in exactly the same detail as intended by the sender.

Communication role   The specific functions an individual serves in an organization's communication network.

Comparison level   The standard by which people evaluate the rewards and costs of a relationship. The average value of all outcomes of past relationships of a particular type.

Comparison level of alternatives   The standard an individual uses in deciding whether to maintain or terminate a relationship.

Complementary transaction   In transactional analysis, a relationship between two people that is predictable.

Compliance   An individual's acceptance of an influence attempt in the belief that rewards will follow or punishment will be avoided.

Compromising   A style of conflict management that strives for partial satisfaction of both sides' desires.

Conditioned response   In classical conditioning, a reflexive response evoked by a conditioned stimulus.

Conditioned stimulus   In classical conditioning, a neutral stimulus that has attained the capacity to evoke a conditioned response.

Conflict   A form of interaction between individuals or groups in situations that occur when one or both sides perceive that the other has thwarted or is about to thwart an important concern.

Conformity   An individual's change of attitudes or behavior in response to real or imagined pressure from others.

Confrontation meetings   An organizational development technique in which conflicting groups are brought together in a structured situation designed to enhance cooperation.

Consideration   A factor referring to the extent to which a leader exhibits concern for the welfare of the group members.

Content theories   Theories that focus on the specific factors that motivate people to perform. Examples are the theories of Maslow, Herzberg, and McClelland.

Contextual dimensions   Characteristics of the entire organization and its external environment, such as size, technology, and external constituents (e.g., customers, suppliers, and competitors).

Contingency approach   An approach to organizational behavior stating that there is no one best way to manage every situation, but that management must find different ways to deal with different situations.

Contingency model of leadership effectiveness   A theory suggesting that leadership effectiveness is determined both by the characteristics of the leader and by the level of situational favorableness that exists.

Continuous reinforcement   A schedule designed to reinforce correct behavior every time it is exhibited.

Correlational method   A method employed by OB research that examines the relationship between two variables, particularly whether changes in one variable produce changes in the other.

Cosmopolite   An individual whose communication network extends into the organization's external environment.

Culture Assimilator   A culture-specific, programmed learning exercise designed to provide the learner with feedback on his or her responses to hypothetical situations.

Decentralization   The degree to which decision making occurs lower down in an organization.

Decentralized network   A communication network in which each member has an equal opportunity to obtain and pass on information.

Deduction   To infer something about a particular case from a general principle that holds for all such cases.

Deficiency needs   The lower-order needs (physiological, safety, and social) in Maslow's hierarchy that must be satisfied to ensure a person's existence.

Delphi technique   A technique for improving group decision making in which the opinions of experts are solicited by a mailed questionnaire and then compiled. The consensus of opinions is used to make a decision.

Demand characteristics   In laboratory experiments, the cues and signals of an experimental setting that indicate to the subject how to respond to the experimenter's wishes.

Dependent variable   An outcome or consequence that is attributable to the independent variable.

Differentiation   A concept that refers to the degree of difference in orientations and perspectives among an organization's subunits.

Diffusion of responsibility   A concept, often used to explain the risky shift, that holds that individual responsibility is shared among a group's members.

Directive leadership   In path–goal theory, a leader behavior that involves giving specific guidance to subordinates and asking that they follow standard rules and regulations.

Dogmatism   A system of beliefs insisting upon the existence of certain truths and opposed to skepticism.

Downward communication   Communication that flows from higher to lower levels within an organization.

Employee growth need strength   The strength of an employee's desire for personal growth experiences in the work setting.

Employee orientation   A style of leadership referring to the extent a leader shows concern for the welfare of the group members.

Enacted role   The actual set of behaviors exhibited by an individual in a position.

Equity theory   A theory that suggests that a person will strive to maintain a ratio of input to outcome that is equal to the ratio of a comparison other.

Evaluation research   Techniques of research design used to evaluate a program's success. The three major designs are preexperimental, experimental, and quasi-experimental.

Expectancy theory   A theory suggesting that behavior is a function of a person's expectancies about the future and the value of future outcomes.

Expected role   The formal set of behaviors conveyed both by a job description and by members of the work unit.

Experimental method   A method employed by OB research that manipulates one variable (the independent variable) in the hope of observing resulting changes in another variable (the dependent variable).

Expert power   Individual power based on the possession of expert, job-relevant knowledge.

External validity   The extent to which a study's results can be generalized beyond the immediate situation.

Extinction   The decline in response rate that occurs when reinforcement is removed from behaviors that were previously rewarded.

Extrinsic reward   A reward external to the job, such as pay or promotion.

Faceted approach   An approach to studying job satisfaction that breaks down an employee's reaction to a job into several facets (e.g., one's supervisor, pay, or working conditions).

Feedback interview   A meeting between manager and employee in which the results of a performance appraisal are conveyed to the employee.

Field experiment   A type of OB research in which an investigator attempts to manipulate and control variables in a natural setting rather than in a laboratory.

Fixed interval schedule   A schedule in which a reward is applied only after a fixed amount of time has passed since the last reward was given.

Fixed ratio schedule   A schedule in which a set number of responses must be performed before a reward is applied.

Fixed schedule   A reinforcement schedule in which the amount of time or number of behaviors performed is fixed.

Flat structure   Describes an organization with fewer levels of authority and larger spans of control.

Flextime   A work schedule that gives employees some discretion in arranging their working hours, specifically their starting and ending times.

Forced comparison   An evaluating technique in which the rater assigns employees to categories on the basis of performance, but limits the percentage of employees placed in any one category.

Forcing   A form of conflict management that attempts to overwhelm an opposing side with formal authority, threats, or the use of power.

Formal group   A group formed within an organization to accomplish the goals of the organization.

Forming   The earliest stage of group development, in which members determine behaviors that are acceptable and unacceptable.

Four-fifths rule   In discrimination cases, adverse impact is said to exist if a protected group's selection rate for employment decisions is less than four-fifths (80%) of the rate for the nonprotected group.

Functional form   A basic type of organization design that groups personnel and activities according to resources that are essential to the production process.

Functional turnover   The assumption that high turnover among poor performers can benefit an organization.

Gain sharing   An incentive scheme that ties an individual's bonuses to the performance of a business unit.

Game playing   Forms of patterned social interaction based on giving and getting "strokes" in the transactional analysis view.

Gamma change   A shift in response that reflects a change in the way an employee conceptualizes the construct being measured.

Gatekeeper   An individual in an organization who controls the flow of information to others.

General Adaptation Syndrome Refers to the three stages of stress identified by Selye: alarm, resistance, and exhaustion.

Global approach   An approach to studying job satisfaction taking into account an employee's overall reaction to a job.

Goal acceptance   The degree of a person's acceptance of the goal.

Goal difficulty   The degree of proficiency or level of job performance that is being sought by the goal.

Goal specificity   The degree of precision of the goal.

Grapevine   Informal channels of communication that exist within an organization and short-circuit the formal channels.

Graphic rating scale   An evaluation technique in which the rater checks the point on the scale that best represents the performance level of the employee.

Graphic scale   A method of measuring attitudes in which an individual checks the point on a scale that best represents his or her degree of agreement with a statement.

Grid analysis   A technique for improving creativity in which ideas are listed on the sides of a two-dimensional grid and all possible combinations of ideas are examined.

Group   A collection of two or more individuals who interact with each other, share common beliefs, and perceive themselves as being in a group.

Group polarization   The tendency for members of a group to move to extreme positions (in the direction they originally favored) following group discussion.

Groupthink   The tendency for members of a highly cohesive group to seek consensus so strongly that they fail to explore alternative, possibly correcting, courses of action.

Growth needs   The higher-order needs (esteem and self-actualization) in Maslow's hierarchy that are concerned with the realization of one's potential.

Halo effect   An overall favorable or unfavorable impression of a person that is used as a basis for performance evaluation, regardless of the actual performance level.

Halo error   Occurs when a rater assigns the same rating to all aspects of an employee's performance, regardless of the actual level, because of an overall favorable or unfavorable impression of the employee.

Harshness error   The tendency to rate all ratees unfavorably.

Hawthorne effect   A phenomenon seen in test situations, in which enhanced employee performance largely results from the employees' awareness that they are being observed.

Hawthorne studies   A series of studies of worker behavior conducted at the Hawthorne plant of Western Electric near Chicago from 1927 to 1939. The studies, which demonstrated the effect of social processes on job performance, provided the impetus for the human relations approach to organizations.

Hedonism   One of the earliest views on motivation, hedonism argues that people will seek pleasure and comfort and try to avoid pain and discomfort.

Hersey–Blanchard situational theory   A theory proposing that optimal leader behavior is related to the maturity of subordinates.

Heuristics   Simplified decision rules (rules of thumb) that are used to make quick decisions.

Hierarchy of needs   Maslow's theory that there are five sets of needs arranged in such a way that lower-level, more basic needs must be satisfied before higher-level needs can be fulfilled. The needs are physiological, safety, social, esteem, and self-actualization.

Horizontal communication   Communication between individuals at the same level in an organization.

Human relations approach   An approach recognizing the importance of social factors and processes in explaining worker behavior.

Human resources management   A field of study that applies princi-ples of behavioral sciences to design and implement ways of attracting, developing, and moti-vating individuals in an organiza-tion.

Hybrid form   A type of organiza-tion design that combines the functional and product forms.

Hygiene factors   In two-factor theory, the group of variables that pertain to the context in which a job is performed (e.g., job secu-rity, company policies, and work-ing conditions).

Hypothesis   A proposition of how the independent and depen-dent variables are related that is assumed in order to test its logical consequences.

Identification   An individual's acceptance of an influence attempt out of a desire to establish or maintain a satisfying relationship with the source of influence.

Illumination experiments   One of the Hawthorne studies, showing that psychological aspects of the job setting external to the job itself can influence worker behav-ior.

Immediacy   A concept used in interpreting nonverbal communi-cation based on the fact that peo-ple physically approach people whom they evaluate positively and withdraw from those whom they evaluate negatively.

Implicit personality theory   The tendency to perceive a trait in a person because he or she exhibits a linked trait.

Impressionistic prediction   An approach through which we com-bine intuitive or subjective infor-mation about others when at-tempting to predict behavior.

Independent variable   A factor or event believed to influence or cause a change in another variable (the dependent variable).

Induction   A process in which a principle is inferred from observ-ing many cases.

Influence   Efforts by individuals to change the behavior of others in situations in which they do not possess formal power or authority over their targets.

Informal group   A group in which membership is voluntary and based on interpersonal attrac-tion.

Informal leader   An individual who lacks formal authority but possesses substantial influence in a group.

Information overload   A situation occurring when the information-processing capacities of a member of a communication network are saturated.

Initiating structure   A factor referring to the extent to which a leader initiates activity in a group, organizes it, and defines the way that work is to be done.

Instincts   Predispositions that are inborn or innate.

Institutionalized arrangements   An organization's "way of doing business," exemplified by formal policies, reward systems, and lines of authority and communication.

Integrating department   A formal and permanent mechanism with a goal of integrating the efforts of other departments.

Integration   A concept that refers to the degree of unity of effort among an organization's subunits.

Intensive technology Uses skills or services to transform an object; a hospital exemplifies intensive technology.

Intergroup conflict Conflict that exists between groups.

Interlocking directorates A situation created when a company places board members of another corporation on its own board.

Internal validity The extent to which the independent variable had the intended effect in a study.

Internalization An individual's acceptance of an influence attempt in the belief that the resulting behavior is correct and appropriate.

Interpersonal conflict Conflict that exists between two individuals.

Interval schedule A schedule that reinforces behavior on the basis of time elapsed.

Intervening variable An unobservable state or process that helps explain the link between the independent variable and the dependent variable.

Intrapersonal conflict Conflict that exists within an individual.

Intrinsic reward A reward that is a part of the job itself, such as degree of challenge or responsibility.

Isolate An individual in an organization who has very little or no contact with other members of the organization.

Japanese management A management approach incorporating informal control of employees, an emphasis on quality and productivity, intensive socialization, slow evaluation and promotion, commitment to the worker, and consensus seeking.

Job characteristics theory A model of job enrichment in which the presence of five job characteristics — skill variety, task identity, task significance, autonomy, and feedback — leads to three critical psychological states that in turn result in positive work-related outcomes.

Job description A concise summary description of the duties performed by an employee.

Job diagnostic survey A series of questions designed to determine the extent to which workers view their jobs as possessing the five characteristics of job characteristics theory.

Job enlargement Expansion of a worker's job to include more and varied tasks at the same level; the horizontal expansion of a job.

Job enrichment Efforts to make jobs more satisfying by providing the workers that perform them with greater autonomy and decision-making responsibility; the vertical expansion of a job.

Job maturity The component of subordinate maturity that is defined in terms of subordinates' technical knowledge and job-related skills.

Job rotation Systematically shifting workers from one job to another with the goal of increasing motivation and interest.

Job satisfaction An individual's attitude toward his or her job. One of the more widely studied aspects of the field of organizational behavior.

Laboratory experiment A type of OB research in which the investigator creates an artificial setting in which variables can be tightly controlled and manipulated.

Last-chance meeting A technique for countering groupthink in which a meeting is held where members are encouraged to voice any nagging doubts or hesitations about a decision.

Law of attraction A finding that the greater the proportion of similar attitudes that two people share, the greater the degree of interpersonal attraction.

Law of Effect A law that proposes that behavior that produces pleasant outcomes is more likely to recur, whereas behavior that produces unpleasant outcomes is less likely to recur.

Leader–member relations A factor in the contingency model referring to the degree of confidence, trust, and respect that the leader obtains from the group members.

Leadership The process through which leaders influence the attitudes, behavior, and values of others.

Leadership neutralizer Individual, task, or organizational characteristics that may prevent the leader from being effective.

Leadership substitute Individual, task, or organizational characteristics that may make leadership superfluous.

Learning A fairly permanent change in behavior that occurs as a result of experience.

Least preferred coworker (LPC) A questionnaire that measures how respondents characterize their feelings about a person with whom they work least effectively. A high LPC score (favoring the least preferred coworker) is considered to indicate a relationship-oriented individual, while a low LPC score is considered to indicate a task-oriented individual.

Legitimate power   Individual power based on the belief that the individual has a legitimate right to exert control over others.

Leniency error   The tendency to rate all ratees favorably.

Liaison   An individual in an organization who serves as a communication link between groups but is not a member of either group.

Locus of control   The extent to which a person believes that his or her behavior has a direct impact on the consequences of that behavior. People with an internal locus of control believe they control their lives themselves. People with an external locus of control view their lives as guided by external factors.

Long-linked technology   Sequential, or serially linked, operations.

Long-run process production   A technology in which the entire manufacturing process is continuous and mechanized.

Mach scale   An attitude scale that measures the extent to which individuals agree with Machiavelli's views (and are thus assumed to be domineering and manipulative).

Management-by-objectives (MBO)   A process in which superiors and their subordinates set goals for a specified time period, at the end of which they meet again to assess the subordinate's performance in terms of the previously designated goals.

Mass production   A technology based on long runs of standardized parts or products.

Mass psychogenic illness   Group outbreaks of physical illness that are psychological in origin and are suspected to be triggered by work-related stress.

Matrix design   A form of organization design in which a product form is superimposed on a functional form, creating a dual system of authority.

Maximize   The attempt to find the best or optimal solution to a problem.

Mechanistic or statistical prediction   An approach to predicting behavior that employs the mathematical manipulation of data.

Mechanistic organization   An organization characterized by a high degree of formalization and centralization.

Mediating technology   Joins otherwise effective, independent units of an organization or different types of customers.

Medium factor   A factor in attitude change attempts that involves the effects of the channel employed.

Message factor   The specific content and structure of what is transmitted in an attitude change attempt.

Method-bound   A term describing a theory that can be supported only by a particular method.

Moderating variable   A factor influencing the nature of the relationship between the independent and the dependent variables.

Modified workweek   A shortened workweek. The most common form involves working 4 days a week, 10 hours each day (called a 4-40).

Moral involvement   Organizational involvement in which members are committed to the socially beneficial features of the organization.

Moral maturity   Refers to one's stage of ethical judgment. Kohlberg identifies six stages of moral development, grouped into three categories: preconventional level, conventional level, and principled level.

Motivator factors   In two-factor theory, the group of variables that pertains to the content of the job (e.g., career advancement, degree of responsibility, and feelings of achievement).

Need for achievement   The need to excel or to accomplish a goal or task more efficiently than others.

Need for affiliation   The need for human companionship.

Need for power   The need to control or have an impact on others.

Negative reinforcement   The use of stimuli to weaken undesired responses, leading to their elimination.

Networks   Patterns of relationships.

Nominal group technique (NGT)   A technique for improving group decision making in which a small group of individuals presents and discusses its ideas before privately voting on its preferred course of action. The group's decision is derived by pooling the votes into a single preferred alternative.

Noncomplementary transaction In transactional analysis, a relationship between two people that is unexpected or unpredictable.

Nonprogrammed decision A decision made about a unique, complex situation for which there is no pre-established course of action.

Nonverbal communication The transmission of information through facial expressions, eye contact, body language, and the use of physical objects and space.

Nonverbal cues Messages sent with facial expressions, posture, shifts of tone or pitch of voice, and eye and head movements.

Normative power Organizational power that relies on its members' sense of affiliation with the organization and its values.

Norming The third stage of group development, in which group cohesiveness develops.

Norms Written or unwritten rules of conduct that guide group members' behavior.

OB Mod The application of operant conditioning principles to individuals in organizational settings, usually aimed at increasing desired behaviors through the use of positive reinforcement.

Observational learning The learning that occurs when an individual witnesses the behavior of another and vicariously experiences the outcomes of the other person's actions.

One-group pretest–post-test design A pre-experimental evalua-

tion design that provides a baseline comparison measurement by testing before and after a program, but does not control many confounding variables, i.e., other change-producing events or the testing process itself.

Open group A group that frequently changes its membership.

Open system A system that has some degree of interaction with its external environment. All organizations are open systems, though they vary in degree of environmental interaction.

Operant conditioning A form of learning in which behaviors that produce positive outcomes or eliminate negative ones are acquired or strengthened.

Organic organization An organization characterized by a relatively low degree of formalization and centralization.

Organizational behavior (OB) The study of human behavior within an organizational setting. OB borrows many concepts and methods from such fields as psychology, sociology, and cultural anthropology to explore (1) individual perceptions and values, (2) interpersonal and work-group processes, and (3) organizational and environmental forces.

Organizational culture The system of values, beliefs, and norms that exists in any organization and that is transmitted to new employees.

Organizational decision making Decisions that pertain to the problems and practices of organizations.

Organizational decline Cutbacks in the size of an organization's profits, budget, work force, or clients.

Organizational development (OD) The process of introducing and managing changes in organizational settings.

Organizational form In the population ecology perspective, a configuration of an organization's goals, human resources, products, and technology that will be acceptable to the environment.

Organizational politics Activities used to acquire, develop, and use power to attain one's preferred (and usually selfish) outcome in situations in which there is uncertainty or disagreement.

Organizational theory A field of study focusing on the organization (and attributes such as goals, technology, and culture) as a unit of analysis.

Paired comparison A technique for evaluating performance that entails comparing employees two at a time.

Partial reinforcement A situation in which a response is rewarded in a noncontinuous or variable manner. Behavior acquired under partial reinforcement is usually more resistant to extinction than that acquired under continuous reinforcement.

Participative leadership In path–goal theory, a leader behavior in which the leader shares authority and responsibility with subordinates, encouraging their participation in decision making and on matters affecting their jobs.

Path–goal theory A theory based on the expectancy model of motivation suggesting that leaders can affect the satisfaction and performance of subordinates by basing rewards on the accomplishment of performance goals and by clarifying the path to these goals.

Perceived role The set of behaviors that an individual believes he or she is expected to perform.

Perception The process by which the individual receives and interprets information about the environment.

Perceptual distortion The act of altering perception to avoid an unpleasant reality. Forms include denying events, modifying or distorting reality, seeing only what we want to see, and accepting illusions.

Performing The fourth and final stage of group development, in which the group directs its energies toward performance of valued goals.

Personal decision making Decisions that directly affect an individual rather than others.

Personal space zones Culturally defined distances that exist between people.

Personality The set of traits and characteristics that form a pattern distinguishing one person from all others.

Personality inventories A widely used method of assessing personality characteristics that asks respondents to indicate whether statements are applicable to themselves.

Population ecology perspective A view of how organizations relate to their environment contending that the success of an organization depends on its finding a niche in a highly competitive surrounding.

Porter–Lawler model A conceptual framework that attempts to integrate the various approaches to motivation.

Position power A factor in the contingency model referring to the power inherent in a position.

Positive reinforcement The use of stimuli to strengthen desired responses, leading to their recurrence.

Power The ability of a person or group to change the attitudes or behavior of others.

Pre-experimental design A form of evaluation research in which observations are taken after the occurrence of a program. This design omits any baseline comparison measurement and does not control variables.

Prepotency In Maslow's hierarchy of needs, the capacity of lower-order needs to assert themselves over higher-order needs.

Pretest–post-test control group design An experimental evaluation design that adds a control group to the one-group pre-test–post-test design and assigns subjects to either group by a random procedure.

Process theories Theories that focus on the process by which rewards control behavior. Examples are expectancy, equity, and reinforcement theories.

Product form A basic type of organization design that groups personnel and activities according to a product line.

Programmed decision A fairly routine decision that can be made according to pre-established procedures.

Progressive discipline The use of a sequence of penalties for infractions of rules, in which each penalty is more severe than the preceding one.

Projection The tendency to ascribe our emotions and attributes to others; a defense mechanism.

Projective techniques Tests that are based on the idea that people will provide highly individualistic responses to ambiguous stimuli. Projective techniques include the Rorschach test, story-telling, and sentence completions.

Proxemics The study of physical space as a form of nonverbal communication.

Psychological maturity A component of subordinate maturity that is defined in terms of the subordinate's self-confidence, and willingness and ability to take on responsibility.

Punishment The presentation of an unpleasant event that follows an undesirable behavior. It is a negative reinforcer that attempts to eliminate the undesired behavior.

Quality circle Small groups of workers who volunteer to meet regularly to identify, analyze, and solve quality and related problems pertaining to their work.

Quality of work life (QWL) An organizational development approach that seeks to enhance the work climate of an organization. QWL programs are assumed to improve both productivity and employees' psychological experiences at work.

Quasi-experimental design A form of evaluation research in which a control group does not exist, but inferences are cautiously drawn from patterns in available data.

Random assignment A situation afforded by laboratory experiments, in which individuals have an equal likelihood of being placed in an experimental group or a comparison group.

Ratings A device for assessing personality in which respondents rate themselves on scales either with adjectives as endpoints or with specific definitions for each point in the scale.

Ratio schedule A schedule that reinforces behavior on the basis of the number of times a behavior is performed.

Rational–economic model A model that assumes that decision making is and should be a rational process consisting of a sequence of steps that enhance the probability of attaining a desired goal. *See also* Classical decision theory.

Reactivity In evaluation research, a problem occurring when the employees respond to the testing process itself.

Referent power Individual power based on a high level of admiration or respect for the power holder.

Refreezing The third phase of Lewin's model of change, in which newly created systems or behaviors become part of ongoing organizational processes.

Reinforcement theory A theory using operant conditioning principles that views present behavior as a function of the consequences of past behavior.

Relay Assembly Room study One of the Hawthorne studies, which first suggested that increased productivity could be partially attributed to the employees' awareness that they are being observed (the Hawthorne effect).

Representativeness heuristic An assessment made on the basis of the similarity between the specific attributes of a given event or object and the attributes of a class of such events or objects.

Resistance to extinction The persistence of a behavior in the absence of reinforcement.

Resource dependence model A view of how organizations relate to their environment contending that the success of an organization is a function of how well it manages its environment.

Retention A stage in the population ecology perspective in which certain successful organizational forms are institutionalized.

Reward power Individual power based on the extent to which one person controls rewards valued by another. The opposite of coercive power.

Risky shift The tendency for groups to make riskier decisions than individuals.

Role The set of expected behaviors associated with an individual's position in a group.

Role ambiguity A situation occurring when an individual is uncertain about how he or she is expected to behave in a role.

Role conflict A situation occurring when an individual receives conflicting messages regarding appropriate role behavior.

Role episode The process by which individuals receive information about their role and adjust their behavior accordingly.

Role overload A situation occurring when too many activities are expected of an employee given the time available and ability level of the employee.

Rorschach test A projective technique for assessing personality consisting of inkblots that the respondent describes in terms of what they look like to him or her.

Rumors Unverified beliefs transmitted through informal channels within an organization.

Sandwich approach A method of conducting feedback interviews in which positive points of the employee's performance are followed by discussion of negative aspects, and ending on a positive note.

Satisfice A situation in which a decision maker considers alternatives only until one arises that is minimally acceptable and then looks no further.

Scientific management One of the first approaches to managing worker behavior, developed by Frederick W. Taylor, an engineer. Scientific management sought to improve job performance by (1) measuring productivity, (2) emphasizing efficiency in job procedures, and (3) instituting incentive pay schemes.

Selection A stage in the population ecology perspective in which only organizations that possess the needed form survive, and those that do not, fail.

Selective perception The tendency to be influenced by our own interests.

Self-fulfilling prophecy (SFP) A phenomenon in which ratees perform in accordance with a rater's prophecy, or expectations, for them.

Semantic differential scale A method of measuring attitudes that asks for ratings on a scale anchored by a pair of adjectives opposite in meaning.

Sensitivity training An organizational development technique that seeks to enhance employees' understanding of their own behavior and its impact on others. Such enhanced sensitivity is assumed to reduce interpersonal conflict in the organization.

Sentence completion A projective technique for assessing personality in which respondents are asked to supply the endings for a series of incomplete sentences.

Shaping A behavior modification technique in which the individual receives reinforcement for small successive approximations of the desired behavior.

Situational favorableness In the contingency model, the notion of how easy or difficult a situation might be for a leader. Three factors — leader–member relations, task structure, and position power — combine to represent a range of possible situations.

Situational tests A technique involving the direct observation of an individual's behavior in a test situation designed to provide information about personality.

Social exchange theory A theory suggesting that in relationships people continually monitor the difference between rewards and costs, and judge the outcomes against two standards: a comparison level and a comparison level of alternatives.

Social facilitation effect The tendency for the presence of others to enhance an individual's performance.

Social inhibition effect The tendency for the presence of others to impair an individual's performance.

Social learning theory An approach to motivation emphasizing the importance of modeling and self-regulatory processes in learning.

Social loafing The tendency for group members to exert less individual effort on a task the larger the group size.

Sociofugal areas Arrangements of physical space that drive people away from each other.

Sociopetal areas Arrangements of physical space that bring people together.

Sociotechnical system The view that every organization is simultaneously a technical and a social system and that attempts to change either system must take into account their interrelatedness.

Solomon four-group design An experimental evaluation design that attempts to eliminate reactivity to being pretested by adding to the pretest–post-test control group design two groups, one of which is a control group, that are only post-tested.

Source factor A factor involved in attitude change that refers to the individual characteristics of the presenter of an attitude change attempt.

Span of control The number of people who report to a given supervisor.

Status The social ranking or worth accorded to an individual because of the position he or she occupies in a group.

Status incongruence A situation in which all dimensions of an individual's status are not congruent.

Stereotypes Beliefs that all members of a group (e.g., a racial, ethnic, religious, or occupational group) share the same traits and behaviors.

Storming The second stage of group development, in which members wrestle with the division of power and status.

Story-telling A projective technique for assessing personality in which respondents supply stories about pictures they are shown. *See also* Thematic Apperception Test

Strategy A plan of action formulated by top-level management to deal with the future.

Stress Physical and psychological reactions experienced by an individual when confronted with a threatening or excessively demanding situation (such as extreme conflict).

Strokes Positive reactions from others, including praise and recognition. In transactional analysis, the giving and getting of strokes is seen as motivating much of the social interplay of people in organizations.

Structural dimensions An organization's internal characteristics, such as degree of specialization, hierarchy, and decentralization.

Subjective probabilities Estimates of the likelihood that one event will follow another (e.g., that performance will lead to a given outcome).

Subliminal influences Factors influencing perceptions that occur below the threshold of awareness.

Subordinate maturity The critical situational attribute in the Hersey–Blanchard model. It consists of the job maturity and psychological maturity of the subordinate for a given task.

Supportive leadership In path–goal theory, a leader behavior that entails being sensitive to and supportive of group members' needs.

Survey A type of OB research in which a set of written or oral questions is designed to collect personal responses about a topic of interest to the investigator.

Survey feedback An organizational development technique in which questionnaires are used to obtain information on issues of concern, and the results are summarized and returned to employees for consideration and interpretation.

Symbolism Includes rituals and ceremonies. Symbols communicate values, legitimize practices, and help to socialize members and build loyalty.

Tall structure Describes an organization with more levels of authority and smaller spans of control.

Task orientation A style of leadership referring to the extent to which a leader shows concern for getting a job done and helps steer the group to meet its goals.

Task structure A factor in the contingency model referring to the degree to which a job can be clearly specified.

Team building An organizational development program designed to help existing work groups or newly formed special groups improve performance by tackling obstacles and problems.

Technology The knowledge, tools, and techniques used by organizations in performing their work.

Territory A specific physical location toward which an individual has a proprietary attitude.

Thematic Apperception Test A story-telling device for assessing personality composed of 20 pictures portraying situations of ambiguous meaning. The respondent constructs stories that are analyzed for recurrent themes.

Theory Z A management approach developed by William Ouchi that incorporates Japanese management principles.

Time management A strategy for coping with job-related stress through effective self-management.

Time-series design A quasi-experimental research design that allows repeated testing before and after a program.

Transactional analysis Originally a psychotherapeutic device, a set of concepts used in organizations to teach people how to communicate more effectively. In each two-person interaction, the participants are viewed as acting out of three ego states: Parent, Adult, or Child, and such transactions are termed either complementary or noncomplementary.

Transformational leadership A leadership style that implies reshaping the entire strategy of an organization.

Two-factor theory Herzberg's theory of job satisfaction contending that satisfaction and dissatisfaction stem from different groups of variables, termed motivator and hygiene factors.

Type A personality A personality type characterized by impatience, competitiveness, and the drive to succeed.

Type B personality A personality type characterized by a relaxed, easygoing, noncompetitive attitude toward work and life.

Unconditioned response In classical conditioning, a reflexive response evoked by the occurrence of an unconditioned stimulus.

Unconditioned stimulus In classical conditioning, a stimulus that has the ability to evoke a natural reflexive response (an unconditioned response).

Unfreezing The first phase in Lewin's model of change, in which people become aware of the need for change.

Unit production A technology in which products are custom-made in response to specific customer orders.

Unity of command A concept maintaining that employees are accountable to and take orders from only one superior.

Unobtrusive measure A research approach that does not disturb or interfere with the subject's usual behavior.

Upward communication Communication that flows from lower to higher levels within an organization.

Utilitarian power Organizational power that relies on contingent incentives to extract compliance from members.

Valence The value a person places on rewards that he or she expects to receive.

Values Preferences of an organization's members from among activities and outcomes.

Variable interval schedule A schedule in which a reward is applied after a variable amount of time has passed since the last reward was given.

Variable ratio schedule A schedule in which a reward is applied after a variable number of responses are performed.

Variable schedule A schedule for reinforcement in which the amount of time or number of responses performed varies.

Variation A stage in the population ecology perspective referring to the development of organizations with unique attributes.

Verification Determining the truth or falsehood of a hypothesis by gathering data to test whether the prediction holds.

Vertical dyad linkage model A model stressing the importance of individual relationships between leader and subordinates. Each relationship is termed a vertical dyad.

Vertical integration A situation that occurs when one organization acquires another with the goal of controlling forces that affect its production process.

Vroom–Yetton model A model that focuses on selecting the ap-propriate leadership style for deci-sion making, based on situational considerations. The model pro-poses five styles: two are auto-cratic (AI and AII), two are con-sultative (CI and CII), and one is oriented to a group decision (GI).

Wellness program A proactive approach to health management that focuses on prevention of illness.

Work ethic A belief in the dig-nity of all work, especially the belief that hard work brings suc-cess.

Name Index

Abelson, R.P., 137
Abraham, L.M., 137
Adams, J. Stacy, 36, 37, 63, 189, 192, 202
Adizes, Ichak, 579
Adkins, C., 575
Adler, N.J., 576
Adorno, T., 103
Alderfer, C.P., 180, 201
Aldrich, H.E., 545
Aliotti, N.C., 374
Allen, L.A., 102, 433
Allen, R.W., 299
Altman, S., 28
Alvares, K.M., 205, 265
Amend, Patricia, 221
Andresky, Jill, 256
Andrews, Edmund L., 68
Andrisani, P.J., 103
Apple, W., 101
Argyris, C., 524
Aristos, 10
Arndt, Michael, 503
Arnold, H.J., 137
Arolio, B.J., 338
Aronoff, C.E., 472, 485, 496, 497
Aronson, E., 116, 137, 336
Arvey, R.D., 137, 258, 266
Asch, Solomon E., 75, 102, 286, 299
Ash, Mary Kay, 155
Asimov, Isaac, 434
Atkin, R.S., 265
Atkinson, J.W., 201

Ball, George, 349
Bamforth, K.W., 407, 524
Bammer, K., 461
Bandura, A., 169, 202
Barbere, Lawrence, 609
Bares, Jack A., 7
Barnes-Farrell, J., 265
Baron, R.M., 103
Barrett, D., 496
Barron, Robert, 434, 498
Bartocci, Barbara, 580
Bartol, K.M., 266
Basaszewski, J., 607
Basen, J.A., 265
Baskin, O.W., 472, 485, 496, 497
Bass, Bernard M., 302, 336, 338

Bateman, T.S., 63
Bauer, R., 137
Bauers, Sandy, 450
Baum, Laurie, 22
Bavelas, A., 496
Beall, Donald R., 528
Beatty, J.R., 264
Beatty, R.W., 264
Beer, M., 607
Bekkers, F., 433
Bell, C.H., 233, 588, 593, 607
Bell, N.E., 137
Bennis, W.G., 601, 607
Benson, H., 461
Bentham, Jeremy, 174, 175
Bentley, Randy, 33
Berdie, R.F., 201
Berg, P.O., 598, 599, 600, 607
Berkowitz, L., 137, 202, 407
Bernardin, H. John, 246, 250, 265
Berne, Eric, 480, 497
Berry, R.C., 375
Bhagat, R.S., 138
Bierce, Ambrose, 498
Billingsley, K.R., 596, 607
Black, C.H., 375
Blades, J., 336
Blair, J.D., 398, 407
Blake, Robert R., 310, 311, 312, 336, 607
Blanchard, K.H., 317, 318, 330, 337
Blau, G.J., 136, 137
Blau, P.M., 524
Block, P., 299
Blood, Milton R., 222, 234
Blum, M.L., 121, 137
Boehm, V., 259, 266
Borman, W., 265
Bortner, R.W., 438
Bouchard, T.J., 137
Bowan, M.L., 265
Bowen, D.D., 497
Bowen, M.G., 374
Boyatzis, R.E., 177, 201
Bramel, D., 30
Bray, Rosemary L., 378
Brayfield, A.H., 137
Breaugh, J.A., 137
Brett, J.M., 137
Bridwell, L.G., 201

Brief, A., 460
Briggs, Katherine C., 72, 90, 103
Briggs-Myers, Isabel, 72
Brittain, J., 545
Brockner, J., 407
Broome, Dean, 22
Brown, H.A., 266
Brown, Paul B., 160
Brugholi, G.A., 265
Brunelle, E.A., 375
Bryne, D., 406
Buchanan, R.D., 170
Buck, R., 101
Buetow, Richard, 206
Burger, Michael, 483
Burke, R.J., 265
Burns, T., 536, 545
Buros, O.K., 102
Burtt, H.E., 138
Busch, August A., III, 72
Bush, George, 273, 423
Buss, D., 138
Busse, W.E., 265
Butterfield, D.A., 266
Byars, L., 496
Byham, W.C., 265
Byrne, John A., 4, 107, 292

Calley, William, 288
Campbell, D.T., 63, 607
Campbell, E.Q., 103
Campbell, J.P., 201, 202
Campion, J.E., 265
Candee, D., 104
Caplan, R.D., 460
Carli, L.L., 137
Carlsmith, J.M., 102, 116, 137
Carrell, M.R., 202
Carrico, William, 442
Carrol, S.J., 252, 265
Carroll, A.B., 103
Carroll, S., 234
Cartwright, D., 299
Case, E.L., 337
Cashman, J.F., 337
Cassel, J., 460
Castro, Fidel, 351
Cavanagh, Gerald F., 284, 285, 299
Chandler, Alfred D., Jr., 540, 541, 546

Chapman, Charles, 100
Cherner, Paul, 256
Cherns, A., 234, 607
Cherrington, O., 89, 103
Child, John, 509, 524, 575
Chollar, S., 101
Chouinard, Yvon, 462, 463
Chung, K.H., 489, 497, 561, 575
Christie, R., 282, 299
Clark, R.A., 201
Clausen, J.A., 137
Clemens, John, 3
Clines, Francis X., 535
Clore, G.L., 406
Coch, L., 590, 607
Cohen, A.R., 225, 226, 234
Cohen, B.M., 265, 461
Cohen, Daniel, 409
Cohen, D.S., 524
Cohen, S.L., 398, 407
Cohon, George A., 611, 613
Colarelli, S.M., 137
Cole, R., 407
Coleman, J.S., 103
Coleman, Michael, 503
Colligan, M., 460, 461
Confucius, 204
Conlon, E.J., 265, 374
Connolly, T., 233
Cook, T.D., 607
Coolidge, Calvin, 470
Cooper, C.L., 460
Corry, Charles, 269
Cosby, Bill, 273
Costello, T.W., 102
Cox, Robert G., 3
Craib, D., 497
Cranny, C.J., 250, 265
Crawford, Karen, 312
Cronbach, L.J., 102
Crow, Trammel, 72
Crowne, D.P., 102
Crump, C., 461
Cukor, George, 307
Cummings, Larry L., 6, 30, 201
Cummings, T.G., 460
Cunningham, D.A., 460
Cunningham, John F., 409, 410
Curtis, Rebecca, 82
Cutler, R.L., 102

Daft, Richard L., 508, 524, 531, 533, 545,
    585, 607
Dale, E., 396, 407
Dalkey, N., 374
Dalton, D.R., 138
Dalton, M., 433
Dampier, W.C., 63
Daniell, Robert, F., 511
Danserau, F., 337
Darwin, Charles, 70, 101
D'Aveni, R., 607
David, L.E., 607
David, R.V., 137
Da Vinci, Leonardo, 85
Davis, K.E., 488, 497
Davis, L.E., 234
Davis, S.M., 516, 524
Davis-Blake, A., 137
Dawes, R.M., 374

Deci, E.L., 157, 170
DeGeorge, Richard T., 584
DeJung, J.E., 264
Delbecq, A.L., 360, 374
DeNisi, A.S., 264, 337, 575
Dessler, G., 337
DeVries, David, 246
DeVries, Manfred F.R. Kets, 554
Dickson, P., 234
Dickson, W.J., 30, 407
Dienesch, R.M., 337
Dillon, L.S., 575
DiNatale, Antonio, 11
Dion, K.L., 407
Dittrich, J.E., 202
Doe, Susan Stites, 63, 431
Domanick, Joe, 416
Dowling, W.F., 202
Downey, H.K., 337
Downs, C.W., 265
Drew, Richard G., 549
Drucker, Peter, 234, 502
Dubois, P.H., 265
DuBrin, Andrew J., 299, 364, 375, 445,
    461, 489, 497, 500, 607
Duchon, D., 337
Duffy, Susan, 584
Dumaine, Brian, 500
Duncan, Robert B., 501, 524, 528, 529,
    530, 545
Dunham, R.B., 137
Dunn, Keith, 471
Dunnette, M.D., 103, 201, 202, 265, 373
Durand, D.E., 201
Durocher, Leo, 268
Dvorkin, B.R., 170

Eagley, A.H., 137
Earley, P.C., 233
Eason, Henry, 117
Eden, D., 216, 234
Eichmann, Adolf, 288
Ekegren, G., 233
Ekman, P., 70, 101
Elbing, A., 373
Elder, G.H., Jr., 201
Ellis, Roy, 535
Ellsworth, P.C., 102
Engel, B.T., 170
England, G.W., 137, 575
Epicurus, 175
Erez, M., 265
Esposito, J.P., 103
Esrig, F., 265
Estrin, Judith, 442
Etzioni, A., 274, 275, 276, 277, 299
Evans, Martin G., 316, 337
Ewen, R.B., 138

Faber, Sharon, 188
Faden, J.A., 202
Falkland, Lord, 340
Farmanfarmaian, Roxane, 587
Farmer, R.N., 575
Farr, J.L., 264
Faucheux, C., 475, 496
Fay, C.H., 265
Fayol, Henri, 478, 496
Fazio, R.H., 137
Fein, M., 234

Feldman, D.C., 137
Feldman, J., 30
Ferris, G.R., 63, 337
Feshback, S., 102
Festinger, Leon, 115, 116, 137, 433
Fiedler, Fred, 305, 311, 312, 314, 315,
    316, 324, 336, 337, 576
Field, R.H., 337
Filley, A.C., 219, 234
Fishbein, M., 137
Fisher, C.D., 265
Fishkin, Harris, 450
Fisk, Jim, 434, 498
Fleishman, E.A., 138, 336
Fletcher, G.J., 30
Flynn, W., 104
Fode, K., 234
Forbes, Malcolm, 268
Ford, D.L., 266
Ford, Henry, II, 503
Freedman, S., 202
French, John, 41, 63, 271, 276, 299, 460,
    590, 607
French, W.L., 588, 593, 607
Frenkel-Brunswik, E., 103
Freud, Sigmund, 175, 201, 480
Fribush, Barry, 160
Friedman, A., 202
Friedman, M., 438, 460
Friend, R., 30
Friesen, W.V., 70, 101
Froggatt, Jack, 477
Frost, Robert, 300
Fry, Arthur L., 549
Fry, L.W., 30
Fudge, Kim, 205

Gadon, H., 225, 226, 234
Gadsby, Polly, 219
Galbraith, John Kenneth, 201, 433, 534
Galen, Michele, 51
Galler, V., 101
Galvin, Bob, 205
Gamboa, V., 170
Gandhi, Mahatma, 304
Ganz, R.L., 103
Garcia, J.E., 336
Garfield, Charles A., 301, 302
Garmezy, N., 169
Garrett, J., 103
Gaugler, B., 265
Gebhardt, D., 461
Geis, F.L., 282, 299
Gemmel, G.R., 299
George, Claude, S., 10, 30
Gergen, K., 137
Gerwitz, J., 104
Getman, J.G., 126, 138
Getty, John Paul, 526
Ghiselli, E.E., 104, 336, 558, 559, 575
Giannantonio, C.M., 266
Gibb, C., 336
Gibran, Kahlil, 236
Gill, Mark Stuart, 206
Gobdel, B.C., 338
Goldberg, S.B., 126, 138
Golden, Vincent P., 292
Goldstein, A.P., 170, 202
Goldwater, Barry, 89
Goleman, Daniel, 387

Golembiewski, R.T., 234, 596, 607
Goltz, S., 374
Goodman, P.S., 202
Gorbachev, M., 610
Gordon, Judith, 522
Gordon, M.E., 63
Goshen, C., 497
Gowan, J.C., 375
Grady, J., 407
Graeff, C.L., 337
Graen, George, 265, 321, 322, 337
Gray, M.A., 561, 575
Green, J.A., 407
Green, S., 337
Greenberg, J., 63, 103
Greiner, Larry, E., 581, 582, 607
Greller, M.M., 265
Griffeth, R.W., 202, 338, 461, 575
Griffin, R., 404, 522
Gross, B.M., 390, 406
Guetzkow, H., 299
Guion, R.M., 138, 375
Gumbel, Peter, 535
Gupta, Udayan, 442
Gustafson, D.H., 374
Gutenberg, Johannes, 562

Hackett, E., 407
Hackett, R., 138
Hackman, J. Richard, 207, 208, 222, 223,
    224, 225, 234, 392, 407, 536, 545
Haga, W.J., 337
Haire, M., 557, 559, 575
Hakel, M.D., 71, 101
Halcrow, Allan, 34
Hall, D.T., 201
Hall, Edward T., 484, 497
Hamner, E.P., 154, 156, 170
Hamner, W.C., 126, 138, 154, 156, 170
Hanada, M., 407
Hand, H.H., 461
Haney, W.V., 486, 497
Hardy, George, 464
Hare, P.A., 406
Harkins, S., 386, 406
Harris, E.F., 138, 336
Harris, P.R., 576
Harris, Thomas, 480, 497
Hartley, E.L., 299
Hatfield, J., 202
Hawken, Paul, 463
Hawkins, B.L., 496
Hawkins, Kathleen L., 396, 407
Henderson, A., 524
Heider, Fritz, 78, 102, 136
Heisler, W.J., 299
Hellriegel, D., 103
Hendrix, W.H., 460
Heneman, H.G., II, 265
Herman, J.B., 126, 138
Herrick, N., 138
Hersey, P., 317, 318, 330, 337
Hershey, R., 497
Herzberg, Fred, 4, 180, 181, 182, 183,
    184, 185, 193, 194, 201, 220, 221,
    234
Hess, T., 407
Hickey, C.O., 299
Hills, Carla A., 423
Hinkin, T., 299

Hinrichs, J.R., 265
Hippocrates, 72
Hissink, Bob, 612
Hitler, Adolf, 88, 273
Hobson, L.J., 103
Hodgetts, Valenzi, 28
Hoeffel, Bruce, 117
Hoerr, John, 174, 183, 398
Hoffer, Eric, 268
Hoffman, Abbie, 106
Hofstede, Geert, 559, 560, 575
Holden, C., 102
Holden, Ted, 565
Holland, W.E., 433
Hollenback, J., 202, 233
Holmes, T.H., 439, 440, 460
Hom, P.W., 337, 338, 575
Honzik, M.P., 102
Horning, R.W., 460
Horstman, Sanford, 33
House, Robert J., 219, 234, 316, 337, 338
Howard, A., 265
Howard, G.S., 596, 607
Howard, J.H., 460
Howell, J.M., 338
Huberman, John, 22
Huck, J.R., 259, 266
Huffman, P.E., 103
Hughes, J.L., 104
Hughes, L., 460
Hulin, Charles L., 137, 222, 234
Hunt, J.G., 336, 337, 338
Hunter, J.E., 104
Hurwitz, J.V., 398, 407
Huseman, R., 202
Hyatt, Joshua, 312, 472

Iacocca, Lee, 72
Ilgen, D.R., 265
Imada, A.S., 70, 101
Ingrassia, Paul, 584
Ivancevich, John M., 234, 406, 437, 444,
    455, 460, 461

Jacobson, L., 214, 216, 234
Jago, A.G., 321, 337
James, William, 175, 201
Janis, Irving L., 111, 136, 350, 351, 352,
    374
Jay, Anthony, 396, 407
Jenkins, C.D., 439, 460
Jerdee, T.H., 266
Jermier, John M., 325, 338
Jerrel, S., 353
Jethro, 501
Jobs, Steven, 72
Johns, Gary, 138, 473, 496
Johnson, G., 104
Johnson, H., 103
Johnson, Lyndon B., 349
Johnston, W.B., 234
Johst, Hanns, 548
Jones, H. Bradley, 256
Jones, R.A., 234
Jordan, P.C., 170
Joss, Eric H., 51
Joyce, Robert D., 455
Joyce, W.F., 524
Jung, Carl Gustav, 90

Kahn, R.L., 389, 460
Kahneman, Daniel, 348, 374
Kamata, S., 575
Kanfer, F.H., 170
Kanter, Rosabeth Moss, 45
Kaplan, J., 264
Karoly, P., 170
Karren, R.J., 233
Kasl, S.V., 41, 63
Katerberg, R.D., 136, 137, 337
Katz, D., 389
Katz, M., 265
Kaufman, R.S., 234
Kavanaugh, M.J., 264
Kaye, D., 111, 136
Keller, R.T., 433
Kelley, H.H., 383, 406
Kelman, H.C., 270, 276, 299
Kemelgor, Bruce, 30, 169, 200, 230, 262,
    264, 297, 329, 433, 494, 544, 575,
    607
Kendall, L., 137, 265
Kennedy, Allan A., 3
Kennedy, John F., 351, 408
Kennedy, Robert, 351
Keon, T.L., 537, 545
Kerr, C., 607
Kerr, Steven, 219, 234, 264, 325, 336,
    338, 496
Kiechel, Walter, III, 534
Kilmann, Ralph, 353, 550, 552, 575
Kilminster, Joe, 467
Kimble, G.A., 169
King, A.S., 216, 234
King, B.T., 137
Kipnis, David, 283, 284, 299
Kirkland, Lane, 172
Kirschner, P., 111, 136
Klasson, C.R., 258, 266
Klein, H., 233
Kleinke, C.L., 102
Kleinmuntz, B., 102
Knapp, M.L., 102
Koenig, R., 102
Kogan, N., 374
Kohlberg, Lawrence, 91, 92, 103, 104
Kohn, A., 30
Kohn, D.A., 201
Kondrasuk, J., 234
Konrad, Walecia, 353
Koplin, C.A., 202
Koplow, Harold, 409, 410
Korman, A.K., 264
Kornhauser, A., 461
Koutilya, 282
Krachhardt, D.M., 138
Krauss, R.E., 101
Kraut, R.M., 101
Kreitner, R., 170, 202, 461
Kroes, W.M., 460
Kroc, Ray, 610
Kunin, T., 137
Kurtines, W., 104
Kushner, Malcolm, 483

La Don, J., 460
LaFong, C., 102
Lakien, A., 461
Lambert, W.W., 576
Lamm, H., 374

Landy, F.J., 137, 264, 309
Langer, E.J., 102
LaNoue, Joan, 82
Lappin, M., 264, 265
Larson, L.L., 336, 337, 338
Latane, B., 386, 406
Latham, D.R., 407
Latham, Gary, 233, 249, 250, 259, 265, 266
Lawler, Edward E., III, 128, 137, 138, 193, 201, 202, 206, 207, 208, 209, 210, 211, 233, 234, 264, 497, 536, 545
Lawrence, P., 497, 516, 524, 537, 538, 546, 607
Lazarsfeld, Paul F., 20, 30
Lazer, R.I., 240, 264
Leavitt, H.J., 496, 589
Le Diberder, Alain, 423
Leefeldt, E., 233
Leeper, R., 69, 101
Lefcourt, H.M., 103
Lego, Paul, 477
Lehman, H.C., 374
Leigh, Jason, 72
Leister, A.F., 336
Lenin, N., 408
Leventhal, H., 136
Levin, I., 138
Levine, R., 557, 575
Levinson, D., 103
Levitan, S.A., 234
Lewin, Kurt, 306, 336, 588, 607
Lickona, T., 91
Liden, R.C., 337
Likert, J.G., 524
Likert, Rensis, 109, 136, 406, 509, 510, 511, 524
Lincoln, Abraham, 106, 300, 304
Lincoln, J., 407
Lindzey, G., 336
Lippitt, R., 306, 336
Livingston, J.S., 234
Locke, E.A., 30, 170, 201, 233
Lofquist, L.H., 137
Logan, J.W., 202
Lorenzi, P., 231
Lorsch, J.W., 497, 537, 538, 546
Lott, B.E., 406
Lott, H.J., 406
Lowell, E.L., 201
Lowell, J., 433
Lubben, G.L., 258, 266
Luce, R.D., 433
Lundstrom, W.J., 407
Lupton, D.E., 265
Luthans, Fred, 170, 202, 481, 497, 571
Lyons, H.C., 234

MacArthur, Douglas, 89
Maccoby, E.E., 299
MacCrimmon, K.R., 373
Macfarlane, J.W., 102
Machiavelli, Niccolò, 10, 274, 282–283
MacKenzie, K., 475, 496
MacKenzie, R.A., 461
MacKinney, A.C., 264
MacKinnon, D.W., 102, 374
MacRury, King, 237, 238
Madison, D.L., 299

Magnusson, Paul, 423
Maher, B., 103
Maier, N.R.F., 388, 406
Maler, Mark, 468
Maloney, P.W., 265
Malyshkov, Vladimir, 611, 613
Mandel, Michael J., 528
Maney, Kevin, 613
Mann, F.C., 336
Mannari, H., 546
March, J.G., 347, 374
Marcus, E.H., 497
Margolis, B.L., 460
Mark, Reuben, 269
Markerich, Sam, 470
Marks, M., 407
Marlowe, D., 102, 137
Marples, D.L., 304, 336
Marrow, A.J., 460
Marsh, R.M., 546
Martin, J.G., 103
Marting, B., 497
Martinko, Mark J., 481, 497
Martocchio, J., 460
Marx, Karl, 12, 119, 219
Maslow, Abraham H., 4, 32, 178, 179, 180, 184, 185, 193, 194, 201, 277, 380
Matteson, Michael T., 406, 437, 444, 455, 460, 461
Maurer, E.H., 225, 234
Mausner, B., 201, 234
Maxwell, S.E., 596, 607
Mayer, R., 299
McAuliffe, Christa, 465
McBride, K., 407
McClelland, David C., 50, 63, 176, 177, 178, 193, 194, 201, 299, 558, 575
McClelland, John, 442
McConnell, J.V., 102
McCormick, E.J., 265
McDonald, Al, 465
McGinnis, E., 137
McGrath, J.E., 63
McKnight, William L., 550
McLane, J.T., 126, 138
McLean, Alan A., 439, 448, 460, 461
McLuhan, M., 137
McNamara, Robert, 351
McNeil, E.B., 102
McPartland, J., 103
Mee, J.F., 375, 524
Meeker, F.B., 102
Megginson, L.C., 489, 497
Meglino, B., 575
Mehrabian, Albert, 482, 497
Meng-Tse, 300
Mento, A.J., 233
Merrens, M., 103
Miles, E., 202
Miles, Raymond E., 269
Miles, R.H., 299
Milgram, Stanley, 110, 136, 288, 290, 293, 299
Mill, John Stuart, 174, 175, 201
Miller, Danny, 554
Miller, N.E., 170
Mills, J., 116, 137
Milton, O., 103
Minelo, J.M., 103

Miner, J.B., 201, 234, 322–323, 337, 338, 510, 524, 545, 546
Minkow, Barry, 416
Mintzberg, H., 336
Mirtz, John, 117
Mirvis, P.H., 63, 407
Mitchell, J.L., 264
Mitchell, Russell, 550
Mitchell, T.R., 202, 233, 576
Moberg, Dennis, 284, 299
Mobley, W.H., 445, 461
Montana, Joe, 273
Mood, A.M., 103
Moore, Jesse, 467
Moore, L.F., 524
Moore, Michael, 584
Moore, Tina, 67
Moorhead, G., 404, 522
Moran, R.T., 576
Morgan, Michael, 442
Morgan, Susan, 422
Morse, M.C., 138
Morze, Mark, 416
Moscinski, P., 265
Moses, 501
Moses, J.L., 259, 265, 266
Moskowitz, M., 265
Mouton, Jane S., 310, 311, 312, 336, 607
Mowday, R., 202
Muczyk, J.P., 46, 47, 63
Munsterberg, Hugo, 436, 460
Murphy, C.J., 336
Murphy, Kevin, 246
Murray, Henry A., 102, 175, 176, 178, 201
Myers, D.G., 374
Myers-Briggs, Isabel, 72, 90, 103

Nath, R., 353
Naylor, J.C., 121, 137
Nelton, Sharon, 275
Nemeroff, W.F., 266
Nestel, C., 103
Newberry, B.H., 461
Newcomb, T.M., 299
Northcraft, C.F., 374
Nougaim, K.E., 201
Novak, J.F., 225, 234
Nunnally, J.C., 102, 136

Oberle, R.L., 162
Obrist, P.A., 170
O'Connor, E.J., 63
Okie, Francis G., 549
Oldham, Greg, 222, 223, 224, 225, 234
O'Leary, A., 460
Olsen, Kenneth, H., 501
Olson, C., 101
Oppler, S., 265
Orben, Robert, 483
O'Reilly, C.A., 474, 496, 497
Orwell, George, 350
Osburn, R., 336
Osgood, C.E., 136
Osmond, H., 485, 497
Ouchi, W.G., 561, 575
Ovalle, N.K., 460
Owen, David, 578

Palmer, David, 450
Palmore, E., 137

Parks, J., 374
Parnes, S.J., 375
Parsons, H.M., 30
Parsons, T., 524
Paul, W., 234
Pavlov, Ivan, 146, 147
Pearlman, K., 104
Pedalino, E., 170
Pennar, Karen, 528
Penney, James Cash, 552
Perkins, Charles, 173
Persinos, John F., 7
Peters, L.H., 63
Peters, Lawrence J., 548
Peters, T.J., 170, 502, 524, 607
Petre, P., 524
Pettigrew, A., 497
Pfeffer, Jeffrey, 137, 277, 299, 532, 545
Pinder, C.C., 524
Piotrowski, M., 265
Plumez, Jacqueline Hornor, 377
Pondy, L.R., 474, 496
Porras, J.I., 598, 599, 600, 607
Porter, Lyman W., 128, 137, 138, 180,
        193, 201, 202, 299, 445, 461, 497,
        536, 545, 558, 559, 575
Premack, S.L., 137
Preston, P., 496
Price, M., 561, 575
Pritchard, R.D., 202
Proehl, C.W., 234
Pruitt, D.G., 374
Pulakos, E., 265

Quadracci, Harry, 139, 140
Quick, Thomas L., 215
Quinn, R.P., 138, 460

Rabbie, J.M., 433
Rabin, A.I., 102
Rahe, L.O., 439, 440, 460
Raia, A.P., 234
Raiffa, H., 433
Rammizzini, Bernardino, 119, 436, 460
Ramquist, J., 233
Randall, F.D., 375
Randsepp, E., 362, 373, 374
Rath, R., 497
Raven, Bertram H., 271, 276, 299
Ravlin, E., 575
Rayburn, Sam, 376
Rayner, R., 169
Reagan, Ronald, 465
Rechnitzer, P.A., 460
Reed, Jim, 99
Rehder, R.R., 561, 575
Reitan, H.T., 406
Reitz, H.J., 382
Rhodes, S.R., 138, 445, 461
Rice, Berkeley, 246
Richards, H.C., 103
Ricklees, R., 103
Riecken, H.W., 79, 102
Riley, Walter, 312
Rinehart, Diane, 613
Ringelmann, K., 386
Ritchie, J., 606
Rizzo, J.R., 234
Roach, D., 138
Robbins, S.P., 406, 412, 421, 427, 433

Roberts, K.H., 497, 575
Roberts, N.C., 607
Robertson, K.B., 234
Robey, D., 103
Rockefeller, John D., Sr., 526
Roethlisberger, F.J., 30, 407
Rogers, E.M., 478, 496
Rogers, R.A., 478, 496
Rokeach, M., 89, 103
Rorschach, Hermann, 85
Rosen, B., 266
Rosen, H., 138
Rosenman, R., 438, 460
Rosenthal, Robert, 214, 216, 234
Rosow, J.M., 607
Ross, J., 123, 137, 350, 374
Rossiter, Winston G., 578
Rothe, H.F., 137
Rothfeder, Jeffrey, 51
Rotondi, T., 374
Rotter, Julian B., 87, 88, 102, 103
Rubin, I.M., 201
Rucci, Anthony J., 435
Rudolph, E., 497
Rue, L.W., 496
Ruffin, William R., 477
Runkel, P.J., 63
Rusk, Dean, 351
Russell, A., 30

Saari, L.M., 265
St. John, W., 497
Salancik, Gerald R., 202, 532, 545
Sanford, N., 103
Scanlon, Joseph, 210
Schein, Edgar, 550, 551, 552, 575
Schein, V.E., 225, 234, 266
Schiemann, W., 322, 337
Schlesinger, Arthur, Jr., 351
Schmidt, F.L., 104, 170
Schmidt, Stuart M., 283, 284, 299
Schmitt, N., 63, 126, 138, 264, 265
Schneider, J., 201
Schneier, C.E., 253, 264, 265
Schriesheim, C.A., 126, 138, 299, 336,
        337
Schuler, R.S., 460
Schultz, T., 461
Schwartz, R.D., 63
Schwenk, Charles, R., 353
Scott, K.D., 138
Scott, W.E., 460
Scott, W.G., 406
Sears, S.S., 102
Seashore, S.E., 63, 394, 407, 607
Seaverson, Linda, 442
Sechrest, L., 63
Seeman, M., 103
Segal, H.L., 137
Selye, Hans, 436, 460
Semler, Richardo, 341, 342
Shanah, M.E., 299
Shang (Lord), 282
Shani, A.B., 216, 234
Shaw, George Bernard, 268
Shaw, M.E., 374, 406, 407, 496
Sheelen, Donald D., 292
Sheffield, F.D., 234
Shepard, H.A., 607
Sheppard, H.L., 138

Sheridan, J.E., 337
Sheridan, John H., 146
Sherif, M., 420, 433
Silverstein, M., 497
Simon, Herbert A., 343, 347, 373, 374
Simonetti, Jack L., 369
Sims, H.P., Jr., 231, 337
Singer, R.D., 102
Singh, J.P., 266
Sink, D. Scott, 359
Siu, R.G., 448, 461
Siwolop, Sana, 436
Skinner, B.F., 4, 150, 170, 202
Slade, L.A., 63
Slevin, D., 353
Slocum, J.W., 103, 337
Slusher, E.A., 231
Smale, John, 499
Smith, Adam, 12, 219, 234
Smith, B., 337
Smith, C.G., 553, 556, 575
Smith, Emily T., 436
Smith, Frank J., 125, 126, 137, 138
Smith, L., 575
Smith, M.M., 460, 461
Smith, P.C., 137, 265
Smith, Roger B., 584
Snarey, J.R., 104
Snyderman, B., 234
Sollman, H.M., 201
Solomon, R.L., 170, 607
Sorcher, M., 170, 202
Sorokin, P.A., 103
Stack, Jack, 357
Stagner, R., 30, 138
Staines, G.L., 138
Stalker, G.M., 536, 545
Stark, E., 607
Staw, Barry M., 123, 137, 138, 202, 349,
        350, 374
Stayer, Ralph, 269
Steel, R.P., 233
Steers, R.M., 138, 153, 202, 386, 406,
        445, 461
Steiner, G.A., 201
Steiner, I., 103
Stephani, Diana, 183
Stewart, L.H., 102
Stewart, R., 336
Stewart, Thomas A., 270
Stogdill, Ralph M., 304, 305, 309, 336,
        407
Stokes, J., 138
Stoner, James A.F., 354, 374
Stratton, W.E., 104
Strauss, Gary, 463
Streeter, L.A., 101
Strickland, L.H., 102
Strube, M.J., 336
Suci, G.J., 136
Sundry, Arthur, 205
Susnjara, Ken, 145, 146
Sussman, M., 201, 202, 276, 277, 299
Suttle, J.L., 201, 207, 208
Synderman, B., 201
Szilagyi, A.D., 337

Tabor, T., 337
Taft, R., 102
Taggert, W., 103

Tannenbaum, A., 497
Tannenbaum, Jeffrey A., 613
Tannenbaum, P.H., 136
Tavris, Carol, 82
Taylor, D.W., 375
Taylor, Frederick Winslow, 3, 12, 13, 25, 30, 156
Taylor, G.S., 138
Taylor, M.S., 265
Taylor, R.N., 103, 373
Teel, K.S., 264
Teger, A.F., 374
Teigen, Karl Halvor, 22
Terborg, J.R., 266, 596, 607
Terpstra, D., 607
Thibaut, J.W., 79, 102, 299, 383, 406
Thomas, Ken W., 353, 422, 424, 425, 433
Thompson, D.E., 258, 266
Thompson, James D., 528, 540, 545, 546
Thompson, P., 606
Thompson, V.A., 524
Thorndike, E.L., 149, 170
Thornton, G.L., 264, 265
Timmons, J.A., 201
Todor, W.D., 138
Torrance, E.P., 374, 391, 406
Tosi, H., 234
Treffinger, D.J., 375
Trevino, Linda K., 92, 104
Triandis, Harry C., 102, 136, 566, 576
Trist, E.L., 407, 524
Troxler, R.G., 460
Trumbo, D., 101, 309
Tubbs, M., 233
Tuckman, B.W., 384, 385, 406
Turla, Peter A., 396, 407
Tversky, Amos, 348, 374
Twain, Mark, 66, 236

Ulrich, L., 101

Valentine, Charles F., 565
Van der Ryn, S., 497
Van de Ven, A.H., 360, 374
Van Sell, M., 460
Van Zelst, R.H., 394, 407
Vassiliou, V., 102
Vecchio, R.P., 30, 63, 103, 137, 138, 201,

202, 234, 276, 277, 299, 336, 337, 338, 374, 407, 537, 545, 553, 556, 575
Velasquez, Manuel, 284, 299
Vernon, R., 575
Vogel, A., 496
Vogel, Todd, 511
Voltaire, 35
Von Oech, Roger, 364, 375
Vroom, Victor, H., 103, 127, 138, 185, 187, 202, 319, 320, 321, 336, 337

Wada, T., 407
Wahba, M.A., 201
Wainer, H.A., 201
Wallace, A., 234
Wallace, I., 234
Wallace, R.K., 461
Wallach, M.A., 374
Wallechinsky, D., 234
Walster, E., 202
Walton, E., 497
Wang, An, 409, 410
Wang, Frederick A., 409, 410
Wanous, J.P., 137
Warren, J.R., 102
Waterman, R.H., Jr., 170
Waters, L.R., 138
Wates, Oliver, 613
Watson, John, 147, 148, 169
Webb, E.J., 63
Webb, Max, 506, 507, 511, 524
Webster, W., 461
Wedley, W.C., 337
Weick, K.E., 63, 201
Weinfeld, F.D., 103
Weir, T., 265
Weiss, D.J., 137
Weiss, R.S., 124, 138
Weitzel, W., 265
Wells, L.T., 575
Westie, F.R., 103
Wexley, Kenneth N., 249, 250, 259, 264, 265, 266
Whetten, David, 583, 607
White, J.K., 234
White, L., 265
White, R.K., 306, 336

White, R.W., 169
White, S.E., 233
Wholey, D., 545
Whyte, G., 374
Whyte, W.H., Jr., 406
Whyte, William F., 485, 497
Wiener, M., 497
Wiggins, Jerry S., 73, 102, 374
Wikstrom, W.S., 240, 264
Wiley, Kim Wright, 155
Williams, C., 233
Williams, K., 386, 406
Williams, Patsy, 155
Wilson, Earl, 66, 144
Winget, C.M., 460
Winter, D.G., 201
Wise, S.L., 63
Withers, Bruce, 22
Witte, J.F., 44, 63
Wolf, G., 374
Wolff, E., 557, 575
Wolins, L., 264
Woodward, Joan, 538, 539, 540, 546
Woodworth, R.S., 84, 102
Wool, H., 138
Worthy, James C., 504, 524
Wozniak, Steve, 72
Wren, D.A., 30
Wright, Michael, W., 67
Wright, P.M., 233
Wright, Richard F., 275
Wrightsman, L.S., 103

Yahya, K.A., 299
Yeager, E., 407
Yetton, Philip W., 319, 320, 337
York, R.L., 103
Young, T.E., 202
Yukl, G., 233, 266, 306, 325, 336

Zahra, S.A., 407
Zajonc, R.B., 136, 406
Zalesny, M.D., 138
Zalkind, S.S., 102
Zander, Alvin, 392, 407
Zanna, M.P., 137
Ziller, R.C., 406
Zimmer, F.G., 337
Zwerman, W.L., 546

Subject Index

Absenteeism, 119, 124–125
  and flextime, 225
  and stress, 445
Abstract, 54
Accommodating style, of conflict management, 422–423, 425
Achievement
  need for, 176–178
  and religion, 177
  of women, 82
Achievement levels, national need for, 558
Achievement motivation, 175–178
  McClelland's work on, 50
Achievement-oriented leadership, 316
Acquiescence/defiance, as research bias, 45
Actions, attitudes and, 117–118
Administrative model, 346
Adult ego state, in TA, 480
Adversarial relationships, 209
Adverse impact, 257–258
Affective component, of attitude, 108, 109
Affiliation
  with groups, 380
  need for, 176
Age, and persuasibility, 111
Age Discrimination in Employment Act (1967), 256
Alarm stage, of stress response, 436, 437
Alcoholism, and stress, 444–445
Alienation, and bureaucracy, 508
Alienative involvement, 275
Alpha change, 596
Alternate ranking technique, 246–247
American Psychological Association, Publication Manual of, 55n
Annual reviews, of employee performance, 239
Antisemitism, 8
Appraisal. See Performance appraisal
Approach-approach conflict, 415–416
Approach-avoidance conflict, 418
Archival research, 49–50
Asch experiment, 286–288
Asia, business with, 564
Assessment centers, and performance appraisals, 251–253

Atrocities, and obedience, 290–292
Attitudes
  and actions, 117–118
  change in, 111–116
  component of, 108
  formation of, 110–111
  and job satisfaction, 107–141
  measuring, 109
  nature of, 108–118
Attraction, law of, 383
Attribution theory, 78–79
Audience factors, and attitude change, 112, 115–116
Authoritarianism, 88–89
Authoritarian Personality, The, 88
Authoritative organization, 510
Authority, 270
  in bureaucracy, 508
  obedience and, 288–293
  and unethical orders, 292
Authority levels of organization, tall and flat structures for, 502–505
Authority/obedience management, 310
Autocratic leadership style, 306–307
Autonomy crisis, 582
Availability heuristic, 348
Avoidance-avoidance conflict, 416–418
Avoiding style, of conflict management, 423–424, 425

Baby boomers, and stress, 435
Balance theory, 112–113
Bank Wiring Room Study, 15–17
BARS system, 248–249, 259
Bay of Pigs, 351
Behavior. See also Discipline; OB Mod; Organizational behavior; Punishment; Rewards
  and attitudes, 108, 117–118
  causes of, 35
  changing employee, 145–170
  and conflict, 414–415
  ethics and, 285
  generalities about, 35
  predictability of, 34–35
  punishment and, 158–163
  supervisor, 277
  territory and, 485

Behavioral approach to leadership, 305–311
Behavioral component of attitude, 108, 109
Behavioral element, 5
Behavioral expectation scales (BES), 248n
Behavioral observation scales (BOS), 249–250
Behavioral tests, 83–84
Behavioral theory of decision making, 346–349
Behavior modification (OB Mod), 150–157. See also OB Mod
  and reinforcement theory, 187
Beta change, 596–597
Bias
  and communication, 487
  in research, 45–46
Black market, 535
Blacks, and job satisfaction, 921
Boards, use of, 395
Bonus plans, 208, 209
Bootstrapping (expert systems), 360–361
BOS, 249–250, 259
Boundary-spanning positions, 426
  and external environment, 532–533
Bounded discretion, 347
Bounded rationality, 346
Brainstorming, 363–364
Brand management system, at Proctor & Gamble, 499–500
Brayfield-Rothe Job Satisfaction Questionnaire, 119, 120
Bureaucracy
  drawbacks to, 507–509
  as organizational life cycle, 579
  size of organization, performance, and, 509
  Weber's views of, 506–509
Bureauotics, 509n
Burnout, and stress, 446
Burns and Stalker's model, 536–537
Bystanders, 284

Calculative involvement, 275
Case studies, 44
Category management organizational structure, 499–500

Cautious shift, 355
Centralization, of organizational structure, 503
Centralized networks, 476
Central tendency error, 245
Central traits, 75
Chain of command, 506
Challenger disaster, 464–468
Change, 146. *See also* Employee behavior
  organizational, 579–610
  readiness for, 590
  resistance to, 589–590
Change process, phases of, 588–589
Charismatic leadership, 323
Child ego state, in TA, 480
China, 564
Civil Rights Act (1964), 256
Class consciousness, 209
Classical approach, to organizational design, 506–509
Classical conditioning, 146–148
  and operant conditioning, 150
Classical decision theory, 344–346
Cliques, 281–282
Closed group, 380
Closed systems, 534
Coalitions, 278
  eliminating, 281–282
Coal mining, Tavistock studies of, 511–512
Coercion, and change, 590
Coercive power, 272, 274
Cognitive component of attitude, 108, 109
Cognitive dissonance, 116, 416n
Cognitive resource theory, 305
Cognitive styles, 90
Cohesiveness, in groups, 393–395
Collaborating style, of conflict management, 422, 425
Collaboration, growth through, 583
Collectivism, 560
Command
  chain of, 506
  unity of, 505–506
Commission, use of, 395
Commitment, escalation of, 349–350
Committees, use of in organizations, 395
Common sense, 21
Communication, 471–497
  and conflict, 412
  definition, 472
  direction of, 476–478
  furniture arrangements and, 485–486
  humor in, 483
  improving, 489–490
  individual barriers to, 486–487
  informal, 488–489
  in Japan, 562
  nonverbal, 482–486
  organizational barriers to, 487–488
  roles in, 478–480
  and transactional analysis, 480–482
  types of, 474
Communication networks, 474–476
Communication process, model of, 472–473
Communications gangplank, 478–479
Comparison level, 383
Compensation, role of, 206–211

Competition, and conflict, 410–411
Competitiveness, rating, 82–83
Complementary transaction, in TA, 480–481
Compliance, 271
Compromising style of conflict management, 424, 425
Compulsive organization, 554
Conditioned response (CR), 147, 148
Conditioned stimulus (CS), 147, 148
Conditioning
  classical, 146–148
  instrumental (operant), 149–150
Conflict, 410–411
  intergroup, 424–427
  international trade, 423
  reducing, 420–424
  review of, 415–420
  sources of, 412
  stimulating, 427
  views of, 411, 412
Conflict management, 409–433
  styles of, 422–424
Conformity, 286–288
Confrontation meetings, 592–593
Congruency, 537
Conservatism, 88
Construction firm, organizational structures for, 505
Consultative organization, 510
Content theories, 193
Content, and attitude formation, 111
Contextual dimensions of organizations, 535
Contingency approaches
  to leadership, 311–323, 324
  1945–present, 17–19
  to organizational design, 534–540
Contingency model of leadership effectiveness, 311–316
Contingency research, 537–538
Control
  locus of, 87–88
  as research goal, 39
Control crisis, 582
Cooperation, and groups, 381n
Coordination, growth through, 583
Corporate Cultures, 3
Corporation
  group dynamics in, 377–378
  neurotic, 554
Correlational method, 41–43
Cosmopolite role, 479–480
Costs, of relationship, 383
Country-club management, 310
Coworkers, performance appraisal by, 241
Creativity
  and decision making, 361–365
  enhancing, 363–364
  measuring, 362
  steps in creative process, 363
Credibility, and communication, 487
Crises
  of autonomy, 582
  of control, 582
  of leadership, 581
  of red tape, 583
Cross-cultural research, 556–563
Cross-cultural training, 566–568
Cuban Missile Crisis, 351n

Cultural differences, 557–559
  dimensions of, 559–561
Cultural influences, 549–576
Culture. *See* Organizational culture
Culture assimilator training method, 566–567
Customer service, at United Technologies Corporation, 511

Death, organizational, 583n
Decentralization, 500–501
Decentralized communications network, 474–475
Decision making 341–375
  behavioral view of, 346–349
  classical view of, 344–346
  creativity and, 361–365
  democratic, 341–342
  devil's advocate and, 353
  improving, 355–361
  individual vs. group, 355–358, 359
  judgmental strategies for, 348–349
  obstacles to, 349–355
  organizational, 342–344
  personal, 342
  by workers, 357
Decisions, programmed and nonprogrammed, 343–344
Decision theory, classical, 344–346
Decline, organizational, 583–585
Decoding, 472
Deduction, 36
Defense Department, 508
Deficiency needs, 178–179
Delegation, 582
Delphi technique, 358–360
Demand characteristics, 48
Dependency, 586–587
Dependent variable, 39–40
Depressive organization, 554
Description, 38
Dialectical inquiry, 353
Differentiation, 538
Diffusion of responsibility, 354, 387n
Directive leadership, 316
Discipline, 257
  administering, 160–163
  conducting meeting for, 162–163
  as management technique, 22
  progressive, 161–162
Discrimination, 257
  and performance appraisal, 244n
Division of labor, 219, 507
Dogmatism, 89
Dow Jones Industrial Average, and Super Bowl, 42
Downward communication, 476
Drug abuse, and stress, 444–445
Duncan's model of environmental uncertainty, 529, 530
Dyads, 322

Early retirement, 126
East Asia, business with, 564
EDGE advanced negotiations system, 477
Education, and change, 589–590
Effect, law of, 19n, 149
Effort-performance expectancy, 185
Ego states, in TA, 480–481

Emotional conditioning, and attitude formation, 111
Emotions
and attitudes, 108
perception of, 70
Employee behavior, changing through consequences, 145–170
Employee growth-need strength, 225
Employee motivation
enhancing, 205–234
rewards and, 206–211
Employee orientation, 307
Employee performance, and expectations, 214–218
Employees. See also Annual reviews; Behavior; Job satisfaction; Performance appraisal; Punishment; Rewards
corporate programs to keep, 117
legal aspects of performance appraisals, 256–259
turnover of, 119
Enacted role, 388
Encoding, 472
Encounter groups, 592
Entrepreneurs, couples as, and stress, 442
Environment
external, 479–480
and organizational success or failure, 585–586
Environmental forces, 527–546
resource dependence model, 532–533
simplicity-complexity, 528–529
and static-dynamic environments, 529
Environmental uncertainty, 529
Duncan's model of, 529, 530
Environment vs. heredity, 80
Equal Pay Act (1963), 256
Equity, and workers' performance, 37
Equity theory, 189–192
and expectancy theory, 191
ERG theory, 180n
Escalating commitment, and decision making, 349–350
Esteem, and groups, 380–381
Esteem needs, 179
Ethics
intrapersonal conflict and, 416
and order taking, 292
in managing decline, 584
and organizational politics, 284–286
in research, 53–54
and space shuttle Challenger, 464–468
Ethnocentrism, 88
Eustress, 437
Evaluation research, 594–598
Evans-House path-goal theory, 316–317, 324
Exercise, and stress, 447
Exhaustion stage, of stress response, 436–437
Expectancy theory, 186–187
and equity theory, 191
Expectations, 214–218
Expected role, 388
Experimental method, 43
Experiments
field, 46–47
laboratory, 47–49
Expert power, 273

Expert systems, 360
External environments
dimensions, 528–533
managing, 533–534
of organizations, 479–480
External locus of control, 87
External sources of change, 580–581
External validity, 52–53
Extinction
and behaviors, 158
and OB Mod, 151
resistance to, 151
Extrasensory perception (ESP), research on, 218
Extremism, as research bias, 45
Extrinsic rewards, 206

Faceted approach, to job satisfaction measurement, 119–120
Facial expressions, 70
Failure, organizational, 586–588
Faking scales, 84n
Familiar stranger, 110
Fascism, 88
Fast-food restaurants, 531–532
Fatalism, in Latin America, 564
Fayol's gangplank, 478, 479
Fear, and attitude change, 114
Federal government, as bureaucracy, 508
Feedback interview, 253–356
Feminism, 534
Fiedler's contingency model, 311–316, 324
Field experiments, 46–47
Fight or flight, and stress, 437, 447
Firing practices, 256
Fixed interval schedules, 151–152, 153
Fixed ratio schedule, 152, 153
Flat structure, 502–505
Flextime, 225
Forced distribution ranking technique, 247–248
Forcing style, of conflict management, 422
Forecasting, 527
Formal groups, 378–379
Forming stage of group, 384
Four-fifths rule, 257
Functional form of organization, 513
Functional turnover, 126
Furniture arrangements, and interpersonal communication, 485–486

Gain-sharing plans, 210–211
Game playing
organizational, 481–482
in TA, 481–482
Gamma change, 597
Gangplank, 478–479
Gatekeeper role, 478–479
Gender bias, and cross-cultural attitudes, 559
General Adaptation Syndrome, 436–438
Genetics, and job satisfaction, 123
Global approach, to job satisfaction measurement, 119
Global marketplace, 398
GM Faces Scale, 119

Goal acceptance, 211
Goal difficulty, 211
Goal setting, 211–214
managerial pitfalls and, 215
Goal specificity, 211
Goldilocks point, 411
Gossip, 488
Government
policies and spending of, 528
regulations, and performance appraisals, 256–257
Graen's vertical dyad linkage model of leadership, 321–323, 324
Grapevines, 488
Graphic scales
and attitude measurement, 109
as performance appraisal device, 245–246
Greiner's model of organizational growth, 581, 582
Grid analysis, 364
Grievances, 119
Group decision making, and nominal group technique, 358
Group development, stages of, 384–385
Group dynamics, 377–407
Group illusions, 387
Group polarization, 355
Groups
and cognitive dissonance, 116
cohesiveness in, 393–395
communications networks. See Communications networks
composition of, 387–388
decision making, 355–358, 359
formal vs. informal, 378–379
and interpersonal attraction, 381–384
linking pin view of, 379
nature of, 378–380
norms in, 391–393
open vs. closed, 379–380
and organizational development, 591
performance impact of, 385–395
reasons for joining, 380–381
risk taking within, 354–355
roles in, 388–390
size of, 385–387
status in, 390–391
use of in organizations, 395–400
Groupthink, 350–353
Growth
crisis in, 581
patterns of, 581–585
Growth needs, 178, 179

Halo effect 74
Halo errors, 245
Handbook of Leadership, 302
Haney's "Buzz Phrase Generator," 486–487
Harshness errors, 245–256
Hawthorne effect, 15, 399
Hawthorne studies, 13–17
Hedonism, 174–175, 188
Heredity vs. environment, 80
Hershey-Blanchard situational theory of, 317–319, 324
Heuristics (rules of thumb), 347
Hierarchy, 506–507
Hierarchy of needs, 178–180, 194
and two-factor theory, 185

Hiring practices, and linkages, 533
Histrionic organization, 554
Holocaust, obedience and, 290–292
Horizontal communication, 478
Human element, 5
Humanistic approach, to employee treatment, 180
Human relations approach (1927–1945), 13–17
Human resources, 3
    management of, 7–8
Humor, use of, 483
Hybrid form of organizational design, 514–515
    and matrix design, 515–517, 518
Hygiene factors, 181
Hypotheses, 40

Ideal generation, 472
Identification, 271
Identity, and groups, 380–381
Illness, and stress, 443–446
Illumination experiments, 14
Imitation, 192–193
Immediacy, and nonverbal communication, 482–483
Implicit personality theory, 75
Impoverished management, 310
Impressionistic prediction approach, 73
Impression management, 278
In-basket exercise, 252
Incentive pay schemes, 12
Incentive plans, 209–210. See also Pay schemes; Rewards
Incentives, for hourly workers, 221
Indefinite layoff, 164–165
Independent variable, 39
Individual decision making, 355–358, 359
Individualism, 560
Induction, 36
Industrial democracy, 44
Industrial Revolution, 11–12, 219
Influence, 270
    interpersonal, 270–271
    power and, 269–299
Influence tactics, consequences of, 283–284
Informal communication, 488–489
Informal groups, 378–379
Information management, 279
Information overload, 387
Ingratiation, 278
Ingratiators, 284
Initiating structure, 308
Inkblot test. See Rorschach test
Inputs, in equity theory, 189
Inquiry into the Nature and Causes of the Wealth of Nations, An, 219
Instincts, 175
Instinctual theories, 175
Institutionalized arrangements, and organizational culture, 555
Instrumental leadership, 325
Instrumental (operant) conditioning, 149–150
Integrating department, 427
Integration, 538
Intelligence, and leadership, 305

Intensive technology, 540
Intergroup conflict, 424–427
Interlocking directorates, 533
Internal-External Control Scale, 87
Internalization, 271
Internal locus of control, 87
Internal sources of organizational change, 581
Internal validity, 52–53
International business, 398, 424, 503, 535, 563–568
    and uninformed travel, 565
International organization, McDonald's structure as, 610–613
International teamwork, 398
Interorganizational conflict, 415n
Interpersonal attraction, 381–384
Interpersonal communication process, 473. See also Communication
Interpersonal conflict, 418–420
Interpersonal influence, 270–271
Interval schedules, 151
    fixed, 151–152
    variable, 152
Intervening variable, 39, 40
Intraorganizational conflict, 415n
Intrapersonal conflict, 415–418
    in ethical decisions, 416
Intrinsic rewards, 206
Involvement, 274–276
    Etzioni's model of, 274–276
Isolate role, 479

Japan, 564, 565
    quality circles in, 397, 398
    and trade conflicts, 423
Japanese management, 561–562
Job characteristics theory, 222–225
Job description, 244
Job Descriptive Index (JDI), 119–120
Job diagnostic survey, 224
Job enlargement, 220
Job enrichment, 221–222
    job characteristics model of, 223
Job level, 121
Job maturity, 317
Job redesign, 219–227
    and job characteristics theory, 222–225
    methods of, 220–222
    obstacles to, 226–227
    and stress, 447
Job-related stress, 436–438
Job rotation, 220
Job satisfaction, 118–129
    attitudes and, 107–141
    causes and consequences of, 121
    and dissatisfaction, 124–127
    expectations and, 122–123
    intrinsic and extrinsic sources of, 122
    and performance, 127–128
    and productivity, 127–129
    at Quad Graphics, 139–141
    and race, 45–46
    in 1600s, 119n
    sources of, 121–123
    trends in, 123–124
    and two-factor theory, 182, 184
Job security, 357
Job simplification, and productivity, 220

Job specialization, 219
Job turnover. See Turnover
Journals, about organizational behavior, 55
Judgmental strategies (judgmental heuristics), for decision making, 348–349

Kirkland v. New York Department of Correctional Services, 244n
Korea, 564

Labor, division of, 219, 507
Laboratory experiments, 47–49
Laboratory training, 592
Labor dispute, earliest recorded, 10n
Labor force, productivity in, 45
Labor movement, 219
Laissez-faire management, 210
Last-chance meeting, 353
Latin America, business with, 564
Law of attraction, 383
Law of Effect, 19n, 149
Lawrence and Lorsch's contingency research, 537–538
Layoffs, and termination, 164–165
Leader-member exchange model of leadership, 321, 324
Leader-member relations, 313, 314
Leaders. See also Leadership
    behavioral dimensions of, 307–309
    informal, 303
    traits and skills of, 306
Leadership, 301–338
    behavioral approach to, 305–311
    charismatic, 323
    comparison of models, 323–324
    contingency approaches to, 311–323, 324
    crisis of, 581
    Evans-House path-goal theory of, 316–317, 324
    Graen's vertical dyad linkage model of, 321–323, 324
    Hershey-Blanchard situational theory of, 317–319, 324
    House's types of, 316, 324
    instrumental, 325
    nature of, 302–303
    Ohio State studies of, 307–311, 323, 324
    path-goal theory of, 316–317, 324
    style of, 312
    substitutes for, 325–326
    supportive, 325
    team, 307
    trait approach to, 304–305
    transformational, 323, 324
    Vroom-Yetton model of, 319–321, 324
Learning
    and classical conditioning, 146–148
    and employee behavior, 145–146
    nature of, 146
    observational, 148–149
Least preferred coworker (LPC) scale, 311, 314–315
Legal aspects of performance appraisal, 256–259
Legitimate power, 272–273
Leniency errors, 245–246

Liaison role, 479
Life changes, and stress, 439, 440
Life cycles, of organization, 579–580
Liker's six systems of organizational design, 509–511
Line responsibility, 279
Line-staff conflict, reducing, 421
Line-staff distinctions, and conflict, 413–414
Linkages, 535
  with external environment, 533
Listening, 472
Live-in assessment centers, 251
Locus of control, 87–88
Long-linked technology, 540
Long-run process production firms, 539–540
LPC scale, 311, 314–315

Machiavellianism, 274, 282–283
Machismo, 564
Mach Scale, 282–283
Macro aspects of organizational behavior, 500
Magazines, organizational behavior, 55
Malaysia, 565
Management. See also Contingency approach; Hawthorne Studies; Organizational behavior
  of conflict, 408–433
  and organizational success or failure, 585–587
  at Wang Laboratories, 409–410
  zero-defects, 205–206
Management-by-objectives (MBO), 212–214, 250–251, 259
  field experiment and, 46–47
  programs, 241
Management style, in changing environment, 534
Management techniques, discipline as, 22
Management training programs, 301–302
Managerial Grid, 310–311
Managers. See also Decision making
  activities of, 303–304
  cross-cultural studies of, 558–559
  in Japan, 561–563
  and leadership, 302–303
  measuring performance of, 301–302
  middle, 107
  traits of, 559–561
Mānana concept, 564
Manipulation of opinion, and change, 590
Masculinity vs. femininity, and cultural values, 560
Maslow's hierarchy of needs, 178–180
  and two-factor theory, 185
Massage, and stress, 450
Mass media, and attitude change, 115
Mass production firms, 539–540
Mass psychogenic illness, 445
Matrix organizational design, 515–517, 518
Maturity, in Hershey-Blanchard theory, 317, 324
Maximizing (optimizing), 346–347
MBO. See Management-by-objectives
Mechanistic organizations, 536

Mechanistic prediction approach, 73
Mediating technology, 540
Medium factors, and attitude change, 112, 114–115
Meetings, effectiveness of, 396
Mental dissonance, 116
Mental Measurement Yearbook, 84
Message factors, and attitude change, 112, 113–114
Messages, 472–473
Method-bound theories, 183
Micro aspects of organizational behavior, 500
Middle East, business with, 565, 566
Middle managers, 107
Milgram studies, 288–293
Minnesota Satisfaction Questionnaire, 119
Modeling, 192–193
Moderating variable, 39, 40–41
Modified workweek, 225–226
Moral maturity, 91–92
  developmental stages, 91
Motivation, 173–202. See also Expectancy theory
  comprehensive model of, 193–195
  enhancing employee, 205–234
  nature of, 174–193
  Porter-Lawler model of, 193–195
Motivator factors, 181
Motives, in intrapersonal conflict, 417
Multiple advocacy, 353
Multiple pay system, 211
Myers-Briggs Type Indicator, 90

NASA, and Challenger disaster, 464–468
Needs
  Alderfer and, 180n
  Maslow's hierarchy of, 178–180, 185
  McClelland studies of, 176–178
Negative reinforcement, 149–150
Negotiation, and change, 590
Network Computing Devices, 442
Networks, 278
  communication, 474–476
Neurotic corporations, 554
Neutralizer, leadership, 325–326
Nominal group technique (NGT), 358
Noncomplementary transactions, in TA, 481
Nonprogrammed decisions, 343–344
Nonverbal communication, 474, 482–486
Nonverbal cues, 70–71
Normative power, 275
Norming stage of group, 384
Norms
  in groups, 391–393
  of organizations, 555
Notions of balance theory, 273n

Obedience, as response to authority, 288–293
OB MOD, 150–157
  controversies about, 156
  and extinction, 151
  setting of program for, 154–157
  and shaping, 151
  success of, 156
  and technology, 188
Observational learning, 148–149

Office of Strategic Services (OSS), and assessment centers, 251
Offices, layouts of, 382
Ohio State leadership studies, 307–311, 323, 324
One-group pretest—post-test design, 594–595
Open group, 379–380
Open systems, 534
Operant conditioning, 149–150
  applying, 154
  and classical conditioning, 150
  criticism of, 157
  in organizational settings, 150–157
  and reinforcement theory, 187
Opposition, promoting, 279
Oral communication, 474
Organic organizations, 536
Organization
  life cycles of, 579–610
  size and conflict, 412–413
  success and failure of, 585–588
  use of groups in, 395–400
Organizational behavior, 4. See also Behavior
  applications of, 4–5
  criticisms of field, 19–22
  definition of, 6–7
  development of, 9–19
  framework for study of, 22–23
  and increased knowledge, 6
  journals and magazines about, 55
  modification (OB Mod), 150–157
  and personal growth, 5–6
Organizational behavior research, 33–63
  assumptions of, 34–35
  goals of, 38–39
  methods of, 41–43
  scientific method in, 35–38
  strategies and settings, 43–52
  terminology and, 39–41
  theory in, 36–38
Organizational change
  growth and decline, 581–585
  sources of, 580–581
Organizational culture, 3, 550–553
  analyzing, 553–555
  creation and maintenance of, 552–553
  in different cultures, 556–563
  measurement and change of, 551–552
  and strategy, 555–556
Organizational decisions, types of, 342–344
Organizational decline, 583–585
  ethics in managing, 584
Organizational design, 499–524
  behavioral approach to, 509–511
  Burns and Stalker's model of, 536–537
  classical approach to, 506–509
  contingency view of, 534–540
  functional form of, 513
  hybrid form of, 514–515
  integration and differentiation, 538
  Likert's six systems of, 509–511
  matrix, 515–517, 518
  mechanistic and organistic forms, 536
  product form of, 514
  and pyramid structure, 518
  Sociotechnical systems approach to, 511–513

Organizational design (*continued*)
structure and strategy and, 540–541
at United Technologies Corporation, 511
Organizational development (OD), 8, 588–593
changes from, 600
conditions for, 593
effects of on outcome and process variables, 598–599
evaluating, 594–598
at Lakeway Resort, 608–610
in McDonald's Soviet enterprise, 610–613
phases of, 588–589
techniques of, 590–593
value of, 598–599
Organizational factors, in stress, 439–443
Organizational form, 530
Organizational politics, 277–286
coping with, 281–282
ethics of, 284–286
Organizational power, 274–276
Organizational sciences, fields in, 8
Organizational theory, 7
Organization management, 310
Organizing, principles of, 500–506
Outcomes
in equity theory, 189
and social exchange theory, 383

Paired comparison ranking technique, 247
Paranoid organization, 554
Parent ego state, in TA, 480
Participation, and change, 590
Participative leadership, 316
Participative organization, 510
Path-goal theory of leadership, 316–317, 324
Pavlovian conditioning, 146–148
Pay-for-performance schemes, 208–209
Pay incentives, 221
Pay schemes, 206–211
Pay systems, multiple, 211
Peers, performance appraisal by, 241
Penalties, for discriminating, 258
Perceived role, 388
Perception
biases in, 487
obstacles to, 74–78
perceiver and, 69–70
and personality, 67–104
selective, 78
and success, 82
Perceptual distortion, 76
Performance
bureaucracy, organization size, and, 509
group performance and, 385–395
and job satisfaction, 127–128
leadership and, 301–338
and OB Mod program, 154–156
and operant conditioning, 154
rewards and, 206–209
of top managers, 301–302
Performance appraisals, 237–266
accuracy of, 246
and assessment centers, 251–253

behavioral expectation scales (BES), 248n
behaviorally anchored rating scales (BARS), 248–249
behavioral observation scales (BOS), 249–250
factors assessed, 244
and feedback interview, 253–256
legal aspects of, 256–259
legal systems, 258–259
and management-by-objective, 250–251
and performance measures, 244–253
personnel conducting, 240–243
rankings and, 246–248
reasons for, 238–240
sources of, 243
Performance-outcome expectancy, 185–186
Performing stages of group, 384
Permissive organization, 510
Personal decision making, 342
Personality
definition of, 79–80
determinants of, 80–81
dimensions of, 87–92
implicit theory of, 75
managerial, 67–68
perception and, 67–104
predicting behavior from, 73
ratings, traits, 81–83
trait assessment, 81–86
Personality inventories, 84
Personality measures, predictive utility of, 92–93
Personality traits, 71–73
Personality types, and stress, 438–439
Personal space, 484–485
Philosophers, utilitarian (hedonistic), 174–175
Philosophy of life, and stress, 448
Phyligistin, 183n
Physical disorders, and stress, 443–444
Physiological needs, 178–179
Political blunders, 280–281
Political tactics
devious, 279–280
Machiavellianism, 282–283
Politics, 277–286. *See also* Organizational politics; Tactics
tactics of, 278–282
Population ecology perspective, 529–532
Porter-Lawler model of motivation, 193–195
Position power, 313, 314
Positive reinforcement, 149
Post-decision regret, 416n
Posthypnotic suggestion, 77
Power. *See also* Politics
bases of, 271–274
coercive, 272, 274
and conflict, 414
distinguishing, 270
expert, 273
and influence, 269–299
and involvement, 274–276
legitimate, 272–273
need for, 176
in nonverbal communication, 484
normative, 275

organizational, 274–276
referent, 273
reinforcement and, 274
reward, 271–272
utilitarian, 275
Power bases, interplay among, 273–274
Power-distance, 559
Power models, 274–277
Prediction, 38–39
Preemployment programs, 123
Pre-experimental design, 594
Prepotency, 179
President of the United States, traits of, 305n
Pretest—post-test control group design, 595
Prisoner's Dilemma, 418–420
Problem solving (cognitive) styles, 90
Process theories, 193
Product form, of organizational design, 514
Productivity, 219–220
job satisfaction and, 127–129
and performance appraisal, 238
Professional associations, 275
Programmed decisions, 343
Progressive discipline, 161–162
Projection, 75
Projective techniques, 84–86
Proxemics, and communication, 484–485
Psychological maturity, 317
Punishment. *See also* Discipline
and behavior, 158–163
effective, 159–160
and employee behavior, 145
Pygmalion in the Classroom, 216
Pyramid organizational design structure, 518

Quality circles, 394–400
Quality of work life (QWL), 593
Quasi-experimental designs, 596

Race, and job satisfaction, 45–46, 121
Random assignment, 49, 595
Rankings, and performance appraisals, 246–248
Ratings. *See also* Projective techniques; Tests
of personality, 81–83
scales. *See* Rating scales
Rating scales
behaviorally anchored, 248–249
graphic, 245–246
Rational-economic model of decision making, 344–346
Rationality, bounded, 346
Ratio schedules, 151
fixed, 152
variable, 152
Reactivity, 595
Reception, of message, 472
Reciprocal influence view of strategy and environment, 556
Reciprocity principle of interpersonal attraction, 19n
Red tape, 508
crisis of, 583
Referent power, 273

Refreezing phase, 589
Reinforcement, 149–150
    continuous, 151
    partial, 151
    and power, 274
    schedules of, 151–153
    and strokes, 481n
Reinforcement theory, 187–189
Relationships, predictions about, 384
Relaxation techniques, and stress, 448
Relay Assembly Room Study, 14–15
Religious organizations, 275
Representativeness heuristic, 348
Research. *See also* Organizational
        behavior research
    archival, 49–50
    ethics in, 53–54
    and OD, 594–598
    organizational behavior, 33–62
    strategies and settings, 52
    unobtrusive measure and, 50–52
Research methods, 41–43
Research report
    reading, 54–55
    writing of, 55n
Research strategies and settings, 43–52
Resistance stage, of stress response,
        436, 437
Resource dependence model, 532–533
Resources, and conflict, 414
Response, to message, 473
Responsibility, diffusion of, 354
Responsibility for others, and stress, 439
Retention, 531
Retirement, early, 126
Reward power, 271–272
Rewards, 154, 206–211, 383
    and behavior, 158
    conflict and, 414
    and employee behavior, 145
    extrinsic, 206
    intrinsic, 206
    and observational learning, 149
    organizational, 207
Risk taking, in groups, 354–355
Risky shift, 354
Rituals, 551
Roger & Me, 584
Role ambiguity, 389
    and stress, 443
Role conflict, 389
    and stress, 441–442
Role episode, 389
Role overload, and stress, 443
Roles
    communication, 478–480
    in groups, 388–390
    list of employee, 390
Rorschach test, 84–85
Rowe v. General Motors, 258
Rubic's cube, 517n
Rumors, 488–489

Safety needs, 179
Salary rewards, 208
Sandwich approach to feedback
        interview, 255
Satisfice, 346
Scales
    for authoritarianism, 88–89

behaviorally anchored rating, 248–249
behavioral observation, 249–250
    graphic, 109
    graphic rating, 245–246
    for job satisfaction, 119–120
    semantic differential, 109, 110
Schedules, of reinforcement, 151–153
Schizoid organization, 554
Schizophrenia, 81
Scientific management (1900–1945), 3,
        11–13
    and OB Mod, 156–157
    period before (before 1900), 9–11
Scientific method
    in organizational behavior research,
        35–36
    in practice, 36–38
Securities and Exchange Commission,
        395
Security, in groups, 380
Selective perception, 78
Self-actualization needs, 179
Self-appraisal, 240–241
Self-feedback, 157
Self-fulfilling prophecies (SFP), 214–218
    constructive management of, 217–218
Self-rewarding, 149
Semantic differential scale, 109, 110
Sensitivity training, 591–592
Sentence completions, 86
Sex, and persuasibility, 115
Sexism, and management style, 534
Shaping, 151
Shift work, and stress, 443, 444
Shotguns, 284
Similarity, and groups, 382–383
Simplicity-complexity, of environments,
        528–529
Simulation, and cross-cultural training,
        567–568
Situational assessment, 251n
Situational favorableness, 313
Situational tests, 83–84
Six Sigma plan, 205
Social communication, and attitude
        formation, 110
Social desirability, as research bias, 45
Social exchange theory, 383
Social facilitation effect, 385
Social influence
    conformity as response to, 286–288
    and supervisor behavior, 277
Social inhibition effect, 385
Social learning theory, 192–193
Social loafing, 386
Social needs, 179
Social norms, and managerial consis-
        tency, 350
Social status, 79
Social structure of organization, 554
Social support, and stress, 447
Societal changes, and employee motiva-
        tion, 210
Sociofugal areas, 485
Sociopetal areas, 485
Sociotechnical system of organizational
        design, 511–513
Solomon four-group design, 595–596
Source factors, and attitude change,
        112–113

Sources of organizational change, 580–
        581
Soviet Union
    business with, 565–566
    McDonald's in, 610–613. *See also*
        McDonald's
Space
    furniture arrangements and, 485–486
    personal, 484–485
Span of control, 503–504
Specificity, goal, 211
Staff heterogeneity, and conflict, 413
Static-dynamic environments, 529
Status
    and communication, 486–487
    in groups, 390–391
Stereotypes, 74
Stimuli, 85n. *See also* Projective tech-
        niques
Stimulus-response, 147–148
Stories, and organizational culture, 551
Storming stage of group, 384
Strategy, and structure, 540–541
Stress, 435–461
    causes of, 438–443
    coping with, 446–450
    job-related, 436–438
    by job type, 441
    reactions to, 443–446
    weighted list for, 440
    wellness programs and, 450–451
Strokes, in TA, 481
Structural approaches to conflict reduc-
        tion, 420–421
Structural dimensions of organizations,
        535
Structure
    and organizational success or failure,
        585–586
    and strategy, 540–541
Subjective probabilities, 186
Subliminal influences, 76
Subordinate maturity, 317
Subordinates, performance appraisals
        by, 242
Substitute, for leadership, 325–326
Success, organizational, 585–586
Super Bowl, and Dow Jones Industrial
        Average, 42
Superordinate goals, and conflict reduc-
        tion, 420–421
Supervisor
    behavior of, 277
    and performance appraisal, 240
Supportive leadership, 316, 325
Survey feedback, 590–591
Survey measurement method of organi-
        zational culture, 551–552
Surveys, 44–46
Symbolism, and organizational culture,
        555

Tacticians, 284
Tactics
    consequences of influence, 283–284
    devious political, 279–280
    Machiavellianism, 282–283
    political, 278–282
Tall structure, 502–505
Tardiness, 125

Task analysis, and Taylor, Frederick, 12–13
Task forces, 395
Task orientation, 307
Tasks, accomplishing in group, 381
Task structure, 313, 314
TAT, 85, 86, 175–176
Tavistock studies, 511–512
Teams
  building, 591
  leadership, 307
  management, 311
Teamwork, 7
  in global marketplace, 398
Technological change, 387
Technological systems, and social systems, 511–513
Technology
  and OB Mod, 188
  and privacy, 51
  Thompson's typology of, 540
  Woodward's studies of, 538–540
Termination, 163–165
  meeting for, 256
Territory, and personal space in communication, 485
Test ability, of theories, 38
Tests. See also Ratings
  projective techniques, 84–86
  situational, 83–84
Tests in Print, 84
T-group (training group), 3, 591–592
Thematic Apperception Test (TAT), 85, 86, 175–176
Theories, in organizational behavior research, 36–38
  See also specific theories by name
Theory Z, 561–562
Thorndike's Law of Effect, 149
Time, and nonverbal communication, 486
Time-and-motion study, 12–13

Time management, and stress, 448–450
Time-series design, 596
Trade, conflicts in, 423
Trade associations, 534
Traits
  approach to leadership, 304–305
  of leaders, 304–305
  personality, 71–73, 81–86
  and personality dimensions, 87
Transactional analysis (TA), 480–482
Transactions, in TA, 480–481
Transformational leadership, 323–324
Transmission, of message, 472
Turnover, 125–126
  and flextime, 225
  and stress, 445
Two-factor theory, of Herzberg, 180–184
Type A personality, 438–439
Type B personality, 438–439

Uncertainty, avoidance of, 559–560
Unconditioned response (UR), 147, 148
Unconditioned stimulus (UCS), 147, 148
Understanding, of messages, 472
Unfreezing process, 588
Unions, 119
  and job satisfaction, 126–127
  and quality circles, 399
United States
  managers' traits in, 560–561
  peace economy of, 527–528
Unit production firms, 539–540
Unity of command, 505–506
Unobtrusive measures, 50–52
Upward communication, 477–478
Urbanization, and job satisfaction, 222
Utilitarian philosophers, 174–175
Utilitarian power, 275

Valence, 186
Validity, 52–53
Values, of organizations, 555

Variable interval schedule, 152, 153
Variable ratio schedule, 152, 153
Variables, 39–41
  and attitude change, 112
  in job satisfaction, 121
Variation, 530–531
Venetians, management techniques of, 10–11
Verification, 36
Vertical dyad linkage model of leadership, 321–323, 324
Vertical integration, 533
Vocational Rehabilitation Act (1973), 256
Vroom-Yetton leadership model, 319–321, 324

Wall Street crash (1987), 435
Weber's bureaucracy, 506–509
Wellness programs, 3, 450–451
  and stress, 435
Withdrawal behaviors, and job satisfaction, 124–127
Worker behavior, 33–34. See also Organizational behavior research
Workers. See also Employees; Job satisfaction
  motivation of, 173–202
  safety of, research about, 33–34
Work ethic, 89–90
Working conditions, and stress, 441
Women
  and achievement, 82
  and attitude change, 115
  and job satisfaction, 121
  and semantic differential scale, 109, 110
Written communication, 474

Zero-defects management, 205–206

Organization Index

Aid Association for Lutherans (AAL), 183
Allstate Insurance Company, 490
American Airlines, 397
American Dental Association, 275
American Hospital Supply Corporation, 435
ARA Services, 358
Association of Information Systems Professionals, 587
AT&T, 177, 251, 593, 601

Bache and Company, 292
Baker and McKenzie, 503
Baxter Travenol Laboratories, 435
Bethlehem Steel, 12, 13
Black and Decker, 213
Blue Cross-Blue Shield, 451
Bubbling Bath Spa and Tub Works, Inc., 160
Burger King, 531
Byrnes, Elsom, Mirtz, Morice, Inc.; 117

California Factors and Finance, 416
Campbell Soup, 451
Chicago Museum of Science and Industry, 50
Chouinard Equipment, 462–463
Coca-Cola, 553
Colgate-Palmolive, 269
Control Data Corporation, 451
Cummins Engine Company, 210

Data General, 45
Digital Equipment Corporation, 501
Dolce Corporation, 608–610
DuPont, 51, 541

European Economic Community (EEC), 423
Equal Employment Opportunity Commission, 257
Exxon, 242, 447

Federal Trade Commission, 395
First Security Service Company, 7
Ford Motor Company, 391
  centralized structure at, 503

General Accounting Office, 398
General Electric Company, 51, 107, 119, 213, 358, 398
General Foods, 221
General Motors, 107, 258, 357, 397, 421
  decline of, 584
Georgia-Pacific Corporation, 107
G.O.D. Inc., 312
Great Pacific Iron Works, 462
GTE, 253

Herman Miller, 210
Hewlett-Packard, 119
Honeywell, 397
Hughes Aircraft, 397

IBM, 251, 593, 601
Internal Revenue Service, 508
International Harvester, 397

Johns-Manville, 447
Johnson & Johnson, 451
Johnsonville Foods, 269

Kepner Tregoe, 321

Lakeway Resort, 608–610
Leaseway Transportation, 119
Lincoln Electric, 208
Lost Arrow, Inc., 462

Maid Bess Corporation, 125
Management Recruiters, Inc., 51
Manufacturers Hanover Trust Company, 107
Mary Kay Cosmetics, 155
McDonald's, 489, 531
  in Moscow, 535, 610–613
McGuffey's, 471–472
Mead Corporation, 591
Metropolitan Economic Development Association, 178
Metropolitan Life Insurance, 448
Milbar Corporation, 7
Minnesota Mining and Manufacturing (3M). See 3M
Mitsubishi Chemical Industries, 400

Morton Thiokol Inc. (MTI), 464–468
Motorola, 205
MTEC Photoacoustics, 442

NASA, 464–468
National Opinion Research Center, 46
National Training Laboratory, 592
NEC, 205
New York Department of Correctional Services, 244
New York Telephone Company, 44
Nissan Motor Manufacturing, 123
Northrop, 397

Office of Strategic Services, 251

PA Executive Search Group, 3
Parsons Pine Products, Inc., 221
Patagonia, 462–463
PepsiCo, 553
Performance Sciences Institute, 301
Personnel Decisions Inc. (PDI), 67–68
Polaroid, 221
Procter & Gamble, 489, 593
  brand management system at, 499–500
Prudential Insurance, 451

Quad Graphics, Inc., 139–141

Rand Corporation, 358
Regina Company, 292
Rockwell International Corporation, 527–528
ROLM, 210

Sandoz Pharmaceuticals, 188
Sears, 119, 125, 127, 164, 541
Securities and Exchange Commission, 395
Semco, 341
Smith, A.O., Corporation, 173
SNI Companies, 450
Softview, Inc., 442
SOHIO, 251
Springfield Remanufacturing Corporation, 357
Standard Oil of New Jersey, 541
Super Valu, 67

Tandem Computers, 591
Tavistock Institute, 511–512
Tenneco, 447, 451
Texas Instruments, 221, 397, 593
Thermwood Corporation, 145–146
3M, 549–550
  employee programs of, 117
  organizational culture of, 549–550
Toshiba, 205
Toyota, 83, 400
Trans Australia Airlines, 591
TWA, 210

Union Carbide, 601
United Auto Workers, 399
United Technologies Corporation, organizational structure of, 511

Volvo, 221

Wal-Mart, 499
Wang Laboratories, 409–410
Wells, Fargo, 119, 213
Wendy's, 531

Western Electric Company, and Hawthorne Studies, 13–17
Westinghouse, 397
  communication at, 477
Weyerhauser, 242, 447

Xerox, 45, 593

ZZZZ Best Company, 416